AF228487

The Grand Debate

THE GRAND DEBATE

THE REASONS PRESENTED BY THE DISSENTING BRETHREN AGAINST CERTAIN PROPOSITIONS CONCERNING PRESBYTERIAN GOVERNMENT

AND THE PROOFS OF THEM VOTED BY THE ASSEMBLY OF DIVINES, SITTING BY AUTHORITY OF PARLIAMENT, AT WESTMINSTER; TOGETHER WITH THE ANSWER OF THE ASSEMBLY OF DIVINES TO THOSE REASONS OF DISSENT

Edited by Chris Coldwell
Introduction by Rowland S. Ward

NAPHTALI PRESS &
REFORMATION HERITAGE BOOKS

Naphtali Press
P. O. Box 141084
Dallas, Texas, 75214
www.naphtali.com
naphtali@naphtali.com

Reformation Heritage Books
3070 29th St. SE
Grand Rapids, Michigan, 49512
616-977-0889
orders@heritagebooks.org
www.heritagebooks.org

ISBN 979-8-88686-120-4

CONTENTS

I. Presbyterian Government: Jerusalem

Reasons Against The Third Proposition Concerning Presbyterial

Assertion 1: The Church of Jerusalem consisted of more congregations
    than one.

II. Presbyterian Government: Ephesus

III. Subordination of Synods

IV. Ordination

V. Committee for Acommodation

Appendix, Bibliography and Indices

Foreword to this Second Edition

THIS WORK CONTAINS a lesser known set of documents produced by the Westminster Assembly of Divines, arguing for and against the Presbyterian form of church government. Discontented with the majority's Presbyterian views, the Congregationalist members produced dissenting papers to which the Assembly replied, giving a more detailed view of the matters debated than the information recorded in the Assembly's Minutes.

Presented in five sections, *The Grand Debate* includes the following exchanges between the Congregationalist 'dissenting brethren' and the Presbyterian majority of the Assembly: I. Reasons against the proposition that many churches may be under one Presbyterial government from the example of the church at Jerusalem, and the Assembly's reply; II. Reasons against … from the example of the Church at Ephesus, with the Assembly's reply; III. Reasons against the subordination of church synods, with the Assembly's reply; IV. Reasons against the Assembly's limitation on the power of individual congregations to ordain, with the Assembly's reply; V. Four papers by the Congregationalists presented in the committee formed to come to an accommodation, with answers by the representatives of the Assembly.

The text was first published in 1648 under the original title, *The reasons presented by the Dissenting Brethren against certain propositions concerning presbyteriall government: and the proofs of them voted by the Assembly of Divines, sitting by authority of Parliament, at Westminster. Together with the Answer of the Assembly of Divines to those reasons of dissent* (Printed by T.R. and E.M. for Humphrey Harwar). This printing was reissued by the printers with a new title page as *The Grand debate concerning presbitery and independency by the Assembly of Divines convened at Westminster by authority of Parliament* (Printed [by T.R. and E.M.] for Anthony Williamson, 1652). The texts are the same. The only surviving manuscript for the text is that of the first exchange, which is preserved in the volume that also contains the Burges manuscript of the Confession of Faith (Braye volume, Confession, Westminster College, Cambridge; see the bibliography, p. 412). This manuscript has been placed online. While a collation was not performed, a browse through the text showed no apparent significant differences, and only incidental variations from the printed form of the text. An occasional key has been placed in the margin for this new edition at the beginning of major sections in the first part, "Presbyterian Government: Jerusalem."

One will not find fully developed arguments or systems for Presbyterian and Congregationalist forms of church government in *The Grand Debate*. On the one hand the Presbyterian argument was shackled by a limitation to reason only from the standpoint of what had been passed by the Assembly, and on the other, the Congregational case was limited by the dissenting brethrens' refusal to articulate their own polity, resting satisfied instead, for political reasons, in playing naysayer to the majority Presbyterian opinion. But despite these limitations, and while these papers did not nor could not evolve into constitutional documents for Presbyterianism as did the Confession of Faith, Larger and Shorter Catechisms, Directories for Worship and Government, and Psalter, they nevertheless are part of the corpus of official writings of the Westminster Assembly of Divines, and they offer further insight into their deliberations.

The text has been edited for modern spelling and usage. With an exception or two, most all of the bibliographical references have been traced. Notes have been added throughout keying the text to the Assembly Minutes, Gillespie's notes, Lightfoot's journal, and other sources. While a new edition of Gillespie's notes are reissued in the third volume of *Shorter Writings of George Gillespie* (2024), referencing herein remains to the original text published in Gillespie's *Works* (1844–46), as the most widely available text. Cross references linking the arguments in the dissenting brethrens' papers to the Assembly's replies and vice versa have been added in the margins. All the Latin has been translated marginally or in footnotes. For this second edition, a few corrections or updates have been made, denoted by "Ed. 2024."

In the original text, the Assembly quotes and often summarizes and paraphrases the Independents' argument without any distinction—all set in the italic face, as was all other emphasis. Much of this over-italicization has been removed for this edition. Any apparent quotations appear within double quotation marks. Obvious paraphrases, proposed objections, or words placed in the mouth of the opponent are set within single quotation marks.

An appendix presents an updated version of research into the theological resources available to the Westminster Assembly, presenting in better form the Assembly's working library borrowed from Archbishop Laud's study, and adding references to the personal libraries of William Greenhill and Lazerus Seaman. It is noted in the Bibliography which referenced works were possibly in these two private collections and other public libraries of the time. Some facts based on the Map of London are revised (pp. 394, 396).

As to those who assisted with the 2014 edition of this work, I reiterate my thanks expressed more fully therein, and also thank Reformation Heritage Books for their interest in reprinting this important and certainly the largest production of the Westminster Assembly of Divines.

Chris Coldwell
Dallas, Texas
April 1, 2024

Introduction

I. Background to the Westminster Assembly

In 1533 King Henry VIII of England sought the annulment of his marriage to Catherine of Aragon as it had only produced Mary and not the male heir he desperately desired. The Pope was unwilling to get on the wrong side of Catherine's nephew, the powerful Emperor Charles V, and so refused Henry's request. Henry thereupon broke with the pope and proclaimed himself as head of the Church of England. In other respects he remained of Catholic belief, but the Protestant movement was impacting English society. The attempts to secure further reformation of the English church after Henry's death were very much dependent on the views of the monarch, given the absence of widespread popular support for change. Edward VI, who came to the throne at age 9 in 1547, was the child of his third marriage and was the male heir Henry had been seeking. Edward was raised a Protestant and had a sincere interest in religious matters despite his youth. During his reign the Protestant faith was established in England, the Book of Common Prayer of 1549/1552 and the Forty-two Articles (1552/53)—later reduced to thirty-nine—being significant milestones.

Advised by Thomas Cranmer, the architect of the English Reformation and since 1533 the Archbishop of Canterbury, Martin Bucer and Peter Martyr Vermigli were invited to England to serve the universities at Cambridge and Oxford respectively. Bucer had influenced Calvin's views on worship and church polity when Calvin ministered to a congregation in Strasbourg 1538–41.[1] Essentially Presbyterian in his polity, Bucer wrestled with the tension between a gathered church and a church coextensive with the community. In his Strasbourg ministry in 1546/47 he encouraged within the larger parish what we might call 'house groups' of the more spiritually committed, whose ultimate aim was to energise the larger parish church. This met with significant opposition. Bucer related the church and its offices in a mutual way with a strong pastoral orientation. In regard to the church as the body of Christ, he held that "the church's power, to the extent that the Lord wishes to exercise it through human beings, rests with the entire people of God. Authority in its administration, however, rests with the ministers of the church."[2] The classic expression of Bucer's vision for church and

---

1. Willem van't Spijker, "Bucer's influence on Calvin: church and community," in *Martin Bucer: Reforming Church and Community*, ed. David F. Wright (Cambridge University Press, 1994), 32ff.

2. Willem van't Spijker, *The Ecclesiastical Offices in the Thought of Martin Bucer* (Leiden: E.J.Brill, 1996), 295.

community is seen in the work written shortly before his death in February 1551. It was entitled *De Regno Christi* (On the Kingdom of Christ), prepared in manuscript for King Edward.[1] The death of Edward in July 1553 interrupted the progress of reform, and Mary's five-year reign brought a reversion to Roman practice. Elizabeth, the daughter from Henry's second marriage, succeeded to the throne in 1558. By and large she maintained the position Edward had set out, but declined to carry this compromise 'Elizabethan Settlement' further.

The endeavour to reform church polity in a Presbyterian direction was constantly frustrated by Elizabeth, and the attempt of Robert Browne in 1581 to establish a separatist church on congregational principles was also suppressed. The Presbyterian interest, whose discipline had been spreading in Church of England parishes, was silenced in 1592. Elizabeth died unmarried and childless in 1603 and the English Crown passed to her cousin James VI, King of Scotland, who became also James I of England. King James, who wanted to completely unify the two kingdoms, something that only came about in 1707, stated at the Hampton Court Conference in 1604 that (a Scottish) Presbytery agreed as well with Monarchy as God with the Devil. Robert Browne was only a separatist from 1579 to 1585, but there were those who continued his original approach and who therefore believed in reformation 'without tarrying for any' and denied that the Church of England was a true church. Many of those who emigrated to America on the *Mayflower* in 1620 were separatists. Others unhappy with the Church of England continued within it as supporters of congregational independency or presbyterianism, and still others recognised the Church of England as a true church, but sought to establish separate congregations, beginning with Henry Jacob at Southwark in 1616. While it has been common for historians to suggest minimal or no continuity between Elizabethan presbyterianism and the presbyterianism that came to the fore in 1640, Polly Ha has produced what is overall a convincing argument that a body of Presbyterian opinion, though small, continued after 1592 in Puritan circles.[2]

Although the direct impact of *De Regno Christi* on the subsequent 16th century debates on English church polity is not apparent, Bucer's views on ministry expressed in this and other works, his influence on significant friends and the contributions of fellow Reformers elsewhere, formed a pool of ideas that would be debated and refined in a number of ways in

---

1. For the Presbyterian dimension of the reforms under Edward VI the older work of A. H. Drysdale may be consulted, *History of the Presbyterians in England: Their Rise, Decline and Revival* (London: Publication Committee of the Presbyterian Church of England, 1889), 29ff. For the text of *De Regno Christi* in English translation see Wilhelm Pauck (ed.), *Melanchthon and Bucer,* Library of Christian classics, v. 19 (Philadelphia: Westminster Press, 1969), 155ff.

2. Polly Ha, *English Presbyterianism 1590–1640* (Stanford: Stanford University Press, 2011).

the course of time,[1] and ultimately erupted in the debates of the 1640s between Presbyterians and Independents.[2]

The period 1638–1660 was one of the most tumultuous in British and Irish history. It embraced six wars. The two Bishops' Wars of 1639–40 arose out of the desire of King Charles I to impose Episcopal rule on the Scottish Church through the instrumentality of William Laud, the Archbishop of Canterbury. Charles believed in the Divine Right of Kings and that he was answerable only to God. The Scots covenanted together to reject Charles' policy. The first war ended as a stalemate in June 1639 (the Pacification of Berwick). Charles prepared for a second war, and raised an army in Ireland. Charles, who had ruled England personally since 1629, was forced to recall the Parliament in April 1640 to secure funds for the war. Although the Lords and the Convocation of the Church of England approved, the House of Commons refused to vote to approve money until grievances in church and state were addressed. The King promptly dissolved Parliament on 5 May, and went to war anyway. Hostilities began in July with a pre-emptive invasion of England by the Scots who easily defeated the English. The Treaty of Ripon was signed on 26 October 1640. Alexander Henderson, the highly esteemed minister at Edinburgh and a Scottish Commissioner to deal with peace negotiations, much impressed the King. In 1641 the King approved the establishment of presbyterianism in Scotland.

In April 1640 a Convocation of the Church of England had been called by authority of the King to pass canons to legitimise Laud's reforms. Canon VI was an oath to be taken by every clergyman, every Master of Arts not the son of a nobleman, all who had taken a degree in divinity, law, or physic, all registrars, actuaries, proctors and schoolmasters, all persons incorporated from foreign universities, and all candidates for ordination. The oath-taker had to declare

> … nor will I ever give my consent to alter the government of this Church by archbishops, bishops, deans, and archdeacons, &c., as it stands now established, and as by right it ought to stand, nor yet ever to subject it to the usurpations and superstitions of the see of Rome.

The ambiguity arising from the "&c," had led to much contention. The Bishop of Gloucester objected and Laud ordered his arrest.[3] The ambiguity, as well as the suggestion the Convocation was not legally constituted, had resulted in the King disallowing this 'Etcetera Oath' in August 1640, but the

---

1. *De Regno Christi* was printed (in Latin) in Basel in 1557 and German and French translations appeared the following year.

2. The more familiar term, Congregationalists, came into use in the 1640s.

3. Godfrey Goodman (1582/1583–1656). Goodman did not object on Puritan grounds; he was sympathetic to Romanism and later converted. After a few months, he repented of his objection and was released from prison, but was later arrested again when Laud was imprisoned.

damage was done. Its presupposition was divine-right (*jus divinum*) episcopacy, which in effect challenged review of the evidence for such a claim.
According to Baxter, many, including himself, "were roused by the terrors
of the Oath to look about us and understand what we did."[1] From being
complacent they became opponents of divine-right episcopacy while ac-
cepting a moderate episcopacy based on grounds of utility and good order.

The King recalled the English Parliament on 3 November 1640, as he
needed funds to pay the Scots. Charles had to make some concessions. The
so-called 'Root and Branch' petition was presented to the Long Parliament
on 11 December 1640 on behalf of 15,000 signatories from in and around
London. In a conscious reflection on the Etcetera Oath it sought a reduction to a more moderate limited episcopacy.

> That whereas the government of archbishops and lord bishops, deans,
> and archdeacons, &c., with their courts and ministrations in them, have
> proved prejudicial and very dangerous both to the Church and Com-
> monwealth.... We therefore most humbly pray, and beseech this hon-
> ourable assembly, the premises considered, that the said government
> with all its dependencies, roots and branches, may be abolished, and
> all laws in their behalf made void, and the government according to
> God's word may be rightly placed amongst us:...[2]

There were various other petitions to similar effect. Alexander Henderson, who was also later a Commissioner to the Westminster Assembly of
Divines, published a nineteen-page pamphlet early in 1641 about the dan-
gers of a moderate episcopacy. It was entitled *The unlawfulness and danger
of limited prelacie, or perpetual precidencie in the church, Briefly discovered.*
Robert Baillie, another of the Scottish Commissioners, responded to criticism of Henderson's work later in February.[3] Various reforms were passed:
Parliament had to meet at least every three years; the present Parliament
could not be dissolved without its consent (and hence became known as
the Long Parliament 1640–48); Laud was impeached and imprisoned; the
Star Chamber was abolished in July 1641; taxation without Parliamentary
consent was declared illegal, &c. A Grand Remonstrance listing some 200
points of grievance was narrowly passed by the House of Commons in
November 1641 and presented to the King. Many of these were concerned

---

1. Richard Baxter, *Reliquiæ Baxterianæ: or Mr Richard Baxter's Narrative of the Most Memo-
rable Passages of His Life and Times* (London 1696), Book I, Part 1, §22 §23, 16.

2. *Documents Illustrative of English Church History*, ed. Henry Gee and William John Hardy
(New York: Macmillan, 1896), 537–38.

3. *The Unlawfulness and danger of Limited Episcopacie: whereunto is subjoined a short reply to
the Modest advertiser and examinator of that treatise* (London: printed for Thomas Underhill).
See also Robert Baillie, *Letters and Journals of Robert Baillie, AM*, ed. David Laing (Edinburgh:
Bannatyne Club, 1841), 3.303. Hereafter Baillie, *Letters & Journals*.

with the risk of Romanism, heightened because the King was married to
a Roman Catholic. The King rejected it, although on 14 February 1642 he
assented to an Act to exclude bishops from sitting in the House of Lords.
The Remonstrance included a call for an Assembly of Divines to deal with
the "peace and good government of the Church." On 1 June 1642 a Bill for
the Assembly was passed by Parliament, but the King, who was readying
for war, refused his assent. The King raised his standard at Nottingham in
August 1642. The major battle of Edgehill on Sunday 23 October 1642 was
indecisive. An Assembly of Divines became imperative since, while the Act
for the Abolition of Episcopacy was not passed until 9 October 1646, the
effective government of the Church of England was already in disarray.
The conflict between Parliament and the King was to run until June 1646

Those of Presbyterian sympathy were prepared to negotiate a settlement
with the King, while the Independents wished to achieve military victory.
However, neither approach succeeded, so Parliament desperately sought
the help of the Scots. Knowing the religious concerns of the Scots, on 12
June 1643 the English Parliament ordered an Assembly of Divines to address religious questions. The key terms of the summoning ordinance were:

> Whereas amongst the infinite blessings of Almighty God upon this
> Nation, none is, or can be more dear unto us than the purity of our
> Religion; and for that as yet many things remain in the Liturgy, Disci-
> pline and Government of the Church, which do necessarily require a
> further, and more perfect Reformation then as yet hath been attained:
> And whereas it hath been Declared and Resolved by the Lords and
> Commons assembled in Parliament, That the present Church-Gov-
> ernment by Archbishops, Bishops, their Chancellors, Commissaries,
> Deans, Deans and Chapters, Archdeacons, and other Ecclesiastical Of-
> ficers depending upon the Hierarchy, is evil, and justly offensive and
> burthensome to the Kingdome, a great impediment to Reformation
> and growth of Religion, and very prejudicial to the State and Govern-
> ment of this Kingdome, and that therefore they are Resolved that the
> same shall be taken away, and that such a Government shall be settled
> in the Church, as may be most agreeable to Gods Holy Word, and most
> apt to procure and preserve the Peace of the Church at home, and
> nearer Agreement with the Church of Scotland, and other Reformed
> Churches abroad, and for the better effecting hereof, and for the vindi-
> cating and clearing of the Doctrine of the Church of England from all
> false Calumnies and Aspersions, It is thought fit and necessary to call
> an Assembly of Learned, Godly, and Judicious Divines, to consult and
> advise of such matters and things….[1]

---

1. Cf. *The Confession of Faith, the Larger and Shorter Catechisms…* (Edinburgh: Johnstone &
Hunter, 1855; repr. FPP, 1990), II. The 12 June Ordinance (with those appointed) and vow (and

The Assembly commenced work on 1 July 1643, in the relatively safe matter of revision of the Thirty-nine Articles, which were already Reformed in theological character. However, in August the situation was dire, and the English Parliament sent seven commissioners 300 miles north to Scotland to seek military assistance. These included two members of the Assembly of Divines: Stephen Marshall (Presbyterian) and Philip Nye (Independent) as well as Sir Henry Vane, the younger.

The English wished for a civil league but the Scots insisted on a religious covenant, and the English did not have much choice given the desperate military situation. Terms were readily agreed in Edinburgh on 18 August.[1] The proposal was presented to the English Parliament ten days later. Parliament promptly referred it to the Assembly of Divines. Certain changes were made and sent back to Parliament. Parliament made certain other changes, principally including the Kingdom of Ireland, and these received the approbation of the Assembly on 15 September.[2] The Solemn League and Covenant, as it was now known, was approved by Parliament on 21 September 1643. It was subscribed by the House of Commons and by the Assembly of Divines on 25 September 1643, and by the House of Lords four days later.

The changes in the wording agreed in Edinburgh of the Solemn League and Covenant are indicated in the text of the key sections that follows. The bracketed words are those dropped from the Edinburgh text and the words in italics are additions. After the words 'the Reformation of Religion in the Church of England' the Edinburgh text had '(this Explication to be at the end of the Covenant, *As far as we do, or shall in our consciences conceive to be according to the Word of God*);' it was dropped in the final version.

---

list of those actually attending) was first published in Rothwell's 1658 edition of the Confession of Faith and Catechisms. The ordinance in modified form appears in the 1728 Lumisden and Robertson edition, the form of which became the model for all subsequent Scottish printings of the full Westminster Standards. See Chris Coldwell, "*Antiquary*: The Traditional Form of *The Westminster Standards*," *The Confessional Presbyterian* 1 (2005), 170.

1. *The New Oath or Covenant, to be taken by All Persons within the two Kingdoms of England and Scotland. Agreed upon at Edinburgh by the General Assembly, the Convention of Estates, and the Commissioners for THE PARLIAMENT in the Kingdom of England, the 18. Day of August, 1643. And sent to the Parliament of England for the like Approbation* (London, printed for Philip Lane at Grayes-Inne Gate, September 4, 1643). For more notes on publications of the covenant and textual issues see *The Solemn League & Covenant* (Large broadside, printed for Westminster Letter Press by Golgonooza Letter Foundry & Press in handset type on handmade paper, in an edition of no more than one hundred and twenty-five, including twenty-five signed and numbered copies, 2009) and S. W. Carruthers, "The Solemn League and Covenant: Its Text and Its Translations," in *Records of Scottish Church History Society*, VI (1938), 232–251.

2. Incidentally, this was the same day that Charles, through his military commander, made a truce with the Irish rebels with a view to bringing his army there back to England to help his forces. This act united Parliament which was fearful that Papist soldiers from Ireland would also come to England.

I. That we shall [all and each one of us] sincerely, really and constantly, through the grace of God, endeavour in our several places and callings, the preservation of the [true] Reformed [Protestant] Religion in the Church of Scotland, in Doctrine, Worship, Discipline and Government, [according to the Word of God] *against our common enemies*; the reformation of Religion in the *kingdoms* [Church] of England *and Ireland*, in doctrine, worship, discipline and government, according to the [same holy] Word [of God], [and] the example of the best reformed Churches; and [as may] *we shall endeavour to* bring the Churches of God in [both nations] *the three kingdoms* to the nearest conjunction and Uniformity in Religion, confession of Faith, Forme of Church-government, directory for Worship and Catechizing; That we, and our Posterity after us, may as Brethren, live in Faith and Love, *and the Lord may delight to dwell in the midst of us.*

II. That we shall in like manner, without respect of persons, indeavour the Extirpation of Popery, Prelacie *(that is, Church government by Archbishops, Bishops, their Chancellors and Commissaries, Deans, Deans and Chapters, Archdeacons, and all other ecclesiastical officers depending on that hierarchy)*, Superstition, Heresie, Schisme, and Profaneness, and whatsoever shall be found to be contrary to sound Doctrine and the power of godliness [in both nations], lest we partake in other men's sins, and thereby be [endangered] *in danger* to receive of their plagues, and that the Lord may be one, and his Name one in [both] the three Kingdoms.

At the request of Sir Henry Vane, "League" was introduced into the title, his motive being the thought that a league was easier to break than a covenant. The wording concerning reformation "according to the word of God" was rearranged to have direct reference to the Church of England, so offsetting in a measure the Church of Scotland as the standard of conformity to Scripture. While the Scots thought the change supported their Presbyterianism (surely Scotland was the example of the best reformed church?), it suited other parties too, for they thought their understanding of church government was in accordance with the Word of God also. Some among the Divines took exception to the word 'prelacy' in the second article as lacking definition and capable of excluding a moderate episcopacy. The Scots wished all forms of episcopacy rejected, but the ancient moderate episcopacy had significant support in England. Featley, Gataker, Cornelius Burgess and others expressed their concern.[1] According to John Lightfoot, the debate was heavy and at times acrimonious, mainly due to the 'captiousness' of Dr Bur-

---

1. Richard Baxter, *Reliquiae Baxterianae*, Book I, Part 1, §70, 48–49; Daniel Neal, *The History of the Puritans*, ed. Joshua Toulmin (Boston: Charles Ewer, 1817), 3.91. For an overview see

gess.[1] It was eventually resolved by incorporating the words in brackets in the text above which were taken over from the summoning ordinance for the Assembly. The interpretation became that only a certain kind of prelacy was excluded from consideration. The Parliament made further minor adjustments, particularly including the Kingdom of Ireland, as already stated. It is of note that Thomas Coleman, in preaching before the Lords at the time they subscribed the Solemn League and Covenant, argued that only the kind of prelacy described in it was proscribed.[2]

It is evident from the above outline that the Solemn League and Covenant was not exactly the unambiguous Presbyterian standard of much popular Presbyterian thought. If it was a sincere religious document, it was also one with political dimensions. A new government for the Church of England was an urgent necessity given the close relationship between Church and State and the importance of stability in society. Archbishop Laud had been imprisoned in the Tower of London in 1641 and would be executed 10 January 1645. His kind of episcopacy was out, but, at the other end of the spectrum, the many sects that were on the rise were of increasing concern, and fears of Roman Catholic intrusion real. The situation in the parishes was disordered, the need to examine and ordain ministers pressing, the Parliamentary military forces not fully effective. If English opinion in early 1643 was not quite sure about any radical change to the traditional pattern of ecclesiastical organisation, other than rejecting Laudism, the options became more limited as the political and military position worsened.

The agreement to *preserve* the reformed religion in Scotland and to pursue the *reformation* of religion in England and Ireland suggested conformity to the Scottish pattern, and the Presbyterian pattern had many examples in Europe. It could also provide a helpful unity through its graded system of assemblies by which the part was subordinated to the whole. But the expression "according to the Word of God" could extend to several possibilities. Thomas Case urged the London ministers that the Covenant was so mutual that "we are no more bound to Scotland, than Scotland to us," and that there was a pledge to preserve Scottish practice, not observe it.[3]

The five 'dissenting brethren' who were members of the Assembly of Divines, were influential Independents[4] whose fortunes would rise with

---

James C. Spalding and Maynard F. Brass, "Reduction of Episcopacy as a Means to Unity in England 1640–1662," *Church History* 30.4 (December 1961), 414–432.

1. *The Whole Works of the Rev. John Lightfoot, D.D.*, ed. J. R. Pitman, 13 vols. (London, 1824) 13.11 (hereafter Lightfoot); Robert S. Paul, *The Assembly of the Lord* (T&T Clark: Edinburgh, 1985), 93.

2. Richard Baxter, *Reliquiae Baxterianae*, 49.

3. Thomas Case, *The Quarrel of the Covenant, with the Pacification of the Quarrell, Delivered in Three Sermons on Levit. 26.25 and Jere. 50.5* (London: printed for Luke Fawne [licensed by Joseph Caryl, 5 December 1643]), 42, 44.

4. There were another five to eight supporters of these men. Cf. Paul *Assembly of the Lord*, 232, fn. 47.

the success of the New Model Army in 1645, but who argued that their position was of divine mandate, as the Scots did for their position. The four Eraſtians, two divines (Lightfoot and Coleman) and two MPs (Selden and Whitelocke), did not think there was a rule for church government prescribed in Scripture, and essentially were supporters of a Presbyterian settlement with ultimate control in the State. It is to be remembered that the Assembly of Divines was the creature of Parliament, and Parliament retained the dominant position in so far as the acceptance or otherwise of the Assembly's work. In that sense Parliament was taking Eraſtian ground. Parliament also appointed the prolocutor (chairman) and the scribes, and had parliamentary representatives present. Only the texts of the two catechisms escaped unscathed from changes by the Parliament.[1]

Since the King had not assented to the Assembly, about 20 of those appointed did not attend, moſt notably James Ussher, Archbishop of Armagh, a ſtrong Royaliſt. He was the primary author of the Irish Articles of 1615 which in several reſpects influenced the Weſtminſter Confession. He had sympathised with and protected Presbyterian miniſters who had served in the Episcopal Church in Ireland, argued for the ancient origin of episcopacy in a series of works from 1641, and contemplated a compromise of Episcopal and Presbyterian positions in the same year.[2] He was much esteemed on all sides, but a ſtrong representation of advocates of a moderate Episcopal position would not be found in the Assembly. So the remaining members were not likely to be ſtrong representatives of a moderate episcopal solution. Convinced divine right Presbyterians at the commencement in July 1643 were not numerous, but support for, even if not entire agreement with, that position became the default viewpoint of the majority by the close of January 1644. They feared the chaos that Independency might provide and recogniscd that with the imperative need for Scottish military help, there was no other practical option. The eleven Scots werc non-voting treaty commissioners able to participate in any committee.[3]

---

1. For an excellent introduction see *The Minutes and Papers of the Weſtminſter Assembly 1643–1652* ed. Chad Van Dixhoorn, 5 vols. (Oxford: Oxford University Press, 2012), vol. 1. Hereafter, *Minutes*.

2. *The reduction of episcopacie unto the form of synodical government received in the ancient Church: proposed in the year 1641 as an expedient for the prevention of those troubles, which afterwards did arise about the matter of church-government. By the moſt reverend and learned father of our Church Dr. James Usher, late Arch-Bishop of Armagh and Primate of all Ireland. A true copy set forth by Nicolas Bernard, D.D. preacher to the Honourable Society of Grayes Inne occasioned by an imperfect copy lately printed* (London: Printed by E.C. for R. Royston at the Angel in Ivie-lane, 1656).

3. Those appointed Scottish commissioners from the Church of Scotland were: Robert Baillie (attended 1643–47), Robert Blair (did not attend), Robert Douglas (did not attend), George Gillespie (1643–47), Alexander Henderson (1643–45, d.1645), Samuel Rutherford (1643–47). Those Scottish peers and gentry appointed were: Archibald Campbell, marquess of Argyll (1646), John Campbell, first earl of Loudoun (1644–46), John Elphinstone, second

When on 12 October 1643 the Assembly of Divines was directed by Parliament to enter on the pressing issues of worship and the reform of church government, a major debate was likely on the latter, but not the former. The matters of the reform of worship did not prove greatly controversial. This was not surprising given those with strong commitment to episcopacy did not attend, other than Featley (who was later expelled for breaching the confidentiality rule by corresponding with Ussher).[1] The principle of keeping strictly to the regulative principle[2] meant an outline of a reformed worship service was provided which was very similar to the form practiced in Scotland, except that the suggested content of prayer rather than the actual wording of such was provided. The longest debate was actually over whether or not communicants should sit at the table or remain in their seats.[3] It was resolved by way of a compromise wording which did not decide that point.

Lord Balmerino (1644–47), Sir Charles Erskine of Alva (1645), John Kennedy, sixth earl of Cassillis (did not attend), John Maitland, Viscount Maitland, earl of Lauderdale (1643–1648), Robert Meldrum (did not attend), George Winram of Liberton, Lord Liberton (1644, 1647). See *Minutes*, 1.[170], 175.

1. Those attending the assembly were "not to divulge" assembly matters, "by printing, writing, or otherwise, without the consent of both or either Houses of Parliament." See *Ordinance*, ibid. "An intercepted Letter from Doctor *Feateley* to the Archbishop of *Armagh*, laying great Imputations upon the Proceedings and Members of the Assembly, and upon divers Members of the Parliament; and whereby it appears, that he is an Espy and Intelligencer to *Oxon*; the which Letter was examined before a Committee, and the Doctor called to his Answer; and confessed all the material Points of it. *Resolved*, &c. That Dr. *Feately* shall be discharged from being a Member of the Assembly." "House of Commons Journal Volume 3: 30 September 1643," *Journal of the House of Commons: volume 3: 1643–1644* (1802), 259. Featley had made it clear he would not disown episcopacy in the assembly and this letter incident may have been a "sting operation" to remove him from the scene. He was charged with treason for trying to correspond with the King. See Arnold Hunt, "Featley, Daniel (1582–1645)," *Oxford Dictionary of National Biography* (Oxford University Press, 2004 online edn, Jan 2008 http://www.oxforddnb.com/view/article/9242, accessed February 11, 2014) and the biographical entry in *Minutes*, 5.117. The second volume of Baillie's *Letters & Journals* is made up largely of violations of this confidentiality rule. *Minutes*, 5.108.

2. See a succinct explanation of the regulative principle of worship drawn from the Westminster Standards in Richard A. Muller and Rowland S. Ward, *Scripture and Worship* (Phillipsburg, NJ: P& R Publishing, 2007), 97–98. The term derives from Scottish and American Southern Presbyterian usage and though "it may have been used earlier, the term … apparently was coined from or at least popularized by usage in the 1946 report of the OPC," "Report of the Committee on Song in Worship Presented to the Thirteenth General Assembly, on the Teaching of Our Standards Respecting the Songs That May Be Sung in the Public Worship of God," specifically section 'A' by John Murray (*Orthodox Presbyterian Church, Minutes of the General Assembly* [1946] 101–107). [Chris Coldwell,] Introduction, "Reframing Presbyterian Worship: A Critical Survey of the Worship Views of John M. Frame and R. J. Gore," by Frank J. Smith, Ph.D., D.D. and David C. Lachman, Ph.D., *The Confessional Presbyterian* 1 (2005) 116. See also Frank J. Smith with Chris Coldwell, "The Regulative Principle of Worship: Sixty Years in Reformed Literature [Part One] (1946–1999)," *The Confessional Presbyterian* 2 (2006), 89ff.

3. For the Directory for Public Worship see Muller and Ward, *Scripture and Worship*, 83–175. For discussion of the debate over the use of a table in communion see pp. 130–131 and *The Book*

The debate on church government would be a different matter and ultimately a debate between Presbyterian and Independent models. However, trying to get off to a positive start, it was decided that the matter of church officers, about which there was general agreement, should be discussed first before proceeding to consider church government proper. The critical period of discussion was 2 February 1644 to 14 May 1644.

II. Prelude to the Grand Debate

Why was the debate on the disputed points of church government by the Westminster Assembly published as *The Grand Debate*? Was it because the debate was long, on a grand scale? Was it because it was splendidly impressive? Was it because the debate became famous? Was it because it aimed to give a comprehensive and well-integrated statement of the subject? Was it from Parliamentary usage in respect of the four grand committees which the House of Commons appointed each year prior to 1832 to deal with religion, grievances, courts of justice and trade? Was it because it was the chief subject debated at the Assembly, or the matter of most importance? In a measure all these reasons are relevant yet, judged from the amount of the Assembly's time spent on church government (about 25%), it was not the longest: that honour belongs to doctrinal matters (36%), as Van Dixhoorn has convincingly shown.[1] However, the shape of the polity of a reformed Church of England was of immense practical importance: it was a 'Grand matter'.[2]

---

of Common Order of the Church of Scotland commonly known as John Knox's liturgy and The Directory for the Public Worship of God agreed upon by the Assembly of Divines at Westminster, With historical introductions & illustrative notes by George W. Sprott and Thomas Leishman (Edinburgh, Blackwood, 1868), 346–358, and C. G. M'Crie, *The Public Worship of Presbyterian Scotland: Historically Treated* (Edinburgh; London: William Blackwood and Sons, 1892), 441–450.

1. "The arrival of the Scottish commissioners on 15 September 1643, an event celebrated in the minutes, turned the assembly's attention away from the Thirty-nine Articles and towards church government—a subject on which the assembly would ultimately spend a quarter of its plenary sessions, a fifth of its ad hoc committees, and a quarter of its texts—perhaps less time than has been traditionally assumed, but a staggering number of hours nevertheless" (*Minutes*, 1.27). "In 508 sessions theology was the or a main subject of debate. The preponderance of sessions dedicated to deliberating theology does not in itself indicate that theological debates were of primary importance at the Assembly. But the fact that 36% of the Assembly's sessions were spent debating theology suggests that there may be doctrinal issues which the divines considered both important and difficult to state. Sadly most of these doctrinal debates take place in the later sessions of the Assembly where Byfield's record keeping is parsimonious" (Chad Van Dixhoorn, "Reforming the Reformation: Theological Debate in the Westminster Assembly," 7 vols., unpublished University of Cambridge Ph.D. thesis, 2004], volume 1, p. 89; hereafter, Van Dixhoorn, "Reforming the Reformation"). Cf. Robert Letham, *The Westminster Assembly: Reading its Theology in Historical Context* (Phillipsburg, NJ: P&R Publishing, 2009), 105–160.

2. Compare the record of the Savoy Conference of 1661 on the liturgy of the English

It is worthy of note that the first decades of the 17th century coincided with the rise of interpretation of Scripture which focused on a future millennium rather than a past one typically running from 300 to 1300, as had been the case previously. Joseph Mede's *Clavis Apocalyptica* [Key to Revelation] of 1627 was published in English translation in 1642 with a recommendatory preface by William Twisse, the first chairman of the Westminster Assembly. It predicted a future millennial reign of the saints beginning no later than 1715. The same year John Archer's 59 page booklet *The Personall Reign of Christ on Earth* appeared. Thomas Goodwin had been co-pastor with Archer at Arnhem in 1639–40 and had similar views. He believed antichrist (the papacy) would be overthrown in 1666. Reformed teacher at Herborn, Johnann Alsted's quite brief and sober *Diatribe de mille annis apocalyptic* issued in 1627, was published in English in 1643 as *The Beloved City,* advocates a full future millennium beginning about 1694, with Christ in heaven but the resurrected martyrs governing for him on earth.[1] It was a time of considerable ferment.

> The collapse of censorship saw a fantastic outpouring of books, pamphlets and newspapers. Before 1640, newspapers were illegal; by 1645 there were 722. Twenty-two books were published in 1640; over 2,000 in 1642.[2]

The Scots were generally more sober in their prophetic views and rejected the distinctives of the pre-millennial scheme characteristic of many Independents. Baillie seems in the Augustinian mould so far as the millennium is concerned.[3] Nevertheless, Gillespie thought the reign of the beast (the papacy) would shortly end and he counts the time of a more glorious and peaceable condition for the church to have begun in his own time, most probably in 1643.[4]

The relevance of the views on eschatology for our present purpose is that each party tended to see the future glory in terms of the elevation of their particular view of the church. Presbyterians looked for a national church, Independents one to which only the regenerate would belong. It is no

---

Church which resulted in the Act of Uniformity: *The grand debate between the most reverend bishops and the Presbyterian divines…* (London, 1661).

1. Johann Alsted, *The Beloved City* (London, 1643), 13, 17.

2. Crawford Gribben, *The Puritan Millennium, Literature and Theology, 1550–1682* (Dublin: Four Courts Press, 2000), 195, quoting Christopher Hill.

3. Robert Baillie, *A dissuasive from the errours of the time: wherein the tenets of the principall sects, especially of the Independents, are drawn together in one map, for the most part, in the words of their own authours, and their maine principles are examined by the touch-stone of the Holy Scriptures* (London: printed for Samuel Gellibrand 1645 [i.e. 1646]), 79.

4. *Sermons Preached Before the English Houses of Parliament by the Scottish Commissioners to the Westminster Assembly of Divines 1643–1645,* ed. Chris Coldwell (Naphtali Press: Dallas, 2011), 341–342. Gillespie's sermon was preached before the House of Commons on 27 March 1644.

accident that pre-millennial and extravagant views of the future belonged mostly to Independents and Baptists, and it is no accident that the Fifth Monarchy men of the 1650s, who talked of helping God bring in the reign of the saints by force, would be drawn from their ranks.

A Pivotal Decision
The discussion leading to the Grand Debate began on 17 October 1643, five days after the Assembly received an order from both Houses of Parliament as follows:

> Upon serious consideration of the present state and conjuncture of the affairs of this kingdom, the Lords and Commons assembled in Parliament do order, that the Assembly of Divines and others, do forthwith confer and treat among themselves, of such a discipline and government, as may be most agreeable to God's holy word, and most apt to procure and preserve the peace of the church at home, and nearer agreement with the church of Scotland and other reformed churches abroad, to be settled in this church instead and place of the present church-government by archbishops, bishops, their chancellors, commissaries, deans, deans and chapters, archdeacons, and other ecclesiastical officers, depending upon the hierarchy, which is resolved to be taken away.

> And touching and concerning the directory of worship or liturgy hereafter to be in the church. And to deliver their opinions and advices of and touching the same to both or either House of Parliament with all the convenient speed they can.[1]

The Independents wished to first debate the proposition that Scripture contained a system of church government, but the majority opposed this as likely to make "too sudden a trial of the differences of opinion that are like to show among us."[2] These differences were not simply between erastian and divine-right positions,[3] but were differences among the presbyterian majority as to the precise seat of church power.[4] These differences focused on the Petrine promise in Matthew 16:18–19 in which Christ says to Peter: "You are Peter and on this rock I will build my church and the gates of hell shall not prevail against it. I will give you the keys of the kingdom

---

1. Lightfoot, 18.

2. Lightfoot, 20.

3. Contra Robert S. Paul, *Assembly of the Lord*, 138.

4. See Hunter Powell, "October 1643: The Dissenting Brethren and the *Proton Dektikon*," in *Drawn into Controversie: Reformed Theological Diversity and Debates Within Seventeenth-Century British Puritanism*, ed. Michael A. G. Haykin and Mark Jones (Göttingen: Vandenhoeck & Ruprecht, 2011), 52–82 and the literature there cited, particularly Chad Van Dixhoorn, "Reforming the Reformation: Theological Debate in the Westminster Assembly."

of heaven, and whatever you bind on earth shall be bound in heaven, and whatever you loose on earth shall be loosed in heaven."

Was the promise personal to Peter so that the keys of church power were given to him and to those to whom he conveyed it, a theory congenial to Roman Catholics, although certainly not the universal position? Or was it to Peter as representative of office-bearers, a view congenial to those, such as Seaman, Gataker, and Gouge, who shrank from the separatism and disorder they associated with independency? Or was it to Peter as a representative of all believers in Christ, so that "tell it to the church" in Matthew 18:18 referred to the local gathered church? And if this last was so, were elders mere representatives of the local church to do the bidding of the church (the view of the separatists and independents properly so called)? Or should one hold rather that the elders of the church also received power directly from Christ, not from the church, the view of the dissenting brethren, which went somewhat toward the Presbyterian position although not granting authority or jurisdiction to assemblies of elders beyond the congregation? And then there was the question of the meaning of 'church' in the Petrine promise. Some held the promise was to the universal visible church considered as a political body but divided as to how that power was spread to each level: some thought it ascended from the congregation, others (Seaman, Gataker, Gouge) that it descended from the universal church, while the dissenting brethren did not allow the universal church to be a body politic and so did not derive the particular church from it.

The Scottish commissioners had a matured view of church government, the more definite as it had been tempered in the fires of Stuart absolutism. To the Scots, Presbyterian government by sessions, presbyteries, synods and assemblies was of divine right, and Andrew Melville's doctrine of two kingdoms was dear to them.[1] The magistrate could not intrude into the

---

1. In 1596 Melville had addressed James the Sixth of Scotland (and First of England) thus: "Sir, we will always humbly reverence your Majesty in public; but since we have this occasion to be with your Majesty in private, and since you are brought in extreme danger both of your life and crown, and along with you the country and the church of God are like to go to wreck, for not telling you the truth and giving you faithful counsel, we must discharge our duty, or else be traitors both to Christ and you. Therefore, Sir, as diverse times before I have told you, so now again I must tell you, there are two kings and two kingdoms in Scotland: there is King James the head of this commonwealth, and there is Christ Jesus the King of the church, whose subject James the Sixth is, and of whose kingdom he is not a king, nor a lord, nor a head, but a member. Sir, those whom Christ has called and commanded to watch over his church, have power and authority from him to govern his spiritual kingdom both jointly and severally; the which no Christian king or prince should control and discharge, but fortify and assist; otherwise they are not faithful subjects of Christ and members of his church. We will yield to you your place, and give you all due obedience; but again I say, you are not the head of the church: you cannot give us that eternal life which we seek for even in this world, and you cannot deprive us of it." Thomas McCrie, *The Life of Andrew Melville* (Edinburgh: William Blackwood, 1824), Vol. 1, 391–392.

ſpiritual jurisdiction of the church, but he was bound to support and encourage the true religion and to provide the conditions in which it might be free to flourish.[1] The church had the ultimate power of excommunication, while the magistrate could not command religious acts as service to God but could forbid the opposite as harmful to Christian societies.[2] That the Westminster Assembly was not a proper church Assembly, but could only offer advice to the Parliament, was something endured for the sake of the end in view, but otherwise it was an anomaly to the Scots.

The few Erastians at the Assembly did not believe Scripture held out a particular form of church government. They were happy to acquiesce in a presbyterian form but with the ultimate power of discipline in the hands of the civil authority, since they could not countenance the idea of two kingdoms as in the Melvillian Presbyterianism of Scotland. Further, to argue for toleration in the church seemed to threaten the stability of the state.

Having resolved to leave aside the question whether Scripture contained a system of church government, the Assembly had effectively ensured a Presbyterian outcome to the Grand Debate. The Assembly proceeded, through its existing three committees, to investigate the officers mentioned in the New Testament, and which were temporary and which permanent. Over the next month discussion strayed several times beyond the initial subject. On 26 October, when discussing the office of apostle, the majority held that the power of the keys belonged to the office as such, and not, as the dissenting brethren held, to the officeholder as representing the congregation. This debate again effectively anticipated the Grand Debate.[3] On 13 November, when discussing the rules to be used in the examination of candidates for ordination, the Independents wanted to restrict the term 'church' to the local congregation and thus there was significant discussion as to whether the Church of England in all her parishes was a true church. The rest of the Assembly found doubt on this point a dangerous notion, and it only confirmed them in belief that Independency was not the way for the Church of England to be a united, national body.

On 14 November a report from the Scots' commissioners was introduced, and the following day Henderson addressed the Assembly on the Scottish contention that there were four offices warranted from the New Testament: pastors, teachers (or doctors), ruling elders and deacons. He was the first of the Scots' commissioners to speak in the Assembly. The Scots argued that the pastor and the doctor were separate offices. The latter was for teachers of theology and the Scots would have been happy to add catechists to their

---

1. See Henderson's statement of the two kingdoms in his 27 December 1643 sermon before the Commons in *Sermons Preached Before the English Houses of Parliament by the Scottish Commissioners to the Westminster Assembly of Divines*, 88–89.

2. Wm. M. Campbell, "The Scottish Westminster Commissioners and Toleration," in *Records of the Scottish Church History Society*, IX (1947) 11, referring to Rutherford's way of stating the case.

3. Hunter Powell, "October 1643: The Dissenting Brethren," 81.

number. The Independents argued that every church should have both a pastor and a teacher, while Stephen Marshall and those English of Presbyterian leanings were not convinced that Scripture taught an office of teacher (doctor) distinct from that of pastor. However, on 21 November the matter was settled with agreement on six propositions:

1. That there be different gifts, and different exercises, according to the difference of those gifts in the ministers.
2. Those different gifts may be in and exercised by one and the same minister.
3. Where there be several ministers in the same congregation, they may be designed to several employments [ie. assigned to different tasks].
4. He that doth more excel in exposition, doctrine, and convincing them by application, and accordingly employed therein, may be called teacher or doctor.
5. A teacher or doctor is of excellent use in schools or universities.
6. Where there is but one minister in a particular congregation, he is to perform, so far as he is able, the whole work of the ministry.[1]

The debate had shown that while some considered there was a divine right for a distinct office of doctor, there was no consensus, while the Scots acknowledged the office of pastor and doctor was in essence one.[2] Baillie was happy that the absolute necessity of a teacher (doctor) in every congregation and the divine institution of this office were in formal terms in this way avoided.[3]

The Scots also intervened in the debate concerning the office of ruling elder on 22 November. Here the Independents supported the Scots and the English Presbyterians, but a good number, including the Erastians, were not convinced that the office was of divine right, although they were prepared to admit the office on practical grounds so long as coercive discipline ultimately belonged to Parliament. This was not satisfactory to the Scots. The debate continued until 14 December when it was laid aside for the time being, and other matters, including concerns about the forming of gathered churches in existing parishes taken up.

On 29 December 1643 a 31–page pamphlet was registered at the Stationer's Company licensed by Charles Herle, a Presbyterian member of the

---

1. Lightfoot, 58. The grammatical construction of Ephesians 4:11 has led some to the view that one ministry of pastor-teacher is being described, others that the functions were not always exercised by the same people. Thus A. T. Lincoln, *Word Biblical Commentary on Ephesians* (Dallas: Word Books, 1990) 251: "It is more likely that they were overlapping functions, but that while almost all pastors were also teachers, not all teachers were also pastors.... The one definite article is therefore best taken as suggesting this close association of functions between two types of ministers who both operate within the local congregation."

2. Lightfoot, 43.

3. Robert Baillie, *Letters and Journals*, 2.110.

Assembly. It was entitled *An apologeticall narration, humbly submitted to the Honourable Houses of Parliament. By Tho: Goodwin, Philip Nye, Sidrach Simpson, Jer: Burroughes, William Bridge.* The authors were the five dissenting brethren and their narrative set out their views on church government in a modest way that distanced them from the sectaries that were becoming increasingly prominent. It is not entirely clear when this pamphlet was generally available since the available sources are silent on that point. Whilst George Thomason, the bibliophile of the time, dated his copy 3 January,[1] Robert S. Paul argues that it cannot have become known until somewhat later, perhaps 26 January, since the discussion in the Assembly, so far as we know it, suggests no heightened animosity between the Independents and the Scots Presbyterians until later, and there is a reference in Lightfoot's Journal for that date that indicates something was distributed to each member.[2] Yet, regardless of the precise date of distribution, Herle was certainly aware of the content, and in his licence printed in the front of the pamphlet stated:

> *This* Apologeticall Narration *of our Reverend and Dear Brethren the learned authors of it, 'tis so full of peaceablenesse, modesty, and candour; and withal at this time so seasonably needfull, as well towards the vindication of the Protestant party in generall, from the aspersions of Incommunicablenesse within it selfe, and Incompatiblenesse with Magistry; as of themselves in particular, both against misreportings from without, & some possible mistakings from within too: That however for mine own part I have appeared on, and doe still incline to the Presbyteriall way of Church Government, yet doe I think it every way fit for the Presse.*

It does not seem unreasonable to suppose that *An Apologeticall Narration* was prepared in advance of the impasse the authors thought inevitably would come in the debate on church government. Baillie says as much.[3] The Independents were a minority and regardless of the outcome it would be a polity that did not conform to their model. The succession of Sir Henry Vane the younger to leadership in Parliament following the death of John Pym on 8 December 1643 looks to be relevant as he was, unknown to the Scots, supportive of Independency. In these circumstances the dissenting brethren obviously thought a direct appeal to Parliament and thus also to community

---

1. *Catalogue of the Pamphlets, Books, Newspapers, and Manuscripts Relating to the Civil War, the Commonwealth, and Restoration collected by George Thomason, 1640–1661,* 2 vols. (London: British Museum, 1908), 1.304. Perhaps Thomason was able to obtain a copy from the printing which the dissenting brethren were holding in reserve?

2. Paul, *Assembly of the Lord,* 206–209.

3. "At last, forseeing they behooved, ere long to come to the point, they put out in print, on a sudden, an Apologeticall Narration of their way, which had long lyen readie beside them, wherein they peition the Parliament, in a most slie and cunning way, for a toleration…." Baillie to William Spang, 18 February 1644, in *Letters and Journals,* Vol. II 129f.

discussion was a good strategy even though it seems inconsistent with the procedural rules Parliament had established for the Assembly. Rule 7 read:

> No man to be denied to enter his Dissent from the Assembly, and his reasons for it, in any Point, after it hath first been debated in the Assembly; and thence, if any dissenting Party desire it, to be sent to the Houses of Parliament (not by any particular Man, or Men, in a private Way) when either House shall require it.[1]

The content of the pamphlet was modestly expressed. It reminded readers that the authors had been exiled for their opinions in time past but had only sought to establish all practice on the basis of Scripture. They sought to disassociate the Independents from any revolutionary attitude toward the civil magistrate, to distance them from sectaries and simply to plead for toleration for their position within any new government that might be established for the Church of England. They note that they were not opposed to presbytery and synods as advisory gatherings but rejected any binding power beyond the local church, and limited powers of discipline to admonition and withdrawal of fellowship. They did, however, give a power to the magistrate in religious matters. They claimed that power was as great if not greater than the Presbyterians would allow.

The strong reaction against *An Apologeticall Narration* was because it rejected the idea of uniformity aimed at in the Solemn League and Covenant. When the Scottish army entered England on the side of Parliament on 18 January 1644 the commitment in the Covenant was only highlighted and the prestige of the Scots boosted. The day of the announcement of that event to the Assembly (29 January)[2] was also the day in which the stage was set for the Grand Debate since it marked the continuation of a debate urged by Parliament on the power of preaching presbyters in London to ordain. The nub of the issue was whether the London ministers were to ordain as, in effect, a regional presbytery, a position opposed by the Independents. On Friday 2 February this was put to one side and the fundamental issue of Presbyterian government began to be addressed.

III. The Grand Debate

The debate began on 2 February 1644. Three propositions had been brought forward by the Grand Committee which had been established to facilitate Parliament overseeing its obligation to the Scots. The Committee consisted of the Scots' commissioners and representatives of Parliament and the Assembly. The three propositions were:

---

1. Lightfoot, 4.
2. Lightfoot, 130.

1. That there is a presbytery holden forth in the New Testament.
2. That it consists of pastors and other church governors [ie. elders].
3. That the Scripture holds forth that many particular congregations may be under one presbyterial government.

The Independents did not object to the first two propositions since they could interpret them in accordance with their view about the local church. The third proposition brought the issue very clearly into the open.

Timeline of the Grand Debate[1]

The Grand Debate is made up of five sections. Sections one and two debate proofs of the third proposition just noted, the third debates a proposition concerning subordination of synods, the fourth concerns the power of ordination, and the last contains papers from the committee for accommodation.

    I. Presbyteries proved from the churches at Jerusalem.
    II. Presbyteries proved from the churches at Ephesus.
    III. Subordination of Church Synods.
    IV. Ordination (specifically that it should be done by a presbytery).
    V. Committee for Accommodation.

The debate of these subjects do not follow a neat outline and are interwoven, as the divines had to often change and/or go back to topics due to the dictates of Parliament. The discussion in the *Minutes* are as follows:

17 October 1643. The Assembly voted to take up the question of church government. It was agreed over the objections of the Independents to begin with the offices of the church, to stave off the contention over Presbyterianism as long as possible.[2]

January 1643/44. There is a gap in the minutes from 21 December 1643 until 14 February 1643/44,[3] making invaluable the notes of Gillespie[4] and Lightfoot. Because of the need to begin filling the many pulpits vacated by defectors to the King and those sequestered by the Parliament, the

---

1. The contribution of Chris Coldwell to this section down to and inclusive of the section entitled "The Publication of *The Grand Debate*" is gratefully acknowledged.

2. John R. de Witt, *Jus Divinum. The Westminster Assembly and the Divine Right of Church Government* (Kampen: J.H. Kok, 1969; repr. Naphtali Press, 2010), 63–64.

3. At this time England (but not Scotland) was still using the Julian Calendar, which set 25 March as the first of the year. Dates from 1 January to 25 March for this time period are given showing both year designations (e.g. 13 March 1644/45).

4. "Notes of Debates and Proceedings of the Assembly of Divines and other Commissioners at Westminster, February 1644 to January 1646," ed. David Meek, *The Presbyterian's Armoury, The Works of George Gillespie* (Edinburgh: Robert Ogle, and Oliver & Boyd, 1846).

Assembly began debating the subject of ordination. However, it quickly became apparent that the subject of Presbyterian government had to be addressed first.

19 January 1643/44. It was during the disputation on ordination that "Dr. Burgess reported out from the first committee two propositions concerning the wider question of a classical presbytery." 1. That the Scripture holds out a presbytery in a church (1 Tim. 4:14; Acts 15:2, 4, 6). 2. That a presbytery is made up of ministers of the word, "and such other public officers, as have been already voted to have a share in the government in the church."[1]

22 January 1643/44. A third proposition was added to the previous two, "That there may be many congregations under one presbytery, as in the church at Jerusalem."[2]

2 February 1643/44. After more than a week with "the urging of Lord Saye the Assembly set aside the matter of the 'London ministers' ordination' and began to treat of the proposition brought in by the committee 'concerning many churches under one presbytery.'"[3] It was voted to begin debate on Monday, 5 February 1643/44.

I—THE CHURCH AT JERUSALEM

5 February to 13 March 1643/44. The Assembly debated the third proposition from the proof of the church of Jerusalem. On 8 March a committee was formed to see if an accommodation could be reached between Presbyterians and Independents over whether "many congregations may be under one presbiteriall government,"[4] and permitted it to keep meeting to seek such an accommodation on 14 March.[5] This committee reported some progress on points of agreement on 21 March.[6]

IV—ORDINATION

15 March 1643/44 to 3 April 1644. In Session 178 the subject of ordination came up again and on 3 April Cornelius Burges presented "twelve propositions which summarized the Assembly's votes on the subject." A House of Lords order came in urging "the assembly to begin a directory for ordination, and a committee was appointed to review the work of the grand committee on the subject. The assembly's doctrinal propositions concerning ordination were set aside as the gathering turned its attention

---

1. de Witt, 101; cf. Lightfoot, 115–116.
2. de Witt, 101; cf. Lightfoot, 115–116.
3. de Witt, 102.
4. *Minutes*, 2.599.
5. *Minutes*, 2.617.
6. *Minutes*, 2.636.

to presbyteries."[1] The Assembly had voted 25 March "that 'The power of ordering the whole act of ordination is in the whole presbytery' and that this ordination should be conducted by preaching presbyters from neighbouring churches."[2]

I—THE CHURCH AT JERUSALEM (CONTINUED)

4 April 1644. The Assembly reviewed what they had resolved concerning presbyteries and ordered the scribes to arrange them logically. In a change of argument, the Independents dismissed the proofs from the church of Jerusalem because the members and officers were fluid, while the British context was one of fixed membership and officers. This held the Divines in debate until 10 April when the majority voted the question was irrelevant. "In Session 197 the assembly was presented with its votes on presbyteries."[3] The Independents "threatened to send a minority report if the votes were submitted to parliament." Another committee for accommodation was established.[4]

11 April 1644. The subject returned to whether the churches of Jerusalem were fixed or fluid and if that was material to Presbyterian ordination. They put off sending their "votes on Presbyterian church government to the two houses of parliament until its directory for ordination" was finished.[5] The partial draft for a directory for church government (those resolutions logically ordered by the scribes) apparently dates to this time. This partial draft was not sent to the Parliament until 8 November 1644.

II—THE CHURCH AT EPHESUS

15 April 1644. The Assembly "voted that the fixed or not fixed nature of the congregations in the New Testament church is all one with respect to the truth of the proposition that presbyteries are to ordain ministers."[6] William Bridge brought up Acts 20 to prove the Independents' argument regarding fixed versus unfixed congregations. This brought the example of the church at Ephesus into debate, which the Presbyterians were keen to address. Herle remarked, "I am glad we are fallen upon this argument. It grants that of Ephesus to have many congregations."[7] The Scottish views had been communicated on 14 November 1643, before they had taken their seats as commissioners to the Assembly. On 24 January 1643, the Scots had presented a book to the Assembly clearing Scottish Presbyterianism from

---

1. *Minutes,* 2.662.
2. *Minutes,* 2.643.
3. *Minutes,* 2.665–680.
4. *Minutes,* 2.678.
5. *Minutes,* 2.681.
6. *Minutes,* 3.15.
7. *Minutes,* 3.16.

"miſtakes and prejudices,"[1] and the next day presented a paper "concerning their government," which amongſt other things defended presbyteries from the examples of "Jerusalem, Antioch, and Ephesus, Corinth, Rome."[2] On 14 February, Coleman had given a report from committee of "other three inſtances from Scripture for a Presbytery beside Jerusalem" (Corinth, Ephesus, and Antioch). At that time Gilleſpie noted: "These inſtances we had given in our second paper about church assemblies to the Committee of the Assembly, having firſt given only the inſtance of Jerusalem."[3]

IV—ORDINATION (CONTINUED)

17 April 1644. The doctrinal ſtatements on ordination were put in final form. Some of the Divines "argued that the votes [on ordination] should not be sent to parliament unless requeſted, or unless the assembly decided to submit them with a completed directory for ordination."[4]

18 April 1644. The directory for ordination was approved and voted to be sent to Parliament along with the twelve propositions on ordination. It was determined not to send up the votes regarding presbyteries.

II—THE CHURCH AT EPHESUS (CONTINUED)

25 April 1644. The Assembly voted to affirm that the church at Ephesus "proves many particular congregations may be under one presbytery."[5]

IV—ORDINATION (CONTINUED)

6 May to 13 May 1644. In debating additional propositions concerning church government, the Divines took up a twelfth proposition, "that no single congregation can assume sole power in elections, ordinations, censures, and judicial cases,"[6] which held their attention until 13 May. On 10 May, the majority voted "that no single congregation, which can conveniently join with others in association, may assume to itself all and sole power in ordination."[7] The topic of suſpension and excommunication held the Divines' attention, 20 May to 24 May, and the directory for worship from 27 May to 9 Auguſt.

14 Auguſt to 4 September 1644. The topic of ordination came up again because the Commons revised the Assembly's directory that had been given in to them and the two bodies argued over amendments and wording. On

---

1. *Reformation of Church Government in Scotland, cleered from some miſtakes and prejudices, by the Commissioners of the … Church of Scotland, now at London* (London: January 24, 1643/4).
2. Lightfoot, 119.
3. Gillespie, 18.
4. *Minutes*, 3.25.
5. *Minutes*, 3.33.
6. *Minutes*, 3.51.
7. *Minutes*, 3.72.

29 August it was urged that the Divines complete debating the directory for church government. On 4 September final votes on ordination were made and the Assembly resolved to take up church government by various levels of synods (which they did from 6 September to 23 September). Wording issues were resolved on the ordinance for ordination on 16 September.

V—COMMITTEE FOR ACCOMMODATION

Because of the sharp divide with Presbyterian views in the Assembly, there were private meetings initially, and then committees formed at various times to seek to accommodate the views of the Independent brethren. Gillespie records one formed by the Assembly in his entry for 8 March 1644 and reports six points agreed upon by both sides.[1] That early agreement was deceptive, as de Witt notes, "because the propositions stop short of that authoritative spiritual power which the presbyterians [*sic*] insisted appertained to the higher courts and assemblies of the church and by virtue of which discipline was possible, but which the Independents denied."[2] The Divines trudged on as outlined above when things came to a head once again.

13 September 1644. Parliament ordered "the Committee of Lords and Commons appointed to treat with the Commissioners of Scotland, and the Committee of the Assembly, to take into consideration the differences of the opinions of the members of the Assembly in point of church government, and to endeavor a union: and in case that cannot be done, to endeavor the finding out some way how far tender consciences, who cannot in all things submit to the same rule which shall be established, may be borne with according to the Word, and as may stand with the public peace; that so the proceedings of the Assembly may not be so much retarded" (*Infra*, 305).

20 September 1644. "At the meeting of the Grand Committee, after Mr Marshall had read the order of the House of Commons for endeavouring a union, and, if that be not possible, to consider how far tender consciences may be borne with.... It was put to the question, and concluded, To appoint a Sub-Committee for bringing in to this Committee the agreements and differences."[3] These agreements/differences make up the first pages of the last section of *The Grand Debate*.[4]

---

1. Gillespie, 36–37.

2. de Witt, 102.

3. Gillespie, 103–104.

4. While not noted in the *Minutes,* Dr. Van Dixhoorn confirmed to the editor that the reason these committee papers are not noted in his Calendar of Papers (*Minutes,* volume 5), is because they are technically not assembly productions (though written by a sub-committee made up of some of the divines), but a hybrid, being drawn up by a sub-committee of the Grand Committee (made up of representatives from both house of Parliament, the assembly and the Scottish commissioners).

The Assembly majority was not happy about this order. This committee met through mid October and produced nine points concerning church government as well as eight concerning classes and synods, all of which at the key points of difference the Independents registered their views and how they would understand or limit them (307–310). Through this committee the Independents nearly pulled off a complete subversion of the Assembly in settling the question of church polity by a direct appeal to parliament; it was only waylaid because the Commons suspended the committee when the Scots succeeded in taking Newcastle and applied political pressure.[1] For a time the Divines were able to avoid another attempt at accommodation. Shaw writes, "The fortunes of the war had for the moment declared in favour of presbytery, and for a time things went merrily on with the Assembly. That body even managed by a ruse to get rid at once of the presence and the opposition of its Independent members. On the 4th of April, 1645, it appointed the Dissenting Brethren to be a committee to bring in the whole Independent frame or platform of Church government. The Independents accepted the commission with averted faces, and for months practically withdrew from the Assembly on the pretext of being engaged on the drafting of this platform."[2]

III—SUBORDINATION OF CHURCH SYNODS

23 September to 2 October 1644. The Divines debated the subordination of ecclesiastical synods (congregational, classical, and synodical), concluding the scriptures teach such a subordination.[3]

THE DEBATES OVER CHURCH GOVERNMENT END

14 October to 25 October 1644. The Assembly took up again debating the draft directory for church government and the subject of excommunication. On the 25th an order came from the Commons to "send the directory for public worship and whatever had been voted about church government, even if incomplete."[4]

---

1. Shaw sketches how close the Independents through this committee came to subverting the Assembly and how events cut the attempt short. Shaw, 2.37–44. "On the 19th of October, 1644, Newcastle was taken by storm. Four days later, 23rd October, the Scotch Committee wrote an almost peremptory letter from the captured town, pressing upon the Parliament the prosecution of the matter of Church government and the repression of sectaries…. Under the incentive of it, the House of Commons ordered … the Treaty Committee should surcease [*cease*] to sit upon the order of the previous 13th September, concerning an accommodation, until the House should take further order therein. In Baillie's phrase 'the Commons voted over the Independents bellie [swollen body] the dissolving of that dangerous committee which these five weeks has vexed us.'" Shaw, 2.43–44. See more details in Baillie, *Letters & Journals*, 2.235–237.

2. Shaw, 2.44.

3. *Minutes*, 3.329–366.

4. *Minutes*, 3.426.

6/7 November 1644. Parliament again insisted the Divines send up what it had by way of a directory for church government. "The assembly, unwilling to send up its directory in progress, decided to send up its votes about Presbyterian church government which it completed on 11 April 1644. The congregationalists registered their negative votes to this decision."[1]

8 November 1644. "Cornelius Burges reported on his summary of the assembly's 'Third Proposition' on Presbyterian church government. The assembly voted to submit the paper under the title, 'Concerning some part of church government.'" The Congregationalists registered their dissents and requested permission from the Commons to submit a minority dissent on Presbyterian government.[2]

13 November 1644. The Commons informed the Assembly the Independents would be submitting a "minority report" regarding the third proposition (which they did on the 14th) and asked that it be forwarded to them upon delivery. The assembly decided to send Parliament the votes on church government and the additional proofs based upon the churches at Ephesus.[3]

PRODUCTION OF THE PAPERS MAKING UP THE GRAND DEBATE
The Assembly and Independents presented their several papers and dissents as follows (as presented in the five sections of *The Grand Debate*):

> I. The reasons of the dissenting brethren against the third proposition concerning presbyterial government, submitted to both houses of parliament, 14 November 1644.[4] This was published 5 February 1644/45 (the House so ordering at the assembly's expense).

> II. Reasons of the dissenting brethren against the proofs from the instance of the church of Ephesus, submitted to both houses of parliament, 12 December 1644.[5]

> III. The arguments of the dissenting brethren against the subordination of synods, submitted to both houses of parliament, 12 December 1644.[6]

> IV. The reasons of the dissenting brethren concerning the power that is in congregations [for ordination], 12 December 1644.[7]

---

1. *Minutes*, 3.439.
2. *Minutes*, 3.441.
3. *Minutes*, 3.446.
4. Document 38, MS extant, WCL Braye, fos. 63r–108r, Calendar of Papers, *Minutes*, 5.111.
5. Document 47, MS not found, Calendar of Papers, *Minutes*, 5.141–142.
6. Document 48, MS not found, Calendar of Papers, *Minutes*, 5.143.
7. Document 49, MS not found, Calendar of Papers, *Minutes*, 5.144.

The Assembly submitted their "Draft directory for church government" to Parliament, 11 December 1644,[1] and submitted responses to the four papers of the dissenting brethren as follows, with the latter three well spaced out, with the urgency/pressure to bring in their answers subsiding:

> I. Answer to the reasons of the dissenting brethren against the third proposition concerning presbyterian government, submitted to both houses of parliament, 20 December 1644.[2]

> II. Answer to the reasons of the dissenting brethren against the instance of the church of Ephesus, 13 October 1645.[3]

> III. The Answer of the assembly of divines to the reasons of the dissenting brethren against the proposition concerning the subordination of congregational, classical, provincial, and national assemblies, 19 August 1646.[4]

> IV. An answer to the reasons of the dissenting brethren against the proposition concerning ordination, 19 April 1648.[5]

COMMITTEE FOR ACCOMMODATION REVIVED

17 November 1645. "In Session 536 the assembly received an order from the Lords and Commons to revive the committee for accommodation on church government (a committee comprised of members of the Lords, Commons and assembly, along with the Scottish commissioners)."[6] V. The papers produced for this committee take up the last section of *The Grand Debate*.

July 1645. The tide turned in the dissenting brethren's favor again with the victory of the New Model army at Naseby. The Presbyterians' hope lay in the dilemma facing the Independents between declaring only for a toleration for themselves or for every sect and heresy in the City of London.[7] They "evaded the dilemma by simply doing nothing at all."[8] When the Assembly asked on 22 September 1645 for the brethren to bring in their model for congregational church government, they instead brought in a paper giving

---

1. Document 45, MS extant, WCL Braye, fos. 1r–6v, Calendar of Papers, *Minutes*, 5.127

2. Document 52, MS extant, WCL Braye, fos. 63r–108r, Calendar of Papers, *Minutes*, 5.152–153.

3. Document 91, MS not found, Calendar of Papers, *Minutes*, 5.250–251.

4. Document 111, MS not found, Calendar of Papers, *Minutes*, 5.307.

5. Document 134, MS not found, Calendar of Papers, *Minutes*, 5.340.

6. *Minutes*, 3.709.

7. "If they declare against them [the sects] they [the Independents] will be but a small inconsiderable companie; if for them all honest men will cry out upon them for separating from all the Reformed Churches to joyne with Anabaptists and Libertines." Shaw, 46; Baillie, 2.299.

8. Shaw, 2.46.

reasons why they would not do so. The Assembly appointed a committee to answer what was viewed by the majority as a libel against Presbyterianism, which subsequently involved drafting a public reply to the 'unauthorized' publication of the Independent's reasons.[1] However, this contention was soon overtaken by events with the reviving by Parliament of the Committee for Accommodation.[2]

31 October, 1645. The Commons ordered the reviving of the 1644 Committee for Accommodation concerning church government with all the powers that had been given it at that time. This committee produced four papers by the brethren with four corresponding replies from the Assembly. Shaw sketches the history and unfolding of this last exchange on the subject of church polity between the dissenting brethren and the Presbyterian majority of the Assembly.

> The outline of this renewed committee's history may be briefly drawn.
> It met on the 17th of November, 1645, for a first time in the Jerusalem
> Chamber, and ordered the Divines of the Assembly who had formerly
> been a sub-committee to again act in that capacity, and to draw mat-
> ter for debate. A week later (24th of November) the sub-committee
> reported that they had not succeeded in preparing matter for debate,
> because the Dissenting Brethren, waiving or rejecting the first part of
> the order which concerned an accommodation, insisted on the second

---

1. The brethren's paper was published as *A copy of a Remonstrance lately delivered in the assembly.... Declaring the grounds and reasons of their declining to bring in to the assembly, their model of church-government* (London: 1645). The answer was published as *The answer of the Assembly of Divines.... Unto the reasons given in to this assembly by the dissenting brethren, of their not bringing in a model of their way* (London: John Field for Ralph Smith, 1645). See papers 92 and 99, Van Dixhoorn, 5.252–256, 264–296. Though soon overtaken by the reviving of the Committee for Accommodation, this exchange was important. "Delivered to the House of Lords and to a committee of the House of Commons, this answer [Document 99] presents a lengthy counter-narrative to the *Remonstrance* of the dissenting brethren (Document 92). The assembly found the *Remonstrance* galling and the majority argued that the congregationalists constantly criticized the Presbyterian system without producing one of their own.... Document 99 is important, among other reasons, for providing chronologies of events and for preserving responses and position papers of the assembly as well as papers of individual congregationalists and a congregationalist committee." Ibid., 5.264.

2. See de Witt's detailing of the *Remonstrance* and *Answer*, 155–161. "Following hard upon the *Remonstrance*, and while the Assembly was in a dangerously divided state on this account, came an order from Parliament setting in motion once more the machinery of accommodation after a lapse of more than a year. The committee of Lords, Commons, and divines had the now almost hopeless task of bringing together two parties apparently irreconcilably sundered. Its mandate was the same as before: *i.e.* to endeavour a union if possible, and if that could not be done to find out some way by which tender consciences might be borne with according to the Word. The first meeting was held on 17 November in the Jerusalem Chamber, and the same sub-committee that had functioned during the previous negotiations a year before was appointed to prepare materials for the debate of the committee...." Ibid., 161.

part of it which concerned a toleration [first paper, 311], and that not only for themselves but for the other sects. Thereupon Goodwin, Nye, Simpson, Bridge and Burroughs were requested to bring in their desires Concerning Church government. On the 4th of December they accordingly presented such their desires [Second Paper, 311–312]:

1. Ordination to be permissibly performed by sufficiently qualified persons in case there be no presbytery.

2. Their congregations to be exempt from Classical, Provincial and National Synods in respect of jurisdiction.

3. Liberty to form congregations.

After a whole day's debate, this paper of the Dissenting Brethren's desires was referred to the sub-Committee of Divines [for the committee]. On the 15th of December, the latter body presented an answer to the paper of desires [sub-committee's answer to the second paper, 307–315]. This answer was handed to the Dissenting Brethren, and on the 23rd they in turn brought in their answer to that answer [Third paper, 315–324].[1] After debate of this latter paper, the committee resolved that those who agreed with the Directory and the doctrine of the Reformed Churches should have the benefit of the indulgence, otherwise not.

The sub-committee was ordered as before to consider the Dissenting Brethren's answer, and then the committee itself adjourned. It did not meet again for nearly a month, until the 23rd of January, 1645–46....

On the 23rd of January the committee sat again, and received from the sub-committee its reply to the Dissenting Brethren's answer [answer to the third paper, 324–353].

At the succeeding meeting of 2nd of February, 1645–46, the Dissenting Brethren brought in a reply and a second part of the answer of the sub-committee of 15th of December preceding [Fourth paper, *Infra*, 353–356].

The committee met again, and for the last time, on the 9th of March,

---

1. "We have had many bickerings with the Independents in the Grand Committee about ane indulgence for their separate congregations. We have spent many sheets of paper on both sydes. They have given us wryte thrice and we have also oft answered in wryte. They are on their fourth wryte; to that we must give a fourth rejoinder and then come to debate verbally. For this point both they and we contend *tanqtuam pro aris et focis* [as for home and hearth]. Baillie, *Letters & Journals,* 2.349–350.

1645–46. The sub-committee presented an answer to the laſt-named paper of the Dissenting Brethren [reply to Fourth Paper, *Infra*, 357–376].

17 March, 1645/46. The laſt notice of this famous Committee for Accommodation is given by Robert Baillie.

> The Independents has the leaſt zeale to the truth of God of any men we know. Blaſphemous heresies are now ſpread here more than ever in any part of the world; yet they are not only silent but are patrons and pleaders for libertie almoſt to them all. We and they have ſpent many sheets of paper upon the tolleration of their separate Churches. At the laſt meeting we concluded to ſtop our paper debates and on Thursday next to begin our verball diſputation againſt the lawfulness of their desired separation. When we have ended, the Houses will begin to consider this matter. The moſt there and in the armie will be for too great a libertie; bot the Asemblie, the city and the body of all the miniſtrie in the kingdome are passionatelie opposite to such an evident breach of our Covenant. What the Lord will make the issue a little time will now declare.[1]

The verbal debate that was to proceed never happened. "After the delivery of this paper, the committee of Lords and Commons, and the Assembly of Divines adjourned to a day, but being diverted by other occasions, have not since had any meeting, and so there was no further proceeding in that business" (p. 376).

PUBLICATION OF *THE GRAND DEBATE*

The Lords ordered on 24 January 1647/48 that the collection of papers that would make up *The Grand Debate* be published,[2] ordering 3 February that Goodwin and Whitaker have liberty to look over and approve the same. The laſt paper answering the dissent on ordination apparently had not been produced yet; it was a couple of months before it came from committee before the Assembly to approve, which they did on 19 April 1647/48. The papers from the committees for accommodation were published in a volume of 123 pages on 5 May 1644, without a printer noted on the title page ("*London*, Printed *Anno Dom.*" 1648).[3] The dissents with the Assembly's answers were published in a volume of 212 pages on 6 May 1648 by T.R. and

---

1. Baillie, 2.361.

2. *Minutes*, 4.726.

3. *Papers Given in to the Honorable Committee of Lords and Commons and Assembly of Divines with the Commissioners of Scotland, for Accommodation, 1644, by a sub-committee of Divines of the Assembly and Dissenting Brethren* (London: Printed *Anno Dom.*, 1648). Except for the first few pages, the book is made up of papers prepared for the revised committee of 1645.

E.M. for Humphrey Howard[1] (211 pages plus a final page of errata).[2] The 1648 publication was reissued in 1652 with a new main title page as *The Grand Debate concerning Presbitery and Independency by the Assembly of Divines convened at Westminster by authority of Parliament.*[3]

THE SUBSTANCE OF THE DEBATE

The background already given will provide an orientation to the debate. Before providing an overall assessment the following brief overview of the main stages of the debate is provided.[4] It is important to recognise that at this period there were recognised rules of scholastic debate which did not include being gentle with your opponent. Powell rightly notes that the "methodology of scholastic disputation utilising Aristotelian syllogisms as a preferred rhetorical tool, heightens the complexity of studying the Westminster minutes."[5] The Divines were not scholastics in the strict sense but they used the scholastic tools almost universal in disputation in their day.

The Grand Debate is made up of four sections dealing with propositions passed by the Westminster Assembly, and a fifth containing papers drafted for the committee of accommodation. The first and second sections concern the famous Third Proposition.

I. The dissenting brethren begin by offering the negative case to this proposition, **"That the Scripture holds forth that many particular congregations may be under one presbyterial government."** Their argument proceeded on the basis that every pastor and elder must know, watch and care for the

---

1. *The Reasons Presented by the Dissenting Brethren against certain Propositions concerning Presbyteriall Government. And the proofs of them voted by the Assembly of Divines, sitting by authority of Parliament, at Westminster. Together with the Answer of the Assembly of Divines to those Reasons of Dissent* (London: Printed by T. R. and E. M. for Humphrey Harward, 1648).

2. Thomason, 1.617. While some libraries apparently hold examples of the committee papers as a separate publication, the majority of examples held are noted as one volume (cf. www.worldcat.org). It is clear that, though they were produced separately, the two volumes were intended to be a set. Apart from the order of the Parliament which implies this, the signature letters indicate they were to be considered in series. While Thomason bought the 211 page work second, its signatures are lettered A through Fff. The committee papers Thomason bought on the fifth begin the signature lettering with Aaaa. Though not consecutive (picking up at Ggg), if it were a separate publication the last section would have begun with A. This numbering indicates the anonymous printer knew the last section could begin with Aaaa.

3. *The grand debate concerning Presbitery and independency by the Assembly of Divines convened at Westminster by authority of Parliament concerning first the assemblies propositions (with the proof of them from Scripture) concerning the presbiteriall government, secondly the Dissenting Brethrens reasons against the said propositions, thirdly the answer of the assemblies to those reasons of dissent / examined and perused by Jer. Whitaker, Tho. Goodwin* ([London]: Printed for Anthony Williamson ..., 1652). While the title page is dated 1652, the text is the 1648 printing.

4. For more detailed coverage see Robert S. Paul, *Assembly of the Lord*, 249–357; John R. de Witt, *Jus Divinum*, 100–138.

5. Hunter Powell, "October 1643: The Dissenting Brethren," 54.

flock over which the Holy Spirit had made him an overseer. In other words the primary relationship between elder and congregation of worship and discipline could not be separated, and one was not required to obey someone who did not sustain this direct pastoral relationship (pp. 63–74).[1]

The response of the Assembly was that this argument proved too much, and did not properly recognise the unity of the body of Christ, and that association of congregations—not to hurt or destroy but to help and strengthen for the common good—is consonant with Christ's institution, and without such association much division and confusion arises. The authority of elders is ministerial, not lordly, and their commission is not only for the congregation over which they are appointed but also for those duties for the whole church wherever and so long as they have a call. Clearly there is a measure of reaction from the episcopal system, under which the dissenting brethren had suffered in exile. In that system there were many who demanded obedience who had no real relation to the people of the parish, and they were treated as servants and vassals rather than brothers and friends (pages 99–114).

After presenting their negative case to the proposition, the brethren presented objections to the first proof of the third proposition, **the example of the church at Jerusalem.**

The first assertion was that there was more than one church in Jerusalem, which the dissenting brethren denied and the Assembly affirmed.

The dissenting brethren argued that the church at Jerusalem, consisting of at least some 5,000 persons, could have met as one church, since it was not proven that such a number could not meet in one place, while, in any event, the scattering of believers as a consequence of the persecution mentioned in Acts 8:1 reduced the number of believers in Jerusalem considerably. Further, it was no argument that the apostles would not have had much preaching to do if there was only one congregation at Jerusalem, for the apostles are recorded as constantly involved in preaching and teaching not only in the temple but 'from house to house', not just on the weekly day of worship. And finally, the diversity of languages evident at Pentecost and later does not mean there was not a common language. Indeed, the fact that the church, including both Greek and Hebrew speaking Jews, met together and elected deacons must mean that the speakers of the different languages had enough in common for a distinct congregation for each to be unnecessary (pages 74–82).

The Assembly responded that all the dissenting brethren offered was evidence that at some times and some places all the believers met together as one congregation, such as for electing deacons (Acts 6) or to resolve a problem (Acts 15), but this does not prove that they did not meet in separate

---

1. Robert S. Paul, *Assembly of the Lord,* 261.

congregations at other times. Indeed, we read that they 'broke bread', generally taken as a reference to the Lord's Supper, from house to house (Acts 20:7). The language concerning the persecution cannot be pressed to conclude that only one congregation was left after the scattering. Public gatherings may have been limited, but meetings in private homes would have continued, and increased once the persecution ceased, if we may judge from Acts 9:31; 12:24. The activity of the apostles is acknowledged but for the more efficient instruction of the converts it is only reasonable to suppose the many thousands were divided into several congregations, and that preaching in the temple was to the crowds who gathered, whereas the proper church meetings were in private homes. That the gift of tongues was not given simply to instruct the hearers is granted. Greek was the common tongue and it is denied that the Hebrew language was generally understood by ordinary people. In any event, the distinction between the two sections mentioned in connection with the election of deacons is in essence a cultural one not a language one: Grecian Jews and Hebraic Jews. In that election there is no proof that the actual choice occurred at a single meeting of all the believers. Given the number of the believers and the diversity of their background, it is more reasonable to think that the candidates were first nominated after consultation with the congregations to which they belonged (pages 114–142).

The second assertion was that all those congregations at Jerusalem were under one presbyterial government. This was affirmed by the Assembly and denied by the dissenting brethren.

The dissenting brethren agreed there was one presbyterial government but insisted that this did not prove the assertion since the number of believers was not greater than could meet as one congregation, and formed in fact only one church. There was no mention of elders prior to the dispersion recorded in Acts 8, and the Assembly had not positively affirmed proof from evidence after the dispersion (pages 82–83).

The Assembly responded that, even supposing the number of believers was such as all could meet as a single congregation, this was no proof they did so, since for practical reasons they may have met in smaller congregations. As regards the presence of elders, the examples after the dispersion prove the case, while the lack of express detail about the appointment of elders before the dispersion does not prove there were none. There are reasonable grounds to conclude that the apostles did set apart elders very early (pages 142–144).

The third assertion was that the apostles did the ordinary acts of presbyters as presbyters in the Jerusalem church which proves a presbyterial government in that church before the dispersion. The dissenting brethren denied this and the Assembly affirmed it.

The dissenting brethren argued that what the apostles did, they did as apostles, so that no pattern for eldership is provided. While apostleship included eldership, the latter was based on the former. The apostles had a universal ministry, and if made the pattern for eldership this would infer that elders have the same. Indeed, episcopacy would have a better case than presbytery (pages 83–86).

The Assembly responded that it was really enough to prove many congregations and one presbyterial government. However, the apostles are elsewhere called elders, the acts of the apostles concerning the church at Jerusalem did not go beyond the power of elders, and the power of the apostles was not based on their power over all churches but on the union of congregations in one church. The insistence that what the apostles did they did as apostles, so as to provide no example to us, proves too much, for then elders would not be able to preach, take care of church funds or ordain office-bearers (pages 144–151).

The fourth assertion was that the elders of the Jerusalem church met together for acts of government proving the several congregations were under one government. The dissenting brethren denied it and the Assembly affirmed it.

The dissenting brethren rejected the argument brought from Acts 11:30 and Acts 21:17ff. on the grounds that receiving alms and greeting Paul are not acts of government. As regards the meeting in Acts 15:4, 6, 22, no meeting of elders can have authoritative power over other than the church to which they belong. The meeting was not a synod, for a synod only has jurisdiction in regard to churches that have sent commissioners. If it had authority it was from the apostles as apostles not the elders. In fact it appeared merely to provide an opinion, not deliver an authoritative judgment (pages 86–93).

The Assembly responded that the argument from the passages in Acts had been misconstrued, the mere receiving of alms was not the only act as its distribution would have to be decided, while Acts 21:17ff sufficiently proves there was a presbytery in Jerusalem. If the presbytery met to welcome Paul how much more for acts of government! As regards Acts 15 it is clear that the apostles did not act as apostles but as elders, and in such a way as provides an example for us. The meeting was a synod and its decisions bound the churches, and attempts to prove otherwise are unavailing (pages 151–162).

Two other statements for the proof of the fourth assertion were included in the proof of the Third Proposition. (a) *And whether these congregations were fixed or not fixed, in regard to officers or members, it is all one to the truth of the proposition.* (b) *Nor does there appear any material difference between the several congregations at Jerusalem, and the many congregations now in the ordinary condition of the church, as to the point of fixedness in regard of officers or members.*

The dissenting brethren claimed that the church at Jerusalem consisted of people with a verifiable conversion experience with elders over them, and that this was considerably different from an organised church based on a parish system. They also argued that before the election of elders the apostles would have been in a very anomalous position if they were each tied like parish ministers to particular congregation. They added some comments as to the impropriety of a regional presbytery over a congregational presbytery since there is no express specification of such in Scripture (pages 93–98).

The Assembly responded that the principle of presbyterial government over a number of congregations is the point contended for and not whether congregations were territorial or of gathered visible saints. If there were parish elders in Jerusalem it does not follow that the apostles were also tied to a parish. Nor does the absence of a specific title prove that there are not two kinds of presbyteries, congregational and regional (pages 163–174).

It was therefore concluded from the example of the church at Jerusalem that many congregations may be under one presbyterial government.

II. The second section of the Grand Debate concerns the second point of proof to the Third Proposition to similar effect, namely, **"That there were more congregations than one in the church of Ephesus under one presbyterial government &c."** The Assembly advanced three propositions—1. the multitude of believers made more than one congregation; 2. over those multiple congregations as one flock, there were many elders; 3. these multiple congregations were one church in one presbytery. The dissenting brethren only addressed the first of these propositions. The Scripture proofs adduced by the Assembly for that first proposition were: the effect of Paul's three year stay at Ephesus (Acts 20:31), the great effect the Word had at Ephesus with converts destroying books worth 50,000 pieces of silver (19:18–20); that there were both Jewish and Greek converts (19:10, 17); the reason given for Paul's stay until Pentecost, that "a great and effectual door was opened" (1 Cor. 16:9–9); and the mention of another church in the house of Aquila and Priscilla (18:19; 24:26). The dissenting brethren in brief arguments rejected the assertions: 1. that the effect of the Word would be so great that even if there were several thousand converts, they could not all meet as one church, 2. that the 50,000 pieces of silver was for many rather than a few valuable books, 3. that the church in the house of Aquila and Priscilla was distinct from one single congregation, and 4. that there needed to be more than one church due to the different languages of the Jews and Greeks. They then concluded by making a case contrary to the proposition "That the multitude of believers were not more than could meet in one place" (pages 175–178).

The Assembly responded to the brethren's brief rebuttals, 1. regarding the number of believers at Ephesus (180–186); 2. the price of the books burned

(186–189); 3. the church in the house of Aquila and Priscilla (189–193); and 4. the diversity of languages (193–194). They then spent the remaining sixty percent of their answer addressing the brethren's case that the number of believers were not more numerous than could meet in one place, and there was not one body of elders caring for several congregations (195–204).

III. The third section of the Grand Debate concerns the Assembly's proposition regarding **the existence of provincial, nation and ecumenical synods and the subordination of congregations to superior assemblies.** The dissenting brethren allowed occasional synods for encouragement and advice but rejected the ordinary use of synods because they lacked the very express warrant in Scripture that such would need in their view. They further rejected belief that synods had authority or jurisdiction over congregations. Four syllogistic arguments were presented by the dissenting brethren: 1. that such courts must have an express warrant from Scripture; 2. such courts necessarily imply there is no independency except in an ecumenical council (since on Presbyterian principles such a council as final court of appeal may err); 3. a "church power which cannot show a constant divine rule for its variation and subordination, and ultimate independency, is not of God"; and 4. there is no Scriptural warrant for a polity which must produce "representations of spiritual power out of other representations, with a derived power therefrom." The brethren conclude with specific arguments rejecting the proofs from Acts 15 and Matthew 18 (pages 207–223).

Clearly weary, the Assembly began their response with eight premises which noted that much of the brethren's argumentation was common to that concerning many congregations under one presbyterial government; that they only denied the standing use of synods (yet none of their arguments were directed toward that, but toward the subordination of synods); that they acknowledged enough concerning synods to give *sufficient* warrant for them, that such are agreeable with Scripture (the Assembly's argument was not for synods by express *jure divino* institution); and that their arguments actually undermine their own allowance of elective synods. The Assembly's stance was that if it was granted that occasional use is lawful then, considering the many common issues that arise, there was justification for the regular use of synods. The substance of the brethren's argumentation was misdirected. The question was not whether synods are expressly instituted *jure divino,* but whether they are *agreeable* to the word of God, and thus warranted. They then proceed with answering the four arguments presented by the brethren before concluding with two sections answering their objections to the use of Acts 15 and Matthew 18 as proofs for the proposition for the subordination of church courts (pages 224–272).

IV. The fourth section of the Grand Debate concerns the Assembly's proposition that **"it is very requisite [appropriate], that no single congregation that can conveniently associate [with other churches] should**

assume to itself all and sole power in ordination." This was a vital question given the pressing practical circumstances in England. The dissenting brethren argued that a sufficient body of elders, even two or three, in a single congregation may ordain and that while they may associate with other elders, that does not change the power of the elders in the single congregation (pages 275–277).

Before responding to these arguments, the Assembly again prefaced their remarks, this time noting with clear disapproval the apparent disingenuousness of the brethren's method in objecting to the proposition by putting forth the arguments of others not of Congregationalist views, rather than their own.[1] The Assembly then answered the arguments at some length by pointing out inconsistencies in the position of the dissenting brethren. They also considered that ordination of ministers was of such importance to the general good of the church that where more elders could be had it was appropriate; that to ordain without consulting with or even against the opinion of neighbouring churches was inappropriate; and that even if a congregational eldership was sufficient the opportunity for appeal should exist to a wider body of elders (pages 278–302).

THE DEBATE IN THE COMMITTEE FOR ACCOMMODATION.
The fifth and last section of the Grand Debate contains the papers created by the dissenting brethren and a sub-committee of the Assembly for the committee of accommodation. The Independents' first paper was simply a notification they rejected an accommodation and would press for a toleration of their separate churches. They were then ordered to bring in a paper expressing what they desired "to be borne with in point of church government, in all those things wherein they cannot submit unto the common rule that is established" (page 311).

The desires of the brethren expressed in their second second paper were 1. Freedom to ordain where there is no presbytery. 2. Freedom of their congregations from the jurisdiction of the Presbyterian system of presbyteries and synods. 3. Freedom to form congregations without restriction (pages 311–312). The Presbyterian reply to this second paper (313–315) opens with a preface chastising the brethren for choosing schism over an accommodation, followed by three premises: 1. That whatever forbearance is given, all would be under the same Confession of Faith and Directory for Worship. 2. That those sects not agreeing with these or the doctrine of the Reformed

---

1. The assembly expected their brethren to "prove, that 'every single congregation' (whether there be in it a sufficient or insufficient presbytery, or none at all) 'have the whole power of ordination within themselves;' and that none but themselves may ordain for them (for we suppose our brethren, or at least some of them, are of this opinion), but this they are pleased to decline" (p. 278). It should be noted that the passage of this proposition involved one of the most contentious debates of the assembly, and passed by only eight votes (de Witt, 125–126).

churches should not be given a forbearance of toleration. 3. Any person opposing the settled doctrine of the church should face the same discipline as those not separated from the established church. The reply then goes on to address the brethren's third proposition requesting to not be under the authority of any presbytery, desiring that the brethren not be simply granted this on their own terms, 1. because it is "a plain and total separation" from settled government; 2. grants the gathering of churches from out of other true churches; 3. would destroy what parliament was endeavouring to build up; 4. grants greater privileges to those outside the settled church than those under it; 5. countenances a standing "schism and division in the church"; and brings "all manner of confusion in families where the members were of several churches." Secondly, they pled that none over simple matters of church government be allowed to separate from the worship wherein they are otherwise in agreement. Thirdly, they suggested that those with scruples who cannot partake of the Lord's Supper after conference with the minster and elders, not separate from the other parts of worship, concluding, that common folk (not officers) who cannot resolve their scruple over Congregationalist church government, "shall not be compelled to be under the power of censures from classis or synods: provided that they continue under the government of that congregation, and that no man who hath submitted to classis and synods shall decline them, in any case, *pendente lite* [*pending litigation*]."

This first round of relatively brief papers set the contents for those that followed as the debate expanded in points and counterpoints. The second round contains the brethren's third and longest paper (pages 315–324), which received a 30 page reply from the Presbyterian divines (324–353), and a fourth four page paper received a 20 page reply (357–376). The topics in dispute included the nature of the Solemn League and Covenant, schism and separatism, uniformity in doctrine, worship and government, and the integrity of the Dissenting brethren, who were charged with crass political maneuvering rather than an honest engagement; with employing delaying tactics (i.e. trusting that in time Cromwell would deliver a win for the minority over the majority of the Westminster Assembly); with catching at words rather than engaging in the substance of matters; and with refusing to actually put forward a Congregational model of church government for debate.

ASSESSMENT

As one reads the record of the debate both in the published form and in the Minutes, it is evident that to some extent both Independents and the various groups of Presbyterians tended to read Scripture in the light of their own experiences and backgrounds. The five dissenting brethren had gone into exile under episcopacy and naturally enough were wary of any authority beyond the congregation. The Scots had their Melvillian system of Presbyterianism well worked out, so that the situation in Jerusalem on the Day of Pentecost as described by Gillespie bore "an uncanny resemblance to seventeenth century Presbyterian Edinburgh or Glasgow."[1] Many of the English Puritans were extremely wary of the power of the people and the role of elders, and in this sense protective of the privileges of the 'clergy.' The few Erastians were concerned for the unity of the state so that in their thinking Royal supremacy was replaced by Parliamentary supremacy. All sides had a great deal invested in the outcome. Ultimately, Presbyterianism won out in the Assembly because episcopacy was excluded, the rise of various sects was extremely concerning on all sides, and there seemed no alternative that would meet the needs of a church for the nation. The Independents pled for tolerance within a Presbyterian structure but this was denied.[2]

So far as the substance of the debate is concerned, the Presbyterians clearly had the superior case since, while particular exegetical points might be strained, it was impossible to ignore the general principles arising from the nature of the church as the body of Christ, as well as the binding (and not just advisory) nature of scriptural decisions of synods on the churches. Of course the differing views on the nature of an Established Church to which all citizens would belong was very relevant in the participants' thinking. In a different political context there would have been a greater possibility of an accommodation between the Presbyterians and the Independents/Congregationalists. Thus, there are few Presbyterians today who would suggest that membership in a local church should be held by other than 'visible saints' (so long as we do not profess to read the heart but the profession), and they would agree with Jeremiah Burroughs and William Bartlett that birth into a nation with an Established Church should not automatically make one a member of the Church entitled to baptism.[3]

The final efforts towards the close of 1645 to achieve an accommodation in the end accomplished nothing.

> "In simple truth," says Shaw, "the same rigorous logic of events which had reduced the Presbyterians to entertain this negotiation at all had made the Independents too arrogant for it" [2.50]. Assessments of the

---

1. W. J. D. McKay, *An Ecclesiastical Republic: Church Government in the Writings of George Gillespie* (Carlisle: Paternoster Press, 1997), 271.

2. James Bannerman's comment is noteworthy: "In recoiling from the extreme and often dangerous positions taken up by not a few of the Independents, it was not unnatural that men should be tempted to lean rather too much to High Churchism" (*The Church of Christ* [1869] Edinburgh: Banner of Truth, 1974, vol. 1, 266fn).

3. William Bartlett, *Ichnographia, or a Model of the Primitive Congregational Way* (London: H. Overton, 1647), 51–52, who cites Burroughs on this point.

controversy have been different according to the point of view taken up by the historian. Hetherington deals severely with the Independents and their *Remonstrance,* declaring that the *Answer* "certainly exposes their duplicity in a manner altogether unanswerable…."[1] Considered from the standpoint of party interest, the actions of the dissenting brethren were no doubt wise and foreseeing. Their political prospects were improving every day. Since the great victory of Cromwell and his New Model Army at Naseby on 14 June, 1645, the royalist cause was doomed—and that at the hands of the Independents! Parliament was not yet subservient to Cromwell, nor would it be till the presbyterians were thrust out in Pride's Purge, December, 1648, which deprived 143 members of their places. Hence, as they had long perceived, delay was in their favour, and any measure which tended to such delay served their cause. But the Westminster Assembly was not, despite its dependence upon Parliament, a political body met for political purposes, but an assembly of divines convened for religious purposes, according to the parliamentary ordinance calling it into existence and the Solemn League and Covenant. Before one praises Thomas Goodwin and his fellows for political perspicacity, therefore, one must remember the reason for their part in the Assembly and the work the Assembly had been assigned to do. Their task was not to seek political advantage, but to re-settle the English church. When that is remembered, perhaps the more credence can be given to the at first glance excessively harsh judgment of Hetherington than that of the enthusiastic Masson and others like him.[2]

The doctrine of the church embodied in the Assembly's *Confession of Faith* represents a careful statement. The influential Martin Bucer, mentioned at the beginning of this essay, did not define church polity so as to usurp the role of the state to be a nursing mother to the church, and this was a common position shared by those of Presbyterian persuasion, as well as Congregationalists.[3] There was thus no threat to proper royal supremacy even

---

1. See W. M. Hetherington, *History of the Westminster Assembly of Divines*, third edition (1856), 224. On the *Remonstrance* and *Answer* see the previous footnote 1 on page 39.

2. J. R. de Witt, *Jus Divinum*, 163–164.

3. Note *Savoy Declaration* 24.3: "Although the magistrate is bound to encourage, promote, and protect the professors and profession of the gospel, and to manage and order civil administrations in a due subserviency to the interest of Christ in the world, and to that end to take care that men of corrupt minds and conversations do not licentiously publish and divulge blasphemy and errors, in their own nature subverting the faith and inevitably destroying the souls of them that receive them: yet in such differences about the doctrines of the gospel, or ways of the worship of God, as may befall men exercising a good conscience, manifesting it in their conversation, and holding the foundation, not disturbing others in their ways or worship that differ from them; there is no warrant for the magistrate under the gospel to abridge them of their liberty." Note the parallel (not exact) in WCF 23.3. "Civil magistrates may not

though the argument that the church derived its power directly from Christ as king of the church, and that elders elected by the congregation governed alongside the ministers, were seen as hostile to that supremacy. Bucer had also emphasised that office in the church and the believing community were intimately related: the power of the church was granted to the universal people of God, but its administration rested with the teaching and ruling elders.[1] Reflecting his temperament as a man who avoided extremes and sought to reconcile polarised positions where possible, Bucer recognised a balance that in subsequent debate was not always maintained by others, but is countenanced by the *Confession* and in the *Form of Presbyterial Church Government*. Neither congregational independency or high-church presbyterianism receive endorsement in these documents, although there is a measure of compromise in the *Form* on the standing of the ruling elder so that he might be regarded as a lay representative rather than a true presbyter.[2]

Presbyterianism rightly rejects the idea that church power belongs exclusively to the church members, but it can readily admit that it belongs both to the office-bearers *and* to the whole body of believers: it is not either/or, but both/and, although for different purposes. In the *ordinary* course the office bearers administer church power, but in *extraordinary* cases the body of believers may exercise the power they have to, for example, call and ordain office-bearers when there are none. Bannerman considers this distribution of church power to be the position sanctioned by the Confession of Faith 25.2–3,[3] and it fits comfortably alongside Bucer. A comparison of the cited sections of the Confession with the corresponding sections in the Congregationalist *Savoy Declaration of Faith and Order* of 1658, drawn up by a Committee of John Owen, Thomas Goodwin, Philip Nye, William Bridge, Joseph Caryl and William Greenhill, bears out Bannerman's interpretation (see facing page and page LIV).[4]

---

assume to themselves the administration of the Word and sacraments, or the power of the keys of the kingdom of heaven: yet he hath authority, and it is his duty, to take order that unity and peace be preserved in the Church, that the truth of God be kept pure and entire, that all blasphemies and heresies be suppressed, all corruptions and abuses in worship and discipline prevented or reformed, and all the ordinances of God duly settled, administered, and observed. For the better effecting whereof, he hath power to call synods, to be present at them, and to provide that whatsoever is transacted in them be according to the mind of God." Cf. *Reformed Confessions of the 16th and 17th Centuries in English Translation, Volume 4: 1600–1693*, ed. James T. Dennison, Jr. (Grand Rapids: Reformation Heritage Books, 2014) 482–483, 262, .

   1. Willem van't Spijker, *The Ecclesiastical Offices…*, 295, 304, 470; cf. also R. E. H. Uprichard, "The Eldership in Martin Bucer and John Calvin," in *Evangelical Quarterly*, 61.1 (1989), 21–37.

   2. The Church of Scotland regarded the ruling elder as a true presbyter as in her *Second Book of Discipline* of 1578. Many of the English were not familiar with the working of the eldership hence a compromise wording. The *Form* secures the practical end leaving the theoretical underpinnings somewhat ambiguous. A useful overview is W. D. J. McKay, *An Ecclesiastical Republic*, 199–229.

   3. For an important discussion of the seat of church power see James Bannerman, 262–275

   4. Cf. The Westminster Confession of Faith (1646) and The Savoy Declaration (1658) in

WCF (1647) 25.

1. The catholic or universal Church, which is invisible, consists of the whole number of the elect, that have been, are, or shall be gathered into one, under Christ the head thereof; and is the spouse, the body, the fulness of him that filleth all in all.

2. The visible Church, which is also catholic or universal under the gospel (not confined to one nation as before under the law), consists of all those throughout the world that profess the true religion, together with their children; and is the Kingdom of the Lord Jesus Christ; the house and family of God, through which men are ordinarily saved and union with which is essential to their best growth and service.

3. Unto this catholic and visible Church, Christ hath given the ministry, oracles, and ordinances of God, for the gathering and perfecting of the saints, in this life, to the end of the world; and doth by his own presence and Spirit, according to his promise, make them effectual thereunto.

4. This catholic Church hath been sometimes more, sometimes less, visible. And particular Churches, which are members thereof, are more or less pure, according as the doctrine of the gospel is taught and embraced, ordinances administered, and public worship performed more or less purely in them.

5. The purest Churches under heaven are subject both to mixture and error: and some have so degenerated as to become apparently no Churches of Christ. Nevertheless, there shall be always a Church on earth, to worship God according to his will.

SDFO (1658) 26.

1. The catholic or universal Church, which is invisible, consists of the whole number of the elect, that have been, are, or shall be gathered into one, under Christ the head thereof; and is the spouse, the body, the fulness of him that filleth all in all.

2. The whole body of men throughout the world, professing the faith of the gospel and obedience unto God by Christ according to it, not destroying their own profession by any errors everting the foundation, or unholiness of conversation, are, and may be called the visible catholic church of Christ; although as such it is not entrusted with the administration of any ordinances, or have any officers to rule or govern in, or over the whole body.

3. The purest churches under heaven are subject both to mixture and error, and some have so degenerated as to become no churches of Christ, but synagogues of Satan: nevertheless Christ always hath had, and ever shall have, a visible kingdom in this world, to the end thereof, of such as believe in him, and make profession of his name.

WCF 31.

1. For the better government, and further edification of the Church, there ought to be such assemblies as are commonly called synods or councils.

2. As magistrates may lawfully call a synod of ministers, and other fit persons, to consult and advise with, about matters of religion; so, if magistrates be open enemies to the Church, the ministers of Christ, of themselves, by virtue of their office, or they, with other fit persons upon delegation from their Churches, may meet together in such assemblies.

3. It belongs to synods and councils, ministerially to determine controversies of faith, and cases of conscience; to set down rules and directions for the better ordering of the public worship of God, and government of his Church; to receive complaints in cases of maladministration, and authoritatively to determine the same; which decrees and determinations, if consonant to the Word of God, are to be received with reverence and submission; not only for their agreement with the Word, but also for the power whereby they are made, as being an ordinance of God appointed thereunto in His Word.

4. All synods or councils, since the apostles' times, whether general or particular, may err; and many have erred. Therefore they are not to be made the rule of faith, or practice; but to be used as a help in both.

5. Synods and councils are to handle, or conclude nothing, but that which is ecclesiastical: and are not to intermeddle with civil affairs which concern the commonwealth, unless by way of humble petition in cases extraordinary; or, by way of advice, for satisfaction of conscience, if they be thereunto required by the civil magistrate.

SDFO (1658) The Institution of Churches, and the Order Appointed in Them by Jesus Christ.

5. These particular churches thus appointed by the authority of Christ, and entrusted with power from him for the ends before expressed, are each of them as unto those ends, the seat of that power which he is pleased to communicate to his saints or subjects in this world, so that as such they receive it immediately from himself.

6. Besides these particular churches, there is not instituted by Christ any church more extensive or catholic entrusted with power for the administration of his ordinances, or the execution of any authority in his name.

26. In cases of difficulties or differences, either in point of doctrine or in administrations, wherein either the churches in general are concerned, or any one church in their peace, union, and edification, or any member or members of any church are injured in, or by any proceeding in censures, not agreeable to truth and order: it is according to the mind of Christ, that many churches holding communion together do by their messengers meet in a synod or council, to consider and give their advice in, or about that matter in difference, to be reported to all the churches concerned. Howbeit, these synods so assembled are not entrusted with any church-power, properly so called, or with any jurisdiction over the churches themselves, to exercise any censures, either over any churches or persons, or to impose their determinations on the churches or officers.

27. Besides these occasional synods or councils, there are not instituted by Christ any stated synods in a fixed combination of churches, or their officers in lesser or greater assemblies; nor are there any synods appointed by Christ in a way of subordination to one another.

The Grand Debate is at times both complex and tedious reading to us who come 370 years later and who live in an age of religious freedom and diversity. We may think that at times the members of the Assembly sought to prove too much or to use Scripture somewhat atomistically. We will recognise that the contentious political setting impacts the language and style, generally not for the better. Nevertheless, we cannot but admire the serious endeavour to base polity on the Word of God, and recognise that in leaving no stone unturned in their argumentation they have provided a great help in appreciating the issues at stake. We should also realise that the principles which the Puritans debated and the impact that they had on the politics of the day, laid the basis for the many of the freedoms we enjoy today.

AFTERWORD

Although Presbyterian polity was established in London and Lancashire in 1646, the Royalist assault on the Long Parliament in 1648 halted further organisation. Charles I was executed 30 January 1649, following his impeachment by the Rump Parliament, and Oliver Cromwell ruled as Lord Protector 1653–58. In 1650 the Scots declared Charles II king, and Cromwell invaded and subjugated Scotland in the following year. Oliver's ineffective son Richard succeeded him as Lord Protector but resigned in May 1659. Shortly before Charles II returned to England in May 1660, Parliament declared Presbyterianism the polity of the Church with toleration for tender consciences, but almost immediately it was a dead letter as the naïve Presbyterians soon found to their cost. Meanwhile, the followers of the Congregational way had not ignored the obligations of a wider fellowship. As early as 1652 Associations were formed in England for mutual fellowship, particularly among ministers, and for the purpose of ordaining ministers, although such associations were still voluntary and advisory in nature.[1] At least 1,760 ministers (20% of the total) were ejected from the Church of England in 1660–63, under the harsh Episcopal regime Charles somewhat stealthily re-introduced.[2] Of those ejected following the restoration of the monarchy, almost all were Puritans and the majority Presbyterians, with significant numbers of Congregationalists and Baptists as well. Let Richard Baxter have the last word. He wrote "… as far as I am able

---

Reformed Confessions of the 16th and 17th Centuries in English Translation, Volume 4: 1600–1693, 264–265, 270–271; and 484, 490, 494. At WCF 31.2, it should be remembered that the Church of Scotland in adopting the Confession in 1647 limited this section to churches that were not organized.

 1. Alan P. F. Sell, *Saints: Visible Orderly and Catholic. The Congregational Idea of the Church* (Geneva: World Alliance of Reformed Churches, 1986), 55–56.

 2. A. G. Matthews, *Calamy Revised: Being a Revision of Edmund Calamy's's Account of the Ministers and Others Ejected and Silenced, 1660–1662* (Oxford: Clarendon Press, 1988), xii–xiii.

to judge by the information of all history of that kind, and by any other evidences left us, the Christian world, since the days of the apostles, had never a synod of more excellent divines (taking one thing with another) than this [Assembly at Westminster] and the Synod of Dort." While faulting all sides, Baxter lays the blame mostly and severely on the dissenting brethren, who preferred to rend Christ's garment "all to pieces, rather than it should want their lace." [1]

Rowland S. Ward
Presbyterian Church of Eastern Australia
Melbourne
June 2014

---

1. *Reliquiæ Baxterianæ*, 73, 103.

THE GRAND DEBATE

REASONS AGAINST THE THIRD PROPOSITION
CONCERNING PRESBYTERIAL GOVERNMENT

THE ANSWER OF THE ASSEMBLY OF DIVINES UNTO THE
REASONS OF THE SEVEN DISSENTING BRETHREN, AGAINST
THE PROPOSITION OF DIVERS CONGREGATIONS BEING
UNITED UNDER ONE PRESBYTERIAL GOVERNMENT

Abbreviations

Baillie, *Dissuasive*	Robert Baillie, *A Dissuasive from the Errours of the Time*. London, 1645.
Baillie	*The Letters and Journals of Robert Baillie*, ed. David Laing, 3 volumes. Edinburgh: Printed for Robert Ogle, 1841–1842.
Beza, *Annotationes*	*Jesu Christi Domini Nostri Novum Testamentum, sive Novum Foedus … Annotationes….* Cambridge: Roger Daniel, 1642.
Calvin, *Commentaries*	*Calvin's Commentaries*, 45 volumes. Edinburgh: Calvin Translation Society, 1844–1856; repr. Grand Rapids: Baker Book House, 1983.
Cotton, *Way of N.E.*	John Cotton, *The way of the churches of Christ in New-England*. London, Matthew Simmons, 1645.
De Witt	J. R. De Witt, *Jus Divinum, The Westminster Assembly and the Divine Right of Church Government*. Kampen: Kok, 1969.
WFOG	"The Form of Presbyterial Church-Government and of Ordination of Ministers." In [Westminster] *The Confession of Faith*, etc. Edinburgh: Johnstone and Hunter: 1855.
Gillespie	"Notes of Debates and Proceedings of The Assembly of Divines and other Commissioners at Westminster. February 1644 to January 1646," ed. David Meek. In *The Presbyterian's Armoury, The Works of George Gillespie*. Edinburgh: Robert Ogle, and Oliver & Boyd, 1846.
Goodwin	Thomas Goodwin, *The Constitution, Right Order, and Government of the Churches of Christ*. In *Works*, volume 11. Edinburgh: James Nichol; London: James Nisbet, 1865.
Lightfoot	"The Journal of the Proceedings of the Assembly of Divines: From January 1, 1643, to December 31, 1644." In *The Whole Works of the Rev. John Lightfoot, D. D.*, vol. 13, ed. John Rogers Pitman, 13 volumes. London: Dove, 1824.
32 Questions	Richard Mather, et al., *Church-government and church-covenant discussed in …two and thirty questions*. London, 1643.
Minutes	*The Minutes and Papers of the Westminster Assembly 1643–1652*, ed. Chad Van Dixhoorn. 5 volumes. Oxford University Press, 2012.
PG	*Patrologiae cursus completus, series Graeca*, ed. J. P. Migne. 166 volumes. Petit-Montrouge, Apud J.-P. Migne, 1857–1866.
PL	*Patrologiae cursus completus*, series Latina, ed. J. P. Migne. 217 volumes. Petit-Montrouge, Apud J.-P. Migne, 1844–1855. Citations are from the original Migne printing; the pagination in the later Garnier reprint may vary.
NPNF1	*A Select Library of the Nicene and Post-Nicene Fathers, first series*, ed. Philip Schaff. Buffalo: The Christian Literature Company, 1886–1890.

THE PROPOSITIONS AS VOTED IN THE ASSEMBLY OF DIVINES

THE THIRD PROPOSITION

Concerning Presbyterial Government, as it was voted
in the Assembly and sent up to both the Honourable
Houses of Parliament

The Scripture does hold forth that many particular congregations may be under one Presbyterial government.

This Proposition is proved by instances.

[I.] 1. Instance, of the church of Jerusalem, which consisted of more congregations than one, and all those congregations were under one Presbyterial government.

This appears, thus,

i. The church of Jerusalem consisted of more congregations than one, as is manifest.

1. By the multitude of believers, mentioned in divers texts collated: Both before the dispersion of the believers there, by means of the persecution (mentioned in the Acts of the Apostles, chapter 8, in the beginning thereof). Witness Acts 1:11, and Acts 2:41, 46, 47, and Acts 4:4, and Acts 5:14 and Acts 6:1, 7. And also after the dispersion, Acts 9:31 and Acts 12:24, and Acts 21:20.

2. By the many apostles and other preachers in the church of Jerusalem. If there were but one congregation there, then each apostle preached but seldom, which will not consist with Acts 6:2.

3. The diversity of languages among the believers, mentioned both in the second and sixth chapters of the Acts, does argue more congregations than one in the church.

ii. All those congregations were under one presbyterial government, because,

1. They were one church, Acts 8:1 and Acts 2:47, compared with Acts 5:11, Acts 12:5 and Acts 15:4.

2. The elders of that church are mentioned Acts 11:30 and Acts 15:4, 6, 22 and Acts 21:17, 18.

Doc. 35. Third Proposition
Doc. 45. Draft Directory for Government
Minutes, vol. 5, 90–92, 134–136

3. The apostles did the ordinary acts of presbyters as presbyters in that church; which proves a presbyterial church before the dispersion, Acts 6.

4[/5]. The several congregations in Jerusalem being one church, the elders of the church are mentioned, as meeting together for acts of government (Acts 11:30 and Acts 15:4, 6, 22 and Acts 21:17, 18, and so forwards); which proves that these several congregations were under one presbyterial government.

[6.] And whether these congregations were fixed or not fixed, in regard of officers or members, it is all one as to the truth of the proposition.

Nor does there appear any material difference between the several congregations in Jerusalem, and the many congregations now in the ordinary condition of the church, as to the point of fixedness[1] in regard of officers or members. [7][2]

Therefore the Scripture does hold forth, that many congregations may be under on presbyterial government.

[II.] II. Instance of the church of Ephesus; for,

i. That there were more congregations than one in the church of Ephesus, appears by Acts 20:31, where is mention of Paul's continuance at Ephesus, in preaching for the space of three years; and Acts 19:18, 19, 20 where the special effect of the Word is mentioned, and verses 10 and 17 of the same chapter, where is a distinction of Jews and Greeks, and 1 Corinthians. 16:8, 9 where is a reason of Paul's stay at Ephesus until Pentecost, and verse 19 where is mention of a particular church, in the house of Aquila and Pricilla then at Ephesus, as appears, chapter 18, verses 19, 24, 26, all which laid together do prove that the multitudes of believers did make more congregations than one in the church of Ephesus.

ii. That there were many elders over these many congregations as one flock, appears, Acts 20: 17, 25, 28, 30, 36.

iii. That those many congregations were one church, and that they were under one presbyterial government, appears, Revelation 2:1–6 joined with Acts 20: 17, 28.

Concordat Cum originali.
Adoniram Byfield, Scriba

---

1. *Fixed*: elders are assigned to particular churches. *Unfixed*: elders are shared between local congregations. See *Minutes*, Session 199, April 12, 1644, summary, vol. 3, p. 7.

2. Numbers have been added in square brackets to conform to the outline in the Contents. The brethren add what is numbered in this edition as a seventh section, "other reasons against the main proposition."

[III.] The Propositions concerning the Subordination of Assemblies as they were voted in the Assembly of Divines.

1. Synodical assemblies may lawfully be of several sorts, as provincial, national, and ecumenical. *Minutes, 5.136*

2. It is lawful and agreeable to the Word of God that there be a subordination of congregational, classical, provincial and national assemblies for the government of the Church. *Gillespie, 84*

\{Proof of it, Matthew chapter 18 holding forth the subordination of an offending brother to a particular church, it does also by a parity of reason hold forth the subordination of a congregation to superior assemblies. *Minutes, 3.360–366 Gillespie, 86*

3. In the several sorts of assemblies of the government of the Church, it is lawful and agreeable to the Word of God that appeals may be from the inferior to the superior respectively. *Gillespie, 23, 81*

The proof brought for the subordination of Assemblies, proves the lawfulness of appeals from the inferior to the superior.

*It is agreeable to the light of nature, that he who is wronged and deprived of his right by one power, should have recourse to another power, which may restore unto him his right again, and rescind the sentence whereby he was wronged; else there would be no powerful remedy provided to remove wrong and to preserve right.\}** *Minutes, 2.503 Lightfoot, 162 Gillespie, 84*

*The text in braces does not appear in the draft Directory of December 11, 1644, and the three points without proofs are condensed to one with an additional paragraph added, in the final version of the Directory (see *Minutes*, 5.212).

[IV.] The Proposition concerning Ordination, as it was voted in the Assembly of Divines.

It is very requisite that no single congregation that can conveniently associate, do assume to itself all and sole power in ordination. *Minutes, 3.51–77; 5.138*

1. Because there is no example in Scripture that any single congregation which might conveniently associate, did assume to itself all and sole power in ordination; neither is there any rule which may warrant such a practice. *Lightfoot, 262 Gillespie, 58–64*

2. Because there is in Scripture, example of an ordination in a presbytery over divers congregations; as in the Church of Jerusalem, where were many congregations; these many congregations were under one presbytery, and this presbytery did ordain.

Concordat Cum originali.

Adoniram Byfield, Scriba

To the first of these [Propositions], 1. The Dissenting Brethren gave in after the debate reasons against the proposition itself. 2. Against the proofs of the proposition, 1. From the instance of the Church of Jerusalem. 2. Of Ephesus, in this order as follows.

THE PROPOSITIONS AS VOTED IN THE ASSEMBLY   61

Die Lunæ 24. January 1647.

Ordered by the Lords in Parliament assembled, That Master Adoniram Byfield, one of the Scribes of the Assembly, do take special care in the printing of these things following; And that no other shall presume to print the same, *viz.* The Reasons of the Dissenting Brethren against the third proposition concerning Presbyterial Government, and the Answer of the Assembly to those Reasons, as well those formerly printed for the use of the Houses, as any other reasons and answers never formerly printed. As also the papers and answers of the Dissenting Brethren, and the Committee of the Assembly put into the Committee of Lords and Commons and Assembly of Divines for Accommodation. And that none shall presume to print or reprint any of the particulars above recited, but such as shall be thereunto appointed by the said Adoniram Byfield, as they will answer the contrary at their peril. John Browne Cler. Parliamentorum.

I do appoint Humphrey Harward, and no other perforce to print the reasons, answers, and papers above mentioned.
Adoniram Byfield, Scriba

Die Jovis 3. February 1647

Ordered by the Lords in Parliament Assembled, That Mr. Thomas Goodwin and Mr. Whitaker, shall have the oversight and perusal of such papers and writings as Mr. Byfield hath order to print; and that the said Mr. Goodwin and Mr. Whitaker have free liberty to peruse the originals of the said papers and writings before they go to the press.
John Browne Cler. Parliamentorum.

The papers and writings above mentioned have been examined and perused, this we testify.
Tho. Goodwin.
Jer. Whitaker.

****

The Dissenting Brethren entered their dissent with reasons in writing to be presented to the Honorable House by the Assembly, only to those propositions. *Viz.*

1. The third proposition concerning Presbyterial Government.
2. The propositions concerning the subordination of assemblies.
3. The proposition concerning the power of ordination, whether in a particular congregation, though it may associate.

Reasons Against
The Third Proposition

Concerning Presbyterial Government, and the
Principles thereof: *viz.* The Scripture holds forth that
many particular Congregations may be under one
Presbyterial Government. Humbly Presented[1]

[MAIN ARGUMENT]

If many congregations having all elders already affixed respectively unto {See p. 99}
them, may be under one presbyterial government: Then all those elders Braye, 35r
must sustain a special relation of elders to all the people of those congregations as one church, and to every one as a member thereof.

But for a company of such elders already affixed, etc., to sustain such a relation, carries with it so great and manifold incongruities, and inconsistencies,
with what the Scripture speaks of elders in their relation to a church committed to them, and likewise with the principles of the reformed churches
themselves, as cannot be admitted.

And therefore such a government may not be.

THE FIRST PROPOSITION

That according to the Scriptures, such a presbyterial government necessar- {See p. 106}
ily draws such a special relation, is evinced [*shown*] by parts thus.

1. They must have the relation of elders to all and every one of the members; for church and elders are relative. And the argument for the presbyterial government is taken by the presbyterial divines from this, that many
congregations in Scripture, are made one church, and the elders thereof
elders of that church.

2. That relation they have must be a more special relation, as is evident
from the practice and principles of this government. For when the congregations in shires are divided into several presbyteries or deaneries, the elders (though neighbors) of a bordering presbytery, intermeddle not with

---

1. [*The Reasons Presented by the Dissenting Brethren against certain Propositions concerning
Presbyteriall Government and the Proofs of them voted by the Assembly of Divines, sitting by au-
thority of Parliament, at Westminster. Together with the Answer of the Assembly of Divines to those
Reasons of Dissent* (London: Printed by T. R. and E. M. for Humphrey Harward, 1648).]

the congregations under another presbytery, and yet neighbor elders. It is therefore a ſpecial relation puts the difference, that those of these presbyteries do judge the congregations under them, as having a ſpecial relation to them, such as not to other congregations.

THE MINOR PROPOSITION [INCONGRUITIES]

For the proof of which, we present these incongruities as follow.

I. Firſt, this breeds many incongruous diſproportions to the order set by Chriſt, about the officers of the church.

{See p. 108}
Goodwin, 221

1. To extend a paſtor's power of ordinary ruling beyond the extent of his ordinary teaching, is againſt the order which Chriſt has set (and all extent of power muſt as well have an inſtitution of Chriſt, as the power or office itself, the difference of evangeliſts and ordinary paſtors lay in extent of power). But the extent of a paſtor's ordinary ruling power, is but to that flock as his whole flock which he is able to feed. The firſt proposition is confirmed, (1) by Scripture; (2) by Reason.

Feb. 5, 1644
Gillespie, 10, 11

(1) Firſt, by Scripture (Acts 20:28), "Take heed to yourselves, and to all the flock over the which the Holy Ghoſt hath made you overseers to feed the flock of God, which he hath purchased with his own blood." Whence [1] we see the ſpecial limitation of their extensive power and relation *to a flock* and *ALL in that flock* is by the Holy Ghoſt, and not by man, and therefore is not to be extended by man, further than the Holy Ghoſt has appointed.

[2] The extent of that relation to that flock, and the whole flock they feed, and to feed all that flock alike. And if they be preaching elders, then to feed by preaching, and therefore are overseers to them to feed them, and this because they feed them.

[3] He ſpeaks to preaching elders eſpecially that feed by doctrine. For he propounds his own example to them (v. 27): "That he had revealed the whole counsel of God." And Peter seconds Paul in this (1 Peter 5:2): "Feed the flock of God which is among you, taking the oversight thereof." The flock ἐν ὑμῖν—among you—is that flock any of them had relation to as his flock reſpectively. Peter here writing unto the churches in several nations (1 Peter 1:1), whereas in Acts 20:28, the charge is to the particular elders of Ephesus to that whole flock. Therefore that note of reſpectiveness is here put ἐν ὑμῖν—among you—that is, the flock which reſpectively belongs to you, as Colossians 1:7: "Who is for you a faithful miniſter"—that is, your proper paſtor. So the flock ἐν ὑμῖν is your several proper flocks that belong to you. And hereby it appears that their oversight is not extendible beyond their feeding.

Minutes, 3.18

Thus also Hebrews 13:7: "Remember them that have the rule over you, and have ſpoken to you the Word of God." Which he ſpeaks of preaching elders, and of ruling elders (of whom he ſpeaks, verse 17), "Obey them that have the RULE over you, for they watch for your souls, as those that muſt give an account." And whether these places note out two sort of offices, preaching

          I: REASONS OF THE DISSENTING BRETHREN AGAINST

elders (verse 7), and ruling elders (verse 17), or but one sort, and so but several acts of the same office, however, if but one, yet still the ordinary rule over them was not further extendible than their ordinary preaching. If two sorts of officers, they being officers together in the same church, if the pastor's power of ruling extends no further than his preaching, then the mere ruling elder's power (or his that is assistant to him), must extend no further than the pastor's also. This is the natural obligation to obedience, and so is the measure to set the bounds of the extent of ordinary church power. It is one argument used against episcopal power, that they are enforced to obey him that speaks not the Word to them, nor watches over their souls; and this holds as well against these presbyterial officers. When a man to be excommunicated comes before such, if he say, "I am not bound to obey you in such an authoritative way, nor do I owe a subjection as to a power of censure in you, for many, yea most of you, never spake the Word unto me, nor did watch over my soul;" nay, perhaps the man can say, he never saw their faces before.

And it avails not to say that they may occasionally preach; for take two places more: 1 Thessalonians 5:12, speaking of respect to their officers, "Know them that labor among you, and are over you in the Lord, and admonish you." These two, "labor" and "are over you," are commensurable. That is, who make it their calling to have a care of you, which the many pastors and elders in a common presbytery cannot. And "labor" in what? 1 Timothy 5:17 expounds it, "That labor in Word and doctrine." The elders that rule well, are worthy of double honor, especially those that labor in the Word and doctrine. And expound this latter known place, whether of teaching elders only, or ruling and teaching both (as the reformed churches do) however it affords this to us; that the extent of ruling in either the one or the other, is but as large as teaching. And if it be meant of teaching elders only, that both rule and labor in the Word and doctrine, yet if they be limited in laboring in the Word (as they are being fixed pastors to their own congregations), then in ruling. And if it be meant of ruling elders (as distinct from them), yet their ruling is but of the same extent that the other's laboring in the Word is, and that is extended but to one congregation.

And (2), reason is for this. For in a pastor's office in which preaching and ruling are joined, yet his power of ruling flows in him, from, and is the adjunct of his power to preach, and to be sure it is not extendible further. And however, yet there is the same proportion of either, and then by just reason, the extent of the church, which is the subject of his ordinary ruling, cannot be extended larger than what is the ordinary subject of his preaching. And so these relations are of equal limits; if a father has the power of governing, as a father, then it is extendible only to those he is a father to. And that a pastor has his ordinary ruling powers annexed to his ordinary power of preaching, is proved by these reasons:

[1] If not upon this ground, then upon some other. Not by any special

faculty and office, over and above this of preaching, for then he should be ordained a ruling elder over and above his being first a preaching elder as a new faculty given him; or by being made a ruler first, and then this of preaching superadded, as the bishops first made deacons, then presbyters. But,

[2] All the keys are given him at once, the keys of ruling with the keys of knowledge, the power of the staff intrinsically follows, his being a pastor or shepherd; and though the one is a power of mere order, namely, that of preaching, and that of his ruling be a power of jurisdiction (to be exercised with others and not alone), yet still his receiving power to join with others in those acts of rule of jurisdiction is from this his power of order, and the ordinary extent of his authority therein, is extendible no further than his ordinary call to preach. Yea,

[3] The extent of the power of the apostles themselves, in ruling in all *Minutes, 2.579,* the churches was founded upon, and extendible with their commission to *582, 588, 3.420* preach in all churches, and their very call and obligation being not to preach in a set fixed relation, as ordinary pastors' calling is, but to all churches in all nations. Hence their power of ruling was answerable. It was their very call to be universal pastors, and therefore universal rulers; yea and in reference to those that are without, their authority of ruling was narrower, in the extent of it, than of their preaching. The apostles might preach to heathens, and their call was so to do, to convert them, but they had not power to rule all men [1 Corinthians 5:12]: "What have I to do to judge them that are without?" But in this way of presbyterial government, though they also may occasionally preach where they may not rule, yet the proportion of their ordinary ruling, is extended beyond the proportion of their ordinary preaching, which it was not in the apostles themselves.

2. It breeds an incongruous disproportion between the offices of ruling and preaching elders compared among themselves. For this government makes this extent of the ruling elders office and relation to be larger than that of their teaching or pastors. For the pastor, *quâ* [*as*] pastor, is limited to his particular congregation he is fixed to, for the ordinary performance of his office, as the deacons also are; but the ruling elder's office, *quâ* ruling elder, is extended over all these congregations in the presbytery. The ruling elder performs his office in the highest perfection of it, as to admonish, excommunicate in all these churches, but the pastors are limited in the highest work of their callings (preaching being more excellent than ruling, yea than baptizing is), unto one congregation. That in 1 Timothy 5:17 (interpret it as you will) justifies this.

3. It perverts the order and distinction of teaching elders, and mere ruling elders (as the reformed churches call them) or church governors (as *Minutes, 2.426* the assembly); that whereas Christ has made some teaching elders, and *WFOG: other* some ruling elders, and these distinct in this, that the preaching elder's of-*church governors* fice is to preach and rule, the ruling elder's office only to rule. This frame *De Witt, 84* of presbyterial government, makes one person, not only to do both these

works (which in a particular congregation every pastor does), but formally to bear both those offices, in respect of a double relation he does sustain, namely, of a pastor, to be a preaching elder to the congregation where he is fixed, and a mere ruling elder to the rest of the congregations of the classical church. For it is demanded, when a pastor in a particular congregation is in this common presbytery, what sort of officer he is to that presbyterial church? An elder he is, because he does the work of an elder; a teaching elder to that church he is not, for to that whole church he labors not in the Word and doctrine (1 Timothy 5:17). Therefore a mere ruling elder he must be, and so the same man bears two sorts of offices, and by this means there are two sorts of mere ruling elders: whereas in a particular congregation, a pastor though he rules, yet he rules as a pastor to that congregation. And this disorder and confusion is further set out, in that, by this means the same officer has a full relation to one church, but half a relation to another, and causes him to perform the whole of his office to one church (the particular church he has relation to) and but the half thereof to the other.

4. It makes an incongruous disproportion between the extent of the relation of those two offices of elders and deacons unto a church. If the Scrip- Gillespie, 10
tures had intended many churches making one church, and the elders of those many churches to have been elders in common to those churches as one church, then in like manner the deacons of all those churches should make up a common deaconry, and be deacons in common unto all those churches in an ordinary way as the other are elders. But this is contrary to the practice of the reformed churches, though subject to the presbyterial government, in which the deacons have the ordinary relation of deacons in no respect extended further than to a particular congregation, nor do they exercise acts of that office in an ordinary way to other congregations, nor otherwise to neighbor congregations than to any other; much less is there a common deaconship of them all. And why should not the latter be erected over all those churches as one church, as well as a common eldership? especially if in matters of this nature, *par ratio* should carry it; every church, *"like reason"*
quâ church, being a body, has a relation to all its officers as organic members thereof (Romans 12:4). And the apostle writing to Philippi, a church in a city, he writes to the bishops, *the elders* and the deacons as both alike officers of that church. And Acts 6, the deacons of the church of Jerusalem (if there were many congregations as our brethren suppose) were chosen by the whole multitude when gathered together by the twelve, and therefore were deacons of the whole church as well as the elders, elders thereof.

Now if the deacon's office should thus be extended to all the congregations as the elder's is, then why should not each church be bound to bring contributions to the deacons of each church, and to be distributed in common? And so our purses should be subject to the deacons in common, as far as our persons to the elders in common, and they might challenge the same power in their office over the one, that the elders do over the other; and then also each congregation were in an ordinary and standing obligation bound to relieve all the poor in those churches, as well as those in their own parishes, not only by the common law of charity, but by virtue of special relation of their being one church, which relation in all these things, does beget the like obligation that it does in government. And so all things of this nature should be alike common to all and each, and there should be a common treasury for this one great deaconate church, as we may in a parallel allusion to that other name of presbyterial, call it.

[SECOND HEAD OF INCONGRUITIES]

{See p. 110}

Goodwin, 228

Braye, 38r

II. A second head of incongruities, and inconsistencies which will follow upon it, are in the mutual duties required, and that do necessarily follow upon this standing relation for a constant government of these elders to all this people of these churches, and of the people to those elders.

Gillespie, 11

1. From the people to all these elders. According unto what the Scripture speaks of, as due to standing elders, they owe at least honor and esteem; yea, maintenance to all their elders, whether those that ordinarily rule them or preach to them; and they owe it for both. 1 Timothy 5:17–18: "Let the elders that rule well, be counted worthy of double honor, especially those that labor in the Word and doctrine." Which honor is expressed by the analogy of that law (verse 18), not to "muzzle up the mouth of the ox that treadeth out the corn." And this is certainly due to elders, for all that is the work of elders, whether performed apart, or together, by way of jurisdiction in a presbytery; and it cannot be denied that their constant ruling in the presbytery, is one great part of the work of elders, and so must be here intended, for which a special honor is due. And as they are to feed all and every one in the flock (as Acts 20:28), so maintenance and honor is due from all people to all and every one of these elders, as well to those that rule, as those that labor in the Word and doctrine.

And in reason, if the elders that rule well (and perform the lesser acts of ruling) in their particular congregations, and the presbyteries thereof are to have this honor in their relations, then all those elders that rule well in the common presbytery (and perform the greatest acts of ruling) are to have the like from all that classical church—the emphasis being put upon ruling well, and in those acts done by them the excellency of ruling consisted, and the precept is not to honor presbyteries in some abstract notion, but elders; because the particular persons of the elders are to be the object of it, and those most who excel most in that rule, that rule well or best. But when there are many congregations that have their proper fixed pastors and elders whom they maintain for performing one part of the elders' work (for they perform but one part of it), how shall they perform this due to all the rest for that other part of it? and it is due from every person as he is able, or he cannot perform his duty. How burdensome, how confused would this be? And then how to proportion this, suppose it should not be maintenance, but honor and esteem, this people will not be able to judge; not only for that they cannot be present at their work, and so cannot judge of it; but because either it must be proportioned to them as constant preaching elders, or as ruling? Not as to preaching elders, for they labor not to them as such (the ground upon which it is required is, that they tread out their corn); and to honor and esteem them as ruling elders only, were to honor preaching elders below the rank and degree of their office. So,

2. It brings the like incongruities upon the performance of those duties of elders, which the New Testament indifferently requires of all those that it acknowledges to be elders unto a people, and therefore no such constant relation of elders to so many churches may be. As (1) Praying with the sick—"Send for the elders of the church to pray for them" (James 5:14). What? Are these elders of a presbyterial church bound hereto? This duty lies in common upon elders of churches, and how shall we distinguish when the Scripture does not? (2) "Visiting from house to house," as Paul in his example instructs the elders of Ephesus (Acts 20:20). (3) "Watching over men's souls, as those that must give account" (Hebrews 13:17). To watch, is not to stay [*halt*] till causes are brought by appeals or so, from the congregations, but personally to observe and oversee them, as souls committed to them, which they must give an account for. (4) Of preaching (if preaching elders), in season and out of season. The bishops, they said the flock was theirs, and the whole care committed to them. And to salve the incongruity of not being able to preach themselves to them, they professed a derivative delegated power to inferior pastors, whom they called their curates. This was plain dealing. But *these* elders make all the whole flock theirs and this from those Scriptures that speak of elders and flock, and themselves not curates, and so personally obliged according to the rules in Scripture, and yet cannot perform it, which is a worse incongruity.

It is said, that they may part these duties among them.

Ubi Scriptura non distinguit, nec nos debemus distinguere. Now all those duties that are spoken of elders to the flocks, they are without distinction, as in respect of the object to whom they are extended. Paul said to those of Ephesus, "Feed the flock." Peter, the like to those he writes to "the flock," ἐν ὑμῖν, respectively, "To feed and to take the oversight of them." The author to the Hebrews, "To watch over their souls;" and to the Thessalonians, he describes them to be those that "are over them," and "labor and admonish them." When those injunctions are thus laid upon all, how shall the consciences of elders be able to part and distinguish their discharge of them, and to say, "Though I am an elder in common to all in these congregations, yet I am bound but to govern them in greater matters, and to admonish them as with others, when publicly met in a consistory, and am bound to no

Braye, 39r

Where Scripture does not make a distinction, neither should we

Gillespie, 11

other acts of eldership; and yet to this particular congregation, I am obliged to private admonition, rule, watchfulness," etc. Where has the Scripture set these bounds, or thus parted them? And therefore certainly all these places hold forth singly, only the elders and their duties of a particular church fixed thereto, as knowing no other. It was necessary [that] Christ should have set the bounds and given the distinction, and not indifferently lay all these upon all. And either in these places the duties of elders in a common presbytery are contained, and that under the notion of elders to those, or they are not to be found in the New Testament. And all these may be brought in several arguments alone by themselves against the main proposition, though here they come in only as branches of the minor.

[THIRD HEAD OF INCONGRUITIES]

{See p. 112} III. Lastly, this is inconsistent with the ordinary way of the call of elders held
Gillespie, 11 forth in the Word, and the principles of the Reformed churches.

Goodwin, 231   There are two parts of this call. First, choice. Secondly, ordination.

First, for choice, Chamier in the name of all the reformed churches, allows
Braye, 39v the people this, the approbation of their elders, and so in Scotland.[1] And if the apostles themselves allowed them the choice of the deacons, that had the charges of the church treasury and took care of their bodies; then much more of their elders that have to do with their consciences. Look what ever the right of the people is in the choice of them that should preach to them, there is as much reason they should have the exercise of it in the choice of those elders that in a common presbytery do rule over them, for they perform one part of the elders' duty, namely ruling, as the preaching elders do the other; and therefore by the equity of the same law, that speaks of elders indefinitely, if they choose any elders as elders to them, they are to choose these also, there being no distinction put on choosing preaching elders only, but elders indefinitely. And further, the greatest and highest acts of power over them, are committed in an ordinary way unto them, as of excommunication, of all punishments the most formidable: there is put as much, if not more than every man's life (that is a member of the classical church) into their hands, the enjoyment of all ordinances forever. And so the power of deposing their ministers already fixed to them, and by refusing to ordain them, they shall approve: And therefore in antiquity, of all other the persons of the bishops, who had the power of all those, were chosen by all the people, and by panegyrical meetings.

And it is strengthened by this further parallel. A minister's call has two

---

1. [Daniel Chamier, French Protestant divine (1565–1621). No citation was given. Cf. *Panstratiæ Catholicæ sive controversiarum de religione adversus pontificios corpus*, 4 vols. (Geneva, 1626), 2.289. "… præter electorum Ministrorum approbationem vel improbationem, plebis nullas esse partes censemus in Ecclesiastico regimine." Pages 64–71 are reproduced in Goodwin, "Constitution, Right, Order, and Government of the churches of Christ." *Works*, vol. 11 (1865), pp. 221–1231. For Scottish practice see Gillespie's *Assertion*, part 2, chap. 1.

parts: first, ordination, which belongs to the elders; secondly, choice, in which the people have some interest. These elders, as elders in common, and these congregations as one church be relatives, and so that interest which a church, *quâ* [*as*] church has, is commensurable to the interest of these elders, *quâ* elders. If therefore in ordaining, all the elders in a common presbytery do join to ordain an officer, then all the people, *quâ* church, must join in choosing or approving him. Neither can their common right of choosing be swallowed up by the interest of their elders' ordaining him.

And if it be said "they all chose by virtue of the general law of combination, as the shires' parliament men"—the constitution of the state makes the one; if the like be found in Scripture it will be sufficient. But if not, but that this interest must be common to the people of the classical church, it is asked, when a fixed pastor is to be chosen to a particular charge, what office he shall be chosen to by the people of the other congregations? Not to a pastor's office; he is not to be such to them. If to be a ruling elder only, then besides that he has two offices (as before), so now he must have two choices, and two ordinations. "We choose him for our pastor," says the particular church he belongs to, and "we," say the other, "to ruling." And besides, in his ordination, the people have an interest of presence and joining in the fasting and prayer at his ordination. And this therefore must be performed, either in panegyrical meeting of all (which cannot be), or in all the several churches, which will multiply the ordination of them.

THE MAJOR PROPOSITION CONFIRMED

In regard that the main argumentation of such as contend for a presbyterial government (as in their writings and otherways appears) is from the mention of the elders of such and such a church (as Jerusalem, etc.) having many congregation (as they suppose). The consequence of the major was taken so much for granted as on all sides agreed on, as it was less insisted upon the first day; but being denied and answered thus, that they bear not the relation of elder, but of a presbytery, because, *quod convenit toti quâ toti, non convenit cuilibet parti;* and that elders, yet *in sensu composito non diviso,* as a colonel is a colonel to a particular regiment, but in a council of war, not so to all regiments. A head of a particular tribe is an head to his own tribe divisively, but not so to all the tribes, and the like.

For that logical axiom: it is true, *quod convenit toti quâ toti, non convenit cuilibet parti:* and so here, that which does *competere toti*, to the whole of these elders, belongs not to every part. For take them all as met together, they are a presbytery, and accordingly each elder is not a presbytery to all these congregations, nor does the argument suppose it, but only that if they be a common presbytery to all these congregations, that they then bear the relation of elders. As take an heap of stones—it is true, each stone is not a heap of stones, but each stone is a stone in that heap. So this company of

Braye, 40r

{See p. 106}

Gillespie, 12

Lightfoot, 135

In a sense composite not divided

Goodwin, 215

That which belongs to the whole body as a whole can not be applied to each part

apply to the whole

elders must be supposed [to be] both a presbytery, and also elders to this whole people and every member of them: which is further proved thus:

1. The Scriptures would have the people look at them and honor them as elders in all acts of ruling as well as the preaching, and especially wherein the most and chief of ruling lies, and wherein the excellency of their ruling is seen; they rule most and best when met in this common presbytery. Upon that relation we are to honor them, as performing this rule, and under that relation they must be said to perform it: "the elders that rule well, are worthy of double honor, especially those that labor in the Word and doctrine" (1 Timothy 5:17). And besides, otherwise we destroy the relation of elders, *quâ* elders, in the highest acts of governing, which are exercised only in a presbytery.

2. The New Testament does indifferently and promiscuously use the word "presbytery," and the word "elders," of the same persons in relation to the same people; and therefore to whom these elders are supposed to be a presbytery, they must bear the relation of elders (Matthew 21:23 [Braye, 21:33]), those that are called "elders of the people," are called (Luke 22), πρεσβυτέριον τοῦ λαοῦ, the "presbytery of the people: so as if they related as a presbytery to the people, to the same people they related as elders.

Secondly, for that distinction of their being elders only in a community to all those congregations as one church, *in sensu aggregato* [*in an aggregate sense*], but not *in sensu diviso* [*in a divided sense*], to every person thereof, as was instanced in burgesses, etc. First, this church as it is *totum aggregatum* [*an aggregate whole*], is but an abstract notion, but the rule and government of the elders in a presbytery, falls upon persons in particular, and every member of the church; if therefore they be elders to every person therein. Again, it must be remembered where we are, namely upon "what the Scriptures hold forth," so the proposition runs. And if there had been those differing relations of elders (which from those similitudes in commonwealths, armies, and the universities are given), it were necessary the Scripture should have held it forth by like differing names and respects, or by differing charges, whereby it might appear that this relation obliges them to this duty, and this other relation to that, which being not done is therefore to us a fiction. That it was necessary appears from the instances themselves, as in that of the tribes, there were general elders of all the tribes, and there were (and perhaps some of them the same men) that were heads and elders of the particular tribes. But as this was a differing relation and respect in the same, or divers persons, so they had names and titles of difference and distinction: For the heads general (as we may call them) were called "elders of the people." The particular elders of the tribes, were called by the way of distinction from them, elders of such cities, families, etc. And there were as distinct laws given in such cases. The elders of the several tribes did such and such particulars in their tribes respectively, and the general elders had reserved cases of blasphemy etc., set

Goodwin, 216

Goodwin, 216
Braye, 41r
Feb. 7, 1644
Lightfoot, 136
Gillespie, 13

Feb. 6, 1644
Gillespie, 12
Lightfoot, 132
Goodwin has revised this section, see 218, distinction 4,

                    I: Reasons of the Dissenting Brethren Against

down by the law. So in that instance of the heads of colleges, and heads of the university, there is as a differing, so a distinguishing character. The names are changed, the particular bodies are called colleges, the general body the university, and their several special relations to their colleges is expressed by the title of masters of such and such colleges, and the other by the title of heads to the university. Yea, and accordingly there are differing statutes, and local statutes for each college apart, or the colleges as colleges, and the duties of masters in their several relation. And there are statutes for the university and their duties as heads thereof. And this distinction and difference was necessary, if there were this differing relation.

But for the case in hand, if we come to the New Testament to find out these {See p. 105} several jurisdictions and relations of elders, therein we still read but simply and singly elders and churches as relatives, no such note of distinction. And also speaking of the duties of elders to the people, and people to elders, it speaks similarly and univocally—so as whoever will take upon them to be elders, all those duties fall upon them, let them distinguish how they can. And to confirm this, the instances in the minor serve. And where the Scripture does not distinguish, we are not to distinguish. And if the elders of a particular congregation are elders to that church, both *in sensu diviso,* and every member thereof, and also *in sensu composito,* in their presbyteries unto the whole, *in a composite* then those general elders must bear the like relation to that classical church *sense* and every member of it; else the difference is so vast, and the consequent difference of duties thereupon depending such, as it was necessary a distinction should have been made in Scripture, that each might know their duties.

If all the records, laws, and ruled cases of this kingdom, should in setting Braye, 41v down the ordinary government thereof, have made mention only and singly of burgesses (as the rulers) and of corporations (as the correlate to them) and used no other distinguishing word—and there were undeniably burgesses of every incorporate town continued from antiquity—if any would afterwards pretend that this word "corporation" was intended by our ancestors to import an association or community of many of these corporations into one shire, and that by burgesses of those corporations were meant a community of all those burgesses in one body for government, and so pretend the same names without distinction, and say they were also meant; yea, and further, if the laws and charters concerning such burgesses in each corporation, the duties given them in charge by the law in their relations to their corporations, did run without any distinction of what the burgesses in the supposed greater corporation should do in that relation and community, from what the same burgesses in their lesser corporations in a more proper relation do; yea, and if the duties set down in those laws mutually between corporations, and those burgesses should argue an inconsistency with the government of burgesses over many corporations in common (as the minor here shows it to be in our case), but all naturally fall in with that of burgesses over single corporations—in this case to say that therefore this kingdom did hold forth, there might not be (that is, according to the laws thereof) such a government of the burgess of corporations over many corporations, were not this a right way of arguing to overthrow such a pretence?

And if in answer to such arguments it should be said, that both these might be consistent; for, that in foreign states and kingdoms and societies, there are burgesses of particular corporations, and there are burgesses in an assembly of parliament (so called by way of distinction) met in common, for the ordinary government of all those corporations in common and therefore the like may be here in this, the reply were easy. That whatever such distinction there is in other states, yet the question is of such burgesses as the laws of this state hold forth, the question is of such burgesses as this kingdom has set up where there is no distinction of burgesses of corporations, and burgesses in parliament mentioned. But on the contrary only, one single uniform style and title in the laws, namely burgesses of the corporation and duties suited thereunto. Now parallel to this case are our arguments, and the answers given thereto.

Lastly, if they be elders only *in sensu aggregato,* yet so far as they are acknowledged thus elders, so far will many of the incongruities in the minor follow them, and fall upon them, as that still they are but merely ruling elders, and that there by deacons *in sensu aggregato.*

Minutes,
Sess. 160–162
2.534–552

1a. Reasons against and exceptions to the first proof of the first assertion: *viz.* That the church of Jerusalem consisted of more congregations than one, from the multitude of believers

Braye, 42r
{See p. 114}
Goodwin
omits 1a; cf.
vol. 11

Minutes,
Sess. 161, 162
2.540–552

First, reasons to show there were not more than could meet in one place.

The Holy Ghost has from first to last as one purpose shown this, as if his scope had been beforehand to prevent and to preclude all reasoning to the contrary.

1. In the beginnings of that church, their meetings are set out to us by two adjuncts. (1) That they met ὁμοθυμαδὸν, with one accord in the same duty of prayer (Acts 1:14). And (2) ἐπὶ τὸ αὐτὸ together in one and the same company (verse 15). Which therefore is there and usually translated "in one place." And that here by these words the intent of the Holy Ghost is to show their meeting in one and the same assembly is evident. For whereas in the 15th verse it is said Peter stood up in the midst of them (as therefore being present together in one company), he adds, "And the number of them that were ἐπὶ τὸ αὐτο, that is "present together in company, were an hundred and twenty."

2. Then Acts 2:1, another meeting of theirs for worship at Pentecost is continued to be expressed in the same phrases a second time, "They were all with one accord in one place."

                    I: Reasons of the Dissenting Brethren Against

3. Then when about three thousand, yet still some of their meetings then for some acts of worship are recorded to have been as before "with one accord," as joining unanimously in the same duty, and instead of that former expression ἐπὶ τὸ αὐτο (used of the former meetings) there is the mention of the place itself, where they met, set down to supply it, and so to interpret it, and shows it was still in "one assembly" (Acts 2:46). "They continued daily with one accord IN THE TEMPLE," as mentioning the very place where they had their most frequent meetings which were for hearing, as being there altogether in one assembly; and not as coming thither only for Jewish worship. For it is said of these as of the former meetings mentioned, which were proper to themselves, "That they continued with one accord." And though they held these meetings in this place for preaching, that the Jews might be present to hear, etc., yet that hindred not, but it was a church meeting to them; wherein they continued with one accord; which expression is still used of all their Christian meetings throughout this story (Acts 1:14; 4:24; 5:12; 15:25).

4. When there was a further addition to these (Acts 5:1, whether to five thousand or no, is spoken to afterwards), yet in that chapter, he making a description of their state, in almost all the very same particulars by which he had done it before (Acts 2:43 unto the end—as by the parallel comparing of these two passages of the story will appear), he lastly speaking of a meeting of theirs (which is the point in hand), as carefully puts in, as in the former (verse 14), "And they were ALL with one accord in Solomon's Porch," the same words he had used in 2:46. Their union and joining together "with one accord" being carefully indigitated, and *the place* named instead of ἐπὶ τὸ αὐτο, as was observed before. And that the *All that met* were not the apostles only, appears not only by the aforementioned parallel of this with 2:46, where their being "with one accord" in the Temple, is spoken of all the multitude, and so here—but secondly, that all the apostles should be met with one accord in any duty, and not the people who are said to continue in the apostles' doctrine and prayer, and ὁμοθυμαδὸν (or "with one accord") still in this story of this church referring to communion in some holy duty, as 1:14 and 4:24 is most unlikely. And Solomon's Porch was a place large enough to hold them, and fitted for preaching and to hear, which in John 10:22 is called "the Temple;" and so is the place intended in Acts 2:46: "They met in the Temple," that is, in the Porch of Solomon. It was the outer court, as Josephus (lib. 20. cap. 8). It was the place where Christ used to walk and preach, and the apostles also (Acts 3:11). The multitude ran to Solomon's Porch.

Lightfoot, 175
Minutes, 2.545

5. When again upon mention of this multiplication of disciples, the deacons are to be chosen, the apostles called the multitude (Acts 6:2), and not persons selected, but "all." For (verse 5) they are called *the whole multitude* and are spoken to, as together, "For the saying pleased *the whole* and

the *whole* chose seven men out from among them, and set them before the apostles" (verse 6), as being in one place together, and they prayed (in which the multitude had an interest to join with them) and laid on them hands. And this meeting was certainly a church meeting, and yet still in some one place; and therefore though it might fall out that always they should not have met together in one, yet they both did and could.

6. After that great dispersion mentioned in Acts 8:1, then as they might more conveniently meet in one place and assembly, so that they did so, it is as carefully recorded, that so the Holy Ghost might hold forth this from the first unto the last mention of this church (Acts 15, Acts 21:22): "The multitude musts needs come together." And to interpret ὁμοθυμαδὸν, or with one accord, which the Holy Ghost carries through all, to be intended of the joining of the same persons in the same act of worship (for which they still did meet) is genuine. For it imports that which is the spirit and life of public worship, which of all other actions done by a multitude, is to have the nearest union of spirits, as that wherein the communion of saints in worship consists. And then naming the place where they met also, it must needs import oneness of assembly which also hold forth in this example this duty: that as saints when met in worship should join with one accord, so living in a place together, should as far as possibly may, join themselves to one assembly. And this carries with it such an appearance as is not in the other sense. And that the Holy Ghost should in the same story of the same church set forth the unity of their first meetings, as in one and the same individual assembly, by this expression of being in one, and with one accord (Acts 2:1), and in the next mention not far off, carry along one of the same expressions, namely *with one accord* and together therewith shall name the place of their meeting, and yet in the latter intend not one, but meetings in several companies in that place, this we humbly submit to better judgments.

Secondly, Exceptions.

1. For the mention of five thousand (Acts 4:4), this cannot be evinced [*shown*] from that place that the five thousand were a new number added to the three thousand. The words are these, "Howbeit many of them that heard the Word, believed; and the number of the men was about five thousand." But that this number of five thousand should refer to them that believed, is not certain; seeing both the Greek will bear it and favor it, as well to be meant of the number that heard, as of the men that believed; and of the two, that former is the more probable, that he should say of the men that heard they were five thousand, and that of them that heard many believed, this sounds well, and is no way forced. But five thousand men to be converted at once, is that which was never before nor since. And the great conversion that our divines have instanced in, is the three thousand (Acts 2) and not in this five thousand. And if the scope of the Holy Ghost therein, why the number of the men that heard should be here reckoned to be five

Minutes,
Sess. 165–167
2.564–575

ὁμοθυμαδὸν
Minutes, 2.548

Braye, 43v
Lightfoot,
171–180
Minutes,
2.534–548 thousand, be asked after, it was to show what had occasioned the persecution, which he had spoken of, in the verse before. Namely this, that such a multitude of the people should be taught and preached to; this fretted the Pharisees that came upon Peter and John. And with this agrees the second verse, that "they were grieved they taught the people," the effect whereof is, that "many of them that heard believed," notwithstanding this persecution. But how many of these is not certain. And Beza and Calvin[1] and many other of our Protestant writers judge this number not to be of this new accession of converts, but the total number including the former; and the ἀνδρῶν although translated "men," is when put alone (as there) all one with ανσθρώπων, females as well as males; which especially may be so taken, because it is spoken of such a promiscuous auditory. And if any should affirm it meant of males only, and then now converted, it would make a greater miracle than any other recorded, especially when the people are said to be converted (verse 2), that did alike run to see the miracle.

2. Exception is, that it may be supposed that all that are mentioned to be converted, remained not constant members of that church abiding at Jerusalem until the dispersion; and so, though the Holy Ghost's scope may be to show the increase of converts to the faith, yet not as such as continued all that while at Jerusalem; and our reason for that are these:

First, those three thousand who where converted (chapter 2), were not settled dwellers at Jerusalem, but strangers, commorants [*sojourners*] of the ten tribes, which were dispersed in all those countries mentioned in [Acts] 2:9, who came up to the feast of Pentecost, as the manner of the Jews was (Acts 21:20, 27, 28). Jews that lived in Asia came to the feast of Pentecost as Paul also did, compared with Acts 20:16. And the word which is translated "dwellers at Jerusalem" is interpreted by an eminent critic[2] "sojourners at Jerusalem" during this feast (although the word signifies both) and to that end he quotes the Septuagint in 1 Kings 17:20 where Elijah cries unto the Lord, saying, "O Lord my God, hast thou also brought evil upon the widow—μεθ' ἧσ ἐγὼ κατοιηῶ [κατοικῶ][3]—with whom I sojourn only?" and that which confirms it is, that they are said to be dwellers or inhabitants of Mesopotamia and Judea and Cappadocia (verse 9). They could not

Minutes, 2.541
Gillespie, 28
Lightfoot, 173

---

1. Beza in 1 Cor. 1[?] 13 [*sic ?*]; Steph.; Budaeus; Eustath. [Calvin, cf. *Commentaries*, vol. 18, book 2, 167. Beza.* Henri Estienne *Thesaurus Linguæ Graecæ*, vi-pt2 (Geneva: 1572–1573; Paris: 1831–65), p. 666. Guillaume Budé, *Commentarii Linguae Graecæ* (1529; Basil: 1556). Eustathius of Thessalonica, *Commentarii in Homeri Iliadem et Odysseam* (Rome, 1542–1550; Lipsiæ: Weigel, 1827). *Ed. 2024. The Braye MS (44r) reads "2 Cor. 1:23" Both are incorrect. There is no note at Acts 4:4 in Beza, *Annotationes*, p. 458. See a possible solution in "*Antiquary:* The Identity of W. A. & Other Bibliographical Mysteries in *Jus Divinum Regiminis Ecclesiastici* (1646–1654), *The Confessional Presbyterian* 16 (2020): 258, and *Jus Divinum Regiminis Ecclesiastici* (2020), p. 258 n18.]

2. Mede Diatribe. [Joseph Mede, *Diatribæ. Discourses on Divers Texts of Scripture: delivered upon severall occasions* (1642), On Acts 2:5, "Of the old dispersions of the Jewish Nation," pp. 314–315. While the *Minutes* do not, Lightfoot notes Goodwin adduced Mede in debate (173).]

3. [The 1648 Errata page, in correcting the Greek here, introduced an η for a κ.

fixedly belong as dwellers to both. They were therefore rather sojourners in Jerusalem now at the feaſt, though fixed dwellers in all those places. For if they were fixed dwellers in Jerusalem, to what end while they were at Jerusalem should the evangeliſt tell us they were sojourners in Mesopotamia? And they muſt needs rather be dwellers there, because they are said to underſtand every one his own language. And that which ſtrengthens this is, that the Greek there is this difference in the words in verses 5 and 9, in that they are said κατοικοὶν ἐν ᾽Ιερουσαλὴμ, *in Hierusalem*, as for the present there. Yea, and as to come, ἀπὸ παντὸς ἔθνους from out of every nation. But in the ninth verse he changes it, and says, κατοικοῦντες τὴν Μεσοποταμίαν, as inhabiters of Mesopotamia, and those other countries where their fixed possessions were. And therefore verse 14, he calls them men, Jews and dwellers at Jerusalem, as two sorts; and (verse 22), men of Israel, the ſtyle given those of the ten tribes scattered; men devout (as verse 5), who came up at those solemn times, having wives and children and their families at home, to whom they used after a time to return.

Minutes, 2.539
Lightfoot, 173

Now although these were added and made members of that church, and are said to continue in the apoſtles' doĉtrine; yet that will not necessarily imply that they continued all the time till the diſpersion at Jerusalem. But while they were there, they were προσκαρτεροῦντες, that is, they cleaved to the apoſtles. But to think that many of them coming as ſtrangers should not go down to their wives and children, which nature taught them to provide for, and religion taught them to take care of their souls, or to fetch them up to them—so as this might well be a fluid church, ebbing and flowing as touching the residence of its members. Yea, some of these were of Judea (verse 9) and so of the country about; and of them might be churches ereĉted in their proper dwellings is rationally suate. For in that persecution in Aĉts 8:1, it is said that Paul persecuted disciples in other places than at Jerusalem (Aĉts 26:10). "Which things I also did at Jerusalem," (says he) and in other places, at Damascus. And also it is confirmed by this, that upon the ceasing of Paul's persecution it is said (Aĉts 9:31), "then had the churches reſt through Judea and Galilee," and are said to be at reſt in diſtinĉtion from the persecution raised (Aĉts 8:1).

3. Exception is, that they in those countries and times had often great assemblies consiſting of many thousand hearers at once, that did and could hear (Luke 12:1). Chriſt preached to myriads, many thousands; and (Aĉts 13:44) almoſt a whole city came to hear the Word of God by Paul. And at Charenton [France], how many thousands may and do hear, is well known; and so in many places of England. And Moses sometimes ſpoke "in the ears of all the people," and so Ezra (10:9–10). And it is known by experience, that as in hot countries they may see as far again, through the pureness of the air, so they may hear at a far greater diſtance, than in our colder climate.

4. Exception is, that this being the firſt church, and whereof all the apoſtles

were the officers, those therefore that dwelt there, would certainly abide together as one church without parting or dividing, even till they came to the
utmoſt proportion that the conſtitution of a church was capable of—and
so *maximum quod sic*—and continue together in one, for the more united *The largeſt as*
ſtrength and glory of holding forth the name of Chriſt in one body, united *such* or *of its*
for the honor of religion and communicating in ordinances together.   *kind*

   5. Exccption is, that they had during all this time of their multitudes until the persecution of Paul arose, the greateſt freedom and liberty even to
the utmoſt; "for the people magnified them" (5:12); "they had favor with
all the people" (2:47). Insomuch that although the rulers fell upon two of
them, John and Peter, yet they were enforced to let them go, "finding nothing how to punish them, because of the people" (4:21). Besides that, it was
no new thing among the Jews for seĉts to have great multitudes to follow
and cleave to them, and to preach in any place (as in Spain and Italy), and
to baptize openly as John and Chriſt did.

**1b. Reasons and Answers to the Appendix[1] added to the former
proof, *viz*. That the dispersion mentioned in Acts 8:1 does not
simply prove such a scattering, as that there might not remain more
congregations than one in that church (Acts 9:31, 12:24, and 21:20)**

Thus having showed the multitudes not arising to that number, but that {See p. 126}
they might meet in one; now after the diſperſion much less. And to that *Minutes,*
end let the greatness of the persecution be considered to demonſtrate the Sess. 167
greatness of this diſperſion. It is called not a persecution only, but a great 575–576
persecution, both extensively and intensively; for the extent of it to all sorts Braye, 45v
of persons, "entering into every house" (verse 3), and for the height of it, it Lightfoot,
being to "imprisonment, even unto death" (22:4; 26:10). It is also called "a 190–192
making havoc of the church" (8:3). The objeĉt of this persecution was not Gillespie,
preachers only, but Chriſtians of all sorts indifferently, for it is said indefi- 32–34
nitely to be "upon the church" (8:1–2). It is called "an entering into every Goodwin
house, haling men and women." And in chapter 26 Paul ſpeaking of this omits 1b
very persecution (wherein he had a ſpecial hand) says (verse 10) "that he
imprisoned many of the saints" (not preachers only) and (verse 9), his aim
was promiscuously againſt the "name of Jesus," and so any that professed
his name. Unto this end compare the varying expression used by the Holy
Ghoſt, when ſpeaking of this persecution, and of another mention (Aĉts
12:1) there it is said, "Herod ſtretched forth his hand to vex certain of the
church;" but here it is againſt the church in Jerusalem, men and women in
every house. And "all except the apoſtles" (the word πλὴν "except" there is
to show, that none of the apoſtles) "were scattered," though the generality

---

1. The Congregationalists apparently call this the Appendix, because the three proofs
were added to Acts 8:1. "Dr. Smith added, Acts ix. 31; xii. 24; xxi. 20…." Gillespie, p. 33.

of others were; if men gifted fled away, then others also, except we suppose the people more courageous to ſtay by it than the teachers.

And whereas it is said, that these that were diſpersed, "went about preaching the Word" (verse 4). Firſt, it argues not that preachers only or chiefly were diſpersed; for (as Calvin said) it comes in to show what was the fruit of the diſpersion; and we may well suppose women and whole families to have been scattered abroad, who yet preached not. And secondly, it was ordinary in those times, for men that were not by office miniſters, occasionally to teach the Word in private ways of converse, yea and otherwise; and that is not called teaching only, which is by way of sermon to a multitude, for verse 25 of this chapter, Philip in private conference taught the Eunuch, as Aquila and Pricilla taught Apollos; and they are not called εὐαγγελισαι as having an office, but εὐαγγελιζόμενοι, as referring to the act—the work they did; and that the word seems to sound as if they made it their work. It may well be attributed to the zeal of those days to gain proselytes, and not to an office committed to them; they went not forth by mission but persecution. And here the many congregations are brought but to an "it might be" and the grand proposition itself, is but an "it may be" and how can "it may be," be proved by an "it might be" eſpecially in such things as need have a ſtrong foundation for matters, upon which so great alterations are like to be made.

"But it is said, that it appears that there were multitudes of believers 'there after that time'" by Acts 9:31, and 12:24, and 21:20.

Firſt, for Acts 9:31, ἐπληθύνοντο signifies not ordinarily a great number made up, but an increase (Matthew 21:12 and 1 Peter 1:2 "Grace be multiplied," is the same word), not in number, but in measure. Again, they are the churches of Judea, Galilee, and of Samaria. But what is all this to prove that there were so many in the church of Jerusalem as could not meet in one?

For Acts 21:20, πόσαι μυριάδες, how many thousands does not argue it. For firſt it was the feaſt of Pentecoſt: when Paul came now up to Jerusalem in Acts 20:16, it is said of this journey, that "he haſted if possible to be at Jerusalem upon the day of Pentecoſt:" when the Jews out of all quarters came to Jerusalem, and the great concourse that then would be there at the feaſt, moved him to aim to be there at that time. And by the journal of Paul thither, from his firſt setting out from Philippi (chapter 20:6, which was when the Passover was ended, eight weeks before this ensuing feaſt of Pentecoſt), and also by computing the days of his traveling, which the Holy Ghoſt has recorded (verses 16, 21; 21:2), it appears he came in few weeks unto Tyre (but forty miles off from Jerusalem). Time enough to come to the feaſt; and no wonder if at the feaſt he found thousands of the Jews. And this is confirmed by the 27th verse, for the Jews which laid hold on him in the temple, were as it is said, "Jews of Asia," not of Judea. Secondly, the word μυριας, being put without any other word of numbers, signifies no more than a great multitude, as μύριον πλῆθος; or a greatness, as ἐν μυρια πενία as Plato has it; and being put indefinitely, is all one to say "thousands" or "many;" as the Latins also use a definite for an indefinite, as *sescenta possum proferre decreta,* as Tully speaks.[1]

I can produce six hundred decrees in which…

Braye, 46v

2. To the second proof of the first head, by the many apostles and other preachers in this church of Jerusalem; for if there were but one congregation, then each apostle preached but seldom, which will not stand with Acts 6:2

First, for the apostles.

They took all opportunities to fill their hands with work, "preaching daily in the temple and in every house" (Acts 5:42, 2:46). Paul also taught in Ephesus, as, publicly in the congregation, so "from house to house" (Acts 20:20). Also when any in the places abroad in Judea, or elsewhere, were converted (and many churches were then erected in Judea) the "apostles went abroad," as chapter 8 shows; and besides, how were the twelve employed, when for forty days they met in an upper room (Acts 1), and had but an hundred and twenty for their flock.

{See p. 132}

Minutes,
Sess. 163
2.553–556

Gillespie,
29–30

Lightfoot,
181–182

Secondly, for the many teachers.

In those times there were many gifted men that were not officers, who occasionally instructed others, as Aquila did Apollos. Yea those gifts were so plentiful, that in one church of Corinth (1 Corinthians 14:23), almost all of them had doctrines, prophesying, speaking with tongues, and yet these were not officers, so as if congregations should be multiplied according to the number of such gifted men, then there would have been almost as many teachers as members of congregations. And the pouring out of the Holy Ghost, which was more ordinary then, did not make every man a teacher by office, for then all those in Samaria should have been made teachers (Acts 8). And that not any of these were in office, seems evident by this— that when the deacons were chosen (chapter 6) there is no mention made of elders in their ordination, in which if any elders had been they had had an interest. We read Acts 15, when there were elders, though apostles were also then in that church, both are mentioned together. And it appears that apostles had managed all the affairs of that church until then—those deacons being the first choice of any sort of officers; the work of administration of all sorts having laid on the apostles' hands.

3. To the third proof of the first head, the diversity of languages among the believers (Acts 2:8–11 and Acts 6) does argue more congregations than one in the church of Jerusalem

First, it is true, there were in that second of the Acts, out of all nations that heard the apostles speak in the several languages of the countries they

{See p. 134}

Goodwin
omits §3

---

1. [Plato, cf. Apology of Socrates, IX; Cicero, *Orationes.* "In Verrem," 1.47.125]

Minutes,
Sess. 164
2.557–563
Gillespie,
30–31
Lightfoot,
183–186
were born in; but yet these were all either Jews or Proselytes, εὐλαβεῖς, worshippers (as verse 5), who came up to worship, and some parts of the worship were audible; and though born in other countries (the Jews being diſpersed), yet all were generally learned and underſtood the Hebrew tongue, the language of their own nation, even as to this day the Jews and their children do. Which seems evident from the ſtory in the twentieth, twenty-firſt and twenty-second chapter of the Aᴄts, Paul came up with divers Grecians to the feaſt of Pentecoſt (Aᴄts 20:4), unto which the Jews out of all quarters came, and being all at a solemn meeting in the temple (Aᴄts 21:27). The Jews out of Asia, ſtrangers, ſtirred up all the people againſt him, and when (Aᴄts 22:2) "He made a ſpeech to them, and they heard he ſpake the Hebrew tongue, they kept silence and heard him patiently." And further those mentioned (Aᴄts 2), did underſtand all of them Peter's sermon; and though others ſpoke to them in their own languages the wonderful things of God, besides Peter, yet that was but a preparatory sign to them (as 1 Corinthians 14:22) making way for their conversion (verses 11–13). But the means of their conversion was Peter's sermon after; and it was he also, that gave direᴄtions to them all what to do to be saved. And therefore it muſt be ſpoken in some one common tongue, they all underſtood; and those gifts of languages given to the apoſtles, were not out of a necessity to inſtruᴄt these new converts only, but to fit them when they should go abroad into all the world, and to be a sign to the Jews at present to convince them.

Secondly, for the Grecian widows (Aᴄts 6), the Helleniſts that lived among the Jews, might well be supposed to underſtand Hebrew; and that these had not several congregations from the reſt, appears by this, that the whole multitude together met and chose the deacons. It was a joint aᴄt. And if of differing languages, wherein the one underſtood not the other, occasioning such a diſtinᴄtion of congregations (as the proof would hold forth), how could they all have agreed in one meeting on the same man? But the argument as well holds againſt the presbyterial association of these congregations into one church, people and elders, unto which and in the communion and exercise whereof such correſpondences and intercourses are needful, as they require one common language.

1. [Reasons against and exceptions] to the Second branch of this argument that all these congregations were under one presbyterial government [because one church, 2. Elders of it are mentioned]

{See p. 142} Proof 1. Because they were but one church.

Braye, 48r
Goodwin
omits
  Though it be one, yet they not being more than could meet in one, the argument concludes not.

Proof 2. The elders of that church are mentioned.

  There is no mention of any elders in this church, until after the aforesaid dispersion (Acts 8). And so the weight of this argument will depend upon the proof of this—that after the dispersion there were many congregations, which the reverend assembly does not so positively affirm. The proof of their being such a presbytery (as the proposition intends) does depend upon this their being called elders to that church. We nowhere read them called a presbytery and that therefore they are elders, but they are therefore a presbytery (as here it is argued) because they are elders to that church. Now if they be elders in common, because a presbytery (as was said in answer to our first argument), then they are not to be argued a presbytery only, because they are elders in common. For then the argument runs *in circulo*. And the chief and first reason of their being elders (for no other is mentioned) is accordingly held forth in their being elders to that church in common, whereas according to presbyterial principles, there is a primary relation of elders, *quâ* elders, to their particular fixed congregations.

Minutes,
Sess. 165–166
2.564–574

Gillespie,
31–33

Lightfoot,
186–190

3. Reasons against the third proof of the second branch, *viz*. That the apostles did the ordinary acts of presbyters as presbyters in the church of Jerusalem, does prove a presbyterial government in that church before the dispersion

Braye, 48v

The proof of the whole depends upon this proposition; for though before the dispersion there had been many congregations, yet not under elders, but apostles.

{See p. 134}

Now it is granted that the substance of ministerial acts were one and the same in apostles and evangelists who were extraordinary, and in other ordinary ministers. But first, though for the acts of ministerial power, it was the same in the apostles, and them, yet in the extent of power (which is the point in question) therein the apostles' jurisdiction over many congregations is not the pattern of presbyterial elders over many. For the apostles' power was universal over all churches, and upon that was founded their power over those congregations, supposed many; and episcopacy may as strongly argue and infer, that because in Crete (by apostolical warrant) one man, Titus, did ordain elders, etc., that therefore there may be one man, *a bishop*, that has power to ordain, etc., in and over several churches. And this argument will be stronger from the instance of an evangelist for episcopal power, than this of apostolical government, for the presbyterial, by how much it is the more inferior office, but that of the apostles is more immediate and transcendent, and so the power of an evangelist is nearer to an ordinary succession; and it will as well follow, that any one presbyter alone might govern many congregations, because one of these apostles might, as that because the apostles did govern these jointly, that therefore many presbyters over several congregations may.

Secondly, each of these apostles, as he had by virtue of his apostolical

Minutes,
Sess. 169–171
2.817–592

Gillespie,
34–36

Lightfoot,
199–203

Goodwin,
96; generally
omits §3

commission the power of them all, so he had relation of ministry unto all these supposed congregations, unto every person thereof for the performance of all sorts of duties, of preaching to them, admonishing them, etc. But thus in the presbyterial government over many congregations fixed, and their pastors and elders fixed to them, the several elders are denied to have the relation of elders to each congregation, but make up only an eldership in common as united over all these. But the apostles here have the relation to both. And therefore if this apostolical frame be made a pattern, then it follows that all the elders of these congregations were directly and immediately elders to each congregation and every member of them, and not only of a common presbytery, for so the apostles were.

Minutes, 2.579, 582, 588, 3.420 If it be alleged that those acts of government, performed by them in that church, were for the substance of them ordinary acts, such as presbyters perform, and that therefore answerably their persons themselves are in them to be considered as elders, because that the apostles were not only apostles, but elders also (as 2 John 2 and 1 Peter 5:1); and therefore might and did act as elders in ordinary acts of church government—and are therefore therein to be looked at, as a just pattern to us, and to have ruled these congregations at Jerusalem as a college or body of elders united, condescending so to act as common presbyters taking the consent of the church (as Acts 6), as likewise they did in every church were they came joining with the eldership thereof, as elders, and not as apostles, and therefore that they might give a pattern, and example of an ordinary presbytery, especially seeing that what they thus did, they did as an united body to many congregations considered as one church—

It is answered to the first, that although the apostles are called elders, yet they are so called virtually, not formally, and but because apostleship contains all offices in it; so they are elders but upon this ground, that they are apostles. And therefore John in the very epistle where he styles himself an elder, he yet writes canonical scripture as an apostle, and takes on him to threaten Diotrephes, as an apostle, to remember him, which as a formal elder he could not have done. And surely those offices which Christ distinguishes (Ephesians 4), he gave some apostles, some pastors and teachers, the same person is not formally both, though virtually he may be. All that they did in that church of Jerusalem they are said to act as apostles. Their preaching is called the apostles' doctrine; their bringing their monies to them, as to the officers of that church, is to them not as elders, but as apostles. They laid it down at the apostles' feet, yea in that act of ordaining the seven deacons, it is said, they set them before the apostles (Acts 6:6) and they laid on their hands. And it is very hard to distinguish and say that the men were apostles, but the power they acted by, was as elders, when the name of an apostle imports the office. Yea in that the very act of government about deacons they must needs act as apostles: for they do not simply ordain the men, but do anew, by virtue of apostolical authority, institute the office of deacons by declaring Christ's mind, which none but apostles could immediately and at first have done. So as the same persons in this same act instanced in, must act partly as apostles, and partly as elders, and by what infallible rule shall we distinguish?

To the second, *viz.* that they acted here as it were in a joint body or *in collegio* over these many congregations, it is answered, that an association of elders in an eldership over many is not argued from hence. For first, they had all singly the same power which they exercised jointly, and that they should exercise it jointly here to that end to give a pattern for eldership, is not easy to prove. They exercised it together, because it fell out that they were together; and it was fit none of them should be excluded. But it depended not upon this union of all in a body, as acts of elders in a presbytery do. As parliamentary power is not the result of parliament men, but as assembled in parliament; yea and the authority of jurisdiction thence arises. Not so here—one apostle might have done that which all here did. Yea may it not be said that because two apostles, Paul and Barnabas, ordained elders in every church (Acts 14) as joined in the same act, and so acting not as apostles, but jointly, that therefore two elders associated may do the like? Secondly, it is hard to suppose that these apostles, when all together, should act with an inferior power to what they put forth in a like case alone. If Peter had been himself alone in a church new planted; then, and there, he must be supposed to act as an apostle, because he alone governed. And shall these apostles, when they are all in one and joined all together in one act, be yet supposed to fall lower in their power under the formal exercise of it? Thirdly, if they had acted as elders in a college, they might miscarry as elders do; and so the minor part of them have been subject to excommunication of the greater. And what power was there on earth to have excommunicated an apostle who held his office immediately from Christ, and who while he was in that office had power over all churches?

To the third, *viz.* that they in their proceedings did join with others, as in this choice of the deacons they did join with the multitude, as also when they came to any other churches they used to do; neither does that argue, that they acted not as apostles, but as elders. For first, they joined in acts with others, and joined others with themselves, wherein they yet acted as apostles. Thus in writing scriptures they joined others with them, as Paul joined Silvanus and Timotheus in his epistle to the Thessalonians; and not merely in the salutation, for the expressions run in their names also in that epistle. And Acts 15, the apostles, elders, yea brethren, joined in a letter to the churches; but these as apostles (therefore so called in distinction from the elders), and the rest according to their several interests; as the brethren did all according to their interests, so the elders and apostles in theirs. So in ordaining Timothy the presbytery laid on hands, yet they as a presbytery and Paul as an apostle. For else a presbytery had not had power to ordain an evangelist. Yet secondly, the apostles did wherever they came leave the elders and people to the exercise of that right belonged to them, although they joined with them; neither did therein lie their apostolical authority, to do all alone; for then they seldom or never acted as apostles in churches. Paul alone excommunicated not that Corinthian, and yet as an apostle wrote to have it done by them (for it was canonical scripture), and therefore although that this church at Jerusalem should choose their deacons, is a just example of the privilege of a church (for if the apostles when they were present allowed this interest to churches, then elders should much more), yet what the apostles did by an apostolical power in these congregations, cannot be drawn into example for officers, in that thing where their apostolical power lay, which was to exercise acts of jurisdiction in several churches.

Neither fourthly, will that help it, that they exercised this government in these congregations (supposed many) as considered to be one church. For if they acted not as elders, then the correlate to it, namely, church, could not be considered as presbyterial.

4. Reasons against the fourth and last proof of the second branch, *viz*. That the elders did meet together for acts of government (Acts 11:30; 15:4, 6, 22; 21:17, 18)

{See p. 151}

Minutes,
Sess. 172–175
2.593–610

Gillespie,
36–38

Lightfoot,
203–210

Goodwin generally omits §4 to the end

First, the argument from Acts 11:30 lies thus: There were elders in Judea that received alms (verses 29 and 30 compared); therefore the elders of Jerusalem did meet together of acts for government. In this argument, as the persons are mistaken, so the acts. For the elders of Jerusalem are not mentioned, but of Judea, as by comparing verse 29 and 30 it appears. And by this it might be as well argued that the elders in Judea met for presbyterial government, as that the elders of Jerusalem; seeing their alms were carried to the elders of Judea, as it is there said. The receiving alms (which is the only act that is mentioned) was not an act of government, for the deacons may meet to receive alms, and yet met not for acts of government.

For the second place mentioned (Acts 21:20), where it is said Paul came to James, and all the elders were present—although we read that all the elders were present, yet that they met for acts of presbyterial government, appears not. The occasion of the meeting was Paul's entertainment, whom some of the brethren had received at his first coming (verse 17) and now the elders meet to receive him also—a Christian duty of love and respect due to so great and famous an apostle. And Paul went not as cited, but to visit and salute them (as in verse 19). Secondly, the acts that passed were none of them presbyterial, for Paul gave them an historical relation of what things God had wrought by his ministry, the matter of which relation was intended to provoke them as brethren and fellow-laborers, to glorify God (as verse 20 is said they did), and not to give them an account, as to a consistory,

          I: Reasons of the Dissenting Brethren Against

that met for government. Such narrations, the apostles made even to the whole churches, as Paul and Barnabas at Antioch (Acts 14.27). When they had gathered the whole church together (which church was of not more than to meet in one assembly) they rehearsed in like manner, as here, all that God had done by them, and how he had opened a door of faith to the Gentiles. Neither will the advice they gave to Paul to prevent the scandal and offence the people would take at him, argue authority, much less government, neither was there any act of government put forth over their own churches if supposed many.

5. **Reasons against the alleging [of] Acts 15 for the meeting of the elders of Jerusalem, for presbyterial acts of government**   Braye, 51v

1. If it were a meeting of elders for acts of government, then it was a presbyterial meeting for acts of government; but that it was not such [a] meeting appears, because there was nothing done in it, that may seem to have any bond in it, but such as bound the churches, as Antioch, Syria, Cilicia, as much as Jerusalem. This cannot be any presbyterial meeting, for acts of government; for such meetings have only authoritative power over their own church.   {See p. 153} *Minutes,* Sess. 175–176 2.604–616 Lightfoot, 207–208 Gillespie, 38–42

2. The scope and end of this meeting was to give satisfaction to the offended brethren of Antioch, and dogmatically to declare their judgments in a difficult case of conscience, not to put forth any acts of juridical power upon any, as appears in the matter of their debate, and the issue of all. Of which more fully afterward. And if it be said that Peter reproved some of their own members present, such as had taught the necessity of the ceremonial law, "Why tempt you God," etc., this was not delivered as an act of government formally, by any vote of the presbytery, but in the way of discourse.

But it was affirmed to be sufficient to confirm the proposition, if it be a synodical meeting.

Presbyterial and synodical both it cannot be. For synods, they are (or ought to be) extraordinary and occasional. Presbyteries are standing and ordinary. Synods are made up of commissioners sent from presbyteries, and presbyteries are made up of the elders of particular congregations. The members of synods are elders of such churches which are (according to the principles of presbyterial government) complete churches, having full power of jurisdiction for all acts of government with themselves. But the members of presbyteries are elders of such congregations which are neither complete churches, nor have within themselves full and complete power. And these cannot be one. The elders of the presbytery at Jerusalem (when this once became a synod by the addition of the elders of other churches), ceased to be any longer a presbytery to that church, and must become with them a new body to all the churches, these other elders did come from. And then to argue these acts done by these (because the elders of Jerusalem were present and members of this synod) were presbyterial acts of the elders of Jerusalem, is all one as to go about to argue from the acts of government put forth by a Parliament at Westminster, to the power of the burgesses and common counsel of the city of Westminster, because there the Parliament sits, and the burgesses of that city are parts and members of that Parliament. Or, as if all the kingdom were governed by county courts; and out of those country courts, knights and burgesses should be chosen to make up a Parliament, when the Parliament is met, there can be no argument drawn from the power of a Parliament to prove the power of the county court. Or from the power of a county court to prove the power of a Parliament. Thus synods are made out of presbyteries, therefore we cannot argue from the power of presbyteries to the power of synods.

But secondly, we deny it to have been such an ordinary formal synod. The jurisdiction of synods is founded upon this necessary requisite thereunto, that there be commissioners from all those churches representing them, present, or called to be so. And the power of the jurisdiction cannot reach nor extend further than to such churches as have sent commissioners thereunto. The weight then of this synodical power depends on the proof of this, that all those churches sent commissioners to this assembly, which if either it be not proved, or the contrary thereunto found true, the authority of those decrees (as from those elders here) well prove, not to have been acts of government, further than the apostles' authority, who joined in it, was stamped on it. To affirm that commissioners from them all were present, because the decrees did bind them, is to beg what is denied, when another just reason may be given of their binding, if any such authority were in them. Our reasons to the contrary are these.

1. We find a deep silence about it. For we read but only of two churches between whom it was transacted, they of Antioch sending to Jerusalem, and their elders there (Acts 14:27–28 compared with Acts 15:2–3), and the messengers which were sent from this assembly going only to Antioch (verses 30 and 31), as those who were chiefly troubled. Only the benefit redounded to all they wrote to. Yea, although Paul came through Phœnice and Samaria (verse 3), yet we read not a word of any of the churches of those parts, their sending of any commissioners unto this synod, as had it been intended such, certainly they would. And there was this special reason, why those of this church were thus electively sent unto, because they were the mother church from whom the Word of God came, and from whom those men that troubled them had gone forth, and had pretended to teach what they had received from them. And besides, they were in an especial manner versed in this question, it being about the observation of their law; and there also some of the apostles were present (how many we

Goodwin
"deep silence,"
489

know not, for dispersed they had been long before). And if any number of others out of those other parts of Judea, had come up hither, it would have been said, as Acts 11:30, the elders of Judea, not only of Jerusalem. Yea, it is not so much as said that they that were sent from Antioch, were of the elders of that church, but that they sent Paul and Barnabas, and certain others of them.

2. The contrary seems clear. Namely, that those letters and decrees were written and sent only from the elders of Jerusalem, and not from all those churches. For (1) The decrees are everywhere attributed to the elders in Jerusalem (so 16:4—the decrees of the apostles and elders in Jerusalem, πρεσβυτέρων τῶν ἐν ʼΙερουσαλήμ). Now the usual style of the New Testament, is by way of distinction of churches to say the church in such a place, the elders in such a place, as the church of Antioch (Acts 13:1) and the church at Corinth (1 Corinthians 1:1), and by the like reason the elders in such a place do signify the proper elders of the church in that place or city, while but one, and therefore, if by the elders in Jerusalem, had been meant in this place only the elders met from all quarters at Jerusalem, as the place of that assembly, there had been a great ambiguity, seeing the more usual and proper import of that expression is to note out the fixed standing elders of a place, and the church in a place.

(2) Again, in the fourth verse Paul and Barnabas are said to be received of the church and apostles and elders, namely of Jerusalem, as in particular relation to it.

(3) Yea, the standing elders of that place assumed to themselves to have written the decrees (Acts 21:25, "As touching the Gentiles we have written and concluded.").

(4) And accordingly the conclusion of their letter is made the special act of that church, and the elders thereof (Acts 15:22, "It pleased the apostles and elders with the whole church"—that is of Jerusalem), to send chosen men, and the letters run thus, the apostles, elders and brethren (as verse 4).

(5) The matter of the letter argues it (Acts 15:24, "Forasmuch as certain that went out from us have troubled you with words, to whom we gave no such commandment.") How could this be said by a synod of elders of those churches, which were themselves troubled by them? It is manifest therefore they came out from this church of Jerusalem, who wrote this, and they pretended the apostles doctrine; which is called a commandment, because the apostles taught no other than what Christ commanded (as Matthew 28:20). And to say the denomination was from the more eminent part, namely, the elders of that church, had been derogatory to the synod, if it had been such a meeting.

(6) If the elders of all those churches had been present, there had been less need for the apostles and elders of Jerusalem to have sent chosen men to carry the letters, and withal to show the grounds of those their judgments

by word of mouth (Acts 15:27, 31). This needed not, if their own elders had been present, and so had been to have returned; and if they were sent as messengers from the synod, then to all the churches as well as to Antioch, and why do they then go no further than unto Antioch (Acts 15:33)? Yea, and although Paul and Barnabas delivered those results to all the cities, yet, as it should seem accidentally and not principally intended, they go not on purpose chiefly to deliver those decrees, but (Acts 15:36) it was Paul's motion upon other grounds to go visit the churches in every city, where they had preached, and so but occasionally delivered these decrees (Acts 16:4). So as they came to them, not as sent in a mandatory way, as to churches subject to that synod by a synodical law (as such canons are used to be sent), but as the judgment only of this church; and the apostles delivered them for their edification.

3. And in the third place, if there were any further authority or jurisdiction in their decrees, it was from the apostles, who were present and concurred in it, and who had power over all the churches. And accordingly, though the elders in the whole church were present and joined with the *as far as it per-* apostles, *quantum in se*, to consent and approve their decrees with that sev-*tained to them* eral respective kind of judgment proper unto them, yet all the authority put forth over these churches was that transcendent authority of the apostles, which is not now left in all the elders of the world joined together; and that therefore these decrees made, and the decision of these questions here, were by infallible apostolical authority. And to that end thy subjoined that apostolical seal, "It seemed good to us and the Holy Ghost." And although the ordinary elders, yea, and the whole church joined in this, yet but according to their measure, analogy, and proportion of their faith (even as in writing some epistles Timothy and Silvanus joined with Paul, but yet only Paul wrote apostolically, and the authority in them is looked at as his). Or else because perhaps they having the Holy Ghost fallen on them through the apostles' doctrine then delivered (which was then usual), persuading their hearts unanimously (though before dissenting, as verse 25) to accord; in that respect they might speak this in such a sense, that no assembly of men wanting apostolical presence and instruction, may now speak. And although it may be objected, that then this letter and these decrees should be formal Scripture, and so bind us still, it is answered; that they are Scripture, and written for our learning; and if the case were the same upon which they obliged them (*viz.* matter of offense), that then they would bind us now. But the things being enjoined, but as ἐπάναγκες [Acts 15:28], things of a super-added casual necessity and not absolute, in case of offense only and not simply for the things themselves, therefore now the necessity being ceased, the obligation ceases. Yet so as the equity of the rule and ground these were commanded upon, to abstain from things that offend our brethren does hold in like cases to the end of the world.

4. And laſt of all, there is no act of such authority and government put   Braye, 54r
forth in it, which the propositions intend; which will appear, if we either
consider the occasion and rise of it, or the issue and result of it.

It was not a set ſtated meeting by common agreement of the churches,
but Antioch sends to Jerusalem unknown to them; there are no summons
sent to send up delinquents, nor can we find these diſturbers are sent to
Jerusalem to be censured by those ecclesiaſtical punishments in which gov
ernment does properly lie and consiſt. The subject matter sent to them for
their decision was mercly mattcr of doctrine, about this queſtion (verse 2),
and about this word (verse 5). Namely, whether the ceremonial law was to
be observed? Concerning which they wrote their judgments dogmatically,
which they were called to do, being thus sent unto. Neither does it argue
that it was more than to determine this queſtion doctrinally they came up
for, because that Paul and Barnabas could have decided that before (being
themselves apoſtles), and that therefore their coming up was for discipline
againſt delinquents. For as the case ſtood, they liſtened not to Paul and
Barnabas as apoſtles, but pretended the judgment of the other apoſtles.
For indeed Paul and Barnabas did declare their judgments (the στάσισ, or
contention, verse 3, being attributed unto them as contending againſt the
false teachers for the truth), and so even the church of Antioch reſted not
in their decision. Otherwise Paul and Barnabas might have as apoſtles censured those delinquents without coming to Jerusalem, as well as by apostolic authority have decided the queſtion. For apoſtolical power extended
to discipline as well as doctrine.

If it be said, that even doctrinally to deliver the truth when it is done by
a company of elders, has authority or power in it, as when Chriſt said, "Go
and teach, all power is given me"—it is granted an authority exercised in
doctrine and so to be in synods, but yet not jurisdiction, which the proposition intends, which is when doctrines are delivered *sub pæna*, under the   *under the*
penalty of that ecclesiaſtical punishment of excommunication, if not re-   *penalty*
ceived. One miniſter alone has a dogmatical authority as a miniſter to rebuke, exhort, and yet acts of jurisdiction are not his alone, but of others
conjoined with him.

Neither, secondly, do the titles given to these results of theirs argue a
jurisdiction in that they are called τὰ δόγματα and τὰ κεκριμένα (Acts
16:4). For although the word δόγμα is used for an imperial decree (Luke
2:1), yet rarely, and more commonly (as Stephanus and Budaus observe)[1] for
doctrine and opinions in matters moral or ſpeculative, as *Platonis Dogma*,   *The Doctrines*
etc., and thence is translated to import the judgments of divines given, in   or *Dogmas of*
matters theological, although delivered with certainty. And so the using of   *Plato*
this word implies the subject to have been doctrinal only and so delivered.

---

1. [Stephanus (Henri Estienne), *Thesaurus linguae graecae* (Geneva: 1572–1573; Paris: 1833),
2.1602. Budé, *Commentarii Linguae Graecae* (1529; Basil: 1556), p. 255.]

And further the subject matter of this decision being about rules and ceremonies, and the not observing of them, the *Dogma* is elegantly, and perhaps on purpose, given to these apostolical canons by way of opposition and contradiction to those that taught and observed such rules, who are said—δογματίζειν—in so doing (Colossians 2:20), being led away by the false *Dogmata*, or *Heterodox* theses of false teachers that enjoined them.

And for that other word κεκριμένα translated "ordained," it plainly notes out but this, that these doctrinal "theses" were the joint declared and avowed judgments and conclusions of these (and so answers to those other words in their letters—"It seemed good unto us," "being with one accord" etc.—apostles and elders thus met with one accord agreeing therein, and particularly, and unanimously so judging. And therefore when James gives his judgment, he uses the same word κρίνω (15:19). "This is my judgment," which being voted and agreed upon by the rest they are called κεκριμένα. Neither does this argue any act of authority that the things here declared to be observed are indifferent, for some of them come under a moral consideration, and all come under the case of offence.

Neither does the language they commend these to them in, sound of that jurisdiction or government intended in the proposition. For although they seem to speak as guided infallibly in their resolutions—"it seemeth good to us and to the Holy Ghost"—yet their expressions are carried so, as to avoid jurisdiction. Those words "to lay no other burden," if any, must import this jurisdiction. But these words, as Ludovicus de Dieu has well observed,[1] are (as they may be) taken passively, therein agreeing with the Syriac translation, "It seemth good to us and the Holy Ghost that no other burden be laid on you." That whereas these teachers of the circumcision had gone about by their doctrine to bind the law of Moses upon men's consciences, and to put on them a burden too heavy for them to bear, as Peter speaks (verse 9), and had taught this to be the command of Christ and his apostles, and the judgment of the church of Jerusalem, they disclaim this, and profess they would have no such burden put upon them, and they gave these teachers no such commandment; that is, never delivered or uttered any such doctrine to be commanded. And if it be taken actively, yet the declaring it to be the command of Christ is the imposition here intended, for the same words are used of the teachers, who yet had not assumed by virtue of an ecclesiastical authority to impose these things, but by way of doctrine so, verse 10, "Why tempt you God to put a yoke upon the neck of the disciples?" And it is well known that in the Scripture phrase to teach and to declare, though by way of doctrine, and to press men's consciences with things as the commands of God, is said to be a binding and imposing a burden on

Minutes,
Sess. 175
2.578, 605,
607

---

1. [Louis (Lodewÿk) de Dieu, *Animadversiones in Acta Apostolorum* (1634) 147. Cf. Emmanuel Tremellius, [H Kainê Diathêkê] ... *Syriaca Novi Testamenti* (Stephanus: 1569), p. 378v; *Biblia Sacra*, vol. 6 (London: 1592), p. 100r. Cf. *Novum domini nostri Jesu Christi Testamentum Syriacè* (1621/1622).]

                I: REASONS OF THE DISSENTING BRETHREN AGAINST

them (verse 5). So of the Pharisees (and these were of the sect of the Pharisees, or whom, and to whom that was spoken, verse 5), it is said (Matthew
23:4), that the Pharisees "bind heavy burdens and grievous to be borne, and
lay them on men's shoulders;" which is spoken but of a doctrinal declaring and pressing men's consciences with the rigor of the law; and this is so
well known to be the language of the Jews, that it need not be insisted on.

Neither does it follow that if they may lay these burdens by way of doctrine, they may censure for the neglect of them, for every minister in his
sermon imposes those burdens, while they urge and declare these duties to
men, and yet have not power ecclesiastically to censure them. For though,
it being a command of Christ, they could not but hold it forth as such and
so urge it; yet not by way of jurisdiction, but with these soft words—"which
if you observe you do well."

Lastly, although these false teachers had subverted their faith, and, against
their own light, had vouched their doctrine to be the doctrine of the apostles, which deserved the highest censure being a sin so scandalous, yet they
proceeded not to censure them, by way of admonition or excommunication (which are acts of government), but only do declare their sin and error, and give their judgment of it.

[6.Reasons against the two last assertions of the assembly,   Braye, 56r
concerning the instance of the church of Jerusalem

Assertion. Whether these congregations be fixed or not fixed, in regard of   {See p. 162}
officers or members, it is all one as to the truth of the proposition.   *Minutes,*

Our reply.][1] Whereas in the close of the proof from the church of Jerusa-   Sess. 198, 199
lem, for many congregations to be under one presbyterial government, it   2.681–684;
is asserted, "Whether these congregations be fixed or not fixed, it is all one   3.7–14
as to the truth of the proposition," this reason is offered against it: Lightfoot,
245–247

There is this difference. Every congregation having elders fixed to it, is a   Gillespie,
church; for the relation of elders and church is mutual (Acts 14:23). "They   49–51
ordained elders in every church." This relation of elders to a church is a
special distinct relation to that congregation of which they are elders, so as
they are not related to other congregations. And these congregations are
Ecclesiæ primæ; churches formed up though incomplete, as being according   *the first*
to our brethren's opinion, members of a more general presbyterial church.   *churches*
But if congregations have no fixed officers, they are not churches according to their principles.

Now it makes a great difference as to the truth of the proposition, whether
many churches may be under the government of one, or whether many congregations (which to them are no churches), may be under the government
of one? Whatsoever our brethren show of divers congregations to be under

---

1. [The Braye MS omits the text between brackets. Braye, 56r.

the government of a church presbyterial, yet they nowhere show any one pattern or example in Scripture wherein many churches were under the power of one, nay, nor where any one church was under the power of another.

Assertion. That there appears no material difference between the several congregations in Jerusalem, and the many congregations now in the ordinary condition of the church, as to the point of fixedness, in regard to officers and members.

Our reply. And lastly, if there were many congregations in Jerusalem, having their officers fixed to them, and not in common, then during the time before the dispersion, the apostles must be those officers, that were thus fixedly disposed of to those several congregations, some over one, others over another, as ordinary elders now are. Now suppose this number of believers to have been as many thousands as is argued, as 10,000 or 12,000 souls, and these to be divided into as many congregations as might be divided to twelve apostles, severally to watch over; or suppose the several congregations made up of 2,000 (which is an allotment small enough to be set apart for the pains of two apostles).

Hereupon this great incongruity does follow, that apostles are brought to the state and condition and work of parish ministers, to whom, yet it was committed, and inseparably annexed to their office, yea, and constituted it, as apostles to have the care of all churches. And if when the churches were multiplied and dispersed into several countries, they were to have the care of them, then much more when they were in one city. Some of the writers against episcopacy (when those that write for it, allege that instance of James abiding at Jerusalem, as the bishop of the church), have judged it as debasing the apostolical power to limit it to one diocesan church. But this position does debase all the apostles at once much more. It makes them not bishops to many churches, but ordinary elders; in that one or two of them (perhaps) are over one single church. Yea, and which is yet more incredible, if these churches and their government were like to those under the presbytery, and no material difference between them and ours, these apostles were in their parishes not only subordinate in their government to the common presbytery of all the apostles, but limited to lesser acts of government. For so the lesser elderships in the churches under the presbyterial government are; confined only to examine, and admonish, and prepare for the greater presbytery, and therein not enabled to ordain elders over the congregations, or excommunicate a member. Peter and John joined together were by this principle not enabled to it. And yet, if we do not suppose such a limited government in those several congregations, here can be no pattern for the presbyterian government as it is practiced. Or if otherwise, we should suppose them fixed officers for teaching only, to one of those congregations, and to have no government at all over it, but to bring all to the common presbytery of apostles, that is a greater incongruity than the former. For this casts them below the condition of our parish elders, for unto them, the greater presbytery does allow some measure and part of the government, but such a supposition would allow apostles none in their several congregations.

7. Other reasons against the main proposition, the Scriptures holds forth, that many congregations may be under one presbyterial government

Braye, 57r

By particular congregations either first an assembly of Christians meeting for worship only, as to hear, pray, etc., or secondly, an assembly so furnished with officers as fit for discipline having a presbytery, is meant. In the latter sense, which is *that* the proofs are brought to confirm, and *that* that is practiced where this government is set up, the proposition is equivalent to such an assertion as this; many presbyteries may be under presbyterial government, as thus, parochial presbyteries may be under one classical, many classical, under one provincial, etc., which is the same as to affirm that one presbytery may be over another, as the bishops affirm, that one presbyter may be over another. This is evident, if you assert a presbyterial government may be over a congregation that is composed of a presbytery and people. For it cannot be said to be over a congregation, if it be over the people only, that is not over their presbytery also, for then the presbytery will be independent, and the people under two presbyteries coordinate, and not subordinate, which stands not with common reason.

{See p. 164}
Gillespie, 18

This then being the assertions, it is thus argued against. A presbytery over a presbytery, or power over power necessarily implies two sorts of presbyteries, or ecclesiastical jurisdictions, specially distinct or at least more than numerically. A greater or lesser vary not the kind in a physical or theological consideration, but in a political it does. He that has a greater power than I have, that is a power over my power, a power to order, direct or correct the power I have. This man's power and mine differ as two sorts or kinds of power. And although this superior presbytery be made up of presbyters sent as commissioners from the congregational or parochial presbyteries, yet this hinders not at all but that they may be thus distinct. For some cities and towns corporate, their officers are sent up, and sit as members of Parliament, yet this Honorable House has a power distinct, and superior to that which is in London or York. Though the superior presbytery be made up of presbyters from several congregations, yet it is made up of presbyteries. It has the persons materially considered, but not that power formally considered. For as while the Parliament sits and certain burgesses from borough towns sit as members in it, these towns notwithstanding still retain all the power those corporations were ever invested with, so particular congregations while some of their elders sit in the classical presbytery,

Minutes, 2.523
Lightfoot, 166
Gillespie,
25, 70

have elderships or a presbytery still. Now that it is very probable the Scriptures hold not forth two sorts of presbyteries thus specifically distinct, may be thus argued.

I. Where the Scripture holds forth distinct sorts in any kind, there will be found either distinct and proper names and titles, or at least some adjunct or difference added to that which is common or general. In the apostles' times there were presbyters over presbyters, apostles were superior to prophets, and prophets a distinct order from teachers. Therefore in 1 Corinthians 12[:28], "God hath set some in the church: first apostles, secondarily prophets, thirdly teachers, after that miracles, then gifts of healings," etc. They have not only particular names and titles, but special notes of distinction added, πρῶτον ἀποστόλους, δεύτερον προφήτας, as in Genesis 1, where no distinction of names is given, the sun, the moon, and stars of heaven, are all called lights, yet there are terms of difference added. They are called first, "great Lights," and then the "greater to rule the day," and the "lesser to rule the night."

Minutes, 2.523
Gillespie, 25

Throughout the New Testament we find this word πρεσβυτεριὸν, but in three places, whereof there is but one that holds out the government in hand, and in that place you have the naked word only without the addition of any such expression, greater, lesser, superior, inferior, or any kind of adjunct, that can possibly put a thought in us, of more presbyteries than one. Notwithstanding so useful are particular distinct names where there are distinct sorts or kinds of administration, as it is not omitted by any church in their ordinances for government; in Scotland the lowest is termed a consistory, the next a classis or presbytery, the third a provincial synod, the fourth a general assembly. The French in these terms, consistories, and colloquells [*colloquys, conferences*] and synods: so in the episcopal republic there was the like variety.

II. As the Scriptures hold forth nothing in any title or name to distinguish, no more can we thence discover any sorts of government different in nature. For trial of this, let it be supposed there is a parochial or consistorian presbytery for one sort, there is another sort we call classical, what Scripture gives light by any kind of reasoning to warrant the setting up one of those above or over the other? Do you read any where God has set in his church, first presbyteries, secondarily, classes, then consistories? Or is there anything in the Word directing a different composition or constitution in these?

1. For the material, the persons that these presbyteries are made up of, are the same. The consistory has gifted men set apart to the office of the ministry. Those that are in a classical presbytery are no otherwise qualified, nor indeed does the Scripture require anything but a "presbyteration" to qualify men for any sort, if there were sorts of presbytery.

That there is a greater number of presbyters in the one than in the other, this alters not the state in respect of the matter. For if the number be competent, that is, so many as two or three may agree (Matthew 18), it suffices. The Honorable House of Commons, is to all parliamentary purposes as much a house, when but two or three above forty, as when four hundred. Nor does this always fall out that all classical presbyteries have a greater number than some parochial. Scriptures have determined neither how few will constitute a classical presbytery, nor how many may be in a parochial. Practice many times makes them equal.

2. Now for the formal, the uniting of this matter into a *consessus* or *cœtus*. Presbyters become united into a presbytery in the classical, by having pastoral charges in such a division, whosoever comes so to be disposed of, he is no sooner pastor to such a parish, but he is *eo nomine*, member of such a classis. The presbyters of a parochial presbytery are as nearly united and more. They are united in the choice and call of the same congregation they govern, and united in the whole work of the ministry over the same people; so that they are not only fellow governors, but fellow laborers in the same vineyard. There is therefore no just ground for such a distinction of difference between presbytery and presbytery in respect either of the matter or the form.

> *gathering or assembly*
>
> *by the very name/title*

III. Nor thirdly, do we find anything in the Scriptures making them, as from different employments, or functions, to differ. 1. We pretend and so it is in the proposition, the one is superior, the other is inferior; but how can you say the Scriptures have made this difference, when there is not a word spoken this way in any place? Presbyterian writers themselves in some expressions seem to take away utterly such difference as this. In one place you shall read the classis can do nothing, *renitente ecclesia*, but it is null and invalid; thus *The Assertion for Discipline*, and avouches Zepperus, Zanchy, and others as of this opinion.[1] The congregation, though but *minima Ecclesiola*, yet may reform, that is suspend, excommunicate, etc., *renitentibus correspondentiis*—So Voetius in his *Theses* and *Desperata causa Papatus, lib. 2. Sect. c. 12.*[2] Surely according to what these reverend divines have expressed, it is hard to be said, which of these presbyteries has the greater or superior power.

> *with the church resisting—the least little church —with the correspondents resisting*
>
> *Minutes*, 2.499
>
> Gillespie, 21
>
> Baillie, 2.65, 165

2. The employment or work of a presbytery is to ordain, excommunicate,

---

1. [George Gillespie (1613–1648), *An Assertion of the Government of the Church of Scotland, in the points of ruling elders, and of the authority of presbyteries and synods* (Edinburgh, 1641), Part Two, chapter 1, p. 121. Also *Works: A Presbyterian's Armoury*, ed. William M. Hetherington (Edinburgh: Ogle and Oliver & Boyd, 1846), p. 42. Cf. *An Assertion* (Naphtali Press, 2008), p. 113. Wilhem Zepper, German Reformed theologian (1550–1607), *De Politia Ecclesiastica* (Herbornae, 1595), lib. 1. cap. 19. Jerome Zanchi, Reformed Theologian (1516–1590), *Operum Theologicorum* (Geneva, 1605; 1613; 1618), 4 Præl., col. 756.]

2. [Gisbertus Voetius, Dutch Calvinist theologian (1588–1676). As is clear in the response (p. 170), the Independent divines' reference is to two works: *Disputatio Theologica ex Politiâ Ecclesiasticâ de Unione Ecclesiarum earumque Regimine in Classibus & Synodis* (Ultraiecti: ex officinâ Aegidii Roman, Academiae typographi, 1641); cf. *Gisberti Voetii Tractatus selecti de politica ecclesiastica Series Prima*, edited by F. L. Rutgers (Amsterdam, 1885), 2.257; and *Desperata Causa Papatus, novissime prodita a Cornelio Jansinio, ubi imprimis magna illa præjudicia de Reformatorum vocatione: de Magia, aliisque abominationibus Papatus* (Amstelodami: 1635), pp. 186ff.]

suspend, admit members, appoint times for worship and the like. The classical presbytery reserve ordination and excommunication to themselves, but the other are left to parochial presbytery. Thus some Presbyterians divide the work, others possibly otherwise. But how can we affirm any such designment from the Scriptures, if you have not two sorts, either in name or nature to be found there? And none of these acts or administrations but may be done by that one, the Scripture mentions, which doubtless they may, seeing ordination seems to be specified in the text. If the greater, then doubtless the lesser. The pastor in one place is said to exhort, in another to comfort, in another to visit the sick. This will not warrant distinct sorts of pastors, for there being but one sort spoken of in Scriptures, we must interpret all these several administrations to belong to that one.

It was not found as easy work in this assembly to find two sorts of elders, teaching, and ruling. Notwithstanding all the Scripture has said on these, and in some places, so plain, as if of purpose to distinguish them. If it be so hard a matter by Scripture light to hold forth two sorts of presbyters, it must needs be more difficult to find out two sorts of presbyteries, especially seeing (as it is generally granted, and this by the presbyterians themselves) that for above fifty years after Christ, and in the apostles times, there was but one kind of presbytery.

It has been the wisdom of states to keep and preserve the bounds and limits of their judicatures evident, and distinct, and as free from controversy as *mine* and may be. If laws and ordinances above matters of *meum* and *tuum*, and such *thine* inferior claims should not be so evident, the authority of these courts will be in a readiness to relieve wrongs and injuries through such mistakings. But controversies and clashings about these high and public interests are no other in the issue than the dividing of a kingdom within itself.

Is a man wiser in his generation than Jesus Christ? He is our Law-giver; Braye, 59r the government is laid upon his shoulders; he is the Wonderful Counselor, the Prince of Peace. And therefore surely though other matters of practice and duty should have obscurity in the rule, yet it is most probable, He has ordered authority and jurisdiction with the officers and offices for the managing of it, so evident, as not to put us to search in a dark corner for directions. We cannot be said to be clear in our rule when we are thus enforced out of one word, and but once used, to raise so many thrones, or forms of government, especially it being foreseen by Christ that such is the nature of man as nothing occasions more bitter contention than the lusting which is in us to have authority and jurisdiction over others.

Sic Subscribitur: Thomas Goodwin, William Bridge, Philip Nye, William Greenhill, Jer. Burroughes, William Carter, Sidrach Sympson.

Concordat cum Originali. Adoniram Byfield, Scriba.

The Answer of the Assembly of Divines

Unto the Reasons of the Seven Dissenting Brethren, against the Proposition of Divers Congregations being United under one Presbyterial Government[1]

[OBSERVATIONS ON THE INDEPENDENTS' MAIN ARGUMENT]

And first, to their first and main argument. Concerning which we observe: {See page 63} First, that:

This first main argument is equally strong against all government by synods, which the whole Christian church has ever acknowledged unto this day.

Secondly, it is as strong (though they intended it not) against elders doing any acts of elders out of their own particular congregation, what need *Braye, 65r* soever there be of it. So that if any particular congregation cannot preserve itself, it must be left in corruption and to perdition, rather than any act of the elders of an other congregation may be exercised for their relief, by any ecclesiastical or presbyterial power. As suppose a minister should administer the sacrament in another congregation upon any exigent, all the incongruities and absurdities of this argument fall upon him. It may be alleged against him, then he must stand in relation to them as an elder of that flock; church and elder are *Relata*, as well as church and elders, and then he must watch *Things related* over their souls, etc. Then his whole work must be ἐν ὑμῖν, then may he rule them, his preaching and ruling power must be commensurable; then may they challenge to elect him, then may the deacons of his parish come and collect alms among them, etc. And so of all the rest of the incongruities, and disproportions. This argument therefore carrying with it so much mischief to the whole church, must needs be false either in the major, or minor, or both, which to discover, we premise these few *præcognita*.

1. The whole church of Christ is but one, made up of the collection and aggregation of all who are called out of the world by the preaching of the Word, to profess the faith of Christ, unto the unity thereof. From which union there arises unto every one such a relation unto, and dependence upon the catholic church, as parts have to the whole, and are to do all Christian duties, as parts conjoined unto the whole, and members of the same commonwealth and corporation (Ephesians 4:3–14).

---

1. [*The Answer of the Assembly of Divines to the Reasons of the Dissenting Brethren against the Third Proposition concerning Presbyteriall Government and the Proofs thereof* (London: for Humphrey Harward, 1648). The Braye MS has 11 blank leaves and a title page between 59r and 65r.]

2. All the ministers and officers of the church are given to the whole church for the gathering and building of it (1 Corinthians 12:28, Ephesians 4:11–12). And they are all to teach and rule, and perform all other ministrations with reference to it, and the best advantage of it.

3. When this whole number of called men, and their officers were no more than might meet together in one place, they taught and ruled, and did all other ministerial and Christian works in one undivided body respectively.

4. Their number increasing, so that they could not with edification meet all together according to the will of Christ, they divided into several companies for their better ordering and increase, and such several companies joined together in one external fellowship and communion of the same public profession, and rule of faith, worship of God, and ecclesiastical discipline, and practice of love, and the duties of it, are in the Scripture called churches, and to some one of these should every believer join himself.

5. And being thus joined, the officers and members should not act or work, as if they were independent corporations, but only as parts of Christ's body, and are all to regard the common good of the whole, and all things in these smaller bodies are to be managed for the greatest advantage of the whole (Ephesians 4:1, etc.).

6. As it is the will of Christ that particular Christian men and families should be associated into some particular assembly, for their own and others' edification, so (as many as may be) should such particular assemblies associate with other assemblies, for the common and mutual good of them all— sometimes they standing in need of others, or others of them; sometimes themselves singly are insufficient to their own business; sometimes divisions grow between the people and their elders; sometimes the people rent from their elders; sometimes the elders miscarry in their administrations to the people; sometimes a whole church grows corrupt in doctrine or conversation; sometimes it is not commodious and expedient to use their power without assistance and counsel—in all which cases they stand in need of the help of others, and when other congregations are in the like condition, they stand in the like need of them. Some things also [are] of common concernment to them all, as when sometimes error, heresy, schism, overrun many of these congregations; sometimes divisions grow betwixt church and church; sometimes ministers are to be translated from one congregation to another, and many the like things fall out, which are of common concernment, and cannot be done by any of them alone—and in all such cases, and for all such ends they are tied to associate, as much as particular men are tied to associate with a congregation if it may be obtained. And no excuse can be pleaded for a congregation and their officers, which may not be pleaded for a particular person, the unity of the body of Christ being as strong for the one as for the other, and the necessity and benefits of the one as of the other.

7. In such associations, as the mutual consent of particular men and

Braye, 65v

families orderly regulated joining in one congregation gives them power and authority one over another according to the rule of Christ, without hurting or destroying, but rather helping and strengthening of the liberty of their several persons and families; so in this association of congregations their mutual consent orderly regulated gives them a sufficient call for the elders to exercise their power of elders (which is nowhere any other than ministerial) and the people their interest in such things as are above mentioned, without impairing or hurting the liberty and privileges of the congregations, but rather preserving and strengthening of them; this association of congregations, as that also of families being such a joining as proceeds *ex charitate, ex debito mutuæ societatis colendæ* as is between friends and equals, *non ex debito inferioris conditionis ad præstandum obsequium*, as between masters and servants.[1] This is most clear in the continual intercourse held in the churches of the New Testament betwixt several churches or congregations, one with another, even while they enjoyed the personal presence, direction and authority of the apostles (2 Corinthians 8:14, 19 with Romans 15:26; Colossians 4:16; Acts 11:29, 30; Galatians 6:1, 2, 5, 9 with Galatians 1:2; Acts 13:1–5; 15:1, 3–4), sometimes by letters written to many churches as one body, sometimes by commissioners, sometimes by synods, sometimes in a particular matter concerning one church, sometimes in matter of common concernment to many churches. And it is impossible the common good of the whole church should be preserved without these associations; it being clearly the will of Christ that the communion of saints not only internal, but also external among them all should be maintained and increased; all being tied to "strive together in one spirit, to help one another, to strengthen the weak, to admonish the unruly, to withdraw from them that walk inordinately." The institution of Christ making His church one, and appointing all these as means proportionable to attain that end, and nowhere limiting them to be as means to particular and individual men only, but left them to be applied according to the present condition of times, places, persons, of one, or more, or many, whether men or churches; the very light of nature requiring, that all due and lawful means should be used for the attaining of some necessary end, warrants us to conclude, that the means appointed or commanded for particular Christians, should be as appliable to whole companies of them, unless God's Word has somewhere forbidden it.

If it be demanded whether it be not left free to congregations and their officers, whether they will join in such association or not; because their mutual consent is that which is pleaded as the next foundation of it? We *answer:* It is here as it is in the case of joining with a particular congregation. All are enjoined to it by Christ to be members of some congregation. But when they join to this congregation rather than to that, the mutual

Braye, 65v

from love, from the obligation of cultivating mutual society… not from the obligation of the inferior condition to furnish obedience

---

1. [This is a quotation from Robert Parker (1564–1614), *De Politeia Ecclesiastica Christi, et hierarchica opposita, libri tres* (Frankfurt: Basson, 1616), lib. 3, c. 22, p. 329 (second pagination).]

consent between them, and the congregation with whom they join, is that which immediately gives them that ſpecial relation to one another. So it is here. What further rules are about the regular settling of congregations or such associations as these are? what is the magiſtrate's power or duty in settling the bounds of congregations of such presbyteries or what he has to do with such [as] refuse either to associate with particular congregations, or classical presbyteries or what the duty of the churches is about it? belongs not to this present queſtion. It is sufficient here to show that such as are willing thus to associate may see a warrant for it.

8. Such proofs and evidences muſt be admitted by our brethren in this point, as are acknowledged and allowed by them in other parts of church government, wherein they agree with us, which are not always immediately out of Scripture sufficiently clear to convince pertinacious adversaries; and yet the Scripture grounds compared with light of nature are sufficient to satisfy pious and moderate men.

{margin: Braye, 66r}

[REPLY TO MAIN ARGUMENT]

These things premised, we proceed to this their main argument, *viz.* If many particular congregations, having all their officers fixed, etc.

{margin: {See p. 63}}

Where firſt in general we note, that they have framed this argument only againſt the joining of those many congregations into one presbyterial government, who have all their officers fixed, which is not our proposition, nor was our inſtance brought to prove it. We determined not whether all congregations can have all officers fixed, not whether they muſt have them if they could, whether the several congregations so united muſt have each their own particular presbytery, or whether they muſt all *coalescere in unum tantum presbyterium*; nor do we find it certain, whether in Jerusalem the officers were fixed or not fixed.

{margin: *coalesce/unite into one presbytery*}

We doubt not to affirm that there may be divers congregations joined in one presbytery only, and the officers to teach and govern in common, when it shall be found moſt for their edification, and so it is in some reformed churches at this day. And the truth thereof was also acknowledged by one of these dissenting brethren, who refused to enter his dissent againſt the proposition if taken in this sense. And we doubt not also to affirm, that where there is this joining of many congregations, there may be diſtinct presbyteries in the several congregations, who may have either some or all officers fixed, and they may do what belongs to that congregation, only so far as they are able, and their joining into a common presbytery is for their helping and ſtrengthening.

{margin: Jeremiah Burroughs *Minutes,* 2.440, 441}

So that our proposition may ſtand true, though their whole argument were granted, and the whole ſtrength of it is by their new framing of it appliable only againſt the Appendix in the inſtance of Jerusalem, *viz.* That "it is all one as to the truth of the proposition," etc.

{margin: {See p. 93}}

And unless the fixing of officers do wholly alter the ſtate of the queſtion, their argument muſt fall to the ground. For inſtance, suppose in Jerusalem there were ten congregations and twenty officers feeding and ruling them in common, no one of them fixed to any one congregation. This kind of presbytery would pass for a lawful government, and none of these incongruities or absurdities are charged upon it by this argument. But if they should find by experience that it would be more for the edification of the congregations to have two of the officers fixed to each congregation to teach and govern them in such things which concern themselves, and yet all of them agree in a common college with mutual advise and consent to transażt all things which should be of difficulty or common concernment, such a presbytery should make them liable to all these incongruities and absurdities by this their argument. Yet notwithſtanding we shall examine it, as themselves have framed it, *viz.*:

"If many congregations having all elders already fixed reſpeżtively unto them may be under a presbyterial government, then all those elders muſt suſtain a ſpecial relation of elders to all the people of those congregations as one church, and to every one as a member thereof." But this 'carries with it great and manifold incongruities and inconsiſtencies with rules of Scripture, and principles of reformed churches themselves; therefore it may not be.' {See p. 63} Braye, 66v

We *answer:* Firſt to the consequence of the major by denying it, that in such a government the elders do the work of elders, is granted, and that in that work, and because of the work there done, they bear a ſpecial relation of presbytery to the churches, is as readily granted. But that therefore they muſt be judged singly elders of these churches, tied to do all the offices of elders to them as to the congregations where they are fixed, or that all the congregations who joined in such an association muſt necessarily be one church, one particular firſt church (as it is called) is utterly false. When many elders of several congregations meet in a synod and do such ażts as our brethren grant they may do in relation to many congregations, we suppose they will not deny that they do these ażts of elders as elders; yet they are not thereby every one argued to be elders of every one of these congregations, or these congregations argued to be one church. Or when a miniſter adminiſters the sacrament to another congregation, he does it as an elder, and as having a ſpecial relation to that people at that time, and in that work, he being called to it; yet it follows not that he is, or therefore muſt be an elder of that church, bound to perform all offices of an elder publicly and privately to every one of them. Gillespie, 12

And if it be excepted againſt this, that 'such an occasional ażt does not indeed prove it, but to do it ſtatedly or ordinarily will prove it.' We *answer:* That which is lawful for him to do once or twice, is not made unlawful to do oftentimes when the same call and occasion requires it. He may not once do that which is unlawful; he may not once do that ażt of an elder out of his own place which should needlessly disable him from his work in his own place. But supposing him faithful in that, he may and ought to put forth any act of an elder for the good of other churches, yea for all the churches in the world (if he be able and thereunto called) as well as to pray and write books for the benefit of all. If he be able without prejudice to [do] his own work at home, he may keep a weekly lecture in another congregation for the benefit thereof. Or in administration of sacraments—suppose a minister, who has but a small congregation (it may be a hundred souls), should live by another minister who had a congregation of two or three thousand souls, he may ordinarily assist that other minister in the administration of the sacrament of the Lord's Supper when it may be done without prejudice to his own little flock.

If any should say, 'It is not lawful for a minister to administer the sacraments in another congregation, because it is a church act, but yet may receive the people of another congregation to receive the sacrament with his church,' as the practice of some is:

We *answer:* If by a church act be meant, that they who receive together must be one church, that is false. And we think our brethren will not own it. For if so, none may receive the sacrament in any church, but those that are members of that church. And if it be granted, that they still are members of another church; then it is granted that an elder may do an act of an elder among those to whom he is not a fixed officer. And surely he may as well do it when he goes to them, as when they come to him for it. A man does as truly lend money to his neighbor, who comes to fetch it at his house, as when he carries it to his neighbor's house, though his courtesy is more in the latter.

If it should be yet further said, that though all this should be granted, that 'elders may preach and administer sacraments to others, yet it will not follow that they may exercise acts of discipline towards others, though they should call them thereunto in such an association.' We *answer:* First, where is that limitation in the Scripture for the one and not for the other? Neither can our brethren object it, who acknowledge the elders' power of teaching, ruling, and administration of sacraments to be commensurable. And we further say, that of all the acts of an elder (wherein he is to apply the will of God to others) none are so safe for him to perform as those belonging to discipline, both because they are to be performed *in collegio,* with the advice and assistance of others, and are all to be performed *secundum allegata & probata* only. We say therefore clearly, that when many congregations do mutually agree, that the elders of their several congregations should join by mutual advice, counsel, and authority of elders to manage all matters of common concernment, difficulty, etc., among themselves: all these thus joined in a body or an eldership to those congregations, and each one does the acts of elders in the presbytery to those congregations in all those things for which they are thus associated; yet every one of them

Gillespie, 12, 13

in assembly
according to
what is alleged
and proved severally, and particularly, is not to be looked upon as an elder of every one of those congregations, and bound to do the whole work of an elder to every one of them.

And thus it is likewise in human affairs, in the Jewish commonwealth, the heads of the several tribes, when all joined together, were as a parliament to all Israel, and might in that associated body do many things which could not be required of particular elders, or heads of the tribes. So is it with us, the knights and burgesses assembled in parliament may in that body do many things, in relation to the whole kingdom, which none of them may do severally and singly. So may colonels associated in a council of war, so may particular heads of colleges joined in the consistory, so may the alder-men of several wards, when joined in the court of aldermen.

And whereas they reply to this, page 8,[1] that in all these instances, these {See p. 72} have their distinct names, laws, and work set out by their several states— for example, the Scripture held out in that of the tribes, that there were general heads of the tribes who were called elders of the people, the others were called elders of such and such cities, of such and such families, and so forth, and had their several work set out by law; the general heads had reserved cases of blasphemy, etc., and the like, they say, is in the other in-stances found among ourselves, colonels, masters of colleges, aldermen of cities, burgesses of towns, and parliament, have both their titles, and works set down respectively, what they may do in their lesser sphere, and what they may do in their greater associations. But for ours the Scripture hold forth no such thing, they are called elders similarly and univocally, and we shall read but simply and singly, elders and churches, as relatives, without any such note of distinctions.[2]

We *answer*: (Not to dispute how hard it would be for our brethren to Braye, 67v prove clearly that distinction of the several names and work of these elders in Israel, etc.) We inquire not after names, but things. And as for the thing in question, we have already cleared that the Scripture holds out that as the church is one, and all the elders given for the good of that one church, so their officers (when orderly called for) should be exercised in any part of it for the good thereof. And that a mutual consent and agreement, is a sufficient warrant and call for the exercise of this power, whether in one

---

1. [This must be the page reference in the manuscript used by the assembly (it is the twelfth leaf in the Braye MS, or 40v) as the copy as printed in 1648 has this on pages 10–11.]

2. [The Assembly is summarizing and paraphrasing the Independents' argument at this point. There is no distinction in the original between the Assembly's quotation of the Inde-pendents' reasons, given in italics as are all other emphasized words, and their summation or paraphrase of these reasons. Much of the italicization has been removed in this edition and any apparent quotations appear within double quotation marks. Summations or loose para-phrases have been converted to Roman type without quotation marks. Clear paraphrases, proposed objections or words placed in the mouth of the opponent, are placed within single quotation marks.]

congregation only, as suppose in Cenchrea, or in many, as suppose in Jerusalem, or yet more, as suppose when Antioch and Jerusalem joined (Acts 15), that in any of these, or all of these, they may, and ought, upon such a call, exercise any of their gifts and offices, as the church, or any part thereof shall stand in need. As in a country or kingdom, when the state sets many commissioners for preserving the peace of that country or kingdom in all their meetings, whether in parishes, in relation to the parish only, or in hundreds, in relation to the hundred only, or in their quarter or general sessions; while in all these meetings, they regularly seek to preserve the common peace, they are warranted to all by their commission. So is it here.

As for the allusion of burgesses in several corporations, and their arro-
{See p. 73} gating greater power, or power of larger extent than the laws allow, under pretense of their names of burgesses and corporations, because in some other state or kingdom, there were burgesses who had such power as those would claim, which allusion they largely prosecute.

We *answer:* it would fully confute us, if we challenged any other power, or extent of power than Christ has given to all His ministers to exercise in any part of His church upon a call.

We say again, that this power of ministers is nowhere any other than ministerial, and [it] is not to be exercised anywhere at their own wills, but according to His direction, and the call of His church, and then they may do it.

But we also answer secondly, that it would suit the question in hand far better, to suppose that all and every parish in London, yea, in all England, were every one of them such an absolute corporation, and the several inhabitants such burgesses, that they had not only all power in themselves to do their own business, without any others claiming any authority over them, how bad soever they should grow; but that also it should be pretended to be against their fundamental liberties to associate with any others for matters of difficulty, miscarriages, or common concernment to do anything for suppressing any enormities among themselves or others, otherwise than by taking or giving counsel and advice, which if they refuse to follow, they may deny familiarity to them, but use no other authority to reclaim them. Such a comparison would truly set forth the state of the controversy; by which we might conjecture what rents, divisions, mischiefs, confusions, all cities, towns, and parishes would quickly be filled and overrun withall.

Thus your honors[1] see with what clear evidence and upon what just
Braye, 68r grounds and reason we deny the consequence of their major proposition, which is the only foundation upon which all the rest is built.

[PROOFS OF THE FIRST (OR MAJOR) PROPOSITION ANSWERED]
{See p. 63} We now proceed to examine the proofs of their major. 1. They say "they must

---

1. ["Your honors"—The Houses of Parliament.]

have relations of elders to all and every one of the members: for church and elders are relatives."

(1) We *answer*: If by church there be meant a particular church, we deny the truth of that proposition, *relata* do *se mutuo ponere & tollere*. And a minister of the gospel is so made a minister to the catholic church of Christ, that he does not always cease to be an elder when his relation to a particular church does cease. *relatives do mutually establish or abolish themselves*

(2) When they stand in relation to a particular church; yet if the meaning be, that they are relatives, so that every act of an elder must argue him to stand in relation to an elder in all duties of an elder to that church or people to who he performs one act—we have already shown the falsity of it. An elder in his work is not limited by the law of God to one congregation, as the office of a parent or husband, are limited by the law of nature to their own children or wife, to whom they must perform the duties of these relations whole and only; or as a constable is limited by our laws to one parish. But rather, as in the former comparison of commissioners for the peace, who though they ordinarily exercise their authority in some one certain division, where their residence is, yet occasionally extend it to all parts of the county, as a call requires them; so we say the elders receive their power and commission for the whole church of Christ, and may exercise it wherever they have a call, and nowhere without a call; and the mutual assent and agreement of the persons among whom, and to whom they should exercise it, it is the *proximum fundamentum hujus exercitii*. *proximate foundation of this exercise*

And whereas they further say; "That the argument of the presbyterial government, is taken by the presbyterial divines from this, that many congregations in Scripture are made one church, and the elders thereof elders of that church:"

We *answer*: When a multitude of believers (though many thousands), agreed together in one presbyterial government, who had but one only presbytery, and who probably did all in common, for feeding and governing; they were usually called by the name of one church, and the elders were the elders of that church. So it may be still in the like condition. They found it best, in those times of persecution, and public unsettledness, to have one common treasury for all their poor, and one common consistory for all matters of censure. But doubtless had the number of believers grown to such a multitude, as that it would have bred confusion to have all their ecclesiastical affairs managed in one court, and took them off from the rest of their work, the light of nature teaches us to conclude, that they would have had more consistories than one for government, as well as upon the former increase of believers, they grew to have more meeting places than one for Word and sacraments, and yet would have held such a correspondency as matters of difficulty and common concernment should have been managed by common consent. But whether all those congregations growing so numerous, and those presbyteries thus divided should have been called one church still; we know not, nor is it of any moment. We say again, we {Cf. p. 105} are not inquiring for names and [*sic* but] things.

2. Their other proof is "from the practice of the elders, who do thus {See p. 63} join in a presbyterial government; because when congregations in shires are divided into several presbyteries, the elders (though neighbors) of a bordering presbytery, intermeddle not with the congregations under another presbytery."

We *answer:* It is true, they do take themselves bound in a special relation to those congregations who are associated in the presbytery, in those things for which they are associated, and their mutual consent and agreement gives them that relation and calling to those things. And the case is here as it is in particular congregations. All believers are tied to join to some congregation or other, to whom they bear a special relation, besides that which they owe to the whole universal church, yet peradventure their habitation is nearer to some who are of another congregation, than to some of their own.

And we add yet further, that those several classical presbyteries may have the like association and correspondencies among themselves as matters of difficulty and common concernment may occasion and require.

[INCONGRUITIES OF THE MINOR PROPOSITION ANSWERED]

Braye, 68v Their major, and the proofs of it being thus found insufficient, we need not insist longer upon the pretended incongruities, and disproportions, which they have so largely prosecuted in their minor, and the proofs of it. Yet so far as there is anything in them of any seeming weight, we shall take them into consideration, wherein we shall discover some things to be false in themselves, other things not to be prejudicial to our assertion.

As 1. "For extending the power of ordinary ruling, beyond the power of {See p. 64} ordinary preaching."

We *answer:* This extends not his ordinary power of the one, beyond the ordinary power of the other, but only the ordinary exercise of the one, beyond the ordinary exercise of the other, having herein a call to the one, and not to the other; which is no incongruity or absurdity (as we have before shown). And as for their alleged Scriptures (Acts 20:28; 2 Peter 5; Colossians 1:17; Hebrews 13:17; 1 Thessalonians 5:12; 1 Timothy 3:17), none of them prove the contrary. They only show that all these things belong to their office, and that this is the ordinary and usual practice and work of elders where their work lies, but none of them prove it unlawful for an elder upon a call to do one of these, where they have not occasion, and a call to do the rest.

And as for the comparison, "that this was made the usual argument Gillespie, 11 against bishops, that people were forced to obey him, who preached not to them, nor watched over their souls," etc. "This argument," they say, "holds as well against the presbyterial way."

We *answer*, that the exceptions against [the] episcopal way, were, that they challenged these things as belonging to them, as men of a higher order, challenge that to one which belongs to a college, spoiled both pastors and people of their power and liberties, associated not congregations with them, but subdued them unto them; were not mutually subject to the presbytery, whom they would have subject to him. Things were not carried in a way of confederation as *inter pares*; they and their power being wholly *among equals* extrinsical to them, business not being of mutual concernment. These and the like were the exceptions against the episcopal way. But not that it was unlawful for him being a presbyter to exercise an act of government, upon association toward them to whom he ordinarily preached not. And this is apparent, because even the nonconformists who pleaded thus against him, *regarding the* yet judged ordination received by imposition of their hands to be valid *substance of* *quoad substantiam actus*; because they were presbyters. *the act*

To the reasons, "first, because the ruling power flows from their power *Gillespie, 11* of preaching, and therefore must be extendible no further; as the power of a father is extendible only to his children."

We *answer:* First, it is false that his ruling power flows from his preaching power. Some have the gifts and power of ruling who have not of preaching. Secondly, were it granted, yet it follows not that he must do the one wherever he does the other. Both are given him together, but neither to be exercised without a call, and sometimes he may be called to exercise the one and not the other, as we have shown before.

To the reason of their reasons, first, they say, if it flow not from his power of preaching, it must flow from something else. We *answer:* All his office and authority is conferred together by Christ's gift, as the fountain, and the church's call, as the means.

To their second, all the keys are given together, etc. *Answer.* We grant it {See p. 66} (and this confutes their former reason, that the power of ruling flows from their power of preaching), and we grant also that the one is extendible as far as the other, even to the whole church of Christ, but ever as he shall be called, and as the good of the church requires; yet the exercise of the one is not necessary to be extended actually as far as the exercise of the other.

To their third, the instance of the apostles, that their power was extend- *Minutes, 2.579,* ible with their commission to preach, etc. *582, 588, 3.420*

Answer. Very true; so was their power to administer the sacraments, yet Paul took not himself bound to exercise his power of baptizing in all places, where he took himself bound to preach, but attended chiefly to that which might most benefit the church. And our brethren seem to us not a little to weaken their own argument, and strengthen our answer, in their alleging in the same place, "that though the apostles' power of ruling (as apostles) was extendible with their preaching;" yet grant that "they might exercise the one, where they might not exercise the other." For if an apostle, as an apostle, my exercise one act of his ministry, where he may not exercise another, then may a presbyter, as a presbyter exercise one act of his ministry, where he may not exercise another.

2. To their second head of incongruities, that it makes a disproportion between the works or offices of ruling and preaching officers compared between themselves, because a pastor, *quâ* pastor, is limited in the highest work of preaching to one congregation, and not in his ruling.

We *answer:* The pastors are given to the whole church, and are not limited in their highest office of preaching to one congregation. His ordinary exercise of preaching may possibly be limited to one congregation, yet not necessarily, for he may keep an ordinary lecture in another.

3. Nor does it (as their next head of incongruities imports) make him a ruling elder to some, and a preaching elder to others. These two make him not two officers, but are two branches of his one office, either of which he is to exercise as a call requires. And it is no incongruity or absurdity to say that he may have a relation to one congregation to do some acts of his office upon a call, and yet not tied to all.

4. To the next head concerning the extent of the deacon's office, the sum whereof is that then the deacon's office might be extended to more congregations than one; we *answer:* So it was in Jerusalem, and so it may be still, as the like condition of the church may require. Were the poor saints to be maintained now as then, only by voluntary contributions, divers congregations might be associated in this work also, for the common care of their poor. And with us (where God in mercy has otherwise provided for the poor) the law has ordered, that if one parish be not able to maintain their own poor, the neighbor parishes are to join with them in it. So that neither by God's law, nor man's law, does this carry any incongruity with it. Yet neither from hence does it follow that therefore it must be so, that the deacon's office must extend in the exercise of it, as far, and no further than the preacher's. The deacon's office in the churches of Asia, was extended to send relief to the churches of Jerusalem in a time of famine; when yet they sent not their preachers to preach to them of Jerusalem, because there was no famine of the Word. And the churches at Antioch sent some of their elders to preach, where they sent none of their deacons to distribute alms. All these things are to be managed and exercised as the common good of the church requires.

[ANSWER TO SECOND HEAD OF INCONGRUITIES]

Braye, 69v
{See p. 68} To their next head of incongruities, from the mutual duties which necessarily follow upon this standing relation, first, that the people must honor and esteem, yea, yield maintenance to those who thus ordinarily rule them, which they prove by 1 Timothy 5:17–18, and if that the elders of a particular flock, are to have their maintenance for their preaching there, and performing the lesser acts of ruling there, much more should they be maintained

                    I: ANSWER OF THE ASSEMBLY TO THE REASONS

for performing the greater acts in the classis. What reason (say they) is there that particular congregations should maintain their own elders for performing one part of the elder work, and that they should yet be bound to maintain the rest for all the other part of the work and yet it is due from every person as he is able; how burdensome and confused a thing would this be?

To all which we *answer:* That it is most true that elders are to be honored and maintained for their work's sake, even because they are wholly set apart to this work. And where they do the whole work of an elder to a particular congregation, it is requisite that they should receive a sufficient maintenance; but yet it follows not that all must necessarily contribute to their maintenance who receive any fruit of their ministry. Suppose the state, or some able and well-affected person in a place, should set apart a plentiful and honorable maintenance to a minister, for the service of his ministry in such a congregation, so that he might live plentifully upon it, without the people's contributing anything to him. Are the people notwithstanding bound to contribute another honorable maintenance to him, because of his work among them? Or if a combination of ministers should associate freely to bestow a weekly lecture in some great town or city; yea, suppose they should do it every day of the week, are the people to whom they are willing freely to preach, bound to maintain all those?

Again, it is a mistake that our brethren say, that ministers united in classical presbyteries have maintenance for performing one part of their office. We say they perform all which belongs to their office, which concerns their congregation only, if they are able; their joining in the classis is for matters of common concernment, and to help them, wherein they are insufficient to do their own work belonging to their own congregations.

To their second, wherein they say, that those who are thus associated, must then be bound to all other offices of elders, as to visit the sick, to visit the people from house to house, to watch over them all, to preach to them in season and out of season:

We answer as before: they are bound only by their association to the duties for which they associate. And as for the gravamen [*grievance*] of theirs to make the Presbyterian way to appear worse than that of the bishops:

We *answer:* We are sorry our brethren delight so much in this comparison. The bishops arrogated to themselves to be the only pastors of the diocese, robbed the pastors of their authority, spoiled the people of their liberty, made all their servants and vassals. The Presbyterian way is not as that of masters over servants, but social, as between equals, between brethren, friends, colleagues, confederates, etc., where all judge, and all are judged, where no congregation is above another congregation, no minister above another minister, where every elder is left to enjoy the whole office of an elder, and each congregation left to the freedom of a congregation in what belongs to them, and they able to perform it; and the classis, to corroborate, strengthen and help them. We are not willing to say more of this odious comparison.

To their objection which they suppose may be made, that they may part the work between them of which they endeavor a large confutation:

We *answer:* We never made this absurd objection. We say not that men may part that work among many, and leave but one part of it to one, when God would have one do all. We say every elder must endeavor to do all his own work, and be assistant to his brethren in helping forward their work. But what strength soever there be in their objection, sure we are, the instances brought by our brethren to confute it, are very improper to give a satisfactory solution. When the elders among the Hebrews are said to watch over the souls of the people, and the same elders are charged by Peter to feed the flock of God among them, the same charge which was given to the elders of Ephesus (Acts 20) and this flock contained all the strangers scattered throughout Pontus, Galatia, Cappadocia, Asia and Bithynia, surely these elders were compelled to part the work among them.

And further, whereas they demand where has the Scriptures parted that work, so that he who is fixed in one congregation to do all the work of an elder, should part with others in some of their work, and leave part of his to them?

We *answer:* We affirm no such thing. But on the other side we desire our brethren to show where the Scripture has made such a fixing of an elder to one congregation, as that it should be unlawful for him to do any act of an elder to any part of the rest of the church of Christ, to whom he is yet given by Christ as an elder. For our part we conceive that both the division of the church into congregations, and of fixing particular elders to them, is no further of divine institution than order and edification did first occasion, and do still require it should be so; we conceive, it is here as it was in the church of the Jews, to whom the whole tribe of Levi were given as their ministers. When all the Israelites lived together in one body (though many hundred thousands) as when they were in the Wilderness, the whole tribe of Levi were but as one body or college of elders to them all, and for aught we know fed them all in common, and afterwards when the tribes came to be fixed in their several divisions, the wise providence and grace of God ordered it so that the Levites were also scattered, and fixed among them.

[ANSWER TO THIRD HEAD OF INCONGRUITIES]

To their last head of incongruities, that this is inconsistent with the ordinary way of the calling of elders, both for their choice and ordination; first, then all the people of those congregations must choose all these elders who rule them, as well as those that are to preach to them, as this they largely insist upon, desiring to know under what notion or consideration they are to choose him who is to be their ordinary fixed elder, and the other, who are only to rule them:

Braye, 70r
{See page 70}

Gillespie, 11

We *answer:* Whatever the peoples' right be in choosing their elders, this association is no abridgment of it in any kind. We say clearly, that the several congregations singly choose or accept of the one to be their paſtor to do all offices which concern a paſtor or miniſter among them. And all the congregations jointly in this association do choose or accept of, or associate with all the reſt to be a presbytery, to transaᷓ with themselves all matters of difficulty and common concernment.

And as to that aggravation added to this reason, that if the higheſt acts be committed to them, as that of excommunication ("of all punishments the moſt formidable," a matter of as great, if not more concernment, as life itself) the enjoying "of all ordinances forever," together with the deposition of their miniſters, that then there is so much the more reason, that all the people should have the election of them:

We *answer:* Firſt, if all who are liable to excommunication, and enjoyment of ordinances, and miniſter, etc., muſt therefore elect them, then women muſt elect as well as men. Secondly, the censure of excommunication, which the formidable consequences of it are far more dangerous in our brethren's way, than in this of the Presbytery, because in this way, if any man be wronged, he may have the benefit of his appeal, and be cleared by more righteous judges (a course ever followed by the church, and agreeable to the light of nature), but in their way, if two or three (it may be) ignorant or corrupt elders, prevailing with the major part of (it may be) a very small congregation, do once deliver a man to Satan, and will not be induced by counsel to reverse their unrighteous sentence, the innocent wronged man muſt lie under this doom all the days of his life without any remedy, and muſt be held by all the churches of Chriſt (to whom their sentence does but *innotescere*) as an excommunicate person, *become known* and shunned accordingly, none having power to absolve him. Thirdly, neither is the sentence of excommunication so dreadful as they make it (for as the apoſtle said of the magiſtrate's sword, Romans 13, "If thou do well," etc.) good men need not fear it. If men deserve it not, either it shall not touch them, or if it do, *clavis errans non ligat.*[1] And if it be juſt, it was done in heaven before, and they only on earth declare and apply the will of Chriſt to him, and that for the deſtruction of the flesh, that his ſpirit may be saved; and upon his repentance be received again into the bosom of the church. And therefore excommunication should be embraced as a soul-saving ordinance of Jesus Chriſt, as well as the Word and the Sacraments. And as to that of ordination, we shall not need to say much, because our brethren say little of it; and do in their judgments not look upon it as a matter of any great weight, eſteeming the whole essence of

---

1. [An errant exercise of the key (of discipline) is not binding. For a discussion of the keys, and specifically of discipline, see James Bannerman, *The Church of Chriſt: A Treatise on the Nature, Powers, Ordinances, Discipline, and Government of the Chriſtian Church* (1868), 2.189ff.]

the ministerial calling to be in the people's choice, and his ordination at sometimes not at all requisite; and when it is used, it is looked upon only as a solemn admitting of him into his place.

[1a.   Answer to the Reasons against the first proof of the first assertion of more churches in Jerusalem than one from the multitude of believers]

Braye, 71r
{See p. 74}
Minutes,
Sess. 160–162
2.534–552
Gillespie,
27–29
Lightfoot,
170–181

To their reasons against, and exceptions to the first proof of the first assertion, *viz.* that the church of Jerusalem consisted of more congregations than one, from the multitude of believers, against which they bring first reason to show there were not more than could meet in one place, "The Holy Ghost has from first to last" (they say) "as on purpose shown this, as if his scope had been before hand, to prevent and preclude all reasonings to the contrary."

We incline to believe that the Holy Ghost intended rather to show the early accomplishment of the promise (Jeremiah 32:39), of "Giving one heart and one way," by his so frequent mentioning of ὁμοθυμαδόν and ἐπὶ τὸ αὐτὸ as adjuncts to the first Christian church meetings, than (as our brethren suggest) to prevent and preclude all reasonings against this assertion of theirs, *viz.* that the believers in Jerusalem were not more than could meet in one place.

Reason One. To the first branch of their argument brought from the forementioned adjuncts as they stand upon record (Acts 1:14, 15).

Answer 1. We answer first, that their being ὁμοθυμαδόν (which properly signifies consent of minds), does not all argue their being in one place; a thousand congregations may be said upon a Sabbath or feast day to be ὁμοθυμαδόν in prayer, and yet may be met in several and far distant places.

2. That their being assembled ἐπὶ τὸ αὐτὸ does not necessarily enforce it, because here the words may, and in some places must admit of another translation, as Acts 4:26–27, where ἐπὶ τὸ αὐτὸ signifies not a convention of persons in one place (who can make it appear that ever Herod, Pontius Pilate, and the Gentiles, and the people of Israel were so assembled against Christ?), but only a consent of minds in one thing. Accordingly in Symmachus, his translation of the second Psalm out of which these words are taken, instead of the Septuagint's ἐπὶ τὸ αὐτὸ, we find the word ὁμοθυμαδόν.[1] Montanus renders it *in idem.*[2] And such as meet in consultation to carry on the same business, may well be said to be gathered together ἐπὶ τὸ αὐτὸ, though they meet in several places; as with

Gillespie, 28
Lightfoot, 175
Seaman cited
Symmachus in
debate

---

1. [Symmachus, 2nd century translator of Old Testament into Greek. Likely cited from either Joannes Drusius (*Veterum interpretum graecorum in totum V. T. fragmenta, collecta* {Janssonius, 1622} 869) or *Novum Jesu Christi Domini Nostri Testamentum* ({1586; Paris: Boun, 1628} vol. 2, p. 3). Cf. Fridericus Field, *Origenis Hexaplorum* (Oxford: 1875), 2.88.]

2. [Benito Arias Montano (1527–1598), *Biblia Sacra Hebraice, Chaldaice, Graece & Latine* [Antwerp polyglot] (Antwerp: Plantin: 1569–1573) vol. 7, "Acta Apostolorum," vol. 7, p. 88.

us, the Lords and Commons assemble themselves ἐπὶ τὸ αὐτὸ, and are but one parliament, though met in two houses.

3. Not denying those [in] Acts 1:15 to have met together in one place (though we deny the two adjuncts of ὁμοθυμαδόν and ἐπὶ τὸ αὐτὸ to prove it), our answer to the argument is that it falls short of what our brethren intend to assert. Because it does not appear from hence, that the whole church was there assembled, but rather the contrary. We will not insist upon the word ὀνομάτουν (the number not of men, but of names) which according to some is to be restrained to men of chief note and eminence (so Revelation 3:4 and chapter 11:13). Nor will we urge that possibly these were such, every one whereof was capable of election to an apostleship, which was the τὸ ἐργον of this meeting (for that this was a different meeting from that spoken of in verse 14 is evident by the transition, "and in those days," etc.). But this we say, that however taking in only men of note and disciples of longest standing in Christ's school (even those that companied with the apostles all the time that the Lord Jesus went in and out among them, beginning from the baptism of John unto the day of our Savior's ascension, of whom verse 21, 22), it is very probable that the number of such did not exceed one hundred and twenty. Yet that there were then no more believers in Jerusalem cannot well be imagined by any that shall duly consider the preparation made for Christ by John's baptism and ministry, the years of Christ's own preaching and miracles, the commission he gave to the twelve apostles and seventy disciples, together with the operation which his death, resurrection, and ascension had upon the beholders. Who can but think that by all these many more than one hundred and twenty were converted to the faith? When the Lord Jesus had but begun his ministry, the Pharisees heard that he made and baptized more disciples than John (John 4:1), of whom notwithstanding it is said (Mark 1:5), "There went out unto him all the land of Judea, and they of Jerusalem, and were all baptized of him." The same men afterwards took up this complaint against Christ (John 12:19), "Behold, the world is gone after him." What ground had there been either for a report or a complaint of this nature, if the whole multitude of his disciples, or of the converts in Jerusalem had come within the narrow compass of one hundred and twenty? [In] 1 Corinthians 15:6 we read of five hundred brethren before Christ's ascension.

4. Suppose it should be granted that the whole multitude of believers in Jerusalem were here met in one place, it will not from thence follow, that so they might do, and did afterwards when the church was multiplied.

Reason Two. 'But afterwards (Acts 2:1) another meeting of theirs is expressed in the same words, "They were all met with one accord," etc. {See p. 74}

To which we answer still, that it is not proved that they all there mentioned were "all the church." Beza said that in two ancient copies he finds *Minutes*, 2.578
οἱ Ἀπόστολοι οἱ Ἀπόσολοι, and brings probable reasons why they "all" Lightfoot, 195

should be meant of the apostles only.[1] As first, the coherence with the very last words of the fore-going chapter mentioning the eleven apostles. Secondly, their being filled with the Holy Ghost, and speaking in tongues (verse 4) which was promised to the apostles, and they commanded to wait at Jerusalem for it (Acts 1:2, 4, 8). Thirdly, the multitudes calling them Galilaeans (verse 7). Fourthly, the not mentioning of any other in the whole chapter but the *apostles only*, "Peter stands up with the eleven" (verse 14), "they said unto Peter and the rest of the apostles" (verse 37), "in the apostle's fellowship" (verse 42), "signs were done by the apostles" (verse 43). From all which it is likely that this meeting was of the apostles only, and if so, it is then nothing to our brethren's purpose. However, if it be a meeting of the whole church, the church was not then multiplied to a greater number than in the first chapter.

Reason Three. 'But when they were about three thousand, yet still some of their meeting for some acts of worship are recorded to have been as before ὁμοθυμαδόν, and instead of the other expression ἐπὶ τὸ αὐτὸ, the place itself where they were is set down, to supply and interpret it, and to show, it was still in one assembly, as verse 46. They continued ὁμοθυμαδόν in the temple, where they most frequently met, not for Jewish worship, but for hearing the Word, at which though the Jews were present, yet it hindered not, but that to them it was a church-meeting,' etc.

{See p. 74}

By all which this only our brethren undertake to prove, that some of their meetings for some acts of worship were in one place, wherein they seem to yield the cause. For if they could not meet together for all acts of worship, and especially for those which are peculiar to church-communion, our assertion is not at all infringed. They met indeed in the temple to hear the Word, which (though no Jewish worship) yet was common to Jews and Christians, as themselves confess. But can they prove that in the temple they administered the sacraments, which are the distinguishing ordinances of the Christian church? Interpreters of all sorts from the very next words collect the contrary,[2] *viz.* that the Lord's supper was administered in more private congregations, "they continued daily with one accord in the temple," but it was from "house to house" that they brake bread, which was sacramental breaking of bread, as that phrase is understood generally by all (Acts 20:7)[3] and by our brethren themselves in the 42nd verse of this second chapter, where the Syriac has the very word *Eucharistia*,[4] which is expressly said (verse 46) to be κατ' οἶκον in opposition to ἐν τῷ ἱερῷ. And for the phrase κατ' οἶκον, we find it used for a house appointed for church meeting (Romans 16:5;

Minutes, Sess.
162, 2.551

---

1. [Beza, *Annotationes*, p. 298.]

2. Brentius, Aretius. [Johann Brenz, *Operum … D. Joannis Brentii …* (Tübingten, 1576–1590, 8 vols.); vol. 7, *Commentarij in Acta Apostolorum* (1588), p. 60. Benedictus Aretius, *Commentarii In Sacram Actuum Apostolicorum Historiam* (1579; le Preux, 1607), p. 33ff.]

3. [Beza, *Annotationes*, p. 303.]

4. [Cf. Tremellius, *Biblia Sacra*, vol. 6 (1592), p. 88; Syriac N.T. (1569), p. 332.]

1 Corinthians 16:19). However it is not rationally supposable that the whole multitude of believers met in the temple to receive the Lord's Supper. For first the sacrament was no temple ordinance, and therefore not to be administered in the temple. Nor secondly, could it have been done with safety. For if the apostles were so quarreled for preaching Jesus and the resurrection in the temple (Acts 4:2, though never challenged for administering the sacrament in it), and Paul so assaulted for being supposed to bring a Greek into the temple, what would it have been to have brought in a new ordinance, and a new worship into the temple? Our brethren themselves are sensible of this, and therefore although in the assembly some of them disputed for their receiving the sacraments in the temple, yet now they wave it, and content themselves to say, they met there sometimes for some acts of worship.

Reason Four. Fourthly, they say, when there was a further addition (Acts 5:1—in which chapter is a parallel description to that [in] 2:43 *ad finem*) speaking of another meeting, the same words are used (verse 41). That they were ηομοτηυμαδον, as in Acts 2. And instead of the temple there, is Solomon's Porch here: which was a place large enough to hold them, called the temple (John 10:23), the outward court by Josephus,[1] where Christ used to walk and preach, and the apostles also (Acts 3:11). And that the apostles did not only meet here, first is apparent from the parallel place (Acts 2). Secondly, it is unlikely the apostles should meet and not the people, who are said to continue in the apostles' doctrine and fellowship.

Answer. 1. That this was another meeting cannot be denied, but that it was a meeting of "all the church" for "all acts" of worship is not proved, nor can be, which if not proved, this makes nothing against our proposition.

2. If this place be so parallel to that of Acts 2:43 etc., the same answer will serve here, which was made there, to which we refer them.

3. What Solomon's Porch in our Savior's time was, and why so called, is thought by some too difficult a question to be resolved.[2]

4. In that place of Josephus we find no mention of the outward court, but he is conceived by Pineda to be contrary to himself in the description of the temple, and the same author conceives it was most unlikely to be *Atrium Populi*.[3]

5. That they all that met here were "all the church," will not be proved from the pretended parallel of Acts 2. And that the apostles should meet with one accord without the church is not so unlikely as it is imagined, why might not the Twelve go to the temple without the church as well as Peter and John did (Acts 3:1)—specially it not being said that they were

---

1. Josephus, lib. 20, cap. 8. [Flavius Josephus (37–c.100) *Antiquities of the Jews*, 20.8.]

2. Pinedæ, *de rebus Salomonis*, l. 3. c. 5. l. 5. c. 19. [Juan de Pineda, *De Rebus Salomonis Regis vel Salomon Prævius* (Moguntiæ: Antonij Hierati, 1613), p. 129, [lib. 5, cap. 6, §19?], pp. 450–451. Where space affords fuller bibliographical data is given; otherwise see the Bibliography for details.]

3. Maldonat. in John. 10:23. [Joannes Maldonates, Spanish Jesuit (1534–1583), *Commentarii in Quatuar Evangelistas*; ed. Franciscus Sausen (Franz Sausen), vol. 5 (Moguntiæ: 1844), p. 256.]

preaching there, but working miracles; nor can the "all" here spoken of be referred to the church in the 11th verse more than to the "many which heard," who were not of the church expressed in the same verse, but rather appears to be meant of the apostles only, they being mentioned in this 12th verse.

Reason Five. Further, when they chose deacons (Acts 6), which was cer-
{See p. 75} tainly a church meeting, they were yet no more than could meet in one place. For the apostles called the multitude, and verse 5 they are called the whole multitude, and verse 6, they as in one place chose seven men, and set them before the apostles, who prayed, in which duty the whole multitude had an interest to join, etc.

Answer. 1. That this was a meeting for church business, we deny not. 2. But we do deny that the mentioning of the multitude and the whole multitude proved that all and every one of them that believed in Jerusalem were at that meeting. For it may signify either a great multitude—as Luke 8:37, "the whole multitude of the Gadarens besought him to depart from them," and Acts 25:24, Festus says, "all the multitude had dealt with" him about Paul—not every individual Gadaren or Jew, but a great number of them, or the generality, which the Greeks use to express by πανδημεὶ. Or it may signify, as Luke 1:10, where it is said "the whole multitude of the people were without, praying," that is, *præsentium*, of them that were present, and not of all that were in Jerusalem. So here the saying pleased the whole multitude, implies not that the whole multitude of all the believers were present, but that so many as were present the saying pleased, and our brethren themselves grant that by multitude sometimes is understood not "all" but "select persons," as Acts 15:12, "Then all the multitude kept silence," which even themselves will not expound of "all" the church, but only of such as were men of age and discretion, excluding women and children, who if excluded from the multitude there, why not here? Especially considering that this meeting was for the choosing of church officers, wherein we suppose our brethren will not allow women and children their suffrages. And indeed if we consider the five thousand (4:4) and besides the great additions and multiplications (5:14), believers were the more added to the Lord, multitudes both of men and women, and chapter 6:1, again it is said the number of disciples was multiplied, we cannot in reason conceive that they all could meet in one place to be one assembly, but must be distributed into several divisions, as the 400,000 men of Israel were (Judges 20). Else how could the Levite have told his sad story to them all together and at once. The like we may conceive of that congregation (Nehemiah 9:5), where eight Levites spoke to them all, which unless it had been done to them divided into several companies, would have confounded both the people and themselves.

And whereas our brethren urge their choosing of officers, and presenting them before the apostles to prove their being assembled in one place, let them but consider how the city of London choose their Common-Council, and present them to the Court of Aldermen. So that our answer to their fifth reason is this, it is not proved, nay, it is not probable that all the believers there met. 2. Not in one company. 3. Or were both proved, yet we say, more may meet for choice of officers than can meet to receive the sacraments.

Reason Six. After all this (Acts 15), they are said to meet ὁμοθυμαδὸν, and naming the place, where still it imports one assembly, and after Acts 21:22, the multitude must needs come together, etc. {See p. 76}

We *answer:* It is to be proved that that ὁμοθυμαδὸν relates to the whole body of the church. We say [it relates] to the synod of the apostles and elders, as we shall show hereafter. And secondly, ὁμοθυμαδὸν alone will never prove their meeting in one place, though we deny not, but here they were met in one. For that other text (Acts 21:22), "the multitude must needs come together" etc., how does that prove there were at that time no more in the church of Jerusalem, than might meet in one place? We may say of London, the multitude will come together upon such and such an occasion, does this import no more in London than may meet in one place? Besides the meeting there spoken of was like to be rather a concourse of a mis-informed multitude, than of a congregation for worship; but however, we are glad our brethren understand this multitude to be of the church of Jerusalem—we are afraid they will forget it anon.

And for conclusion, we humbly desire it may be observed, that all our brethren have endeavored to prove, is that the believers in Jerusalem were no more than could meet together in one place at some times, for some acts: as for choosing of officers, so their first instance, and their fifth; for making of decrees, so the sixth (out of both which assemblies, women and children, a better half of the company, are excluded); for hearing, so the second and third; but not a word brought to prove that they all met in one place to receive the sacrament, as to that they were several congregations. So that should we grant all these their instances, what would follow, but this?—That the believers at Jerusalem who receive the sacraments in several places and assemblies, and so were several congregations, did yet meet in one place, and one assembly to choose officers (Acts 1:6) and to perform other acts of government (Acts 15), and therefore it is evident that although they were several congregations, yet they were under one Presbyterial government.

Exception One. We come now to their exceptions against our proofs. The first whereof is to the instance of five thousand (Acts 4) against which they object, first, that it cannot be evinced [*shown*], that these five thousand were a new number added to the three thousand (Acts 2). Beza and Calvin think those three thousand are included here. Secondly, nay it is not certain that the five thousand here were believers; the Greek will as well carry it to express the number of hearers. Thirdly, ἀνδρῶν when put alone (as here) includes females as well as males. Fourthly, if to be understood of {See p. 76} *Minutes,* 2.534–548 Gillespie, 27–29 Lightfoot, 170–180 present converts and of males only, it would be a greater miracle than ever was before or since, etc.

We *reply* to the first, though Calvin and Beza think the three thousand formerly converted to be included here, yet divers both ancient and modern interpreters are of another mind.[1] And we have not only testimony but reason to induce us to be of the same opinion; not to insist upon that which some observe, that as the three thousand (Acts 2:41) did not comprehend the one hundred and twenty mentioned Acts 1. So it holds proportion that the three thousand mentioned there, are not comprehended here. But this we affirm, that the latter part of this fourth verse of Acts 4 is exegetical of the former. Now the former part must needs be meant of those that were won to the faith at that sermon, and therefore the latter part must be understood of them also. Besides, this sermon was not *ex intentione* to the church, but upon occasion of the multitude flocking together to behold the miracle, to whom Peter and John preached in the temple, while the church, or a great part of it, might, it is likely, be attending in private upon the ministry of the other apostles, of whom no mention is made in this passage but of Peter and John only.

To the second we say, that the true syntax of the Greek carries the number to believers, and not to hearers; Πολλοὶ δὲ, many of them that heard the Word believed. And if you ask how many, the Holy Ghost tells that the number of those many believers was about five thousand. Secondly, the Spirit of God does not use to compute the number of bare hearers. Thirdly, we know no interpreters that so expound the place.

As for the reason they seem to allege, why it should be meant of the number of hearers, *viz.* because that such a multitude should hear the apostles was the thing that fretted the Pharisees, we *answer:* 1. That the grieved persons mentioned (verse 1 and 2) were Sadducees and not the Pharisees. Secondly, it

1. Augustine. *In tract. 31* [*Sic 39.5*] *in Joan. Acesserunt corpori Domini, i.e. numero-fidelium tria millia hominum, item alio, facto quodam miraculo acesserant alia quinque millia.* ["There were added to the Lord's body, that is, to the number of believers, three thousand people. And so also by the working of another miracle there were added other five thousand."]. So is the text [Acts 2:41] understood by Jerome, Chrysostome, Oecumenius, Lyra, Lorinus, Salmeron; and of ours by Aretius and Pelargus; Bullinger makes it doubtful. [Augustine, Bishop of Hippo (354–430), Tractate 39.5, Migne, *PL* 35.1684. Saint Jerome (c.345–c.419), *In Isaiam*, 18, 66, 7–9 (*PL* 24.658D). Chrysostom, Greek Father (347–407), *Homilies on the Acts of the Apostles* (*NPNF*1 11.10, 89, 249, 481). Oecumenius (10th century), *Commentaria* (*PG* 118.78A). Nicholas de Lyra (1270–1340), *Biblia Latina*, 4 vols. (Nuremberge: Anthonij Kobergers, 1497) vol. 4, p. CCLXXIII. Jean de Lorin, French Jesuit commentator on Scripture (1559–1634), *In Actus Apostolorum Commentaria* (1607; Colonia Agrippina; 1621), p. 107. Alphonso Salmeron, papal theologian at Trent (1515–1585), *Commentarii in Evangelicum Historiam et in Acta Apostolorum* (Coloniæ, 1612–15) 12.88. Benedictus Aretius, *Commentarii in sacram Actuum Apostolicorum historiam* (Bernæ Helvetiorum: 1607), 33. Christoph Pelargus, German Protestant theologian (1565–1633), *Historiae Sacrae quam Liber Actuum Apostolicorum* (Francofurti, 1602), p. 72. Johann Heinrich Bullinger, Swiss Reformer (1504–1575), *In Acta Apostolorum* (Zurich, 1533), p. 33. In debate, Gillespie cited Chrysostom and Oecumenius; *Minutes*, 2.538; Lightfoot, 172.]

was not so much the multitude of hearers, as the doctrine taught that so vexed them, as is expressed [in] verse 2. Because they preached through Jesus the resurrection which the Sadducees denied; and thirdly, should we grant that the multitude was the thing that fretted them, certainly it would vex them more that five thousand believed that doctrine, than that five thousand heard it.

To the third, though we contend not much that by ἀνδρῶν here, males only should be meant, yet it may seem probable, if first we consider that the custom of the Jews was to number only the males. Secondly, if we compare John 6:10 with Matthew 14:21, ἄνδρες set alone in John, it is expounded to be besides women and children in Matthew. But thirdly, take women and children and all in, yet add those other new multitudes mentioned (Acts 5:14; 6:1; 6:7, etc.), we yet affirm they were more than could meet together in one place to receive the sacrament.

Minutes, 2.537, 538

To the fourth, *viz.* that this (if thus understood) would be a greater miracle than any before or since. We *answer*: 1. That the like may be said of the three thousand converted (Acts 2) that it was such a thing as was never before nor since, if (as they think) there were not 5,000 converted here, shall we question the truth of that therefore? Secondly, it was the day of Christ's power, in which his willing people from the womb of that morning (it was foretold) should be multiplied as the dew upon the earth (Psalms 110:3).

Minutes, 2.548
Lightfoot, 178

Exception Two. 'The second exception is that it may be supposed that those that were converted at Jerusalem remained not constant members of that church. For first the 3,000 (chapter 2) were not dwellers at Jerusalem, but strangers out of all those countries mentioned in that chapter who came up to Pentecost. Secondly, and therefore were (as some interpret it) sojourners at Jerusalem, not dwellers, as Elijah in 1 Kings 17:20 sojourned with the widow of Sareptha, μεθ' ἧσ ἐγὼ κατοικω, says the Septuagint, the very word here used. Thirdly, they are said to be dwellers of Mesopotamia, Cappadocia, etc. (verse 9) and dwellers of Jerusalem and those countries too, they could not be. And fourthly, that which strengthens this, is that (verse 5) they are said to be κατοικοὶν ἐν ʼιερουσαλὴμ, but (verse 9) κατοικοῦντες τὴν Μεσοποταμίαν. Therefore fifthly, the 14th verse calls them men Jews and dwellers at Jerusalem, as two sorts, and verse 22, men of Israel, the style given the ten tribes, and verse 5, devout men who used to come up at those solemn feasts, and after a time to return to their families again.'

{See p. 77}
Minutes, 2.541
Gillespie, 28

Lightfoot, 178

Minutes, 2.539
Lightfoot, 173

Answer. To all which our reply is this: First we find it not elsewhere said in Scripture, that those who came up to the feasts at Jerusalem were κατοικοὶν ἐν ʼιερουσαλὴμ, and though κατοικῶ sometimes possibly may be put for παροικῶ, and so may signify to sojourn, yet by our brethren's own confession, it may signify to dwell. Elijah's sojourning with the widow was, ימים, a year, so in the margin the word is rendered, and so Judges 17:10 and Judges 11:40 and 1 Samuel 7:16. And let our brethren grant these but so long abode at Jerusalem, it might be long enough to make them members of that church.

And why it should signify to sojourn at Jerusalem (verse 5) and to dwell in Mesopotamia (verse 9), we see not. For their criticism of ἐν Ἰερουσαλήμ will not prove it, seeing that Acts 16:4 themselves will needs understand by, τῶν πρεσβυτέρων τῶν ἐν Ἰερουσαλήμ, not the elders that were present at Jerusalem, but the elders fixed in, and officers of the church of Jerusalem.

To that of Acts 2:14 (men Jews and dwellers at Jerusalem) we *answer:* The words need not imply two sorts, at least in our brethren's sense, namely of some Jews living in the country, and others dwelling at Jerusalem. But all may be of Jerusalem notwithstanding that expression, thus: Men Jews, may be understood of those of the Jewish nation—all ye that dwell at Jerusalem of the proselytes, who being converted to the Jewish religion, had for religion's sake there taken up their dwelling. So for that of the 22nd verse, men of Israel, the style, they say, given to the ten tribes, we *answer:* That phrase is not proper to the ten tribes, but applied to the Jews, nay to the dwellers of Jerusalem, as Acts 3:12 and Acts 5:35, where Gamaliel speaking to the council of Jerusalem, said, "Yea, men of Israel." And for the appellation of devout men (verse 5) that makes nothing against us, but what is there added, *viz.* that these devout men were dwelling at Jerusalem is much for us.

2. But granting secondly, that many of those of whom this chapter speaks had been formerly dwellers in Mesopotamia and Cappadocia, etc., what hinders but that they might now be dwellers at Jerusalem? The occasion of their coming up thither at this time, being not only the feast of Pentecost (which was a feast but of one day) but also the great expectation that the people of the Jews then had, of the appearance of the Messiah in his kingdom (as we may collect from Luke 19:11, where it is said, they thought the kingdom of God should immediately appear) so that now they might choose to take up their dwellings at Jerusalem, and not return as they had been wont at the end of their usual feasts.

But nature taught them (say our brethren) to provide for their wives and children, and not desert them.

And how know we but they might bring up their wives and children with them, which some did in those ordinary feasts, and therefore might be more likely upon this extraordinary occasion? 2. Or why might they not fetch up their families to them? which is more probable than that they would leave the apostles' fellowship to go back to their families, especially considering that their hearts were inflamed with such an abundant love to the gospel, and church of Christ, as that they sold their possessions, and parted them to all men, as every man had need (Acts 2:45; 4:34–35), thereby outing themselves of their former possessions, and providing for their own subsistence at Jerusalem, and the support of others that had need, who upon the same ground continued there with them. Nor is it very probable that men thus spirited, should mind returning to their own possessions, in case they had not sold all. Thirdly, but however we have light enough from Scripture to prove (and that according to our brethren's principles and assertions) that they were all members of the church of Jerusalem, thus: They which are added to the church, continue in church communion, put their estates into the church's common treasury, choose officers for the church, are members of the same church. But these multitude of believers were added to the church (Acts 2:47, etc.). Therefore all that whole multitude were members of that church; yea our brethren themselves take that fellowship of theirs (Acts 2:42) for a pattern of ordinary church communion. And should we grant this church to be ebbing and flowing, as our brethren speak, in point of residence of members, yet those members that were not resident, were for all that members of that church. Are not some members of our brethren's congregations so? yea have they not their dwellings sometimes at greater distance from the usual place of their church-meeting than the utmost borders [of] Judea were from Jerusalem, and members still? and yet according to our brethren's assertion, the number of members, whether resident or not, must not be more than that they might (did they all reside) meet together in one place.

Objection. But some of these were of Judea, the country about, and that of these might be churches erected in their proper dwellings is rationally supposable. For (Acts 8:1) it is said, Paul persecuted disciples in other places besides Jerusalem, as Acts 26 at Damascus, and upon the ceasing of the persecution it is said, "the churches had rest throughout all Judea" (Acts 9:31).

Answer. Our answer to this, shall be no other than what our brethren make their fourth exception, *viz.* that this being the first church, and whereof all the apostles were the officers, the believers who dwelt there (we add and who dwelt near) would certainly abide together as one church, without parting or dividing, till they came to the utmost proportion that the constitution of a church was capable of, to a *maximum quod sic.* And *The largest as* therefore it is not so rationally supposable, that those that lived so near *such or of its* Jerusalem, would so soon erect churches in their proper dwellings; nor *kind* will Paul's persecuting the saints in other places besides Jerusalem, prove churches in Judea. For the very text cited (Acts 8:1), expresses, that those of the church of Jerusalem, were scattered abroad throughout all Judea Gillespie, 28 and Samaria, so that still they whom Paul persecuted unto strange cities, Lightfoot, 191 were members of the church of Jerusalem. And this Paul himself tells us (Acts 26), yet we deny not, but that they who were thus scattered abroad, preaching the Word (Acts 8:4). Churches were erected in Judea, Galilee and Samaria, of whom it is said (Acts 9:31) that the persecution ceasing, they were edified and multiplied.

Exception Three. Their third exception is, 'that they in those countries had {See p. 78} great assemblies, consisting of many thousand hearers at once, that could and did hear; so Christ [in] Luke 12:1 preached to myriads, many thousands: So [in] Acts 13:45 [*sic* 44] almost the whole city came to hear the Word of God by Paul; at Charenton many thousands hear in one place, as is well known, and so in many places in England. Moses sometimes spoke in the ears of all the people, so Ezra 10:9–10. And it is known by experience, that in hot countries, as men may see further by reason of the pureness of the air, so they may hear at a greater distance than in cold."

We *answer:* First, that we read (Luke 12) of "myriads" (or as our English translation renders it), an innumerable multitude gathered together, so that they trod one upon another, but not, first, that they all heard, nor secondly that Christ preached to them all. The text is express—"Jesus began to say to His disciples;" and though upon occasion of a question made by one of the company (verse 13), He speaks something applicable to the people (verse 14), yet He returns to preach to His disciples again (verse 22). As for that in verse 54, it is questionable whether that be part of the same sermon. To that Acts 13:45, "the whole city came together to hear," etc., we *answer:* That city was Antioch of Pisidia, and how do they prove that to be so populous a city? Or secondly, that all they that came together heard the Word. It is said, indeed, they came together to hear the Word, but many more might come together intentionally to hear, than actually did or could hear, as in many assemblies in this city. Thirdly, the text makes equal mention of Paul and Barnabas, as both speaking to the people, and why then might they not be in distinct assemblies or divisions?

As to that of Charenton, where they say, "it is well known many thousands hear," we *answer:* First, that the number of the members of that church does not (probably) arise to the number of them in Jerusalem, when at highest before the dispersion. Secondly, that their meeting place (as it is well known) has such accommodation of seats and double galleries, as they had not either in the temple or Solomon's Porch. The like answer will serve in part for England. There do not meet so many (that can hear) as were of the church of Jerusalem. Secondly, they have better accommodation than they had. And thirdly, more may hear at once than can at once receive the sacrament: and therefore in great congregations, they are necessitated to receive some at one time, and some at another.

For that of Moses, it is true, we read he spoke in the ears of the people, but do our brethren in good earnest believe, that Moses had such a strong voice as could reach to all Israel at once? who the last time before this that they were numbered, were six hundred thousand, one thousand, seven hundred and thirty (Numbers 26:51), besides twenty three thousand Levites, and they males only (verse 62). That phrase therefore of speaking in all their ears, must necessarily be some other ways understood; as first, either in their presence, to them being present, as Diodati renders it (Genesis 20:8; Genesis 44:18) *in loro presenza.*[1] Or secondly, mediately, he to some, and they to others, as is probable (Exodus 11:1), where Moses is commanded to speak in the ears

---

1. [Giovanni Diodati, Reformed divine (1576–1649), Bible translations: *La Sacra Biblia* (Italian, 1607), *La Sainte Bible* (French, 1644). Genesis 20:8: "in lot presenza;" "en leur presence."]

of the people, that every man and woman borrow jewels, etc., who were not (in all likelihood) suffered to leave their tasks to meet all together to hear that proclamation. Or thirdly, *turmatim & successive*, they were ſpoken to in several companies, Moses to one, and some others joined with him to others; as Deuteronomy 32:44, it is said, "And Moses ſpake in the ears of the people, he and Hoshea the ſun of Nun." Or fourthly, by all the people, is meant all the heads and rulers of them, as Deuteronomy 31:30. Moſes is said to ſpeak in the ears of all the congregation; yet verse 28, the elders of the tribes only were gathered together for him to ſpeak to. The like answer may be given to that inſtance of Ezra. *by groups and successively*

To that experiment, which our brethren mention of hearing at a farther diſtance in pure air and in hot countries than in cold, we oppose the judgment of that great maſter of experiments in this kind, the Lord of Verulam, who in his *Centuries* expressly said, "The thinner or drier air, carries not the sound so well as the more dense," etc.[1]

The queſtion is not, how many may meet together to hear, but how many may met together to partake in all ordinances of church fellowship, eſpecially in the sacrament of the Lord's Supper. And in this we appeal to our brethren, whether they think the "Myriads" (Luke 12:1) so thronged that they trod one upon another, could in that throng have received the sacrament? and so for those other vaſt multitudes, in whose hearing (as they say) and in their sense, Moses, Ezra and Paul ſpoke? or whether more thousands in one assembly may receive the sacrament in a hot country, than in a cold? and whether the heat of the climate and pureness of the air they ſpeak of, will help more to meet in one room, as well as to hear, as they conceive, at a more remote diſtance?

Exception Four. The fourth exception is a ſtrong argument for us; 'that this being the firſt church, and whereof all the apoſtles were officers, those therefore who dwelt there' (we add upon the same ground, who were converted there, and joined the church-fellowship with them) 'would certainly abide together as one church, till they came to the utmoſt proportion, that the conſtitution of a church is capable of, *maximum quod sic*, for the more untied ſtrength and glory of religion and Chriſtian communion in holding forth the name of Chriſt in one body.' {See p. 78}

We grant this, and therefore say that when the number of believers was so increased, that they could not hold visible communion together there in one assembly in all acts, they were enforced to divide themselves into diſtinct congregations for acts of worship. Yet that they might hold communion as far as it was possible, for acts of government, they continued one church, one body; and supposing more congregations there than one (which we conceive abundantly proved) judge whether it make more for the *Minutes, 2.536–552*

---

1. *Nat. Hiſt.* cent. 2. n. 143. cent 3. n. 217, 218. [Francis Bacon, *Sylva Sylvarum, or, A Natural Hiſtory: in ten centuries* (1627; 1661), pp. 98, 128.]

united ſtrength and glory of religion and Chriſtian communion in hold-ing forth the name of Chriſt in one body, that each of these congregations should be so complete a church as to be independent from all the reſt, or that many of those congregations should be united in one government, *by joint counsel* and so transaċt their affairs, *communi consilio* as one church.

Exception Five. Nor would their fifth exception much prejudice us should {See p. 79} we grant the whole. "They had," they say, till Paul's persecution, 'the greateſt liberty, and freedom even to the utmoſt;' "they had favor with all the peo-ple," and the rulers did not punish Peter and John for fear of the people, etc.

Bate something of 'the greateſt liberty to the utmoſt,'[1] when Peter and John immediately after the miracles, and while they were preaching, were hauled to prison before the people's faces (Aċts 4:1, 3), and all the apoſtles were laid hold of, put in the common jail, threatened and beaten (Aċts 5:17, 18, 40)—if we had such measures, we should not account it the greateſt lib-erty to the utmoſt. The people's favoring and magnifying them, only shows they were not at that time aċtive in the persecution, but all the Sanhedrin were. For their not punishing of them by reason of the people, it was only that they did not put them to death that occasion, the miracle being so fresh and notorious. But secondly, should we grant what our brethren say, they had liberty to the utmoſt, we might from it more probably colleċt the increase of the church to have been so many and great, that they could not but exceed the bounds of one single congregation.

They tell us, it was no new thing among the Jews, for seċts to have great multitudes to cleave to them, and for them to baptize openly, as John Bap-tiſt and Chriſt did.

Surely it is not the honor of Chriſt and His apoſtles, to have the Chris-tian church thus ranked with seċts. And to what purpose is this? Our breth-ren will not say, there were no more of the seċt of the Pharisees than could meet in one place and make one congregation, or that John and Chriſt bap-tized no more than could make one single congregation. And if the liberty granted to other seċts made them so numerous, why may we not think that the number of believers was far greater than any of those seċts, the apoſtles confirming their doċtrine by so many miracles?

[1b. Answer to the Reasons against the Appendix and Acts 8:1]

{See p. 79} The brethren having in the assembly affirmed, that though it should be *Minutes, Sess.* granted that the number of believers in Jerusalem before the diſperſion 167, 575–576 was so great, that they could not meet together in one place; yet the perse-Lightfoot, cution so waſted and scattered them, as that there were no more left than 190–192 might meet in one congregation. This engaged the assembly in a diſpute Gillespie, about it, and after many days diſpute it was resolved upon the queſtion: 32, 34

---

1. ["Bate:" i.e. 'it diminishes the claim of liberty that the apostles were imprisoned,' etc.]

> That the dispersion mentioned (Acts 8) does not prove such a scattering, as that there might not remain more congregations than one in that church. And for confirmation hereof were brought Acts 9:31, Acts 12:24, Acts 21:20.

Minutes, 2.17–18, Votes, Sess. 166–167 Gillespie, 33

Now against this proposition our brethren argue from greatness of the persecution that caused the dispersion, that it was great for intension [*intensity*], reaching to imprisonment and death (chapter 22:4). And for extent, it reached to all sorts both preachers and Christians. [In] Acts 8:1 it is said indefinitely to be against the church, and, verse 3, it is called an entering into every house, and haling men and women to prison, and Acts 20, Paul said he imprisoned many of the saints, not preachers only; and that this is an observable difference between this persecution, and that mentioned, Acts 12, that there it is said Herod vexed certain of the church, but here that Paul made havoc of the church, and that they were all scattered except the apostles.

Braye, 79r.

To which we *answer:* The persecution was indeed great and general against all the saints promiscuously, but therefore we conceive would make more congregations in Jerusalem than there were before, though it made them smaller. They could not now meet in the temple, daily, nor possibly at their wonted meeting hours. But yet certainly even then they had their meetings and congregations. No terrors could make them forsake the assembling of themselves together. In that other persecution (Acts 12) we find the church assembled in several places. They were praying in the house of Mary (verse 12), there was one; to which Peter comes and tells them the manner of his delivery, and bids them go and tell it to James and to the brethren, there was another. So it was in that persecution, and so it might be (nay was likely to be) in this.

No say our brethren, for the text says expressly they were all scattered except the apostles.

To which we *answer:* They all must be understood either of all the believers, or all the teachers and church officers in the church of Jerusalem, except believers. But it cannot be understood of "all the believers," that they all were scattered, and therefore it must be understood of "teachers," and that for two reasons.

First, because the particle πλὴν used with the genitive case in the New Testament, is always exceptive to the utmost; and therefore (according to our brethren's sense) would imply that there was not one believer left in Jerusalem besides the apostles, which cannot be. For the text says that Paul broke into houses, and haling men and women, committed them to prison (verse 3), and this he did in Jerusalem (Acts 26:10). Therefore all the believers were not scattered abroad through the regions of Judea, Galilee, and Samaria, some of them were in prison at Jerusalem. And to what purpose can we imagine did the apostles (who in all their motions and stays were directed by the Spirit of God), tarry at Jerusalem, unless it were to comfort and support the church there, in the rage of this persecution which had scattered their other officers and teachers from them?

Secondly, it appears that they were the teachers who were thus all scattered except the apostles, for it is there said, "They that were scattered, went everywhere preaching the Word" (verse 4).

To this our brethren reply, "That is not only called teaching which is by way of sermon to a multitude; for verse 25 of this chapter, it is said that Philip taught the eunuch in a private conference, and Aquila and Priscilla taught Apollos."

But we *answer:* The text speaks not of "teaching," but of "preaching." They went everywhere εὐαγγελιζόμενοι τὸν λόγον or *preaching* the Word. *Act of love* Teaching may be *Actus charitatis*, but preaching is *Actus officii*. How can they *Act of office* preach except they be sent (Romans 10)?

Objection. 'But they are not called εὐαγγελισαι as having an office, but {See p. 80} εὐαγγελιζόμενοι, as referring to an act. And it was ordinary in those times for men that were not by office ministers, occasionally to teach the Word in private converse and otherwise, and these went out by persecution not by mission.'

Answer. That in those times men not in office did teach by private converse we deny not. But we speak not here of teaching but of preaching, and if εὐαγγελιζόμενοι τὸν λόγον refer to the act, yet to the act as men in office, we desire our brethren to produce one text of Scripture where εὐαγγελιζόμενοι τὸν λόγον is used by any that are not preachers by office. We can bring many where it is used of those that are, even by the penman of this history (Luke 8:1; 9:6; 20:1; Acts 5:42; 8:12; 10:36). So that we conclude that these εὐαγγελιζόμενοι τὸν λόγον had their commission to preach before, though this persecution occasioned their mission into Judea and other places to preach there.

Objection. But can we think (they say) the teachers were scattered, and the ordinary believers were not; except we suppose the people more courageous to stay by it, than their teachers?

Answer. We dare not say that those that are scattered in a time of persecution are less courageous than those that stay and suffer. In Queen Mary's days many preachers fled beyond sea; whether it were that God had present employment for them there, or did it to reserve them for future service in their return home, we do not say. But we dare not say that they were less courageous than those that stayed by it, and died for it. In the late times of prelatical rage and persecution many were scattered into foreign parts, while others that did abide by it had trial of cruel mockings, yea, moreover of bonds and imprisonments. Shall we say, that those were less courageous than those?

2. But should we grant that this dispersion was not only of the teachers,

but of the multitude of believers, we yet might answer, secondly, that though this persecution was great, yet it was but short. And it cannot be imagined, but they who were scattered by the persecution, would upon the ceasing of it return again to Jerusalem, and that upon the grounds laid down by our brethren in their fourth exception.

3. Should we grant they were so scattered that they never returned to Jerusalem again, yet this does not weaken our proposition or the main proof of it; because we must rather look to the first frame of that church, than to their condition under persecution, which was but accidental; so that our brethren either mistake themselves, or wrong us, when they say that we build an "It may be" upon an "It might be."

For we proved our "it may be" by the state of the church of Jerusalem before the dispersion, and only to take off an objection made by them, we say "it might be" that after the dispersion there were more believers in Jerusalem than could meet in one place. And to prove this we bring Acts 9:31, where it is said the persecution ceasing, the churches were multiplied, or according to the original ἐπληθύνοντο, were filled up, and Acts 12:24, the Word of God grew and multiplied. And Acts 21:20, where we read of many thousands of myriads of Jews which believed.

To which our brethren except as follows:

First to that Acts 9:31 they say, that ἐπληθύνοντο does not signify ordinarily a great number made up, but an increase in measure, not in number; so Matthew 24:12, 1 Peter 1:2, "Grace be multiplied," etc. Secondly, they are the churches of Judea, Galilee, and Samaria, that are there spoken of; and what is that to prove more in the church of Jerusalem than could meet in one?

Whereto we reply first, that the word πληθύνω does properly signify to increase in number, and not in measure, and accordingly is translated to be multiplied (Acts 6:1, 7; 7:17). Πλῆθος the noun from whence it is derived, in the whole New Testament is translated "multitude," and this verb that comes of it throughout the whole book of the Acts, when applied to the church, is only so used and accordingly translated. Nor can it being applied to persons, be otherwise understood, whatever it may of *sins* and *graces* in the text by them produced, yet in them the word is capable of this construction, as might easily be shown, were it needful or expedient.

Secondly, though they be the churches of Judea, Galilee and Samaria that are mentioned, yet the church of Jerusalem therein must needs be contained and included. First, if Jerusalem were in Judea; secondly, it being expressed ὅλης Ἰουδαίας all, or whole Judea, of which Jerusalem was a part; and this thirdly, not in contra-distinction to Jerusalem, as in some other places, as Mark 1:5, Matthew 4:25, Acts 26:10, but to Samaria and Galilee, in which construction Jerusalem (not being named) is included, as Mark 3:7, Acts 10:37. Should we say the churches of all England, and Scotland, and Ireland, are in a covenant? Would not any common understanding take the churches of London to be included here? Nay, fourthly, were Judea set alone by itself, yet it may and does include Jerusalem, which our brethren cannot upon good ground deny. In Luke 1:5, Luke 3:1, Acts 28:21, Acts 11:1, 29, 1 Thessalonians 2:14 and which themselves in Acts 15:1 do upon another occasion and less reason assert, where they will have Judea not only to include Jerusalem, but will needs have it put for Jerusalem. Fifthly, if our brethren say that the church of Jerusalem was not included in these churches of Judea, that had rest, and were edified and multiplied, they must show that it then was troubled and lessened. But sixthly, if other churches of Judea were so increased and multiplied, we may conclude the church of Jerusalem, who had a greater proportion of means, even the ministry of the whole college of the apostles, was multiplied much more; so that all the believers there could not for all acts of worship meet together in one congregation.

To Acts 12:24 our brethren except nothing. But to Acts 21:20, they say: First, that it was the feast of Pentecost when Paul came to Jerusalem (as they would prove by his journal) and therefore no wonder if he found thousands of the believing Jews there, that were come up from all quarters; and (verse 17), some of them are expressly said to be Jews of Asia, not Judea. Secondly, the word μυριας being put alone without any word of number, signifies only a greater multitude, as μύριον πλῆθος, etc., and being put indefinitely, is all one, as to say thousand or many.

Answer. To which we *answer:* To the first, that we contend not much whether Paul came to Jerusalem by Pentecost or no, as not making much either against us or for us. Some that say he was at Jerusalem at Pentecost, think he came thither eight or ten days before. But so timely before the feast those myriads were not likely come up, it being the time of their wheat harvest, which needlessly they would not absent themselves from, and which some conceive was the reason why this feast of Pentecost was but of one day, whereas the two other anniversary feasts continued seven days.

Braye, 81v But we suppose our brethren know it is controverted, whether Paul were at Jerusalem at this feast or no? and denied by some. And if we also should deny it, it will be hard for them to demonstrate it, till they can manifest: how long after the days of unleavened bread Paul's journey began (chapter 20:6); how long he was going on foot to Assos (verse 13)[1] and from thence to Mitylena (verse 14); how long he tarried at Trogyllium (verse 15); how long at Miletus, before he sent for the elders at Ephesus (some say of Asia, verse 17); how long it was before they could come (verse 18); how long he continued there before he departed (verse 38); how long in passing thence

---

1. Which Ptolomy makes 25 miles from Troas, some a great deal more. Miletus was from Ephesus according to Ptolomy, 45 miles. Merc. makes it above 50. Chrysostom endeavors a computation of these days, but it is but conjecture. [Gerhardus Mercator (1512–1599, Flemish mathematician, geographer and map maker. *Claudii Ptolemaei Alexandrini Geographiæ …* (Amsterodammi, 1605). Cf. Chrysostom, *Homilies on the Acts of the Apostles and the Epistle To The Romans, NPNF1*, vol. 11, Homily 45, p. 275.]

to Coos (chapter 21:1) and from Rhodes to Patara in the same verse; and how long he stayed there, and then how long from his setting forth from thence, till leaving Cyprus he sailed to Syria, and landed at Tyre (verses 2 and 3); how long in passing from thence to Ptolomais (verse 7); how many those many days were that he stayed at Philip's house (verse 10); and how long he was going thence to Jerusalem, and the very day he arrived there—none of which are in the story particularly expressed. And then adding the many days besides which are set down (20:6, 7, 15; 21:1, 4, 7, 8) show that all these amount not to above 42 days, for Paul had no more to finish his course in from Philippi to Jerusalem. However the brethren to make it probable that he was there at Pentecost, lengthen the time, and shorten the way, for these 42 days they make eight weeks and make it about forty miles from Tyre to Jerusalem, whereas measuring in a direct line, it was 90; but that way which Paul went, coasting by Ptolomais and Casarea, it was very nearly 120.

But secondly, should we grant our brethren that he was there at Pentecost, we must yet put them on another proof of all the Jews among the Gentiles, being bound or wonted to come to this feast (it especially being but of one day) from all quarters, of which we shall speak more hereafter.

Thirdly, Say all did, yet we can by no means yield that the Jews of Asia, mentioned verses 27 and 28, were of this great multitude of believing Jews, mentioned verse 20, seeing the text is plain, that they were persecutors rather than believers.

Fourthly, Nay none of the believing Jews that were among the Gentiles, must be included in these myriads, for they are clearly distinguished from them. The words are plain, that the myriads of believing Jews were informed that Paul taught all the Jews among the Gentiles, etc. They then are informed that Paul had taught others. The Jews among the Gentiles were they whom Paul had so taught, and how could they be in the number of them that were informed, had they need to be informed by others, what Paul had taught themselves?

Fifthly, They therefore must either be the believing Jews of Jerusalem only; and then we have more than we need, or at most they must be the believing Jews in Judea only, and if so, thence we argue, if there were πόσαι μυριάδες, so many ten thousand of believers in Judea, there must be some ten thousands, at least, one ten thousand in Jerusalem for her part, that will make more than one congregation, which might meet for all ordinances in one place. If so many, where less means, than a greater number proportionably must be in Jerusalem, where the apostles were preaching daily in the temple, and from house to house, and that for two and twenty years together. And therefore it cannot but be very strange, that in all that time of the gospel's spring in so populous a city, all of them should convert no more to the faith than might make up but one congregation.

Sixthly, How do our brethren in the sixth reason, whereby they would prove that the number of believers in Jerusalem were no more than might meet in one place, make use of the very next verse 22 to that purpose, where it is said, "how is it therefore? The multitude must needs come together." Sure[ly] the multitude there are no other than the myriads in this verse 21, and we conceive our brethren then took that multitude to be of the church of Jerusalem, whatever they do now.

"But if it be said that nothing can be argued from the word μυριάδες, which as μυριας being put without addition of another word of number, signifies only indefinitely very many." We *answer:* First, our brethren in their third exception out of Luke 12:1 translate this word μυριάδες myriads, and there stretch it to the utmost extent, and thereby prove that one man's voice may be heard by myriads at once, which no man can believe. But here they would shrink the signification of it, to be a less number, when we would improve it's proper sense and latitude, to show the exceeding great numbers of believers in Jerusalem, or in all Judea (for either will serve our turn), which they cannot deny, but might reach to so many.

Secondly, they found in their book the adjective μύριος put indefinitely, as μυρίον πλῆθος and some other such like, which might have been transcribed, but there they found not an instance of the substantive μύριας so used, else it would have been added. Which we could have desired might have been, or any wherein it signifies fewer than ten thousand, sure[ly] it does not in such instances as we meet with (Acts 19:19; Revelation 5:11).

"Thirdly, they seem to intimate that μυριάς without the addition of another word of number might signify fewer than ten thousand," as if such a word added heightened its signification, whereas we find in Scripture that it stints [*limits*] it rather to his precise signification of 10,000 and no more, as Acts 19:19.[1] But when it is alone by itself, it is left free to reach to a greater numberless number, as in those myriads of saints, Jude 12, and angels, Hebrews 12:12.

[2. Answer to Reasons against the second proof of the first head
from many apostles and other preachers in Jerusalem]

{See p. 81} To their answer to the second proof of the first head from the many apostles and other preachers in the church of Jerusalem, etc., our brethren say,

I. First for the apostles. First, they took all opportunities to fill their hands with work, preaching daily in the temple, and from house to house (Acts 5:22; 2:26). Paul also in Ephesus taught publicly in the congregation, and from house to house (Acts 20:20).

Secondly, when any in Judea, or elsewhere, were converted, the apostles went abroad (Acts 8).

Thirdly, how were the twelve employed, when for forty days together,

____

1. [Acts 19:19:] ἀργυρίου μυριάδας πέντε—5,000 [*sic* 50,000] pieces of silver.

                    I: ANSWER OF THE ASSEMBLY TO THE REASONS

they met together in an upper room, and had but one hundred and twenty for a flock?

Answer. 1. We reply to the first.

(1) Because the apostles took all opportunities to fill their hands with work, therefore they distributed their many thousands into several congregations, that they might all be at work at once in an orderly way, otherwise though they might preach occasionally, yet they could have had no settled way, and opportunity of employing themselves in the work of the ministry. *Resp. ad primum*

(2) Their preaching daily in the temple, and from house to house, confirms this. They preached in the temple to the promiscuous multitude, while they had their proper church meetings in more private houses.

(3) This is yet further confirmed by what our brethren say of Paul, who taught publicly, and from house to house. For if Paul could do both these works at Ephesus himself alone; why might not Peter, James and John, do as much at Jerusalem? especially if but one congregation? So that by this argument the rest of the apostles might have been spared, and yet that one congregation sufficiently instructed.

2. To their second, of the apostles going forth to erect other churches, they can give but one instance of it (Acts 8), where the whole twelve went not forth, but only two were sent.

3. To the third, we say (1), our brethren mistake forty days for ten, at most, for no more were there from Christ's ascension (upon which they went up into that upper chamber, Acts 1:13, 14), to Pentecost (Acts 2:1).

(2) As in those forty days which they mentioned, the apostles were employed not in preaching, but in learning from Jesus Christ the things pertaining to the kingdom of God (Acts 1:3), so in those ten days which they meant, they were taken up especially in prayer and supplication (Acts 1:14), waiting for the promise of the Spirit, further to enable them to the work of the ministry—and of them so fitted and filled with the Spirit, we meant in our argument.

II. For the many teachers, they say,

1. "There are then many gifted men that were not officers," which yet "occasionally instructed others, as Aquila did Apollos." Those gifts "were so plentiful, that in that one church of Corinth, almost every one of them had them" (1 Corinthians 14:26), and yet not officers. For else "there would have been almost as many teachers as members, and the pouring out of the Holy Ghost" (more ordinary than) "did not make every man a teacher by office, for then all those in Samaria should have been teachers" (Acts 8). Gillespie, 33 Lightfoot, 191

2. That not any of them were in office, because we find 'no mention of elders in the ordination of deacons (Acts 6), in which elders (had there been any) had an interest, and would have been named as well as the apostles, as they are (Acts 15), when once there were elders, but deacons were the first sort of officers that were chosen, and till their choice the apostles managed all.'

Answer 1. As for the first part of their answer:

(1) We grant in those times were many gifted men that were not in office, which might occasionally instruct others, as Aquila did Apollos.

(2) But, we did never say, the congregations were to be multiplied according to the number of gifted men, or that there should be almost as many teachers as church members, to which our brethren rather propend [*incline*] in the practice of their congregations.

(3) But this instructing occasionally, was either in private, and then it is nothing to the purpose, or in public, and so it cannot be meant, for not only Aquila, but also Priscilla his wife instructed Apollos. And our brethren will not say women may [teach] (no not occasionally) in public.

(4) Our brethren cannot conclude that ἕκαστος (1 Corinthians 14:26) signifies simply "all" or "almost all," but all, or every one that were so qualified, as Luke 13:15, "Doth not ἕκαστος every one of you loose his ox or his ass" etc., and 1 Corinthians 7:2, "Let every one of you have his own wife," etc., not meant of all in general, but of every one that had an ox, etc., or had need of a wife, and so in that place of the Corinth[ian]s.

Answer 2. To the second part of this answer we reply,

(1) That it will not follow, because elders are not mentioned (Acts 6) therefore then there were none. We find no mention of elders in Jerusalem, till Acts 11. Will our brethren therefore say, there were none till then? The truth is, we read nothing at all in Scripture of the time or occasion of ordaining elders in that church, and therefore less can be said about it.

(2) Yet the current of expositors say, that the seventy disciples were at Jerusalem among those hundred and twenty names, of whom we read (Acts 1), who were teachers by office, and if so, then all the work of administration of all sorts did not lie only upon the apostles' hands, as our brethren affirm.

(3) We have already proved that those who were scattered from Jerusalem were preachers by office before the dispersion, and our brethren grant that after the dispersion there were elders there. So that both before and after the dispersion, there were many teachers and officers there, which is an argument of many congregations there.

[3. Answer to the Reasons against the third proof of the first head from the diversity of languages among the believers]

Braye, 85r
{See p. 81}

Unto our third proof of divers congregations at Jerusalem by the diversity of languages there (Acts 2:6), the first answer that our brethren make is, "that it is true indeed that [there] were in the second of Acts, out of all nations, that heard the apostles speak in the several languages of the countries they were born in, but yet those were all either Jews or proselytes—εὐλαβεῖς— worshippers (as verse 5), who came up to worship, and some parts of the worship were audible."

1. We observe that our brethren translate εὐλαβεῖς—worshippers—for their own advantage, not having either the propriety of the word, the use of it in the Scripture, or the concurrence of interpreters to bear them out in such a translation. The advantage they seek for, is, because they would color it the better that these companies now assembled at Jerusalem came up to worship; or as they explain it elsewhere, that they came up to Pentecost. But this follows not, because they were dwelling at Jerusalem at this feast of Pentecost, that therefore they came up to this feast, or to worship only, as we touched before.

(1) For the Jews that dwelt without the land of Canaan were not bound to appearance at the festivals there.

(2) Nor was it possible that they should so do, if they had been commanded, unless they did nothing almost all the year but go up to Jerusalem, and home again, their habitation being some of them so many month's journey distant.

(3) What had the dispersed Jews to do at the Feast of Harvest (for so it is called, Exodus 23:16) when their harvest in very many of those places where they dwelt was not yet begun?

(4) If their distance from Jerusalem made them to choose to come up but to some one of the feasts, and omit the rest, why to Pentecost, which was the least solemn of all the three, rather than to the Passover or Tabernacles, these two being solemnities for a whole week—Pentecost but for a day?

(5) We produce a more probable reason before (as we suppose) of this matchless and unparalleled concourse at this time, for so we doubt not to call it, *viz.* that the Jews had learned by the Scripture, and especially out of the prophesy of Daniel, that this was the time when the Kingdom of Heaven should appear, as it is apparent both out of Luke 19:11, and out of the Jews' own authors, and therefore came in those multitudes to Jerusalem, and there settled to dwell, to see the fulfilling of those things that all the nations so much looked after.

2. Although it were true, that all these dispersed ones came up to worship, and though the worship in some parts of it were audible, yet can it be no sound arguing to infer thereupon, that therefore all that came to worship understood what was said in it; especially seeing that the worship at the temple was not so much to hear, as to offer.

They proceed thus: "And though born in other countries (the Jews being dispersed) yet all were generally learned, and understood the Hebrew tongue, the language of their own nation, even as to this day the Jews and their children do."

1. That the dispersed Jews were so generally learned, is by far, sooner said than proved; even they of Jerusalem were scorned by the learned men there, as ignorant in the law (John 7:49), and Josephus seems to testify the clean contrary to what our brethren assert.

We more wonder at their assertion concerning the Jews dispersed being so learned, unless they can show us some universities, synagogues, schools or some means of raising learning, in Media, Parthia, and other places, which we never yet have seen or heard of.

To what an unacquaintedness with the law, and with that learning we are now speaking of, the people were grown in the seventy years captivity, may be collected out of the book of Nehemiah. And how these dispersed ones now in mention should come to be so learned, when their dispersion was so vastly wider, and the continuance of it so incomparably longer, we confess we cannot apprehend, histories do not evidence, and we suppose our brethren will not be able to demonstrate.

2. By the Hebrew tongue we conceive our brethren understand not the language properly so called, for it is so clear both by writings of learned men, and by the Scripture itself, that that was not the vulgar language of the nation at those times that we are speaking of, that we cannot once suspect that they mean that tongue, but the mixed Syriac, of which we have some small parcels in the New Testament, and some larger pieces in the Jewish writers, which indeed is called Hebrew (John 19:13, 17), and the Hebrew dialect (Acts 21:40 and Acts 22:2), not because it was the proper Hebrew tongue, but the proper tongue of the Hebrews at this time (Acts 1:19).

Minutes, 2.562, n5

(1) We are indifferent whether [*which*] language they mean, for we deny that the Jews born in other countries did generally understand the one or the other.

{1} The Septuagint translation was the Bible they had then in common use, both in their synagogues, and in their studies, as is apparent both by the quotations of the apostles, and of Philo, and Josephus, and is hinted by Tertullian.

{2} The prophets were translated out of Hebrew into Chaldee a little before the coming of Christ, and the law a little after, to make them the more intelligible.

{3} Even Philo himself, one of the learnedest of the nation, and one that was alive at this very time of which we are speaking, does sometimes bewray his unskilfulness, if not his total ignorance in the pure Hebrew tongue.

And whence then came their skillfulness in the Hebrew tongue so common and general as our brethren conceive, if they mean this language?

(2) As for the Syriac, which was indeed the language of the nation at this time, we offer these things likewise.

{1} That there was no part of Scripture written in that language.

{2} That there was but little exposition of Scripture, or indeed none at all in that language that did then go up and down among all Jews that were dispersed.

{3} That it is questionable, whether the audible parts of worship at the temple were in this language, or no?

{4} That though it were, yet will our brethren hardly ever find a reason or argument, that might persuade all the Jews under heaven therefore to study, and get that Syriac language, because it was spoken at Jerusalem.

{5} There is so much difference of language in the two Talmuds, and in the two Targums, and other authors that were near to this time, as may somewhat argue that all the nation did not so generally understand that one language all alike.

{6} Philo himself appears to be unskillful in it, when he translates a most *Minutes, 2.562* common Syriac word, only upon other men's report.

{7} Though it were granted our brethren, that all the men among the dispersed Jews understood the Syriac, obtaining it by study; yet how will they make it good for women, of which there were some store of company there?

{8} Especially, how will they make it good of proselytes? For that Romans, Cappadocians, Cretians, or any of those nations of the western dispersion, whose language had no affinity at all with the Syrian or Hebrew tongue, if they converted to the Hebrew's religion, should also be skilled in the Syrian tongue, requires a stronger reason to evince, than we expect can be yet shown us.

How learned the Jews and their children are at this day our brethren mention, but we see no proof for it. It may be they have met with some that have attained to good skill in the Scriptures, and Hebrew tongue, but this is not proof for the general. It is true indeed they have their prayers and service in their synagogues in the Hebrew tongue, but this no more proves that they generally understand Hebrew, than it argues that the Papists generally understand Latin, because they have their Latin service. And yet also have we seen the Jews' prayers in Spanish and Italian tongues, though written indeed with the Hebrew letter.

The *Assertion*, 'That all the dispersed Jews understood the Hebrew tongue,' our brethren think is evident in Acts 20–22, where Paul coming up with divers Grecians to the Feast of Pentecost (20:4), unto which the Jews out of all quarters came, and being at a solemn meeting in the temple (21:27), the Jews out of Asia, strangers, stirred up all the people against him. And when (22:2), he made a speech to them, and when they heard he spoke the Hebrew tongue, they kept silence, and heard him patiently.

Whether Paul was at the Feast of Pentecost mentioned in this story, we refer to what we have said before, and that the Jews out of all quarters came to that feast we deny. If we should grant all that our brethren speak in this passage, what does it prove of their opinion? Because Paul being accused by the Jews of Asia, to the Jews of Jerusalem, and assaulted by the Jews of Jerusalem, when he makes a speech to them to whom he was accused, and by whom he was assaulted, in the Hebrew tongue, they heard him patiently, because he spake in their own tongue; *Ergo*, all the dispersed Jews of all countries wheresoever understood that tongue, it is a consequence so far fetched, and so strangely inferred, that we can rather wonder at such logic, than find any strength in such argumentation. If we should put them to prove that these Asian Jews that accused Paul (to meddle with none other) understood his apology, we suppose they could give us but little satisfaction in it. Nay, may we not retort their instance and argument against themselves thus? That if the Jews of Jerusalem took Paul for a Jew as it is most probable they did, they expected at first that he could not have spoken their language, which when they heard him do, they gave him the more attention.

A second instance they produce, is the people's understanding Peter's sermon (Acts 2).

"And further" (they say) "those mentioned (Acts 2) did understand all of them Peter's sermon. And though others spoke unto them besides Peter in their own language the wonderful things of God, yet that was but a preparative sign to them. As 1 Corinthians 14:22 making way for their conversation (verses 11, 12, and 13), but the means of their conversion was Peter's sermon," afterwards, and it was he that gave direction to them all what to do to be saved. "And therefore it must be spoken of some common language they all understood. And those gifts of languages given to the apostles were not of necessity to instruct these new converts only, but to fit them when they should go abroad into all the world, and to be a sign to the Jews at present to convince them."

We desire a proof, that Peter alone preached and converted these three thousand. It is true indeed that mention is only made of Peter's speech, yet this does not, in Luke's style, nor indeed *re ipsa*, exclude the preaching of the other apostles. For

in the matter itself (in the nature of the case)

1. Observe in Acts 3:12, it is said Peter answered the people, and his speech is only recorded without any mention at all of John's, and yet Acts 4:1, it is said λαλούντων δὲ αὐτῶν, declaring plainly that John spake as well as he. So again (4:8), it is said Peter spoke to them, and his speech only recorded, and yet in verse 13 it is said they saw the boldness of John as well as Peter.

2. Observe that though Luke in this book of the Acts of the Apostles intended to declare the growth of the gospel, and of the church, by the ministry of all the apostles and disciples that had their share in it, yet does he fix more specially upon the story of those that were respectively ministers of the circumcision and uncircumcision by a more peculiar designation, as Peter and John, more especially Peter; Paul and Barnabas, more especially Paul.

3. When he particularizes so much concerning Peter, and so little concerning the rest of the twelve, he does not thereby intimate any whit less zeal or activity for the propagation of the gospel in them, than in him, but he chooses rather to insist upon, and follow the story of Peter, partly (it may be) because [of] his great fall in the denial of his Master required the greater testimony of his recovery, and partly or chiefly because he was more

singularly designed for a minister of the circumcision, therefore is he the man most spoken of while the story follows the church of the circumcision.

4. Observe that in Acts 2:14, it is said Peter stood forth with the eleven. Now if the eleven were silent in this action, and auditors only as well as others, why are they mentioned?

Again it is said (verse 37), "They were pricked in their hearts, and said to Peter, and to the rest of the apostles, what shall we do?" Why should they ask counsel of the rest of the apostles as well as Peter, if they had not preached to them as well as he? And likewise in verse 42, it is said they continued in the doctrine of the apostles—ἀποστόλων—in the plural.

5. Peter lays to the charge of those to whom he speaks, the death of Christ. Now there were in that number (Acts 2) divers proselytes (verse 10), who had no hand at all in his death.

6. The pointing in verse 41 is considerable, where it is said, "Those that received Peter's words were baptized," and then as speaking of another story, he said, "There were added the same day three thousand souls."

All these things considered, we have good cause to doubt whether Peter alone preached at this time, and whether he alone was the converter of these three thousand, and whether he alone gave them direction what to do.

Our brethren conclude this passage thus: "Those gifts of languages were {See p. 82} not a necessity to instruct those new converts only, but to fit them when they should go abroad into all the world, and to be a sign to the Jews at present to convince them."

Whereas they say those gifts of languages given to the apostles were not of necessity to instruct those new converts only, we say so likewise; but our meaning is, that those gifts were of necessity to instruct those new converts, but not to instruct them only, but to fit the apostles against [*for when*] they should go abroad into all the world. And if our brethren mean not so, let them leave out the word only, and we shall know then what to say to them. But here we cannot tell what to say to them, because we cannot clearly tell what they mean.

It is true indeed that tongues were for a sign, and it is past gainsaying (1 Corinthians 14:22). But that they were given for a sign as for the proper end, we do utterly deny it. For we know that the gift of healing and power of casting out devils were for a sign, but we suppose our brethren will not say that that was the proper end why they were given. But for the benefit of the people in healing and dispossessing. And since the nature of the gift does import a necessity of it in the parties to whom it was applied, as healing and dispossessing argued sickness and possessedness, so since the very nature of the gift of tongues does imply instruction, we cannot but apprehend a necessity of it in those persons to whom it was used. For it seems monstrous to us that the solemn promise of the Father given in so glorious a manner, and so wondrous a thing in itself, should be more for a sign to them that believed not, than for any benefit for those that did. And that that gift which had been so highly prophesied of before, and so highly magnified now, and so great a gift of the Spirit in itself, should be but for this purpose, to ſpeak ſtrange languages to them that could have underſtood all of them one language if it had been ſpoken; what a needless superfluity of the gifts of the Spirit would our brethren have here, who will have such a thing as this only for a sign to the Jews while the apoſtles were among them? We have ever held that the gift of tongues was for calling in of the people to the knowledge and profession of God and religion, as the confusion of tongues had been their caſting out [cf. Genesis 11], and we have ever thought the gift itself to be of an inſtructive nature, and why it should not be so to the Jews here we see no cause.

The apoſtle indeed said in the place cited, "Tongues are for a sign." But he implies also in the verse preceding, that they were given for this end, that the people might hear. "With men of other tongues and other lips will I ſpeak unto this people" [Isaiah 28:11–12; 1 Corinthians 14:21]. And yet for all this will they not hear. Inſtruction was the proper end of languages, as it is of preaching, yea though the wicked receive it not; and the languages now given had no end at all, if the people had no need of them.

The apoſtles indeed were fitted with this gift againſt [the time] they should go into all the world. But let our brethren consider these things.

1. How long it was before any of the Gentiles were gone and preached unto by any of the apoſtles. Let them look either into the ecclesiaſtical histories, or seriously examine the text, and they shall find that it was divers years before they preached to any but the Jews, and then what should they have done with so many tongues for these divers years being to preach only to Jews that underſtood all of them one language? If we should put our brethren to it, to prove that the apoſtles were gone abroad into all the world before the council at Jerusalem, which was at the leaſt seventeen years, or before the apprehension of Paul at Jerusalem (Acts 21:30), which was at leaſt two and twenty years after this gift, they would have much ado to prove it. And why should they think that they should have this gift which was thought a great and glorious one for so long a time (or grant the time to have been shorter) and never put it to any but a kind of needless use, not for any benefit of the people, but that they might as well have been without?

2. Sure[ly] it is, that James lived and died at Jerusalem, and for aught that can be found, never departed from thence while he lived. Now certainly he had the gift of tongues as well as the other apoſtles, and to what purpose had he it if he were continually to preach to those that could have as well underſtood him in the mother tongue?

If, but say they, it was to be a sign to the Jews at present to convince them—to convince them, how? If by the things ſpoken, why those might have convinced them if they had been ſpoken in the Syrian tongue only,

which our brethren say all the people understood? If by the miracle that
those Galileans should speak so many tongues, why some of the people
took this for so little a miracle that they said they were full of new wine?
Now therefore when the apostles had in their hands the power of healing,
casting out devils, killing by a word, and raising the dead, and such like
signs as spake conviction by the very exercise of them, we cannot but hold
it strange to conceive that speaking of divers tongues should be thought to
be added as a bare sign, and for no other use, than what those other gifts
would have done abundantly without it.

Our brethren, to our second quotations of Acts 6 do make this answer:
"Secondly, for the Grecian widows (Acts 6), the Hellenists that lived among
the Jews might well be supposed to understand Hebrew."

Not to spend time upon this expression (the Hellenists that lived among
the Jews) which to divers learned men would appear barbarism, the Hellenists being conceived by them to be Jews themselves that lived among the
Greeks, and not Greeks that lived among the Jews, as our brethren seem to
us to conceive, how well they might be supposed to understand Hebrew by
our brethren we know not. As for ourselves, we know not any such ground
(that considered that has been spoken before) as to suppose for the generality of the Hellenists any such thing.

They conclude thus: "And that these had not several congregations from
the rest appears by this, that the whole multitude together met and chose
the deacons; it was a joint act. And if of differing languages wherein the
one understood, not the other, occasioning such a distinction of congregations (as the proof would hold forth) how could they all have agreed in
one meeting on the same man?"

We *answer:* Here are two things taken for granted by our brethren which
are yet to prove. First, that all the whole multitude of believers in Jerusalem
met to choose the deacons, and secondly, that they agreed in one meeting
on the same man.

We might here *answer* what we have done before, that the whole multitude in Scripture-style does not always signify all and singular persons of
such a company, but sometimes many of that company, and sometimes only
such as were present at the occasion mentioned. Yet if we should take the
whole multitude in the text, in the sense that our brethren do, for all the
thousands of believers, none excepted, yet is their assertion far from being
proved still. For the text indeed says, "The twelve called all the multitude,"
when they propounded the matter of the choice of deacons; but it cannot
be found, that all the multitude met for their choosing, unless they chose
them at that very instant, which is very questionable, and so is it whether
they agreed in one meeting on the same man. For were it granted, that the
people agreed in one tongue, yet certainly were they of several nations;
and how so many nations, so far distant for habitation, should in so short

a time as a festival season, come so acquainted one with another, and all with these seven, as to agree in one meeting on one man, is so difficult to imagine, that we cannot yet be convinced of it. But must rather conceive, that upon the apostles motioning the matter to the whole multitude (take it if you will in the largest comprehension) that they departed, and considered and consulted of the business, every nation whom it concerned, among themselves, or the most neighboring-nations one with another, and chose their men, and all having thus chosen, present them jointly to their ordination. And such choices as these of officers in several companies, yet all those that are chosen, brought at last into one body, has been and is so common, that it needs no exemplifying.

{See p. 82} But in the wrapping up of all, they use our weapon against ourselves, and say, that "the argument as well holds against the presbyterial association of those congregations into one church, people and elders, unto which, and in the communion and exercise whereof, such correspondencies and intercourses are needful, as they require one common language."

Nay, it holds nothing near so well against the presbyterial association into one church, unless it were true, that the elders of the congregation, and the common members were alike learned. And it is no consequence at all, that because the people could not all of them understand one sermon, nor could all join in the sacrament, because they could not understand one another's speech, that therefore the elders could not understand one another to join in government. Nor that a people that understand not one common language, may not join in one body under one presbyterial government, as well as they may join in one corporation, and in one civil government.

{See p. 82}   [1. Answer to the Reasons against] the second branch of this argument, that all those congregations were under one presbyterial government because one church, 2. Elders of it are mentioned]

PROOFS

Minutes,   1. Proof 1. Because they were one church—To which our brethren answer,
Sess. 165–166   "Though it be one, yet they not being more than could meet in one, the
2.564–574   argument concludes not."

Gillespie,   Reply 1. So then it is granted to be a concluding argument, if there were
31–33   more in that one church than could meet in one congregation for all acts
Lightfoot,   of worship, which whether we have not sufficiently proved, we freely leave
186–190   to those who shall impartially weigh our former arguments to determine.

Braye, 89r   Reply 2. Suppose the number of believers there had been no greater than might possibly have met in one, how can our brethren prove that they did not, for better convenience of administrations, or some other ends, meet in distinct and several assemblies? Some of the new gathered churches in London are not so numerous, but that three or four of them might very well meet in one assembly, yea possibly they have met, two churches at a sacrament, three or four churches at a fast or at a lecture, though they are no more than might meet in one place.

Proof. 2 Because the elders of that church are mentioned.—Against which our brethren except, (1) That there is no mention of any elder of that church, till after the dispersion (Acts 8), and so the weight of the argument depends upon the proof of many congregations after the dispersion, which the reverend assembly does not positively affirm: This is the sum of what is argumentative. (2) What follows, tends only to prove, that we dispute *in circulo*, and against Presbyterian principles. *in a circle*

We say: 1. As before (their repeating of exceptions necessitating us to repeat answers) that our not reading of elders before the dispersion, does not prove that there were none before it; the order of existence is not always to be gathered from the order of the history. We find elders in Jerusalem first mentioned, Acts 11, and after, Acts 15. But when they were first constituted, we find not particularly expressed; only we may rationally conceive, that the apostles in their care for the churches good, did ordain elders in that church very early. For they knew their commission was not limited to Jerusalem, but extended to all nations (Matthew 28:18), and though Christ at his departure gave them a charge to tarry at Jerusalem (Acts 1:4), yet it was but for a time, till they received the Holy Ghost, which was shortly after (Acts 2). After which time they knew not how soon any or all of them might have been called thence to preach the gospel to other nations; and therefore we cannot think they would have less care of settling elders there, than Paul upon a like occasion had in the churches of Lystra, Iconium and Antioch (Acts 14).

2. Let not our brethren therefore say, the weight of our argument lies upon the many congregations after the dispersion, till they can prove that the apostles neglected or deferred to ordain elders until then.

3. Yet did the weight of the argument lie where our brethren would have it, we doubt not but we have so fully proved many congregations there after the dispersion, as it would fully carry the cause.

4. Though the assembly did not at first so positively affirm it, it was not because they wanted [*lacked*] proof or evidence of the thing, but because they did not judge it necessary. What was spoken to the state of that church after the dispersion (as before we have said) was rather to remove an objection, than to make it a further proof of our proposition.

In the rest of this paragraph our brethren are somewhat obscure and perplexed. They 'speak of the presbytery the proposition intends.' {See p. 83}

If they know any other kind of presbytery over more congregations than one, besides that which the proposition intends, and which they conceive lawful, they shall do well to hold it forth, and to distinguish of presbyteries, which they deny, and which they grant.

As for that circle which our brethren would drive our argument into, we appeal to all logic, whether to reason thus, there were many congregations in Jerusalem, and many elders; and these congregations were all one church, and these elders all of them elders of that one church; therefore there were many congregations under one presbytery, be to dispute *in circulo*. If there be any other circle in what we have sent up to the honourable houses, or in anything that passed the vote of the assembly, let them show it.

As for that they would fasten upon our answer to their first argument, for the further clearing of ourselves, we refer them thither, where they shall find that elders have a double relation, one to the single congregation where they are fixed, another to the several congregations whereto it is united. Their relation to those thus united, ties them not to all duties of elders to all those united congregations (as our brethren suppose in their arguments), nor all those congregations to all duties unto them, but only to those mutual duties for which they were united, as is more at large declared in that answer. Which of these relations is primary, is no whit material to be insisted upon to our purpose.

[3. Answer to the Reasons against the third proof of the second branch, that the apostles did the ordinary acts of presbyters, as presbyters, in the church of Jerusalem, etc.

Our brethren labor much to invalidate this proof, which were they able to do, neither should their cause gain, nor ours lose much thereby, because (as some of our brethren have acknowledged) if we prove many congregations, yet so as they make one church for government, it suffices. And our brethren never went about to prove, that in case there were many congregations in Jerusalem they had several and independent presbyteries, yet we doubt not, but with God's assistance to make good this proof against all the reasons our brethren bring against it, which are as follows.

1. First, they grant the act of ministerial power to be the same in apostles and elders; but in the extent of that power (which they say is the point in question) the apostles power over many congregations cannot be a pattern for elders, because the apostles had power over all churches, and upon that was founded their power over many congregations.

And our brethren are further pleased to say, that episcopacy may as strongly argued from Titus' being left alone to ordain in Crete, that one man a bishop may ordain alone over many congregations, yea, and more strongly, in regard that the office of an evangelist is not so immediately from Christ as this of an apostle, and so is nearer a succession; or that one presbyter alone may govern many congregations, because one apostle might, as that because the apostles did govern those many congregations jointly, therefore many presbyters, over several congregations may.

(1) We accept what our brethren grant, that the act of ministerial power is the same in apostles and elders, the only difference they seem to insinuate is in the extent. And from thence we infer, that in all affairs transacted by the apostles properly concerning the church of Jerusalem, they did act as elders, because in such acts there was no extent of their power to many, much less to all churches.

(2) Whereas they tell us, "That the apostles power over many congregations was founded upon their power over all churches, and so cannot be a pattern for the power of elders over many," we *answer:* The apostles' power over many congregations as one church, to govern them all as one church jointly, and in common, was not founded upon their power over all churches, but upon the union of those congregations into one church, which union lays a foundation for the power of elders governing many congregations, and the apostles' practice in governing many congregations jointly as one church, is the pattern and precedent of that government, even as our brethren would make the apostles' joint governing one congregation, to be the pattern of many ministers governing one congregation.

(3) Our brethren therefore deal not so fairly, while they say episcopacy may draw a stronger argument for itself from apostolic practice than presbytery, sure[ly] what the apostles acted singly is not so practicable as what they did jointly; we cannot but wonder what should move our brethren to study such occasions (as in these reasonings they seem sundry times to do), to plead the cause of episcopacy (which they and we have covenanted to endeavor to the utmost to extirpate) at least to prefer the bishop's plea for their usurpation, before that which the Reformed Churches bring for their government, which they and we have covenanted to defend against the common enemy.

2. Secondly (say our brethren) each of these apostles, as he had by virtue of his apostolic commission the power of them all; so he had a relation of ministry unto all those supposed congregations, and every member thereof for the performance of all sorts of duties, as preaching, admonishing, etc. But in the presbyterial government over many congregations that have members and officers fixed, the several elders are denied to have the relations of elders to each congregation, but make up only an eldership in common, and therefore the apostolic frame is not herein our pattern.

We conceive our brethren here answer themselves, while they say, that 'That relation of ministry which the apostles had to each of these congregations, they had by virtue of apostolic commission,' for then it prejudices us nothing, if ordinary elders who have no such commission, have no such relation, and the presbyterial government answers the pattern well enough, though it carry not with it those relations which the apostles had by virtue of apostolic commission, which we clear more fully thus:

(1) The apostles intended here to act so, as to be patterns to others

in such things as were acts of ordinary church government, and to be performed by ordinary church officers, which our brethren themselves acknowledge.

(2) There was some kind of division of the charge for the better and more orderly, and edifying performance of the duties of preaching, watching, and other administrations, as the very nature and necessity of the thing makes evident.

(3) Yet by reason of this division, they acting as ordinary elders, were not bound equally to perform all duties to all their congregations, and every member of them.

(4) Notwithstanding, as they were apostles they had power to preach, and admonish, and perform all sorts of duties to each of these congregations, as they had in all the churches in the world.

In the next place our brethren proceed to give a summary of the reasons which moved the assembly to conclude, that the apostles did the ordinary acts of presbyters, as presbyters, in the church of Jerusalem.

But herein they deal not fairly with us. For (1) Some things urged in the assembly, of no less weight than any by them repeated, are omitted. And (2) Those things which in the assembly were twisted together, as one concluded argument, are by them untwisted, and taken in pieces, and so made the weaker, and less convincing.

The sum of our argument, as it is exhibited by them, is as follows, *viz.* (1) That those acts of government, performed by them in that church, were for the substance of them ordinary acts, such as presbyters perform, and therefore answerably they themselves are in them to be considered as presbyters, etc.

To which first piece our brethren answer nothing; indeed they had granted the antecedent before, and they thought not fit here to deny the consequence. But (2) That which they first take hold of is, that the apostles were called elders (1 Peter 5:1; 2 John 1), and therefore might and did act as elders, in ordinary acts of church-government, for a pattern to us in like administrations.

To which they answer, that the apostles are called "elders virtually," "not formally," and only "because apostleship contained all offices in it," 'so that they were elders, but upon the ground that they were apostles,' "and therefore John in" that "very epistle where he styles himself an elder," "writes canonical scripture as an apostle," "which as a formal elder he could not have {See p. 84} done; and surely those officers which Christ distinguishes (Ephesians 4), the same person is not formally both these, virtually he may."

That the apostleship did contain in it virtually and eminently all church offices, we grant; and so, that the apostles were elders virtually, and possibly that term, if fully explicated, would hold out as much as we desire.

But, they say, they were not elders formally.

If they mean, they were not elders really, we deny it. If they mean, they were not elders only, we grant it; they were so elders, as they were still apostles, and so apostles, as they were yet elders. Their eldership did not exclude their apostleship, nor their apostleship swallow up their eldership. But if by formally they mean, they were not made elders before or after they were made apostles, but that being apostles, they might and did act as elders (which they disprove not) that is sufficient for our argument.

Their reason from the distinction of offices concludes nothing, for offices very distinct, may be formally in one and the same person, as, of king, priest, and prophet in one Christ; Melchisedeck was formally a king and priest, and David formally a king and prophet.

Our brethren in the further prosecution of this reason of theirs say, that all which the apostles did in the "church of Jerusalem, they are said to act as apostles. Their preaching is called the apostles' doctrine," 'the money was brought and laid at the apostles' feet, the deacons were brought and' "set before the apostles," 'and they laid their hands on them, yea in that act of ordination' "they must needs act as apostles." 'For they do not only ordain the men, but erect the office,' "which none but apostles could immediately and at first have done, so as the same persons, in" the "same act," "must act partly as apostles, and partly as elders; and by what infallible rule shall we distinguish it?"

We *answer:* The Scriptures related to show that the particulars mentioned were acted by men, *qui erant apostoli*, who were apostles, but not *qua erant apostoli exclusivè*, as they were apostles exclusively; so as they might not act them under another notion. Sure[ly] our brethren upon further thoughts will not affirm it; for if the apostles did preach, take the trust of the goods of the church, ordain officers, *qua apostoli exclusivè*, will it not follow from hence, that none may do any of these things but apostles? Which we are sure our brethren will never say.

As for that ordination (Acts 6), we doubt not to say, that in it they did act partly as apostles, partly as elders. In constituting an office in the church which was not before, they did act their apostolic authority; but in ordaining into that office men whom the church had chosen, they did act as presbyters; and we doubt not, but that our brethren in this will concur with us. For if they will not say that the apostles did herein act partly as apostles and partly as elders, they must say they acted either only as elders, or only as apostles. If only as apostles, then hence is no warrant for any elders, so much as to ordain men unto an office. And certainly it is not so hard for our brethren to distinguish between these two; for look by what infallible rule they make some things in the practice of the apostles to be, not only a pattern for imitation, but even a proof of an institution; and yet decline other things practiced by the same apostles, as things not only by institution not commanded to us, but not permitted to be imitated by us; by the

same rule may they infallibly diſtinguish between what they acted as apostles, and what as elders.

3. The next particular our brethren insiſt on, is that branch of the argu-
{See p. 85}　ment, where it is said, the apoſtles acted jointly, and *in collegio*, over those
in assembly　many congregations; to which they answer three things:

(1) That they had all singly the same power, which they exercised jointly,
and they exercised that power together, because it fell out that they were
together, and it was fit that none should be excluded, but that they should
exercise it jointly to give a pattern for eldership is not easy to prove. Their
authority of jurisdiction did not arise from, nor depend upon the union of
all in a body, as in an eldership and parliament it does. One apoſtle might
have done that, which all here did; yea may it not be said, that because two
apoſtles ordained elders (Acts 14), as joined in the same act, and so acted not
as apoſtles, but elders, that therefore two elders associated may do the like?

We deny not, but the apoſtles acting as apoſtles, had power to act singly, what they did jointly, and yet we say not only as our brethren, that the
apoſtles being together, it was fit they should act together, that none might
be excluded; but further, that they were bound to act together, because as
each of them alone had the power, so they all had the power. And therefore
it was necessary they should act together, both for their own mutual support, as also that their acts might have the more authority in the church,
in reference whereto (in part) they of Antioch may be conceived to have
sent to the whole college of apoſtles and elders at Jerusalem, when yet Paul
and Barnabas, who were with them, by their decisive sentences, might have
ended the controversy.

"But however it is not easy to prove that they exercised their power jointly,
to give a pattern to presbytery."

Sure[ly] as easy, as it is to prove that their taking in the consent of the
people (Acts 6) in the choice of deacons, was to give a pattern for the suffrage of people in the choice of officers.

We have proved already that there were many congregations in Jerusalem; that these congregations were one church; that the apoſtles who were
officers governed this church; and that they governed jointly our brethren
grant. Is not here a pattern for several congregations in a city, or vicinity, to
unite into one church; and for the officers of those congregations to govern that church jointly in a college of presbytery?

[*Objection.*] But their power of government did not result from their
{See p. 85}　being joined together, as the power of a presbytery does; as the parliamentary power which is not the result of parliament men, but as assembled in
parliament.

in the firſt ac-　We *answer:* Parliamentary power *in actu primo* arises from their being
tualization; in　chosen knights and burgesses, but in *actu exercito*, it depends upon their be-
the act exercised　ing assembled in Parliament, according to the conſtitutions of the kingdom

in that case. So here the authoritative power of the apostles in *actu primo*, did arise from their office, but that power which their office gives them, must be exercised according to the constitution of Christ. Now it was the constitution and ordinance of Christ, that the apostles when they were together, and when they could, they should exercise their power, not singly but jointly, as a church or eldership, to be a pattern to others, as appears Matthew 18:17–19, and therefore the exercise of this power did in some sort depend upon their acting jointly.

[*Objection.*] 'But then two elders associated may govern, for Paul and Barnabas did ordain, who acted not as apostles but as elders, for they acted jointly.'

What ever our judgments be of this, certainly our brethren will never deny but two elders may govern, who say that two elders may make a sufficient presbytery.

(2) The second thing they object against the apostles acting as elders when together, is because it is hard to suppose that when they were all together they should act with an inferior power to what they put forth alone; "if Peter had been alone" in "a new planted church," "there he must" have acted "as an apostle," 'because alone, and shall all the apostles when joined together in one act, be conceived' "to fall lower in their power" in "the formal exercise of it?"

We *answer:* That we do not suppose the apostles to fall lower in their power when they acted as elders, when our brethren say, at Jerusalem they acted as elders of a particular congregation. Let them deliver themselves then from the same inconvenience, and they will relieve us. If they did not fall lower in their power by acting as elders in a particular congregation, why should they by acting as elders in a joint presbytery? We have said that their eldership did not exclude their apostleship, and now add, nor did their acting as elders deprive them of apostolic power, nor of that apostolic spirit which guided them even in those things wherein they acted as elders.

(3) And this may take off the edge of their third objection, which is, "if they acted as elders in a college, then they might miscarry as elders do, and so come under the danger of excommunication, and what power was there on earth to excommunicate an apostle?"

We deny the consequence upon the former ground, and therefore need not answer their demand, what power there was on earth, etc., to which yet if they desire satisfaction we refer them to Mr. Parker's *Tractate de Politia Eccelesiastica* (Lib. 3, cap. 12.).[1]

4. The third piece of our argument which our brethren fall upon, is the apostles joining with others in their proceedings, as in the choice of deacons (Acts 6), which also they used to do in other churches.

This say our brethren does not prove they acted as elders.

---

1. [Robert Parker, *De Politica Ecclesiastica Christi et Hierarchica opposita, libri tres, in quibus tom verae discipline fundamenta, quam omnes fere de eadem controversiae summo cum judicio et doctrina methodice pertractantur* (1616), p. 77 (second pagination.]

(1) 'Because they joined others with themselves in acts wherein yet they acted as apostles, as Paul joined Sylvanus and Timotheus with him, not merely in his salutation, but in his epistle to the Thessalonians, so also Acts 15, the apostles, elders, yea, and brethren joined in a letter to the churches; but these as apostles, and therefore so called in distinction from the elders, and the rest; so in ordaining Timothy, the presbytery laid on hands, yet they as a presbytery, Paul as an apostle, for the presbytery had no power to ordain an evangelist.'

We *answer:* Wherever the apostles joined others with them in acts that are to be imitated by other church officers, such a joining of others with themselves shows, that therein they acted as elders; and therefore that instance of Sylvanus and Timotheus is nothing to the purpose, it was a work of quite another nature than those of which we are now disputing.

The next instance of Acts 15 may seem to come nearer, to which we shall give a full answer in its proper place, only for the present (as before to a like Scripture, so here) we say, the text shows the letter was written by men *qui erant apostoli*, who were apostles, but not simply and exclusively, *quâ apostoli*, as apostles.

And for the ordination of Timothy, our brethren must prove that those two texts that speak of Paul's laying on of hands, and of the laying on of the hands of the presbytery, speak of one ordination, and one joint act of imposition of hands, and that Timothy was ordained an evangelist, before they can make anything of it to their purpose.

"Yet," secondly (say our brethren) 'the apostles, wherever they came, left the elders and people to the exercise of that right which belonged to them, although they joined with them.'

We are herein fully of our brethren's mind; only we desire it may from hence be observed, that it does not belong to the people to ordain either deacons or elders, whatever it may do to choose; for the apostles, who, wherever they came, left to the people what right belonged to them, did nowhere leave them to ordain. But in the next words our brethren and we possibly may differ.

'Their apostolic authority' (they say) 'did not lie in doing all alone, for {See p. 86} then they seldom or never acted as apostles in the church.'

We say their apostolic authority did lie partly in doing all alone; and sure[ly] our brethren will not say, that any ordinary church officer might do all alone; how often, or how seldom they acted their apostolic power, we determine not. Their instance of Paul's not excommunicating the incestuous Corinthian alone, we acknowledge. Yet certainly Paul by his apostolic power, might have excommunicated him alone, as well as he did Hymeneus and Alexander. But what does this make for them or against us? "Paul alone excommunicated not" (they say) "that Corinthian and yet as an apostle, wrote to have it done." What then? Had they said, Paul excommunicated not the

Corinthian alone, but joined with the church in excommunicating him, and yet excommunicated him as an apostle, this had come home to the point.

We say with them, that what the apostles did by apostolic power (properly so called) should not be drawn into example. But we deny that which they affirm, that their apostolic power lay in exercising jurisdiction over several churches. No, it lay in this, that they had power to exercise jurisdiction over all; which power no presbytery has, nor can challenge. And for the proof now before us, and Scriptures by occasion thereof now under debate, they speak not of the power which the apostles exercised over many churches (and so by our brethren's own assertion speak not of apostolic power), but over one church consisting of many congregations; nor does the presbytery by warrant of this precedent lay claim to a government over many churches (as our brethren insinuate) but over one church.

But this (say our brethren for a conclusion) 'will not help it, that they exercised their government in those congregations, considered as one church; for if they could not as elders, then the correlate to it, namely church, could not be considered as presbyterial.'

Whether the apostles in their acts of government could be considered as elders, we leave to the wisdom of the Honorable Houses to judge by what has been spoken. (1) They are called elders. (2) They were in our brethren's own confession, virtually so—we say really and indeed. (3) They acted *in collegio* in a joint body, our brethren say it was fit they should so do; nor was this any degradation of the apostles, or diminution of their power, acting jointly as elders, yet they acted as apostles. (4) They took in the consent of the church with them, in things wherein the church had a right of consenting. We might further add, (5) They acted that power committed to them (Matthew 16; 18). And (6) If they acted not as elders, we can draw nothing of theirs into imitation; which last were insisted upon in the assembly, but because not replied to by our brethren we do but touch upon. But from all these particulars we warrantably conclude, that they acted as elders in the church of Jerusalem; and argue with our brethren, from the relate to the correlate. Therefore the church of Jerusalem was a presbyterial church.

[4. Answer to Reasons against the fourth proof of the second branch viz. elders meeting together for acts of government, proved by Acts 11:30; Acts 15:4, 6, 22; Acts 21:17–18]

Our brethren might well have spared all that they have said against this {See p. 86} clause in the proposition, elders meeting together for acts of government, Braye, 94r since they themselves do assert, as much as we do, that the elders of the church of Jerusalem did meet together for acts of government; only they suppose that that church was no more congregations than one. So thus they differ not from us concerning the truth of the attribute, but concerning the

Minutes,
Sess. 172–175
2.593–610

Gillespie,
36–38

Lightfoot,
203–210

sense of the subject of this proposition; the elders of the church of Jerusalem did meet together for acts of government. But since they are pleased to make exceptions, let us examine them.

First, the argument from Acts 11:30 our brethren conceive to be this, "There were elders in Judea that received alms, therefore the elders of Jerusalem did meet together for acts of government." Which is a marvelous mistake, for our proof was laid thus: Acts 11:30 and Acts 21:17–18 and the verses following, shall be brought to prove that clause in the former proposition, elders meeting together for acts of government, so that we did not argue from Acts 11:30 singly, but joined with Acts 21.

Next, had we argued from that place alone, our brethren have excepted nothing which can weaken such a proof. For,

Whereas they say, that both the persons and the act are mistaken, the persons, "because the elders of Jerusalem are not mentioned," but the elders of Judea, as by comparing verse 29 and 30 it appears: the act, because receiving of alms is no act of government. We *answer:* The persons and the act both are mistaken by themselves, not by us. For first, the elders of Judea are not at all mentioned, but only the distressed brethren of Judea. And secondly, if the elders of Judea had been mentioned, this had been comprehensive of the elders of Jerusalem. Thirdly, the messengers of churches abroad, and particularly of Antioch, were ever directed to the apostles and elders of Jerusalem, when they did at all send into Judea. And as Barnabas was sent from Jerusalem to Antioch (Acts 11:22), and the prophets came from Jerusalem to Antioch (verse 27), so it is the sense of interpreters upon Acts 11:30 that Paul and Barnabas were sent from thence to Jerusalem; and it is the more likely, by comparing Romans 15:31. Yea, fourthly, as for the act, we suppose our brethren will not deny but there was much more in it than the receiving of alms, namely the ordering and appointing how it should be best improved and disposed of; which being an act of government, and it being denied by none that the elders did meet together for this act. It must follow that Acts 11:30 does not a little strengthen that clause in the proposition, "elders meeting together for acts of government."

The next place added for proof of the same clause, is Acts 21:17–18 and the verses following; to which our brethren reply thus; "The occasion of the meeting was Paul's entertainment," a "duty of love and respect." Secondly, that the acts which "passed were none of them presbyterial," only they gave advice to Paul for preventing a scandal.

To this we say, first, it is more than our brethren can prove, that the occasion of this meeting was only to receive Paul, for the text admits (if not favors) another sense (verse 18). "Paul went in with us unto James and all the elders were present;" and how do our brethren know, that they were assembled upon no other occasion? Especially it being said that Paul went in to James, it may be not knowing till he came, that all the elders were present. Secondly, if there were no more but the mention of elders meeting together, it does abundantly prove all which we intended to prove from this place, thus, that Scripture which proves a presbytery in Jerusalem, or an association of the elders in that church, proves, that the elders of the church of Jerusalem did meet together for acts of government. But Acts 21 proves a presbytery in Jerusalem, or an association of the elders of that church; therefore it proves that the elders did meet together for acts of government. The proposition our brethren will not deny, because a presbytery cannot do their duty, but must needs neglect the work committed to them, if they do not meet together for acts of government. Neither can they deny the assumption, that Acts 21 proves a meeting of elders in Jerusalem, or a presbytery in Jerusalem, as Tossanus calls it;[1] yea themselves take their warrant from that place, for the presbyteries meeting apart from the multitude to consult and prepare matters. And thirdly, what they themselves say in this place, does not make against us, but for us. For if the elders of Jerusalem did meet together for a salutation, did not they much more meet together for acts of government? So that, fourthly, it is not necessary here to debate whether any authoritative act of government done by these elders, then and there met together, be mentioned (Acts 21:17, 18, etc.). It is enough for us, that this place proves that the elders of Jerusalem did sometimes meet together for acts of government. Lastly, neither do these who have most authority, being met together, always and in every thing peremptorily enjoin and ordain what they would have done, but oft times consult and advise only, howbeit the advice of elders is not lax, but binding and restrictive (verse 23, "Do therefore that which we say unto thee.").

[5. Answer to the Reasons against Acts 15]

In the next place, our brethren allege reasons against the producing of Acts 15 for the meeting of the elders of Jerusalem for presbyterial acts of government; wherein they fight with a shadow; for we said not presbyterial acts of government, but acts of government. But, say our brethren, "if it were a meeting of elders for acts of government, then it was a presbyterial meeting for acts of government." This consequence they could not be ignorant that we deny; yet they have not said one word for proof of it, only they go about to prove, that this meeting (Acts 15) was not a presbyterial meeting, and that synodical meetings differ much from presbyterial meetings. Which makes nothing against us, for we have constantly asserted it to be a synodical meeting. And if it be asked, to what end then do we add Acts 15 as a branch of the proof of the proposition for presbyterial government?

Braye, 95v

{See p. 87}

Minutes,
Sess. 175–176
2.604–616
Lightfoot,
207–208
Gillespie,
38–42

Minutes, 3.301

Gillespie, 12,
71, 74

---

1. [Daniel Toussain (or Tussanus), French Protestant Theologian and commentator (1541–1602). *D. Danielis Tossani S. Theologiae in academia Heidelbergensi doctoris et professoris: primarii operum theologicorum*, "Commentaria in Acta Apostolorum" (Hanoviae: 1604), 1.375.]

We *answer:* 1. It was added to prove that clause in the proposition, elders meeting for acts of government; the meeting together presbyterially being proved by other mediums; as for instance, thus, all the several congregations in Jerusalem were one church (Acts 8:1 and Acts 15:4). And how can many congregations be one political ministerial church, except only because they are united, and associated under one presbyterial government? And 2. If we had proved from Acts 15 a presbyterial meeting for acts of government, the proof had been as strong and valid as this—Here is a brigade,[1] therefore here is a regiment; here is a university, therefore here is a college. A meeting for synodical acts of government, is no weak proof of a meeting for presbyterial acts of government, unless we will suppose that they who were careful to assist other churches, did neglect their own churches committed to their particular charge, and take no care of governing them. Yea, Acts 15:2, 4 does most certainly prove a presbyterial government in Jerusalem, thus, whence the apostles and elders did govern, and many congregations were one church, there we may certainly conclude there was a presbyterial government. But in Jerusalem the apostles and elders did govern, and many congregations were by them governed, yet so, that all those congregations were one church. Therefore we may certainly conclude that there was in Jerusalem a presbyterial government; all this is certain from Acts 15, except that there were many congregations in Jerusalem, for which we refer to the former proof.

But secondly, our brethren deny their meeting (Acts 15) to have been such an ordinary formal synod, or the acts thereof to have been acts of government, as they proceeded from those elders; the jurisdiction of synods reaching no further than to such churches as have sent commissioners thereunto; and to make good what they intend, they bring several reasons, which they have reduced to four heads or classes.

It is to be observed, that our brethren do not simply deny that this was a synod, or that the decrees of it had authority; but that it was not such a synod, nor the decrees of it of such authority; neither do they clearly express what they mean to conclude from these four classes of reasons. For as to that debate, whether it be a formal synod, or not, our brethren might have spared it, as not being *hujus loci*, but belonging to the votes concerning synods, not then sent up to your honors.[2] But however, we shall examine their reasons, as they have propounded them.

1. First, they say, 'we read but only of two churches, between whom the matter was transacted, they of Antioch sent to them of Jerusalem, and that electively, because they were the mother-church, from whom the Word of

March 12, 1644
sic March 11
Gillespie, 37

of this place

{See p. 88}

---

1. [There is space in the *Minutes*, but nothing recorded. "Mr Vines said, Acts xv. proves a presbytery as well as a synod, as where a brigade is, there is a regiments [*sic*]. That there is a government also." Gillespie (37).]

2. [The Grand Debate papers are addressed to the Honorable Houses of Parliament.]

God came, and from whom those men that trouble them had gone forth, and had pretended to teach what they had received from them. Neither is their mention made of any elder sent thither, either from the churches of Phœnice, and Samaria (verse 3), or from the churches of Judea; yea it is not so much as said that the elders that were sent from Antioch, were the elders of that church?

We *answer:* If a synod of two churches, it proves a synod of more churches, even of as many as shall combine, and associate synodically; yea our brethren themselves acknowledge (some of them[1]) Acts 15 to be a warrant for the meeting of elders out of many or all churches, and that it is an ordinance of Christ. Secondly, if the church of Jerusalem were sent to electively, by way of reference or arbitration, as our brethren use to [*commonly*] call it, then the church of Antioch only should have been tied by that decree, they only having made the reference. Besides, those who were sent from the church of Antioch, ought not to have been members of that meeting (as it is certain they were, verse 12 and 22) for they who electively refer the judging of a controversy to others, do not themselves sit as judges of it. Thirdly, not to stand upon the probability either of the church of Syria, and Cilicia, their sending of commissioners to Jerusalem to make known the condition of their churches to the apostles and elders, and to represent those churches in that assembly, whose decrees did therefore bind them more peculiarly than other churches; or of the churches of Phœnice and Samaria, their sending of some along with Paul and Barnabas, to testify their consent in a case of so great and public concernment, which we may rather think, than that they would fail in such a point of duty, and in the improvement of so precious an opportunity; nor yet to stand upon the utter improbability of the sending from Antioch, deacons, or some other of the people, rather than elders; we cannot pass by that reason given by our brethren, for sending to Jerusalem only, because from them did those men go forth that troubled the churches, which is a mistake. For it is not said, they came out from Jerusalem, but plainly, that they came out from Judea (verse 1), and this strengthens us, and weakens them. Those elders from whom the false teachers did go forth, were members of the synods (verse 24), but the elders from whom the false teachers did go forth, were the elders of Judea (verse 1), therefore the elders of Judea were members of the synod.

We know that they who came from Jerusalem came from Judea, but our brethren take it for granted that they who came from Judea came from Jerusalem. The words also admit another exposition, that this going forth was not locally, but doctrinally, as we shall show afterwards.

2. But secondly, to prove that these letters and decrees were written and sent only from the elders of Jerusalem, they allege divers things, as (1) [in]

---

1. Ep. before *the Keyes*, etc. [John Cotton, New England divine (1584–1652). *The Keyes of the Kingdom of Heaven* (London, 1644). Published by and with an Epistle by Goodwin and Nye.]

16:4, they are called the decrees of the apostles and elders in Jerusalem, it being the "usual style of the New Testament" by way of distinction to say, "the church in such a place, the elders in such a place." This they say, but they have not produced one instance where the elders in such a place, is put for the elders of such a place. We rather suppose that if the Holy Ghost had meant (Acts 16:4) to speak of the elders of Jerusalem only, he would have said, the elders of the church of or in Jerusalem, as Revelation 2–3, "The angel of the church in Ephesus," "The Angel of the church in Sardis," etc. And we cannot but put our brethren in mind, that themselves would not acknowledge those who were κατοικοῦντες ἐν Ἰερουσαλήμ (Acts 2:5) dwelling in Jerusalem, to be members of that church. Yet here they will needs understand by τῶν πρεσβυτέρων τῶν ἐν Ἰερουσαλήμ, the elders of that church only; whereas we need not supply so much as τῶν κατοικοῦντῶν, but only συναχσθειτων, not dwelling at Jerusalem, but met together at Jerusalem, or as it is in our Bibles, which were at Jerusalem.

(2) They object (verse 4), "Paul and Barnabas are said to be received of the church, and apostles, and elders, namely of Jerusalem."

True; but that is not to the point, the synod not being then met. Yea, it makes against themselves; for if Paul and Barnabas were sent only to the elders of Jerusalem, there needed no greater meeting than that mentioned (verse 4) whereas there was another meeting in that chapter (verses 8, 22, 23, 25) which was much more full and comprehensive.

(3) The "standing elders of Jerusalem," they say, assumed to themselves to have written those decrees (Acts 21:25).

So may the ministers of London, who are now of this assembly when they are declaring by way of discourse, what the assembly has concluded, say, "we have concluded." So may the officers of one regiment, relating what the army has done, say "we have done such a thing." Nothing [is] more ordinary than such synecdochical speeches, the part for the whole; and that we must needs understand a synecdoche in that place is plain, for otherwise, if the standing elders of Jerusalem had meant that they alone had written and concluded those decrees, then they had excluded not only the elders of other churches, but Paul also and the rest of the apostles, from whom these decrees did proceed, as well as from the elders of Jerusalem.

(4) They object (verse 22) the "the apostles and elders with the whole church," and (verse 23) "the apostles, elders and brethren."

We will not here debate what is meant by the whole church and brethren, which our brethren know is controverted; but how do they prove, that by the whole church and brethren, are meant only those of the church of Jerusalem, and not the whole multitude of those who were come from several churches? And if by the whole church we shall understand the church of Jerusalem only, that proves not that by the elders there assembled we must understand the elders of Jerusalem only. However, by the whole church cannot be meant the whole *cœtus fidelium*, who were many more than could meet in one place, specially in a private house, such as the Centurists think this assembly did meet in;[1] but *Cœtus Synodicus*, that is the apostles, elders, and others assembled from several churches, such as Titus, in the judgment of some, and however, Judas and Silas, who were not fixed to an office or membership in the church of Jerusalem, but were assistants to the apostles in several places, and did the office of evangelists; which is plain of Silas (Acts 15:40; 16:19; 17:4, 14, 15; 18:5) and of Judas (15:22, 32). So that Judas and Silas being members of that meeting (15:22), it follows that it was a meeting not only of the apostles and elders of the church of Jerusalem, nay nor of the commissioners of Antioch joined with them, but of others also distinct from both these.

assembly of the faithful
Synodical Assembly
March 14, 1644
sic March 13
Gillespie, 42

(5) They argue again from verse 24, "certain that went out from us, and to whom we gave no such commandment, etc."

{See p. 89}

We shall not need to help ourselves in answer:

{1} By telling them that those words ἐξ ἡμῶν—from us—in which all the strength of their objection lies, are not in sundry copies which Camero owns and makes no less use of leaving them out, in an answer, than our brethren do of taking them in, in an argument.[2] And the taking of them in, or leaving them out, does not alter the sense of the place. Nor {2} By saying that the churches themselves, which were troubled, wrote not that epistle, but their officers. But reading the text as our brethren do {3} that which we lay weight upon for a satisfactory answer is this, that those false teachers which went out from Judea (verse 1) might be said to have gone out from all the apostles, elders, and others, from several churches assembled at Jerusalem, and that two ways. First, by a synecdoche of the whole, put for an eminent part, which is no derogation at all to the synod; sure[ly] there is a better warrant for this synecdoche, than to expound that which is said of Judea (verse 1) to be meant of Jerusalem only, as our brethren before did, especially considering that Paul and Barnabas were members of this assembly; yet we suppose our brethren will not say, that those teachers went out from Paul and Barnabas. Second, those false teachers might be said to have gone forth from all doctrinally, or by defections from the truth, though locally they went out from Judea only. Divers note upon this place,[3] that it may be expounded by 1 John 2:19, "They went out from

---

1. [*Centuriæ Magdeburgenses*, vol. 2 (Basil, 1559–74). Century one, part two, col. 547.]

2. Plant. A. Mont. collat. cum Tilen. [Apparently: "Plantin, Arias Montanus, Collatio cum Tilen." Cf. John Cameron (or Camero), Scottish synergestic theologian (c.1579–1625), *Amica Collatio de Gratiae et Volunt. Humanae concursu in vocatione … instituta inter … D Tilenam et J. Cameronum* (Leyden, 1621) 179. Benedictus Arias Montanus Hispalensis, *Biblia Sacra Hebraice, Chaldaice, Graece & Latine* [Antwerp polyglot] (Antwerp: Plantin: 1569–1573), vol. 7, 96.]

3. Camerarius, Lorinus, Gorranus. [Joachim Camerarius, German Reformer (1500–1574). *Commentarius in Novum Foedus* (Cambridge: Roger Daniel, 1642), p. 109. Jean Lorin(us), *In Actus Apostolorum Commentaria in Acta Apostolorum* (1607; Colonia Agrippina; 1621), p. 482.

us, but were not of us;" which is meant, not of a local, but doctrinal going forth, as Beza there observes.[1]

(6) They say, "if the elders of all those churches had been present, there had been less need to have sent chosen men to carry the letters," which the elders of those churches returning might have done: And if they "were sent as messengers from the synod," why not to all the churches as well as to Antioch? "Yea although Paul and Barnabas delivered" the decrees to all the cities; yet this was done only "accidentally" (as it should seem) "and not principally intended", nor sent in a "mandatory way" from the synod.

{1} It is ordinary for synods to send synodical epistles and decrees to particular churches, not by the commissioners who came from those churches, but by chosen men, partly to express their great respect to the church, and partly to take off all *odium* from the commissioners of those churches; and for making the general consent of the churches the better known; which was in this case necessary, because the authority of Paul and Barnabas had been questioned at Antioch, and their doctrine excepted against, as not consonant with the judgment of the apostles at Jerusalem.

{2} They sent not to all the churches, but to Antioch, because the other churches were not so divided and disturbed, as Antioch. They apply the plaster where the wound was most dangerous.

{3} Neither need we dispute how those decrees were delivered to all the churches of the Gentiles, whether intentionally or accidentally, as our brethren conjecture; the reason why they were not sent in the way of synodical decree and epistle to all the churches, but only to the churches of Antioch, Syria and Cilicia, is (as some conceive) because no other churches of the Gentiles had commissioner in the synod; so that no other could be formally bound by their decrees, other churches of the Gentiles being bound *by way of* partly *via materiæ*, partly by the authority of Paul and Barnabas delivering *the matter* those decrees unto them (Acts 16:4).

3. In the third place our brethren say, "If there were any further authority" in those decrees, it was "from the apostles, who had power over all churches;" and although the elders did consent and approve the decrees, yet all the authority put forth over those churches was apostolic; neither can any assembly of men, wanting [*lacking*] apostolic presence and instruction, say in such a sense, as they did, "It seemed good to the Holy Ghost and to us."

It is evident, that the apostles in this business did not act as apostles with a transcendent and infallible authority; but as elders, in such a way as makes that meeting a pattern for ordinary synods: For,

(1) Paul and Barnabas were sent from Antioch to go to Jerusalem (verse 2).

Nicolaus de Gorran(us), French theologian (1230?–1295), *In Acta Apostolorum, et singulas apostolorum Jacobi, Petri, Johannis et Judae canonicas Epistolas, et Apocalypsin commentarii, authore R. P. F. Nicolao Gorrano* (Antwep, 1620), p. 40.]

1. [Beza, *Annotationes*, p. 729.]

Now one of the reasons used by divines against Peter's supremacy, is taken from Acts 8:14, where the apostles which were at Jerusalem (that is, the College of Apostles), sent Peter and John to Samaria. Now he that is sent, is not greater than he that sends him; and therefore in this, Paul and Barnabas did subject themselves to the determination of the church of Antioch, which they could not have done, had they acted as apostles, and not as members (for that time) of the presbytery of Antioch.

(2) In that instance of the synod (as Cartwright said rightly against the Rhemists[1]), the apostles were not acted by an apostolic and infallible spirit, as when they were writing Scripture; but they did state the question, and debate it from Scripture in the ordinary way, whereas we never read that they admitted much, or any disputation, what they should write, or what they should judge of the matter, when they were writing Scripture, as here they did (verse 7), and having by searching the Scriptures, found "what was the good and acceptable will of God," thereupon they say (as Doctor Whitaker said any assembly upon like assurance of Scripture warrant, may say[2]), "It seemed good to the Holy Ghost, and to us."

(3) Before the decisive suffrage of that meeting, there were deliberative suffrages and discourses, first, by Peter, then by Paul and Barnabas, and after by James. And accordingly it is to be observed, that though Peter does clear the point of justification by faith, and not by works of the law, yet he speaks not to the remedy of the scandal of the weak Jews, which was well supplied by James, who offered a way for preventing and removing the scandal.

(4) The elders all along do act as authoritatively as the apostles; for as the elders were sent to (verse 2) and accordingly assembled, as well as the apostles (verse 6), so they did decree and write the epistle as well as the apostles (verses 22, 23), and Acts 16:4, they are called the decrees of the apostles and elders, and (Acts 21:25) the elders say, "we have written and concluded" — from which places Protestant writers prove against Papists, that Presbyters as well as Bishops have the power of decisive voicing in synods. But our brethren in this particular desert all the Protestant divines, and join with the Popish opinion, which is that the apostles only had a decisive suffrage in that meeting.

4. We come to the last head of their exceptions. They say, "there is no act of such authority or government put forth" in that meeting (Acts 15) which our proposition intends. For *first*, here is not summoning nor censuring of those disturbers of the church. Again the subject matter sent, and the judgment passed about it, is only a dogmatic decision of that question, whether

---

1. [Thomas Cartwright, Puritan (1535–1603). *A Confutation of the Rhemish Testament*, Number 364, The English Experience (1618; Amsterdam/New York: Da Capo Press, 1971), p. 299.]

2. Controvers. 3, question 6. [William Whitaker, English Calvinist theologian (1548–1595). *Praelectiones … In quibus tractatur Controversia de Conciliis contra … Robertum Bellarminum …* (Cambridge, 1600). *Opera Theologica*, 2 vols. in 1 (Geneva, 1610), p. 610.]

the ceremonial law should be observed. But the proposition intends jurisdiction, which is, when doctrines are delivered, *sub pœna*, under the penalty of excommunication if not received, one minister alone has a dogmatic authority to exhort, rebuke, etc., but acts of jurisdiction are not his alone.

(1) The dogmatic power of the apostles and elders met together presbyterially or synodically, is another thing than the dogmatic power of a single teacher, and our brethren themselves will acknowledge that the dogmatic power of the presbytery of a single congregation is a church power, and that which agrees not to a single teacher.

(2) And they will also acknowledge that the dogmatic decision of a controversy of faith by a synod, is to be received by the churches with reverence and obligation, as an ordinance of Christ.

(3) There were then three great evils, which were the occasion of that meeting together of the apostles and elders. {1} Heresy taught, asserting the necessity of the observing the ceremonial law, and that believers could not be saved without it. {2} The scandal of the weak Jews, and their alienation of mind from the Gentiles, who did neglect those ceremonies. {3} The schism or στασις raised by those who troubled the disciples; and accordingly there was a threefold power or authority put forth in this meeting. {1} The dogmatic power confuting the heresies, and vindicating the truth. {2} The diatactic power, making a practical canon for avoiding the scandal, and abstaining from such things as gave occasion of it. {3} The critic power (verse 24) branding those teachers with the black mark of liars, subverters of souls, and troublers of the church. Now we appeal to our brethren, whether these be not such acts, as if they were put forth by a parochial presbytery upon any of the members of their own church, would be by themselves acknowledged to be acts of ecclesiastical government, and authority.

(4) Neither was it necessary to make any mention of excommunication, it being a clear case in itself (which we suppose our brethren will not deny) that those heretics or schismatics, who could be by no other means reduced, were not to be suffered, but to be cast out of the churches (Revelation 2:2, 14, 20).

Second, [they say] 'whereas those decrees are called τὰ δόγματα τὰ κεκριμένα, the decrees that were ordained (Acts 16:4),' our brethren say, 'though δόγμία is used for an imperial decree; yet but rarely, and more commonly for doctrine and opinion, and so it is here used in opposition to the false dogmas, or heterodox theses of the false teachers, as Colossians 2:20.'

This is the only place which our brethren cite for that sense of the word, but does it not make against themselves? For δογματίζεσθε in that place is expounded by the Syriac, "Are you judged;" in our English translation, "Are ye subject to ordinances." Erasmus and Bullinger read, "*Decretis tenemini*;" Gualther, "*Ritibus oneramini*."[1] Those ordinances were the ceremonial laws

{See p. 91} appears in the left margin beside the line beginning "μένα, the decrees". The left-margin gloss beside the final lines reads: *are ye bound to decrees; are ye burdened by rites*

---

1. [Desiderius Erasmus, Dutch Catholic Theologian and Humanist (1466–1536), *Novum*

imposed, "Touch not, Taste not, Handle not" (verse 21). Therefore interpreters make that place parallel to Matthew 15:9, "In vain they do worship me, teaching for doctrines the commandments of men." And we cannot but take notice, that wheresoever δόγμα is found in the New Testament, it is put for decrees or laws, as [in] Luke 2:1; Acts 17:7, it is put for the decrees of Cæsar, and Ephesians 2:15; Colossians 2:14, for the ceremonial laws of Moses; and so frequently by the Septuagint in the Old Testament, either for decrees, as Daniel 2:13; 3:10, 29; 4:3; 6:9, 12, 15, 26, or for laws, as Daniel 6:8.

As for the "other word κεκριμένα," they say, it notes no more but that these doctrinal theses were the joint declared judgment of those who were met together; therefore when James gives his judgment, he uses the word κρίνω.

But they might remember the authority which is given *uni*, is one thing, *to one* and the authority which is given *unitati*, is another thing. If they had given *to a unity* us a place where the word is used of a whole assembly, and yet noted no authority nor jurisdiction, that had been somewhat to purpose. James might use the word to signify the judgment of discretion, and the whole assembly might use it to signify the judgment of authority. In such a signification the compound is used in the Old Testament, as Esther 2:1, καὶ κατέκρινεν αὐτήν, and what was decreed against here; so also σύγκριμα and σύγκρισις is put for a decree, as Daniel 4:14, 21, so that each word, δόγματα and κεκριμένα holds forth authority, much more both of them put together.

They say, these words, "to lay upon you no greater burden," if any, must prove this jurisdiction.

It is a proof indeed, but not the only proof.

But, they say, these words may be taken passively, that no other burden {See p. 92} then be laid on you, as Lodovic. de Dieu has observed.[1] *Minutes, Sess.* 175

As this is contrary to the general sense of interpreters, so our brethren 2.578, 605, 607 have not given so much as one instance in all the New Testament, where ἐπιτίθεσθαι [Acts 16:4] is used in a passive sense, and they know that ordinarily it signifies authoritative judgment, when used of an assembly's judgment (as John 18:31; Acts 24:6). And if we should take it passively in this place, it does not at all help their cause; for when the text shall be thus translated, "It seemed good to the Holy Ghost and us, that no greater burden be laid upon you, than these necessary things," hence it must follow, that these things are laid upon them as burdens, and as necessary, and this was done by the synod.

Next, they say, if the word be taken actively, yet the laying on of a burden here intended, is but by way of doctrine, and declaring the command

---

Testamentum omne (Basil: 1519), p. 435. Heinrich Bullinger, Swiss Reformer (1504–1575), *In omnes Apostolicas Epistolas* (Tiguri: C. Froschoverum, 1558), p. 490. Rudolf Gwalther, Reformed theologian, successor to Bullinger (1519–1586), *In Divi Pauli Apostoli Epistolas Omnes* (Tiguri: In Officina Froschoviana, 1589), p. 252.]

1. [Louis (Lodewÿk) de Dieu, Dutch Reformed theologian and linguist (1590–1642), *Animadversiones in Acta Apostolorum* (1634), p. 147.]

of Christ, as verse 10 and Matthew 23:4, not by virtue of an ecclesiastical authority.

They cannot prove that the Pharisees laying on of burdens (Matthew 23:4), was but a doctrinal declaring, it rather appears it was an authoritative commanding (Matthew 15:9), from which place our Protestant writers dispute against Papists, concerning the binding power and authority of ecclesiastical canons. Nor yet can they prove, that "the laying on of a yoke" (Acts 15:10), must be understood only doctrinally, and not rather authoritatively; or that those who contended in the synod, for the necessity of observing the ceremonial law, to whom Peter directs that part of his speech, did not endeavor, in their debates, to carry the judgment of all the elders that way, to lay on such a yoke, by their decree, upon the neck of the disciples. However that laying on of the burden, and prescribing some things at that time necessary for the avoiding of scandal (verse 28), is taken as well by Protestant as Popish writers, who have disputed for the binding authority of ecclesiastical canons, for a foundation thereof, with this difference, that Papists will have their binding power to arise from the will and authority of the church—and these Protestants hold that they bind only *per & propter* *by and because* *verbum Dei*, only so far forth as they are founded upon, and warranted by *of the Word* the Word of God, as here the decree of the apostles and elders binds; and *of God* is therefore called "the laying on of a burden." Yet so, that they lay on no other burden, but what was the will of Christ, and what the law of love for removing scandals did at that time make necessary to be imposed.

That which our brethren add, that the apostles and elders did not proceed to censure these false teachers, has been answered before. They did *with a mark/* censure them in some degree, even, *cum notâ infamiæ*; and it was time *note of infamy* enough to proceed to excommunication, when they should be found incorrigibly pertinacious.

[6. Answer to Reasons against the Two Assertions Concerning the Church at Jerusalem]

Braye, 101r Whereas in the close of the proof of the proposition, for many congrega-
{See p. 93} tions to be under one presbyterial government, it is asserted, that whether
Minutes, these congregations be fixed or not fixed, it is all one; as to the truth of the
Sess. 198, 199 proposition, our brethren offer this reason against it.
2.681–684;
3.7–14 "Every congregation having elders fixed unto it, is a church, for the re-
Lightfoot, lation of church and elders is mutual (Acts 14)." 'And fixed elders have a
245–247 special relation to that church whereof they are elders, so as they are not
Gillespie, related to other congregations; but if congregations have no fixed officers,
49–51 they are not churches according to the principles of presbyterial government.' "Now it makes a great difference," they say, "as to the truth of the
proposition," whether many congregations, which are not churches, "may

be under the government of one:" and that no pattern can be showed for many churches being "under the power of one, nay where any one church was under the power of another."

We *answer:* 1. That a congregation having fixed elders, is a church, and has power of government in such things as concern itself only if they be able, we acknowledge. 2. That congregations having officers, though not fixed, are not churches, we never asserted. 3. We are not solicitous of names, if we may agree of the thing. 4. Nor did we ever hold, that divers churches may be under the power of one church; which is a prelatical not Presbyterial principal. It is far from our thoughts to put any one church, though the smallest, under the power and government of another church, though the greatest; the power of a presbytery over particular churches being not extrinsic, but intrinsic to them, and the presbyterial or classical church, not another (as the Cathedral was), but that whole whereof the particular churches are the constituent parts. 5. And whereas our brethren say that elders fixed to a congregation, have a special relation to that congregation, so as they are not related to other congregations, if by "so as," they mean comparative more than to others, we grant it. But if by "so as," they mean exclusive, so related to that congregation, as they have or can have no relation to any other, we have abundantly shown before how false that is.

As for their discourse of supposing the elders to be fixed in Jerusalem, that then the apostles must be these fixed elders, which would be, they say, a great debasing of the apostles, to make them but as so many parish ministers.

We *answer:* 1. It follows not that if they had fixed elders, that they apostles must be fixed elders. There were many other elders besides the apostles at Jerusalem; our brethren grant that there were other elders after the dispersion, and sure[ly] when they had them, the church had need of them. And they think the church was not then so numerous as it was before the dispersion. 2. Suppose the apostles had been pleased to divide themselves to the several congregations, what debasing of them is there in this more than in our brethren's own way? Which opinion will seem to debase them more, they who would argue that ten or twelve apostles divided themselves to do the ordinary work of elders in eight, ten, or twelve parishes? Or they who would thus fix ten or twelve of them to be as the ordinary ministers of one parish only?

As to all the rest of their discourse upon this point, of the several inconveniences which (in their judgment) will follow upon the preparing only of work in the lesser presbyteries for the greater, and the like, which tends only to disparage the presbyterial government; our brethren touch not us, nor other reformed churches, so far as we know. We have not yet in our assembly set forth what all the things are which belong to the parochial presbytery, and what to the classical, much less have we presented anything concerning them to this Honorable House. When we take these things into debate, we shall willingly hear and weigh our brethren's advise and judgment. And if we offer up anything in them, as our humble advice to the Honorable Houses, which in their judgment shall not prove agreeable to the Word of God, it will then be time enough for our brethren to give their arguments against it.

[7. Answer to the Last Reason of the Independents against the Third Proposition]

{See p. 95}
Braye, 103r

Minutes, 5.523

Lightfoot, 166

Gillespie, 25, 70

a single complex

by divine right

by common counsel

In the last reason of our brethren, we observe that in the stating of the question, they limit the proposition only to such congregations as have fixed officers, of which contracting the sense of the proposition, we have spoken before.

But to follow them in their own steps, we do next observe that they distinguish between the presbytery of a congregation, and the congregation, taking them in pieces, which they ought to have considered as *unum complexum*, and this to make the fairer way to their medium of power over power, which (before they come to their argument) they would render the more odious, by comparing it to the episcopal assertion, that one presbyter may be over another. Which comparison, we conceive neither true nor pertinent.

1. Not true; for the bishops ascribed their superiority to an higher degree or order, *jure divino*, distinct from that of a presbyter; making themselves successors to the apostles, and presbyters to the 70 disciples, and accordingly they had a new ordination, or solemn consecration by imposition of hands.

2. Not pertinent. For (1) In a presbytery, all things are done *communi consilio*, whereas the bishops did all by a personal jurisdiction, and so his power was exclusive of the power of all other presbyters. (2) In a presbytery, all who judge are liable to be themselves judged in the same presbytery; whereas the bishops did judge only, but were not judged by their brethren. (3) The bishop's power was altogether extrinsic to those congregations which were under it; but the presbytery is an aggregate made up out of their mutual associations into one.

To that of 'powers specifically distinct from each other,' we acknowledge the power of the classes to be more than numerically distinct from that of particular congregations. Yet such a power, as is the aggregation of coalescence of these several particular powers into one; and so is not altogether another for kind, but only more extensive.

These things being observed upon the form of stating the question; we proceed to examine the reason produced.

They lay the ground of their argument thus, "Where the Scripture holds forth distinct sorts in any kind, there will be found either distinct and proper names and titles, or at least some adjunct of difference added to that which

{See p. 96}

is common or general," as 1 Corinthians 12 where apostles, prophets, teachers, have not only particular names and titles, but special notes of distinction: first apostles, secondly prophets; and Genesis 1, where no distinction in names is given, the sun, moon, and stars, are all called lights; yet there are terms of differences added, greater and lesser.

To which we say, that it is true, something there must be either in the text, or context, or collated with other places, which may give distinction to things distinct. But then we answer, that we looked for such instances as might not only give marks of distinction of things distinct, but might give notes of distinct superiority of one thing or person over another, which the scope of the text (1 Corinthians 12) does tend nothing towards. For though the apostles were superior to all, yet our brethren will find it not so easy to demonstrate the superiority of prophets, teachers, etc., to those mentioned after them. And for that other instance of the luminaries (Genesis 1), they are not so great, as that we can see by them any reason of the consequence, that if luminaries be so distinguished, then presbyteries must be so too.

Secondly, it is not proved that all things that are distinct, agreeable unto, or warrantable by the Scripture, should have distinct names, titles, adjuncts of difference therein set down. Parity of reason from Scripture grounds is sufficient to give distinction. For we do not assert such a formal express mention of the subordination of presbyteries and synods as our brethren require, because they do not *competere* to a church as it is a church, but only *apply* to the well being of it, in such or such times, places and conditions. For sometimes particular congregations may want [*lack*] a competent number of officers, and of men fit for government, and so cannot have a particular presbytery. And sometimes, as in times of persecution, several churches may be so dispersed, or may otherwise live at such distance from one another, as that they may be disabled to associate into a classical presbytery.

This ground being laid by our brethren, they thus enforce it, 'There is no distinction of presbyteries by any name or title; for in the New Testament the word πρεσβυτέριον is but in three places, whereof there is but one which holds out the government in hand, and in that place we have the naked word only, without the addition of any such expression, greater, lesser, superior, inferior, or any kind of adjunct that can possibly put a thought into us of more presbyteries than one.'

To this we *answer:* 1. How can it be proved, that by presbytery in that one place is meant the presbytery of a particular congregation? And if that cannot be proved, how then can the presbytery of a particular congregation be proved?

2. We do not by that word in that one place used, go about to prove distinct sorts of presbyteries, but we say distinct presbyteries may be called by that general name, as every distinct species of animal, may be called animal.

3. As the word πρεσβυτέριον signifying a court among the Jews, was in

assembly   Scripture language the same with πρεσβύτεροι in *consessu*, or in *synedrio*,
sanhedrin   as is most manifest. So the same word in the Christian church, is no other
presbyters in than *presbyteri in consessu*, and then we have it above once in the New Tes-
assembly   tament, as to the government in hand.

4. The several judicatories among the Jews, which were as much and more
distinguished than our presbyteries, had one and the same name, as *gnedah*,
qahal, *zekenim*, *shophtim*, promiscuously given to them all, as the learned
have observed[1] and the like may be affirmed of συναγωγὴ, εκκλησια, and
sanhedrin   other like. So *synedrium* is a common name unto different courts subordinate
to each other. And it is further observed by the learned,[2] that the Jews had
the great *San[h]edri[n]*, and two others besides that in Jerusalem, and every
great city twenty three elders, and every of these courts is called *Hagnedah*.

5. Our brethren know that the thing was in the church before the apostle made mention of it by this name; for he did not in this place institute a
presbytery. And if he had not here called it so, and the word could nowhere
have been found, yet the thing itself was and would have been in being,
as our two distinct sacraments are, though that name be not there found.

6. Our brethren do acknowledge, "That the elders of divers congregations
met together to determine or dogmatically declare matters of faith, are the
ordinance of Christ." And yet our brethren do not anywhere read God has
set in his church, first, presbyteries, then synods. We see no reason, why a
court of judicatory, might not as well be without Scripture name, as an ordinance of Christ is by their own confession.

medium   And therefore we conclude this *nominal[e] medium* with our brethren
pertaining to thus; that as in Scotland and France, and in the episcopal republic, there
name   are particular distinct names for the distinct sorts or kinds of administration in their ordinances for government. So shall we also use distinct names
for them, as well as they; only we conceive, the episcopal republic need not
have been named with Scotland and the French, but that they were pleased
to serve us with variety.[3]

Our brethren say, that as the Scripture hold forth 'nothing in any name
{See p. 96}   or title to distinguish, no more can we therein discover any sorts of government different in nature?' For do you read?' they say, "any where, God has
set in his church, first presbyteries, secondly classes, then consistories, etc?"

To this we *answer:* 1. That this is but recurring to disprove difference in

---

1. Bertram, *De politia Iudaica*, c. 6.9. [Cornelius Bonaventura Bertram, Professor of Hebrew at Geneva and Lausanne (1531–1594) *De Politia Judaica* (Geneva, 1580), pp. 33–39, 44–53.]

2. Selden. [John Selden, jurist and orientalist, and one of the Erastian divines at the
Westminster Assembly, and author of works on Jewish antiquities and history (1584–1654). Cf.
De Synedris et Præfecturis Juridicis veterum Ebræorum 3 vols. (London: Flesher, 1650–1655); *Opera
Omnia*, 3 vols. (London: 1726), 1.1160. It is said Selden had written this work about 1640, and
kept working on it issuing the first volume in 1650, the second in 1653, and the third in 1655.
See Selden's comment, *Minutes*, 2.520–522, Gillespie, 26, Lightfoot, 165–166.]

3. [Episcopal republic: i.e. A prelatical church without a monarchical civil government.]

nature, because there is no difference in name, and so is all one medium with the former.

2. They seem to allude to that place [of] 1 Corinthians 12:1, first, apostles, secondly, prophets, which is not meant of superiority in government, nor is the church spoken of there, any other than the church general, and not in one kingdom or nation.

3. It is not necessary that every aggregation of presbyters for government of the church should have distinct names set down in Scripture. What name in Scriptures have those presbyters that meet dogmatically to determine cases and points of faith? "Yet they have power, and are the ordinances of Christ," they say. Scripture sets not things down as arts do, by artificial definitions or distributions; there are no logical or systematic methods. It says not, 'faith is dogmatic and justifying,' 'the church general and particular,' etc., and yet the things themselves have a being in Scripture.

1. Now to the particulars of this medium, it is first said. (1) They have the same materials, and therefore are not in that respect different. This militates as well against courts civil, where the members are the same, as against ecclesiastical; and we answer them by their own words:

Although this superior presbytery be made up of presbyters but as commissioners from the congregational or parochial presbyteries, yet that hinders not at all, but that they may be offices distinct. And to the illustration they give there, we add, that the officers of several regiments sitting in a counsel of war; the heads of colleges sitting in consistory; the aldermen of wards sitting in council, are materially the same; yet the courts thus made up, are not the same in power with that which these persons have in their particular places of command.

(2) We further answer, that the matter of a particular presbytery is, presbyteries of one congregation alone, respectively, to that alone. But the matter of a classical presbytery, are the presbyters of several congregations respectively unto several congregations. Even as the material of a national synod is not simply commissioners, but commissioners sent from all the churches of a nation.

(3) Where it is said, that presbyteration alone does sufficiently qualify a gifted person to be the matter of any presbytery, we *answer:* That this is not true, without distinguishing of *materia remota*, which makes a man only *material remote* capable of such of relation; and *materia proxima*, whereby a man is actu- *material* ally in such, or such a relation; for unto this, besides presbyteration, there *proximate* is required a special call respectively to those presbyteries, wherein a man acts as a presbyter.

(4) Whereas they say, "That a greater number of presbyters in the one presbytery alters not the state in respect of the matter." We grant it, but it makes as much against distinction of civil judicatures as of ecclesiastical.

2. For the *formale*, the uniting of these persons into a *consessus* or *coetus*,

they say, "That this is the same, because a pastor joined to a particular congregation is *eo nomine*, a member of the classis to which that congregations belongs." To this we *answer*: that the union of person into a *consessus*,
is but *forma generica* to all presbyteries or courts, made up by aggregation
of more members, and so it gives no special difference between presbytery
and presbytery. We cannot but wonder at such a consequence, that if divers courts do agree in this genetic form of union and coalition, therefore
they are not distinct in form; for there is a special form or reason of their
union, which diversifies them. For the pastor is united unto other ruling
officers in a single congregation respectively to that congregation alone.
And he is united to other pastors and officers of divers congregations by
association respectively to all these congregations; which respects are formerly distinct from one another.

And for that the brethren say, "The presbyters of a parochial presbytery,
are as nearly united" or more, as in the choice and call of the same congregation, and in the work of the ministry—that rather argues the union to
be distinct, and the presbyteries consequently to be distinct. As the master of a college has a nearer relation to it in the call of the college, work of
governing, admitting scholars, disposing of revenues, etc.; and yet being
met in a *consessus* of heads, for common government over the whole university, does concur to the making up of a distinct court from that in the
college. So is it here—the special reason of union of the same person with
both making the distinction.

And whereas it is said, that a presbyter by having pastoral charge in such
division, "is *eo nomine* member of such a classis;" granting it to be so, that
would nothing hinder the classical presbytery to be distinct from a parochial, no more than a master of a college being *eo nomine*, a member of the
consistory does prove, that the government of the college and of the university are not distinct; or that every particular judge of the King's Bench,
common pleas, and exchequer, being *eo nomine* of power to argue and judge
cases, as it were *in collegio*, in the Chequer Chamber,[1] would prove that the
judgment in the Chequer Chamber, and that in any of the other courts
were not distinct or different.

So then to the *ultimate form* and constitution of a political body, there
is more requisite than the common uniting of the members thereof, *in
consessum*; for though the persons should be the same, and the manner of
union the same, yet if those persons so united have in one capacity some
ends and objects, and in another others, diversity of these will diversify their
meetings, even as different ends and objects do make the same person being united to the same congregation, to be a pastor in one sense for the
works of ministry; and a ruler in another for works of government: and a

---

1. [*Obs.* "The chamber devoted to the business of the royal exchequer" (exchequer
chamber).]

member in a third, for communion in worship, and yet ministry, jurisdiction, and membership in the same person are things specifically distinct, though he have both the one and the other by virtue of his union unto that particular congregation. And that such diversity is sufficient to make a formal difference in matters political, wherein specific diversity may arise from such reasons as in natural things do not vary the species, our brethren have informed us in this paper of theirs.

Now classical presbyteries have different objects, namely things of common concernment, and different ends, as will appear in the answer to the next branch. And this is therefore sufficient formally to difference them from other presbyteries.

3. "Nor," say the brethren, "Do we find anything in Scripture making them, as from different employments and functions to differ."

(1) We affirm, and so it is in the proposition, "The one is superior, the other inferior: but how can you say, the Scriptures have made this difference, when there is not a word spoken that way in any place?" The sense of their argument lies thus, if we do not find anything in Scripture, how can you say it? To which we *answer:* We can say it, though they do not find it. And they can say, "That particular congregations are independent of any church-power superior to them," though we do not find that there is a word spoken this way in any place of Scripture.

And as to the instances alleged out of some presbyterial writers themselves, whereby they seem utterly to take away such difference of superior and inferior presbyteries; because in one place you shall read, "The classis can do nothing, *renitente ecclesia,* but it is null and invalid, *Assertion of Discipline,*" and in another, "The congregations, though but *minima ecclesiola,* may reform" (that is suspend, excommunicate, etc.) "*renitentibus correspondentiis,* Voetius in his *Theses* & *desperata causa papatus*; and that according to these expressions, it is hard to be said, which of these presbyteries has the greater or superior power;" We *answer*: {See p. 97}

{1} That the renitence[1] of such as are of the *quorum,* and have power of a negative voice to the rest in any *consessus,* does indeed null and make void the act of the rest. But the renitence of them that are not necessarily concurrent to pass an act of power, is no derogation to the power itself, but may give occasion to the governors in prudence to forebear the execution of such an act or sentence. As the council of war should in wisdom suspend the execution of any order, which may endanger mutiny in the army. But such renitence of people to their governors does not null the power; for then they may at pleasure by renitence to whatsoever they dislike, null the power that is over them. And upon this ground, we affirm that the measure or degree of power is not to be estimated by renitence, or non-renitence

---

1. [Renitence (opposition). Resistance; reluctance or unwillingness to be compelled or persuaded; uncooperativeness (OED).]

of them that are subject to it. For the renitence of subjects to a power over them, is either renitence of contradiction to that power, or of appeal from it to an higher, and neither sort nulls the power. So that the case alleged by our brethren is justly thus: the court of war should not in wisdom exercise an act of power unto which the officers and soldiers of a regiment are renitent: but the officers and regiment may reform themselves, though the council of war be renitent. Therefore it is hard to say, whether the council of war or that regiment have the greater power. Whatever they shall answer to this instance, will answer theirs.

{2} The authors which they cite are clear. The *Assertion* does assert, "That the classis should not proceed unto excommunication, *renitente ecclesia;*" but does not say that such renitence annuls the power, and gives the reason, because such excommunication would want [*lack*] its due effect, because the renitent congregation would not cast out a person out of their communion, which the classis had discerned to be cast out. And as for Voetius, he does plainly assert power in a classis to receive appeals from a particular

Braye, 106r congregation, and to judge them. The words which our brethren point us unto (Thes. 5. 8. 9), are these, *Cessantibus, aut male rem agentibus correspondentiis classicis aut synodicis, in casu necessitatis (quae ordinariam legem sæpe non fert) Licet Ecclesiis potestatem suam resumere, & recte usurpare, si non cum correspondentiâ cum aliis completâ, saltem incompletâ, nunquam enim causa Dei deserenda est. Imo quidni etiam uni ecclesiolæ vel minimæ liceat sua suorumque, saluti consulere, & omnibus correspondentiis renitentibus eam præferre? Cum hic teneat illud; charitas & Reformatio incipit a seipso.*[1]

[1. "With the classical or synodical correspondents ceasing, or handling the matter incorrectly, in a case of necessity (which often does not admit of the ordinary law), it is lawful to the Churches to resume their power, and to use it rightly; if not with the mutual agreement with others complete, at least incomplete, for the cause of God is never to be forsaken." Cornelius Poudroyen, Gilles Roman, and Gijsbert Voet, *Disputatio theologica ex politiâ ecclesiasticâ de unione ecclesiarum earumque regimine in classibus & synodis* (Ultraiecti: ex officinâ Aegidii Roman, Academiae typographi, 1641). *Gisberti Voetii, Theologiæ in Academ. Ultrajectinâ Professoris, Politicæ Ecclesiasticæ,* volume 3 (Amsterdam: Johannem Jansonium à Wæsberge 1676) 128. Many theological dissertations were published at Utrecht University from 1636 to this time, for which Voet acted as *præses.* After this period it was common for the præses to compile the thesis and the student only needed to defend it, and this must have been the case here since this was included amongst Voet's tracts. See also *Gisberti Voetii Tractatus selecti de politica ecclesiastica Series Prima,* edited by F. L. Rutgers (Amsterdam, 1885), 2.257. Cf. Section 3, pp. 252–255. Voet's endorsement and aid were sought by both the Independents and the Presbyterians. Baillie was not pleased with Voet's 1641 work, writing prior to attending the assembly, "I confesse I am verie evill satisfied with Voetius's Theses of Presbytries and Synods:… in the matter, he sticks so to Parker's grounds of mutual association and *ecclesia prima,* that I wish he had written nothing in this purpose…" June 2 1643, 2.65. And just prior to the Independents' drafting their dissent to the third proposition, Baillie wrote, "We are informed from thence very credibly, that the agents of the Independents have so farr prevailed with Voetius, as to make him publish his approbation of Cotton's Keyes of the kingdom of Heaven, as consonant to truth, and the discipline of Holland." To Spang, November 1, 1644, 2.240.]

                    I: ANSWER OF THE ASSEMBLY TO THE REASONS

If there be anything here, which may make it hard to be said which of these presbyteries have the greater or superior power, let them show it that can, and will make the reverend author contradictory to himself, and to the title of his book, *De unione Ecclesiarum, earumque, Regimine in Classibus & Synodis.* Surely he gives no more here to a congregation, than he does elsewhere to a particular member in a particular congregation (Section 3), and yet it is easy to affirm, that a particular congregation has more power than any member of it.

(2) Our brethren proceed in their argument thus: The "work of a presbytery is to ordain, excommunicate, suspend, admit members, appoint times for worship, and the like. The classical reserve ordination and excommunication to themselves; but the other are left to the parochial presbytery. Thus some Presbyterians divide the work, others possibly otherwise. But how can we affirm any such designment from the Scriptures, if you have not two sorts, either in name, or nature to be found there? And none of these acts … but may be done by that one … which doubtless they may: seeing ordination seems to be specified in the text. If the greater, then doubtless the lesser. The pastor in one place is said to exhort, in another to comfort, in another to visit the sick. This will not warrant distinct sorts of pastors, for there being but one sort spoken of in Scriptures, we must interpret all these several administrations to belong as to that one." {See pp. 97, 98}

To this we *answer:*

{1} That the argument is *circular*, for they prove there are not two sorts of presbyteries, because not different employments belonging to them: and now they prove, that there are not different employments, because we have not two sorts of presbyteries in name and nature, to be found in Scripture to whom these employments should belong.

{2} There is not such division of the work of presbyteries yet determined, nor in some part yet debated in this assembly.

{3} Admitting that all these acts here mentioned, ought to be done in a parochial presbytery, *quoad speciem actus*, yet it follows not, but that there may be a superior presbytery; for if there be a presbytery, which has power to order, correct, or direct this power of a particular presbytery, then, by the confession of our brethren, *there is a distinct presbytery.* As suppose an inferior court to which appeal is made, can do no more; and yet it is superior, because it has power to correct, order, and direct those acts of the inferior. *with respect to the species of the act*

{4} Our brethren's argument does proceed upon an insufficient enumeration of employments, for that there are many employments, proper to another sort of presbytery distinct from that which is parochial, we show by a more full enumeration of particulars, as 1. In matters of common concernment to more churches than one. 2. In case of an incompetent parochial presbytery. 3. In case of appellation and presumed mal-administration. 4. In case of divisions arising in particular churches and presbyteries. 5. In case of differences between neighbor churches. 6. In case of sects and heresies spreading abroad, and endangering the peace of the church, and truth of God. 7. In case of obstinacy, when the major part of a congregation erring refuse to put the differences among them to reference or arbitration. 8. In case of examination of a minister's learning in tongues, arts, theology, and other things requisite to make him a fit pastor or teacher for such a particular congregation, according to the rules of ordination already established.[1] 9. In case the people, or any of them, reject or slight the admonition or censures of their pastor and officers. 10. In case the pastor be like some Diotrephes, tyrannical and vexatious to the people, and they not able to help themselves, or do subtly deliver and spread among them erroneous doctrine. 11. When the presbytery and people are divided into equal, or almost equal parts. 12. When hard and difficult cases are to be decided. 13. *with spiritual* When some powerful adversaries or persecutors, are to be resisted *spirituali armor* *armaturâ*. 14. To prevent partiality or neglect of censures towards some offenders, such as was in Corinth, towards the incestuous person. 15. In case of the excommunication or deposition of a pastor.

In these cases, said Voetius, *Non puto aliquem negaturum quin [in his casibus] Salubris sit Autoritas multarum Ecclesiarum, uno animo, unis Consiliis [& operis] conjunctarum; quidni necessaria[?]*[2]

{5} When it is said, that ordination seems to be done by a particular presbytery, and therefore all other things may be done there too.

For the antecedent, it is *gratis dictum*, and being granted, the consequence *freely granted* is denied. Neither does the degree of greater or lesser make any proof of it; for to preach the Word, and administer sacraments, are as great works, as to excommunicate, yet it does not follow, because a minister may do those alone, therefore he may do this alone too.

And besides, it is also *gratis dictum*, to say that ordination is the greatest work belonging to the presbytery, especially for our brethren to say so, who sometimes think it not all requisite, and when it is, make it only a solemn admitting him into his place.

Surely our brethren look upon the delivering of a man unto Satan as a work of a higher nature.

---

1. [On April 19, 1644, the assembly gave the House of Commons a draft directory for ordination, the text of which is given as document 20 in "The Calendar of Papers of the Westminster Assembly," *Minutes*, 5.63–69. The Assembly was dismayed by the revised/redacted version returned by the Commons, and they added to this thirteen amendments (document 28), the text of which is lost, but the amendments recovered (5.75–77) by examining the MS of document 29, which is the directory for ordination first printed in early October, 1644 (*Minutes*, 5.78-84). "On 3 October the assembly withheld further protests against changes made by the House of Lords to the directory and agreed to proceed with printing the text." The rules in the October 1644 printed document are those to which the assembly refers here.]

2. ["I do not think that anyone is going to deny that [in these cases] the Authority of many churches, conjoined in one spirit, in united Counsels [and works], is wholesome; why not necessary? Cf. *Gisberti Voetii Tractatus selecti de politica ecclesiastica Series Prima*, 2.261.]

As for that which our brethren say; "It was not found so easy in this assembly to find two sorts of elders, teaching and ruling; though the Scripture in some places ſpeak so plain of them, as if of purpose to diſtinguish them. And therefore it muſt needs be more difficult to find out two sorts of presbyteries."

We *answer:* 1. That it is no right way of argumentation to diſpute from the difficulty of finding a thing to the denying of it. Many points in divinity are of difficult discovery, and yet not to be denied.

2. As it seems to have been easy and clear in the apprehensions of our brethren, that there are several sorts of presbyters, though they say it was a difficulty to the assembly, so they may be pleased to allow the same clearness of apprehension to the assembly in the point of presbyteries, though it seem difficult to themselves.

3. If the assembly found it hard to find out that which is plain in Scripture, then the pains of the assembly in discussing and searching the Scriptures, argues not inevidence of the thing itself, but their care to find a good foundation of that advice they should give to the Honorable Houses, and their care to satisfy if it were possible their dissenting brethren.

4. The consequence which they infer is denied, that it "muſt be more difficult to find out two sort of Presbyteries;" for admitting there were but one sort of presbyters, yet it is easy to compound of them two sorts of presbyteries, as easy as it is of juſtices of the peace, heads of colleges, aldermen, burgesses, to form diſtinct meetings in regard of power, and the adminiſtration thereof, which is confessed by the brethren in their inſtances of burgesses of cities and towns corporate, sent up unto, and sitting in parliament.

And whereas they say, that it is "generally granted" by "presbyterians themselves" that "for above fifty years after Chriſt, and in the apoſtles times, there was but one kind of presbytery," we desire our brethren to tell us, what sort of presbytery that was, parochial or classical, as we now call them. If parochial, who are these presbyterians that so grant? If classical (which they know those presbyterians mean, who from undoubted antiquity aver, that the church was governed, *Communi Consilio Presbyterorum*) then it helps *by the Common* them not at all, for if the brethren grant parochial, and the Presbyterians *Counsel of the* grant classical, then there are two diſtinct sorts by grant on this part, and *Presbytery* on that. However the rules and reasons which the presbyterians go upon, were as valid in these former times as now.

To the inference made from the wisdom of ſtates to the wisdom of Chriſt, in clearly bounding out the judicatories of his church, we shall not go one syllable less in our attributions to Jesus Chriſt than our brethren. But though unwilling to make such comparison of things, which are of no degree of comparison, we answer to that which is argumentative in this rhetoric:

1. If the light of nature have directed all ſtates to appoint superior courts for relieving of men in case of appeals from the miscarriages of inferior,

we apprehend it no less wisdom in Christ, to appoint or warrant such authority in His church, as may relieve wrongs through mistakings or miscarriages of inferior presbyteries. For otherwise the ecclesiastical republic
were in worse case than the civil, which confessedly does afford relief of
wrongs about inferior claims.

2. What is it that the brethren would assume? Is it that Christ has set
such bounds of church judicatures for relief of wronged persons? Then
they grant the question. Or has He set no such? Then, how do they vindi-
cate His wisdom!

And whereas it is said, that "controversies and clashings about these high
and public interests, are no other in this issue, than the dividing of a kingdom within itself" (thereby haply intimating some formidableness of the
government to the civil state) that this observation of theirs is true, we have
too sad experience. But that a presbytery over a presbytery does thus divide
a kingdom within itself, the experience of all the reformed churches where
this government has obtained, does plainly witness the contrary.

3. We shall not easily grant what our brethren insinuate, that matters of
practice and duty, should rather have obscurity in the rule, than authority
and jurisdiction; since the former being matters of faith, worship and obedience, do more immediately relate unto salvation itself; the other, though
it be subservient thereunto, yet in an inferior and remoter degree.

Neither are we enforced out of one word, but once used, to raise up so
many thrones (as they call them) or forms of government. For the form of
government is but one; and for the warrantableness thereof, we have shown
it out of other places of Scripture, not so much as mentioning this to prove
our proposition, which our brethren so much insist upon.

And lastly, we cannot but wonder, that all the churches of Christ until
this present age, should never before have discovered this frame of government, by our brethren contended for, as so clear and evident; especially considering, that the nature of man is very inclinable to search out diligently,
and easily to assert such ways of liberty, whereby they may be independent
upon superior authority and jurisdiction over them.

Cornelius Burges, Prolocutor *pro tempore.*
John White, Assessor.
Henry Robroughe, Scriba.
Adoniram Byfield, Scriba.

REASONS AGAINST

And Answers to the Proofs from the Instance of the Church of Ephesus alleged by the Reverend Assembly, to prove that the Scripture holds forth that many Congregations may be under one Presbyterial Government

THE ARGUMENT OF THE REVEREND ASSEMBLY from the church of Ephesus, is laid down in these three propositions:

First, *The multitude of believers did make more congregations than one in Ephesus.*

Secondly, *There were many elders over those many congregations, as over one flock.*

Thirdly, *Those several congregations were one church, and under one presbyterial government.*

The proofs brought by the reverend assembly to prove the first proposition, *viz.* that the multitude of believers did make more congregations than one, in Ephesus, are these:

Acts 20:31, where there is mention made of Paul's continuance at Ephesus preaching for the space of three years.

Acts 19:18–20, where the special effect of the Word is mentioned, *viz.* many that believed came and confessed their deeds, many also of them which used curious arts, brought their books together, and burned them before all men, and they counted the price of them, and they found it to be fifty thousand pieces of silver, so mightily grew the Word of God, and prevailed.

Acts 19:10, 17, where mention is made of Jews and Greeks.

1 Corinthians 16:8–9, where a reason is given of Paul's stay at Ephesus until Pentecost, *viz.* because "a great and effectual door was opened."

1 Corinthians 16:19, where there is mention of a particular church in the house of Aquila and Priscilla, who were then at Ephesus, as appears [from] Acts 18:19 and Acts 24:26.

To these proofs, the answer is:

1. As for such of them which are brought to prove the number of believers in Ephesus, the consequence is denied, because that notwithstanding what is said of the "apostle's being three years at Ephesus, and a great and effectual door was opened, and so mightily grew the Word of God, and

Minutes,
Doc. 45, 5.136
Sess. 200–205,
3.15–34

Gillespie, 51–55
Lightfoot,
247–254

Goodwin, 106

prevailed, etc.," it follows not that the converts in Ephesus were so many as could not meet in one place.

For (1) Suppose it be granted there were two or three thousand (though there is no sufficient ground to say there were near so many), yet they all might meet in one place; and yet this were enough to show that there was a large and effectual door opened to the apostle, and a comfortable fruit of his so long stay and preaching there.

(2) Because this efficacy of the Word preached by Paul, has reference not only to Ephesus, but also to all Asia (Acts 19:26), "Not only in Ephesus, but throughout all Asia; this Paul hath persuaded and turned away much people." And where he said (Acts 20:31), for the space of three years he ceased not to warn every one night and day with tears, the words are not to be restrained to his being at Ephesus; but to be understood of his being in Asia, as appears by verse 18. "Ye know from the first day that I came into Asia, after what manner I have been with you at all seasons, serving the Lord with all humility of mind, and with many tears."

2. As for the price of the books of the converts.

The *answer* is, that when there was no printing, a few men's books, yea, a few books of so curious and gainful arts, might well be worth that money. For that fifty thousand pieces of silver, Calvin upon the place,[1] computes to be but nine thousand pounds French, which is six hundred seventy five pound sterling, or thereabouts, at eighteen pence the franc. Beza reckons it less,[2] *viz.* eight thousand, seven hundred pound French. And our own countryman Brerewood in his first chapter *de nummis*,[3] interpreting this very place, accounts every ἀργύριον [ἀργυρίον] at 7.d.[ob.] according to which rate, the sum amounts to about £1,406 sterling. Some one man's study [*library*] now of common books, though not manuscripts, as they were, is worth as much; and how can this argue such a multitude of believers, or several congregations, as could not meet in one place, we cannot see.

3. As for the church in Aquila's house, which is supposed by the reverend assembly to be a congregation distinct from the Ephesians, and therefore more congregations than one making that one Ephesian Church, so much spoken of in the New Testament, the *answer* is:

(1) The church in his house is not necessarily to be understood of a congregation, such as the proposition intends, but of a family church, as most of our divines say.

(2) Suppose it were such. It does not appear that the church in Aquila's house was at Ephesus, but in Asia. We read that Aquila and Priscilla traveled with Paul to Ephesus, and were left there, not that their church

Gillespie, 18
Lightfoot, 151
Goodwin, 99;
otherwise not
addressed

---

1. [Calvin, Acts 19:20. Cf. *Commentaries*, vol. 19, on Acts, volume second, page 221.]

2. [Beza, *Annotationes*, p. 354. "Francicis libris 8,750."]

3. [Sir Edward Brerewood (or Bryerwood), *De ponderibus et pretiis veterum nummorum, eorumque cum recentioribus collatione liber unus* (Londin: Apud Ioannem Billium, 1614), p. 5.]

was there; for themselves might travel where their church traveled not with them.

(3) Grant they were such a church, and at Ephesus, yet the *answer* is, they were strangers that were driven from Rome by Claudius (Acts 18:2 compared with Romans 16:4 where also we read of a church in their house), and therefore kept themselves a distinct church from the Ephesians, as the English do in the Netherlands, and the Dutch in England, who choose rather to join with their own country people, whose dwellings are more remote, than with those of another nation nearer to them. And if the difference of their language may argue different congregations, and that they could not join in one (as is alleged), it will argue as strongly that this church, and the other congregation of Ephesus, could not be under one presbyterial government. And ordinary officers had not ordinarily the gift of several tongues (1 Corinthians 12:8, 9—to one is given the word of wisdom, to another, knowledge, to another, divers kinds of tongues). Goodwin, 194

4. As for Jews and Greeks being mentioned; it makes nothing for the number, nor yet that for difference of language, there must needs be more congregations than one. For the Jews that lived among the Gentiles understood their language, else they would make so many independent congregations.

That the multitude of believers were not more than could meet in one place

The contrary to this first proposition, *viz.* "that the multitude of believers were not more than could meet in one place"[1] is proved thus:

It is apparent that the number of believers there when Paul came first to Ephesus was but about twelve (Acts 19:7, "All the men were about twelve.") And when the number was increased, yet then the church of Ephesus is called one flock, in relation to those elders which were at Ephesus (Acts 20:28), which were willed by Paul to "feed that flock" by doctrine as he had done, by which it is evident they might and did meet in one; for elders are pastors only for one congregation.

"It was said that the feeding of this flock is to be understood *partitivè*, *viz.* some, one congregation, some another, and so among them the flock was fed." *divided into parts*

But if it be understood *partitivè* with reference to their feeding, it must be also with reference to their overseeing, because it is so expressed in the text. "Take heed to yourselves," etc., "to the whole flock over which the Holy Ghost has made you overseers, to feed the church of God." For no reason can be given why these words "feed the flock" should be understood *partitivè*, and not these other words "take heed to the flock over which the Holy Ghost Minutes, 3.23
Gillespie,
50–52
Lightfoot, 158

---

1. [Goodwin would still maintain that English and Scottish writers against episcopacy concede that it cannot by manifest argument be proved that at the first congregations contained more than could meet in one place, p. 106]

has made you overseers." And if their overseeing and ruling are to be understood *partitivè*, then how does this place argue a presbyterial government
over many congregations? And if it be said the many congregations were
not fixed ones, then that distinction of feeding *partitivè* falls to the ground.

Whereas it is replied that the same phrase as used [in] 1 Peter 5:2, "feed
the flock of God among you, taking the oversight thereof," must be understood *partitivè*, because those believers and elders to whom the apostle Peter writes, were scattered through[out] Pontius, Galatia, Capadocia, Asia,
and Bithinia, which could not meet in one congregation. It is answered:

1. That in this place of Peter there are no such words, whereby the relation of the whole flock is equally carried to all those elders, as there are in
that speech of the apostle to the elders of Ephesus (Acts 20:28), "Take heed
to the whole flock over the which" (whole flock) "the Holy Ghost has made
you overseers."

2. In this [in] 1 Peter 5:1, 4, there are words which plainly point at such
a distribution, namely ἐν ὑμῖν—among you—applied both to the elders,
and to the flock: "the elders" ἐν ὑμῖν "among you, I exhort to feed the flock"
ἐν ὑμῖν, that is, 'each elder feed your flock respectively wherever they are
among you in each country.' Therefore though it be understood *partitivè* in
Peter, yet it follows not it should be so understood [in] Acts 20:28.

And if it be said further, 'that although ruling and teaching be applied
to the same flock, the elders need not be in both alike understood *parti-*
in assembly *tivè* to perform their office, because elders when they rule do it in *consessu*,
and all join in every act; but when they teach they do it severally, each by
himself; therefore where ruling and teaching are applied to elders as over
one flock, as they are [in] Acts 20, they may well be supposed to do the one
partitivè, the other not.'

The *answer* is, it is true, where elders rule, they do it in *collegio*, whether
collectively over more or few, and when they teach they do it severally, but still both
ruling and teaching are to be within the same compass, in respect of them
who are ruled and taught. For when elders rule one congregation in *colle-*
gio, yet each of these elders oversee and rule the whole flock as truly as he
can be said by teaching to feed that whole flock.

As for the second and third propositions, "that there were many elders
over that people as one flock, and one church, and that they did govern this
one flock," the former proposition not being proved, they make nothing
to the proof of that conclusion, that the Scripture holds forth that many
congregations may be under one presbyterial government.

> *Sic Subscribitur:* Tho. Goodwin, William Bridge, Philip Nye, Wil-
> liam Greenhill, Jer. Burroughes, William Carter, Sidrach Sympson.
>
> *Concordat cum Originali.* Adoniram Byfield, Scriba.

The Answer of the Assembly of Divines

Unto the Reasons of the Dissenting Brethren against the Instance of the Church of Ephesus

OUR ARGUMENT FOR MANY CONGREGATIONS under one presbyterial government, from the instance of the church of Ephesus, consisted of three propositions.

I. That the multitude of believers there, did make more congregations than one.

II. There were many elders over those many congregations as over one flock.

III. Those several congregations were one church under one presbyterial government.

Of which our brethren insist only upon the first, which was proved from:

1. Paul's continuance and preaching for the space of three years (Acts 20:31, 19–20).

2. The special effect of the Word there, that "many that believed came and confessed their deeds. Many also of them which used curious arts brought their books together, and burned them before all men, and they counted the price of them, and found it to be 50,000 pieces of silver. So mightily grew the Word of God and prevailed" (Acts 19:18–20).

3. The mention made of Jews and Greeks (Acts 19:10, 17).

4. The reason of Paul's stay there, because a great and effectual door was opened (1 Corinthians 16:8–9).

5. Mention made of a particular church in the house of Aquila and Priscilla (1 Corinthians 16:19), who were then at Ephesus (Acts 18:19, 24, 26).

All which laid together do prove the proposition.

[Answer to the Independent Brethrens' Replies to the Assembly's proofs from the church at Ephesus]

For the right understanding of which proof, we desire that [that] may be considered which our brethren do not mention, but in the debate was often expressed, and therefore in the vote carefully added, *viz.* "That all these laid together do prove, etc.," arguments of necessity being answerable to the thing they prove. And so though the several particulars of this proof should be singly but probabilities, yet being joined together make a sufficient proof, as many concurring likelihoods in courts amount to a good evidence, and many lesser stars make up a *galaxia* [*galaxy*]. Our argument therefore may hold, though their answer (while they take it asunder) should seem to make the several particulars of it less demonstrative. But how do they endeavor that?

[I. ANSWER REGARDING THE NUMBER OF BELIEVERS AT EPHESUS]
First, in a fair way of answer, they join divers of them together, the apostle being three years at Ephesus, and his having there a great and effectual door opened, and that expression, "so mightily grew the Word," etc., to all which {See p. 175} they answer, by denying the consequence, that therefore the converts in Ephesus were more than could meet in one place, and that for two reasons.

1. "For suppose it be granted there were two or three thousand (though {See p. 176} there is no sufficient ground to say there were near so many), yet they might all meet in one place, and this were enough to show, that there was a large and effectual door opened to the apostle, and a comfortable fruit of his so long stay and preaching there."

In our answer to which assertions, we shall consider what they say to the number of believers there, and then how they could all meet in one place.

As to the first, those words of theirs, "There is no sufficient ground to say there were near so many as two or three thousand" in our ordinary use of the phrase, "not near so many," import, that in our brethren's judgments, the number fell far short of three, nay of two thousand, which in the general, gives us just occasion in the spirit of meekness to desire them to be wary how they use such arguments, or without clear evidence pitch upon such tenets as force them to make use of them, which as before in the church of Jerusalem, so here again in the church of Ephesus, do laboriously endeavor to straiten [*restrict*] the number of believers, that they might get them all into one room, so as not to exceed the bounds of one congregation, which not only at first blush, but we fear if more nearly looked into, weakens the power of the gospel in those first most powerful dispensations of it, and lessens the goodness of God in that his plentiful redemption by laboring to make the number of converts as few as possibly may be. Which the Scriptures and both ancient and modern Christian writers are wont frequently and studiously to set out to the full, and amplify to the greater glory of Christ and his gospel, which we believe our brethren will [*should*] be very tender of.

But to the particular in hand, we conceive that we have sufficient ground to think that there were more than three, or at least two thousand believers in Ephesus in Paul's time (and much rather afterward when Christ by John writes to them in the Revelation, when yet but one church, Revelation 2:1), and that, had we no more for it, than what the three particulars by them repeated, may rationally persuade.

The last of which, *viz.* that expression "so mightily grew the Word of God," etc., they say nothing to, and therefore it stands for us still in its strength, for anything that is said against it.

The second, *viz.* that large and effectual door opened to him, being an extraordinary expression, must needs hold forth something more than ordinary and therefore may reasonably make that great door wide enough, to let in more than three or two thousand.

But the first is that which our brethren most insist on, *viz.* the apostle's long stay and preaching there, and here, though whilst we consider the worth of one soul, we cannot but confess that the conversion of two or three thousand were (as they truly say) "a comfortable" fruit of it. Yet we cannot say or think it answerable to that abundant blessing, which God in that first plentiful harvest vouchsafed to the endeavors of those his chief laborers, who in the short course of their ministry were to convert the world, especially of Paul, who durst affirm of himself, that he labored more abundantly than they all (1 Corinthians 15:10), and this the rather:

(1) If we compare Paul's ministry with Peter's, which he himself at least equals in the success of it (Galatians 2:8), "He that wrought effectually in Peter to the apostleship of the circumcision, the same was mighty in me toward the Gentiles." Now then if Peter alone preaching (as our brethren in their former reasons conceived), or say with the rest of the apostles, did in one day bring in about three thousand souls (Acts 2:41), and day by day, many more (verse 47), so that within some few days, the number was grown up to five thousand, or rather (as we have shown in our former answer), was increased by the accession of five thousand more, it is very probable that Paul's preaching with his assistants (for he had some or other ordinarily with him, Acts 15:40; Acts 16:3) so many days and months as made up three years, should within that space bring in near (if not more than) three, or at least two thousand.

(2) If we compare his stay, and constant pains at Ephesus, with the whole course of his own ministry: For if in three years abode, and incessant preaching and warning night and day, and that with tears (Acts 20:31—the like expression we find not elsewhere), he converted not near two thousand souls (as our brethren think there is no ground to say), than by the rule of proportion, his harvest among the Gentiles in all the rest of his ministry and life, will be far short of what we conceive the Acts of the Apostles, and his own epistles do hold out, and divines have generally conceived of it.

(3) If we shall consider the happy success of Paul's ministry in the other particular places, as that he wrought upon a great part of a whole city at one sermon (Acts 13:42, 44), on a great multitude of Jews and Greeks at another (Acts 14:1), at another on some of one sort, and on a great multitude

of another, and of a third not a few (Acts 17:4), and the like we have [in] Acts 18:8—from which it will not be groundless to conceive that he might convert near two or three thousand in three years constant course of a settled ministry in Ephesus.

(4) If we consider what Ephesus was—

{1} An exceeding great city; the metropolis and greatest mart [*market*] town of all Asia, within Taurus, as we read in Strabo,[1] and which he said was every day increasing when he wrote that, which was about thirty years before Paul's being there. And therefore by that time grown much greater, in the very temple of Diana that was in it, having a quarter of a mile round about it for an asylum or sanctuary, which must needs make the compass of the whole city very great.

{2} As populous as great, by reason of the great and general concourse of people thither, partly because of Diana, whom all Asia and the world worshipped (Acts 19:27), and partly for traffic, it being by reason of the convenience of its situation, the greatest mart town (as was before said of Strabo), not only of Asia the less, but also of the half of Asia the greater.

{3} More superstitious and idolatrous than it was either great or populous, it being the place where by reason of idolatry, sorcery and other sins that usually accompanied them (as it is said of Pergamos, Revelation 2:13), Satan had his seat, Diana her temple, which they were so brutishly mad upon (Acts 19:1; 1 Corinthians 15:32).

All which put together add a great advantage to the success of the apostle's ministry there, it being better fishing in so wide a sea, and though by reason of the third particular, he might there find many adversaries, yet he makes account that made not his door there opened any whit narrower, or less, but rather more effectual, it being the end [*goal*] of Christ's coming to dissolve the work of the Devil (1 John 3:8), and so usually having proved his greater glory, there most to advance his scepter, where Satan has had his highest throne, and the mad profane Ephesus idolater and sorcerer not harder to be wrought upon, than the malicious Jewish Pharisee and justiciary, nor did it less redound to the glory of God to redeem the one from idolatry, than the other from ceremonies. So that if in Jerusalem in few days so many thousands were gained, there may be some ground (though our brethren think not), to say that in so many years there might at least near two thousand be converted in Ephesus.

And should we delight in drawing parallels, as our brethren did in their former reasons between Acts 2 and Acts 5, we might here do it between

---

1. Lib. 14. In the reign of Tiberius [A.D. 14–A.D. 37], as appears from the conclusion of his sixth book. And Casaubon conceives about twelve years before Tiberius's death. [Cf. *The Geography of Strabo*, trans. H. C. Hamilton and W. Falconer, 3 volumes (London: Bohn, 1854–1857), 3.14. See the end of the sixth book, where Hamilton dates Strabo's *Geography* to A.D. 18 (1.441). Cf. Isaac Casaubon, French humanist scholar (1559–1614), *Strabonis Rerum Geographicarum libri XVII* (1587; Paris: 1620).]

what is said of Jerusalem and Ephesus. It is said of Jerusalem that the Word was preached there daily in the temple, and from house to house (Acts 5:42). So at Ephesus Paul taught publicly and from house to house (Acts 20:20). The apostles at Jerusalem spoke the Word with boldness (Acts 4:31). So it is said Paul did at Ephesus (Acts 19:8), and Apollos (Acts 18:26). At Jerusalem, many wonders and signs were done by the apostles (Acts 2:43 and Acts 5:12), in so much that even the shadow of Peter seemed to have cured the sick (Acts 5:15). At Ephesus God wrought special miracles, δυνάμεις οὐ τυχούσας, no ordinary ones, by the hand of Paul (Acts 19:11–12), so that from his body were brought handkerchiefs and aprons, which did great miracles, and as some think, greater than Peter's shadow did. And if upon the one, great multitudes were brought in, as it is said there were (Acts 5:14), why then not upon the other?

And as these wonders struck fear upon the church of Jerusalem, and upon them that heard of them (Acts 5:11), so also at Ephesus (Acts 19:17).

The extraordinary effect of the Word at Jerusalem was expressed by extraordinary acts of believers, as in selling their goods, etc. (Acts 2:45, Acts 5:34). So at Ephesus in confessing their deeds, and openly burning their books (Acts 19:18, 19).

In the church of Jerusalem it is said the Word of God increased (Acts 6:7) and grew (Acts 12:24); so at Ephesus (Acts 19:20).

So that if Jerusalem and Ephesus in all these particulars were parallel, and if in bigness equal, why should we judge that in the number of converts they should be so unproportionable, that when in the Scripture we read that in one of them there were in two days brought home at least five thousand, our brethren should think that there is no ground to say that in three years time of Paul's constant incessant preaching and weeping, there were near three or two thousand converted in the other?

(5) If lastly we take notice of the fair way and great advance that was made for the happier progress of Paul's settled ministry in Ephesus, by the foregoing labors of Aquila and Apollos, both able and faithful, and the latter set out to be very powerful and diligent, and earnest in the work, and this for some longer time, to the bringing in of disciples of note with foreign churches (Acts 18:19 *ad finem*), who whether they were but about the *unto the end* of number of twelve (as our brethren afterward say), we shall consider when the chapter we come to that place, and hope we shall make it appear to be otherwise. Meanwhile, comparing this fifth particular with all the former, and taking in those first fruits of Ephesus before Paul's settled ministry there, with the rich and plentiful harvest of his three years after-labors, we conceive (under favor) contrary to what our brethren peremptorily assert, that there were near two or three thousand believers in the church of Ephesus.

[Secondly] But they supposing there were no more, add that "so many as two or three thousand might all meet in one place."

We *answer:* But if there were more (as from what has been said may be gathered), than we have more cause to say they might not; no not though they were but two or three thousand.

Partly in regard of Ephesus, it being an heathenish city, mad upon their idol Diana, and her worship, and therefore not likely either to assign, or allow them a public meeting place for the ordinary and constant exercise of a contrary religion.

And partly in regard of some special duties of church communion, particularly of receiving the sacrament, especially if sitting at a table (as the manner then seems to have been), which no room in a private house would have been large enough for. And if it be said, that they met in the school of Tyrannus (Acts 19:9), which was a more public place, and might be capacious enough for such a number, in such a service, we *answer:* We cannot say how large it was, nor can they prove that it was so large. But this we can say, that we read not of the disciples receiving the sacrament, but only of Paul's disputing there; that school being of that use then and there to Paul, which the temple at Jerusalem was before to the other apostles, *viz.* not the place of their select church meeting for such ordinances, of which the disciples were only partakers, but where (having indeed separated from the Jews, and left their synagogue) he disputed or reasoned (διαλεγόμενος) with others as well as Christians (Acts 19:9–10).

2. Their second reason of denying the consequence, is because "this efficacy of the Word preached by Paul, has reference not only to Ephesus, but also to all Asia," as they gather from the words of Demetrius (Acts 19:26) and when Paul (Acts 20:31) said for the space of three years, he ceased not to warn every one both day and night with tears. "The words are not to be restrained to his being at Ephesus, but to be understood of his being in Asia, as appears by verse 18, 'Ye know from the first day that I came into Asia,' etc."

(1) We readily grant that the efficacy of Paul's ministry was not confined to Ephesus, but reached to all Asia, which we take up, not upon Demetrius's truth (Acts 19:26), but from the Holy Ghost's own words (Acts 19:10), Ephesus being the place of greatest resort from all quarters, both for traffic and the worship of Diana. And so the filling of Asia with converts, was not so much by Paul's going abroad out of Ephesus, as by those multitudes flocking thither, and hearing him at Ephesus; whence we may infer two things to our purpose from this instance of Ephesus, as we did in our answers to their former reasons, from that of Jerusalem:

{1} That many coming from all quarters, and being converted by hearing Paul in Ephesus, it is very likely that diverse of them might change their habitations, and come and sit down at Ephesus by the apostle's constant ministry there, and so add to the increase of that church.

{2} That if his doctrine filled all Asia, then much more proportionately it filled Ephesus, where it was constantly by the apostle himself preached, and from whence it spread into other parts abroad.

(2) Whereas they say this efficacy of the Word, has reference not only to Ephesus, but also to all Asia, we *answer:* That this efficacy, namely that which we proved out of Acts 19:18–20, in those many converts confessing their deeds, and burning their books, so mightily grew the Word, etc., does so plainly and clearly relate to Ephesus where the thing was done, that it needs no other proof than the very looking on the text.

(3) For that speech of Demetrius (Acts 19:26) as we did not cite it, so need we not much to heed it. He would be sure out of his malice to take in, and snatch at all he could, *ad invidiam & odium exaggerandum,* and *to magnify* what though the efficacy of Paul's doctrine reached all Asia, as Demetrius *ill will and* speech (which they allege) asserts, does that hinder it to have a more spe- *hatred* cial efficacy in Ephesus, which our proof plainly manifests? they being two distinct things, and their allegation not crossing, but confirming ours? If the efficacy of Paul's ministry was so great in all Asia, as they truly affirm, then was it much greater in Ephesus as we inferred upon the grounds before mentioned.

(4) For that of Acts 20:31, by us alleged for Paul's three years abode and preaching at Ephesus, which they say must not be restrained to Ephesus, but intended to Asia, which they prove from verse 18 we say,

{1} That in Acts 19:8–10, there seems to be express mention of his abode at Ephesus for two years, and three months, which is a great part of the three years, nor is it unlikely but the business in that chapter further re- lated, might help well to make up the rest. Or should we take in (as some do) that passage of his through the upper coasts (Acts 19:1), before his first coming to Ephesus, within the compass of those three years, and grant also that while he remained at Ephesus he looked sometimes abroad (though that we read not of), yet no constant abode, nor any longer stay of his do we find anywhere else for that time, which should it fall short of some weeks, or two or three months of three years, yet *rotundatio numeri* are no stranger in Scripture accounts, and it is sufficient for the purpose which *rounded* we brought it for; namely to show that his so long abode at Ephesus, and *numbers* his constant instant preaching there with tears, might in all likelihood convert more than could for all acts of worship be but one congregation, to meet in one place.

{2} For that which is urged from verse 18, "from the first day that I came into Asia," etc., we say, true indeed the precise first day that he came into Asia, he might not come to Ephesus, as Acts 19:1, yet:

First, that phrase—ἀπὸ πρώτης ἡμέρας—from the first day, by an He- braism, may be very well taken in some latitude, and put for the beginning of his access into those parts, as if he had said, 'from my first coming into Asia, in a manner, I have been with you all the while.'

Secondly, this makes more for our purpose, that he tells the elders of Ephesus that he had been so constantly with them, that in a manner from the first day of his coming into Asia, he had not been absent from them, so that the more that our brethren stand to the precise first day of his coming into Asia, the more they gratify us, thereby allowing him the more time for his being at Ephesus, which we plead for.

Thirdly, but in case it be objected that this follows not, because our brethren here expressly affirm that the apostle's meaning is of Asia, and not only of Ephesus, and so his speech is directed to the elders of all Asia, and not of Ephesus only, we confess that in our answers to their former reasons, we said that some so thought, but did never think that our brethren would. Which because here they do, they will give us leave to remind them, that in their former answers they were of a contrary judgment, that they were the elders of the church of Ephesus only, and that which was included in the bounds of one only congregation. But if now they be the elders not only of Ephesus, but also of Asia, that he speaks to (verse 18 and in verse 17), we have them expressed, by πρεσβυτέρους τῆς ἐκκλησίας, elders of the church in the singular number, then upon this supposition we have here found an Asian National Church, and a further proof of the proposition we are upon, that very many particular congregations may be under one presbyterial government.

{See p. 64}
Lightfoot, 248
Minutes, 3.23
Gillespie, 52

[II. REGARDING THE PRICE OF BOOKS BURNED]

{See p. 176}
Gillespie, 18
Lightfoot, 151

But having thus far in their answers more fairly put three of our arguments together, in what follows, they otherwise than we intended, take the rest asunder, and here single out that out of Acts 19:18–20, and pitch only upon the price of the books: to which they answer,

'That according to Calvin's account, the 50,000 pieces of silver amount but to £9,000 French, which is about £670 sterling at 18 pence the Franc, according to Beza, but to £8,700 French, and according to Brerewood (who estimates every ἀργύριον [ἀργυρίον] at 7.d.ob.) but to £1,406 which some one man's study now of common books, and not manuscripts (as they were) is worth, and therefore then, when there was no printing, a few men's books, yea, a few books of so curious and gainful arts, might well be worth that money, and then how does this argue such a multitude of believers as could not meet in one congregation?'

To which we reply, and complain herein of a double wrong, that not only this whole proof from Acts 19:18–20, that it may be the more easily broken is plucked as a single arrow out of the sheaf, whereas as we had bound it up with the rest it had more strength, but also that whereas there were four things in it argumentative to our purpose, all which we looked at, our brethren pitch only upon this third of them, which we least of all regarded.

1. The first was, that many of several sorts of persons are there expressed,

"many that believed came, and confessed" (verse 18) and again, "many of them that used curious arts, brought their books" etc. (verse 19), which words seem to distribute the believers there into three ranks. (1) Such as had used curious arts, and there were ἱκανοι sufficient store of them. (2) Other believers that came and confessed their deeds, and there were πολ- λοί many more of them. And (3) They imply that there were other disciples that did believe, but did not then come, for it is said that πολλοί τῶν πεπιστευκότων, many of them that believed came, which argues there were other believers, that did not, which might be a greater number.

But all three sorts put together, might make a number so great as may be considerable to our present purpose.

2. The second thing we looked at in that place, was their bringing of their books and burning them before all men, which as Mr. Cartwright observes,[1] they durst not have done, had they not been, if not the major part, yet such a sufficient number, which might even in that populous city have carried out that action, which could not but by the opposite party be deeply distasted. In Queen Mary's time a small number of Protestants durst not have burnt their mass-books in Cheapside; it was when Luther's doctrine began generally to be received, that he burnt the Pope's Decretals in Wittenberg.

3. The third thing was the price of the books burnt, amounting to 50,000 pieces of silver, which because we found in the text, we set down in our proof, but did very little insist upon in our debate. And yet this only our brethren pitch upon in their answer, as hoping to overthrow our argument in wounding of it, in what they conceive to be the weakest part of it. But we have seen the strength of what they say against it. In our reply whereto, we shall not need to trouble the Honorable Houses, nor ourselves, either in calling our brethren to account for casting up £9,000 French to about £670 sterling, at 18 pence the franc, which if it be 2 shilling the franc (as some say), will amount to £900 sterling. Or again for casting up 5,000 pieces of 7.d.[ob.] the piece to about £1,406, which comes to £1,562 10 shilling. Or in examining Calvin's or Beza's or Brerewood's account,[2] though the last of the three in the same place cited acknowledges a *duplex Argenteum Hebræum* (Matthew 27:15), and that he acknowledges 2 shilling 6 pence *Græcum*, which he rates at 7.d.[ob.] and though he pitches upon the latter, as

a twofold silver coin of the Hebrews

---

1. [Thomas Cartwright, *The Second Replie of Thomas Cartwright: agaynst Maister Doctor Whitgiftes second answer, touching the Churche disciplineline* ([Heidelberg]: Imprinted [by Michael Schirat], [1575]), p. CCXXXVII, line 25. Item 34 on the books taken from Laud's library for use by the Assembly was "Cartwright agt Whitgift 4°". See the Appendix, "Westminster Abbey Library and other Theological Resources of the Assembly of Divines (1643–1645)," *Infra, p.* 384.]

2. [Calvin, Acts 19:20. Cf. *Commentaries*, vol. 19, On Acts, volume second, page 221. Beza, *Annotationes*, p. 354. Brerewood (or Bryerwood), *De ponderibus et pretiis veterum nummorum, eorumque cum recentioribus collatione liber unus*, page 5.]

meant in this place, yet we want [*lack*] a cogent argument to evince [*show*] it. For though the thing were done in Ephesus, where they would reckon it according to their coin; yet what hinders, but that while Luke relates it, he might express it according to the coin of his own country, as an English man writing of what was sold in the Low countries for so many ſtivers, or dollars, according to our English coin, may say it was sold for so many (proportionably) pence or shillings?

And if so here and the *Argentium Hebræum* be meant, and that were of the value before mentioned, these 50,000 silverings will amount to £6,250 ſterling, which would help well to furnish many of our ſtudies. And surely there are not now, when the world is so full of books, many particular men, who have in their greateſt overgrown libraries, books of that value, being all of the same art or faculty as these were, eſpecially of such a kind of ſtudy as this was, which indeed was curious, and it may be gainful as our brethren say; but such as either few ſtudied, and so they had few chapmen [*traders*] for their books, and so their price was less, or if many did as the text implies (the Εφεσια γραμματα[1] being then famous), then there was more ſtore of them, and so they were not such rarities as our manuscripts now are, which raises their price among us. But as we will not say, how much such ſtuff as they were, was well worth, as our brethren's words are, so can neither they nor we tell what was the rate of their written books then, that the books were not few (as our brethren seem to think they might be), the text implies, but that the men were many (which is the thing that we moſt ſtand upon) it plainly expresses, and this price of the books helps to prove both, unless our brethren can show that the books were great volumes, and that of many and several arguments and authors. For should they be but small books, there muſt be many of them that should arise to such a sum. They would be very many primers or grammars that would amount to £6,250, or till it be but to their £1,460, and should they not be many, but moſt what the same authors and arguments (as generally all ſtudents in a science, have the same principal and fundamental books of it), then many books would argue many owners, and so many books that should amount to such a sum, would prove very many praĉtitioners, whom if you consider either as learned, many of which are not called (1 Corinthians 1), or as deeply engaged in Satan's depths and myſteries,

---

1. [Ephesus "was one of the free cities, governing itself. Its trade in shrines and idols was very extensive, being spread though all known lands. There the margical arts were remrkably prevelant, and notwithstanding the numerous converts made by the early Christians the Ἐφέσια γράμματα, or little scrolls upon which magic sentences were written, formed an extensive trade up to the fourth century. These 'writings' were used for divination, as a protection against the 'evil eye,' and generally as charms against all evil. They were carried about the person, so that probably thousands of them were thrown into the flames by St. Paul's hearers when his glowing words convinced them of their superstition." William Blades, *The Enemies of the Book* (London: Trubner & Co., 1880), pp. 5–6. Revised and Enlarged by the Author (London: Elliot Stock, 1888), p. 6.]

and so less hope of their learning to know Jesus Chriſt, you muſt needs conclude, that if so many of them, then very many more of other sorts and ranks,
in that populous city were converted unto Chriſt, that might fill more than
one congregation. And this particular, however our brethren seem to under-   *Minutes, 3.22*
value, yet the Holy Ghoſt pleases to set a ſpecial mark on it, in his epiphone-   *Lightfoot, 248*
matical acclamation, which thereupon he makes (verse 20).

4. Which is the fourth branch of this proof that we insiſted on, "so mightily grew the Word of God and prevailed," which plainly shows, that the Holy
Ghoſt summed not up the value of those ungodly books only, to show the
dearness of them, but the multitude also of those that had burnt them. For
had He said only that the Word of God prevailed ἴσχυεν, it might have related to the great power it had to make those men willingly to put themselves to so great a loss, and so the fewer the men had been, their loss had
been the greater, and the Word had prevailed with them the more. But there
is added also the ηὔξανε, "the Word of God increased," which Calvin said,
relates to the number of the men that had done that thing, and which in
those two other, Acts 6:7 and Acts 12:24 (where alone this kind of ſpeech is
used), expresses the great increase of multitudes of believers, as we showed
in our answers to our brethren's former reasons.

[III. REGARDING THE CHURCH IN AQUILA'S HOUSE]

To our inſtance of a particular church in Aquila's house, our brethren   {See p. 176}
answer:

1. That [it] is not necessary to be meant "of a congregation, such as the
proposition intends, but of a family church, as moſt of our divines say."

(1) For the judgment of divines, though divers think as our brethren say;   *they had a do-*
yet many are of another mind. Bullinger and Erasmus on Romans 6:5 [*sic*   *meſtic Church,*
16:5] read it, "the congregation in their house."[1] Lyra so expounds it,[2] on   *i.e. they con-*
which place Gualther thus, *"Ecclesiam habuerunt domeſticam, i.e. domum*   *secrated their*
suam Ecclesiæ consecrarunt, ut in eâ haberentur sacri cœtus."[3] And Oecumenius,[4]   *own house as a*
though he alleges both interpretations, and so does Diodati, yet he sets this   *Church, so that*
in the firſt place, and for 1 Corinthians 16:19, the interlinear gloss has *"Con-*   *in it might be*
gregatione fratrum."[5] And though Beza would have it underſtood of a fam-   *held sacred*
ily, yet both he and Diodati note on this place, that in one and the same   *assemblies*
   in the congrega-
   tion of brethren

---

1. [Erasmus, *Novum Teſtamentum omne* (1519), p. 348. Bullinger, *In omnes apoſtolicas Epiſtolas* (Tiguri: C. Froschoverum, 1558), p. 118.]

2. [Nicholas de Lyra (1270–1340), *Biblia Latina*, 4 vols (Nuremberge: Anthonij Kobergers,
1497), vol. 4, CLXXVIII, verso.]

3. [Rudolf Gwalther, Reformed theologian, successor to Bullinger (1519–1586), *In Divi Pauli
Apoſtoli Epiſtolas Omnes* (Tiguri: In Officina Froschoviana, 1589), p. 84.]

4. [Oecumenius, Bishop of Tricca (fl. 600), *Oecumenii Commentaria in Hosce Novi Teſta-
menti Tractatus* (Paris: 1630), p. 408.] So Occumenius expounds this like saying of Nymphas.
Col. 4. 15. [Cf. *Commentaria … Pars Altera* (Paris: 1631), p. 146. Cf. *PG* 118.630, 119.54.]

5. [Lyra, *Bibliorum Sacrorum Glossa Ordinaria*, 6 vols. (Venice: 1603), 5.354.]

city there were more assemblies or congregations of the faithful than one.[1] Peter Martyr on Romans 16 and 1 Corinthians 16 said,[2] the words may suffer a double exposition, either of a congregation, or of their own family; but he said the former is more probable. And so does M. Mede,[3] "which I understand not to be spoken of their families, but of a congregation of the saints there, wont to assemble for the performance of divine duties τὴν συνερχομενην κατ᾽ οἶκον αὐτῶν ἐκκλησίαν."[4]

(2) For reasons which may persuade us to continue still in this our judgment, we have these.

{1} We find the same word before, so used in the same verse. The apostle in the beginning of it had said, "the Churches of Asia salute you," and after adds the church in Aquila and Priscilla's house, as one of that number, and of note, for forwardness and love to the saints, and if the story of Acts 18 be well considered, their opinion will be probable, who make it the first church that was in Ephesus.

{2} We find not elsewhere in Scripture, the name of a church given to a family. But on the contrary in that very chapter, where the apostle means the persons of anyone's family, he uses another phrase, as τήν οἶκιον (verse 15 [sic 5]), not ἐκκλησίαν; and (Romans 16:10, 11) τοὺς ἐκ τῶν and τοὺς σὺν αὐτοῖς (verse 14), and the like.

{3} The church in their house is distinguished from themselves, so that it must then be meant of their children or servants, or some strangers that lodged in their house, but these to be so saluted, and as a church, seems no way probable.

{4} This of having a church in their house is only spoken of three. Of Nymphas (Colossians 4:15), of Philemon (Philemon 1–2), and of Aquila and Priscilla (Romans 16:4–5; 1 Corinthians 16:19). But shall we think, that in those prolix catalogues of salutations, none had Christian families but these three that are thus remembered? No! We read besides, of them of

---

1. [Giovanni Diodati, Reformed divine (1576–1649), Cf. *Giovanni Diodati, I Commenti Alla Sacra Biblia Con Le Introduzioni E I Sommari* (Firenze: 1880), 2.1169. Beza, *Annotationes*, p. 454.]

2. [Peter Martyr Vermigli (1499–1562), *In Epistolam S. Pauli apostolic ad Romanos … commentarii* (Heidelberg: Andreae Cambieri, 1613), p. 613. *In … S. Pauli Priorem ad Corinth[ios] Epistolam commentarij* (Tigvri, 1572), p. 240 verso.]

3. [Joseph Mede (1586–1638), *Churches, that is, appropriate places for Christian worship both in and ever since the Apostles times: a discourse at first more briefly delivered in a colledge chappell and since enlarged* (London, 1638). Cf. *Works* (1648), separate pagination, 43–44; (1672), Book 2, p. 324.]

4. [Since this section is particularly heavy in citing the Greek, it should be noted that for books printed up into the eighteenth century, the typefaces created for Greek letters were based on the abbreviations and ligatures of Renaissance incunabula. The text here reads in the 1648 edition: τ̄ συνερχομϕύlω κατ᾽ οἶκον αὐτϖ̄ ἐκκλησοϡαν. Renaissance Greek with Ligatures font (RGreekL2) copyright © Vernon Eugene Kooy, Ph.D. The Greek throughout has been set to modern conventions, with any necessary corrections in square brackets [].]

the household of Aristobulus (Romans 16:10), and Narcissus (verse 11), and
of them that were with Asyncritus, Phlegon, Hermas, Patrobas, Hermes
(verse 14), and of the household of Onesiphorus (2 Timothy 4:19), and yet
no mention of churches in their houses, which expression therefore, must
not hold out a godly family, which was common to many, but some special thing peculiar to them, to whom it is applied. And what should this
be, but what we now plead for? Namely, a congregational church used to
meet in Aquila and Priscilla's house.

{5} Which agrees well with their qualifications, the man being a preacher,
and both Paul's helpers in Christ (Romans 16:3), and instructors of Apollos (Acts 18:16), in the fore-rank of believers, and therefore in their house
rather than another's might be the meeting of the disciples.

{6} The phrase κατ' οἶκον also is the same with that [in] Acts 2:46, which
speaks of a congregational meeting, and that word is in all the four places.

{7} This exposition also agrees with other places where we find church
meetings in private houses, because of the persecution of those times (Acts
12:12; 20:8; 19:9; 28:23), but we pass over this, and come to their second answer. It is,

2. 'Suppose it were a congregation, yet' "it does not appear that the church {See p. 176}
in Aquila's house was at Ephesus, but in Asia. We read that Aquila and
Priscilla traveled with Paul to Ephesus, and were left there; not that their
church was there, for themselves might travel, where their church traveled
not with them."

(1) We hope our brethren do not intend to deny Ephesus to be in Asia
(as their words seem to imply) when they say that it appears not that the
church in Aquila's house was at Ephesus, but in Asia; nay, if in Ephesus,
then in Asia, but if they mean in some other place of Asia, we say,

(2) It no where in Scripture appears that Aquila seated himself in any
other place of Asia, but in Ephesus; or that the church in his house was
anywhere in Asia, if not in Ephesus.

(3) We may not suppose that they and their church parted without great
cause. Now we read not of any such particular cause why they should part,
or that *de facto* they did. At Rome we find them together (Romans 16:4, 5),
and at Corinth, as it may seem from their acquaintance with the church of
Corinth, as appears from the salutation (1 Corinthians 16:19), which place
does more clearly prove that they were together at Ephesus also. For thence
it appears they were at that place, from whence the apostle wrote that epistle, which though the spurious postscript said was from Philippe, yet both
the Syriac and Arabic translators, Occumenius, and generally both Protestant and Popish writers agree,[1] that it was from Ephesus, and prove it from

---

1. Beza, Deodate, Thorndike, Cudworth, and Baronius, C. a Lapide. [Diodati, ibid., on
1 Corinthians 16:9, p. 1209. Beza, ibid., p. 513. Herbert Thorndike, English Caroline divine
(d.1672), "Of the Government of Churches; a Discourse Pointing at the Primitive Form," in

1 Corinthians 16:5, 8 with Acts 19:21, 22, and by diverse other arguments, there then both Aquila and his household, and the church in his house *in whose place* were, and Paul with them as sojourning with them, if we give credence to *I am a guest* the addition that we meet with in Ambrose, "*apud quos hospiter,*" and which Beza said he found in some ancient Latin copies.[1]

But our brethren as it seems, not much trusting to these two first allegations, pass on to that which they say is the answer—and what is that?

3. "Grant they were a church, and at Ephesus; yet the answer is, they *{See p. 177}* were strangers that were driven from Rome by Claudius (Acts 18:2 with Romans 16:3, 4), and therefore kept themselves a distinct church from the Ephesians, as the Dutch in England, who choose rather to join with their own country people, whose dwellings are more remote, than with those of another nation nearer to them. And if the difference of their language may argue different congregations, and that they could not join in one (as is alleged) it will argue as strongly, that this church and the other congregation at Ephesus could not be under one presbyterial government, and ordinary officers had not ordinarily the gift of several tongues (1 Corinthians 12:8, 9, 'to one is given'" etc.).

But the answer perhaps may prove none:

For (1) Not to insist on that (which yet we cannot but take notice of) *viz.* that by what they here say they make account that Aquila and Priscilla, and the church in their house, being first at Rome (Romans 16:4–5), and expelled thence by the edict of Claudius, came to Ephesus, and were then that church mentioned (1 Corinthians 16:19), which is a foul mistake in chronology, that first epistle to the Corinthians, though set after in our Bibles, being written before that to the Romans, and so that church of theirs then at Ephesus, when mentioned in 1 Corinthians 16, was before that being of it at Rome, mentioned in Romans 16.

(2) There is no likelihood that Aquila and Priscilla, though strangers, would yet estrange and withdraw themselves to a peculiar church dissevered from the presbytery by the apostles there settled. Their Christian

---

The Theological Works, Volume 1, Part 1 (Oxford: John Henry Parker, 1844), p. 13. Ralph Cudworth, English divine and philosopher (1617–1688). See Cudworth's comment on this (where he also cites Baronius), and on other postscripts to Paul's Epistles naming the place of writing, in his supplement to Perkin's commentary on Galatians. *A Commentarie or Exposition, upon the Five First Chapters of the Epistle to the Galatians .... Now published for the benefit of the Church, and continued with a supplement upon the sixth chapter, by Rafe Cudworth* (Cambridge: John Legat, 1604), p. 655. Cardinal Caesar Baronius, ecclesiastical annalist (1538–1607), *Annales ecclesiastici*, volume 1 (1614; Paris: 1666), p. 43. Cornelius à Lapide, Roman Catholic commentator (1567–1637). This is addressed at the close of the opening argument. *Commentaria in omnes Divi Pauli Epistolas* (Antwerp: Nutii and Meursium, 1617), p. 205. Cf. *Commentarii in Sacram Scripturam*, 10 vols. (Melitæ: 1843–1851), vol. 9; *The Great Commentary of Cornelius à Lapide*, vol. 7, 1 Corinthians, trans. W. F. Cobb (Edinburgh: John Grant, 1908), page 4.]

1. [Cf., Ambrosiaster, *Commentaries on Romans and 1-2 Corinthians,* translated and edited by Gerald L. Bray (Downers Grove: InterVarsity Press, 2009), p. 205.]

wisdom, charity, and zeal for the promoting of God's glory, and their own and other's good, would not suffer them to withdraw themselves from that communion of saints, and rob themselves of such a blessed advantage and opportunity, especially the partition wall between Jew and Gentile being known now to be broken down, which the apostle speaks so fully to in his epistle to these Ephesians. And therefore for some reasons, they might be a distinct congregation, which our argument asserts; yet for these reasons they would not be such a distinct church, as to sever themselves from so useful an association in joint government.

(3) There was not the like reason for their severing themselves from the church in Ephesus, as is and has been for the French or Dutch churches, keeping themselves distinct from the English, namely, difference of church government, which was the special cause of their earnest renitence, when the bishops' strong hand would have violently bowed them to it.

(4) The difference of language we showed might be an argument for several congregations in the instance of the church at Jerusalem, because the Jews' language was not in such common use, and yet not so even there, but that they might well be under one presbyterial government, as appears from our answer to our brethren's first reasons, where this part of their argument is answered, to which we refer. But it was not alleged by us here in this instance of the church of Ephesus, the Greek tongue being then of more common use, and the Jews that lived among the Gentiles understanding their language, as our brethren themselves tell us in their next and last answer, which is this:

[IV. REGARDING THE MENTION OF JEWS AND GREEKS]

"As for Jews and Greeks being mentioned, it makes nothing to the number, {See p. 177} nor yet that for difference of language there must needs be more congregations than one. For the Jews that lived among the Gentiles, understood their language, else they would make so many independent congregations."

1. As to that first clause, wherein they say, the mentioning of Jews and Greeks makes nothing to the number, we say, yes sure[ly], we doubt not but our brethren will grant us it makes something if they consider:

(1) That in both the verses cited (Acts 19:10, 17) there is an "all" mentioned—"all" Jews and Greeks—and we hope that "all" is something to the number.

(2) That there is an addition of one "all" to the other, of Greeks to Jews πᾶσιν Ἰουδαίοις τε καὶ Ἕλλησι, the bare adding of Greeks to Jews speaks an addition of number, and when the Holy Ghost joins them with a τε καὶ, He tells us He would have us take notice of it, that He intends an addition of an "all" of the one, to an "all" of the other (which was very great in so large and populous a city). Such a great increase, as (at least joined with other proofs) may make something for our purpose, even to make up

more than one single congregation. Paul for certain intended to express some enlargement of the number of them to whom he was a debtor, when he said he was debtor Ελλησι τε καὶ βαράροις, σοφοῖς τε καὶ ἀνοήτοις, in the same phrase (Romans 1:14) and of that "all" of believers, when he said the gospel was the power of God to salvation, παντὶ τῷ πιστεύοντι Ἰουδαίῳ τε καὶ Ελληνι, in the same word (verse 16) it would be taken to make much for the increase of the number, if when we had said all English men should take the covenant,[1] we should add, all Englishmen and Scotsmen also, and this was all that we meant, by producing the mention of all both Jews and Greeks.

2. For as for that which in the second clause our brethren add, as though we here meant, "that for difference of the language of Jews and Greeks there must needs be more congregations than one," we again say, it was alleged by us to that purpose before, in the instance of the church of Jerusalem, but not in this of the church of Ephesus for the reason aforesaid, and therefore this part of their answer, is to a supposition of their own, but to no argument of ours now in hand.

3. And therefore that reason which they add, "For the Jews that lived among the Gentiles understood their language," confutes nothing that we said, but serves to answer to what they themselves objected a little before in their third answer, and to clear this truth, that though Aquila and Priscilla were strangers, and of a different language, and so might be in a distinct congregation, yet this difference of their language from that of Ephesus, seeing they understood it, could be no hindrance, but that they with the rest of the Ephesian believers, might well be under one and the same presbyterial government.

4. Though for that which they add in the close, that "unless they understood their language, they would have made so many independent congregations," we might justly deny the consequence. For though upon that ground of different language they might well make several distinct congregations, yet it follows not that therefore they should be independent ones, but not withstanding it might be under one common ecclesiastical government, as suppose the Welsh should not generally understand our English, yet thy might be (as they are) under the same civil government with us. All of Aquila and Priscilla's church might not understand the Ephesian language, and so it might be necessary they should be preached to in a distinct congregation, by such of their own whose language all might understand, whereas so many only as might join with the rest of the common presbytery in point of common government, had need to have understood the Ephesian language. Nay two men may be fit to join in a common government, though they do neither of them understand one another's native speech, if they did both understand a third language.

---

1. [A reference to the Solemn League & Covenant.]

[Answer to the Independents' Reasons that the multitude of
believers were not more than could meet in one place]

Our brethren having thus endeavored to answer our argument from this {See p. 177}
instance of the church of Ephesus, for the proposition that there were more
believers there, than did make one congregation, in the next place, they
bring their arguments against it.

The first whereof is this: They say it "is apparent that the number of believers there, when Paul came first to Ephesus, was but about twelve (Acts
19:7, 'And all the men were about twelve.')"

1. It is an apparent mistake of our brethren to say that it was Paul's first
coming to Ephesus, when he met with those twelve men mentioned in Acts
19:7. If they had but minded the foregoing chapter (Acts 18:19–21) they might
have found him there, and departed thence, before this his after coming
and return thither, mentioned in this nineteenth chapter.

2. It is apparent that all men there particularly spoken of, were but about
twelve, but it is nothing less than apparent that there were then no more
disciples at Ephesus, but the contrary rather is apparent.

(1) From what we read (verse 1) that Paul found there τινας μαθητάς,
not τοὺς μαθητάς, disciples indefinitely, or the disciples that were there,
as we have that phrase (Acts 21:4), but τινας μαθητάς, certain disciples by
way of distinction from the rest (for τινὲς and πάντες are not *termini con-* *interchangeable*
vertibiles), as either being the first that upon his coming thither he met with, *terms*
or that afterward he had this special intercourse with, the story whereof is
there related, some certain special disciples that were of that judgment and
way, which would argue rather that there were some of another, at least does
not argue there were not any besides, no more than if it should be said that
one in Queen Mary's days coming to Frankford found τινὰς, some that Minutes,
stood for the book of Common Prayer, it would be thence concluded that 3.545
all there were of that judgment.[1]

(2) From that great space of time, which came between Paul's first being at Ephesus (chapter 18), and this finding of those twelve at this second
coming in the nineteenth chapter, and the means of conversion and salvation which they enjoyed in that interim. In that time Paul goes from

------

1. [A reference to the controversy in the English exile church at Frankfurt at the time
John Knox was a pastor, during the reign of Queen Mary. While no work was cited, item 31
of the list of books taken from Laud's library for the use of the Assembly was "Troubles of
Frankfort about the English Liturgy 8," which is William Whittingham, *A brief discours off the
troubles begonne at Franckford in Germany A. Domini 1554. Aboute the book off common prayer
and ceremonie.* Cf. *A Brief Discourse of The Troubles Begun at Frankfort in the year 1554* (London:
1846), and in Knox's *Works* edited by Laing, volume 4. See the Appendix: "Westminster Abbey
Library and other Theological Resources of the Assembly of Divines (1643–1645)," p. 384.]

Ephesus to Cesarea, and so from one place to another in order, strengthening the disciples (Acts 18:22, 23), and after through the upper coasts (Acts 19:1), which journeys and his stays in some of the places mentioned, would take up some longer time. And in that time, Aquila and Priscilla were at Ephesus,[1] and there not idle, as appears from what they did to Apollos, who also came thither in that time, that eloquent man, and mighty in the Scriptures, who being instructed in the way of the Lord, and being fervent in the Spirit, taught diligently the things of the Lord, and this, as may seem, to the disciples in their church meetings (verse 25)—it being added after as a distinct thing (verse 26) that "he began to speak boldly in the synagogue." Now what a poor harvest would it have been only to have gleaned up about twelve new ignorant disciples by the pains of such faithful and earnest laborers so long continued, in those growing times, wherein the Word had another kind of success than now it has usually. And yet even in our days, meaner men and women than Apollo[s], Aquila, and Priscilla, if they bestir themselves as they did, in a less time can tell how to gain more than above twelve followers.

(3) Answerably in the third place, this appears from the success that Aquila's and Apollos' labors had in that interim. For [in] Acts 18:27 we read that there were brethren so considerable, that when Apollos was disposed to go to Achaia, they were able to commend him to the disciples there, exhorting them to receive him (Acts 18:27), with authority: so few and ignorant disciples, were not likely to rise up with the Corinthians in Achaia, who were so enriched with all utterance and knowledge (1 Corinthians 1:5).

(4) These twelve were raw and ignorant (Acts 19:2), and only instructed in John's baptism (verse 3), as Apollos was when he first came to Ephesus (Acts 18:25). But Aquila and Priscilla better instructed him (verse 26), and so certainly would they have done these twelve also, if they had been of their congregation. So that they could not be all the disciples that were there; there was Aquila and his church besides, of which some conceive those brethren (Acts 18:27) were. But Calvin is confident they were not these twelve.[2]

(5) He also conceives they might be special men, and such as Beza conceives were made officers there,[3] which way that passage (Acts 19:6) of Paul's imposing of hands on them, and their thereupon speaking with tongues and prophesying, seems something to propend [*propound*]. Now if so, it will be no sound reasoning of our brethren, that because there were about twelve whom the apostle ordained for officers, that therefore there should be no more disciples.

3. But grant there had been but about twelve then, yet because then a handful of corn on the top of the mountain was so mightily to increase, as

---

1. Acts 18:18–19.
2. [Calvin, Commentary on Acts 19:2, Commentaries, vol. 19, p. 207.]
3. [Beza, *Annotationes*, p. 353.]

after to shake like Lebanon (Psalm 72:16), there might soon be more, than to make up one only congregation, before John's writing his Revelation, which was so many years after, and yet then Ephesus but one church (Revelation 2:1)—nay, in Paul's time, after his own three years ministry there, as was before shown, together with the assistance of divers others, his fellow-labors there in this work (which was the assembly's second proof, but our brethren touch it not): as Luke, who was with Paul in all these his travels (Acts 16:16–17 compared with Acts 20:5–6); Sosthenes for he is joined with him in the front of the first epistle to the Corinthians (1 Corinthians 1:1), which was written from Ephesus, as we showed before; Aquila (Acts 18:19 and 1 Corinthians 16:19); Timotheus and Erastus, whom he sent not from Ephesus till towards his own departure thence (Acts 19:22); to whom he might add Gaius and Aristarcus (Acts 19:29 and 20:4), if they were preachers, as is probable they were: all which must have more than one congregation to be employed in.

"And when the number was increased, yet then the church of Ephesus is called one flock, in relation to those elders which were at Ephesus (Acts 20:28), which were willed by Paul to feed that flock by doctrine as he had done, by which it is evident they might and did meet in one, for elders are pastors only to one congregation." {See p. 177}

Minutes, 3.23

Lightfoot, 248

Gillespie, 52

1. It was but even now that these both elders and flock were made by our brethren to be of all Asia, and not only of Ephesus, when it would help them to deny the consequence of our argument, but here to make out their own argument, they must not be of all Asia (for then we should hope there would be more congregations than one), but must be confined to Ephesus only; so they were in their former reasons, but extended to all Asia in the former part of this answer, and now in the third place contracted again to Ephesus. This, if an inadvertency, may easily be pardoned, but such a liberty to contract and extend at pleasure for present advantage (if we may call it an advantage) must not be granted.

2. There is no sufficient reason why our brethren should restrain that feeding, which the apostle there gives, in charge to feeding by doctrine only, which yet they do, when they say, that "they were willed by Paul, to feed that flock, by doctrine as he had done." For (1) It is well known, that as in Homer's, so in Scripture language, ποιμνεῖ and ποιμαίνειν holds forth feeding by ruling, as well as teaching (Matthew 2:6).[1] (2) Paul fed them by ruling as well as teaching, and so must they, if they must do as he had done. (3) Some expressions both in Acts 20 and Revelation 2 concern government as well as doctrine, and if our brethren cannot deny but both

---

1. [Homer repeatedly uses the phrase "shepherds of the people" for kings and military leaders. Socrates explained: "Isn't it because a shepherd must see to it that his sheep are safe and have food…." Cf. Timothy Laniak, *Shepherds After My Own Heart: Pastoral Traditions and Leadership in the Bible* (Downers Grove, IL, InterVarsity Press, 2006), pp. 72, 73.]

belonged to those elders, which the apostle there spoke to, what reason is there that when he exhorted them to their duty, he should be thought to exhort them to one part of it, and say nothing to the other, especially when the word and expression he uses, do in their true signification reach both?

3. But the true reason why our brethren do here single out teaching, and leave out ruling, is because that would best fit their present argument, which in brief is this: At Ephesus it is evident there was then but one congregation, because but one flock (Acts 20:28), and that in reference to feeding elders or pastors, and pastors are only of one congregation, to which we reply and say that:

(1) Our brethren here, and elsewhere in this paper, use too confident expressions. Here, "it is evident;" a little before, "it is apparent;" and a little after, "no reason can be given;" and again, "plainly point at," etc., which we humbly convince [*assure*], is not so, nor so. And if this they here say, that all believers in Ephesus, "might and did meet in one," be not made more evident than that (as they before said), it was "apparent" that there were but about twelve believers when Paul came first to Ephesus (Acts 19:7), in which they hold out that to be his first coming, we hope we shall not be convicted by such evidences.

change of number

(2) Should we say, that by an *enalage numeri* flock is put for flocks, as there is nothing in that place (we conceive) that crosses it, so many instances thereof in other Scriptures may justify it.

collectively

(3) But take it (as it is) in the singular number, flock, yet why may it not be taken *collectivè* for such a flock, as contained in it diverse particular flocks, as we read expressly, Genesis 33:13, Jacob said of his, "The flocks are with me, and if men should over-drive them one day, all the flock would die." Here is a full parallel to Luke's παντὶ τῷ ποιμνίῳ [Acts 20:28], ἀ πᾶν ποίμνιον,[1] all the flock in the singular, is said to have several particular flocks, as parts of it. And so Christ's little flock, and one fold, μικρὸν ποίμνιον (Luke 12:32), and that μία ποίμνη (John 10:16), though both in the singular number, and so expressing one flock and fold in general, namely the church catholic; yet comprehends many particular flocks and churches contained in it, and under it, as we have in our former answers shown, there were many particular congregations in Jerusalem, and yet it [is] but one church, and governed by one common presbytery.

(4) Whereas upon occasion of the word "feed," the word "pastor" is urged, "elders being pastors to one only congregation," we *answer:* That the word "pastor" is not in the text, but only the word "feed," and that we have already

---

[1. The divines are making the specific instance of Acts 20:28 (παντὶ τῷ ποιμνίῳ) into a general statement, by switching it from its dative neuter singular form to its standard nominative neuter singular form. But the ἀ should be τὸ, a possible miss-reading of the scribe's hand by the typesetter. The old abbreviation for το is Ｔ and τὸ, is ϛ or δ. My thanks go to Samuel Renihan and Matthew Winzer for assistance regarding the Greek text.]

shown, reaches to governing as well as teaching, and therefore that although use has obtained, that the word "pastor" is commonly taken for the minister of one congregation (the bishop having injuriously appropriated that title to himself, and to his single inspection over many congregations), yet according to that signification of the word (as it relates to government), there is no inconveniency, that many elders associated for government, may be *eatenùs*, called "pastors" of the many congregations that are under *in such an* their joint inspection. *extent*

But whereas it was said in the assembly, that the feeding of the flock (especially as it related to teaching), was to be understood *partitivè, viz.* some one congregation, some another, and so among them the flock was fed—our brethren object,

That "if it be understood *partitivè* with reference to their feeding, it *{See p. 177}* must be also with reference to their overseeing, because it is so expressed *Minutes, 3.23* in the text, 'Take heed to yourselves, and to the whole flock, over which the *Gillespie,* Holy Ghost has made you overseers to feed the flock of God.' For no rea- *50–52* son can be given why these words, 'feed the flock;' should be understood *Lightfoot, 158* *partitivè*, and not these other words, 'Take heed to the flock, over which the Holy Ghost has made you overseers;' and if their overseeing and ruling be to be understood *partitivè*, then how does this place argue a presbyterial government over many congregations? And if it be said the many congregations were not fixed; then that distinction of "feeding" *partitivè* falls to the ground."

1. We do not say that those many congregations were not fixed, but rather hold that they were, as not conceiving how Paul's long residence there should not form them into such a more orderly settlement, that so they might feed their several flocks *partitivè*, as in the assembly was said they did.

2. Whereas our brethren do here seem to make these two words, ἐπισκόπους and ποιμαίνειν, to signify the two distinct parts of a pastor's duty; the first his ruling, and the latter by feeding and teaching; it is to be conceived rather, that all these three words in the text, ἐπισκόπους, προσέχηειν and ποιμαίνειν, have all of them reference both to their ruling and teaching. For in both, they ought ἐπισκοπεῖν, προσέχηειν and ποιμαίνειν, to oversee, take heed, and feed.

3. Suppose then, that ποιμαίνειν or feeding, does contain the exercise of all their duty, as they are ἐπίσκοποι, or overseers; yet it is not necessary that the feeding in the several branches or offices of it, should in the same manner be executed. As suppose (for example) the king should charge the justices of the peace in a whole country, being convened, that they carefully govern and do justice, to the people committed to their charge; their power and office being such, as it is known to be, must needs be conceived, that for that part of it, in taking examinations, binding over to the sessions, and the like, he means they should do it *divisim*, within their several precincts. *separately*

But for that other part of executing of justice on persons so bound over, in-
jointly dicted and arraigned, they should do it *conjunctim, in concessu* [*sic consessu*],
in assembly at the sessions or assizes, and so the like here.

4. But suppose (according to our brethren's sense) this over-sight and feeding, should express the two distinct parts of their office, the one their ruling, the other their teaching; yet such manner of joining them together as we find in the text, does not imply that they should both be exercised [in] the same manner and way, it being usual in Scripture to speak of things put together indifferently and alike, which yet are to be considered differently according to their diverse capacities. And so though these two be thus joined together, yet the one may be *divisim*, and the other *conjunctim*. As suppose in a like manner of speech, it should be said to the ministers of one congregation, being many, "Take heed to the flock, over which God hath made you overseers, that you preach the Word to them;" and take the word "overseers," as our brethren do, for their ruling power, that (they will say) must be exercised *conjunctim*, and yet this preaching they will not deny, but must be done *divisim* and *partitivè*.

5. Whence it appears, that in case overseeing be taken for ruling, and feeding for teaching, this may be a sufficient reason why these words "feed the flock" should be understood *partitivè*, and not that other word "oversee-ing;" the one being (as by us both is granted) to be performed *conjunctim*, and the other *divisim*, though our brethren too confidently say no reason can be given of it, which yet it seems they afterward suspected might. And therefore in the latter end of their paper, they suggest this very reason to themselves, to which they there frame this answer, which we do here insert as coming in most fitly in this place. Their answer is this:

That although elders of a congregation, though "they do it *in collegio*,"
{See p. 178} "and when they teach they do it severally," yet "both ruling and teaching are to be within the same compass, in respect of them who are to be ruled and taught," etc. "For when elders rule one congregation *in collegio*, yet each of those elders oversees and rules the whole flock, as truly as he can be said by teaching to feed that whole flock."

And so they make account it will make nothing for a presbyterial joint ruling of them in a classis, whom they do not teach in a congregation. To which our answer is, that to this we have already answered in our answer to their former reasons, now with the Honorable Houses, in which we deal
{See p. 104} with that commensuration of ruling and teaching, which they there pleaded
waste time for; to which (that we may not *actum agere*) we refer them, and therefore
repeating say nothing more here to that paragraph, and only add to this in hand.

6. That whereas towards the close of it, they ask, "How does this place (of the Acts) argue a presbyterial government over many congregations, if this overseeing and ruling be to be understood *partitivè*?" We answer, that presbyterial government stands as well with *partitivè* governing, as *partitivè*

                    II: ANSWER OF THE ASSEMBLY TO THE REASONS

teaching, though not confined to it. For it grants the elders a particular interest in their several congregations, by virtue of which they there govern *partitivè, viz.* as to the elders of other congregations who have not there that particular interest and power, though that hinders not but that they may govern both them and the other congregation *conjunctim* with those other elders in an association, which is our presbyterial government.

That of their paper which remains, is their answer to what was said in the assembly, *viz.* that that feeding (Acts 20:28) might be understood *partitivè*, because the same phrase used (1 Peter 5:2, "Feed the flock of God among you, taking the oversight thereof") must be understood *partitivè*, because those elders and believers to whom the apostle Peter wrote, were scattered through[out] Pontus, Galatia, Cappadocia, Asia and Bythinia, which could not all meet in one congregation, to which they give this answer,

"1. That in this place of Peter there are no such words, whereby the rela- {See p. 178} tion of the whole flock is equally carried to all those elders, as there are in that speech of the apostle to the elders of Ephesus (Acts 20:28). 'Take heed to the whole flock over which' (whole flock) 'the Holy Ghost hath made you overseers.'"

"2. In this 1 Peter 5:1, 2, there are words which plainly point at such a distribution, namely ἐν ὑμῖν, among you, applied both to the elders and the flock. The elders ἐν ὑμῖν, 'among you, I exhort, feed the flock,' ἐν ὑμῖν, that is, 'each elder feed the flock respectively, whereever they are among you in each country.'

"Therefore though it be understood *partitivè* in Peter, yet it follows not it should be so understood [in] Acts 20:28."

To which first in general we answer.

1. That when it was said in the assembly that that feeding the flock (Acts 20:28) might be understood *partitivè*, it was said in reference to their feeding by teaching, and specially their ordinary fixed teaching in those several fixed congregations, and so it was *partitivè*. But by so saying we never meant that it was simply and only *partitivè*, as feeding contained all their office and duty in ruling as well as teaching, for so it might be, and was *conjunctim*, as of the elders of a congregation in their consistory, so of associated elders in a classical presbytery. We dare not go in this sense against the *conjunctim* in the Acts, nor the *partitivè* in Peter, which we averred, and therefore our brethren need not have taken so much pains to prove. But we are for both in both places, that as in both places they did feed by teaching severally, in their several congregations, so they fed by ruling jointly in their united respective associations, so far as that διασπορὰ in Peter would admit. So that these two places, which our brethren set at such an odds, may for all this very well agree.

2. And especially if we look into the expressions of both places, they seem to look very like parallels, and so interpreters make them, ἔθετο ἐπισκόπους

ποιμάινειν in Acts to ποιμάνετε [ποιμάνατε] ἐπισκοποῦντες in Peter, and there a ποίμνιον in both places to be overseen and fed, and for God's church in the one place, there is God's heritage in the other, though we must not dissemble, that the word is τῶν κλήρων [1 Peter 5:3], in the plural number, which some expound of particular congregations, which has a show of a better proof for the understanding of this of Peter *partitivè* (which as even now we said, we deny not, but allege it for), than our brethren's criticism of ἐν ὑμῖν, as we shall see when we come to it by and by. However, the places are so parallel, that from a "must be" in the one, we may rationally infer at least a "may be" in the other. But our brethren say no, in regard of the difference which they observe between those two places.

1. For first, they say that in "the place of Peter, there are no such words, whereby the relations of the whole flock is equally carried to all those elders, as there are in the place of Acts. 'Take heed to the whole flock, over which (whole flock) the Holy Ghost hath made you overseers.'"

We *answer*: (1) Whatever the sense is, or the thing was, yet consider whether the words in the place of the Acts, which our brethren insist upon, do necessarily hold forth the relation of the whole flock, and that equally carried to all these elders as our brethren affirm. For the word is not ὅλῳ τῷ ποιμνίῳ, which answers to our brethren's translation of it, "the whole flock;" which, to lay more weight on it, they repeat the second time, and put in a parenthesis, the more to be taken notice of; but it is παντί τῷ ποιμνίῳ, and that word, παντὶ, we doubt not but they know, does not always necessarily infer a collective sense, that it must needs be read "all the flock" as our translators render it, or the "whole flock," as our brethren would. But that it is taken ofttimes distributively, as πᾶσαν νόσον καὶ πᾶσαν μαλακίαν (Matthew 4:23; 9:35) and πᾶσάν ἡμέραν (Acts 5:42; 1 Thessalonians 5:18), and so if it be read to every flock, over which the Holy Ghost has made you overseers, it is taken *partitivè*, and so all of them spoken together to feed their several flocks in their several divisions. And where is then that collective whole that our brethren make account must necessarily be hence inferred? Suppose this should have been the meaning of Paul, to have said, 'I charge you all that you take heed to every flock, which severally God has given you the oversight of;' we ask whether that very sense might not have been expressed in these very words προσέχετε παντὶ τῷ ποιμνίῳ ἐν ᾧ τὸ πνεῦμα ἅγ[ι]ον ὑμᾶς ἔθετο ἐπισκόπους.

Or if it be said, it should then have been παντὶ ποιμίνῳ, without the article τῷ, which makes it collective, and not distributive:

We say it is not so necessarily nor always, especially when this τῷ is answered by the relative ἐν τῷ following. The article is without this observation sometimes left out, when the sense is collective (as 1 Peter 1:24). Nay in one clause left out, and in another taken in, in the same sentence, and when spoken in the same sense πάσῃ τῇ μνείᾳ, καὶ πάσῃ δεήσει (Philippians 1:3–4).

For the equal carrying of the relation of the whole flock to all those elders which they mention, it is nothing for them nor against us. For we say that the elders in a classis have an equal relation to the whole flock in their association, as the elders in a consistory have to all the flock in their congregation. And besides such a speech as that in Acts to "feed the flock," may be made to such as in any measure or degree have an interest in the feeding of the flock, to wit, in their several capacities, yea though they should not be equal.

(2) Consider whether that be true which they say, that there is no such word in that place of Peter, whereby the relation of the whole flock is equally carried to all those elders which be spoken to. Here we say,

{1} If there be no word in Peter that expresses that παντὶ which was in the Acts, yet it is necessarily to be understood when he said ποιμαίνετε [ποιμαίνατε] τὸ ἐν ὑμῖν ποίμνιον, he means πᾶντὸ ἐν ὑμῖν ποίμνιον, feed the flock of God among you, *i.e.* all (or the whole) flock of God among you, unless he would give leave that some part of the flock should be left unfed. Nay therefore,

{2} These words τὸ ἐν ὑμῖν ποίμνιον do hold out and express the whole flock, for some of the flock, or part of the flock, is not in propriety of speech, but by a trope, the flock.

2. But they say positively that in "Peter there are words which plainly point out such a distributive, *viz.* that ἐν ὑμῖν applied both to elders and flock: and so he exhorts each elder to feed the flock respectively, where they are among them in each country."

(1) Then by their own interpretation, if it be understood *partitivè*, yet not *partitivè* of several congregations, and what then have they gained? But *partitivè* of each country, as they speak, and that will hold out classical, synodical, provincial or national partitions, and so we may rather gain something by that bargain.

(2) That pointing out such a distribution by that double ἐν ὑμῖν, is not so plain either to us, or in itself, as our brethren would make it.

{1} If we compare it with that place of the Acts in which they say there is no such thing, and therefore, not "plainly pointed out," and yet let indifferent readers judge whether τοὺς πρεσβυτέρους ἐν ὑμῖν in Peter do more plainly point out a distribution, then πρεσβυτέροις [πρεσβυτέρους] τῆς ἐκκλησίασσ (Acts 20:17), especially as our brethren interpret that for one congregational church. Or whether τὸ ποίμνιον ἐν ὑμῖν, "the flock of God amongst you," be more distributive, or rather not all one, as to this purpose, with τῷ ποιμνίῳ ἐν τῷ ὑμᾶς τὸ πνεῦμα τὸ ἅγιον ἔσθετο ἐπισκόπους, "over which the Holy Ghost made you overseers," and this rather,

{2} If we consider that phrase ἐν ὑμῖν singly by itself, in which we can find no ground of our brethren's criticism that it should so plainly point out such a distribution as they plead for, for it plainly points out what it plainly signifies, and that is, "in you" or "among you," and let all judge whether such an expression then, may not be used.

{1} Where there is no such distribution as our brethren mean, namely into several congregations; for it may be said of one individual congregation. As suppose in Yarmouth, where but one congregation, and there divers elders, a minister from some other parts may properly write, "I exhort the elders ἐν ὑμῖν to feed that flock of God, ἐν ὑμῖν."

{2} Whether there are such distributions, but as collectively knit together in a joint association and government, as in case one should have said to the Sanhedrim at Jerusalem, ποιμαίνετε τὸ ἐν ὑμῖν ποίμνιον, it had been most proper and sensible speech, for they did ποιμαίνειν τὸ ἐν αὐτοῖς ποίμνιον, all the several divisions in Jerusalem, yea of all Israel appealing to them. And yet it is well known they never governed *partitivè*, but *conjunctim*, as a highest national synod or assembly.

And thus far in answer to what our brethren have said against the first proposition of our argument, for many congregations under one presbyterial government, *viz.* that the multitude of believers there, did make more congregations than one. Our brethren add in the close of all:

"As for the second and third, that there were many elders over that peo{See p. 178} ple as one flock, and one church, and that they did govern this one flock, the former proposition not being proved, they make nothing to the proof of that conclusion, etc."

To which we say only two things.

1. That if the former proposition (of more believers at Ephesus than could meet in one congregation) had not been proved, yet this second of many more elders being there then could have been employed in one congregation, might of itself have made something to the proof of the conclusion of the congregations under one presbyterial government.

For those many elders might have argued several congregations, which they might have been divided into, for convenience of habitation, and for preventing of many and great inconveniences in that idolatrous and heathenish city, and those times of persecution, which might possibly, nay probably have come to pass, if they had all met in one place, though they had been no more than might have possibly met altogether in one congregation.

2. But what if that proposition has been proved, and our brethren's objections against it answered? as (we hope they are) then it so joined with the other two following propositions might make enough for the proof of the main conclusion, that many congregations may be under one presbyterial government.

Concordat cum Originali.

Adoniram Byfield, *Scriba.*

THE GRAND DEBATE

*ARGUMENTS OF THE DISSENTING BRETHREN
AGAINST THE SUBORDINATION OF STANDING SYNODS,
PROVINCIAL, NATIONAL, ECUMENICAL, AS JURIDICAL,
ECCLESIASTICAL COURTS*

*THE ANSWER OF THE ASSEMBLY OF DIVINES UNTO THE
REASONS OF THE DISSENTING BRETHREN AGAINST THE
SUBORDINATION OF ECCLESIASTICAL ASSEMBLIES
FOR GOVERNMENT*

Propositions of the Assembly concerning Synods

1. The Scripture doth hold out another sort of assemblies for the Government of the Church, besides classical and congregational, which we call synodical, Acts 15.

2. Synodical assemblies may lawfully be of several sorts: as provincial, national, and ecumenical.

3. It is lawful and agreeable to the Word of God, that there be a subordination of congregational, classical, provincial, and national assemblies{: that so appeals may be made from the inferior to the superior, respectively. Proved from Matthew 18, which holding forth the subordination of an offending brother to a particular church, it doth also, by a parity of reason, hold forth the subordination of a congregation to superior assemblies.

And it is agreeable to the light of nature, that he who is wronged and deprived of his right by one power, should have recourse to another power, which may restore unto him his right again, and rescind the sentence by which he was wronged: else there would be no powerful remedy provided to remove wrong, and to preserve right.}

 To the latter proposition about the subordinations of synods, the Dissenting Brethren entered their dissent, after the debate, and their reasons in writing, as follows.[1]

---

1. This text differs from that on page 61, but all the text there and above appears in the draft directory of December 11, 1644 except for the texts in braces (see *Minutes,* 5.212). The phrase in proposition 3 in the directory, "for the government of the church" is not reproduced above or in the other iteration on page 61. The propositions appear in some form in Gillespie whose arguments during debate are often reproduced in the Assembly's replies, and who was the framer of the wording of proposition 3 above. For #1 see September 16, 1644 (pp. 71–72), for #2 see September 23 (p. 78), and for #3 see October 1 (pp, 78, 84, 86). For the final paragraph arguing from the light of nature, the argument dates back to February 16, 1643/44, and is adduced in part one (pages 67, 127), but this exact text is not found in Gillespie, Lightfoot, nor the Minutes, but probably dates to October 2 when the Assembly voted that Matthew 18 holds "forth the subordination of an offending brother to a particular church, it doth by parity of reason, prove a subordination of a congregation to superior assemblies. This was voted as a proof of the proposition" (Gillespie, 86). Or it may have been worded and added later, sometime before the Assembly's answer was finalized and printed in August 1646, as the exact phrasings do not occur in the dissenting brethren's reasons, nor in the Assembly's reply.

Arguments of the

Dissenting Brethren Against the Subordination of Standing Synods, Provincial, National, Ecumenical, as Juridical, Ecclesiastical Courts[1]

Although we judge synods to be of great use for the finding out and declaring of truth in difficult cases; and encouragement to walk in the truth; for the healing offenses; and to give advice unto the magistrate in matters of religion; and although we give great honor and conscientious respect unto their determinations: yet seeing the proposition holds forth, not only an occasional, but a standing use of them; and that in subordination of one unto another, as juridical, ecclesiastical courts; and this in all cases: we humbly present these reasons against it.

Minutes,
3.329–366

Gillespie,
78–86

Lightfoot,
313–314

First Argument[2]

All such subordinations of courts, having greater and lesser degrees of power, to which in their order, causes are to be brought, must have the greatest and most express warrant and designment [*plan*] for them in the Word. Whence it is argued thus:

{See pages
224–226}

> *Those courts that must have the most express warrant and designment for them in the Word, and have not; their power is to be suspected, and not erected in the Church of God.*
> *But these ought to have so, and have not.*
> *Therefore, etc.*

THE FIRST PART OF THE MINER IS THUS PROVED

There ought to be the greatest and most express warrant, and that for two things belonging to them. First, for their subordination and number. Secondly, for their bounds and limits of power. And because this principle is made use of, both in the point in hand, and other of like nature, *viz.* to argue, *à pari ratione*, from like and parallel reason, the argument to establish

{See p. 227}

---

1. [*Arguments of the Dissenting Brethren Against the Subordination of Standing Synods, Provincial, National, Ecumenical, as Juridical, Ecclesiastical Courts* (London: Harward, 1648).]

2. [The five arguments given here cover similar ground to what Goodwin presented during debate, Session 292, September 27, 1644, *Minutes,* 3.337–340. Gillespie, 79–81. Goodwin is apparently the main author as this material was edited and published as chapters IV–VII of Book Five of his *Constitution, Right Order, and Government of the Churches of Christ,* pp. 232–260.]

this proposition shall proceed accordingly, from the strength of like reason in other cases and instances: *That there ought to be a warrant and designment for them in the Word.*

{See p. 227} 1. From like reason in the case of subordination of officers in the church, one over another: there was a special institution, and it is required, or we own them not; and that for intensive power, and extensive power: and therefore for the subordination of such courts also. The rule of proportion holds: for a government of and by several subordinations, whether of one church officer or person over another, and of him over others, or of "a many" in the like degree of subordination, are but several forms of government, of which there is the like reason in common; as of subordinations in a monarchical way, wherein still but some one person is superior to another downwards; or in an aristocratic way throughout, in this they come all to one, that if there is to be an institution or warrant for the one, there is to be for the other; whether God or men are to be the institutors of them. Now in the government of the church, for the subordination of officers, there was an express institution, or men ought not to have assumed it. 1 Corinthians 12:28, "God has set in his church, first apostles, secondarily prophets and evangelists" (who were of a parallel order), "thirdly teachers:" and the difference of power in apostles and evangelists is by subordination. But Christ has not set the like subordination of courts.

{See p. 229} 2. It is proved from what the presbyterial principles themselves reject. An institution is required by them in the case of subordination of bishops, archbishops, popes, in their arguing against them and their power. Yea and by the episcopal writers themselves, who when it is objected, that if there may be a bishop, and an archbishop over him, why not a patriarch over archbishops, and a pope over all? They deny this, and reject a patriarch or pope (although with renouncing of infallibility) as not warranted by the Word. They say a higher and more universal subordination alters the case. And the usual exception against this subordination of church governors is, that in Scripture we read neither of the name of an archbishop, nor the thing; and therefore not of a subordination of them. The like may be said of these. Where read we of councils provincial, national, names or things? Yea, and in this way of arguing (in this respect) the disadvantage {See p. 230} is on this side rather: for we are sure that once there was in the church such a subordination in church officers, evangelists over pastors, apostles over evangelists (only they were extraordinary, and so no patterns); but of such a subordination of councils in an aristocratic way, there is nothing to be found.

3. It is argued from like and just reason in other societies and bodies politic. In all kingdoms and commonwealths well ordered and constituted, there is and ought to be a set and express order by the laws, both of the number and bounds of courts of judicatory, from whom and to whom appeals are

made, and in what cases, etc. And that this subordination should be set forth and fixed by the law is as necessary, as the laws or rules by which men in a kingdom are to be governed. The wisdom of the law does judge it not enough to appoint several sorts of officers, as to say counselors, sergeants, judges; but designs also and appoints several courts with their power and bounds. The designment [*plan*] of which, especially of standing courts (being made up of these), is a matter of much more moment than the other. Yea, and still the greater and higher such courts and assemblies are, having amplitude of power over others, the more express evidence and warrant for their power there is, and ought to be: as for parliamentary power, and the privileges thereof.

And this is evident, as from the examples of all kingdoms, so from what the Scripture speaks of the constitution of them; each part of the subordination of such power in all government, both is, and also was called a creation of men, in things human, whether it be in a monarchical or aristocratic way. 1 Peter 2:13, "Submit yourselves to every human creation," ἀνθρωπίνη Gillespie 82 κτίσει, and he speaks there evidently of (and therefore thus styles) the subordination of powers in a commonwealth, whether officers or courts: for it follows, "whether unto the king as supreme, or unto governors, as those that are sent by him," etc., and so here subordination of power under him. Now parallel spiritual and ecclesiastical government with this. As in the rearing a human fabric and contignation [*framework*] of power, there must be an ordinance or creation from man, when God has left the framing of it unto him (as in this case he has), so this subordination, being in divine power, there must be a divine institution for it, besides that of the distinction of the officers themselves.

4. It is argued from like reason with Christ's institution (Matthew 18). {See p. 231} If in a particular church, Christ has prescribed the several subordinations of proceedings, and set forth the degrees, bounds and order of them; then much more it is required in these; by how much a larger extent of power is committed to them. The first rule in Matthew 18 is: 1. "If they brother offend thee, tell him thyself." Then 2. "Take two or three, and if he hear not them:" Then 3. "Tell the church." If there were a thousand brethren in a congregation, a man were not bound, nor were it orderly, in an ordinary and set way, to take, as the church shall please, first two or three, and then ten, and then twenty, and still the like proportion of a greater number, ere he comes to the church itself: but Christ has set the order, and his wisdom saw it meet [*suitable*], thus to design and limit the proceedings in a particular church. And it had been much more necessary to have appointed the like, about these general and greater assemblies; because every one of these courts (intended) have the power of a sentence and judgment, whereas those two or three proceed but in a way of admonitions, in order to a superior court. Shall Christ take care for congregations (which are esteemed

the meanest) and not for these? Of which, if Christ should not have set the bounds of power and subordination thereof, none would know what belongs to them; who is in fault, if offenses be not corrected; nor would any know whom first to appeal unto. 'I will appeal unto the national assembly first,' says one, 'and am not bound to the classical or provincial;' another would say, 'I will appeal to a general council,' which can best judge, and will be sure to make an end of it. Why should any be hindered for going *per saltum*,[1] if Christ has not set forth and obliged us to these subordinations, in their order?

{See p. 233} 5. In the church of the Jews, the subordinations that were, were set forth and determined by institution or example; how many courts there should be, and where to rest [cases]. There were the courts of the cities, and the towns; and then their Sanhedrin, to which the case was to be carried, if it were too hard for their particular courts: and no other courts, between, appointed (Deuteronomy 17). In the New Testament we have for removing scandals, a congregational standing court and government (or be it a classical standing presbytery over many congregations as our brethren say), and we have an example also of going out from a particular standing church (whether the one or the other) *electively*, to another church or churches, when divisions are therein (which Acts 15 holds forth), but still, for such standing subordinations and courts as these, out of the church, nothing at all. If there had been any national sanhedrin, a set and constant judicatory, then Christ would have appointed it, as he had done before; but he has not; no example, no institution holds it forth. Which is:

THE SECOND PART OF THE MINOR PROPOSITION, THUS PROVED.

{See p. 234} 1. The New Testament is silent in it. And if it be said, that all nations were not then converted when the apostles wrote, it is answered that God in the Old Testament took care to set the order aforehand, when they had no cities, nor were settled in the land; and accordingly if the apostles had not lived to see that which might occasion such an institution or precept, yet they would some way have left order, for time to come.

But 2. Though the apostles lived to see many famous particular churches {See p. 235} erected in a province, as well as in cities; in a nation, as in Judea; in Asia, in Crete, there were many cities and churches in each: and although all the people in these countries were not Christians, nor members of churches, yet there was matter for the molding and casting them into these subordinations, as well as now in France, where not the third part are Protestants, or in the Low Countries, where not a tenth part of the inhabitants are members of their churches. And sure[ly] if these superstructions had been so absolutely necessary in the government of the churches, it had been as

---

1. [*Per saltum*—"Leaping ahead." i.e. Passing over the normal order of proceedings; 'without intermediate stages.']

necessary to have appointed them. They set up and appointed all needful remedies for ordering the churches after them, when they should be gone. And it is more strange, that in the case of the spreading of errors, they should not write to churches as gathered into synods, and as having the standing power to prevent and suppress them (if such ordinary standing assemblies armed with coercive power had been then, in that existence, as now), that upon no occasion this should be done, when yet they had occasions. Take the seven churches in Asia, Ephesus, Thyatira, Smyrna, etc., with the rest of the churches therein—a province—and though therein we find many great disorders, and some in doctrine (the more proper work of these standing synods), yet we see that Christ writes only to each of those churches apart, and reproves each for their disorder in each. Whereas had they been one church in such a standing association for government, and had had ordinary provincial and national assemblies extant, as now, the reproof would have been especially directed thereunto—as if errors and disorders were in the classical churches (as those all are pretended to be) of Scotland, the chief rebuke would now more justly fall upon the national and provincial assemblies, as their constitution is.

Yea thirdly, the Holy Ghost would have at least vouchsafed to these, or some other churches (that were in like manner in a nation, or province, as Galatia, etc.), in respect of such a combination, the name of a church, who {See p. 237} must (according to the principles of this government) have had so much of the power of a church. But nowhere are the churches in a province called a church, but churches in the plural. And if the *lesser* churches, then *these;* yea rather these, having most of the power, should therefore have had most of the name. Yea, and by how much the church power thereof, should have been most independent (as a nation is) and so come, most eminently, within that rule, "tell the church" (from which words these pretend their power, and yet cannot show so much title thereto, as to have the name "church" given them). Let a rational account be given of this.

Second Argument

If there be such a subordination of synods in the church of Christ, then {See p. 238} there is no independency but in an ecumenical council. Goodwin, 252

Which first, would bring in a foreign ecclesiastical power over each state {See p. 239} and kingdom. *Minutes,* 2.651

And secondly: Therefore of all other should have its designation and existence in the Word; and is more needful, than the other two sorts of synods mentioned. For if any should be extant, then that, which is *remedium effica-* *the most effec-* *cissimum.* It is said, there is wanting *remedium efficax,* if these subordinations *tive remedy;* be not; but according to these principles that is wanting that, which is the *an efficacious* *most efficacious* remedy, if a general council be not extant in the world. For if *remedy* there be not a resting in a classical presbytery, but provincial also must be, and appealed to; neither are they reckoned efficacious enough, but there muſt be national also (upon this supposition, that the greater assembly has more of the promise and assiſtance of Chriſt than the lesser), then of all others a general council muſt be supposed in a transcendent manner, above all the reſt, to have the promise of assiſtance made to it; and so to be the moſt eminently efficacious (if not the *only remedy*) on earth; yea and only to be reſted in, being that which only is the ultimate. Some of the papiſts, they gave this to such a general council, that it cannot err. But according to these principles of presbyterial divines, though it might err, yet it is supposeable to be transcendently more infallible than all the other under it; and God more with it than with all the reſt. And therefore God in His Word would have given eſpecially order for this, above all other. And the same God that suits His providences to His inſtitutions, would not have failed, in what is the moſt sovereign remedy of all other, that it might have been exiſtent in all ages: as we see his promise was to the Jews, to keep their land when the males thrice a year went up to the general assembly at Jerusalem. But 300 years the churches wanted [*lacked*] them, and could not enjoy them; and they were judged therefore not necessary to the government of the church, which yet (according to these principles), muſt have been the moſt necessary of all the reſt.

Yea, and further also, thirdly, there muſt be an injurious independency {See p. 241} set up in a national synod: for when a man has appealed from one court to another, and comes to this national, that is the ultimate [court] exiſtent; and upon the sentence thereof, comes next to be banished out of a nation, to have his eſtate forfeited, to the ruin of himself and poſterity. Then it is, that he moſt of all needs the relief of an higher remedy, more efficacious than all these [courts] he has gone through, if such an one may be; yet then he is left remediless, and he (according unto these principles) left more unsatisfied than ever; because thinks he, there is by God's appointment a court that has more of God, and of Chriſt in it, than all these, to judge of the truth and right, and lo, it is not; and can never be expected.

Let it be withal considered, that when God appointed a subordination of ſtanding courts, He withal designed out which should be the supreme and made it the ultimate; and the supremacy and independency of it, in a set and ſtanding way, was His inſtitution, as much as the appointment of the court itself; so that he was to be put to death that obeyed not the sentence of it, and all appeals were thereby cut off. Therefore if a national church does take upon it to be an independent church, upon the sentence thereof, to have the extremiſt punishment executed (but that of death) that in a nation men are capable of; it had need, for the quieting of all men's ſpirits that muſt submit to it, not only [to] show a warrant from God for it to be an ecclesiaſtical judicatory, but also to be the supreme court, as the Sanhedrin was, that appeals should be made to.

THIRD ARGUMENT

To that end let it be examined, what set rules there are, or may be supposed {See p. 243} to be of these subordinations, and their bounds; and the ultimate independency in a national church: which should be fetched from some standing considerations, which the Word warrants; God never having constituted a church, but He gave the bounds thereof. All variation of church power is from God. The alteration of the government of His people the Jews, from family government (which had been under the law of nature), to national, in Moses' time, was by express appointment. And as Himself made and constituted it a national church, so there was an ecclesiastical government framed by Himself suited thereunto. And in the New Testament there is a "reed to measure the temple" (Revelation 11:1)—a rule to set out the limits of church power, as well as under the old; and therefore the arguments is framed thus:

That church power which cannot show a constant divine rule for its variation and subordination, and ultimate independency, is not of God, and so may not be.

But this variation of church power into these subordinations, cannot show any such steady and constant rule for these things.

Therefore, etc.

The Major is evident from what has been said.

The Minor is made good by a removal of all particulars, that may be sup- {See p. 245} posed to be the square of framing these subordinations, etc.

I. Not that rule, *that the greater number of company of churches should rule the less, and that the whole should rule the part.* For then,

1. There would be as many several subordinations as there can be supposed variations of greater numbers; and that will arise to more than these three only. Every new greater company would constitute a new synod.

2. Where is the promise of God that He will be more with the greatest {See p. 245} part of them that profess Christianity, rather than with a few, so far as to constitute a new power and government? Yea,

3. The greater number of churches professing religion are more cor- {See p. 246} rupted; the pure churches are fewer. It had been ill for Philadelphia and the angel [i.e. minister] and elders thereof, if those seven churches in Asia had been cast into such a subordinate association for government, to be exercised by the angels and elders of all the other six churches, with the rest in Asia. And the like may be said of the purer Reformed churches in Germany. If the greater number of those, that yet were true churches, should have ruled the lesser, then the Lutherans and Calvinists being bound to this government, the Lutherans being also true churches, and the more in number, would by virtue of this law, have soon corrupted the purer. And what reason can be pretented [*pretended*] (according to this

rule, and the principles of this government) to leave any true churches out of an association?

4. Suppose there should be as many elders and churches more purely reformed, in one province or shire than in the rest of a whole nation besides (as instance might be given in some of the Reformed churches, *that there are*). Why should not God be thought to be as much with them, as with the national assembly? And if all are to give themselves up to this law, how [many ways] will the greater which is the worse, either corrupt the purer or oppress them?

5. If *qua* [*as*] greater; then the decrees of greater, *viz.* general councils, in former ages, should bind us more than national or provincial now: for they should have had more of church in them, by this rule, and so more of Christ. And then all general councils that set up popes and bishops, and all other superstitions, are still binding.

If it be said, "we chose them not;" yet still that is not the ground which makes their decrees less divine or obliging to us, but it lies in the authority of God's ordinance, that they were the greater and more general councils. And however still, if this be the rule, that the greater number of churches rule the less; then take the measure of this greatness and number of the churches from time, stretching the line over all ages past, as well as from the more number of churches in such or such a place, or nations in the present times; and so look what general councils for most ages of the world did establish, should by virtue of this law, oblige the present times, and have more force upon us, than the universal church in this present age; much more than of any national assembly, if either be simply considered under a mere ecclesiastical obligation, that is, *qua* greater and more of church. Time varies not the case: so: but that all their acts, having been acts of the church universal, in all ages should, comparatively, stand more in force. The acts of any the last general councils will stand in force, until a general council of like extent repeal those acts; as the statutes of parliament of our ancestors do, if not repealed, by like and equal authority.

II. Secondly, it is not the notion or consideration of their being churches {See p. 247} in such or such a nation or province, that can be the rule of making this obligation or setting of these bounds. It must be considered the question is of a mere ecclesiastic obligation by virtue of church principles, such as should have been a just rule and measure to the primitive churches (ere princes turned Christian) to have reared up the like subordinations. Now then the limits from hence must either rise from being first one church in a kingdom under the same civil government; or secondly, one church in a nation; that is, either from a national respect or political.

First in general from neither. For that instance [in] Acts 15, of the council there, its rise or the bound of its authority was founded upon neither. For if either national or political respects should have obliged them, they should have sent to Syria and Cilicia, and not to Jerusalem, who were both under a differing civil government, and of another nation.

But more particularly.

First, not *qua* church in one kingdom, for that is *per accidens* to a church, *accidental* that it grows up to a kingdom, or that the whole nation is converted to Christianity. And therefore a set rule for all times cannot be fetched from hence; this could not be the certain measure of the independency of church power in the apostle's times.

Secondly, this makes the bounds of ecclesiastical independency and jurisdiction uncertain, varying as the bounds of kingdoms do vary. When the Roman Empire had all kingdoms under it, all the churches must then have been obliged to have had general standing councils suited to the extent of the empire, to have been the next unto the provincial, such as the national are now to the provincial; or else before the empire turned Christian, there was by this rule even as many independencies as churches. And then again, when this empire was broken into the kingdoms, yea and many more, there arose instead of the former, many new independent boundaries of church power (of which only the question is, and not of that power which a church does come to have, and simply and alone holds of [*from*] the magistrates, which will be merely civil). And then as kingdoms vary by conquests, the like alteration the bounds of church power must receive. Among the Jews it did not; for when the church was broken into two kingdoms by God's appointment; yet the church state, by God's institution, varied not, but was still one church. All these things are therefore mere accidentals to church power, and how can they be the foundation of the bounds of it?

III. Lastly, if this independency arises from the magistrates, then there is *{See p. 249}* no need of such subordinations; which is proved by experience in Reformed *Minutes, 3.353* churches abroad, who are well enough governed without these subordinations. Geneva has no appeals, yet is governed but by one classical church. And why may not all other churches be governed as well without them, if the magistrate oversees them, and keeps each to their duties? The churches of the Low Countries want [*lack*] national synods, and yet are peaceably governed. Yea, some for a long time are without provincial [synods], and say if they can, they will never have more; and yet are peaceably and quietly governed. It is as the civil magistrate will terminate the independency, and himself over look [*watch over*] it. Or,

IV. Secondly, if these bounds be fetched from national respects: Then 1. *{See p. 250}* In Germany, Calvinists must be subject to the greater number of Lutherans; and in this kingdom, all ministers must make up this association, and the greater number will be the worser, and malign and oppose the good. If because the Calvinists profess a further reformation, they are disobliged from associating with the Lutherans, then those in any nation that profess a further reformation than others, are free by the same law also. Surely uniformity of principles is a more intimate bond of such association than any such outward extrinsical respects. 2. If *qua* [*as*] nation, or principality, then Wales must be independent. 3. If *qua* nation, then if nation is taken for a people of the same tongue and kindred, then all the Christian Jews in the primitive times, when scattered into a nation, were bound to have made one church distinct from all the churches they cohabited with. If nation be taken for a people dwelling in the same national bounds, then the same Jews being dispersed into several countries and nations, must have made one church with the several nations where they lived; whereas Peter in his epistles, and James in his, and Paul to the Hebrews, write unto the Jews apart, as churches in all nations.

FOURTH ARGUMENT

{See p. 251} *That government which necessarily produces representations of spiritual power, out of other representations, with a derived power therefrom, there is no warrant for.*

But these subordinations of synods, provincial, national, ecumenical, for the government of the church, do so.

The major shall be spoken to, after the minor proposition is both cleared and proved, which is done by putting two things together.

[MINOR OF THE FOURTH ARGUMENT]

First, that if there be an authoritative subordination of all churches in the provinces to a national assembly, and so of many nations to an ecumenical, binding unto subjection; that then all in the provinces must be interested in that national, and all in the nation in that ecumenical; so as it may be said, that they are all involved and included, and so obliged; as it is in parliamentary power, wherein the shires are involved.

Secondly, that this interest in this subordination cannot arise, but either by immediate choice of those elders, which shall represent each church and congregation immediately (which is the case of our parliament men chosen immediately by those they represent), or else that the provincial elders sent by the congregations, shall choose out of themselves some few, that shall represent the provinces, and so likewise the national assemblies shall choose out some few which shall represent the whole nation in a general council. Now the first of these is not, nor can be, in the choice of a national assembly. Congregations meet not for any such immediate choice, but the elders of them all chosen out of themselves. So as the obligation of all the churches to be subject to a national assembly (arising out of those other subordinations) is not, because they are a greater number of elders or divines (for in a provincial synod there may be assembled as many as in the national), but it arises from hence, that some out of all, do represent the rest. And if they did not meet and vote as representers of the whole, then when a national assembly sits in a great city, all other neighbor miniſters might come and vote with them, and out-vote them, who are the repreſenters of the whole.

MAJOR [OF THE FOURTH ARGUMENT]
Now that such a representation having derived ſpiritual power from other representations, is not in matters ſpiritual, warrantable. Besides, all argu- {See p. 253} ments againſt delegated power in matters ſpiritual, all miniſters being immediately *Chriſti vicarri:* and that all such representations grow weaker, as *vicars of Chriſt* reflections use to do; elders represent the churches in classical and provincial assemblies as being immediately chosen by them, but the elders in national assemblies, are the representations of elders in provinces, and so are a shadow of that firſt shadow; whereas yet, they have the moſt of power, even all that can be supposed to belong to the whole subſtance. Besides such considerations, it is argued thus:

1. If these few out of nations in a general council, should bind all those nations in matters ſpiritual, and a few out of provinces the nation, they muſt be supposed to have the promise and the assiſtance answerable. But where {See p. 253} is either the promise, or can gifts in a few be supposed to produce such an obligation? It is true, where two or three are gathered together, His promise is to be in the midſt of them, and so suppose with more, when more are met; but that His promise should be, to be with a few out of a nation, as with the whole nation, and these not chosen immediately by the nation, and but the representers of them, cannot be expected. It is granted, that each so met has the gifts and assiſtance of an elder, and so the whole as of so many elders met (as we in this assembly met together, are to be looked upon, and the judgments thereof accordingly reverenced), but that as they are elders representative of hundreds of other elders, who themselves are representers of churches, that any such addition should arise to them, by virtue of this duplicated representation, over and above what is in their single gifts and office, let either a warrant be produced or a promise. Two things are allowed them, but a third denied them. Firſt, it is granted they may have assiſtance to judge, as elders, which is their office. Secondly, assistance to judge according to their personal abilities, being thus called to give their advice. But thirdly, such a superadded assiſtance as holds proportion to that ſpiritual bulk and body which they represent is denied them. For suppose that always it falls out, that the beſt and choiceſt of a nation are chosen; yet ſtill not to hold proportion to the whole nation, there muſt be more than an ordinary promise for it; and therefore had need be express and evident. When the Jesuits say that the Pope may err, as *persona privata*; *private person* but not as *pontifex*, when he is in his chair, representing the whole church; *pope* Davenant confutes them thus: *officium* [...] *dat* [dabunt] *authoritatem judicandi, sed privatæ personæ conditiones, dant* [dabunt] *modum et facultatem*

[facultatem & modum judicandi].[1] That it is otherwise in commonwealths, is because they being human creations, the represented can set up a power which shall represent them. But this power we speak of is supernatural, and muſt be from God and His inſtitution. The Sanhedrin of Jerusalem had a special assiſtance above all courts else; and therefore God appointed *causes* to be brought to it; which special assiſtance is intimated twice in the inſtitution of it. Deuteronomy 17 by this, "That they should go up to the place which God shall choose" (verse 8), and "do according to the sentence which they of that place" (which the Lord shall choose) "shall show thee." An emphasis is put upon that blessing, which by God's choice and election did accompany that place, which God had chosen to put his Name, and promised to be in an eminent manner present in; and to accept their sacrifices there offered (which was a representative worship of that nation) and not elsewhere. Now, as it was the representative worship of the nation, so these governors were the representative governors of the nation; and both sanctified in that place, as the gift was by the altar, as that which God had chosen. If the like inſtitution were found with the intimation of such a blessing, from a peculiar choice of God's, of national assemblies, all ought to subject to them in matters spiritual.

2. If there be such representations as these, in one or few persons of {See p. 254} many churches, they have each for that time, while in such an assembly, archiepiscopal and episcopal power; and their case is parallel (parallel then, as for that time and occasion, and as met in a synod) with that of so many bishops met in a council; whose episcopal power as then, and therein met, lies in this, that they are so many churches representative: especially this would fall out, if these synods should ſtill consiſt of the same men, or if some few should be always chosen to them. And why may there not be ſtanding persons that are more skillful in such affairs, through exercise, as well as ſtanding assemblies themselves? And then as touching matters of jurisdiction, in such an assembly, they are for the present the same with so many bishops met in a convocation.

3. If these representations having the power of all the churches in the {See p. 255} nation, were warrantable, they muſt be a church. Now besides, that they

---

1. *De Judice et Norm de fidei*, Pref. [John Davenant, Bishop of Salisbury (1576–1641), "De Judice ac Norma Fidei et Cultus Christiani Disputatio," in *Prælectiones de duobus in theologia controversis capitibus: de judice controversiarum, primo; de juſtitia habituali et actuali, altero: per Reverendissimum virum Joannem Davenantium, S. Theologiæ doctorem (nunc Episcopum Sarisburiensem) ante aliquot annos in celeberrima academia Cantabrigiensi theologiæ professorem pro domina Margareta, in scholis theologicis autitoribus suis dietatæ. Quibus jam accesserunt quæſtionum quarundam theologicarum, quæ.* (Canterbury: Thomam & Joannem Buck, ac Rogerum Daniel, celeberrimæ academiæ typographos, 1631/1634), Præfatio ad Academicos, B2. Missing words/corrections are in square brackets. "The office ... gives [will give] authority to judge, but the conditions of the private person give [will give] the means and ability [ability and means of judging]."]

are nowhere so called and if they were called so, then they are a body to Christ; for so every church is; and where is Christ said to have a representative body of his body? They are a company of elders personally gathered, but a representative church they are not, nor can be; and yet must be, or they have not the power of all the churches in a nation in them, nor otherwise do their acts oblige them to subjection.

Reasons against the allegations of Acts 15 for the subordination of synods, provincial, national, ecumenical

Besides what has been said against this example, alleged to prove presbyterial acts of government by the elders of the church of Jerusalem, in the reasons formerly presented; proving first, that this one example cannot serve to prove both the presbyterial government and synodical; but that if the reverend assembly will lean to the one, the other must be quitted; and secondly, that that assembly was not a formal synod, but only a reference by the particular church of Antioch of their differences among themselves, unto this particular church of Jerusalem and no other; it may be moreover observed, that the example of it is here further extended, to prove all sorts of synods and subordinations thereof; both provincial, national, ecumenical; and so it must suit all these so great varieties, whereas it is not fit for any one of them. {See pp. 63–98

{See p. 256}

Gillespie, 82

Minutes,

3.344–350

But if it had been a synod: Yet 1. Neither provincial, nor national, for Antioch consults not with the churches of her own nation, but seeks to Jerusalem, a church of Judea of another nation, and another province. Neither 2. Is it the instance of a standing synod (which the word subordination in the proposition, does necessarily infer, or else the links of those chains will not hang together), but elective; for they sent out of election, and choice of them, and to them but about this one question, at this time, without any obligation to refer all other matters to them in an ordinary way. Nor 3. Was there a multiplication of synods, but only one in whose judgment those of Antioch rested. 4. Much less is it the instance of rearing up of a subordination and contignation [*framework*] of synods, superior and inferior; which is a further thing. For though, when offenses are not healed, and one reference to other churches is not sufficient to cure them, there should be a seeking to others; yet the example obliges the churches that are in difference, [and obliges] not to take and choose the churches of that province; either as of that province, or as the greater number, to whom both those among whom the controversy is, and these to whom it was afore referred, must be subordinately subject. Much less does it hold forth, that the churches of that province may judicially challenge a right of authority, to decide it, and oblige them subpoena to their determination; Gillespie, 79

{See p. 257}

{See p. 258}

and then, the churches of that whole nation challenge the like over all. But still it runs in this way only; that those who shall be judged [most] meet and [most] able and [most] faithful to determine and compose it, by those who are to refer it, shall have the hearing of it.

The argument of the reverend assembly was drawn from like reason, and let there be found like reason, and it is granted. And though the instance is {See p. 261} not the pattern of a formal synod; yet it holds forth this rule of equity, that when offenses arise among churches, references ought to be made from out of themselves to churches abroad to heal them. But the question is, to what churches these references are to be made and how? (Let the like reason held forth in the example, be kept unto, and decide it). Say we still, to those churches, the churches offended or divided shall choose as fittest and ablest to determine it. This is clear in the example. Antioch was not bound to refer it to the church of Jerusalem, as greater, or as a neighbor church, or of the same province, but as best able to judge of the differences. And this way agrees with the law of nature, and of arbitration, so usual among men, which God has there set up as an ordinance and pattern of proceeding in such cases. But this subordination of synods the proposition intends, holds so differing a course from this, as first, instead of elective synods and occasional, it sets up standing and set, to be the judge of the churches under them forever. Secondly, not in one case (as Antioch to Jerusalem), but in all cases, whatever shall fall out. Thirdly, not in a way of multiplication or diversification, as need shall be; but of subordination and settled superiority. and the grounds of this to be, because the greatest must rule the less: and that they are neighbor churches in the same province or nation. And this [in] Acts *an equal jus-* 15 is so far from countenancing by a *par ratio*, that in all things it is unlike: *tification; the* and so there is a differing constitution and rule of these synods thus subor-*same grounds* dinate, and what the reason drawn from Acts 15 will warrant, and therefore does make a differing formal reason in the government.

And human prudence added, will not rectify it, when the reason of the institution is so much varied from. For instance:

If the fundamental law for remedy of wrongs and deciding controversies in any kingdom, were by arbitration elective, to take them to be their judges whom the parties in difference judge [most] apt, every way, for the present controversy;

and that the precedents and ruled cases hold forth no more; and if the government of another kingdom were, that the greater should rule and determine the causes of the less; and according to the proportion thereof, to have subordinate standing courts erected, to which (by appeal from one to the other) all causes should be brought:

—whether were not these two, such differing frames of government, so as that he that would mold the first to the second, might not be challenged to set up a new government, differing from the fundamental law of that kingdom; and whether the first is not a liberty to be stood upon, against the second, if it were vouchsafed to any kingdom (and that is the case here), is humbly submitted.

And the bounds of such elective assemblies, need no set or standing rule: because they arise from emergent occasions, in cases of controversy and offense; and the extent of them, and so the condition and nature of the things themselves, do hold forth their own rise; like as the bounds of particular congregations to be of such, as live so, as conveniently to meet in one place, arises from the nature of the thing itself, and the necessary requisites thereunto.

Reasons against the argument drawn from the analogy of Matthew 18

1. The strength of the argument runs, that because there should be this remedy, that therefore there is such a remedy. {See p. 262}

2. It is granted there is a remedy, which is a going forth to other churches, which Acts 15 holds forth; but that excommunication (which is the remedy held forth, Matthew 18) of the offending church or churches should be the remedy, is not there held forth as has been shown. There is remedy of coordination, such as between two nations, and as between *pares*, as churches are, proceeding in a way suitable to their condition; but not this of subordination, that the greater number of churches should become standing courts, and have power to excommunicate the lesser; but that all churches have a power to declare offense, and withdraw the communion from those churches. And in reason, how is it possible for a national church to excommunicate all the churches of a province? And how ineffectual would that be? Or for a general council to excommunicate a nation? And if they cannot use this remedy; to what end is the subordination of synods, having this authority pleaded for?

Gillespie, 84–86
Minutes, 3.360–366

equals
{See p. 263}

And whereas it is said, "that there must be the same remedy that is in a congregation, for an offending brother; or else where the disease is strongest, the remedy is weakest." It is answered,

Gillespie, 85.
Minutes, 361
Goodwin, 259

I. First, that where the disease is strongest, there, this which is called the strongest remedy, cannot be applied; or with an apparent inefficaciousness. For when the churches in a province err, or a national church, here the disease is strongest; and yet it would be in vain to interdict them, *communion among[st] themselves,* or *deliver them unto Satan.* Yea, when it comes to the highest, namely, a national assembly, wherein (if erring) the disease is greatest and strongest; there is not only no remedy, but the highest and greatest power to do hurt upon all under them; as when the generality of the clergy were Arians. And if they err, the error is worse than of a Pope's erring, or a bishop's: he is but one, and may be deposed. And in the greater

{See p. 265}
{See p. 267}

bodies of the clergy, the greater part are, and have been still the worse, and more corrupt; as is apparent in this kingdom at present; in which, by virtue of the presbyterial principles, all ministers must be taken in. And if you will put them out, where will others be had in their room? Convert men we cannot; and if not converted, ministers of all others, are the worst and greatest opposites to religion. And if a national assembly be chosen *by these*, the greater number are like to be of the worst; and such as may alter all that you now have done.

And if it be said, "that this will hold against great politic bodies as well, who may undo the commonwealth;" the answer is, that the common and equal interest of all, and the common principles of preserving the rights and liberties of a state, and seeking the common good, is natural unto the generality of men; but the truths of the gospel and purity of religion, and the power thereof, is contrary to the principles of all natural men; and in all ages, the most of the clergy have been [most] apt to corrupt the one, and oppose the other. And in those ages when such councils began to be standing and in most credit, after the first 300 years, then was it that the mystery of popery did work most powerfully, and those superstitions, and corrupt opinions grew up, which made way for that man of sin, and that body of popish doctrine, that has overspread the world.

And, if there should be no danger of corrupting the truth; yet the churches, though reformed, coming all out of popery, and not being fully enlightened in all things; and the first notion of anything further in matters of theology usually falling into the hearts and spirits but of a few, we should have no further truth taught, but oppressed, till a whole nation is enlightened in it.

II. Secondly, the efficacy of all remedies does depend, first, upon Christ's blessing on them, which depends upon his institution of them; and *par ratio*, [f]or like reason will never set up an ordinance, unless Christ has himself appointed it. And in the example, Acts 15, there is not this way of proceeding held forth. Secondly, it lies in suitableness to the condition of those that are to be dealt with. Now when many churches deal with an erring church, the churches in a province, with any erring churches, or of a nation with a province, they must be in reason dealt with, suitably to the condition of churches, and of a multitude. And surely, a brotherly way of admonition, etc., withdrawing communion, is more suitable unto such. As in the civil government, if a province rebels, or a great multitude of subjects, should the state presently hang up [*execute*] all in that province? Although unto partticular persons, rebelling, this is efficacious to suppress rebellion. Thirdly, Christ has suited his remedies, to all times, and unto all conditions; and how national and provincial assemblies could be, during the first 300 years, when yet churches were well governed, is submitted.

[III] And lastly, if the analogy of this 18th of Matthew be argued. Then

First, let the analogy be kept. And then, when a church has offended other churches, they are not to bring them to a set court of judicature at first; for Christ's rule is otherwise in dealing with an offending brother— electively to take two or three other churches to admonish them (which is more suited to that way aforementioned, Acts 15). As for the proceedings against a brother in a congregation, there is not a set appointed number of two or three standing persons to be the admonishers of all persons offending ere it comes to the church; nor have they power to excommunicate. And thus by this proportion, instead of these set and standing provincial assemblies, to whom causes are next brought; and these armed with power of excommunication; there should only be two or three, or more neighbor churches to admonish the offending church, and not a standing court to bring it unto. And then, {See p. 271}

Secondly, let it be shown where a standing synod of elders is called the church; and how then can the analogy hold, when it holds not in the name, *tell the church*? The like reason holds not, unless these particular congregations have the power of excommunication; for otherwise, if these greater assemblies' power be argued from the analogy of the lesser, and the same remedy excommunication, and the particular congregations have not that allowed them; then by the principles of this analogy, it is nowhere to be found. But as the congregational churches have power only to admonish and suspend from sacraments, so the greater assemblies should have no more also. And though the church universal is called a church and one body to Christ; yet as materially considered, and not as a politic body in respect to government, which was never yet asserted by this assembly. {See p. 271}

Sic Subscribitur:
Tho. Goodwin, William Bridge, Philip Nye, William Greenhill, Jer. Burroughes, William Carter, Sidrach Sympson.

Concordat cum Originali.
Adoniram Byfield, Scriba.

The Answer of
The Assembly of Divines,

Unto the Reasons of the Dissenting Brethren Against the Subordination of Ecclesiastical Assemblies for Government, viz.[1]

It is lawful and agreeable to the Word of God, that there be a subordination of congregational, classical, provincial and national assemblies, for the government of the church.

Before we make answer particularly to their arguments, we desire these few things may be premised, to give light to the whole business.

1. That this question is of the same nature with that against which our {See p. 63} brethren did give in their former reasons {whether many particular congregations may be under one presbyterial government},[2] especially as themselves stated the question. For they there dispute only against joining of such congregations under one presbytery, as have their officers particularly fixed to them (and such a classical presbytery is a kind of synod); but they professedly decline the dispute in case those officers do all in common take care of those several congregations.

2. That the *præcognita* before our answer to those reasons, have the same {See p. 99} use here that they had there.

3. That most of these arguments of our brethren, are the same for substance with some of their former arguments, and only put now to another dress, as will appear further in scanning of them.

4. Our brethren here deny not synods (which they say frequently are a holy ordinance of God), nor the several sorts of synods; but only the standing use of them (as the prelates did against the non-conformist; see Parker, *De Polit. Eccles.*,[3] lib. 3. c. 25), and their subordination one to another; not the subordination of congregations to them.

---

1. [*The Answer of the Assembly of Divines to the Reasons of the Dissenting Brethren Against the Proposition concerning Subordination of Congregational, Classical, Provincial, and National Assemblies, for the Government of the Church* (London: Printed for Humphrey Harward, 1648).]

2. [Unless noted otherwise, braces are original to the text (originally square braces).]

3. Parker [chapter XXIIII, De Classibus, *sic* XXV]. [Cf. Robert Parker (d.1614), *De Politica Ecclesiastica Christi et Hierachica opposita, libri tres* … (Frankf., 1616), p. 353. The chapter number 24 is repeated for 25, which is "De Classibus." Chapter XXVI is De Synodorum potestate, pp. 367–370. The Parker is item 58 on the list of books taken from the personal library of

5. Though our brethren here deny the ſtanding use of synods; yet none of their arguments are framed againſt their ſtanding use, but only againſt the subordination of them. Only they except sometimes againſt their ſtanding use, because the causes to be judged there are occasional, which can be no juſt exception; for there may be ſtanding civil courts, yet such controversies are occasional. And there may be not only ſtanding physicians, but colleges of them, though diseases be occasional; and there may be not only ſtanding presbyteries in congregations, but also set times of their meetings, and yet their business be occasional.

6. Our brethren acknowledge (in their diſputes and otherwise) so much concerning synods and their usefulness, as is sufficient to warrant not only the lawfulness of their use, but also the ſtanding use of them. As for inſtance: (1) That they are an ordinance of God upon all occasions of difficulty. (2) That all the churches of a province being offended at a particular congregation, may call that single congregation to an account; yea all the churches in a nation, may call one or more congregations to an account. (3) That they may examine and admonish, and in case of obſtinacy, declare them to be subverters of the faith. (4) That synods are of use to give advice to the magiſtrate in matters of religion. (5) That they have authority to determine concerning controversies of faith. (6) That their determinations are to be received with great honor and conscientious reſpeĉt, and obligation as from Chriſt. (7) That if an offending congregation refuse to submit to their determinations, they may withdraw from them and deny church communion and fellowship with them. (8) That this sentence of non-communion may be ratified and backed with the authority of the magiſtrate, to the end it may be the more effeĉtual. (9). That they may convent and call before them any person within their bounds, whom the ecclesiaſtical business before them does concern; and may hear and determine such causes and differences as do orderly come before them (besides many other things which have in the assembly been voted concerning synods; to which they have entered no dissent). And surely such things as these, wherein there will be occasion of the use of synods by our brethren's acknowledgment, are so ordinary, and likely to fall out so often, as will afford occasion enough for set and frequent meeting of synods.

Minutes, 3.350
Gillespie, 106
See Oct. 15,
1644, Accommodation, 309

7. That whereas our proposition and proofs concerning the several sorts of synods and church assemblies, do only hold out an agreeableness to the Word, and a warrantableness by the Word, of these several sorts of assemblies and their subordination: our brethren's arguments do only endeavor to

{See p. 165}

Archbishop Laud for use by the Westminster Assembly ("Parker de Politia Ecclias 4°"). See Appendix: "Westminster Abbey Library and other Theological Resources of the Assembly of Divines" (1643–1645), page 385. In the version of this research published in *The Confessional Presbyterian* (2010) 266, my note incorrectly reads "libro duo." The 1638 edition of Parker only contains the first two books (libri duo), lacking book three, "De ejus subjecto, i.e. Ecclesia." The edition is not noted in the MS list of books; both are quarto size.]

prove, that the Scripture does not express or design them; that is, that they have not an express institution: which is not our assertion, and to which we spoke sufficiently in our answers to their former reasons now before the Honorable Houses. For though we agree with our brethren, that synods are an ordinance of God; yet [we] do not plead an express institution that each synod must necessarily be thus and thus bounded, according to the division of shires or provinces, so that there may not be more or fewer than such a number, nor otherwise bounded or divided (no more than either we, or our brethren, can plead for the number and bounds of particular congregations); though yet we do affirm that synods thus bounded are agreeable to, and warranted by the Word of God.

{Answers to the exceptions to Jerusalem and Ephesus, pp. 99–174, 179–204}

8. That the arguments of our brethren against such synods as we assert, do in many things militate as strongly against such elective synods which themselves allow, as against our assertion, as will appear in the particulars.

THE ANSWER TO THEIR FIRST ARGUMENT

{See p. 207} These things being premised, we come to their first argument, which they form thus; 'those courts which must have the most express warrant and designment [*plan*] for them in the Word, and have not; their power is to be suspected, and not erected in the church of God. But these ought to have so, and have not. Therefore,' etc.

{Minutes, 3.329–366}

{Gillespie, 78–86}

Answer. 1. Our brethren here lay out their strength in proving the minor, and show that these assemblies are not instituted; but wave that which is in question: whether they be *agreeable to* an institution or the Word of God. For things which are not in every particular of them instituted, may yet be agreeable to an institution and the Word of God. But if they would have concluded against the proposition, they must have argued thus: those assemblies which (though for the general they have an institution, and are an ordinance of God, yet in particular) have not the greatest and most express warrant and designment for them in the Word, and that both for their subordination and number, and also for their bounds, and limits of power, are not agreeable to, or warranted by the Word of God. But if they contend only that what has not such express designment has not in those particulars an express institution, and may not therefore be erected as so instituted, they contend about that which is not now in question.

{Gillespie, 83}

2. Their argument if it have any strength at all against our proposition, proves more than our brethren pretend to strive for; for they profess here to dispute against the subordination of them, and not against the being and existence of them; which they grant to be lawful and useful. If our brethren can show such a particular express designment for the being of them, we shall be glad to hear it. If they cannot, but say only (as we do) that they are agreeable to and warranted by the Word; then either their argument hurts not us, or else it overthrows what [they] themselves grant.

{Gillespie, 80}

                    III: ANSWER OF THE ASSEMBLY TO THE

But we will examine the *reasons* our brethren bring to prove their minor; yet muſt tell them withal, that their major (of which they offer no proof at all) may admit of an exception. For though it were granted, that such things as have express designment in the Word, ought in the practice of them to be conformed to that designment (in their bounds, limits, number, etc., if any such designment be), yet we muſt not therefore infer that, if there be any failure in any of these, the thing were better not be at all, yea, ought not at all to be; which is the sense of their major proposition. The Passover had particular designment for the time, place, persons, etc. Yet Hezekiah thought fit to keep a Passover, though varying in some particulars from that designment, rather than not to keep a Passover at all. Yet say our brethren in this argument, that synods which [they] themselves call a holy ordinance of God, and grant that they have an express warrant and designment for them in the Word (or else, by this argument, they muſt not, as here they do, grant them lawful, and of great use), may not yet be at all erected, unless we can find out the greateſt and moſt express warrant and designment for their subordination, and number, and for their bounds, and limits of power. In civil courts, we are sure they may be agreeable to, and warrantable by the Word of God, though they have no such express particular designment in all those circumſtances. But, say our brethren, in the church of God, courts may not be erected unless there be such designments of those particulars, though the courts themselves be designed.

TO THE FIRST PART OF THE MINOR

To prove the firſt part of their minor (that synods ought to have such ex- press warrant and designment [*plan*] in these particulars), they bring five reasons, and in all of them profess to argue *à pari ratione*.

{See p. 207}
Minutes, 3.335,
337, 360

But we ask them, whether *argumentum à pari ratione*, is a sufficient argument in the point in hand, and others of like nature? If it is, then they muſt not blame us for using such arguments, but grant our arguing (*à pari ratione*) from analogy, though in matters of inſtitution, to be a good way of arguing. If it is not; then they ought to have brought other arguments themselves. For it is not enough to plead that *we use* such arguments, unless they say too, that *we do well* in using them. For if *argumentum ad hominem* only, be a sufficient argument againſt our proposition; then is *reſponsio ad hominem* a sufficient answer to their argument and we need say no more to these five arguments, than that it is a way of arguing which themselves allow not. But we will consider them particularly.

Gillespie, 84

arguing to the man; i.e. abusing the arguer rather than the argument; reſponse to the man

I. Their firſt reason *à pari ratione* is this; that in "the government of the church, for the subordination of officers, there was an express inſtitution. I Corinthians 12:28, 'God has set in his church, firſt apoſtles, secondarily prophets and evangeliſts' (who were of a parallel order), 'thirdly, teachers:'" (they should have added after that, miracles, then gifts of healing, helps,

by like mode of reasoning

governments, diversities of tongues). But, say they, "Chriſt has not set the like subordination of courts." (They should have said, therefore there ought to be the like for the subordination of courts; for they are now proving the firſt part of their minor, that such ought to be, not the second part that such is not).

In *answer* to this we say.

1. That they do not in this argument undertake to prove that synods are not of ſtanding use, much less that they may not be erected, but that they may not be subordinate.

2. That whatever subordination there was of an officer of one kind to an officer of another kind, and whatever power and authority apoſtles had over others, yet no such subordination of officers can be proved out of this place. A diversity of officers may be proved from hence, and perhaps a difference in dignity (that greater is he that prophesies, than he that ſpeaks with tongues), but not a subordination of officers for government. And we do not believe that our brethren will say, that ruling elders (whom they grant to be included in governments), are subordinate to those that work miracles, and those to teachers; those to prophets, and those again to apoſtles; and that appeals might be made from the ruling elder to him that works miracles, from him to the teacher, etc.

3. How does his [*sic?* this] text prove a subordination of evangeliſts to apoſtles and of teachers to them? For the evangeliſt is not mentioned in the text. As for what they add (who were of a parallel order): (1) This is but *gratis dictum*; they do not prove it. If they allege that in Ephesians 4:11,

gratuitously evangeliſts are reckoned after apoſtles, after and before paſtors and teach-
ſtated; mere ers, and therefore muſt be of the same order with prophets; we *answer:*
assertion (2) That the method there used does not prove a subordination, which is the point in queſtion; for if so, then muſt evangeliſts be subordinate to prophets, nor coordinate and of a parallel order. And they might as well, for ought there appears, be of a parallel order with paſtor and teachers, as of a parallel order with prophets. And (3) If it be granted that they are of a parallel order with prophets, yet that there muſt be therefore the same subordination of them to apoſtles, and of teachers to them, is not an express inſtitution, but only an argument *à pari ratione*, because there is the same reason for the subordination of evangeliſts, that there is of prophets. (4) We hence observe that our brethren make use of an argument only, *à pari ratione*, to prove a positive inſtitution. For their argument is to this purpose; for the subordination of prophets there is an express inſtitution, and there is the like reason for the subordination of evangeliſts, *ergo*, evangeliſts are also subordinate. We might as well argue, that for the subordination of officers there is an express inſtitution, and there is the like reason for subordination of courts. Therefore courts also are to be subordinate. And if they will not allow this to be a juſt exception, {that

for the subordination of prophets there was a special institution, or else it might not have been owned, but there is the same reason of the subordination of evangelists, therefore there must be also an express institution for that too (and not only an argument *à pari ratione*), or else it must not be owned,} they must not then make use of this argument against us, but do themselves deny the strength of it.

4. They might as well argue, there was an express institution for subordination in the church, or else it might not be owned; and therefore (*a pari ratione*) there must be as express an institution for taking it away, or else it must be owned still. Yea, that there was an express institution for setting apostles, evangelists, prophets, miracles, tongues, etc. in the church: and therefore (*a pari ratione*) there must be as express an institution for removing them, or else they continue still. For there is the same authority requisite to remove an institution, that there is to establish it. And when our brethren have well considered these things, together with the practices of their own ways, and so stated, interpreted, and limited what they say here, as that themselves will be willing to stand to it, and their own principles and practices not vanish before it; we doubt not but to show better and clearer warrant for synods, for their subordination, and for their standing use (though yet our proposition speaks nothing of the standing use of synods), than they can do for many practices of their own, which yet they believe, not only to be agreeable to, and warranted by the Word, but to have the nature of institutions.

II. Their second reason is this: That presbyterians require an institution "in the case of the subordination of bishops, archbishops, patriarchs, and popes;" but as we read not in the scripture "of the name of an archbishop, nor of the thing;" so we read not in Scripture "of councils, provincial and national, names or things." Yea, and the "disadvantage" is rather on this side; "for we are sure that once there was in the church, such a subordination of officers, evangelists over pastors, and apostles over evangelists," "but of such a subordination of council in an aristocratic{al} way there is nothing to be found." {See p. 208; see also 99, III, 145, 164, 254, 265}

Answer. 1. Still we note our brethren's pleading for episcopacy; yea, for papacy (which both they and we have covenanted[1] to extirpate), rather than the government of the Reformed churches, which both they and we have covenanted to maintain, at least against the common enemy.

---

1. [The Solemn League and Covenant (1643), "II. That we shall … endeavor the extirpation of Popery, Prelacy…." Goodwin first made the comparison in the debate over Presbytery (Feb. 22, 1644). Gillespie retorted "to Mr. Goodwin's twit of Episcopal arguments, that Parker lays it to the charge of the bishops, that there is no appeal and remedy against their errors and injustice" (Lightfoot, 172–173). Goodwin drew parallels again over synods (Sept. 27), with Rutherford replying in a heated September 30 session, that like the pope, Congregationalism had no judge above them. Gillespie and Goodwin contended again in the next session, October 1, 1644 (Gillespie, 81; *Minutes*, 3.337–359.]

2. Of prelacy among ministers, we find nothing in Scripture, but much against it; and therefore presbyterians do not only call for a warrant or institution for the subordination of bishops, archbishops, but for the *being* of them as our brethren themselves observe. The usual exception against this subordination of such church officers is, "that in Scripture, we read neither the name of an archbishop, nor the thing; and therefore not of a subordination to them." But of synods, our brethren will not say that we find nothing in Scripture, either *name* or *thing*; for themselves acknowledge them a holy ordinance of God. And for the bounds of them, whether they may consist of the ministers of one province, or more provinces, or less than a province; is no more a matter of institution, than whether a particular congregation may consist of 40, 50, or 100 members; and those inhabiting within one mile, two miles, or three miles distance; but is to be regulated by general rules of the Word, and particular circumstances of times, places, and persons. And for their subordination, we have already shown (in our former answer, and the proofs of our propositions) sufficient warrant from the general rules of the Word, the light of nature, and parity of reason; besides what is strongly argued from the precedent of the Jewish church in matters of ecclesiastical concernment. But our brethren should have remembered that they are but proving the first part of their minor (that synods *must have* such institution); and therefore most of this discourse is not to the purpose in this place.

{See p. 208} III. Their third instance, *à pari ratione*, is this: 'As in other societies and bodies politic, in the rearing of a contignation [*framework*] of power, there must be an ordinance or creation from man; not only of the several kinds of officers, but of the several courts; and a set and express order, "both of the number and bounds of courts of judicatory, from whom and to whom appeals are to be made, and in what cases," etc.; 'which courts the greater and higher they be,' "the more express evidence and warrant for their power there is and ought to be, as for parliamentary power and the privileges thereof;" 'so must there be proportionably a divine institution for the contignation and subordination of spiritual power, besides that of the distinction of officers themselves.'

Answer. Not to dispute the principles of polity here laid down—Whether a state may not give power to the justices of peace in such or such a county to preserve the peace there, and see that the known laws of the kingdom be observed, without setting down expressly how often, at what places, and in how many divisions they shall meet for that purpose, and how many sorts of committees or subcommittees they shall make of themselves for the better effecting of it; or whether they may not give commission to a general to command an army for such and such purposes, without prescribing expressly into how many companies, regiments, brigades, etc., they shall be divided, and in what proportions and subordinations; or whether a parliament must have more express evidence and warrant for all particulars of power or authority that they exercise, or privilege that they challenge, than inferior judicatories need to have?—We *answer* (to their argument, *à pari ratione*, upon this supposition):

1. That our brethren oft except against such arguing as this; thus it is in civil ſtates, therefore thus it ought to be in church government.

2. That this argument for subſtance is the same with that in their former discourse of power over power, which we then answered at large.   {See p. 164}

3. We here add, that there ought not to be *here* required such an express and plain designment out of the Word, as in civil and human inſtitutions for civil courts and their subordination, the Scripture not being written syſtematically, nor delivered in the manner as human laws are, but as a golden mine to be diligently searched in all the veins, and therein we may find sufficient for our warrant and direction, together with the light of nature and reason, to apply these rules to particular cases. And by such rules our brethren themselves will not refuse to go in many particulars in the government of their churches.

IV. Their fourth inſtance is; 'If in a particular church Chriſt has prescribed {See p. 209}
the several subordinations of proceedings, with the degrees, bounds, and order of them' (Matthew 18), 'so that it were not orderly in a set way to make any more ſteps or degrees of admonition, besides those which Chriſt has designed:' "it had been much more necessary to have appointed the like about these" "greater assemblies," 'which have the' "power of a sentence of judgment;" 'and of which, if Chriſt has not set them forth their bounds and order, none can tell what belongs to them, or which of them firſt to appeal unto.'

Answer. 1. Our brethren here say not, that Chriſt has set a ſtanding fixed order and subordination of proceeding in a particular church, which is *always to be held unto;* but only, that in *a set ordinary way* we are to make no more; tacitly yielding (as some of them did in the assembly expressly), that Goodwin, cf.
after one or more admonitions by one, then by two or three, there may Gillespie, 82
sometimes (if there be hope of gaining him thereby), be an admonition by eight or ten, before they tell it the church.

2. Our brethren should have shown what method, terms, bounds, or subordinations of proceedings, Chriſt had prescribed to the church when offenses are public and openly scandalous, as well as when private and known but to a single brother. Unless they would give leave to argue, as here themselves do: {'That if Chriſt has prescribed the several subordinations of proceedings, and set forth the degrees, bounds, and order of them, in case of a private offense, and how the church may come to take cognizance of it: then much more should this have been done in case of a public offense and scandal, if He had intended the church should at all proceed upon it; which if He has not done, the church (it seems by this argument), may not take notice of that at all.'} For if they say that the directions here given concerning a private offense, will *pari ratione* serve for direction and

the necessary changes having been made warrant to proceed in a just proportion (*mutatis mutandis*) in case of a public scandal; we may say the like concerning synods: that the directions here given concerning the manner of proceeding in a particular church, will afford a sufficient direction and warrant to proceed in a like proportion in a synod, or combination of churches.

3. Our brethren should have shown that by church is there meant a particular congregation, and that only. For if telling a synod, or a church of churches (as Mr. Cotton calls it),[1] may be said to be a telling the church; and if those that refuse to hear a synod may be said to refuse to hear the church; and if the presence of Christ promised to two or three gathered together in his name, may be applied to a synodical meeting, as well as to a meeting in a particular church; and if that ratification in heaven of what the apostles (and those who succeed them in that power), do bind or loose on earth, may as well be meant of their power in synods, as of their power in a particular congregation (and that it may not be so, our brethren have not yet shown); why may we not then believe that the bounds and limits, and order of proceedings in a synod (which themselves grant to be lawful, and an ordinance of God), have as sufficient direction and warrant from this place, as the proceedings in a particular congregation? Nor have our brethren yet shown that the synodical proceedings (Acts 15) were not in pursuance of, and obedience to this order of Christ in Matthew 18.

4. If our brethren had shown that it is meant (properly and immediately) only of a single congregation, and that the manner and degrees, and subordinations of proceeding, both in cases of private and public scandals, had been so distinctly set down, as not to admit of any variation, either in the number of admonitions, or steps of proceeding by way of gradation, before they come to the highest degree in that particular church, or in the manner of proceeding there, to be more or less slow or expeditious in proceeding, before they come to the last sentence, according as the nature of the crime, or quality and disposition of the person might require; yet there might be reason why the same particulars should not be so precisely determined for associations or combinations of churches in their bounds and limits; because, though where they can be had, they much conduce to the well being of particular churches; yet our Lord knew that it would not be alike easy at all times, and in all places to obtain them, in the like extent or proportion, in regard sometimes of persecution, or at least for want of countenance from the magistrate, sometimes by reason of the paucity and distance of churches; and sometimes for other difficulties and obstructions

---

1. ["Look as in the case of the offence of a faithfull brother persisted in, the matter is at last judged and determined in a church, which is a Congregation of the faithfull: so in the case of the offence of the church or congregation, the matter is at last judged in a congregation of churches, a Church of churches: for what is a Synod else but a Church of churches?" Cotton, *The Keyes of the Kingdom of Heaven* (1644; Boston: Reprinted by Tappan and Dennet, 1843), p. 94.]

                    III: ANSWER OF THE ASSEMBLY TO THE

that may hinder: so that where they can be had, they have the authority and blessing of a divine inftitution, being an ordinance of God; yet are not so precisely determined as that they muft be so many, so often, and so many subordinations or gradations in them. Sometimes no more churches perhaps may have that opportunity to associate, then may all join in one classis; sometimes no more classes than to make one synod: and yet elsewhere, or at other times, there may be opportunity, not only of particular churches combining in classes, but of classes in synods, and many synods in one, or more larger associations.

5. The order and degrees of elective synods (which yet our brethren allow as an ordinance of God) are no more set down, or limited in Scripture, than the order or degrees of ftanding synods. And the same inconveniences which our brethren here object (and many more), will fall as heavy upon such elective synods. For, if when a difficulty falls out in a particular congregation in our brethren's way; some should plead to have the aide of one sifter church, some of another; some of two or three, some of all in the province or nation; because in the multitude of counselors there is safety. Or, if they would go firft to one, then join two or three others, then call in the reft if need be; or firft one *per saltum*[1] to them all; what have our brethren here to plead but general rules, Chriftian prudence, light of nature? Even the same with us.

V. Their laft inftance, *à pari ratione*, is from the Jewish church. In the {See p. 210} church of the Jews, they say, "the subordinations that were, were set forth and determined by inftitution or example, how many courts there should be, and where to reft."

Answer. 1. We shall not need here to difpute whether all the courts in Israel are set forth and determined in Scripture; or whether no court there, either was or might be set up before they had either inftitution or precedent example for it. But we suppose it will be hard for our brethren to prove it.

2. Suppose them so to be; yet there is not a like reason that there muft be now a like particular determination; because all churches under the New Teftament are not of a like extent, and alike capable of associations.

3. The Jewish subordinations, being no temple ordinances, nor typical or ceremonial, do in the moral equity of them concern us,[2] as well as them;

---

1. [*Per saltum*—"Leaping ahead." i.e. Passing over the normal order of proceedings; 'without intermediate stages.']

2. [While it does not come up explicitly in the minutes in the debate over subordination of assemblies, Gillespie said during the debate over church officers, wherein the Scottish commissioners and the Independent divines were united in supporting the office of ruling elder: "For that of nationall churches, & apeales, sorry to fall at this time upon anything of this kind. If we goe on unanimously in the poynt of officers, we may agree better in the other questions. I wish controversyes of that kind be not started before the time. Rather hold only upon the poynt of officers & ruling elders. Whether we be bound to follow things in the Jewish church which had noe ceremoniall reason, but a morrall equity." *Minutes*, 2.459-460.]

Gillespie, 78 at least we may with much more reason urge an argument, *à pari ratione*,
Minutes, 3.332 from subordinations in the Jewish church to prove a subordination *still*, than our brethren can argue from thence against it. For the grounds of that subordination being from moral equity, and the ends and necessity of it being the same now as then (*viz.* resolving difficult cases, ordering matters of common concernment, reforming offenses in inferior societies, receiving appeals, redressing of injuries and neglects in male-administration [*maladministration*], etc), the same reason still remains, that for the same ends and purposes, there should be subordinations now in the Christian church, that was then in the Jewish.

And thus we have answered their reasons (*à pari ratione*) for the proof of the first part of their minor, that synods must have the greatest and most express warrant and designment in the Word, etc. It is enough for us that if there be but a sufficient warrant, we must not prescribe the Holy Ghost, how great, and how express that warrant must be. And when our brethren shall undertake to prove the practices of their own way (gathering churches out of churches; ordination and deposition of ministers by the people alone; their elective synods; their non-communicating churches in their way; that one single church may denounce the sentence of non-communion against other churches, whether one or more, yea, against all the churches in a province or kingdom, whom that particular church supposes to miscarry; with many other practices, which if need were, we might instance in), we doubt not but they will abate some of these expressions, and will desire us to except of somewhat less than the greatest and most express warrant and designment in the Word, both for the subordination and number, and for their bounds and limits of power. And some of them have told us, that the rule they go by in searching after institutions, is not to rest satisfied with such texts only as do clearly set them down, or must necessarily be so interpreted; but if to their consciences, they seem by any circumstance to incline or lean this way, rather than the other; and that this seems to be the meaning of the Holy Ghost, rather than the other (though the text might possibly admit of another interpretation, yet), it is enough to their consciences to prove an institution.

TO THE SECOND PART OF THEIR MINOR

{See p. 210} The second part of their minor they come next to prove, that these synods have not such express warrant and designment. (They should have proved that they have no designment or warrant at all; or else they hurt not our proposition, which said only, they are agreeable to, and warranted by the word of God).

For proof of it they say, 1. "The New Testament is silent, in it. And if it be said that all nations (we suppose they would have said, whole nations) were not then converted;" they answer, the apostles, though they "had not

                    III: Answer of the Assembly to the

lived to see that which might occasion such an institution; yet [they] would have left order for the time to come."

Answer. (1) The Scripture is no more silent of these, than of elective synods.

(2) The subordination of particular churches to greater assemblies is held out [in] Acts 15, and in Matthew 18 (as we have shown in our proofs of this proposition); such particulars only excepted, which are common with the church to other bodies politic, and are determinable by nature's light: so that, herein there was sufficient order taken, not only for the present, but for the time to come.

(3) Our brethren themselves acknowledge, that there is [in] Acts 15, a going out from a particular church, electively to another church or churches (so that there is not a total silence in this point), but they do not tell us to how many churches they may go out, nor to which first, nor how often they may go out successively, in case their divisions or difficulties be not removed upon their first going out. And our brethren tell us at other times, that a church may not only go out, but may be called out to give an account to a {See p. 225} church or churches offended; yea, to all the churches of a province or nation (which how it can be done without a provincial or national synod, we cannot tell); and this is no going out electively, for it is not at their choice, what churches they shall give account to. But when our brethren undertake to prove this, we believe they will content themselves with some such proofs as we have produced for our proposition.

But 2. Our brethren say, 'the apostles lived to see many particular churches in provinces and nations; and though all the inhabitants were not members {See p. 210} of churches, "yet there was matter for molding … them into these subordinations,… as now in France, where not a third part are Protestants," and in "the Low Countries, where not a tenth part" are church members; so that, "if these superstructions had been so absolutely necessary," it "had been as necessary" that the apostles should "have appointed them."

Answer. Whether in France not a third part be Protestants, or in the Low Countries not a tenth part members of churches, we stand not now to dispute. And whether it were necessary for the apostles to have appointed such subordinations, if they be at all warrantable, does not belong to this place, but to the first part of the minor, where we have spoken to it; only this we add here, that they should have shown that they had a possibility, liberty and opportunity of erecting such subordinations, as well as matter for the molding of them. We have not classical, provincial, national assemblies at present in England, not because we think we ought not to have them, or that we may not have them, but because we have not had opportunity to erect them.

But that which our brethren are now to prove, is that the apostles *did not* appoint them. And how should that be proved, but by this reason? 'We read not of those subordinations in the nations of Judea, Asia, Crete, in which were famous particular churches; therefore there were no such subordinations; and Christ writing to the seven churches of Asia, writes to each church apart, and not to a provincial, or national synod of them.'

Answer. (1) They might as well argue, because we read not that the apostles did appoint in the churches of Judea, Asia, and Crete (or, that those churches did practice), the ordinances of public singing of psalms; reading of the Word; and baptizing of children; the examination and trial of those that were to be admitted members of churches, before their admission; catechizing; visitation of the sick; that the women did eat and drink at the Lord's Table as well as the men, or the like; therefore there were no such things in those churches. If it be said, there was warrant and appointment for those things in other places of Scripture: so say we of synods and their subordination. The Scripture gives not many instances of one particular of church government; we have one instance of excommunication in the church of Corinth, and but that one of a church's excommunicating in the New Testament; and we have one instance of a synod; and why should not that be as sufficient as the other?

(2) Neither do we read of any elective synod for arbitration in these churches, such as our brethren yet hold for an ordinance of God; and we are sure their errors, and divisions, etc., needed the help of every ordinance, as our brethren confess. And Christ writes no more to the seven churches of Asia, concerning such elective synods, than of these subordinations: and the objection lies as strongly against their way, as ours.

{Answers to the exceptions of Jerusalem and Ephesus, pp. 99–174, 179–204}
(3) But this we read sufficiently, that the church of Christ is one body, and the officers given to it, for the good of all the body; and we read of all the churches of Galatia written to as one body, as one lump, and we read of the communion of the churches one with another in many particulars, as we showed at large in our former answer; which is sufficient for our assertion.

And as to what they allege of Christ writing to the seven churches apart, and reproving each of them for their own disorders which of our brethren suppose He would not have done, if they had been in a standing association of government. We *answer:*

Gillespie, 80
(1) If so; yet we need not inquire far for a reason: they were several churches, and had their several faults, and needed several counsels, and consequently several letters: as in a kingdom, where all are associated; yet the several provinces or congregations, may need several reproofs or advices; some being cold, lukewarm, declining, others pure, zealous, growing, etc.

(2) But if our brethren consider better of it, they shall find that all these seven letters (yes, the whole Revelation), were written to all the seven churches *in common*, as appears [from] Revelation 1:4; yet so that each might take special notice of that which did most peculiarly concern them. As when a minister, in a sermon to a mixed congregation, tells some of one fault, some of another; reproves the rich perhaps for pride; the poor,

for envy; the magistrate for negligence in his place; the masters, servants, parents, children, each for their several faults; or perhaps reproves some, commends others, etc.; which does not yet hinder, but that all these make one congregation. Or, to use their own instance, if a letter be directed to a national or provincial synod, it is very proper to show therein, what in one congregation or classis is to be commended; what in another is to be reproved; and not promiscuously to reprove or commend all alike. And our brethren may remember, that in some letters directed to this assembly, there have been sometimes large apostrophes directed particularly to themselves,[1] and not spoken to the whole assembly, notwithstanding they are a part of it, and in a standing association therein with the rest. And so it is evident that the whole epistle or book of the Revelation is directed in common to all those seven churches jointly, though yet there be something spoken particularly to each, besides that which is spoken in common to all.

(3) Our brethren do again herein as much dispute against themselves; for we have no more mention of elective synods, than of subordinate. Pergamus, and Thyatira, though troubled with errors in doctrine, etc., yet are not directed to seek out to an elective synod to redress them; nor are the other churches directed to call them to give an account; nor are any of the churches either commended for so doing, or blamed for not doing it. Yet both of these, according to our brethren's principles, ought to have been done; and this silence about it will not (we believe) be admitted by our brethren as sufficient argument to overthrow either the lawfulness, or the institution, of elective synods.

To what in the last place, our brethren add, that 'they are never called {See p. 211} by the name church, but churches,' we *answer*, as before, whether they be or no, it matters not; we inquire for *things*, not for *names*. Nor (2) Does the name churches prove that they were not one church by association; no more than that the flocks [in] Genesis 30:36–38 were not one flock, as they {See p. 198} are called in verses 31–32. And Peter speaking of many churches, yet calls them the flock (1 Peter 5:2). And (3) The many churches or congregations in Jerusalem, are yet called one church; and so at Ephesus, as we have shown already at large—to say nothing of the church of Antioch, and the church of Corinth, which is likewise called churches, 1 Corinthians 14:34, and the

---

1. [The ministers of the city of London wrote a letter to the Assembly concerning toleration, dated January 1, 1645/46 which addressed the dissenting brethren directly. While the brethren's objection to the subordination of synods was presented December 12, 1644, the Assembly did not formally answer until August, 19, 1646. So this letter or some other or others like it may be in view, such as the earlier and sharp correspondence in 1644 from the Walachrian classis and William Apollonius in Zeeland taking issue with the *Apologetical Narration* (see the notes to documents 14 and 17, *Minutes*, 5.30–31, 49). See *A Letter of the Ministers of the City of London, presented the First of January, 1645, to the Reverend Assembly of Divines sitting at Westminster … against Toleration* (1645), reprinted in *A Fourth Collection of Scarce and Valuable Tracts* (London: 1751), 3.343.]

often mention of the church in such a one's house, which, whether it be meant of a Christian family, or of a congregation ordinarily meeting there; yet were they part of a greater society consisting of many of these, which is also called a church. And when Paul is said to persecute the church of God (1 Corinthians 15:9, Philippians 3:6 and Galatians 1:13), yet were the churches of Judea either this church, or part of this church which Paul persecuted ([Galatians 1,] vs. 21–22). And indeed, whether a family or congregation, or a combination of them are called a church, they are but synecdochically so called, as being all parts of that one church, which is the body of Christ. And Stephanus observes as much in his *Thesaurus* (tom. 2 p. 23). *Hinc fit, ut* ἐκκλησίαι *in numero multitudinis saepe occurrat, quum alioqui unam eandemque omnes efficiant Ecclesiam.*[1] And as Christ the Husband has but one spouse (though yet synecdochically, every believer may be called the spouse of Christ), and Christ the Head has but one body; so but one church, which is the body of Christ (Ephesians 1:22–23). And our brethren themselves in their *Apologetical Narration*, page 6,[2] speaking of parochial congregations in England, call them the true churches and body of Christ, not bodies of Christ, though yet each of them, by the same reason that they are called a church, might have been called the body of Christ; yet all of them together are indeed but a part of that body.

Hence it is that ἐκκλησίαι often occurs in the plural number, while in other respects all make but one and the same Church

THE ANSWER TO THEIR SECOND ARGUMENT

{See p. 211} Their second argument is formed thus; "If there be such a subordination of synods, then there is no independency, but in an ecumenical council." Which we suppose they have therefore set down briefly; because if fully set down, it would not sound so well. For thus it should be: "If there may be a subordination of congregational, classical, provincial and national assemblies; then there is no independency, but in an ecumenical council."

Answer. Our brethren know there is nothing of ecumenical councils in our proposition, or of subordination to them, or dependence on them. For though the assembly had asserted in another proposition (to which our brethren entered no dissent), that there may be an ecumenical synod when it can be had; yet, what the power thereof is, and how far other assemblies depend on it, they have not asserted, but thought fit rather to consider of such assemblies, as through the blessing of God, we may possibly enjoy, and what power they have. But if our brethren will from our proposition infer that by a consequence of their own, they should have added some proof of that consequence; or at least an explication, that we

Gillespie, 79

---

1. ["Hinc etiam fit, ut ἐκκλησίαι numero multitudinis sæpe occurrat, quum alioqui unam eandémque omnes efficiant ecclesiam." Henri Estienne, *Thesauri Linguæ Graecæ ab Henr. Stephano constructi* (1572; 1580?),Tomus II, p. 23. Cf. *Thesauri Linguæ Graecæ*, volume 3 (Paris: Didot, 1835), p. 443.]

2. [Thomas Goodwin, Philip Nye, Sidrach Simpson, Jeremiah Burroughs, William Bridge, *An Apological Narration* (London, 1643).]

might see wherein the strength of their consequence lies: for such a consequence as this, if there *may* be a national, there *must* be an ecumenical synod, and if there *may* be a subordination to that, there *must* be a subordination to this (which seems to be the strength of their argument), had need have some proof. Our brethren grant that there *may* be a going out for advice to other churches; to the churches of a province, to the churches of a nation, if occasion and opportunity serve; yet do not say, that there *must* be a going out to all the churches in the world, whether there can be such a meeting or no; or that God's providence is not suitable to his institutions, if such a meeting cannot be had; or that there must be an injurious confining to the advice of the churches in one nation, if they cannot have the advice of such an ecumenic meeting; which yet, if it *could* be had, were like to be *remedium efficacissimun*, and a holy ordinance of God, as well as any of the rest.

But since our brethren have chosen this discourse about ecumenic synods, and therein let pass the proof of the consequence, and only give some reasons to make the consequent seem improbable, we shall briefly follow them therein: and do first observe how ill their three confirmations of it hang together. In the first they reason against us as holding a national church not to be independent; in the third, as if we held a national church to be independent; and in the second, they argue against the very being and existence of ecumenic synods.

1. First, say our brethren, this "would bring in a foreign ecclesiastical power over each state and kingdom;" to wit, if their consequence be good, and that there be no independency but in an ecumenic council.[1]

Answer. We suppose they would say, over each national church or national assembly, not over each state and kingdom. The church and civil state are differing things; as the kingdom of Christ, and the kingdom of this world. To bring in such a foreign ecclesiastical power as should be over civil states, is popish; but the help of an ecumenic synod, when it may be had, is no foreign power to the church, nor any hurt to the civil state. The ordinances of Christ are none of them foreign to the church, nor any of them hurtful to the state.

2. Secondly, say our brethren, 'such a council being the most efficacious and ultimate remedy, must be supposed to have some special indigitation [*pointing out*] in the Word, and special promise made to it; and that God, who suites his providences to his institutions, would have taken order that it should be existent in all ages; whereas the church wanted [*lacked*] ecumenic councils for 300 years.'

Answer. (1) If we should grant our brethren, not only what they say, that

---

1. [Goodwin may have had his main audience in mind here (the Parliament), as this argument does not appear in his original presentation of five arguments in either Gillespie or the *Minutes* (Lightfoot, absent for some days, has little on the debates over subordination).]

the church wanted them for three hundred years; but, that perhaps, there never yet was an entire complete general council rightly constituted, and God only knows whether ever there shall be one or no; yet this proves not, but that if it can be had, it may lawfully be made use of, and looked on as an ordinance of God, with expectation of God's special presence, assistance, and blessing, as in other ordinances; and that a synod of several nations may be made use of, in such measure as may be obtained. For God having given sufficient warrant for combination and communion of churches for their mutual good, and not having limited it to such and such bounds, beyond which they may not exceed, does sufficiently warrant it in the greatest proportions that may be obtained, even of the whole ecumenic church. And our brethren must admit this in their way; for they having, as they conceive, a warrant for going out to advise with other churches, and not being bounded, either how often they may so go forth, nor to how many churches, they conceive it lawful upon this warrant electively to advise with all the churches in a province, a nation; yea, the Christian world.[1] And they do not think that the defect of opportunity thus to advise, perhaps for some hundreds of years, does make such advising to be unlawful, or not agreeable to God's institution, if it could be had; though it may perhaps render it difficult, if not impossible. For we may not press that principle (of God's suiting His providences to His institutions) so far, as if God were bound in His providence to afford at all times an opportunity for doing of whatsoever by His institution might lawfully be done. We know the Arminians have made an ill use of such a principle in the point of universal grace, *quia*
because God Deus non deficit in necessariis ad salutem. And it were hard either for us, or
does not fail in for our brethren to admit such a principle in the matter in hand, that *noth-*
what is neces- ing is agreeable to, and warranted by the Word of God, but what has had,
sary to salvation and shall have an existence in all ages. Our brethren hold ruling elders to be not only agreeable to, and warranted by the Word of God, but of divine institution; and yet we think they will not say, they have an existence at all times in all their churches. And we suppose also, they will hardly prove that in all the reign of Antichrist, every ordinance of Christ had such existence as they require here to be shown of ecumenical synods.

(2) But if this principle were good, then do our brethren apparently overthrow the consequence of their own argument. For how easy is it to reply to that argument, that though there be and ought to be a subordination of congregational, classical, provincial, and national assemblies in this kingdom, where the providence of God, which is suitable to His institutions, has afforded a possibility and opportunity of them; yet no necessity of their

---

1. Preface to M. Cotton's *Keyes* [John Cotton, *The keyes of the kingdom of heaven, and power thereof, according to the Word of God. By … Mr. John Cotton, teacher of the church at Boston in New-England, tending to reconcile some present differences about discipline* (1644; Boston: Tappan and Dennet, 1843), p. 6ff.]

                    III: ANSWER OF THE ASSEMBLY TO THE

dependence on, or subordination to an ecumenic council, which (by our brethren's argument), must not be accounted an institution, because, if so, the providence of God would so have provided that it might be always existent.

(3) Yet withal, we must remember, that our brethren (whatever they here argue), do not deny either the lawfulness of them, or the usefulness of them, but only their standing use, and the subordination to them. Yet this argument, if it proves anything, proves that they may not *be* at all.

3. Thirdly, say our brethren, 'there must be an injurious independency set up in a national synod, because when a man has appealed from other courts to it, and upon the sentence thereof, comes to be banished, and have his estate forfeited to the ruin of himself and his family; then most of all, he needs such an effectual remedy as a general council, and lo it is not. And if the national assembly be independent, and upon the sentence thereof, the [most] extreme punishment, but that of death, be to be inflicted, it had need show a designment and warrant from God, to be the supreme and ultimate court.'

Answer. (1) Why did our brethren except that of death? When as national synods have [i.e. 'when have national synods had'] as much power to inflict death, as they have to inflict these punishments which they reckon up: banishment, forfeiture of goods, the [most] extreme punishments but that of death. For they know that we do not assert a power of inflicting either one or other of these, to be in ecclesiastical judicatory at all; nor is it practiced in the Reformed churches. And why our brethren should go about to cast such odious insinuations, without a cause, both on us and them, we cannot tell.[1] If it be because that, after the church has passed their censure, the magistrate does sometimes, when he sees cause, and according as the offence deserves, add his sentence too (yea, death itself, if he see cause, and the crime deserve it), this does no way concern the national assembly (or inferior assemblies), at all; to which no more belongs under a Christian, than under an heathen magistrate. Nor does it more concern us, than it does concern their way. For their *Apologetical Narration*, page 19,[2] informs us, that their sentence of non-communion may be afflicted and backed

{See p. 212}

Minutes, 3.338

Gillespie, 80

---

1. [As with the parallels to episcopacy and the like, this gratuitous charge seems intended to prejudice the parliament against presbyterianism. "The Independents hes no considerable power, either in Assemblie or Parliament, or the Generall or Waller's army; but in the city and countrie, and Manchester's army, their strength is great and growing; yet by the help of God and our friends, if once we had the Assemblie at ane end, and peace, we would get them quieted." Baillie to Spang, May 31, 1644, 2.186. Regardless, prospects would shift to the Independents' favor considerably, with the ultimate power moving from Parliament to Cromwell. "These men, just now coming into a position of supreme power [summer, 1646], were not absolutely opposed to a reorganization of the national church into a presbyterian form. They did oppose an exclusive presbytery supported by the state to the disadvantage of other sects and groups of Christians" (de Witt, p. 234).]

2. [Thomas Goodwin, Philip Nye, Sidrach Simpson, Jeremiah Burroughs, William Bridge, *An Apological Narration* (London, 1643), p. 19.]

with the sentence of the magistrate, as well as excommunication; and may in that respect, be made as efficacious. And we know that the practice in the churches of New England is consonant to it, where the civil magistrate does with as much, if not more rigor and severity, back their church censures, as in the Reformed churches governed by presbyteries and synods.

(2) The sentence of the national assembly, how dreadful and terrible so ever our brethren please here to represent it, is no other than what they say belongs [to] every particular congregation. For excommunication is their highest censure, and this, say our brethren, every particular congregation may inflict. And if this be independency, yea, an injurious independency, that when this is inflicted by a national assembly, there may be no appeal from it; why do our brethren complain, that that proud and insolent title of independency is affixed to them, as their claim, *Apologetical Narration*, page 23,[1] when as they claim that, which themselves here call an injurious independency? For it is a principle of their way, that from the sentence of excommunication in a particular congregation, there is no appeal, nor is it reversible by any power on earth, but themselves alone. And for the injuriousness of such independency, we desire it may be considered, whether most injury is likely to be done, and remain un-redressed, where in a nation many thousand congregations, shall each of them have an independent power of censuring without appeal; or where the party aggrieved may appeal from them to a classis, from thence to a provincial, and from thence to a national assembly, though when he comes there, he can appeal no further? Especially, when as men are oft emboldened to sin, when they know that none can judicially call them to account. And, on the other side, the very remembrance or fear of an appeal, whereby their actions may come to be scanned, is a great motive to make judges proceed more righteously.

(3) But we do not assert that a national assembly is independent; but though we do not think it fit to trouble an ecumenical council with every particular difference or controversy that may arise in a church (as neither to trouble a parliament with every particularity of civil difference, which may be as well determined in inferior courts), yet in grave and weighty matters, we doubt not but there may be great use of a well constituted ecumenical assembly (if it may be had), and great help by it; and that a national assembly may be accountable to it (at least as much as our brethren hold a particular congregation to be accountable). But if a person conceiving himself to be injured in a national assembly cannot obtain redress, either from another succeeding national assembly, or from a superior assembly, he must commit his cause to God; and so must he that may conceive himself wronged by a classical or provincial assembly, if he cannot have the opportunity of appealing farther. In like manner, as he that thinks himself civilly injured by the parliament, or supreme power in a state, and has no other way to obtain

---

1. [*Apologetical Narration*, p. 23.]

redress. Yet is not this a reason why we may not have recourse to such ways of remedy as God affords, because there may be a further remedy, which God at present affords not; or because we are deprived of an appeal to an ecumenical synod, which seldom, or never, or not without great difficulty can be had; therefore not to make use of provincial or national assemblies, and appeals to them, a remedy which may oft and easily be had; or (in a civil way), because a parliament, which is *remedium efficacissimum*, is not always *most effective* sitting, therefore not to make use of the benefits of inferior courts. And yet *remedy* the complaint may there possibly be as grievous as our brethren here put the case; if a person, by an inferior judge or corporation condemned to die, when he has greatest need of a relief, shall think with himself, "there is yet a more efficacious remedy (a parliament), which both by the law of God and man is more able to relieve me, and lo it is not." Yea, and in our brethren's own way; if a church, after recourse had, first to one, or more neighbor churches, then to all in that province or nation, shall remain as unsatisfied as before; they may as well bewail themselves, that there is yet a further course of having recourse to an elective ecumenical synod, which they might, by Christ's institution have recourse unto, and lo it is not; it cannot be had.

The Answer to their Third Argument

Their third argument is thus framed; that church-power, which cannot show {See p. 213} a set and "constant divine rule for its variation, and subordination, and ultimate independency, is not of God, and so may not be; but this variation of church power into these subordinations cannot show any such steady and constant rule for these things," *ergo*.

Answer. First, to their major. If by a set and constant rule, they mean by a particular and express rule; we deny it. It is not necessary that there be a particular express rule for the local bounds or circumstantial variations in government. If they mean the general rules of the Word, applied and made use of, with the help of prudence and nature's light; we grant it, and it helps not their cause.

And as to the proof of their major—that 'God did never constitute a church, but he gave the bound of it, that the change from family govern- *Minutes,* ment to national government, among the Jews, was by God's appointment, *3.339–344* that in the New Testament there is a reed to measure the temple'—we say, Gillespie, that God never did, either in the constitution or alteration of Jewish church *80–81* government or any other, set out by particular express rules, all the circumstantial variations of it, such as our brethren require of us. And that of measuring the temple with a reed, proves no such thing; for whether that be meant of God's separating the invisible saints from the antichristian apostasy, and preserving them during Antichrist's reign; or of restoring His church again after that time (as men use to measure the ground they intend to build upon); or comprehend an order for the government of the visible political church, as our brethren would have it (which we need not stand now to inquire into); yet it no ways holds out all local and circumstantial variations; which God has no where determined either in the Old or New Testament, but left things of that nature under general rules.

Secondly, to their minor we *answer:* 1. That it is as much against their way as ours. All that they can say for the setting out the bounds of particular congregations and elective synods, will not amount to an express particular rule for all circumstantial variations. All that which they say for the bounds of a particular congregation (in their reasons against our alleging Acts 15 for proof of this proposition), is no more but this: "such as live so, as conveniently to meet in one place" (which yet perhaps will hardly agree with the bounds of some of their congregations); but whether they must be threescore, fourscore, one hundred, two hundred, or a hundred ninety and nine, or more or less; whether they must all live within one mile, two miles, three miles compass, or more or less, or may live twenty, thirty, forty miles or more asunder (as is seen in some congregations nowadays); whether a thousand persons should be divided into three or four, or five, or more, or fewer congregations; and whether this or that man must join himself to this or that, or a third congregation; what is there in all these particulars, and many more, that must determine it, but general rules of the Word, and principles of prudence, and the light of nature, as may best stand with convenience and edification? And for the bounds of elective synods, when a church stands in need of advice or arbitration, there is nothing in the Word of God to determine particularly, whether they must go out to this or that, or a third church first; or whether to one, or more at once, or, if not satisfied upon the first advice, whether they may go out a second, a third, a fourth time; or how often, or to how many churches; or, if one church be offended with the practices of a great many churches, whether they may, or must call them all to account one by one, or two, three, four, or more at once, and how often they may, or must so do; or, if many churches be offended with the practices of one church, whether each of them singly must call that church to an account, or two, three, four, or more together; and whether after account given to some of these churches, they may a second, a third, a fourth time be called to give an account to others. There is nothing in all these cases that can afford a particular express set standing rule to proceed by, but only as by the general rules of Scripture, the light of nature, and principles of prudence, shall appear most to conduce to edification, determining controversies, removing offenses, preserving of peace, etc., the very same rules by which we must go in determining the bounds, number, frequency, gradations of synods. For that synods ought to be, or at least may be (which is all our proposition asserts), we prove: "That such churches, and such a number should associate, as may most conveniently and orderly be united for the best effecting of those ends for which synods are appointed," is but the general rule of Scripture. That they be provincial, national, etc., is according to the different occasions and conditions of times and places; and are to be set up, bounded, circumstantiated, as may be most for edification, and according to the prudent consent and agreement of the churches, together with the help and power of the Christian magistrate when it may be had. And as in other bodies politic, navies, armies, etc., their subordinations are cast for the *good of the whole.* So should it be in the church of Christ, which being the *most perfect republic, does comprehend in it whatsoever is excellent in all other bodies politic.*[1]

I. Next we examine our brethren's confirmation of their minor; wherein they go about to remove all things which they suppose to be the square of framing these subordinations—"not *quâ*[2] greater number of churches," "not *quâ* [*as*] in one kingdom," "not *quâ* in one nation"—wherein they labor in vain, while they take pains to remove those particulars which were in the debate disclaimed in the assembly, from being the square of framing these subordinations; and in the meantime give no reasons to overthrow that which then was, and now is, plainly owned as the rule on which we proceed. Yet since they please to insist upon those particulars, and that the particulars of themselves, be of some weight (*cæteris paribus*), in order to a determination in point of convenience, prudence, edification, etc., though not sufficient absolutely to determine whatever else may counterbalance them; we shall follow them in it.

{See p. 213}
Gillespie,
81–82
Minutes,
3.337–350

all other things being equal

First they say, not *quâ* greater number of churches, for then 1. There must be as many several subordinations, as there can be supposed variations of greater numbers.

Answer. We say not, *quâ* greater number simply (for then a national synod of one kingdom, constituting of a greater number, should bind a national synod of another kingdom consisting of a lesser number), but as the greater number of churches so combined and associated for such ends. As in a congregation, or congregational eldership, our brethren will not say that the greater number, *quâ* greater, binds the lesser, but the greater number of them so united.

2. And whereas they demand—where have we a promise that God will be more present with a greater part of them that profess Christianity, than with a few?—we ask, where has God promised to be more present with the greater part of a congregation, than with a few, suppose two or three gathered together in his name? Or, where have we a promise that God will be more present with an elective synod of many churches, than with the elders

{See p. 213}
Minutes,
3.341–342

---

1. See Robinson's *Justification of Separation*, page 113. [John Robinson (c.1575–1625), *Justification of the Separation from the Church of England against Mr. Richard Bernard his invective, intituled, the Separatists schisme* (Amsterdam, 1639); *The Works of John Robinson: pastor of the pilgrim fathers*, 3 vols. (London: Snow, 1851), 2.140.]

2. [*Quâ*—as; as being; in the capacity of.]

of a single congregation? Or, where have we a promise, that upon a second reference God will be more present than upon a first reference? Yet they tell us afterwards, that when offenses are not healed, and one reference to other churches is not sufficient to cure them, there should be a seeking to others. We are not to prescribe God how much He shall be present with his servants in such or such a way. But either we may expect that God, who promises to be present with every of His servants, will be more present with more of them; or else that the wisdom and graces of many of His servants in His way, will with the same assistance, better do the work, than the wisdom and graces of a few, for God ordinarily works by means (and if it were not so, we might as well refer matters of greatest consequence, and difficulty to a few as to many, to weak persons, as to wise and discreet, upon this ground, "where have we a promise of God's greater presence with the one than the other?"). Or, when God calls to a greater work, we may expect greater assistance. Or at least we are to do our duty in ordering of means, so as may be proportionate to their ends; and trust God to be more or less present as he pleases; and may, upon God's general promises, expect a blessing upon the use of all lawful means; else why should we rather encounter an enemy with a whole army, than with a single brigade or regiment?

3. Whereas they add, 'that the greater number of churches professing religion, are more corrupt, and it had been ill for Philadelphia to be joined in association with Laodicea, or the Calvinists in Germany with the Lutherans.'—we *answer:* If all numbers of men that will call themselves a church, must therefore be admitted into an association (how corrupt or heretical soever), we grant such an inconvenience might follow. And so (say we), it would be in a congregation, if all be promiscuously admitted to power in it; for the greater number of persons that pretend to profess religion, are more corrupt; and yet can they allege no better reason for excluding any true Christian from their church communion, than we for leaving any true church out of association; yea, they profess as much in their *Apologetical Narration* (page 12, 9),[1] that their rule of judging in admitting of members is of "that latitude, as to take in any the meanest, in whom there may be supposed to be the least of Christ;" and their rule for casting out of fellowship (by excommunication), is "for no other kind of sin, than may evidently be presumed to be perpetrated against the party's known light;" as if "in manners and conversation, such as is committed against the light of nature, or the common received practices of Christianity, professed in all the churches of Christ; or if in opinions, then such as are likewise contrary to the received principles of Christianity, and the power of godliness, professed by the party himself, and universally acknowledged in all the rest of the churches; and no other sins." And if our brethren walking by this rule, can yet in a sufficient measure be secured,

{See p. 213}
Minutes, 3.342
Gillespie,
80, 81

---

1. [*Apologetical Narration* (1643), pp. 9, 12.]

that the greater number of persons in some of their congregations may not be the more corrupt, and prejudice those that are more pure; surely we may then hope, that if our synods be made up of such elders as are described [in] 1 Timothy 3 and Titus 1 (to which a tender respect is to be had), we may in a good measure avoid that danger. But there is far more danger in our brethren's way; for if an erroneous heretical congregation may (electively, as our brethren speak), choose their own judges, we have little reason to believe, that they will choose either none at all, or such as they know beforehand, are likely to be of their own judgment.

4. Say our brethren, 'suppose there be as many elders and churches more purely reformed in one province, as in the rest of the nation besides; why should not God be thought to be as much with them, as with the national assembly?'

Answer. So He may (God may be as much present possibly with one regiment, as with the whole army beside); and if He be so present with them, as to enable them to do their work, they need not then bring it to the national assembly; yet even then, the rest of the nation may have need of them. There may possibly be as many able knowing Christians in some one family, as in all the rest of a congregation, yet this hinders not their associating into one church.

5. Say they, 'if *quâ* greater, then the decrees of general councils in former ages (even those that set up bishops and popes), should bind us more than provincial or national synods now, at least till repealed by another general council, as acts of parliament made by our ancestors bind us till repealed.'

Answer. (1) The assembly has not yet debated the power of general councils in making laws, much less of their binding after ages.

(2) Nor do we say that councils (either one or other), do bind absolutely, whatever their decrees be. But when they err, they are no otherwise binding, than as erring eldership.

(3) Nor do the decrees of those councils bind us, except *vi materiæ*, who were not in association with those churches, nor were either actually or virtually consenting to them.

(4) Nor do we grant that such general councils had a like legislative power for these churches, as the Parliament has for the kingdom.

II. Next, say our brethren, 'the bounds and limits of assemblies being ecclesiastical, must not have their rise from national or political respects. Antioch sent to Jerusalem, not of the same province or nation, rather than Syria or Cilicia.'

Answer. 1. We do not bring Acts 15 for a pattern of a synod, either provincial or national, as such; but as an instance of churches associated in a synod. And if not within the same either province or nation, then does it give warrant for association of churches, even beyond the bounds of one nation.

2. We do not say, *quâ* province, *quâ* nation, *quâ* kingdom; but as upon

Gillespie, 81

by virtue of the matter

{See p. 214}

a due weighing of these, and other particulars shall appear moſt for the good of the church.

But we say, 3. That the churches in one kingdom (having more communion with each other, than the churches of another kingdom), are (ordinarily) fitteſt to associate, and to be moſt immediately helpful one to another.

4. We say that the concurrent assiſtance or opposition of the ſtate and magiſtrate, may make associations, either in the same nation, or with other nations, more or less expedient; and variation in expedience may cause a variation in the boundings [*boundaries*] and limits of synods.

And for that queſtion, why Antioch sent not to the churches of Syria and Cilicia; rather than to Jerusalem, which was neither in the same province nor nation?

We *answer:* Whether it were, 1. Because that Aram or Syria being so large and vaſt, containing not only Cælosyria, in which Antioch was, but also Mesopotamia, Phœnicia, and some other regions; and Cilicia likewise (of which Tarsus was the metropolis), being very large (and to which Antioch did not belong, either as a province or nation, as our brethren seem to suppose); those churches could either not at all, or not so conveniently, or not so soon be gathered into a synod.

Or 2. Because those churches being troubled with the same errors (as it appears they were), and ſtood in need, as well as Antioch, of seeking the advice and help of other churches.

3. Or whether those churches being but new planted, were not yet formed into such subordinations.

4. Or whether those churches had already met in synods, and the debates and results at Antioch, were the debates and results not of one church, but of a synod of elders from several of those churches, and yet unable to determine that controversy—For (1) Others besides Paul and Barnabas were sent to Jerusalem. And (2) Other churches were troubled with these errors, and their troubles represented to the synod at Jerusalem. And (3) The return made and letters direĉted to those other churches, to the churches of Antioch, Syria and Cilicia. And 4. Judas and Silas sent to them with these letters; and yet when the letters are delivered and read at Antioch, the messengers sit down and make their abode there, as having performed their whole truſt, without further traveling about Syria and Cilicia, though the brethren of Syria and Cilicia, as well as those of Antioch, are told in these letters, that together with Paul and Barnabas, they had sent Judas and Silas to them, who should tell them the same things, by mouth.

5. Or whether for some other reason; we are not able positively to determine. Only in general we say, the reason why they had recourse unto, or did associate with the church at Jerusalem (and perhaps those of Judea too), for making decrees (in matter of common concernment), obligatory to all those churches of Antioch, Syria and Cilicia, was because this did

appear the most expedient and conducing for those ends, of edifying those churches, composing their differences, and removing their errors. And the same rule are we to observe in our associations.

And as to that of the kingdom of Israel breaking into two kingdoms, while yet the church-state in their subordinations altered not, we *answer:*

1. Whether it did, or did not, is not much material to our purpose; for we do not say that the bounds of a kingdom, *quâ* kingdom, must be the bounds of an association (but that there may be associations larger and lesser than of one kingdom); but, that this is one particular considerable amongst others in point of expediency and edification.

2. As for those services which by God's appointment were to be done only at Jerusalem, the reason is plain of their not altering, because there was but one Jerusalem, the only place which God had chosen to put His name there. But that *nothing* concerning the local bounds, or other circumstances belonging to their government, admitted variations upon that change, is more than our brethren can prove.

III. To what they next add, 'that if this independency arise from the magistrates, then there is not need of such subordinations, because (in experience), Reformed churches abroad are well enough governed without these subordinations; Geneva has no appeals, having but one classis,' "and why may not other churches be governed as well without them, if the magistrate oversees them, and keep[s] each to their duties? The churches in the low countries want [*lack*] national synods, and yet are peaceable governed; yea, some of them are without provincial, and say, if they can they will never have more"—we *answer:* {See p. 215} Gillespie, 83 *Minutes,* 3.353–355

1. If the churches in Geneva and the Low Countries be well enough governed, then are churches under a presbyterial government well enough governed. Yea, then is there no need of elective synods, for those churches have none.

2. We plead not for independency, but for a subordination upon association when it may be had.

3. Our question is not about the power of the magistrate, but about an ecclesiastic obligation, by virtue of church principles, such as might have agreed to the primitive churches, before the magistrate was Christian, as our brethren themselves have noted.

4. If Geneva does not altogether associate with those under another civil government, lest perhaps, they might prejudice their civil liberties; or for some other inconvenience which may over balance it; yet they do associate with the Reformed churches of France, as much as they can, and send commissioners to their national synods. And Beza has been president in some of them.

5. If the Low Countries want [*lack*] national synods, why do our brethren say they are well enough governed without them? If by want, they do

not imply a need of them, but that they have them not; then is it not true. For in the Low Countries they have national assemblies, though of late there have been some interruptions in their meetings, and they have not, as formerly met every three years. And the seldom meeting, either of their national or provincial synods is their prejudice, not their gain; and an affliction of spirit to their godly pastors and people. But whereas our brethren add, that some (churches) of them say, if they can, they will never have more, we know that the Socinians and Arminians have complained of synods, and labored with all their might to hinder the convening of them, but that others, at least that other churches have so said, we do no more believe, than we do what has been said by some others, that some of them have desired the episcopal government; nor are bound to answer for the one, more than for the other.

6. But let it be granted, that some Reformed churches (which could not have them), have not had all these sorts of assemblies. It does not follow, that therefore those who can have them, must yet forbear. Some churches have no ruling elders, some churches have no elective synods; yet our brethren will not say, that therefore no churches may have them.

IV. In the last place, say our brethren, 'as not from political, so neither from national respects are these bounds to be fetched. For then 1. The Calvinists in Germany' "must be subject to a greater number of Lutherans;" 'and all ministers in England must associate, of which the greater number will be the worse.' Or, "if because the Calvinists profess a further reformation, they be disobliged from" 'such an association, then so are those who in a nation profess a further reformation.' And "uniformity of principles is a more intimate bond of such association," 'than such extrinsical respects.' 2. "If *quâ* nation or principality, then Wales must be independent." 3. If *quâ* nation of the same tongue or kindred, then must the scattered Jews have made one church distinct, from those with whom they did cohabit. Or. 4. If *quâ* nation or people, dwelling with the same national bounds, then must those Jews make up one church with those nations; whereas Peter, James, and Paul to the Hebrews writes to them apart, as churches in all nations.'

Answer. These are but light exceptions. For 1. Though the churches in a nation be bound to associate, if they can; yet not *quâ* one nation (that respect of nation or principality being extrinsical to the church, and accidental), but *quâ* such a number, and in such bounds as may be most conveniently joined for the best improvement of synodical government.

2. Nor do we say [that] all ministers must promiscuously be admitted as members in synods, no more than that all pretended Christians may be admitted to all church communion in congregations.

3. Nor do we deny, but uniformity in principles ought among other things, to be dully weighed in reference to associations (and our brethren might as will have showed their reasons, why that may not be a rule to be made

{See p. 215}

Gillespie,81

                    III: ANSWER OF THE ASSEMBLY TO THE

use of in associations, as those that they have singled out); and our brethren know that the reason why the best Reformed churches in Germany (which our brethren call Calvinists), do not associate with the Lutherans (though they do admit amicable conferences and debates with them), is because of the great difference between them, not only in church government, but in weighty points of doctrine.

4. Yet we do not say that a bare profession of a further reformation, will disoblige from association; nor do we believe our brethren will say it; for by the same reason, they must say that if some of their own members profess a further reformation, they may, thereupon, divide from them.

5. That of Wales hurts not us; for if they may conveniently associate, their being a distinct principality, will not hinder it. If by reason of their language, or the like, they cannot; yet this hinders not, but that they, who can, may associate. Their supposed independency touches not us, who hold no independency.

6. The dispersed Jews (for anything our brethren can show to the contrary), might be associated with those churches among which they did co-habit (Christ having taken away the difference between Jew and Gentile). And, for ought we know, when Paul wrote to all the churches in Galatia, as one lump, they might be comprehended with the rest; sure we are, that the errors in the churches of Galatia about circumcision, and other Jewish rites, were too much associated with the errors of Jews who lived among them. And if so, then Peter writing to the dispersed Jews in Galatia, etc., did not write to them as a distinct church not associated. And we think our brethren cannot well say the contrary, unless they intend to grant that in the church of Ephesus (to say nothing of other churches), there were at least two congregations, one of Jews, another of Greeks; for that there were in Ephesus, both Jew and Greeks, we believe they will not deny.

THE ANSWER TO THEIR FOURTH ARGUMENT

Their fourth argument lies thus, "that government which necessarily pro- {See p. 216} duces representations of spiritual power, out of other representations, with a derived power therefrom, there is no warrant for. But these subordinations of synods, provincial, national, ecumenical, for the government of the church, do so." 'For if all churches in the several provinces be subject to the national assembly, and all in several nations to an ecumenical, then must they all be interested in that national or ecumenical assembly, and involved in it, as the shires are involved in the parliamentary power. Which interest must arise, either by an immediate choice (as parliament men are chosen immediately by those they represent), which cannot be here, for the congregations of a province do not meet for such choice of those, who shall represent them in national assembly; or else those chosen by the congregations to represent them in the provincial assembly, choose some few of themselves to represent them in the national; and some of the national assembly to represent them all in the ecumenical. Which may not be, both because there is no warrant for any delegated power at all in *vicars of Christ* spiritual matters, all ministers being immediately *Christi vicarii*; and because representations, as reflections, grow still weaker, the higher they go, and are but a shadow of the first shadow. Yet the whole power that can be supposed to belong to the whole substance, is ascribed to them. But if these few, in a general or national council bind all those nations or provinces under them. Then 1. They must be supposed to have a promise and assistance answerable; not only to judge as elders, which is their office; and according to their personal abilities being thus called to give their advise (which two are granted); but such a superadded assistance as hold proportion to that spiritual bulk and body which they represent. And such *Gillespie, 80,* is twice intimated to be with the Sanhedrin, Deuteronomy 17. *Thou shalt* *82, 83 go to the place which God shall choose, and do according to the sentence which* *Minutes, 3.342, they shall show.* 2. They have each of them in such an assembly, a power *352* parallel to that of bishop and archbishop, who challenge in counsels to represent their churches. 3. They must then be a church, and a body to Christ, which they are not?

Answer. 1. We cannot but observe, that our brethren do neither content themselves with the question as stated by the assembly (who being to advise concerning a church government for this kingdom, speak nothing of a subordination to ecumenic councils); nor yet are constant to their own stating it, but sometimes (as in their third argument), dispute against the assembly, as denying such subordination, and call for proof of an ultimate independency in a national synod; and sometimes (as in this argument), they dispute against subordination to ecumenic counsels, as if the proposition had asserted it.

2. We observe that neither this, nor any of the former arguments, are framed against the subordination of congregational and classical assemblies, to synods (which the proposition affirms), but only of synods amongst themselves, provincial to national, and both to ecumenical; the latter of which the proposition meddles not with.

3. For *answer*, we say: That when several churches send choice men to act thus in a classis; and several classes send choice men to provincial synods, and they to a national, these representations are not (as our brethren suppose), shadows of shadows, but as gold extracted out of gold, which the *Gillespie, 80* oftener it is refined, the purer it is; or as chemical extractions, whereof the last and highest is the most strong and precious.

4. And some representations of this nature our brethren cannot deny, both in their single congregations, and in their elective synods. For

(1) In their congregations, all have not authority to vote, as women and children; yet because the church is said to do it, and all (women as well

as others), are obliged, the voters must necessarily represent the whole church. And when any of those who have power to vote, are absent (which cannot be avoided, by reason of sickness, or the like, especially if persons dwelling at 40 miles distance, or more, are yet standing members of a congregation), the present voters must represent those representers also; and if those present voters do not all agree, the major part of these must represent them all.

(2) And when these representers send any of their delegates to act and vote in an elective synod, these delegates do represent all the former representers; and why may not ten churches meet to delegate some from them all, and send them to a synod of an hundred churches, as well as Antioch send from that one church to Jerusalem? {See p. 217}

5. Nor does this at all hinder it, that they are immediately *Christi Vicarii*. For though the power of such an office be immediately from Christ, yet the designing of such a person to that office, and employing him, *hic & nunc* *here and now* to preach the Word, or perform such an act of government, for the good and edification of those that send him, is not immediately from Christ.

6. But here we must observe likewise, that our brethren dispute not against the subordination or power of these synods, or the standing use of them, but against the being of them; and not of these only, but of their own elective synods; for how can a church or churches go forth electively to one elective synod of all the churches in a province, a nation; yea, of all the world (as our brethren grant they may), without representations, yea, representations of representations? For we do not believe their meaning to be thus; that if ten churches see cause to go forth for light [*knowledge*], to all the churches of a province or nation, by way of an elective synod; then all, and every member of these ten churches must in person repair to a meeting of all the members of those churches in a province or nation in one body. {See p. 217}

As to that demand of our brethren; 'where is there a promise of such an assistance as holds proportion with the whole nation?'—we *answer:* The promise of Christ is one and the same to all the officers; from the apostles to the pastor and teacher; "I will be with you always, to the end of the world," and, "where two or three are gathered together in my name, there am I in the midst of them." [Matthew 28:20; 18:20.] Which He uses to make good in proportion to the work He sets them upon. He does not give a distinct promise to each officer (I will be present with an apostle in such a proportion, with an evangelist in such a proportion, and with a pastor or elder in such a proportion); much less does He give special promises to each act belonging to the same office ('I will be thus far present with a pastor in teaching;' thus far in visiting the sick, thus far in admonishing, reproving, comforting, thus far in ruling his own congregation, and thus far when called to govern or advise in reference to other congregations); but that one promise is sufficient ground for each officer, in every act of his office to expect a blessing proportionable to the work he is employed in. Nor will our brethren we believe, undertake to produce a special promise, how far Christ will be present with an elective synod, more than He was with the church or churches that repair to them; or how much more He will be present with a synod of ten churches than of two.

But if our brethren think, that if a company of ministers be sent to a synod, in the name of so many churches, or to represent those churches, or the ministers in them; they must be then looked upon as having all the light, graces, gifts and consciences of all those churches, and must have as large assistance from God, as if they had so, we acknowledge no such representation as this, either in, or out of synods; and therefore need not seek for a promise of such assistance. If a minister, as the mouth of the people, indite and utter a prayer to God in their name, or on their behalf; though in so doing, he may be said to represent the people (as well, as when the priests offered up sacrifices in the behalf, either of the people, or of particular persons); he is not yet looked upon as having all the gifts and graces of that people, whose mouth he is, and an assistance answerable; but is to employ that light and grace and ability, that Christ has bestowed on him for their good (and so, if he pray to God in the behalf of an absent person, a church, a kingdom). And in the like manner must he do, when in a synod (provincial, national or ecumenical), he acts in the name, and for the good of such churches, by special delegation or appointment of him to that purpose.

Nor was it otherwise in the high priest's offering sacrifices, or making atonement for the whole people; who was not therefore to be looked upon as having gifts and graces equal to those of the whole people (though the sacrifices there offered, and the atonement made, were accepted for the whole); no more than if a king or single minister should make prayers to God, in the behalf of his kingdom or congregation, and be heard in such requests. Neither was the Sanhedrin to be looked upon as having all the grace, justice, wisdom of the whole nation, though they were by God's appointment the highest court; but only an assistance suitable to the work which God called them to. Nor will the text alleged out of Deuteronomy 17 (where they are bid to go up to the place which God shall choose, and to do according to the sentence which they shall show), prove more. And so far is that from making against what we assert, that it makes much for us. For though the place (Jerusalem), and the person (the high priest), were typical, and so ceased; yet the business itself (of hearing appeals, redressing injuries, expediting of difficult cases, etc.), are things of a moral nature, and there is the like need of provision for them now, as there was then.

As to what they next add, 'that this makes them in those assemblies so {See p. 218} many archbishops or bishops,' we *answer:* No more than every elder in one of our brethren's congregations joining in the presbytery may be judged popes in their own parish; nor so much neither, as might be easily shown if it were needful to make retortions of this nature. But we have often spoken to this comparison, which our brethren so much delight in; though yet they would not take it well to be so often told, how near their way comes (and in how many principles), to that of Brownists or Anabaptists; and, what might be said more plausibly for Brownist tenets wherein they differ, than for theirs. Yea, and themselves acknowledging elective synods of elders, who may (authoritatively) teach, and declare men subverters of the faith, fit to be excommunicated, etc. would not yet be willing to be charged to set up so many bishops or archbishops in those branches of authority which bishops challenge to themselves.

To their last exception, 'that if these representations having the power of all the churches in the nation be warrantable, they must be a church, {See p. 218} and a body to Christ,' etc. We *answer* (as often times in this case): That we do not inquire for *names*, but *things*. That there may be synods thus collected, our brethren, do not deny; but say, they are useful for finding out, and declaring of truth in difficult cases, for healing offenses, etc., whether they will say such a synod is a church, or is a body to Christ, we will not contend; if they may be so called, then so may the synods we contend for; if not, then their arguments hurt not us more than themselves, for then (by this argument), neither are their synods warrantable. But their consequence will no way follow; for our brethren assert often that every apostle had the power of all churches, not only in a nation, but in the world, and their acts did oblige them to subjection. Yet will not our brethren say, that every apostle is a church, or is so called, or is a body to Christ. And in every of their congregations, where they suppose the elders and brethren, without the women and children, have the whole church power; we need but turn their words upon themselves, if these representers (elders and brethren, without the women and children), having the power of all the persons in that congregation, were warrantable, they must be a church. Now, besides that they are no where so called, if they were called so, then they are a body to Christ, for so every church is, and where is Christ said to have a representative body of his body? And yet so they must be, or they have not the power of all the members of that church in them, nor otherwise do their acts oblige them to subjection. And when our brethren have thought of an answer in this case, we doubt not but they may see the same answer will serve our turn. That the elders and brethren without the women and children, are a church, we suppose they will not say; for if so, then either the women and children are of no church, or of another church; that they are of no church we believe they will not say; nor can they say, that they are of another church, unless they will say that one church governs another, that the church of elders and brethren, governs the church of women and children. If they say, that the elders and brethren, together with the women and children make but one church; and yet, though the women and children act not, yet the church is said to act thus and thus, when those in the church do thus act, who have authority and commission so to do, we say so to. And then the question will be this, not whether those who act are a church; but who those are in the church that ought to act.

The Answer to our Brethren's Reasons, against the allegation of Acts 15 for the subordination of synods, provincial, national, ecumenical

{See p. 219} We cannot but wonder to see our brethren so frequently run upon gross mistakes, and miss-recitings of our propositions and proofs. We say nothing in any of our propositions concerning subordination to ecumenic synods, but only of congregational, classical, provincial, and national assemblies among themselves; but instead of congregational and classical, our brethren add ecumenical. Nor did we allege Acts 15 for a proof of any subordination at all; nor so much as for the being of provincial or national assemblies, as such, but only for the lawfulness of synods (*That the Scripture holds forth another sort of assemblies for the government of the church, besides congregational and classical, which we call synodical*). A proposition to which our brethren entered no dissent, nor (so far as we can remember), did give any negative vote. For that there are synods held forth in Scripture, our brethren grant (and that they are an holy ordinance of God); and that they are proved by this place; but, whether provincial, national, ecumenical; whether standing, and subordinate; or occasional and elective; whether to excommunicate, or to advise, etc., that proposition speaks not. So that this text is brought by us to prove no more than what they acknowledge to be truth, and what they affirm to be proved from it.

I. But say they, this one example cannot prove both presbyteries and synods, but if we lean to the one, we must quit the other.

Answer. 1. Nor is it brought by us to prove both. We brought it before to prove, that the elders of Jerusalem did perform acts of government over more congregations than one; and it is brought now to prove the lawfulness of synods, which may both well stand together. 2. At least some passages in this chapter may prove the one, and some the other, without any inconsistence. 3. Yea further, if it be sufficient to prove that churches, at so great a distance, may join in a synod; it will prove *à fortiori*, that neighbor churches may join in a classis.

argument *from a stronger reason*

They say further, that this assembly (Acts 15), was not a formal synod, but only a reference by the particular church of Antioch, to the particular church of Jerusalem.

Answer. Whether either Antioch or Jerusalem were a particular church (in our brethren's sense), or whether this reference was made only from

Antioch, and not from any other church or churches assembled there, either in a classis or synod, it is not needful now to dispute. Nor whether this meeting at Jerusalem were a formal synod. Our brethren grant that a synod is a holy ordinance of God; and that it may be proved from this place; but whether the instance be a formal synod, or only a sufficient warrant for a synod, is to our purpose all one.

1. But say our brethren; if it had been a synod, yet neither provincial or national.

Answer. 1. Nor do we say that it was a provincial or national synod. But, though it were neither provincial nor national, yet it might be a synod; which is enough to our purpose, who bring this only to prove that there may be synods.

2. If (according to our brethren's principles), this meeting, though formally not a synod, might yet be a sufficient warrant for a synod (yea, for a multiplicity of synods, in case the first synod be not able to do the work), then this synod, though it were not formally either provincial or national, may yet be a sufficient warrant for both. For if we be bound precisely to follow this example, in all the circumstances of it, without any circumstantial variation, then cannot our brethren approve of elective formal synods under color of this example, which say they, was not a formal synod. Nor may they, in case the first elective synod do not satisfy, have recourse to a second (which yet here they say, they may), because those of Antioch rested in this first resolution.

II. They add, neither was it a standing synod (which the word subordina- {See p. 219}
tion does imply), but elective; and that, but for this one question without obligation to refer all other matters to them in an ordinary way.

Answer. 1. Our brethren should not dispute against the subordination of synods in this place; for Acts 15 was not by us brought to prove the subordination, but the being of synods.

2. Nor does the word subordination prove, that they must needs be standing synods; more than the subordination of inferior courts to the parliament proves, that the parliament must needs be a standing court and not occasional.

3. Nor is there such a material difference between standing synods and *Minutes, 3.348*
occasional, in regard either of their lawfulness, or their power; unless our brethren think, that a triennial or standing parliament be substantially different, in point of lawfulness and power, from occasional parliaments, and that, though the fundamental laws of a kingdom should warrant the one, yet they would not therefore warrant the other. We know not, but that occasional and standing synods are of the like divine authority; and our brethren have as yet made very little objection against it. Nor do those of New England make any such difference (see *Cotton Keyes,* page 48, *Answer to 32 Questions,* page 64[1]).

---

1. [Cotton, *The Keyes of the Kingdom of Heaven* (1644; repr. 1843), chapter six, "Of the Power

They add: III. "Nor was there a multiplicity of synods, but only one, in

{See p. 219} whose judgment those of Antioch rested." IV. 'Much less a contignation [*framework*] of synods, superior and inferior.'

Answer. Yet say our brethren in the next words; when offenses are not healed and one reference to other churches is not sufficient to cure them, there should be a seeking to others; so that this instance of one, is a sufficient warrant for a multiplicity, by their own grant (and if the first synod be able to dispatch the business, we do no more plead for a needless carrying it further, than themselves do). But in case there be reason after the first reference or appeal, to whom should they next go? The text is wholly silent; there is nothing for direction, but general rules of Scripture, together with principles of prudence, and the light of nature, to judge of what is most for convenience, order and edification; which all will persuade rather to seek higher, then lower. And not we only (with other Reformed churches), but Mr. Cotton, with the divines of New England, do argue from hence, by a parity of reason, for a contignation, even to an ecumenical council, as upon a moral and perpetual ground. But, whether this associating must needs be of neighbor churches, and, whether of all churches promiscuously without election; has been spoken to before. Whether they have power to *under a penalty* bind *sub pæna* (as our brethren speak), pertains not to this question, either about the being of synods, or of their subordination; nor do our brethren here object against it.

But because our brethren insist on this, that synods must be elective; we shall speak somewhat more to it.

If by elective, they had meant, an association of churches who meet in a synod, by their own mutual consent and choice, to determine, and manage matters of difficulty, etc. there had been no difference between us. We think that churches should voluntarily agree into such associations, as well as persons ought voluntarily to associate into congregations, so as may be most for general edification; yet is not the one nor the other a matter of choice; but of duty.

But by election, our brethren mean a reference made by a particular church, whose the business is, to some other church or churches of their own choosing, and they to deal in it, only so far, as they refer their business unto them.

To which we say,

1. That we think our brethren are the first that ever held out such a kind of synod.

2. Nor does this place, Acts 15:2, on which they ground it, speak anything of electiveness. It says indeed, when there was a στάσεως, a side or faction in

---

and Authoritie given to Synods," pp. 55–63. Richard Mather (1596–1669), *Church-government and church-covenant discussed: in an answer of the elders of the severall churches in New-England, to two and thirty questions …* (London, 1643), p. 64.]

                    III: ANSWER OF THE ASSEMBLY TO THE

the church that taught errors against the doctrine of Paul and Barnabas, the church concludes that Paul and Barnabas with others of them should go to Jerusalem; but no mention, that it was merely at their own choice, whether to send or not to send, or whether to Jerusalem or any other churches, and about what questions they pleased, and no others.

3. That it should be at the choice of the church whose the business is, is to us most incongruous; partly because it crosses another principle of our brethren's, that neighbor churches offended may (without their reference), call them to an account; and partly because it seems contrary to all principles either of nature or Scripture, that it should be in the power of the offending party, either to choose whether he will be accountable or no, or who alone shall be his judges.

4. Besides that, our brethren do not show, in this church that needs help, who those are that should choose the synod; whether both sides must agree in choice of the arbitrators, or whether one party must choose some and the other party choose others (neither of which they can show in the instance); or, in case a church be divided, whether party shall choose, those in the right, or those that err; if those who be in the right, yet still the question will be, who those are, for both parties pretend to it; or if the major part of the whole, then if either all or the greater part, be in an error, there will either be no choice of a synod at all, or else only of such as will side with them in their error, and confirm them in it. Yea, and by this means, the remedy which our brethren say is an ordinance of God, for the removal of offenses, scandals, errors, will have no place at all where those prevail, for an erroneous church will never make choice (if it be in their own sole power), of such a synod as they know will condemn them.

And whereas our brethren make it a matter of reference, by way of arbitration—

If their meaning be that this reference does give the judges power and authority to determine and conclude them, as elders, who now have authority from Christ (upon this call), to exercise the power of elders to them; then indeed they say something. But should they say thus, then would they fall under all the incongruities and inconveniences of their first argument in their former paper; then must these elders stand related to them as their church, {See p. 99} for church and elders are *relata*, then must they be chosen by them, ordained *things related;* by them, maintained by them; then must they preach to them as well as rule *relatives* them; then must they visit their sick, etc., as our brethren there argue.

If their meaning be but this, that those to whom it is referred, may now declare their judgment upon the case, hold out light to them, exhort them to follow their advice, but have no farther authority. All this they might have done before, or without any such reference made to them. Yea the neighbor churches in the province or nation (whom our brethren would not to have to take upon them the power of a synod), may, without being called, do thus [*this*] much; and such a synod as this would be but a college of advisers, and comes far short of the synod [of] Acts 15, who not only disputed, and declared the false teachers to be perverters and subverters, but made decrees and laid burdens upon the churches necessary to be submitted [unto], and that not only on the church of Antioch, who alone (say our brethren), referred the question to them, but on all the churches in Syria and Cilicia, of whose reference we read nothing. And our brethren cannot well imagine such a reference unless they grant either a synod at Antioch, before the sending to Jerusalem, or a synod at Jerusalem of more than two churches.

But if our brethren say that these referrers have an authoritative power (though not to excommunicate, yet), to declare, command, protest, non-communicate, etc. yet not as elders, but only by virtue of this reference, which power before they had not; then how can our brethren deny all representation or delegation of spiritual power? For what is this but a delegating of somewhat of that power to those arbitrators, which was before entirely in themselves; and that to those who (as to them), are no church officers; yea not only a giving to a multitude of churches jointly to have authority over one of themselves singly, but putting an authority at their own pleasure into the hands of one single congregation, over another single congregation; for a reference may as well be made to one as to many churches. And if they may thus delegate one part of their own power to these arbitrators, why not another part? Why not a power of excommunicating, as well as of declaring to be subverters of the faith?

And if they may thus delegate, either all or part of their church power, what is this but a foreign and extrinsic power to that church, which they so often speak against, with less reason, when in classes and synods, the particular church concerned is part of those that judge, whereas in their way the power is put quite out of their own hands, to the arbitrators. And if they may not be confined herein to the churches of a province or nation, but must make reference at pleasure to any churches in the world whatsoever, as they list [*wish*]; and thereby invest those churches, if not with complete church power, yet at least with a power to judge authoritatively in doctrines of faith, to declare and pronounce the churches of this kingdom to be heretics, subverters of the faith, perverters of souls, and (perhaps), to make and impose decrees and lay burdens; and in all these things to be looked at and acknowledged as an ordinance of Christ—what is this but {See p. 211} an introducing a foreign ecclesiastical jurisdiction, which in their second argument they would charge upon us?

If our brethren say (as sometimes they do), that in this power of making decrees, laying burdens, etc. especially as to the churches of Syria and Cilicia, and as to those points not refereed, the apostles acted by an apostolic authority, and not as elders in a synod:

1. Then (to say nothing at present of the elders joining with them in

these decrees, even to those churches, Acts 15:23 and 16:4), we ask, how can our brethren make this reference to apostles, and decision by apostles, as apostles, to be a warrant for elective synods of those who have not apostolic power? Or how shall we know what they did as apostles, and what as a synod for imitation?

2. How can our brethren say, that this sending to apostles, as apostles, was elective? For it was not elective to the churches of Antioch, whether or not to make the last reference for decision in controversies to the apostles then living; but they were obliged then to stand to their decisions as much as we now to their writings.

3. How can our brethren say, that it was a reference in this case only, without any obligation to refer other matters at other times to their decision? For certainly they were obliged in all matters to stand to their decision as apostles, as much as in this one.

4. We might add, that if the apostles here acted as apostles, then (having authority as elders in all churches), they might not only declare, and censure, but even excommunicate and exercise all church power. And then, if what was here done, or might be done, be a precedent for synods now, the authority of synods will be more than what our brethren allow them.

5. Nor had they then an authority, by virtue of this reference, which before they had not; but only exercised that authority which before they had.

And whereas our brethren add, that though this [of] Acts 15 was not a formal synod, yet it holds out by a rule of equity, that offenses among {See p. 220} churches should be referred by themselves to others who are best able to heal them; and so may be a pattern of elective synods (they should have added, and that they may by other churches be called to give account, in case of offence; for such synods also they acknowledge).

Answer. 1. Our brethren here resolve all into rules of equity; and certainly the rules of equity will as strongly plead for subordination upon association, as for an arbitrary reference for the offending party to chose whether he shall be tried or no, and by what judges.

2. If this only be their warrant for elective synods, then we leave them to answer their own first argument; that such courts as have not the greatest and most express warrant and assignment for them in the Word, both for their subordination and number, and for their bounds and limits of power, are not to be erected in the church of God.

Our brethren conclude, that they have showed sufficiently the difference between the meeting at Jerusalem, and such synods as we contend for; and say, that upon supposition that one kingdom were governed by way of elective arbitration, another by way of subordinate courts, these are such differing forms, that he who would make the first conform to the last, should overthrow the fundamental laws of it.

Answer. Besides that all this is sufficiently answered already; and that this place was not by us alleged to prove either the subordination or power of synods, but only the being of synods (which our brethren grant to be sufficiently proved from it), we only add that since the government of Christ's church is first by brotherly admonition, and if this prevail not, then to cure them by church censure, and neither in the one nor the other the party offending to choose his own judges; they who would bring it to an arbitrary electiveness, so as the parties offending may choose, who shall hear their cause, and submit no further than themselves like, do change the laws of Christ's kingdom.

The Answer to our Brethren's Reasons against the argument drawn from the analogy of Matthew 18

{See p. 221} The strength of that argument (say our brethren), "runs, that because there *should* be this remedy, therefore there *is* such a remedy."

Answer. Why our brethren should take this to be the strength of our argument, we cannot tell. Our argument lies plainly thus: Matthew 18, proving the subordination of a particular person offending, to a particular church, does by a like reason prove the subordination of an offending congregation to greater assemblies. And the reason of it is, because the grounds, reasons, and ends of subordinations are the same in both, that God may be glorified, the offender shamed, humbled, reduced, and sin not suffered to rest upon him, that others may be preserved from contagion and made to fear, that scandal and pollution of the ordinances may be prevented or removed, etc. All which argue as strongly and fully for the subordination of an offending congregation to superior and greater assemblies, as of an offending brother to a particular congregation; for (as our brethren often intimate), there is the same relation between church and church, as there is between brother and brother.

Minutes, Sess. 295, 3.360–366
Gillespie, 84–86

If our brethren were asked, what course were to be taken with a sister offending? We doubt not but they would say, the same that Christ here proposes in case of an offending brother; and they would give this reason, because there is the like reason of both, and therefore Christ supposed to intend both. And if they will then say, the strength of this reason (concerning the offending sister), is this, because there should be this remedy, therefore there is such a remedy, we hope they will then allow that argument to be a good one. And we, not doubting but that it was Christ's meaning to prevent and remove scandals as well of an offending sister, as of an offending brother, and of an offending church, or some number of offenders, as well as of a particular person; and that in case of public scandals, as well as of private offenses; doubt not but it was His meaning while He gives instance in one, that the like course (*mutatis mutandis*), should in a due proportion be used in all the rest.

the necessary changes having been made

Nor is this our argument alone, but (as others, so), Mr. Cotton of New England makes use of it in his *Keyes*, Chapter 6 (a treatise published by two of these brethren),[1] where, having spoken of one cause of synods, that is, when a church desires the help and counsel of other churches, as Acts 15, he adds another distinct ground of synods (which, says he, "just consequence from Scripture" gives us), that is, the case of "any church lying under scandal." "Look then as one brother being offended with another, and not able to heal him by the mouth of two or three brethren privately, it behooves him to carry it to the whole church; so by proportion if one church see matter of offence in another, and be not able to heal it in a more private way, it will behoove them to procure the assembly of many churches, that the offense may be orderly heard, and judged and removed." And more fully in another treatise of his, the same, *Constitution of a Particular Visible Church*, page 12 and 13, where he clearly distinguishes this case (in which he recommends a remedy by proportion from Matthew 18), from that case of Acts 15.[2]

But say our brethren, there is a remedy for congregations, which is a going forth to other churches, held out in Acts 15. A remedy of coordination, {See p. 221} such as between nations, between *pares*, not of subordination. And were it *equals* so, how ineffectual would it be for a general council or national assembly, to excommunicate a nation or province?

Answer. 1. This does not take away the strength of our argument; it shows not, that there is not the like reason of both, or if there be, that the same course (so far as can be), is not proportionably to be used in both.

2. As to that point of ineffectualness; we doubt not but our brethren think that there is an efficacy in subordinations of churches as well as persons, though here should be no proceeding to excommunication of a province or nation. And though they would seem to plead, that such a subordination would be ineffectual and to no purpose, we believe their fear is, it would be too effectual.

3. The parity of church and church does no more hinder the subordination of one church to a combination of many, then the parity of brother and brother will hinder the subordination of one to a congregation of many. And so it was with the parity of tribe and tribe.

4. The remedy themselves propose, as held forth in Acts 15, must have the same foundation with this argument of ours. For (1) They do not say that there was at Jerusalem an elective synod, but a reference which (by a like reason), will give warrant to an elective synod; for if one church may go forth for help, then by the same reason many may so do; and if they

---

1. [*The Keyes of the Kingdom of Heaven* (1644; repr. 1843), chapter six, "Of the Power and Authoritie given to Synods," p. 56.]

2. [John Cotton, *The True Constitution of a Particular Visible Church, Proved by Scripture. Wherein is Briefly Demonstrated by Questions and Answers what Officers, Worship, and Government Christ Hath Ordained in His Church* (London: 1642), pp. 12, 13.]

may go forth to one church for help, they may by the same reason go forth to many, and thus by equality of reason they gather warrant for an elective synod. (2) Nay more, our brethren say here, that all churches (not only those to whom a reference is made), have a power to declare the offence, and withdraw communion from those churches; which power they have not by virtue of that reference (for possibly there was none such made, at least not to all churches), but in themselves, without such reference; and whence can our brethren prove this, but by a like reason, either from Acts 15 or Matthew 18, for it is not express in either? (3) Again, the declaration [in] Acts 15, was not against the church of Antioch, but against some persons in it that were guilty of those crimes; yet hence our brethren infer a declaration against an offending church; which must be on this ground, that this meeting at Jerusalem might by the same reason declare against the church of Antioch, if the church offended, as they did against some persons in it, upon their offence.

5. Whereas our brethren think there is no use of subordination in churches, unless for the excommunicating of whole churches (a thing not known in the presbyterian government), their own instance alleged from Acts 15 shows the contrary. For though the decrees were directed and enjoined to churches, yet not the churches, but particular persons in the churches, are censured as subverters of the faith, etc., and thus may a classis or synod, excommunicate one or more persons in a church, a province, a nation, without excommunicating of whole churches; where as in our brethren's way, their elective synods do non-communicate whole societies for the offence of one or a few persons not redressed.

6. How ineffectual would that be, if according to this notion of elective synods, as our brethren would have it, there were no other course to reclaim or deal with an erroneous offending church, but only upon their own reference to such persons or churches as themselves would choose, and only so far as themselves please? If there had been no course taken with those subverters at Antioch, till themselves had made a reference to Jerusalem; those churches might much sooner have been infested with their leaven, than they persuaded to make such a reference. Our brethren *sometimes* speak of churches offended, requiring an account of churches offending; but we find them *here* very sparing of insisting thereupon, or showing upon what ground they build that practice. For the place of Acts 15 as they interpret it, of a voluntary reference by way of arbitration to other churches, is somewhat different from that of those other churches calling them to an account without such a reference; nor will this be such an elective synod. And that argument which would serve most fairly for warrant of that practice (*viz.* by analogy from Matthew 18 pressed by Mr. Cotton and others), they cannot make use of, without granting our argument. For if the argument from analogy be good so far as they please to urge it; it suffices to our purpose

in this proposition, which asserts only a subordination; but, what power the superior assembly shall have over the subordinate, this proposition asserts not. Yea, though the proposition had asserted that which our brethren here suppose, the power of excommunication in superior assemblies, the argument from analogy would as well hold in that branch of proceeding as in all the rest.

7. And our brethren's exception of the ineffectualness which they urge, {"if they cannot use this remedy (of excommunicating a whole nation)," to what end is this subordination of synod pleaded for?} is of no weight: For (1) There may be occasion of subordination, yea of exercising the power of excommunication of synods, and that to good purpose, against particular persons in a province, or nation, or particular congregation, without excommunicating the whole province, nation, or congregation; as the meeting at Jerusalem censured the false teachers at Antioch without censuring the church of Antioch.

(2) Or, if only the ineffectualness might be a reason why a synod should not proceed to excommunicate a province or congregation; yet this does not prove they have no authority to do it, but only that there may be some cause to stop the exercise of that power or authority. As when a prince or state makes a law against rebels or traitors to punish them with death; in case an army of such rebels or traitors, or a whole province rebels; this multitude does not excuse any one person of them from being obnoxious to that law or the penalty of it. Yet it may be a reason why such a prince or state should not (in prudence), execute that rigor of the law upon every person of them, but only upon some principal offenders; yet is that whole province, or army of rebels, subordinate to the prince or state, and the laws thereof.

Our brethren likewise may remember, that many other things in the assembly were given in answer; as that this gives to a synod of many churches no more power over a particular church (yea, a particular person), than one brother has over another brother, yea over a whole church (for our brethren will not deny, but that he may admonish, declare, and withdraw communion); that independent churches esteem non-communion with other churches their own happiness; and therefore to be non-communing would be to them no punishment at all; or at least, no other than what themselves inflict on all the churches of the world besides. And, that it is not suitable to the wisdom of Jesus Christ to apply the strongest remedy for the weakest and least dangerous disease, *viz.* the case of an offending brother; and the weakest remedy to the most dangerous disease, *viz.* the case of an offending church.

Of this last only our brethren take notice; and give no other answer to it, but only by way of retortion. That in a national assembly, not only there wants [*lacks*] this strongest remedy, but they have the greatest power to do hurt; and if they err, their error is greater than of a bishop or pope, who

Gillespie, 85
Minutes,
3.360–366

{See p. 221}

being but one, may be deposed; and the greater part of the clergy being still the worse and more corrupt, and yet by the presbyterian principles must all be taken in, a national assembly chosen by them, are like to be, for the greatest part of them, the more corrupt.'

To which retortion (omitting their so frequent using of the word clergy, which, for what reasons they do it, themselves best know; and their so frequent comparing the government of the Reformed churches to, and making it worse than, that of popes and bishops), we *answer:*

1. If a national assembly do altogether want this remedy of subordination, then should not our brethren have charged us in their second argument, with bringing in a foreign ecclesiastical power over each state and kingdom; and we know no reason for their so doing, unless thereby (as much as they can), to render this [presbyterian] government odious.

2. We say more of the subordination of general assemblies, than they of particular congregations. We say, not only that they may err, be subject to the advice of a synod, be separated from, non-communicated, etc.; we say they are not more independent than we think less assemblies to be. For, if providence leaves a particular church without the help of neighbor churches, they must needs want the benefit of associations and subordinations (and so must a particular person, if he cannot enjoy the opportunity of joining with any particular congregation), but this is not their privilege, but their loss. The like we say when a national assembly cannot enjoy, *absque gravissimis incommodis,* the help of an universal synod, or an synod of several nations.

without the most serious disadvantages

3. All the remedies that our brethren hold out for particular churches offending, leave them yet more independent than bishops or popes; for these may be not only admonished, prayed for, separated from, non-communicated, but (as our brethren acknowledge), deposed. But their particular congregations offending, are not subject to any such authoritative censure, nor any persons in them, from any but their own congregation. When Bellarmine and others, in the case of an heretical pope, say that though a council may not depose him, yet they may pray for him, and admonish him; and that (said Bellarmine), is sufficient; and though Christ have given no other human efficacious remedies for the evil that may arise by such a pope, we must rest content, the church's condition is safe, because it depends upon God, and not upon man.[1] To this Doctor Ames replies (and may it not be applied to our brethren?), *ecclesia igitur non est republica perfecta sibi sufficiens*

Gillespie, 80, 81

---

1. Bellarmine, *de council,* lib.2. cap 19. [Cardinal Robert Bellarmine, Jesuit apologist (1542–1621), *Disputationes de Controversiis Christiane Fidei* (Lutetiæ Parisiorum, 1620). *Opera Omnia* (Vives: 1870), 2.275. Gillespie adduced this from Bellarmine during debate, citing Whitaker and giving the quotation from Ames: "A passadge of Dr Ames in answer to Belarmine: *ecclesia est Res publica sibi sufficiens* [the church is a commonwealth sufficient to itself] in removing of scandall. If the remedy be not sufficient, then the end is not compassed but loosed." (Gillespie, pp. 81, 85, *Minutes,* 3.365).]

in ordine ad suum finem;[1] nor has Christ provided means for all the churches necessities.

4. For healing the offence or error of a national church, the strongest and most efficacious remedy that can be had, may be made use of; if that of a further subordination cannot be had, the reason then, that it wants [*lacks*] this remedy, is not because, though it could be had, it might not be used; but because, though it might be used, yet it cannot be had. But this will not be a reason why a particular congregation should not make use of such remedies as may be had. No more than, because if a parliament err, there is no higher court to appeal to; therefore there may not be an appeal from inferior courts to it.

5. To what they add, 'that the greater part of the clergy are the more corrupt, and yet must all be taken in;' we say, (1) Though such corrupt ministers, as our brethren suppose, and those congregations that have such ministers, and (as our brethren suppose), can have no better, because there are no other to be had in their name, have as much need as others to be under a government, and not therefore to do what they list [*wish*] without control, because they are corrupt (for we do not think our brethren will own this principle, that because the greater part of men are the more corrupt, therefore there may be no government, but every one be allowed to do what is good in his own eyes); yet that such corrupt ministers must needs be taken into synods, we see no reason, nor does our proposition assert it. (2) And as to their electing of a national assembly; though we doubt not but such corrupt ministers as our brethren suppose, who deserve to be deposed from being ministers, may well be denied their vote in election; yet, if their supposition were granted, they have no better reason to conclude, that the greater part of a national assembly must be corrupt, because chosen by the generality of ministers; than that the greater part of a parliament must needs be corrupt, because chosen by the generality of men, of whom the greater part may as well be supposed to be the worse, as the greater part of ministers. And indeed this argument does not so much oppose subordination of synods, as it strikes at the root of all government, both ecclesiastical and civil. {See p. 222}

But say our brethren, 'the preserving the rights and liberties of a state, and seeking the common good of it, is natural to the generality of men; but the truths of the gospel, and the purity of religion, and the power thereof, is contrary to the principles of all natural men, and has ever been opposed by the most part of the clergy.' {See p. 222}

---

1. [i.e. If this were true, then "the church, therefore, is not a perfect republic, sufficient unto itself in order to its end."] [Ames,] *Bellarmine Enerv.*, Tom. 2. lib. 2. cap. 7. Whitak., *de conc.*, qu. 5. cap. 3. [William Ames, Puritan divine (1576–1633), *Bellarmine Enevatus,* tom. 2 (1625; London: Apud Johannem Humpfridum, 1632), p. 35. William Whitaker, English Calvinist theologian (1548–1595), *Praelectiones … In quibus tractatur Controversia de Conciliis contra … Bellarminum …* (Cambridge, 1600). *Opera Theologica,* 2 vols. in 1 (Geneva, 1610), pp. 600–607.]

Answer. 1. This at moſt would prove only that corrupt men may more safely be truſted with civil liberties. It does not prove, but that according to their argument, the parliament is like[ly] to be the more corrupt, as well as the general assembly.

And 2. Though they might thereupon be truſted with civil liberties, yet (according to these principles), they muſt not meddle with religion at all, more than the national synod.

3. Though the generality of corrupt men may be forward enough to preserve the liberties of a ſtate (yea, and liberty of conscience too); yet they are not forward to have sin punished; yet that is one main work of bodies politic.

4. If the 'truth of the goſpel, and the purity and power of religion, be contrary to the principles of all natural men,' yea, and much more, than the rights and liberties of a ſtate, then is there less reason that every person, or combination of persons should be permitted under pretense of conscience, to believe and praɥice what they please, in matters of religion; than that they should so be permitted in matters of ſtate. For if the generality of men be in matters of religion the more corrupt (and the more apt to corrupt others), they have the more need of government.

5. But why our brethren should thus seek occasion to caſt odious aſpersions upon the miniſtry in general, as here they do ('that in greater bodies of the clergy, the greater part are, and have been ſtill the worse and more corrupt; that miniſters, if not converted, are of all others, the worſt and greateſt opposers to religion; that in a national assembly, the greater number are like to be of the worſt; that in all ages, the moſt of the clergy have been [moſt] apt to corrupt the truth, and to oppose the purity and power of religion'), we cannot tell, unless it be their design to blaſt and vilify (as much as they can), not only the authority and power of synods, but the office and work of the miniſtry or clergy (as they love to call them); eſpecially, when they know that synods in Reformed churches consiſt of others beside miniſters; and that perhaps in a large or larger proportion.

6. But if it be true which they say, that the generality of miniſters are thus apt to corrupt the truth, and oppose religion in the power of it; then of how dangerous a consequence would that be, if every such miniſter muſt be permitted to seduce and gather to himself a company of people at his own pleasure, who should thenceforth plead exemption and independency in reference in any authoritative ecclesiaſtical judicatory whatever? Eſpecially when we may far more truly say, of those that, to obtain liberty, would pretend tenderness of conscience and exemption from ecclesiaſtical judicature, what our brethren here say of miniſters, *viz.* "that of those the greater part are and have been ſtill the worse and more corrupt, as is apparent in this kingdom at present."

7. This reason of our brethren does no way take off the ſtrength of that objeɥion. For we say further, that both parliaments, synods, and particular

churches, have many times dangerously erred; which proves that great care should be had of those who are to be elected and admitted into such assemblies, that no just exception may be made against them; but not that such assemblies should not therefore be. Nor does this answer of our brethren at all take off the strength of our argument *à pari ratione*, that by their *by analogy; by* argument, there must either be punishments for parliaments, or none for *equal reason* inferior courts.

Our brethren add; 'that after the first 300 years when synods began to be {See p. 222} most in credit, the mystery of iniquity grew up with them.'

Answer. 1. So have many schisms and other errors, with independent congregations. 2. So do tares and wheat. 3. The truth is, the mystery of iniquity increased, as well constituted synods did decrease; for as the pope was exalted, so were synods disgraced and disused, much like as it was with us, between prerogative and parliaments.[1]

And for what they fear, that by this means new truths would not be taught, but suppressed, till a whole nation is enlightened in it, we *answer:* That synods ought to suppress new errors, and old ones revived, though they come in the name of new truths; if they do otherwise, it is the fault of men, not the government, and we must not deny all power of suppressing error, for fear lest possibly some men may abuse that power to the prejudice of truth; no more than we may take away all of punishing malefactors, for fear that some should abuse that power to the prejudice of the innocent. It is certain[ly] true that the highest courts, if corrupted, may do the most mischief; but it follows not, that therefore such courts (though uncorrupted), should not be.

Their second answer to our argument, *à pari ratione* from Matthew 18 is this, 'the efficacy of all remedies depends, 1. On Christ's blessing, which {See p. 222} depends upon his institution; but *par ratio* will never set up an ordinance *same grounds* of Christ. 2. The suitableness of the condition of those that are to be dealt with; now it is more suitable for churches to be dealt with in a brotherly way of admonition and withdrawing communion; as if a province, or a multitude rebel, a state will not hang up all, though to particular persons this were an efficacious remedy. 3. Christ has suited his remedies to all times and all conditions.'

Answer. 1. If *par ratio* will not set up an ordinance of Christ, yet it may serve to prove an ordinance of Christ, or at least to warrant a practice, which is enough to our purpose. If not, how will our brethren prove baptizing of infants, or women receiving of the Lord's supper, to be institutions of Christ? How will they prove from Matthew 18 an institution of Christ to proceed in case of a public scandal, as well as of a private offence; or to proceed against a sister offending in the same manner, as with an offending

---

1. [A reference to one of the underlying causes of the civil war, the assertion of the divine right royal prerogative/supremacy claimed by King James I and Charles I.]

brother? How will they prove, that it is an ordinance of Christ that our synods must be now elective, as they suppose it was in the case of Antioch? Or, how will they prove that synods are at all an ordinance of Christ, if (as they say) the meeting at Jerusalem was not a formal synod? How will they prove their non-communion of churches, from the example of Paul's departing from Barnabas (Acts 15:39), which they allege for it, upon this ground, 'that look what power one apostle had in reference to another apostle, the same has one church to another church?'[1] In all which (besides many more instances that might be alleged), our brethren will be very far to seek, unless they will admit a *par ratio* to prove an institution.

Goodwin, 281

2. This way of proceeding with churches is a very suitable remedy; and our brethren's instance will help to make it out. For as if a province rebel, the ringleaders of that rebellion may be hung up, without hanging up all in that province, and the rest reduced by other means (though yet the whole province be subordinate to that prince or state); so may a synod, provincial or national, excommunicate the chief offenders in an erring church without excommunicating that whole church, and reclaim the rest by other means, and yet that whole church be subordinate to that synod. But if they may only admonish an offending church, and if that prevail not, withdraw communion from them; it is much as if that prince or state, who may hang a single rebel, but in case a province or multitude rebel, he may only send them an admonition to lay down their arms, and if that prevail not, declare them rebels and then let them take their own course.

3. To that of 'Christ's suiting his remedies to all times and conditions;' we have answered before (for indeed many of our brethren's arguments are more than once produced). Synods and associations are at all times a remedy to be made use of, so far as may be obtained, and as may most tend to the effecting of those ends for which they are appointed. But, that God's providence is so suitable to His institutions, that whatever may, by His appointment, be made use of at any time, can be enjoyed at all times, and in all conditions, our brethren will never prove. Ruling elders, deacons, elderships are by our brethren acknowledged and professed to be institutions of Christ, yet they will not say that all their congregations (perhaps not any of them), have been so happy as at all times and in all conditions to have them all. Imposition of hands on church officers by an eldership,

---

1. [The argument would seem to be that of the dissenting brethren, not something from printed works by Cotton or other New England divines. It is difficult to date the various parts of Goodwin's *Of the Constitution, Right, Order and Government*, some of which is made up of bits of *The Grand Debate*, but the argument was known to Baxter who mentions it in his *Plea for Congregationall Government: or, A defence of the Assemblies petition, against Mr. John Saltmarsh*, which is entered in the Stationers' register for May 6, 1646 (Eyre, 1.228). The Assembly's answer itself dates to about August, 1646 (*Minutes*, 5.307). Burroughs lays equal fault on Paul and Barnabas and does not so use the example as Goodwin does. Jeremiah Burroughs, *Irenicum* (1646; 1653), p. 232.]

　　　　　　III: ANSWER OF THE ASSEMBLY TO THE

our brethren acknowledge to be an institution of Christ, yet we believe that some of their congregations have not at all times and in all conditions been in a capacity of such imposition of hands, or have had an eldership to do it. To say nothing of excommunication and church censures, which we think that all their churches have not been at times and in all conditions in a capacity to exercise according to their own principles.

Their last answer is this: 'If the analogy of Matthew 18 be argued from, then: 1. Let the analogy be kept, for as a brother is not at first to be brought {See p. 222} to a standing court, but admonished first by one, then by two or three: So by this proportion instead of these set and standing assemblies there should only be two or three or more neighbor churches to admonish the offending church, not a standing court.'

Answer. (1) If not *at first* brought to a standing court, yet there must be a *standing* court by this proposition to which it may *at length* be brought.

(2) Though in private offenses between man and man, there must be first private admonition, to prevent (if it may be), the making of it public; yet our brethren (we think), will not say, that in an open scandal, which is public already, the church may not take notice of it till some private brethren have thus proceeded. We read no such private admonition enjoined by Paul in the case of the incestuous Corinthian [1 Corinthians 5]; nor "in rebuking those that sin openly" (1 Timothy 5:12[1]). But cases brought to a synod, are supposed to be known before; if not, we grant that the same obligation of private admonition lies upon those who shall complain to a synod (either of a church or of a person), as on those that complain to a particular church.

2. To what they next add their (argument so often repeated), and 'secondly, where is a synod called the church?'

We *answer:* That when our brethren have shown us *first*, where the elders and brethren of a particular congregation, without the women and children are so called, and *secondly*, that a synod is not so called in Matthew 18, we Gillespie, 80 shall then besides those answers formerly given (which yet are abundantly sufficient) give them more.

The "church universal" (they grant), "is called a church and one body to {See p. 223} Christ;" but say they, "as materially considered and not as a politic body in respect to government, which was never yet asserted by this assembly."

Answer. Whether the assembly has yet asserted this or no, is not material. There are many truths in divinity, which this assembly has never yet asserted. But, that this church universal is an organical body, in which the members are not all one member but many, and those many members have several distinct functions; that the officers, ordinances, etc., are set in this church, and given to this church universal, and are to exercise their several offices as in relation to the whole, and for the good of the whole; and, that every

---

1. [*sic* 1 Timothy 5:20, "Them that sinne, rebuke openly, that the rest also may feare" (Geneva Bible).]

particular visible church (which our brethren will not deny to be a political body for government), is but a part or member of this church general (and much more to this purpose); we think our brethren will not say, that this assembly has never yet asserted. But whether they will think that this is tantamount as to say, the church general is a politic body, we do not much pass [*care*]; for we liſt [*wish*] not to contend with our brethren for words.

Then 3. To what they laſt objeᴄt, by 'this argument from analogy, no more power muſt be placed in the greater assembly than in the particular congregation,' we *answer:* What power the superior assembly has over the subordinate, is not the queſtion in this proposition. If there be a subordination of the assemblies one to the other, it is as much as this proposition contends for. And let our brethren grant the like power to synods over offending congregations, as we grant a congregation to have over an offending brother, and the controversy will soon end.

Concordat cum Originali.
Adoniram Byfield, Scriba.

THE GRAND DEBATE

*REASONS OF THE DISSENTING BRETHREN CONCERNING
THE POWER THAT IS IN CONGREGATIONS, HAVING IN
THEM A SUFFICIENT PRESBYTERY FOR ORDINATION*

&

*THE ANSWER OF THE ASSEMBLY OF DIVINES TO THE
REASONS OF THE DISSENTING BRETHREN AGAINST THE
PROPOSITION CONCERNING ORDINATION*

Die Jovis 20. April. 1648.
Whereas there is an Order of the right Honourable the House of Peers for the printing of all their Reasons of the Dissenting Brethen, againſt severall Propositions concerning Presbyteriall Government, and the Answers of the Assembly to those Reasons; It is Ordered that the like Order be granted for the printing and publishing of the Answer of the Assembly, to the Reasons againſt the Proposition concerning Ordination, the Reasons being already printed, and the answer of the Assembly to those Reasons, though brought into the Assembly long before their Lordships Order, yet not passing in the Assembly till since the said Order, and so is not included in it.

Jo. Browne Cler. Parl.}

Reasons of the

Dissenting Brethren Concerning the Power
That is in Congregations, Having in them a
Sufficient Presbytery for Ordination[1]

Against the Proposition touching Ordination: *viz.*—

It is very requisite, that no single congregation that can conveniently associate,[2] do assume to itself all and sole power in ordination[3]

We offer these Reasons:

Where there is a sufficient presbytery, all and sole power in ordination {See p. 279} may be assumed, though association may be had: but there may be a sufficient presbytery in a particular congregation.

The major [premise] has two parts: 1. That a sufficient presbytery may assume all and sole power in ordination. 2. That it may do so, though it may associate.

The former part is proved, 1 Timothy 4:14, *by the laying on of the hands of the presbytery,* as is voted by the assembly which, is the only Scripture brought for ordination by ordinary elders.

The second part, [*that they may do this though they may associate*] appears,
1. Because association does neither add to, nor diminish the power of a

---

1. [*Reasons of the Dissenting Brethren Concerning the Power that is in Congregations, having in them a Sufficient Presbytery for Ordination* (London: Humphrey Harward, 1648). "The Reasons," etc., 12 December 1644, Document 49, "Calendar of Documents," *Minutes,* 5.144. "The immediate backdrop to this fourth text of dissent is found in the discussions and recorded dissents in Sessions 337–9 (9–11 Dec. [1644])."[

2. [i.e. Associate with other churches to jointly govern in acts of government such as ordination of officers. While the assembly wondered in their reply why this of all their propositions concerning ordination was disputed by the Independent divines, it was by the latter's account one of the great differences between the two sides (see next note).]

3. [Cf. "Draft Directory for Church Government submitted to both Houses of Parliament, 11 December 1644," *Minutes,* 5.138. See Gillespie (58–64) and the *Minutes* (3.51–75), where this proposition (styled the twelfth) was debated, as well as the assembly's defense against the Independent's *Remonstrance* (Document 92), where this proposition is characterized as one of the greatest points of difference between the two sides, Document 99, "Calendar of Documents," *Minutes,* 5.275–282.]

presbytery: it is by way of accumulation, not privation, as is acknowledged by the Reformed churches.

2. If association be so necessarily required, where it may be had; then neither a classical, provincial, nor national presbytery can assume all and sole power in ordination, if there be any other classical, provincial, or national presbytery, with whom they may associate. And that there is, or may be always some, is necessarily to be supposed in these times of the gospel, if any association ought to be.

The minor, *that there may be a sufficient presbytery* in a particular congregation, is proved,

{See p. 286}

1. By the second proposition touching church government, sent up to the Honorable Houses of Parliament, *viz.* "A presbytery consists of ministers of the Word, and such other public officers, as are agreeable to, and warranted by the Word of God to be church governors to join with the ministers in the government of the church." All which may be in a particular congregation.

Minutes, 5.134

2. Wherein consists *the sufficiency of a presbytery?* The number of how many elders is not set or bounded by institution; suppose two or three; and if more be requisite in a particular congregation, there may be four or five. And a presbytery over many congregations is acknowledged to be sufficient, though it consists of no more. If *they* have this power *as a sufficient presbytery,* why not the other also? *Have they their power only as having relation to many congregations?* Is that the essential requisite to their sufficiency? Here are elders, and as many elders, having relation to a church: and the argument used by the reverend assembly to prove a presbytery over many congregations, is *that elders are mentioned in relation to one church.*

Minutes, Sess. 174–176. 2.18–19; 616

II. That which two apostles being joined together might do in a particular congregation, that ordinary elders may do in a particular congregation. But Paul and Barnabas ordained elders in particular congregations, though they might associate. Therefore, etc.

{See p. 289}

The consequence appears thus: If the argument brought by the reverend assembly holds, *viz.* that when the apostles met together for ordination, or for ordering the affairs of the church of Jerusalem, they met as ordinary elders (which they have voted), then surely when Paul and Barnabas met to ordain elders in particular congregations, it is to be averred they met for that act as ordinary elders.

Minutes, Sess. 171, 2.18, 592

The minor has two parts. 1. Paul and Barnabas ordained elders in particular congregations. 2. That they might associate.

{See p. 292}

1. That these were particular congregations wherein they ordained elders, appears:

Because it is not supposable that the cities, much less the regions round abound [*about*], where the apostles preached and erected churches (as appears by Acts 13:49 compared with Acts 14:6, 21–23), were grown to many congregations before the apostles appointed elders to them. For the apostles who were to preach in all places, would not stay so long in one place; and it was their course when they [*sic* there] were there ἱκανὸι, as at Derbe (Acts 14:21), to set elders to them. [ἱκανοὺς; many]

Again, this was the first ordination of elders to those places, and therefore must needs be to particular congregations, for the classis is made up of elders of many congregations.

Lastly they ordained elders, κατ' ἐκκλησίαν[1] and αὐτοῖς; and at their ordaining they fasted and prayed, commending them to the grace of God; which fasting and praying, being (according to the principles of us both[2]), to be in particular congregations, it follows that the churches to which those elders were appointed, were particular congregations. {See p. 296}

For the second, *that they might associate,* it appears,

Because there were churches in the regions round about, and yet the apostle mentions not association, which they would have done if that had been the way; for when they did things with ordinary elders, it is thus recorded, *the apostles and elders.* But they *commend them to the grace of God,* as Paul did the church of Ephesus (Acts 20:23), as leaving sufficient means to perpetuate succession, and to ordain other elders, if any should die, as also *to build them up to eternal life.* {See p. 298}

> *Sic Subscribitur:* Tho. Goodwin, Philip Nye, Jer. Burroughes, Sidrach Sympson, William Bridge, William Greenhill, William Carter.
>
> *Concordat cum Originali.*
> Adoniram Byfield, *Scriba.*

---

1. [In the errata the printer has erroneously flagged this as a mistake and substituted the genitive (ἐκκλησίας) for the accusative (ἐκκλησίαν), which appears in the Biblical text. The text reads as ἐκκλησίαν throughout the assembly's reply and citations from this place in the brethren's dissent. My thanks to Arnie Robertstad for help regarding the Greek text.]

2. [Both: i.e. the dissenting brethren and the Assembly.]

The Answer to the

Reasons of the Dissenting Brethren Against the Proposition touching Ordination, *viz.*[1]

It is very requisite that no single congregation that can conveniently associate, do assume to itself all and sole power in ordination

Gillespie,
58–64

Lightfoot, 262

Minutes, 3.51–
75; 5.275–282

AMONG ALL THE PROPOSITIONS which the assembly presented to the Honorable Houses of Parliament concerning ordination, our brethren have singled out this one, to which they enter their dissent; as if this alone were opposite to their opinions touching this matter, which whether it be so, or that there was not some other reason of their insisting on this, rather than on any of the rest, themselves best know. We remember that in a proposition not altogether unlike to this, some others of the assembly differed somewhat in the debate from the major part. And we have observed our brethren ready enough to take notice and make use of any such difference (although sometimes but in point of method; as whether of two propositions, this or that should be first debated) and to talk of a third party in the assembly. We observe likewise that the arguments here brought against this proposition are not properly arguments of their own, nor pressed by themselves in the assembly, nor such as are most suitable to their own opinions; but arguments used by others in that debate. And whether that difference were not some reason why our brethren chose rather to insist upon this proposition in their dissent, than on some other, themselves are best able to determine. We expect from our brethren (in a search for truth, not a contest for victory) arguments to prove, that "every single congregation" (whether there be in it a sufficient or insufficient presbytery, or none at all) "have the whole power of ordination within themselves;" and that none but themselves may ordain for them (for we suppose our brethren, or at least some of them, are of this opinion), but this they are pleased to decline.

We must observe also of these borrowed arguments brought by our brethren against this proposition, that neither of them concludes against the

---

[1. *The Answer of the Assembly of Divines to the Reasons of the Dissenting Brethren Against the Proposition concerning Ordination* (London: Humphrey Harward, 1648). "An Answer," etc., 19 April 1648, Document 134, "Calendar of Documents," *Minutes,* 5.340. "In Document 134 the assembly responded belatedly to congregationalist arguments against presbyterian ordination (see Document 49). The assembly states that its answer was 'brought into the Assembly long before their Lordships Order' but not passed in the assembly until later. This answer might be the papers mentioned in Sessions 934 and 935 in October 1647."]

proposition in debate. The first can conclude only this, that "there may be such a presbytery as may assume all and sole power;" not that there is; nor (if they [*sic* there] were) that it is "requisite" they should so do. The other concludes only thus [*this*] much, "that ordinary elders may ordain in a particular congregation" (which we never denied), not that the elders "of one single congregation" may ordain; nor that they may "assume all and sole power in ordination;" nor that it is "requisite" they should so do. But, such as they are, we shall take them into consideration in order.

The Answer to Their First Argument

Their first argument is thus framed: "Where there is a sufficient presbytery, all and sole power in ordination may be assumed, though association may be had. But there may be a sufficient presbytery in a particular congregation." What their conclusion would be we cannot tell, but we think they would conclude, 'therefore a particular congregation may assume all and sole power in ordination though association may be had.' But they must add also, 'and it is requisite that they do assume it, though association may be had, conveniently,' or else they conclude not against the proposition. And were their argument so framed, we must tell them, that besides lesser faults, there would be these two great ones in it. 1. That there is more in the conclusion than is in the premises. And 2. That it apparently consists of four terms. For in the major proposition it is, "where there is a sufficient presbytery;" the minor says only, "there may be;" which is a very material difference.

{See p. 275}

TO THEIR MAJOR
The major, they say, has two parts. "1. That a sufficient presbytery may assume all and sole power in ordination. 2. That it may do so, though it may associate."

Answer. 1. But we think, when they better consider of it, themselves will say that neither of these parts are true. Not the first part; for they do not place the "whole power" in the presbytery, but share it between them and the people; and therein, sometimes they tell us, they go in a middle way between the Brownists[1] and the presbyterians. And if not the first part, much less the second.

Besides that, in thus arguing, they confirm a power of ordination in a

Baillie, July 12, 1644, 2.205

---

1. [Amongst the tenets of the Brownists (named for Robert Browne), were that they "apprehended, according to the Scripture, that every church ought to be confined within the limits of a single congregation, and that the government should be democratical." "The whole power of admitting and excluding members, with the deciding of all controversies, was in the brotherhood. Their church officers, for preaching the word and taking care of the poor, were chosen from among themselves ... the vote of the brotherhood made him an officer, and gave him authority to preach and administer the sacraments…." Daniel Neal, *History of the Puritans*, 3 vols. (1837), 1.247.]

classical presbytery, which they would oppose. For they cannot deny, but that in a classis there may be a sufficient presbytery. Or if they deny it, the proof that they here bring, to prove the sufficiency of a presbytery in a congregation, will much more strongly prove the sufficiency of a presbytery in a classis.

Nor can they help themselves in saying, that by a "sufficient presbytery," they mean a congregation that has a sufficient presbytery (thereby, either to take in the people, or shut out the classis). For (besides that this would not serve their turn to make a major proposition to their argument, and that such kind of expositions would seem too harsh to be justified), the proof they annex would not serve to confirm it. For they could not say that it is proved by 1 Timothy 4:14 (which speaks nothing either of the people, or of a congregation, but only of a presbytery), nor that "it was so voted by the assembly."

2. And as this is inconsistent with their own principles, so neither can we allow it, to be in itself a truth, that "wherever there is a sufficient presbytery" (especially in our brethren's sense, who tell us elsewhere, that two elders, though neither of them be a minister of the Word, are a sufficient eldership), "they may assume all and sole power in ordination," when yet they have opportunity and convenience to "associate" with others; much less, that, "it is requisite for them so to do."

For 1. We think it very possible that there may be so many elders as might be sufficient for number, in some sense, to be called an eldership, and might perhaps be safely entrusted (under the inspection of others) with managing some affairs which concern one single congregation only (at least enough to make such an eldership, as our brethren deem sufficient) whom, yet, to invest with such a power as our brethren here claim for them, would be very unsafe; nor do we believe that Christ has so invested them. For we do not think it to be the will of Christ, that every such member of elders as our brethren account a sufficient eldership (consisting perhaps but of two ruling elders) should be entrusted with such a power, as to be sole judges of the fitness of a person for the ministry, and actually to ordain him thereunto, so as he must thenceforth be owned as a minister of Christ by all other churches, as well as that to whom these elders belong (for we cannot think, as perhaps our brethren do, that a minister is a minister only to his own congregation, and may only there perform ministerial acts). Much less that they are to be trusted with all and sole power therein; and that they *with the neigh-* might do it, not only *inconsultis*, but even *renitentibus omnibus vicinis eccle-* *boring churches* *siis.* And least of all, that they may assume such a power (whether others *unconsulted, but* allow it them or no) so soon as "they deem themselves" such a sufficient el- *even resisting* dership (for who but themselves shall be judges of it?), and that it is requisite that they so do, yea though they might associate, and that conveniently.

2. Nor are we such friends to classical presbyteries because classical, as to

affirm it requisite for every classical presbytery to assume all and sole power
in ordination. For we hold it very possible that in a classis where there may
be elders sufficient for number to be called an eldership (for we liſt [*wish*]
not to diſpute the *minimum quod sic*), their number may be yet so small, or   *minimum limit*
their abilities so weak, or their judgments (at leaſt many of them) so erroneous, or their lives so corrupt, that we should not hold it requisite to en-
truſt them with a power of ordination, when they may with convenience
associate with others better qualified.

And if our brethren say, this is but a particular case and extraordinary;
and that we will not judge it much considerable in making the ordinary
rule, which cannot be supposed to provide particularly for all cases possibly incident; we say the like for their "sufficient presbytery" in a particular congregation. For we think it will be a case as extraordinary, to find
in a particular congregation, a presbytery sufficient to be entruſted with
all and sole power of ordination. We believe that such a presbytery as that
in Charenton near Paris; or such as was supposed possible in the debate
of this point (*viz.* a particular congregation having six or eight preaching
presbyters conſtantly employed in the miniſtry), are not like[ly] to be the
precedents of ordinary congregations, or congregational presbyteries in
this kingdom. And if ever such a thing should happen, it will be *then* time
enough to consider of that extraordinary case, whether it be more *requisite*
for that eldership, to assume the whole and sole power of ordination; or, to
associate with the elders of other neighbor congregations, if (as the proposition supposes) they may with convenience so do, rather than make such
a precedent (though themselves should be thought able for such a work)
for other congregations or presbyteries less sufficient to claim the like, to
the prejudice of themselves, as well as of the neighbor churches.

3. Neither can we allow that even those classical presbyteries who may   {See p. 276}
be conceived "moſt sufficient" to be entruſted with a power of ordina-   Goodwin, 135,
tion, may therefore "assume all and sole power in it," without appeals, or   164
subordination to superior assemblies; at leaſt, when such superior assem-   Cf. Baillie, *Dis-*
blies may conveniently be enjoined. Yet, such is that whole and sole power *suasive,* 23, 39,
which our brethren challenge for particular congregations; and that not   107, 186
only for some particular congregations, but for *all*; not only where there is 32 *Queſtions,*
a sufficient presbytery (as here they ſpeak); that is, any two elders; but also Q. 21.
where there is not. For even a congregation without elders are by them sup- Cotton, *Way of*
posed to have the whole and sole power of ordination within themselves;   *N.E.,* c. 2. §7
so as they neither ſtand in need of any power without [*outside*] themselves   {See p.307}
for the doing of it, nor may there be any appeal from them in it, nor may
any but themselves ordain for them. And if anything less then this be allowed them, they would not think it to be all and sole power. If in government, there be somewhat which themselves alone may not perform, or that
there be appeals from them to superior assemblies, or that any others but

themselves might (in reference to them) exercise it, they would not think that they had all and sole power in government. So for ordination, if either themselves alone may not ordain; or any others ordain for them, they would not think that they have all and sole power in ordination allowed to them.

"The former part" (*that a sufficient presbytery may assume all and sole power in ordination*) "is proved," they say, "1 Timothy 4:14, 'by the laying on of the hands of a presbytery,' as is voted by the assembly."

Answer. By a sufficient presbytery we suppose they mean, every sufficient presbytery, or every number of presbyters, who are sufficient to be called a presbytery (for if their major proposition be not universal, their argument will conclude nothing). And if so, we deny that the assembly has ever voted 1 Timothy 4:14 to prove that every such presbytery (at least according to our brethren's judgment, concerning a sufficient presbytery), may assume all and sole power in ordination. Nor is this at all made out by what they add: {"which is the only Scripture brought for ordination by ordinary elders"}[1] For if it were so; yet it is one thing to vote *that ordination may be performed by ordinary elders;* another thing to vote *that every company of such elders has all and sole power in ordination.* Nor do we think our brethren will allow this to follow from that other.

And we have the less reason to believe that the place alleged will prove, that every particular eldership may assume all and sole power of ordination (even when they might conveniently associate), so as they alone and only they may there ordain. Not only 1. Because of Paul's joining in that ordination (as our brethren elsewhere assert from 2 Timothy 1:6), who was not a fixed member of any particular eldership. But likewise 2. Because even that presbytery there spoken of, by whom Timothy was ordained, seems not to be the presbytery of any particular congregation, having power to ordain officers for themselves only; but a presbytery made up of elders from several places; as Derbe, Lystra, and Iconium, and the region round about, as is probable from Acts 16:1–2 compared with Acts 14:6, as is observed by Apollonius (out of the Belgic interpreters) in a treatise of his directed to this assembly, from the Walachrian churches (cap. 6, question 2).[2] So that, how this place can prove that in every sufficient presbytery there is all and sole power of ordination, so as themselves alone may ordain, and none but themselves have power to join in it; and that it is requisite they

---

1. [Braces are original to the text unless otherwise noted (originally square braces).]

2. Apollonious, *Consideratio Quarumdara Controversiarium*, c. 6. q. 2. [William Apolonius, Dutch Reformed theologian (1600–1657), *Consideratio quarundam Controversiarum ad Regimen Ecclesiæ spectantium, quæ in Angliæ regno hodie agitantur* (London, 1644). *A Consideration of Certaine Controversies at this time agitated in the Kingdome of England: concerning the government of the church of God, written at the command and appointment of the Walachrian Classis, by Guilielmus Apollonii, ... and sent from the Walachrian churches, to declare the sense and consent of their churches, to the Synod at London, October. 16, 1644, stilo novo; translated out of Latine, according to the printed copy* (London 1645), pp. 116–117.]

do assume this power to themselves: we do not discern. Especially when as 3. The apostle Paul (whose authority certainly was as great as the authority of a particular eldership) thought it requisite the others as well as himself should join in Timothy's ordination, and thought it no disparagement to associate with them.

"The second part (*that they may do this, though they might associate*) appears," they say, "1. Because association does neither add to, nor diminish the power of a presbytery; it is by way of *accumulation*, not *privation*, as is acknowledge by the Reformed churches."

Answer. Our brethren taking it now for granted, that the presbytery mentioned [in] 1 Timothy 4:14 (where Timothy, an evangelist, and so not an officer of one single congregation, was ordained), was a particular presbytery, and not classical, or made up of elders of several congregations— and that besides this particular presbytery, there was none else that either did, or had power to join with them; and that they did assume all and sole power in ordination (which perhaps at another time they would not grant, because of the people's interest), and that it was requisite for them so to do; and consequently, that every sufficient presbytery (that is, every presbytery; for our brethren will not say that any presbytery is insufficient, although consisting but of two ruling elders), may assume, yea, and that it is requisite that they do assume, all and sole power, and not associate with others—that which they now attempt to prove, is that an opportunity to associate, even with convenience, does not hinder but that they may thus assume; yea, and that it is requisite so to do. For we are not now disputing what may be done in some possible cases; as if a single congregation were cast upon some remote island, or in the midst of heathens, Turks, pagans, or even amongst papists, or the like, where either there be none to associate with, or only such as would make such association destructive to them (for what power they may assume or exercise in such a case, is not the question now in hand); but whether even there, where they may conveniently associate, it be yet lawful and requisite that every presbytery (at least every sufficient presbytery), do assume all and sole power of ordination?

To the reason they allege ("because association does neither add to, nor diminish the power of a presbytery") we *answer:*

1. We are glad to hear our brethren acknowledge that association does not diminish the power of a presbytery; for if so, then why do they deny that power to diverse presbyteries associated into one classis, which they allow to each of them singly? And why are our brethren so afraid of it, and represent it upon all occasions, so prejudicial to congregations, and to their power? If the power of a presbytery be not diminished by association with others; and this acknowledged by the Reformed churches (as our brethren here intimate), we know little reason why they should be so averse from it.

But 2. That by association, there is nothing *added* to the power of a presbytery, we cannot grant them. For we believe that presbyteries in association have more power (at leaſt extensively, if not intensively), than a single presbytery alone. And though it were granted, that presbyteries associated could do no other aɕts, than each presbytery singly; yet their power might extend further than the power of a single presbytery.

3. If what they allege were true, that by association there were neither addition, nor diminution of power; yet does not this prove aught, but that it may be requisite for them to associate; because though there were no addition of power or authority, yet there would be thereby an addition of sufficiency or ability; and in reference thereunto, it might be requisite, at leaſt for some, to associate; yea, even those who may be thought moſt able, if not for any need of their own (as conceiving themselves so sufficient, that they want [*lack*] no help); yet at leaſt for the good of others, who may ſtand in need of help from them. Though they had singly a like authority to do the thing, yet in association they will have a greater ability to do it well. And therefore, if by association there be no diminution of power (as our brethren here affirm), and withal an addition of ability, it is requisite that where it may be had conveniently, it be made use of; and consequently, it is not requisite that every single presbytery, though some way sufficient, should decline association, and assume to themselves all and sole power.

And that the inconsequence of this reason may be the more appear, we shall propose a case that is like[ly] enough to fall out often in our brethren's way. If in a single congregation of their way, there were no other ruling officers, but one paſtor and one ruling elder, we believe they would say, that these are a sufficient presbytery; and if no more can be had, they may exercise the whole power of an eldership of that congregation. Yet if God afford opportunity to them of having another miniſter to be a teacher, or one or more persons fit to be ruling elders, we believe they would think it requisite to have a larger presbytery than that of two. But we ask, why? Since when two more are added to the former two, it will neither add to, nor diminish the power of the presbytery. For those two (they suppose) had the entire power of a presbytery, and the whole four can have no more, so that there is no addition of power; and why there should thereby be a diminution of power we cannot see. We suppose they would answer, because, though there be no addition of power, yet there is an addition of ability, and these four are now more able to manage those affairs, than those two alone. And the like we say in the case of association; for though (as our brethren affirm) it did neither add to, nor diminish the power, yet diverse presbyteries associated are more able to manage that power, than each of them singly (to say nothing of a multitude of other inconveniences that are thereby likewise avoided).

What our brethren add, that *it is by way of accumulation, not privation, as is acknowledge by the Reformed churches;* we acknowledge likewise; being glad our brethren do acknowledge it too. And we hope that what they here make the foundation of their own argument, they will not afterwards deny, when we shall have occasion to make use of it.

But if they infer that therefore whatever a single church might do alone, when they did not, or could not associate with others, they alone may do now, when they may, or do associate; we deny that consequence. And we give reason for that denial, from a practice that they must needs grant in their own way. For in a single congregation where the eldership consists but of three elders (which according to our brethren's principles is a very sufficient presbytery) any two of these may perform any presbyterial act, because they are the major part of the whole eldership. But in case this eldership be increased to the number of five (as well it may), the act of those two shall not be now accounted the act of the eldership (as before it was), and that because there be now others adjoined to them, who before were not. Yet we suppose our brethren cannot deny, but that this addition of more members to the eldership, is by way of accumulation, not of privation; for the power is not taken from any of the former members by adding of these new ones, but others are admitted to the same power. And the difference which does arise upon it (that those two could before perform a presbyterial act, but now cannot), is merely accidental. Because before, they were the major part of the eldership, but now they are not. For they had not that power, *quatenus* [*as*] two, but *quatenus* the major part. And so it is in association of divers elderships in one classis, for the performing of such acts as they are all concerned in; and yet this difference is by way of accumulation properly, and not of privation; for there is an accumulation of the power of more elders in the same judgment; and if the votes of a few who were before able to have carried the business, be not sufficient now to do it, it is not because their votes are less valid in themselves, than they were before, but only *ex accidenti*, because they are *accidently* not (now) the major part.

They add. "2. If association be so necessarily required, where it may be {See p. 276} had, then neither a classical, provincial, nor national presbytery can assume all and sole power of ordination, if there may be any other classical, provincial, or national presbytery, with whom they may associate. And that there is, or may be always some, is necessarily to be supposed in these times of the gospel, if any association ought to be."

Answer. This does no way hurt us at all.

For 1. We do not say that either classical or provincial assemblies may assume all and sole power; but that there may be appeals from either, where there are higher assemblies to appeal to; no, nor yet the national assembly, if there may be (with convenience) an association larger than it; as we show at large in our answer to our brethren's reason against subordination. A {See pages provincial or national assembly may ordain ministers, as well as a classis; 224–272} yea, and may depose those whom a classis ordains; and we would say the like of a superior assembly to a national, if there were a like opportunity of larger association.

Yet 2. There is less danger in trusting a classis, or synod, with a power of ordination, than in trusting a particular congregation with it (as might easily be shown if it were needful to mention the insufferable mischiefs that would arise, if every eldership in a congregation might ordain for ministers whom they please, without control), and therefore more requisite that congregations do not assume that power. So that neither the thing supposed to follow upon our proposition is any absurdity, nor is the consequence valid.

Especially if 3. We consider that the proposition does not say (as they here suppose), that association is *necessarily* required where it may be had (which yet perhaps might have been said more safely, than what our brethren assert), but that it is *very requisite*, where it may be had with *convenience*.

TO THEIR MINOR

{See p. 276} The minor ("that there may be a sufficient Presbytery in a particular congregation") is proved they say, "1. By the second proposition touching church government sent up to both houses of Parliament *viz.* {*A presbytery consists of ministers of the Word, and such other public officers as are agreeable to, and warranted by the Word of God to be church governors, to join with the ministers in the government of the church.*} All which may be in a particular congregation."

Answer. How this of the assembly should prove our brethren's proposition, we cannot understand. That a presbytery consists of ministers and ruling elders, we think our brethren will not deny; but will our brethren hence infer, that wherever there be ministers and ruling elders, there is a sufficient presbytery to perform all acts that belong to any presbyteries?

If so, then they must not deny classical, provincial and national assemblies to be sufficient presbyteries (at least if they be made up of ministers and ruling elders), and that they may ordain, excommunicate, censure, and do all presbyterial acts lawful for a presbytery to do. If not; then how does this proposition prove their minor? We do not yet see the strength of this consequence, "that if a presbytery consists of ministers and ruling elders, then there may be a sufficient presbytery in a particular congregation unto all acts;" and particularly unto ordination. We say that classes and synods, provincial and national, consist of ministers and ruling elders; but we do not say (nor can our brethren infer it from our words), that therefore there may be in a single congregation, a sufficient classical presbytery, or a sufficient provincial or national synod; either of which might yet with as good consequence be affirmed, as that which our brethren impose. That the assembly's proposition was true, we suppose our brethren will not deny (if they do, they should not have laid that as a foundation of their argument). But if they will argue from it as not only a true, but as a reciprocal proposition, and an adequate definition of a presbytery; we desire they would first own it as such, and we shall make use of it in due time. If not, they must not take that as granted on both sides, which neither the assembly, nor themselves admit.

They add 2. "Wherein consists the sufficiency of a presbytery? The number of how many elders is not set or bounded by institution; suppose two or three; and if more be requisite in a particular congregation, there may be four or five. And a presbytery over many congregations is acknowledged to be sufficient, though it consist of no more. If they have this power as a sufficient presbytery, why not the other also? Have they their power only as having relation to many congregation? Is that the essential requisite to their sufficiency? Here are elders, and as many elders, having relation to a church: and the argument used by the reverend assembly to prove a presbytery over many congregations, is that elders are mentioned in relation to one church."

Answer. "The number of elders," say our brethren, "is not set or bounded by institution." Very true; therefore we say there may be more elders in a presbytery, than those of one congregation. And if there may be, then so often as it may conduce to the general good of the church, and the better edification of the whole body of Christ, it is requisite that there be more, if conveniently they may be had; and consequently, those of one single congregation, not to assume to themselves all and sole power. For where there are {See p. 207} not particular bounds set by institution, there the general rules of Scripture must take place, for the ordering of such particulars so as may tend most to the edification and good of the whole body of Christ. Only (upon this occasion) we desire our brethren to remember what they affirmed in their reasons against subordination of assemblies: that 'there must be the greatest and most express warrant and designment for them in the Word, both for their subordination and number, and for their bounds and power, or else they might not be owned,' and (comparing that rule with their assertion here) to consider whether it had not need of some limitation.

Upon this supposition our brethren argue, that there may be two or three, yea four or five elders in a single congregation; and the number of elders in a presbytery not being set or bounded, it cannot be denied but these may be sufficient to make a presbytery. But this, if granted, does not prove it requisite that there should be no more, where more may be had conveniently; or that all presbyteries must be reduced to the *minimum quod*   *minimum limit* *sic*, and in that capacity, assume all and sole power.

But they say, "a presbytery over many congregations is acknowledged to be sufficient, though they consist of no more."

Answer. If they mean no more than two or three, we hardly believe either that there are any such classical presbyteries; or if there are, that they are acknowledged sufficient. Yea, though they should mean no more than four or five, if that number be made up of preaching and ruling elders together. But if they suppose those four or five to be all miniſters of the Word; we believe that it will be a case so rare, to find a particular congregation furnished with so many able miniſters, as that we need not trouble ourselves much at present to make a rule for such a case, but may defer it, till that case falls out. Only, we think that while that congregation remains so well furnished, they will have no great occasion to ordain more for themselves; and that they assume all and sole power to ordain for others, we suppose our brethren will not affirm.

But, say our brethren, "if they" (a classical presbytery consiſting of four or five) "have this power as a sufficient presbytery, why not also the other" (a presbytery in a single congregation consiſting of as many)?

Answer. If by this power they mean all and sole power in ordination we (for reasons before alleged, both here, and in what we have said about sub-ordinations) deny it, even of such a classical presbytery, if they have opportunity and convenience of associating with others.

And if at any time, either they or a larger presbytery, may assume all and sole power in ordination, it is not *quatenus* [*as*] "a sufficient presbytery;" but *quatenus* the "whole number of those who can conveniently associate."

As if in a remote island (or in a like case) such a classical presbytery as they ſpeak of, where they cannot have opportunity to associate with other churches, may assume all and sole power of ordination for their own churches; we would not say that they do this *quatenus* "a sufficient presbytery," or *quatenus* "so many;" but, *quatenus* "all that can conveniently associate;" and that if they had opportunity of associating with more, they ought, notwithſtanding such a sufficiency, so to do.

In like manner, if in a particular congregation, according to our brethren's principles, there were such a presbytery as our brethren ſpeak of, they would say (we believe), that this presbytery might assume all and sole power of ordination or of government in that congregation; but not *quatenus* a sufficient number, or *quatenus* five, but, *quatenus* all the elders of that congregation; for if to these five there shall be six more added, they will not say that the firſt five have (now) all and sole power; but that the other six have their share in it also: not but that those five be now *as many*, and *as sufficient* as they were before, and as sufficient to conſtitute a sufficient presbytery as before; but because they are not *all*, as before they were. So that what power they had before, they had it not *quatenus* "so many;" but *quatenus* "the whole number."

Therefore the decision of the queſtion, whether a particular congregation, or the eldership of a particular congregation, may assume all and sole power in ordination, does not so much depend upon this, whether that they have *a number sufficient to do the work*; but on this, whether they be the *only persons concerned*, or intereſted in it.

Wherefore, that which follows {"have they their power only as having relation to many congregation?" etc.} might have been spared. For if there were but one congregation of Christians in the world, they should have all and sole power; not as being but one congregation; but as being the whole church.

As for the argument of the assembly (to which the brethren refer), proving one presbytery in Jerusalem over the many congregations there, because they are all mentioned as one church; what advantage it produces to our brethren, in the present business, we cannot yet perceive. But as it served then to prove many congregations to be under one presbytery; so may it be of like use here, to prove that single congregations are not to assume all See p. 276} and sole power in ordination.

The Answer to their Second Argument

Their second argument lies thus: "that which two apostles being joined together might do in a particular congregation, that ordinary elders may do in a particular congregation. But Paul and Barnabas ordained elders in particular congregations, though they might associate. Therefore, etc."

Answer. This argument concludes not at all against the proposition. The proposition says, *it is not requisite that they assume all and sole power in ordination.* The argument concludes that they *may ordain;* not that they may assume all and sole power; much less that it is *requisite* for them to do. Our brethren we think will not deny, but that Paul alone, being an apostle, might ordain; and yet they suppose that Barnabas joined with him. And if he who might alone ordain, did not think it requisite to assume all and sole power in it, but joined with Barnabas therein, having opportunity and convenience so to do; why should it be more requisite now for the elders of a particular congregation, to disclaim the conjunction of others with them, when it may be had conveniently, and to assume all and sole power to themselves? And this we may the better insist upon, because it has been sometime urged (as a ground of our brethren's opinion concerning non-communion of churches), that there was the same relation between apostles, as there is between churches; and therefore that the example of Paul's departing from Barnabas [in] Acts 15 (whom yet he might not excommunicate, because the apostles were all equal, and one had not power over another), may be a precedent of one church's pronouncing a sentence of non-communion against another church, which yet (because of the parity between them) they may not excommunicate. Now, if Paul's denying communion (as our brethren suppose) with Barnabas, may be a precedent for one church to deny communion with another; why should not Paul's joining with Barnabas in ordination, be as good a precedent for a like conjunction of churches? And if Paul, who might himself ordain alone,

Goodwin, 281

Cf. Baxter, *A Plea for congregationall government,* 13.
{See p. 270}
{See p. 309, 334}

thought it requisite to join with Barnabas, when he might conveniently; why should not a particular eldership (though they had, as our brethren suppose, a power to ordain alone), think it as requisite to join with the elders of other churches, when they may conveniently? Can our brethren think that a particular eldership of one congregation has a greater authority and infallibility than Paul had? We have not yet forgotten what our brethren told us (in their reasons against alleging the instance of the church of {See p. 85} Jerusalem, for a pattern of Presbyterial government), that the apostles had singly the same power which they exercised jointly (Acts 6). Yet they exercised it together, because it fell out that they were together, and it was fit none of them should be excluded. Which does not only confirm what we have here said before, upon the former argument, that the sufficiency of a single presbytery to perform the acts of ordination (if that were granted) is no reason why it is not requisite for the presbytery to associate, when they may conveniently, and not assume all and sole power to themselves (for apostles had each of them a sufficiency of power); but it does also confirm that inference, brought from the instance of Paul and Barnabas as joining in ordination (and which might be also brought from the apostles joining together in Acts 6 to ordain deacons, and from Paul's joining with ordinary elders to ordain Timothy, as our brethren say he did, besides many other instances of like nature), that if Paul and Barnabas not only did join together; but it was fit they should do so (because unfit that any of them should be excluded), though each had a sufficient power; then it is not only lawful that elderships of several churches may join, but fit or requisite that they do associate, when they may conveniently do it.

To the particular propositions of the argument we *answer* as follows:

TO THE MAJOR

{See p. 276} For the major proposition {"that which two apostles being joined together might do in a particular congregation, that ordinary elders may do in a particular congregation"}, we appeal to our brethren's conscience, whether they believe it to be true. The emphasis lies in the words ["being joined together"]; for they will not say, that what an apostle might do alone in a single congregation, may be done by ordinary elders in a single congregation; because the apostles did act many things (even in single congregations), by a power apostolical, not imitable by ordinary elders; but what two or more of them did perform, being joined together, may (they say) be performed by *in assembly* ordinary elders; as if whatever the apostles did, *in collegio*, they did as ordinary elders, or by a power common to them with ordinary elders. If this be a truth now, then was it a truth also in the ordination of deacons [in] Acts 6 (which our brethren denied when the assembly made use of that place, as appears in their reasons against the instance of Jerusalem), unless the same proposition which is a truth when it makes for them, be a falsehood when it is alleged against them. If our brethren think it not to be a truth, they should not here affirm it as such, and ground their argument upon it, especially having there denied it. But let us examine their proof of it.

"The consequence," they say, "appears thus: if the argument brought by the reverend assembly do hold, *viz.* that when the apostles met together for ordination, or for ordering the affairs of the church of Jerusalem, they met as ordinary elders (which they have voted) then," etc.

Answer. But what if the argument brought by the assembly does not hold (as our brethren think it does not, for they there deny it)? What then should become of our brethren's proposition, which is built upon no other ground, but a supposition which themselves will not grant?

Yea, suppose the assembly had voted what our brethren here say they have (somewhat like this, we confess, they have voted), and that the argument of the assembly does hold; will our brethren say (as they should have said, if they meant to prove their consequence, as they call it, or major proposition), that then, what two apostles joined together might do, that ordinary elders may do? No. But all they say is this: 'then surely, when Paul and Barnabas met to ordain elders in particular congregations, it is to be averred, that they met for that act as ordinary elders.' But what is this to the proof of the major proposition? There is not a word of Paul and Barnabas in the major proposition (either joining as ordinary elders, or joining at all); but only a general assertion, that what two apostles joined together may do in a particular congregation, that ordinary elders may do in a particular congregation; of which general proposition our brethren give no proof at all. Lightfoot, 243 *Minutes*, 5.135, Doc. 45, Draft Directory for church government

For our own part (though our brethren would seem to ground this assertion upon somewhat voted by us), we cannot assert to the truth of it; because, though we think now as we did before, that the apostles in the ordination of deacons (Acts 6) did act as elders, or by a power common to them with elders; and that they are therein a pattern to be imitated by elderships; yet we neither then did, nor do now believe, that whatever two apostles joined together might perform, that ordinary elders may perform (whether in a particular congregation, or elsewhere). Yea, in that very instance [of] Acts 6 (as we told our brethren then in our answer to those reasons), we doubt not to say, that they did act partly as apostles, partly as elders; something they did by a power apostolical, and not imitable by ordinary elders; something they did by a power common to them with elders. {See p. 147}

{See p. 85}

And we think our brethren are of the same opinion; for they there tell us that in that very act (of ordination) they must needs act as apostles; for they do not simply ordain the men, but do anew, by virtue of apostolical authority, institute the office of deacons, which none but the apostles could immediately, and at first, have done.

But how this consists with their present assertion (that what two apostles together might do, ordinary elders may do), we cannot tell; but leave it to themselves to reconcile. The inserting of the words {"in a particular congregation"} (which, whether they intended as a limitation or no, we cannot tell) will no way help it. For if this erecting of a new office, were not performed by them in a particular congregation (as our brethren think it was); yet doubtless, they cannot deny, but it might have been; and their proposition speaks not only of what two (or more) apostles did, but what they might do.

If our brethren should desert this general proposition (as we think they have cause to do), and urge only thus [*this*] much: that if the apostles at Jerusalem, joining together to ordain deacons (whether it were a church of one or more congregations), did act as elders, then Paul and Barnabas joining together to ordain elders, did act as elders; yet even this inference would not hold. For there is a great difference between the apostles performing ordinary acts of elders, in an ordinary way at Jerusalem, when it was a church already constituted and settled, and that of Paul and Barnabas in the first erecting and constituting of churches in places where before there were none, affixing elders to them. So that the latter being a work extraordinary, and more peculiar to the apostles, whose great work it was to plant the gospel throughout the world, even in places where before it had not been heard of, may with much more reason be affirmed to be the exercise of an apostolical power, than that of performing ordinary acts of government in a ordinary way at Jerusalem, where the church had been settled, an[d] regularly governed for some time before. And thus much for their major proposition; we proceed next to consider their minor.

TO THEIR MINOR

{See p. 276} "The minor," they say, "has two parts: 1. Paul and Barnabas ordained elders in particular congregations. 2. That they might associate."

But there is, or at least there should have been a third thing in that proposition, very material to their purpose (which it concerned them as well to prove as these two); namely that Paul and Barnabas were joined together in that ordination. If not, it serves not their turn; for they do not say that what two apostles might severally perform; but what two apostles being joined together might perform, may be performed by ordinary elders. And yet, for aught our brethren have shown to the contrary, some of these elders might be ordained by Paul, some by Barnabas, and not all by both jointly; and if so, the instance would not be at all to their purpose. But this we do not insist upon.

Yea, there should have been a fourth thing, somewhere added, if they would conclude against the proposition, *viz.* that they were the elders of only one congregation. For we never denied that ordinary elders may ordain elders in a particular congregation; nor that a classis or synod of ordinary elders, may ordain elders for a particular congregation. But the thing in controversy is not what may be done in a particular congregation, but what may be done in it by their own particular elders alone, and is requisite so to be, notwithstanding the convenience of an association with others. And here the instance (in our apprehension) fails them exceedingly; for though it were granted that Paul and Barnabas did ordain as elders; yet who will say they did it as the elders of one congregation only; they being as much elders of all the neighbor congregations, as of that one wherein our brethren suppose them to have ordained? And (if they must be called an eldership), they might as well by styled a classical, or (if you will) an ecumenical eldership, as a congregational.

And then a fifth and sixth thing should have been cast in to all the former; namely, Paul and Barnabas did not only ordain, but did assume all and sole power in ordination; and that it was requisite so to do, so as no others might either challenge an interest, or be permitted to join with them therein. But of these things (altogether very necessary to make out their argument), our brethren say nothing. We proceed therefore to consider those two particulars which they endeavor to prove.

"1. That these were particular congregations wherein they ordained elders appears," they say, "because it is not supposable that the cities, much less the regions round" about, "where the apostles preached and erected churches (as appears by Acts 13:49 compared with Acts 14:6, 21–23), were grown to many congregations before the apostles appointed elders over them. For the apostles who were to preach in all places, would not stay so long in one place: and it was their course, when" there were "ἱκανοὶ, as at Derbe (Acts 14:21), to set elders to them." {See p. 277} [ἱκανοὺς; many]

Answer. When our brethren say in the first part of their minor, that Paul and Barnabas ordained elders in particular congregations, they intend it, we suppose, in one of these two senses: either (first) that the act of ordaining was by Paul and Barnabas performed in particular congregations, referring the words in particular congregations (in their proposition) to the word ordained; and the words κατ' ἐκκλησίαν in Acts 14:23[1] to the word Χειποτονήσαντες, understanding it thus, that Paul and Barnabas did at each of these places (Derbe, Lystra, Iconium and Antioch), fast, pray, ordain elders, and commend them to the grace of God. And it will not at all prejudice our cause to allow them this sense. For we shall say that Paul and Barnabas did ordain elders in each of those congregations, by a power which they had equally respecting all of them (like as when a classical eldership does ordain an elder in a particular congregation), and not that they were ordained by a full and sole power residing in each of those congregations, in which those ordinations are supposed to be performed. And that the rather because it is not said that each congregation or church did ordain elders for themselves, but that Paul and Barnabas did ordain elders for them; and the power of Paul and Barnabas was as much extrinsical to {See p. 277}

---

1. Χειποτονήσαντες δὲ αὐτοῖς πρεσβυτέρους κατ' ἐκκλησίαν.

each of the churches, and as little confined to them, as the power of a classical eldership, to each particular congregation within their limits. But if our brethren thus interpret the words κατ' ἐκκλησίαν, to denote the different places wherein those elders were ordained; they cannot well urge the words κατ' ἐκκλησίαν to be restrictive of their power, as if they were only πρεσβυτέρους κατ' ἐκκλησίαν, each of them elders in their own particular church only, and had not power at all out of their own congregations to join with the elders of other churches to act in common for the good of them all.

Or else (second) they mean it in this sense: that the elders ordained by Paul and Barnabas were settled in particular congregations; referring the words in particular congregations to the word elders; and the words κατ' ἐκκλησίαν to the word πρεσβυτέρους, or to the word αὐτοῖς, understanding it thus, that Paul and Barnabas ordained elders for them (κατ' ἐκκλησίαν) respectivè [*respectively*], *viz.* for each church their own elders. And this seems rather to be their meaning, because that all along in the pursuit of this argument, they do promiscuously use the phrase of *ordaining to them* and *ordaining in them*. And this interpretation also we may without prejudice allow them. For as we conceive it much conducing to edification, that where the numbers of believers are great, or their habitations far distant, they should for more convenience be distributed into several congregations; so we judge it likewise conducing to edification, that each of those congregations should have one or more appointed over them to take the special care of them. But that {See pp. the power of the pastors or elders in those several congregations, should be 63ff, 207ff} so limited each to the peculiar care of his own particular congregation, as that they may not join and act together, in things of common concernment for the good of all of them, our brethren, we suppose, will not be able to prove; and what they have produced to that purpose, in their reasons against the joining of many congregations under one presbyterial government, and against the subordination of assemblies for government; we have in our answers thereunto already considered. But if our brethren would be understood in this latter sense; they do very much vary from the thing in hand; for the thing which at present we are inquiring after is not, for whom, but by whom, these elders were ordained; and this, though granted, will no way prove that they were ordained each of them by a full and sole power residing in one congregation only. We say likewise, that if they understand κατ' ἐκκλησίαν in Acts 14:23 in this latter sense (to denote the charge to which those elders were appointed), then there is nothing in the text concerning the particular place wherein the ordination was performed. Those elders might, for aught appears to the contrary, be all ordained at one time and place, when Paul and Barnabas at their departure out of those parts commended them to the grace of God; at which might be present, if not more congregations, yet at least members of more congregations than one.

We say therefore in general to this first part of their minor, that whether it be taken in the one sense or in the other, it makes nothing to the present purpose. For we are not now inquiring, either in what place or to what charge, but by what authority, elders then were or now may be ordained. And therefore we might spare the pains of examining the three proofs which they bring for the confirmation of it; since that it is no more than what is ordinarily practiced by classical elderships, who do in a particular congregation ordain pastors for a particular congregation; though yet others may be and often are present besides those that are members of that one particular congregation; and those ordained for particular congregations are likewise to take care in common for things that do concern many congregations. Yet the three proofs which they have produced we will examine in order.

For the first reason, wherein they allege that "it is not supposable that those cities and the regions round about were grown to many congregations before the apostles appointed elders to them."

We *answer:* If they mean only, that there were not in each city, and each village of the regions adjacent, many congregations before the apostles appointed elders, we think so too. But if their meaning be, that in those cities and the regions adjacent, taken altogether (*collectivè* [*collectively*]) there were not many congregations before the apostles ordained elders to them; the text is manifestly against them; because, though there be mention of preaching the gospel in Antioch of Pisidia, in Iconium, Lystra, Derbe, and the regions about (Acts 13, Acts 14:49, Acts 14:6, 8, 20), yet we read not of any forming of them into distinct churches and ordaining of elders to them, till they had been at all those places (Acts 14:21–23), and by that time, there was not only a competent number of disciples to make a congregation, but a competent number of congregations too, to make a classis. And it will be hard for our brethren to prove, either that there were no more present at the ordination of each of those several elders, than those of that one particular congregation wherein he was to be placed; or that they were so confined each to the care of his own particular congregation, as that they might not at all join in the common care of all.

2. "Again," they say, "this was the first ordination of elders to those places, and therefore must needs be to particular congregations; for a classis is made up of the elders of many congregations."

Answer. We deny not but that they were appointed to particular congregations as their more peculiar charge; but it does not follow, that therefore the elders of these particular congregations were not as well in common to take care of the whole that concerned them all, as each in particular of his own special charge; or that they were ordained in a particular congregation without the presence or assistance of any others; much less that they were ordained by a particular congregation, assuming all and sole power in ordination. They might be ordained to a particular congregation, though

they were ordained in a meeting of many congregations, and by the elderships of many congregations united. Nor does it follow, that they were elders to particular congregations only; for they might well, as a classis, take
care of the whole in matters of joint concernment, and yet each in their
own congregations deal in those things that did more particularly concern
them. For a classis is made up of the elders of many congregations, as our
brethren themselves ſpeak. But how it should prove that they were not a
classis, because elders to particular congregations, or because it was the
firſt ordination of elders in those places, we do not underſtand? For what
hinders but that, at the same time, they might be appointed both in common to take care of the whole, and in particular, each of his own particular
congregation; and so to endeavor both singly, and jointly, to the utmoſt of
their power, the good of all and every of those congregations, as opportunity and occasion should be offered? Indeed, if as soon as there were disciples converted in one city or village, the apoſtles had affixed elders to
them (and to them only), before there had been any converted in a second
place; and then, at that second place, had erected a church and elders to
them, and them only (independent on [*sic* of] that former church), before
any had been converted in a third or fourth place; and so had conſtituted
in each place a church and elders so diſtinct as to have no dependence on,
or intercourse with any other church, which either was already, or should
afterwards be erected; if thus (we say) they had done, there were some reason why our brethren might bring such a consequence as this. But if they
think it was so, they greatly miſtake; for we read not either of erecting and
forming of a diſtinct church, or of ordaining elders in any of those places,
till there were disciples converted in all of them, as is undeniably manifeſt
by the whole series of the thirteenth and fourteenth chapters [of Acts]. And
therefore, that supposition that it was their course when there were ἱκανὸι
(persons met to make up a congregation or church) presently to set elders
to them, is built upon the sand; and the contrary is evident. For though at
Iconium (Acts 14:1) there were, not only ἱκανὸι, but πολὺ πλῆθος, a great
multitude, yet there is no mention of ordination till afterwards.

    "Laſtly," say our brethren, "they ordained elders κατ᾽ ἐκκλησίαν, and
{See p. 277} αὐτοῖς and, at their ordaining, they faſted and prayed, commending them to
the grace of God; which faſting and praying being (according to the principles of us both) to be in particular congregations, it follows that the churches
to which these elders were appointed, were particular congregation[s].

    Answer. If they would prove what they undertook, they should have said,
"therefore they were ordained *in* those particular congregations;" or rather,
"that they were ordained *by* particular congregations;" not, "that they were
ordained *to* particular congregations." We never denied that the churches to
which they (at leaſt some of them) were ordained might be particular congregations, no more than we do deny that miniſters ordained by classis, or

synods, are ordained to particular congregations; and yet the authority *by* which, and the assembly or meeting *in* which they were ordained, might be more than of one particular congregation. And if the many thousands at Jerusalem, who were converted before the ordination of deacons (Acts 6); yea, all the myriads converted there before Paul's coming to Jerusalem [in] Acts 21 (which was a long time after), were no more than "might conveniently meet together in one place for all ordinations" as our brethren would have us to believe; they will give us leave, we hope, to think it possible, if not probable, that the believers converted by Paul and Barnabas in so short a time, at Antioch, Iconium, Lystra and Derbe, were not so numerous but that they, or at least more than one particular congregation of them, might meet together in one place at the ordination of elders; at least divers brethren from several congregations might be present at it. What they allege ("that fasting and prayer are, according to the principles of both, to be in particular congregations") makes nothing to the contrary; for if they mean no more but this, that there may be fasting and prayers in a particular congregation; or that sometimes a particular congregation is to fast and pray; we do not deny *to accord to our principles*. But if they intend that there *may no more* join together in fasting and prayer than those of a particular congregation; or that several congregations may not lawfully join together in it; it may perhaps be according to our brethren's principles, but not according to ours. That they ordained elders κατ' ἐκκλησίαν, and αὐτοῖς, we grant. They ordained elders for those of Derbe, Lystra, Iconium and Antioch; these being the αὐτοῖς for whom the elders were ordained. And those elders so ordained had their particular congregations assigned them κατ' ἐκκλησίαν, where they were principally to attend; it being most conducing to the general good of believers, that they should be distributed into several churches or congregations, and have particular pastors appointed over them. Nevertheless this does not at all hinder, but that besides that particular care which each had of his own charge, they might all of them jointly have common care of the whole.

But how this or anything else that can be made out of that text, does contribute aught to our brethren's purpose, we do not see. For if it were granted that they were ordained in particular congregations, it would not at all advance their cause, unless they prove withal, that *only a particular congregation* had to do in it; because it is not so much material in what place they be ordained, as by what authority; and if a classical presbytery do ordain elders in a particular congregation, it cannot be therefore said, that the particular congregation does assume all and sole power in it. And so, though Paul and Barnabas (who were as much elders to all these congregations, as to any one of them) did in some one congregation ordain elders, it cannot be thence inferred that this one congregation did either *assume* or *execute* all and sole power in it; perhaps, not *any* power (further than of assent); for it is not said that they did ordain, but that Paul and Barnabas did ordain *for them.*

2. "For the second {*that they might associate*} it appears," they say, "be- {See p. 277} cause there were churches in the regions round about, and yet the apostles mention no association (which they would have done if that had been the way), for when they did things with ordinary elders, it is thus recorded, *the apostles and elders.* But they commend them to the grace of God, as Paul did the church of Ephesus (Acts 20:32), as having sufficient means to perpetuate succession, and to ordain other elders, if any should die, as also *to build them up unto eternal life.*"

Answer. If they mean that the apostles might associate, we think so too; and not only that they might, but that they did associate and join with every church where they came, at least with these churches to whom they actually ordained elders; and we suppose our brethren will not deny it. If they mean that the churches might associate; neither do we in this contradict them; for we believe they might, and did associate. But we think they contradict themselves in it; for they argued even now, that this being the first ordination of elders to those places, it must therefore needs be to particular congregations; whereas, if these churches, even in this first ordination of elders to them, might associate (as our brethren now say), where then lies the necessity of this inference, that it must needs be to particular congregations, because it was the first ordination of elders to those places? They would first prove, that the apostles ordained elders to particular congregations, because it was impossible they should associate; and now, they would prove, that they did not associate, though they might.

"They might associate," say our brethren, "because there were churches in the regions round" about.

Answer. That there were believers in the regions thereabout, we grant; because Acts 13:49 mentions the whole region, ὅλης τῆς χώρας,[1] as well as the town of Antioch; and Acts 14:6 mentions the region round about, τὴν περίχωρον, as well as the cities of Derbe and Lystra; divers of the country people thereabout believed the Word, as well as those that dwelt in the cities mentioned. But it is not said, there were churches in the regions round about, and that there were elders affixed to them, who might join with Paul and Barnabas in ordaining elders for Antioch, Iconium, Lystra and Derbe; nor is it likely that the regions about these cities were by Paul and Barnabas sooner formed into churches, and supplied with elders, then the cities themselves. And when our brethren said before, that this was the first ordination of elders to those places, we suppose they meant that neither the

---

1. [The text reads ὁλίω τίὼ χώραν. Disregarding what appears to be a stray period, this expands to ὁλην τὴν χώραν (ίω=ην). For some reason the author/scribe or the compositor of the type substituted the accusative for the genitive ὅλης τῆς χώρας, which is the Biblical text. My thanks to Arnie Robertstad for his help with the Greek usage here.]

cities mentioned, nor the villages about them, had before this time, elders ordained to them; and not that there had been a former ordination of elders for those villages, though not for the cities themselves. If they think otherwise, they might have done well to have shown the reasons why they think so; for we may as well say, that there is no mention of such churches and elders; as they, that there is no mention of association with them.

As for the *association of these churches;* we believe that the word αὐτοῖς [*for them*] takes in not only the cities of Antioch, Iconium, Derbe and Lystra, but the περίχωρον also—the region round about them, as appendices to them; and that the ordination here spoken of, is the first ordination of elders, either for the cities, or the villages about them. And therefore, though the churches within these confines might, and (as we conceive) did associate among themselves; yet that there were other churches already formed, with whom they might thus conveniently associate, and whose elders might join with Paul and Barnabas in ordaining elders to these churches, does not appear.

Now, if the elders of all these churches were ordained *at once*, either at an assembly of all these churches (if their members or distances were not so great, but that they might conveniently meet); or *of brethren from* all or diverse of them; the reason then is plain, why there is no mention of the elders of some of these churches joining with the apostles in ordaining elders to some other of them; because before this joint ordination of elders to all of them, there were no elders in any of them; and, of any other persons, who are not elders, either ordaining alone, or joining in ordination with others (whatever our brethren's principles about it may be), the Scripture is wholly silent. Nor is there anything in the text to the contrary, but that they might be ordained all at once, if κατ᾽ ἐκκλησίαν is to be interpreted of the charge to which they are appointed, as our brethren seem to take it. For it speaks but once of ordaining elders, and that as one of the last acts done by Paul and Barnabas before their departing out of these coasts; and joined with their commending them to God, or solemn taking leave of them (according as the same or a like phrase is used [in] Acts 20:32 as our brethren observe, and Acts 15:40). Yea, our brethren themselves say they ordained elders, and at their ordaining, they fasted and prayed, commending them thereby to the grace of God; making it as it were, one act. Neither can it be inferred from their having distinct charges, that therefore they were ordained in different places; for it is not necessary that the elders must be ordained either in the presence of that people, amongst whom they are to reside, or in the place of their residence. Nor do we think our brethren will contend for it, if they be still of opinion, that the imposition of hands on Paul and Barnabas, Acts 13:3, was an ordination; for neither was that Antioch the place, nor those then present the people, to which they were then sent forth. And our brethren add here, "they commended them to the grace of God as Paul did the church of Ephesus, Acts 20:32." Yet was not

Paul then at Ephesus, but at Miletus; nor was the whole church of Ephesus there present, but only the elders of Ephesus, and perhaps some brethren accompanying them.

But if our brethren would rather suppose, that κατ' ἐκκλησίαν in Acts 14:33 does denote not so much the distinction of charges to which, as the difference of places in which they were ordained, and that these elders were not ordained all at one time and place, but that Paul and Barnabas did first in one church ordain elders to them and commended them to the grace of God; and then, in a second, ordain elders for them, commending them to the grace of God; and so of the rest; and if upon this supposition, they will ask, 'why those elders ordained for the first, did not assist in ordaining elders for a second church; and the elders of both these, assist in ordaining others for a third, and fourth church, and so of the rest?' We say, that our brethren have not yet shown but that they did so, and none of their three reasons, which they produced to make good the first part of their minor, will prove the contrary.

But they say, "*the apostles mention not association.*" *Answer.* True; nor do the apostles mention that which is mentioned, for Luke was the writer of this history, not the apostles; they are but part of the history. And 2. Suppose it were not mentioned at all in this place. There be many things that the apostles do not mention (either here or anywhere else), which yet our brethren would feign have allowed in their way. The apostles do not mention (no more than Luke) that each of these single congregations did assume all and sole power in ordination; yet our brethren, it seems, think they did. The apostles do not mention that the people without elders may ordain an elder; or that the people may join with the elders in imposition of hands; yet perhaps some of our brethren, if not all of them, think it may be done. The apostles do not mention non-communion of churches; nor a church covenant; nor such elective synods as our brethren contend for (beside many other that might be mentioned); but our brethren will not thence infer, that therefore these things either were not, or ought not to be; because the apostles, without mentioning of these, "commended them to the grace of God, as having sufficient means to perpetrate succession, and to ordain other elders, if any should die, as also to build them up unto eternal life."

{See p. 277} But say our brethren, "this they would have done" (*viz.* mentioned association) "if this had been the way; for when they did things with ordinary elders, it is thus recorded, *the apostles and elders.*"

Answer. Sometimes it is so recorded, but not always. In 2 Timothy 1:6, Paul only is mentioned to have imposed hands on Timothy; and yet our brethren think, from 1 Timothy 4:14, that the eldership joined with Paul in it. And why may not Paul and Barnabas as well be said here to ordain elders for each church (without mentioning others) though others also in some churches might join in the action? Especially considering that in the first of these churches, there could not be a conjunction of other elders, because as yet no other were ordained; and therefore, though the elders first ordained might afterward join in ordaining elders for other churches; yet it could not be said, even upon the supposition, that Paul and Barnabas with the elders of neighbor churches, did ordain elders for each church; because in the first church at least, Paul and Barnabas must be supposed to ordain alone, and not in conjunction with other elders of neighbor churches; but that Paul and Barnabas did ordain elders for each church, might well be said; though in some churches other elders joined with them.

Again, it may be very probably conceived, that not only Paul and a presbytery of ordinary elders joined in this ordination of Timothy; but that Barnabas, or Silas, or some other joined likewise; though neither the first, nor the second epistle to Timothy (nor any other place) do expressly mention it. The first time that we find Timothy mentioned is Acts 16, when Paul and Silas coming to Derbe and Lystra, found Timothy there; but how long he had been there before this time, we cannot tell. Perhaps he might be one of those whom Paul and Barnabas ordained [in] Acts 14:23, and he continued there an elder, till Paul's next coming. And if so; then have we not only Barnabas joined with Paul in this ordination, but also the thing that our brethren inquire after, *viz.* elders associated with Paul and Barnabas in ordaining elders at least to some of these churches. Or if Timothy were not at that time ordained by Paul, it is likely that at his next coming to Derbe and Lystra, chapter 16, finding Timothy there, resolving to take him as a companion of his journey, he would ordain him; and whom can we then suppose to be the eldership then joining with him, but those of Derbe, Lystra and Iconium (of whom express mention is made, Acts 16:1), and probably those of Antioch too. So that at least by this time, we may find these elders associated, if not with Paul and Barnabas, yet with Paul and Silas, which is all one. For why Silas (who was a prophet as appears [from] Acts 15:32) should not be thought to join with Paul in Timothy's ordination, as well as the ordinary elders of those places, we see no reason; and yet we find not him expressly mentioned as joining therein, though we cannot think that he was excluded. Or if Timothy were not yet ordained by Paul, but at some time after (though we see no reason to think that his ordination was longer deferred), yet whenever it was, it is probable that Silas or some other of like quality accompanying Paul in his travels (who did not usually travel without some such companion), did join with him in the ordination of Timothy—so that in a matter of fact, of this nature, it is no good argument to conclude *negatively*, because the history does not in every place make mention of it.

And thus we have answered the arguments produced by our brethren as the reasons of their dissent from this proposition. But whereas the assembly had, to their proposition, annexed this proof, *viz.*

{See p. 61}
Minutes,
3.51–77; 5.138
Lightfoot, 262
Gillespie,
58–64

1. Because, there is no example in Scripture that any single congregation which might conveniently associate did assume to itself all and sole power in ordination; neither is there any rule which may warrant such a practice.

2. Because there is in Scripture, example of an ordination in a presbytery over divers congregations; as in the church of Jerusalem, where were many congregations, these many congregations were under one presbytery, and this presbytery did ordain.

Our brethren are pleased to take no notice of this proof at all, nor do they allege anything against the strength of it. But for what reasons they chose rather to waive it, than to object against it, themselves best know.

Concordat cum Originali.
Adoniram Byfield, *Scriba.*

The Grand Debate

*Papers Given in to the Honorable Committee
of Lords and Commons and Assembly of Divines
with the Commissioners of Scotland, for
Accommodation, 1644, by a Sub-committee of
Divines of the Assembly and Dissenting Brethren*

*The Papers and Answers of the Dissenting
Brethren and the Committee of the Assembly
of Divines given into the Honorable Committee
of Lords and Commons, and Assembly of
Divines with the Scotch Commissioners,
for Accommodation at the reviving of that
Committee. 1645*

Papers Given in to

The Committee of Accommodation 1644–1645[1]

An Order of the House of Commons for a
Committee of Accommodation

September 13, 1644.[2] That the Committee of Lords and Commons appointed to treat with the Commissioners of Scotland, and the Committee of the Assembly, do take into consideration the differences of the opinions of the members of the assembly in point of church government, and to endeavor a *union*: And in case that cannot be done, to endeavor the finding out some way how far tender consciences, who cannot in all things submit to the same rule which shall be established, may be borne with according to the Word, and as may stand with the public peace; that so the proceedings of the assembly may not be so much retarded.

[September 20, 1644.] This honorable committee met according to the order, September 20 following, the appointment of the order being that the differences of opinions of the members of the assembly in point of church government be taken into consideration. The honorable committee appointed a subcommittee of six of the members of the assembly. Mr. Marshall, Mr. Hearle, Master Vines, Dr. Temple, Mr. Goodwin, and Mr. Nye (two

Gillespie,
Grand Committee, 101–107

---

1. [There are separate title pages for the two years. The 1644 is misplaced in the example in Early English Books (EEB, STC #581), and is missing, at the least in the digital copy available at archives. org, of the example owned by Princeton Seminary. *Papers Given in to the Honorable Committee of Lords and Commons and Assembly of Divines with the Commissioners of Scotland, for Accommodation 1644 by a sub-committee of Divines of the Assembly and Dissenting Brethren* (London: Printed Anno Dom. 1648). While relevant and considered part of *The Grand Debate* when published, these are technically papers prepared for "a committee of members of the [House of] Lords, Commons and assembly, along with the Scottish commissioners" (*Minutes*, 3.709). The papers are not given entries in the "Calendar of Papers of the Westminster Assembly" (*Minutes*, volume 5). This section is in different type and neither the printer nor bookseller are noted, and EEB notes it "may also have been issued separately." While Thomason purchased them separately on May fifth and sixth, they were intended to be a set (cf. Introduction, p. xlii).]

2. ["This day Cromwell hes obtained ane order of the House of Commons, to refer to the Committee of both Kingdomes the accommodation or tolleration of the Independents; a high and unexpected order; yet, by God's help, we will make use of it contrare to the designe of the procurers." Baillie, to Spang, September 13, 1644, 2.226. Cf. de Witt, pp. 130–132.]

of the dissenting brethren) to consider of the differences of opinions in the assembly in point of church government: and to bring in what might be matter for that grand committee to consider of.

In pursuance of this, the said subcommittee met, who styled themselves the Subcommittee of Agreements. And after the preface declaring their mutual confidence to agree in one confession of faith, and in one directory of public worship, etc., they prepared several propositions concerning the government of particular congregations and ordination, etc., declaring how far in practical principles they did agree therein, together with the different practices which each according to their principles desired.

October 11, 1644. The honorable committee met again, at which the subcommittee presented the propositions they had prepared, declaring they had further to bring in concerning classes and synods, and what might be the way of accommodation for the dissenting brethren to enjoy congregations amongst us, according to their principles. All which (though they had met many days) was not as then perfected.

Therefore the honorable committee did remit back to the said subcommittee the propositions then brought in, to be further explained, and as much as might to be perfected against the next meeting, adjourning that committee until Tuesday, October 15.

When these propositions that follow were brought in by the subcommittee, as containing both a fuller explication, and the best way to accommodate their own and their brethren's principles in a practique [*practical*] way (which was the end [*goal*] of that honorable committee) both for congregations, and synods, and the government thereof.

October 15, 1644. The honorable committee of Lords, Commons, Divines of the Assembly, with the Scotch Commissioners met. And these propositions were read by Master Vines who was the chairman of that subcommittee.

A vote was passed in the committee to take them into consideration. But *Rule:* form of that debate was not entered upon, because it was the earnest desire of some church polity that the rule should first be made complete by the Assembly and the Houses.

And there was a cessation put upon the honorable committee herein, by the Honorable House of Commons until their further pleasure.

Let the Reader take notice that in what particulars the dissenting brethren do differ from the propositions of the rest of the subcommittee, or do express their desires apart from them, there is a differing character [italics] put in the printing of them for the discerning thereof, and that in other things wherein they express not any difference or further explanation, they agreed to them.

The propositions were as follows.

At the Sub-Committee of Agreements

In confidence that we shall jointly agree in one Confession of Faith, and in one Directory of the Public Worship of God, with the help of a Preface, we come according to our order to points of government, and therein do agree as follows.[1]

1. That a particular congregation having such officers as the Word of God holds out, both for preaching and governing, is a church that has power in all ecclesiastical affairs, which do only concern itself.

2. That these forementioned officers are to be so many in number, in every such congregation, as that three or two at the least may agree together in every act of government. By two at the least, we mean preaching or governing officers. But some of the committee do hold that a preaching presbyter should concur in the sentence of excommunication and suspension.

3. That these officers have power in those things which are voted by the assembly to be due unto them, and in suspension and excommunication: some of the committee meaning that the major part of the officers have power to do it, the congregation not opposing it, in which case of opposition, they hold [it] fit that the officers do suspend the act. *Other of the committee saying that the major part of the officers have power to do it, if the major part of the brethren do consent unto it by their votes: so as the negative lies in the major part, either of the officers or brethren.*

And as for ordination, we all hold that where there are two preaching presbyters at least, that a presbytery may ordain their own elders. *But some of the committee do further say that where there are two ruling elders at least, they have power of ordaining elders for that congregation, and in case there be no elders* {See p. 281} *(as at the first in* ecclesia constituenda*) then the choice of elders by the people, with approbation of the neighboring ministers with fasting and prayer, may suffice.*

4. That the elders of the congregation shall advise with the classis in all cases of excommunication before they proceed to it, and the classis has power to hear and determine: yet so, as the power of the congregation be not concluded thereby in matter of excommunication. *But some of the committee do say that in whatsoever case they find difficult either in excommunication or in any other administration of their power, they shall first advise with some company or classis of neighbor ministers, as at the end of the four following propositions afterwards.*

5. For the associating of churches, let there be in every county of this kingdom, a certain number of select, godly and able ministers of the Word within that county, to hear and determine the causes and differences in every congregation within the same, and let there be a certain number of select church governors assistant unto them: the first choice of these to be made by the Parliament in such a way as they shall determine, and such number to have power of election from time to time of any minister or church governor into any place among them that is void by death or otherwise.

---

1. [Cf. Earlier Propositions agreed upon by an assembly committee for accommodation, Gillespie, 37–40; *Minutes,* 2.593, 600, 617, 636, 678; Lightfoot, 205–207, 214, 215, 229.]

6. That ministers and ruling-governors of every congregation within that county so associated, shall have power to debate and vote in that meeting from time to time in such cases as pertain to that particular congregation, except such of them as are complained of, or are parties in question.

7. A certain number of the aforesaid ministers and ruling-governors as do dwell near together, in the same deanery or division of that county, and who may with convenience more frequently meet together, shall have power to hear and determine the causes and differences within the several congregations of that precinct.

8. Let national assemblies of ministers and others be chosen from time to time, according as shall be appointed by the parliament, as the necessity of the churches' affairs shall require.

To the fifth, sixth, seventh and eighth, the whole committee does assent; *only some of them do desire that the effect of that which hereafter follows may for explanation sake be inserted, viz. that the elders and brethren of each congregation in case they find anything too hard for themselves or have any controversy among themselves, may have liberty to advise with any of those select elders, and others in the province jointly or apart, or with the elders of any other churches, for the determining and composing the controversy or resolving of that difficulty, and in case they cannot be satisfied, then to have recourse also to the advice and help of that classis unto which they appertain, to solve and determine it.*

9. That the members of particular congregations do co-habit and live together within certain bounds and precincts of a parish under preaching and governing officers: *unto which so far as it concerns the mere bounding of congregations, some of the committee do desire that these provisions may be added.*

(1) That they may have liberty to dwell in another parish if the consent of the minister of that other parish be procured.

(2) For country villages that the limits be extended to take in from some one parish immediately adjoining.

We having weighed our brethren's principles, do find no probability of accommodation for them, ordinarily to enjoy congregations, unless when it shall happen in a parish that the minister cannot administer the sacraments to all in the parish, whom possibly the neighbor ministers or the classes may judge fit to be admitted, such persons shall have power to procure to themselves the sacraments, either by the help of a neighbor minister, or some other provision be made by a proportionable allowance out of the tithes of the parish according to the wisdom of the state.

Whereunto our brethren add as follows.

Or otherwise if in a parish it happen that there be a considerable number of such as cannot partake in the ordinances with the minister and people there, they shall have liberty to dispose of themselves as a distinct church, and to choose a minister or ministers at their own charge to be maintained, to be their pastor.

If such a liberty shall seem in the wisdom of the honorable committee to be prejudicial to the peace of the church, as not to be permitted, we humbly desire the doctrinal principles wherein we differ about church-government may be taken into serious consideration, and some other way of accommodation in practice thought upon, as shall seem fit to this honorable committee.

Concerning Classes and Synods

1. At these meetings, let them pray, expound scripture, resolve difficult cases of conscience and preach the Word.

2. They may dogmatically declare what the will of Christ is in such cases as are before them; and this judgment of theirs ought to be received with reverence and obligation, as from an ordinance of Christ. *Some of the brethren (though assenting) yet are bold to add hereunto that the judgment of any other of those elders in the province, or elsewhere, advised with, they do in like manner look at as the ordinance of Christ, and to have the like obligation in them.*

3. If the doctrine or practice of any particular congregation be erroneous, hurtful or destructive to holiness or the peace of that or other congregations, they are bound to give account thereof to the classis or synod. *Some of the brethren add to this that the ground of this obligation to give account to the classis or synod is their being offended, or their churches scandalized thereat.*

4. The classis or synod may examine, admonish, and in case of obstinacy declare against that congregation or any particular member in it, as the nature and degree of that offense shall require. *Some of the brethren assent to such proceedings as towards a church offending and scandalizing of them: but add that no such examination, admonition in any classis or assembly be extended to any particular person in that church, but unto the church itself, for not putting forth the power that Christ has given them for reforming him.*

5. The classis or synod may judge touching any person who deserves excommunication and may charge the several congregational presbyteries whom it concerns to do it.

6. We conceive that in case the particular eldership refuse to do their duty, the classis may and ought not only to withdraw communion from them, but also when need is, exercise the sentence of excommunication themselves. *Instead of this sixth proposition, some of the brethren do insert this, In case the aforesaid particular churches and elderships offending shall refuse to submit to this course that then the classis or synod are to acquaint their congregations respectively, and so withdraw from them, denying church communion* {See p. 289} *and fellowship with them.*

7. In case of appeal if it appear to the classis that the sentence was unjust, they may judge that the particular presbytery ought to reverse it: and in case they obstinately refuse to do it, the classis may reverse it. *Others of the brethren only say that they are to proceed as in the former article.*

8. The classis or synod have power to ordain ministers for such

congregations as have not a sufficient presbytery in them, and let all congregations associated, first advise with the classis, and take their assistance before they ordain a minister. *Some of the brethren do refer themselves for this, to the last clause in the third proposition delivered in.*

The Order of the Lords and Commons for the Reviving of the Committee for Accommodation[1]

Die Jovis 6 November 1645. Ordered by the Lords and Commons in Parliament assembled that the committee of Lords and Commons appointed to treat with the commissioners of Scotland, and the committee of the assembly, do take into consideration the differences in opinions of the members of the assembly in point of church government, and to endeavor a *union* if it be possible. And in case that cannot be done, to endeavor the *finding out some way how far tender consciences,* who cannot in all things submit to the common rule, which shall be established, may be borne with according to the Word, and as may stand with the public peace; that so the proceedings of the assembly may not be so much retarded.

The Lords Committees: Earl of Northumberland, Earl of Manchester, Lord Viscount Say and Seal, Lord Wharton, Lord Howard.

Committee of Accommodation November 14–November 24, 1645

November 14, 1645. Ordered that the said Lords committees are to meet with a committee of the House of Commons, on Monday next at three of the clock in the afternoon in the Jerusalem chamber in the college of Westminster, and that the committee of the assembly be there present.

John Brown, Cler. Parliamentorum.

The members of the assembly who were a committee for to meet with the committee of the Lords and Commons appointed to treat with the commissioners from the Church of Scotland, are as follows:

Master Marshall, Doctor Burges, Master White, Doctor Hoyle, Doctor Temple, Doctor Smith, Master Palmer, Master Seaman, Master Herle, Master Goodwin, Master Nye, Master Bridge, Master Hill, Master Reynolds, Master Arrowsmith, Master Young, Master Vines, Master Tuckney, Master Newcomen, Master Simpson, Master Burroughs, Master Dury.

On the 17 of November, 1645, the committees above mentioned met in [the] Jerusalem chamber, and did then order that those divines of the

---

1. [*The Papers and Answers of the Dissenting Brethren and the Committee of the Assembly of Divines. Given in to the Honorable Committee of Lords and Commons, and Assembly of Divines with the Scotch Commissioners, for Accommodation, at the Reviving of that Committee. 1645.* London, Printed Anno Dom. 1648.]

assembly, members of this committee, who had formerly been a sub-committee for this purpose, should consider and prepare matter for the debate of this committee at their next meeting, which meeting was then appointed to be Monday the 24 of the same month.

November 24, 1645. The committee met again, and the chairman of the sub-committee declared that they had not prepared matter for their debate according to their order, because the dissenting brethren did wave the first part of the order of the Houses touching accommodation, which though the rest of the sub-committee could not assent unto, yet they left it to the dissenting brethren, if they pleased to present their thoughts to this committee, but as their own, and accordingly the dissenting brethren did present a paper which is as follows.

[First Paper of the Dissenting Brethren] November 24, 1645]

The nature of the business puts us upon the second part of the ordinance of Parliament. "The endeavoring to find out some way how far the tender {See p. xlviii} consciences, who cannot in all things submit to the [common] rule which shall be established may be borne with, according to the Word, and as may stand with the public peace, that so the proceedings of the assembly may not be so much retarded;" which we humbly present to the consideration of this committee."

After some debate upon this paper it was

Resolved upon the question that Master Goodwin, Master Nye, Master Sympson, Master Bridge, and Master Burroughs, do bring in unto this committee upon Thursday seven-night, wherein they desire to be borne with in point of church government, in all those things wherein they cannot submit unto the common rule that is established.

[Second Paper of the Dissenting Brethren, December 4, 1645]

December 4, 1645. The committee met again, and the dissenting brethren presented their desires in a paper, as follows.

December 4, 1645. Agreeing in those things that contain the substance of the service and worship of God in the Directory according to the preface; and being confident that we shall agree in the Confession of Faith, for as much as we do agree with the Reformed churches in the doctrine contained in their confessions and writings as our brethren do, who differ from us in matter of discipline,

We humbly crave,

1. In relation to the ordinance for giving power to classical presbyteries to ordain ministers, November 10, 1645,

That where there is a presbytery (that is, two elders at least) in any of our congregations, there may be power of ordination: and where there is not a presbytery, those who are sufficiently qualified and approved for their gifts and graces by godly able ministers, being chosen by the people, and set apart for the ministry with prayer and fasting in the congregations, may *primâ vice* exercise their ministry.

{See p. 281}

at the first opportunity

2. In relation to the ordinance for the settling of the Presbyterial government, August 19, 1645:

(1) That our congregations may not be brought under the government of classical, provincial, or national assemblies, in respect of ecclesiastical jurisdiction; but may be permitted to enjoy liberty as some privileged and exempt places formerly have been permitted to enjoy, in respect of the ecclesiastical discipline then exercised.

(2) That our congregations may have liberty to constitute their own elderships, having a competent number of persons fitly qualified for elders: and that all men who communicate in the Lord's Supper, may have liberty to choose their own officers.

(3) That we may not be forced to communicate as members in those parishes where we dwell; but may have liberty to have congregations of such persons who give good testimony of their godliness and peaceableness, yet out of tenderness of conscience cannot communicate in their parishes, but do voluntarily offer themselves to join in such congregations. Which, how it may best stand with the peace of the kingdom, we humbly leave to the consideration of this honorable committee.

Goodwin, 462

That all such congregations as are made up of such as do voluntarily join themselves, having an eldership which themselves have chosen or accepted of, and submitted to, may have power of all church censures, and of the administration of all ordinances within themselves. Yet so as they submit to give an account of any of their proceedings to whom the Parliament shall appoint.

This paper being read and the day spent in explaining it—

It was ordered that the rest of the divines, members of the committee, be made a subcommittee to consider of the paper of the dissenting brethren given in, and to meet first between themselves, then with the dissenting brethren, and to prepare somewhat against the next meeting of this committee which was resolved to be on Monday seven-night, December 15. The commissioners of the Church of Scotland were desired to assist the subcommittee.

December 15, 1645. The honorable committee met again, and the sub-committee presented an answer to the dissenting brethren's paper, which is as follows.

[The Subcommittee's Answer to the Dissenting Brethren's Second
Paper of December 4, 1645]

Although it would have been a far more comfortable and happy way, and
more agreeable to the peace and edification of the church, and a means
to prevent the danger of schism and many other mischiefs, and which we
have always much rather desired to have pursued the method appointed
by the Honorable Houses; and in the first place to have endeavored an accommodation: yet our brethren professing that an accommodation was
now impossible, and that the nature and present state of the business does
lead them to desire a forbearance (in both which we yet humbly conceive
they are mistaken), upon serious consideration had of their paper to that
purpose, we have found it needful to premise these three particulars.

1. That whatever forbearance we shall agree upon, we take it for granted
upon our brethren's preface that the same Directory for Worship and the
same Confession of Faith, shall be imposed upon them in the same manner, as it is imposed upon us.

2. And therefore whosoever agrees not in those things that contain the
substance of the service and worship of God in the Directory, according
to the preface; and shall not agree in the Confession of Faith, nor with the
doctrine of the Reformed churches contained in their confessions and writing, as we do, who differ from these brethren in matters of discipline, shall
not have the benefit of this indulgence.

3. If any shall practice anything contrary to the Directory, or write, publish, or declare any doctrine contrary to the Confession of Faith, he shall
be liable to the same penalties that we ourselves are for the like offense.

Which things being premised, we have found it needful and most consonant to the business, to take first into consideration the third proposition of our brethren's particular desires under the head of presbytery, unto
which all the rest have so necessary a relation, which they have offered to
this honorable committee.

Concerning which we humbly conceive,

I. That this desire of our brethren is not to be granted to them *in terminis*,[1]
for the reasons which we here withal humbly offer.

1. Because it holds out a plain and total separation from the rule, as if
in nothing it were to be complied with; nor our churches to be communicated with in anything which should argue church-communion; more
could not be said or done against false churches.

2. It plainly holds out the lawfulness of gathering churches out of true
churches; yea out of such true churches which are endeavoring further to

---

1. [*in terminis* (*terminus*, boundary/limit): The divines' usage generally is "in the terms" of the
words exclusively in view. Lightfoot, 232, 286; Gillespie, *Aaron's Rod*, pp. 110, 143, 210, 211, esp. 132.]

reform according to the Word of God: whereof we are assured there is not the least hint of an example in all the Book of God.

3. In granting this, the Parliament should [*would*] grant liberty to destroy and pull down what themselves are endeavoring to set up.

4. The indulgence they seek is a greater privilege than they [i.e. we] shall enjoy, who shall be under the rule, as may appear in several particulars.

(1) Such as own the rule must live in the same parish with the other members of their church. These [of the brethren's way] may live anywhere, and be of any church they please; yea, though a church of their own way were in the place where they live.

(2) If such as live under the rule would better themselves in living under the pastoral charge of another minister, they must remove their dwelling. These need not.

5. This would give countenance to a perpetual schism and division in the church, still drawing away some from the churches under the rule, which also would breed many irritations between the parties going away and those whom they leave; and again, between the church that should be forsaken, and that to which they should go.

6. This would introduce all manner of confusion in families where the members were of several churches; and exceedingly, if not altogether hinder the mutual edification that might be afforded and received among them. And especially in great [*large*] families, it would be impossible for the governors to have a sure account of all their family's attending upon the ordinances, when twenty of them may possibly be of twenty several churches; and much less take account of their profiting by the ordinances.

II. That none are to be allowed upon differences only in matter of government, to withdraw communion from us in things wherein they declare an agreement: but seeing it is confessed in worship and doctrine we are one, and have covenanted to endeavor the nearest conjunction and uniformity, there may be no such indulgence granted to any as may constitute them in distinct separated congregations, as to those parts of worship where they can join in communion with us, but only some expedient may be endeavored how to bear with them in the particulars wherein they cannot agree with us.

III. For this purpose we humbly offer,

1. That such as through scruple or error of conscience, cannot join to partake of the Lord's Supper, shall repair to the minister and elders for satisfaction in their scruples, which if they cannot receive, they shall not be compelled to communicate in the Lord's Supper: provided that in all other parts of worship, they join with the congregation wherein they live and be under the government of that congregation.

2. That such as in this manner are under the government of that congregation wherein they live, and are not officers therein, being of the Independent judgment, shall seek satisfaction as in the former proposition, which

if they cannot receive, they shall not be compelled to be under the power
of censures from classis or synods: provided that they continue under the
government of that congregation, and that no man who hath submitted to
classis and synods shall decline them, in any case, *pendente lite.*   *a pending case*

These papers of the sub-committee in answer to the dissenting brethren's
papers, being thrice read after sundry debates, it was resolved,
   1. That the brethren shall have a copy of the papers in answer to theirs
communicated to them.
   2. That they are to return an answer in writing to this committee, by
Tuesday sevenight [*sennight; week*].

[The Third Paper of the Dissenting Brethren]

December 23, 1645. The honorable committee met again, and the dissenting brethren presented an answer in writing, which was read: first reading
a paragraph of the sub-committee's paper, and then a paragraph of their
answer, in manner as follows.

An Answer to a Paper brought into this Honorable Committee by a sub-
committee of the Divines of the Assembly. December 23, 1645

As to the preface: "Although it would have been a far more comfortable and
happy way, and more agreeable to the peace and edification of the church,
and a means to prevent the danger of schism and many other mischiefs, and
which we have always much rather desired to have pursued the method appointed by the Honorable Houses; and in the first place to have endeavored
an accommodation: yet our brethren professing that an accommodation
was now impossible, and that the nature and present state of the business
does lead them to desire a forbearance (in both which we yet humbly conceive they are mistaken), upon serious consideration had of their paper to
that purpose, we have found it needful to premise these three particulars."
   Answer. As accommodation would have been more advantageous and
safe for us, because it would have set us in the same state with our brethren.
So we have earnestly pursued it, and according to the method appointed
by the Honorable Houses, we did in the first place endeavor an accommodation, and in a sub-committee made a great progress therein, which
was presented to this honorable committee twelve months since. But the
impediment to it was, the insisting on by our brethren that the rule must
first be resolved upon; but now that the rule is resolved on by the assembly,   See the Rea-
and established by the Parliament (we having according to our consciences   sons and An-
entered our dissent unto, and given in reasons to the assembly against it),   swers earlier
we cannot go on in the way of accommodation according to the former   in this volume

method; because accommodation is an agreement in one common rule, and we do not presume to seek a new rule to be made.

That impossibility of accommodation which was spoken of, was then withal explained to be only in respect of the rule, as now it is established: for otherwise as touching the nature of the thing simply considered without a supposition of such a rule, either voted by the assembly, or established by the Honorable Houses, we have from the beginning professed that we thought we and our brethren did agree in common principles enough, and sufficient to have preserved the churches and saints in these kingdoms in peace. And when the Honorable Houses renewed this order, they having not seen (as we humbly conceive) the difference of our judgments in point of sub-ordination of assemblies, and our reasons against them, they might think that we might accommodate with the rule they have set forth.

Neither will such a forbearance as we seek endanger schism. Because there may be a variation in a greater latitude from a government that is established on a divine right, much more from one which is not established upon *Jus* *Divine Right Divinum*: when the government itself has its authority but from the state, a forbearance from it by the state, with laws to prevent contention, cannot be schism, or anyway endanger it; the nature of schism (according to the Scriptures) consisting in an open breach of Christian love, and not in every diversity of opinion or practice. Yea, as both others, and we also have found, the great cause of schism, has been a strict obligation of all to a uniformity beyond that of the Apostle. *That so far as we have attained we should walk by the same rule, and if any be otherwise minded God will reveal it in his time.*

TO THE THREE FIRST PREMISES,

"1. That whatever forbearance we shall agree upon, we take it for granted upon our brethren's preface that the same Directory for Worship and the same Confession of Faith, shall be imposed upon them in the same manner, as it is imposed upon us.

2. And therefore whosoever agrees not in those things that contain the substance of the service and worship of God in the Directory, according to the preface; and shall not agree in the Confession of Faith, nor with the doctrine of the Reformed churches contained in their confessions and writing, as we do, who differ from these brethren in matters of discipline, shall not have the benefit of this indulgence.

3. If any shall practice anything contrary to the Directory, or write, publish, or declare any doctrine contrary to the Confession of Faith, he shall be liable to the same penalties that we ourselves are for the like offense."

Answer. In general we only say affirmatively: that those who do agree in these things that contain the substance service, and worship of God in the Directory according to the preface; and in the Confession of Faith with Reformed churches in the doctrine contained in their confessions and writings (as we and our brethren do, who differ from us in matter of church-government), "may lawfully be tolerated according to the Word of God in such things as we desire:" but we meddle not with the negative; or impositions; or to set the bounds and limits of forbearance unto all tender consciences. Yea, before we brought in this paper, we not knowing but that the Honorable Houses might intend a consideration of "the general rules how far tender consciences might be forborne according to the Word of God, and as might stand with the peace of this kingdom," professed that we presumed not to limit it to our judgments, nor would bring in any other report than about the general rules of toleration, unless the honorable committee did determine and limit us, which accordingly was done. It being also declared that they were sure that we were intended and the matters of difference in point of church-government between us and our brethren in the assembly; yet we, to wipe off such aspersions, prejudices, and suspicions as were upon us, and to make a full and candid declaration of our judgments and agreements in point of doctrine and the substance of worship, did add that preface: which now having done, by these interpretations which our brethren present, we should not only take on us, to call upon the Parliament to exclude other tender consciences from this forbearance and to impose upon them; but make impositions of directory and confessions of faith in the latitude of the body of divinity, and not in fundamentals only; and that not only upon the ministers but upon all the people of this kingdom; and that as a qualification for receiving sacraments. Our brethren's principles may be larger, for power in ecclesiastical assemblies to determine and impose circumstantial orders in worship, as well as in the substance, and therefore for us to join with our brethren to have all those things imposed on us, which they can bear, seems hard to us.

"Which things being premised," (say our brethren) "we have found it needful and most consonant to the business, to take first into consideration the third proposition of our brethren's particular desires under the head of presbytery, unto which all the rest have so necessary a relation, which they have offered to this honorable committee.

"Concerning which we humbly conceive,

"I. That this desire of our brethren is not to be granted to them *in terminis*, for the reasons which we here withal humbly offer.

"1. Because it holds out a plain and total separation from the rule, as if in nothing it were to be complied with; nor our churches to be communicated with in anything which should argue church-communion; more could not be said or done against false churches."

To this first reason:

Answer. 1. A desire to have liberty for multitudes that cannot out of a tenderness of conscience partake as members in your churches, to gather into congregations to enjoy the ordinances; not only professing your churches to be true churches, yea not daring to judge them for that, for which they are in respect of their own consciences enforced to, namely, to preserve themselves from sin against their conscience to remove from that communion with them; and though gathering into other congregations for the purer enjoyment (as to their consciences) of all ordinances, yet still maintaining communion with them as churches (as is expressed in the third paragraph) is far from separation, much less a plain and total separation. The assembly having in what they have given up unto the Honorable Houses said thus, "Nor is it lawful for any member of a parochial congregation, if the ordinances be there administered in purity, to go and seek them elsewhere ordinarily," so as in case the Lord's Supper be not in purity administered, a removal is allowed ordinarily. And this is not setting up churches against churches, but neighbor sister churches of a differing judgment. If the purest churches in the world (unto our judgment in all other respects), should impose as a condition of receiving the sacrament of the Lord's Supper any one thing that such tender consciences cannot join in (as suppose kneeling in the act of receiving, which was the case of Scotland and England), if they remove from these churches, and have liberty from a state to gather into other churches to enjoy this and other ordinances—here is no separation.

2. A plain and total separation from the rule is not in such churches, unless they wholly in all things differ, by setting up altogether differing rules of constitution, worship and government. Now in the churches we desire we shall practice the most of the same things; and these the most substantial which are found in the rule itself. The same ordinances of worship in the Directory; the same officers, pastors, teachers, ruling elders; of the same qualifications required in the rule: the same qualification of members the assembly itself holds forth to have been in the primitive churches, *viz.* visible saints that being of age do profess faith in Christ, and obedience unto Christ, according to the rules of faith and life taught by Christ and his apostles: and these officers to join into one eldership in all acts of government of the church: holding also the same censures, namely, of admonition, and excommunication and absolution and receiving in upon repentance; and who, wherein they differ from the rule, will be accountable of all their ways and tenets unto those, whom the state shall be pleased to appoint. And,

3. Holding and retaining communion with neighbor churches in baptizing our children (as occasion may fall out, of absence of our ministers) in their churches, and by occasional receiving the Lord's Supper in their churches, and receiving such members of theirs, as are above mentioned, unto communion with us also occasionally. Also our ministers to preach in their congregations, and receive theirs also to preach in ours, as ministers of the gospel, as mutually there shall be a call from each other. And when we have any cases difficult and too hard for ourselves, electively to advise with the elders of their churches. And in case of controversy not to refuse to call them in, for the composing of it. Further, in case of the choice of elders, to seek the approbation and right-hand of fellowship from godly ministers of

their churches together with our own. And when an ordination falls out among us, to desire the presence and approbation of their elders with our own. And in case any of our churches miscarry through mal-administration or neglect of censures, to be willing, upon scandal taken by their churches, to give an account as to sister churches offended, and to esteem and account (as we do) a sentence of non-communion by them, as churches, against us, upon such scandals wherein they are not satisfied, a heavy and sad punishment, and to be looked at as a means to humble us, and an ordinance of God to reduce us. All this is more than AS IF IN NOTHING THEY WERE TO BE COMPLIED WITH, NOR THEIR CHURCHES TO BE COMMUNICATED WITH, IN ANYTHING WHICH SHOULD ARGUE CHURCH COMMUNION, more is said and done by these that account them false churches.

To THE SECOND REASON,

"2. It plainly holds out the lawfulness of gathering churches out of true churches, yea out of such true churches which are endeavoring further to reform according to the Word of God: whereof we are assured there is not the least hint of an example in all the Book of God."

We *answer:* That this reason is founded upon this supposition that nothing ought to be tolerated which is unlawful in the judgment of those who are to tolerate: and if so, then by the like reason no state, no assembly, no presbytery is to tolerate any practice or opinion which they account to be in the least erroneous.

2. The way we are to go is not to dispute what is unlawful or lawful in itself, because we are upon the point of forbearance in what is thought unlawful.

3. For that addition ("out of such true churches which are endeavoring further to reform") we say, the reformation which the assembly has ultimately pitched upon, satisfies not our conscience, as our brethren know.

4. For that addition (that "there is not the least hint of an example in all the Book of God"... "for gathering churches out of churches") we shall only at this time humbly present the nature of the thing or case itself, as it lies in our consciences and as in the assembly we also stated it.

The case is this: A multitude of believers after all means used to obtain light to satisfy their consciences in what to them is sin in partaking of the ordinances as members of the churches they live or have lived in, by which, so long as they continue in these churches, they shall be debarred from these ordinances, though it be all their days; and although the opinion be judged an error by those churches they live in, yet of no higher nature than those errors for which they are not to be suspended from any ordinance, by censure, or cast out of the church; and in all other things are such in their opinions and practices as are meet [*suitable*] partakers of communion with Christ in all ordinance, which as their right, as members of His mystical body, He has given to them as to their brethren: In this case, there is no obligation laid by Christ either on the persons themselves, forever to continue in those churches, or on the churches they live in, to withhold them from removing to other churches free of that which would defile their consciences; or, when there are no such churches in the places they live in TO GATHER INTO CHURCHES, wherein they may enjoy all ordinances without sin. This assertion, as thus stated, we are ready to debate, when this honorable committee shall think fit.

TO THE THIRD REASON,

"3. In granting this, the Parliament should grant liberty to destroy and pull down what themselves are endeavoring to set up."

Answer. An exception does not make void a rule; especially such a one as is not founded on a *Jus Divinum*, and where it is in the power of those who make the rule to grant a forbearance from it. The reformed churches grant a forbearance; and yet their general rule stands. And we in our DESIRES, do submit to this honorable committee to find out such ways as may best stand with the peace of the kingdom.

TO THE FOURTH REASON,

"4. The indulgence they seek is a greater privilege than they shall enjoy who shall be under the rule, as may appear in several particulars.

"(1) Such as own the rule, must live in the same parish with the other members of their church. These may live anywhere, and be of any church they please; yea, though a church of their own way were in the place where they live.

"(2) If such as live under the rule would better themselves in living under the pastoral charge of another minister, they must remove their dwelling. These need not."

Answer. The privilege of those ministers who submit to the rule is to be capable of all ecclesiastical preferments, which we are not. They find no need of indulgence to their consciences as touching the rule established, which we do; possibly their consciences may be scrupled in the same or other things hereafter, and they have the privilege of the same addresses for relief, we have.

And as for the two particulars therein expressed, we say first, it is a privilege, and much to be desired to dwell near together, and we also shall endeavor it as much as may be for mutual edification. Secondly, it is the right of every man (we humbly conceive) to choose his own minister, whereas the parishes and their bounds by dwellings, are but of civil right: provided the state be pleased to take some order that it may be known, whither every man does resort.

TO THE FIFTH REASON,

"5. This would give countenance to a perpetual schism and division in the church, still drawing away some from the churches under the rule, which also would breed many irritations between the parties going away and those whom they leave; and again, between the church that should be forsaken, and that to which they should go."

We *answer:* What hurt the abuse of words, and among others this of schism, has done in the churches, our brethren know, and we all have felt; wherefore seeing as yet the assembly has not debated, nor the state determined, what schism is, we desire our brethren that in the seeking to countenance that way which they think is right, they would not seek to cast an odium upon their brethren who differ from them, and yet together with them desire (in faithfulness) to know and obey the mind of Christ, by fastening such a name upon them or their way.

2. What we desire forbearance in, will countenance only this: when men who give good testimony of their godliness and peaceableness, after all means used in faithfulness to know the mind of Christ, they yet cannot without sin to them, enjoy all the ordinances of Christ, and partake in all the duties of worship, as members of that congregation where their dwelling is, they therefore in humility and meekness desire, they may not live without ordinances; but for the enjoyment of them for their edification in their spiritual good may join in another congregation; yet so, as not condemning those churches they join not with, as false, but still preserving all Christian communion with the saints of the same body of Christ (of the church-catholic) and join with them in all duties of worship that belong to particular churches, so far as they are able. If this be called schism, or countenance of schism, it is more than yet we have learned from the scriptures, or any approved authors.

3. And as for that irritation our brethren speak of: as we humbly conceive, it will be according to the temper of men's hearts. If such a practice meets with men whose hearts are gracious, it will only irritate them to search further into the mind of Christ, and to walk before their brethren with more exactness, and to exercise love, meekness and forbearance towards their brethren who differ from them; and such irritation there is no great cause that either we, or our brethren should make complaints of. If this liberty meet with corruption, it is like[ly] enough there may accidentally be an irritation to sin, but the way then to oppose such corruption, is by instruction, prayer, walking convincingly before them: and if they grow turbulent, to call in the help of the civil-magistrate; but not to give that respect to their corruptions, as to deny to men, who give undeniable testimony of their godliness, that use of the ordinances of Christ, that they may with the peace of their consciences enjoy.

To the Sixth Reason,

"6. This would introduce all manner of confusion in families where the members were of several churches; and exceedingly, if not altogether hinder the mutual edification that might be afforded and received among them. And especially in great [*large*] families, it would be impossible for the governors to have a sure account of all their family's attending upon the ordinances, when twenty of them may possibly be of twenty several churches; and much less take account of their profiting by the ordinances."

Answer. I. First in general, our judgments do thus far agree with yours that except upon very weighty considerations, husband and wife, masters and servants, should partake together in the same ministry.

II. Secondly, if it should happen to be otherwise:

1. "All manner of confusion" would not hereby be introduced into families; for can our brethren think that persons agreeing in all the fundamentals of their faith, and in their judgment and practice joining in all the same duties of piety in the family; and also agreeing in the same duties of public worship, for the substance, though not living under the same individual ministry, yet unless they do agree also in an uniformity, both public and private, they must needs run into all manner of confusion? Has either nature, or the gospel put such a necessity upon uniformity in lesser things, to keep families from confusion? If this were the gospel, then except it prevail upon the opinion of those whom it converts to such an uniformity (which it seldom does), it must by this principle, of necessity, subvert human society, by bringing confusion into families, which we conceive to be a great derogation to the gospel.

2. Neither would it "exceedingly," much less "altogether hinder the mutual edification that might be afforded and received among them."

For first, although persons of the same family, not living under the same ministry, may in some respect of family duties, not so fully edify, as otherwise; yet in a great measure, they may. And if there be a zeal, and good conscience in any of the family, to be helpful in good conference, etc., it is no such great hindrance to hear in several places, or several preachers; as scholars reading several books, and then conferring. Many good Christians have for edification purposely practiced it; and it has some advantages for edification, which the other way has not.

Secondly, that further degree of edification, which comes to the persons in a family, by going all to the same ministry, amounts not to that proportion, as to countervail the want [*lack*] of enjoying the public ordinances forever; which compared with family duties, simply considered, have had the preeminence, both in respect to God's glory, and the edification of souls, in all men's concessions; which cannot be enjoyed by many that yet are truly conscientious, except the liberty petitioned be granted.

III. Thirdly, for the account, governors, "in great families" are to take care "of all their families attending upon the ordinances" and "of their profiting" thereby, we *answer:* The churches we desire, being constant and fixed, it is not more impossible, than it was for a godly tutor in the university to take account of his pupils, having liberty to go to several churches. And,

IV. Fourthly, whereas it is heightened that twenty of one family "may possibly be of twenty several churches," we suppose if the state be pleased to grant us the liberty we petition for that they in their wisdom (to which we have referred ourselves) will take into consideration, the limiting such congregations to a certain number; and then there may not be twenty churches in any city or town to divide themselves into.

But the truth is, those that thus plead against this permission (which we desire) as insufferable, must certainly suppose that men are to be tied, throughout this kingdom, to their own parish churches where they live, both masters and servants, and that not only for sacraments, but for constant hearing: which how burdensome it was in former times, the godly people are very sensible of; and now in the time of reformation, it finds many ministers who cannot be cast out, by order of law, though bad and unprofitable, as appears by the leaving them out of the classes; and shall the people be tied to live under them as their minister, who are not worthy to join in government with yourselves? And for time to come, as places are void, they must be supplied by the choice of others for them, or by themselves, *if by themselves,* all parishes are not reformed as concerning the people, and whereas the major part being generally the worst, the ministers chosen by them will be such as the godly cannot live under their ministry. *If by others,* those that are the choosers may also be such as they cannot be denied by law, their right in choosing, and so also unprofitable ministers may be put upon the godly people; and if they be not tied to their parishes, the weight of this reason, and the inconveniences presented, will fall more heavy upon the numerous multitude of parishes in city and country.

For the rules towards an expedient, and the preface thereunto, numbers II and III, we humbly conceive our brethren have not made a complete report in that point of what they intend (as was intimated), and therefore that this honorable committee does not expect that we should speak anything to it, till that part of their answer be perfected.

Let the reader take notice that an answer to the second part of the former answer of the sub-committee of divines, was afterwards given in to the honorable committee, by their command, and comes in printed after the rejoinder (that next follows) made by the sub-committee of divines to this answer of the dissenting brethren, in that order it was given in to the honorable committee.

After some debate upon the cautions premised, in the paper of sub-committee presented December 15, and drawn out of the brethren's preface, it was resolved by the honorable committee:

Resolved that both the affirmative and negative of the second caution, shall be put unto the question; and accordingly it was.

Resolved upon the question that they which agree in the substance of the worship of God in the Directory, according to the preface, and agree in the Confession of Faith, and with the doctrine of the Reformed churches contained in their confessions and writings, as we do, who differ from those brethren in matters of discipline, shall have the benefit of this indulgence.

Resolved upon the question that such as agree not in those things which contain the substance of the worship of God in the Directory, according to the preface; and shall not agree in the Confession of Faith, nor with the doctrine of the Reformed churches contained in their confessions and writings, as we do, who differ from these brethren in matters of discipline, shall not have the benefit of this indulgence.

Resolved upon the question that the brethren's paper this day brought in shall be referred to the sub-committee to consider of it, and they are further to go on with the work begun; and the brethren to go on with their answer to the former paper of the sub-committee.

[The Subcommittee's Reply to the Third Paper, the first part of the Dissenting Brethren's Answer, January 23, 1645]

January 23, 1645. The committee met again, and the sub-committee presented a reply to the answer of the dissenting brethren, brought in December 23, 1645, which is as follows.

A Reply to an Answer brought in to this Honorable Committee (December 23, 1645) unto a Paper formerly tendered by a sub-committee of the Divines of the Assembly

To their Preface: Our Reverend Brethren being charged with an unwillingness to pursue the method prescribed in the order of the Honorable Houses, which was in the first place to endeavor an accommodation, do declare:

1. That in a sub-committee twelve months since, they had earnestly endeavored such an accommodation, and made a great progress therein.

2. That the rule being now resolved on, unto which they had entered their dissent, it is by that means become impossible for them to endeavor an accommodation; which implies an agreement in one common rule; since they do not presume to seek a new rule to be made.

To which we say, that although our brethren had entered their dissent against some particulars of the rule established (for we know not that any dissent was ever entered against the whole), yet the Honorable Houses being pleased in their order to prescribe this method of proceeding, and to require the endeavor of an accommodation, which order, notwithstanding any such dissent of our brethren, they have in their wisdom and zeal for the peace of the church, thought good to renew, we conceive our brethren (as well as ourselves) were obliged first to have endeavored an obedience to it, before they declare that that is in their judgment impossible to be done, which the wisdom of the Houses (notwithstanding they were not ignorant of the cause upon which that pretended impossibility is grounded) have been pleased to require, and therefore we humbly declare that the only stop of endeavoring an accommodation is in our brethren themselves, and not in the Honorable Houses, or in us.

And for the progress which they say was formerly made in a subcommittee towards an accommodation, that should the more have encouraged them at this time in the same endeavor. But indeed we find by the acts of that treaty,

1. That the subcommittee declared that they saw no probability of any accommodation with our brethren, because they could not perceive any willingness in them to take any such congregations, as ours, which some of them have since that time professed they cannot do.

2. That they did not yield anything toward any union with us, but everywhere put in exceptions to the proposals tending thereunto. So that in that accommodation they did in a manner fully demand according to their principles, the same things by way of exception, which they now crave by way of toleration.

3. In that treaty they desired the *liberty of gathering churches,* yet then seemed to doubt whether this Honorable committee would not judge it a thing prejudicial to the state. But now they wholly insist upon it, only referring the manner how it may stand with the public peace to the consideration of this Honorable committee.

They say 'that in the nature of the thing, without supposition of the rule, as now it is established, they and we agree in common principles enough, and sufficient to have preserved the churches and saints in these kingdoms in peace.' Whereunto we *answer:*

1. If so, that again should have encouraged them to proceed in the treaty of accommodation.

2. We conceive those common principles are those only which concern the power of congregations, which they misapply to an independency, and if the peace of the churches must have been preserved by our making the same use of those principles, it is evident it must have been procured not by an accommodation between us, but by our going over to our brethren, and acquiescing in their way.

3. Whatever agreement may be in other things, there is none in that which is fundamental to the very constitution of churches, namely, the qualification of members, wherein their principles are so far from permitting them to join with us, and so to lay any grounds of peace, that indeed they lead them to draw members continually from us unto separation.

4. They make no mention of any mutual bond to preserve churches in truth and godliness for mutual edification, wherein we think their way is much defective.

Nor laſtly, do they tell us how others, whom they look not on as saints, shall be dealt withal, and brought in, they having in their way no paſtoral relation unto any such: and we doubt not but our way will continue to be, as it has been effectual to that purpose, if we be not diſturbed in it by our brethren's opposition.

They say, 'the Honorable Houses not having seen their differences and reasons againſt subordination of assemblies, when they renewed this order, might think that they might accommodate with the rule which they have set forth.' To which we *answer:*

1. That the Honorable Houses cannot be ignorant of their judgment in this point, it appearing evidently in their dissent and reasons againſt classical presbyteries, and in their disclaiming of synods to have power of government.

2. Let our brethren join with us in the reſt, and we doubt not to find out some expedient to ease them to this particular.

They proceed, 'neither will such a forbearance as we seek, endanger schism, because there may be a variation in a greater latitude, from a government that is eſtablished on a divine right, much more from one which is not eſtablished on a *jus divinum*, when the government itself has its authority but from the ſtate, a forbearance from it by the ſtate, which laws to prevent contentions, cannot be schism, or anyway endanger it: the nature of schism, according to the Scriptures, consiſting in an open breach of Chriſtian love, and not in every diversity of opinion or practice; yea as both others, and we also have found, the great cause of schism has been a ſtrict obligation of all to a uniformity beyond that of the apoſtle, that *so far as we have attained, we should walk by the same rule; and if any be otherwise minded, God will reveal it in his time.'*

How far this forbearance may endanger a schism, comes faſter to be considered, nor are we satisfied what great variation may be without schism, than to confess churches to be true, and yet to require separated churches from them of another conſtitution. Their observation that forbearance when a government has its authority from the ſtate only, cannot be schism, does not only lay an aſpersion on the rule, as if it were merely and totally human, and had nothing of the will of God in it; but does clearly open a wide gap for as many as either by them in their way, or by any others in other ways can be persuaded of a divine right elsewhere, to shake off their obedience and submission unto it. Nor can laws to prevent contentions, hinder such a dangerous consequence as this, for who will not hold himself bound upon such premises, to contend earneſtly for the way of God, againſt mere human conſtitution, who will not rather lay hold on the privilege of a toleration, to be among these of the *godly party,* as they call themselves, and in the way of Chriſt, as they ſpeak, than to continue under such a rule, and in such a communion for government as is charged to be merely of an human original? Such a toleration to be provided beforehand, not only for persons already separated from us, but for as many as art and industry for all time to come, can be able to gain unto the same persuasion, from the obedience of the rule established, was we believe, never yet demanded of the Christian magistrate by any in churches confessed by themselves to be true, especially considering that those who demand it, have bound themselves by covenant *to endeavor to bring all the churches of God in these kingdoms to the nearest uniformity and conjunction, and to extirpate schism.* And albeit this schism consists not in every diversity of opinion or practice, but in an open breach of Christian love, yet we see not how our brethren can acquit themselves even by this rule, when they openly profess a necessity to recede from our churches as members, while yet they acknowledge them to be true churches of Christ. Thus to depart from true churches, is not to hold communion with them, as such, but rather by departing to declare them not to be such [*not to be true churches*]. Surely at best we may say of this course as the philosopher did of the Milesians, *Milesii quidem non sunt insipientes, ea tamen agunt quae insipientes.*[1]

And although no uniformity were necessary against schism, yet to our brethren, by virtue of their covenant, it is *aliquot usque* necessary, so far as *something still* the Apostle directs, which *is whereunto we have attained to walk by the same rule.* Therefore agreeing with us in worship and doctrine, and acknowledging our churches, ordinances and ministers to be true, so true, as that they can occasionally join with us in all acts of worship, we conceive they ought in these things to act in joint communion with us by one common rule, and not by different rules, and in separated congregations. And certainly God's way of revealing truth to such as are otherwise minded, is not by setting men at a distance from one another, but by keeping them in *the unity of the Spirit,* to walk together peaceably and regularly in that whereunto they have attained, and more is not desired of our reverend brethren.

TO THEIR ANSWER TO THE THREE FIRST PREMISES,
We need not make any large reply to their answer to our three premises. The first they do not deny, but acknowledge in their explanations. The second is voted in this honorable committee. And the third we doubt not but the Honorable Houses will add. Their reasons moving them to decline the negative, and impositions, and the setting bounds of forbearance to all tender consciences, we will therefore examine.

But when our brethren allege that 'to wipe off aspersions, prejudices, and suspicions' which were upon them, and to make a full and candid declaration of their agreements in point of doctrine and substance of worship, they added the preface: If they mean the agreement of their own persons (who

---

1. [Demodocus of Leros: 'The Milesians are not fools, but they act just as if they were fools;' i.e. 'you couldn't tell it from their behavior.' Cf. Aristotle, *Ethics* (1874), 2.255.]

brought in that paper) in these things, we know not any necessity of so doing, they not having been ever charged with disagreements of that nature: and besides, it would have no relation to the desires of our brethren which are not for their own persons alone, but for all others of their judgment in the matters of difference between them and us. But if they mean all others of that judgment, we conceive it a difficult thing to affirm "that all such do agree in worship and doctrine with the Reformed churches, as we and our brethren do." And therefore except our interpretation of it, which they dislike, be admitted, we cannot look on it otherwise than as a cipher before a number, which is of no signification at all.

In the next place our brethren misinterpret our intentions, when they say we make these impositions upon the people as a qualification of receiving sacraments, for we desire to have not more imposed on our people, than they in that case do on theirs, namely that they appear to us to be orthodox.

Lastly, we wonder at our brethren's conclusion of this point touching the largeness of our principles for power in ecclesiastical assemblies to determine and impose circumstantial matters, seeing our proposition *in termi-* *in the terms* *nis* mentions nothing but agreement in substance, according to their own words; therefore for them to refuse to join with us in settling those things which they declare they agree in, seems hard unto us, and does too much intimate an unwillingness to come to that nearness of conjunction, which may settle us in one body without offense.

[TO THE FIRST REASON]

For the brethren's answer to our first reason, against their desire of toleration as it is by them expressed, we shall premise these few observations to our reply.

1. They seem to grant that "a plain and total separation from the rule, or our churches, as no true churches, is not to be indulged," which strengthens our reason.

2. They suppose some things in our congregations will be so far offensive to multitudes who are of tender consciences, that they will not dare to partake as members therein. This is a hard judgment to entertain against churches, which are under the tie of a solemn covenant, endeavoring a reformation according to God's Word. We desire the particular matters of offense may be expressed, professing our earnest endeavor, so much as in us lies, to remove whatever may hinder comfortable communion that there may be no just occasion of separation.

3. We desire to know whether every person's bare alleging tenderness of conscience shall be sufficient to warrant his deserting of our congregations; or if not, what shall be the rule of discerning, or who the judges in such a case?

4. We conceive that our brethren's ground of separation from one church,

and gathering others, to this end, that men may be preserved from sinning against their consciences, and for the purer enjoyments of ordinances as to their consciences, may to men of other judgments, be a ground to crave toleration for separating from churches which are constituted in all things according to God's Word in the sense of our brethren, and gathering impure and corrupt churches out of them; because upon the dictate of an erring conscience (whereby multitudes may be infected), men may really disallow churches which are pure, in some particulars wherein they are pure, and set up others which are more suitable to their own erring conscience; and consequently, as many several sorts of churches may be set up in a state, as the several dictates of erroneous consciences may suggest. If our brethren conceive this ought not to be done in different cases from theirs, they must give us leave to judge that neither in theirs it ought to be done.

5. Whereas they give a character of those whom they desire indulgence for, 'to be such as acknowledge our churches to be true churches, as dare not judge them in that for which they leave them; and such as maintain communion with those churches, as churches,' which they leave, in several particulars expressed in their third paragraph, we desire it may be declared that none other shall have the benefit of that indulgence which shall be granted, than they who are thus minded.

In this answer our brethren say, 'A desire to have liberty for multitudes who cannot out of tenderness of conscience partake as members in your churches, to gather into congregations to enjoy the ordinances, not only professing your churches to be true churches, yea not daring to judge them for that for which they are in respect of their own consciences enforced to, namely to preserve themselves from sin against their consciences, to remove from that communion with them; and though gathering into other congregations for the purer enjoyment (as to their consciences) of all ordinances, yet still maintaining communion with them as churches as is expressed in the third paragraph, is far from separation, much less a plain and total separation.'

We *answer* not to the English (for whoever called desire of liberty a separation?), but to the matter: 1. We know not whom they mean by multitudes; if congregations, we would gladly know where they are, and how they may be known and distinguished that we may be able to judge whether this character agrees unto them, or whether they will own that which our brethren here affirm of them (for it is dubious unto us, whether there be multitudes of such who are thus minded). If single persons, we have already expressed our sense how far they may be indulged, appearing to be such as are here described. 2. We much doubt whether such tenderness of conscience as arises out of an opinion *cui potest subesse falsum*, when the conscience is *which may be* so tender, as that it may be withal an erring conscience, can be a sufficient *subject to error* ground to justify such a material separation as our brethren plead for. For though it may bind to forbear or suspend the act of communion in that particular wherein men conceive they cannot hold communion without sin (nothing being to be done contrary unto conscience); yet it does not bind to follow such a positive prescript as possibly may be divers [*different*] from the will and counsel of God, of which kind we conceive this of gathering separated churches out of other true churches to be one.

They add an assertion of the assembly in these words, "nor is it lawful for any member of a parochial congregation, if the ordinances be there administered in purity, to go and seek them elsewhere ordinarily;" and then infer, in case the Lord's Supper be not in purity administered, a removal is allowed ordinarily.

We *answer:* 1. It was never the meaning of the assembly to leave the judgment of pure or impure ordinances in this case, unto the alone discretion of a particular person, but before any leave their parochial congregation, upon this pretense ordinarily, he ought to declare the cause of his grievance that if it may be his removal may be prevented, except he think fit to change his dwelling, in which case his removal is without offense. 2. It is one thing to remove to a congregation which is under the same rule, another to a congregation of a different constitution from the rule. In the former case a man retains his membership, though for some defects he seek elsewhere, till those defects be by the care of the officers of the church cured. In the latter he renounces his membership upon difference of judgment touching the very constitution of the churches from and unto which he removes.

It follows, 'If the purest churches in the world unto our judgment in all other respects, should impose as a condition of receiving the sacrament of the Lord's Supper any one thing that such tender consciences cannot join in (as suppose kneeling in the act of receiving, which was the case of Scotland and England) if they remove from these churches and have liberty from a state to gather into other churches, to enjoy this and other ordinances—here is no separation.'

We *answer:* 1. If a church requires that which is evil of any member, he must forbear to do it, yet without separation, and wait on God's providence in the dispensation of that church, till all remedies have been tried. 2. He that is in this kind oppressed, may be relieved by appeal, or change of dwelling. 3. They who thought kneeling in the act of communion to be unlawful, either in England or Scotland, did not separate or renounce membership, but did some of them with zeal and learning defend our churches against those of the separation. 4. Those words, {"if they have liberty from the state to gather into other churches,"} seem to imply that otherwise that liberty may not be taken; else we know not of what use they are. But we think our brethren will not abide by that sense, having now for some years without leave from the state, gathered themselves into separated churches, even then when the state has been and still is laboring to reform the church according to God's Word. 5. The nature of separation is not to be measured by civil acts of state, but by the Word of God. What notion our brethren have of it we know not, but surely to leave all ordinary communion in any church with dislike, when opposition or offense offers itself, is to separate from such a church in the scripture sense. Such separation was not in being in the apostles' time, unless it was used by false teachers. All who professed Christianity held communion together as in one church, notwithstanding differences of judgment, or corruptions in practice.

In their second paragraph they say, "a plain and total separation from the rule is not in such churches, unless they wholly in all things differ, by setting up altogether differing rules of constitution, worship and government."

Of this assertion we expect some proof. We read not the like in any author ancient or modern. Under this pretense, Novatians, Donatists, all that ever were thought to separate, might shelter themselves. The most rigid Separatists, who themselves boast of their separation, hold the same rule of worship and government for substance, with our brethren: and consequently by this rule they must boast no longer of their separation, which is become by this means none, or no plain and total one.

In the next words they say so much of their agreement with us that we cannot conceive any further ground left for their separation from us. We shall practice they say, "most of the same things, and those the most substantial;" we shall have the "same ordinances of worship, as in the directory, the same officers," and of the same qualifications, the "same qualification of members which the assembly holds forth."

But here they leave out infants, which the assembly did express, and amongst censures, suspension, in which they agree not among themselves; but we are glad to hear them profess to agree with us in practice of most of the same things, and those the most substantial in the rule itself; and we are the more sorry to have heard them profess that the nature of the business, and the whole frame and bulk of the rule is such, as that they are not able to endeavor an accommodation with it, but are necessitated to desire a toleration, for gathering congregations under another rule of their own, never yet by them manifested to us.

We desire our brethren to consider, if every small and circumstantial difference among those who agree in most things, and those most substantial, shall be a sufficient ground to gather churches out of churches into a separate and different communion, how the church of God shall ever be kept free from rents and divisions, and how the peace thereof is possible to be preserved?

To these agreements they add that wherein they differ from the rule, they will be accomptable [*accountable*] "of all their ways and tenets unto those whom the state shall be pleased to appoint."

We *answer:* 1. That in this also we agree with them, for all things done by our assemblies; for as we dare not claim an entire, absolute, independent power within ourselves, free from classes and synods, so nether dare we exempt our classes and synods from the power and inspection of the state. 2. Albeit our brethren insinuate much respect and submission to the state, yet we find not that they petitioned the state, or obtained leave from them to practice their own church-way, but did it of themselves, and that by way of anticipation to the state, when it had declared a resolution to reform the church according to God's Word; and we believe they would continue as they have begun, though the state should forbid them. 3. What if the state should at any time be pleased to appoint synods and classes to take an accompt of our brethren's ways and tenets? Would they herein acquiesce? But to proceed,

In their third paragraph they show what communion they will hold with neighbor churches. "Holding and retaining" (they say) "communion with the neighbor churches in baptizing our children, as occasion may fall out of absence of our ministers in their churches: and by occasional receiving the Lord's Supper in their churches, and receiving such members of theirs, as are above mentioned into communion with us also occasionally. Also our ministers to preach in their congregations, and receive theirs also to preach in ours as ministers of the gospel; as mutually there shall be a call from each other: and when we have any cases difficult and too hard for ourselves, electively to advise with the elders of their churches: and in case of controversy, not to refuse to call them in for the composing of it. Further in case of the choice of elders, to seek the approbation, and right-hand of fellowship from godly ministers of their churches together with our own. And when an ordination falls out amongst us, to desire the presence and approbation of their elders with our own. And in case any of our churches miscarry through mal-administration or neglect of censures, to be willing upon scandal taken by their churches to give an account as to sister churches offended: and to esteem and account (as we do) a sentence of non-communion by them as churches, against us, upon such scandals wherein they are not satisfied, a heavy and sad punishment, and to be looked on as a means to humble us, and an ordinance of God to reduce us. All this is more than as if in nothing they were to be complied with, nor their churches to be communicated with in anything which should argue church communion. More is said, and done, by those that account them false churches."

To these things we *answer:* I. First in general: 1. That in most of these particulars they have *de facto* estranged themselves from us hitherto, and therefore we have reason to question in what sense they account our ministers and churches true. 2. If they may occasionally exercise these acts of communion with us once, or a second, or third time, without sin, we know no reason why it may not be ordinary, without sin too, and then separation and church gathering would have been needless. To separate from those churches ordinarily and visibly, with whom occasionally you may join without sin, seems to be a most unjuſt separation. 3. All the communion here ſpoken of is but *ad placi-* *at pleasure* *tum*. We desire to know whether our brethren will be bound to these particulars as conditions of the indulgences to be granted, as,

(1) That no officer be chosen in their congregations without the consent of the churches in that classis.

(2) That they and their members give an account before the officers in the classis, who ſhall as they see occasion, assemble to require it of them. The separatiſts at Amſterdam received none into communion with them out of the Dutch, French, and other Reformed churches there inhabiting; but required them to advertise the elders firſt, and then the whole body of the church[1] whereof they were (if they might be suffered), of the corruptions for which they thought to leave them. But our brethren have taken out of our congregations into theirs, without showing any cause, and their silence in this particular implies they intend to do the like for the time to come, though they cannot be ignorant of the great offense our miniſters and people do take at it.[2]

(3) We desire to know whether they will submit the power of jurisdiction in their particular congregations to the power of arbitration, which they give to synods, or will rescind any sentence upon the determination of a synod, or at the command of the ſtate.

II. To the particulars. 1. 'They say they will baptize their children, and receive the Lord's Supper occasionally in our churches.' It then follows that a miniſter is a miniſter out of the bounds of his own congregation, and {See p. 64} so to the church indefinitely; for members of twenty or more several congregations may occasionally communicate with one miniſter in a diſtinct congregation from all those; this serves much to ſtrengthen our grounds for the presbyterian government, and to weaken independency.

2. 'They can preach in our congregations, and admit us to the like as miniſters in theirs.' No need then of separate churches for the exercise of their miniſtry.

3. 'In difficult cases too hard for themselves, they can electively advise with the elders of our churches.' Ordinarily then they will assume a power to determine controversies and cases of conscience within themselves, and not make use of the advice of others, but at their own discretion. (2) This intimates another and greater power assumed by particular congregations, namely to call synods, more or fewer, smaller or greater, when they please themselves, which liberty of what consequence it may prove to the ſtate, we leave it to this honorable committee to consider.

---

1. ["Unless they had first informed their elders and church (if permitted) of the corruptions they found objectionable and for which they were seeking to leave them." Francis Johnson, *An Inquirie and Answer of Thomas White: his Discoverie of Brownisme* (Amsterdam: 1606), p. 25.]

2. F. Johnson in his inquiry and answer to Th. White, page 25.

4. 'In case of controversy they will not refuse to call our elders in for com-
at one's posing of it.' (1) This is *ad libitum*; they will have no arbitrators but whom
pleasure and when they please. (2) They shall have but a consultative power for
counsel; they will still reserve a liberty of after-debates; and the final determination of every controversy must be by a judicial sentence of their own,
as the bishops who though they allowed of appeals, yet brough[t] back all
to their own courts at last.

5. 'In the choice of elders, they will seek approbation from godly ministers of our churches;' but unless our ministers be judged godly by them,
they intend to excluded them, and herein if they will void their election
upon these ministers' dissent, they say something: but otherwise, it is but a
complement to get countenance from neighbor churches, when it may be
{See p. 281} had, to their proceedings; and when not to be had, to neglect it.

6. 'In an ordination they will desire the presence and approbation of our
elders with their own.' It would please them to have our presence justify
and allow their practice; but they will not permit us to concur with them
in the act of ordaining. They will not receive ordination from our elderships, though they have none of their own: and with them any two elders,
though neither of them be a minister of the Word, makes a sufficient presbytery to this or other purposes. And indeed they look on ordination but
as accidental to the calling of a minister, and place the essence of it in the
people's choice and acceptance.

7. 'In cases of mal-administration or neglect, when scandal is taken by our
churches, they will give an account to them as to sister churches.' We fear
there are many corrupt opinions in the members of their churches, which
they neglect to censure. And we have long professed that we are scandalized
at their practice in drawing away the members of our churches from us,
and gathering churches out of ours. And that boundless liberty and toleration which they do too much favor, and some of their own way plead and
write for, does justly offend us. Yet we have not hitherto been so respected
as churches of God, unto whom offense ought not be given; we would
gladly, to use our brethren's phrase, receive some account of these things.

8 For the sentence of non-communion, we do not well understand it,
nor the grounds out of Scripture for it. We know not how a power to inflict by way of sentence, a heavy punishment, by virtue of a divine ordinance, to humble and reduce, can be severed from all kind of jurisdiction.
If our brethren would clearly state and prove this point, it might haply afford some further light toward an accommodation instead of a toleration.

TO THE SECOND REASON
In their answer to our second reason, they tell us in the first paragraph that
"this reason is founded upon this supposition that nothing ought to be
tolerated which is unlawful in the judgment of those who are to tolerate.

And if so, then by the like reason, no state, assembly, presbytery, is to tolerate any practice or opinion which they account to be in the least erroneous."

We deny this affirmation. Our reason is not founded upon the supposition that nothing unlawful may be tolerated: but upon the supposition of unlawfulness to tolerate the gathering of churches out of true churches; and they do not once endeavor to prove either that such gathering, or the tolerating thereof is lawful.

Next they say, "the way we are to go is not to dispute what is unlawful or lawful in itself; because we are upon the point of forbearance in what is thought unlawful."

We *answer:* 1. This is not the first time our brethren have waved the dispute of the lawfulness of their church-gathering. Upon several occasions it has been pressed on them in the assembly, but they have thitherto declined it. 2. We are here to debate the lawfulness of forbearance, and may insist upon any proper medium to that end: for clearing whereof, the lawfulness or unlawfulness of that point of church gathering is one of the most necessary. 3. We conceive that to judge aright of the lawfulness or unlawfulness of forbearance, will necessarily lead us to consider the lawfulness or unlawfulness of the thing in itself, which is to be tolerated. There are great degrees of danger or mischief in things unlawful, some are more inconsistent with piety, truth, or peace in the church than others, and consequently less tolerable in the nature of the thing than others.

In their third paragraph they say, "For that addition, 'Out of such true churches as are endeavoring to reform,' we say, the reformation which the assembly has ultimately pitched upon, satisfies not our consciences as our brethren know."

We *answer:* 1. That our brethren had such gathered churches before any ultimate resolution of the assembly was known, or in being. 2. What the assembly has done, in great measure does satisfy our brethren; why else profess they so great an agreement with the rule in most things, and those most substantial? 3. If our brethren had brought in their model of government as was ordered April 4, [1645],[1] the assembly would have embraced any light they should have found therein, and consequently have proceeded unto further resolutions consonant thereunto. 4. The wisdom of the Honorable Houses, may find out more for reformation than haply the assembly has advised, or themselves as yet concluded. We have set ourselves no bounds but the Word of God, and example of the best Reformed churches; and therefore we are still reforming, and separation is the more inexcusable.

In their fourth paragraph they thus go on. "For that addition, 'That there

---

1. [On this date the Assembly required the congregationalists "to form a committee for the purpose of outlining a platform for congregational church government." *Minutes,* 3.571 and note 2. See also Document 98, 5.263.]

is no hint of example in all the book of God for gathering churches out of churches," we shall only at this time humbly present the nature of the thing or case itself as it lies in our consciences, and as in the assembly we also ſtated it. The case is this. A multitude of believers after all means used to obtain light, to satisfy their consciences in what to them is sin in partaking of the ordinances, as members of the churches they live or have lived in, by which so long as they continue in those churches they shall be debarred from these ordinances, though it be all their days: and although the opinion be judged an error by those churches they live in, yet of no higher nature than those errors for which they are not to be suſpended from any ordinance by censure, or caſt out of the church, and in all other things are such in their opinions and praĉtices, as are meet [*suitable*] partakers of communion with Chriſt in all ordinances, which as their right, as members of His myſtical body, He has given to them, as to their brethren. In this case there is no obligation laid by Chriſt either on the persons themselves forever to continue in those churches; or in the churches they live in, to withhold them from removing to other churches, free of that which would defile their consciences. Or when there are no such churches in the places they live in, to gather into churches wherein they may enjoy all ordinances without sin. This assertion as thus ſtated, we are ready to debate when this honorable committee shall think fit."

Answer. We desire it may be noted how they wave the main business, whether there be any example in God's Word for gathering churches out of churches. We take it for granted, no inſtance can be given by them, because they produce none. As touching the case which they propound, we are ready to join in the debate, when it is ſtated by mutual agreement. At present we offer these things to consideration.

1. Whether it does not imply that everyone muſt have a liberty allowed him in the right of his being a member of Chriſt to gather a church, or into a church, wherein he may receive the sacrament suitably to his own principles, which opens a gap for all seĉts to challenge such a liberty as their due.

2. Whether from hence it does not follow that an erroneous conscience does bind a man to follow the positive prescript thereof, when indeed (though he see it not) the prescript thereof is contrary to the rule of God's Word. For inſtance: If a man were of an opinion that the sacrament ought to be received at night time, and after his ordinary supper, and could not join in communion with any church which should observe another order, whether he were bound upon the prescript of such an erroneous conscience, to separate from all churches where the ordinance was in truth rightly adminiſtered, and to gather into a church where he might communicate according to the error of his own judgment.

3. Whether this liberty be not denied by the churches of New England, which our brethren think to be the beſt Reformed, and had an eye unto,

in taking the covenant (as some of them have professed), and whether we have not as juſt ground to deny this liberty as they.

TO THE THIRD REASON

To the third reason they thus answer, "An exception does not make void a rule; eſpecially such a one as is not founded on a *Jus Divinum*, and where it is in the power of these who make the rule to grant a forbearance from it. The Reformed churches grant a forbearance, and yet their general rule ſtands, and we in our desires do submit to this honorable committee to find out such ways as may beſt ſtand with the peace of the kingdom."

We *answer*: 1. An exception limited and reſtrained in the extent of it, does not void the rule in all other cases unto which those limits do not extend; but an exception may be of so great a latitude, as by consequence and virtually it may void the rule; and of that nature we conceive this exemption which our brethren desire, to be. For it does actually evacuate it to all such as are for the present of their judgment, and it does the same potentially unto all such who for the future may be drawn unto the same judgment, or any other way to scruple the eſtablished rule in any branch of it, which we have cause to fear, if once tolerated, will be no small number, seeing themselves tell us that multitudes are of this mind already, before they have had the wing of toleration to protect them. He that leaves open one wide gap in a ground at which any cattle that will may go out, does make void the use of the hedge, which is otherwise round about it, unto that purpose of keeping them in.

2. Whether the rule be founded on a *jus divinum* or no, is not our question, though if we would ſpeak *ad hominem*, we conceive our brethren's principles would not allow them to agree in moſt things, and those the moſt subſtantial of the rule, if there were no divine right in their judgment to found [*base*] the rule in those particulars upon; but we find our brethren very willing to insiſt on and wind in that notion on every occasion. We will not busy our thoughts in conjecturing the reasons of it; but surely it is not in this place of such ſpecial use as they pretend; for a rule founded *positive divine* on a *jus divinum positivum* is no more voided by an exception than a rule *right* not founded on a *jus divinum*.

3. Nor is it our queſtion, whether they who make a rule, may not grant a forbearance; but whether a forbearance may not be of such a latitude as in effect to disannul the rule. If this be our brethren's meaning, that an exception will not void a rule, when those who make the rule make the exception likewise, because it may be presumed that the same power will not by an act of favor evacuate a rule of government, which itself has set up; we are of the same persuasion, which makes us humbly suggeſt that such a forbearance as is desired, is of this nature, and therefore not to be granted.

4. We cannot but much queſtion whether any Reformed churches grant

such an unlimited toleration as our brethren desire; that it may be free and lawful for any multitudes of men even of their own natives, who are under a rule, to dispute and declare against it that it is but a rule set up by human power, and that there is another rule appointed by a divine law different from it, unto which men ought to submit, rather than unto the other, and by such arguments to draw as many as can be possessed with so deep a prejudice from the rule established, into separated churches, and such separation to be unto as many as please, as well native as foreigners, as lawful by a toleration, as the rule itself is by a constitution, and all this done by the advice of those churches themselves. We think our brethren cannot find many Reformed churches that tolerate separation at all, nor any one that does it in so unlimited a manner, and that not by connivance only, but by a law.

TO THE FOURTH REASON

To the fourth reason they thus answer: "The privilege of those ministers who submit to the rule is to be capable of all ecclesiastical preferments, which we are not; they find no need of indulging to their consciences as touching the rule established, which we do; possibly their consciences may be scrupled in the same or other things hereafter, and they have the privilege of the same addresses for relief we have, and as for the two particulars therein expressed, we say first, it is a privilege, and much to be desired, to dwell near together, and we also shall endeavor it as much as may be for mutual edification. Secondly, it is the right of every man (we humbly conceive) to choose his own minister, whereas parishes and their bounds by dwellings are but of civil right, provided the state be pleased to take some order that it may be known whither every man does resort."

We *answer:* 1. Our brethren mistake us; we speak of the privileges of the people; they understand us as if we meant ministers and their advantages.

2. Admit this particular privilege were true, yet our reason may be good that in other things their privileges would be more.

3. We know no ecclesiastical preferment but employment and maintenance, and whether our brethren enjoy not these as well as other ministers, we leave to be considered.

4. It is possible as our brethren say that others may be scrupled in other things hereafter, as they are in these now, and then they have the privilege of the same address for relief which now they have; we much doubt this inference, except our brethren would have any scruple whatsoever, which may possibly arise in any men's consciences, to be a just ground.

5. The endeavor which our brethren promise, to have their members live together as much as may be, will indeed be as much as comes to nothing, considering what they next say that it is the right of every man to choose his own minister, which assertion of theirs we will not dispute, but certainly

some would deny, and it will be like[ly] to breed much confusion, and render that, extreme[ly] difficult, if not altogether impossible, which they propound as the only remedy for the magistrate to take account of the people whither they resort to hear.

But granting this assertion, it does not take away our reason. For suppose it be the people's right to chose their minister. Then this is the privilege of those which have the toleration: they shall enjoy their right absolutely, which those who are under the rule cannot do without removing their dwellings.

TO THE FIFTH REASON

To the fifth reason they thus answer: "What hurt the abuse of words, and among others this of schism has done in the churches, our brethren know, and we all have felt; wherefore seeing as yet the assembly has not debated, nor the state determined what schism is, we desire our brethren that in the seeking to countenance that way which they think is right, they would not seek to cast an *odium* upon their brethren who differ from them, and yet together with them desire in faithfulness to know and obey the mind of Christ, by fastening such a name upon them, or their way."

Whereunto we reply, that had the word schism been left out, the reason would have remained strong, *viz.* that this would give countenance to a perpetual division in the church, still drawing away from the churches under the rule: and yet to that (as being manifest in itself) they offer no answer at all, but fastening on the word *schism* labor to divert the *odium* thereof, which yet in the original sense thereof differs no more from division, than Greek from Latin, in expressing the same thing.

That the abuse of words has done much hurt, we willingly grant; but that may be as well by calling evil good, as by calling good evil. So the Papists abuse words, not only by fastening on the orthodox the name of heretic, but by assuming to themselves the name of Catholic; and therefore as we shall be tender in this point toward our brethren, so we desire them that by assuming the name of *tenderness of conscience* to their dissenting from the rule, or of a *church-way* or church-order, to their *way* and *godly party*, they would not reflect an *odium* upon us or the churches under the rule.[1]

And although the assembly has not debated, nor the state determined what schism is, any otherwise than the declaring of what is *rectum*, is the *right* declaring of that which is *obliquum*; yet both have covenanted to endeavor *awry* the extirpation of schism, and so are bound to give no countenance unto any just occasion thereof.

---

1. [*Church way:* The congregational way or "church way" as it was coined in the earliest printed defenses and critiques of the "way" of the churches in New England. Cf. John Ball, *A Tryall of the New Church Way in New England and in Old* (London: 1644). *Godly party:* the appellation which those following Cromwell took to themselves who opposed the imposition of Presbyterianism and the Solemn League and Covenant.]

And however the government which the assembly has advised, and the state already in part established, has had a sufficient load of *odium* and aspersions cast upon it by some who would thereby gain reputation to their own way in so doing; yet we conceive it both unworthy to seek countenance unto that which we think right, by casting *odium* on our brethren who differ from us, and yet together with us desire in faithfulness to know and obey the mind of Christ, and that the cause itself needs no such artifices to gain countenance to it, which has appeared, and we hope shall further appear so agreeable to the Word, and warranted by it, that there will be left no just cause of separating from communion with us therein. And our brethren know that to give countenance to an unjust and causeless separation from lawful church communion, is not far from giving countenance to a schism, especially when the grounds upon which this separation is desired, are such as upon which all other possible scruples with erring consciences may in any other cases be subject unto, may claim the privilege of a like indulgence, and so this toleration being the first, shall indeed but lay the foundation, and open the gap whereat as many divisions in the church as there may be scruples in the minds of men, shall upon the self-same equity be let in.

Our brethren go on in their answer thus; "What we desire forbearance in, will countenance only this: when men who give good testimony of their godliness and peaceableness, after all means used in faithfulness to know the mind of Christ, they yet cannot without sin to them enjoy all the ordinances of Christ, and partake in all the duties of worship as members of that congregation where their dwelling is; they therefore in humility and meekness desire they may not live without ordinances, but for the enjoyment of them for their edification in their spiritual good, may join in another congregation; yet so as not condemning those churches they join not with, as false, but still preserving all Christian communion with the saints as members of the same body of Christ, of the church catholic, and join also with them in all duties of worship which belong to particular churches so far as they are able. If this be called schism, or countenance of schism, it is more than yet we have learned either from the scriptures or any approved authors."

We *answer:* The desired forbearance, which as they say will countenance *only this*, is a perpetual division in the church, and a perpetual drawing away from the churches under the rule; for they desire that they may have liberty to have congregations of persons gathered out of churches under the rule, and that not only for themselves, but for all who are of their way (and indeed upon the latitude of their grounds, for all who are, or may be of any other way, being so and so qualified), and that not for a time, but for perpetuity; and *only this* is a sufficient reason why their desire cannot be granted to them *in terminis.*

in the terms;
see note p. 313

But to show the justness of this desire of theirs, they first put a case, and then conclude, "if this be called schism or countenance of schism, it is more than yet we have learned from the Scriptures or any approved authors."

Whereunto we *answer*: I. In general, that the putting of cases is an usual way of slipping out from the force of a reason, when no other answer can be given; and we desire our brethren to give us their judgment upon their own case propounded, as the face of it may be shown in another glass. Suppose some member of their own congregations have such scruples as that they cannot without sin to them enjoy all the ordinances of Christ, and partake in all the duties of worship as members, as namely, they cannot allow the baptizing of infants; and therefore that they may not live without ordinances, do separate into another congregation, and then again some members of that separated congregation, shall so scruple some other particular doctrine or practice that they cannot without sin to them (as they conceive) enjoy all the ordinances of Christ, or partake in all duties of worship as members, and so shall yet join with them in another congregation which concurs with them in their present principles. Are these divisions and subdivisions as lawful as they may be infinite? Or must we give that respect to the error of men's consciences, as to satisfy their scruples by allowance of this liberty to them? And does not this proclaim an universal liberty to all unto whom the limitations in the case may belong? And does it not plainly signify that error of conscience is a protection against schism?

II. But we come to examine the case particularly.

1. They give the qualification of the persons for whom the forbearance is desired, "They are men who give good testimony of their godliness and peaceableness after all means used in faithfulness to know the mind of Christ."

We shall not mind [*remind; warn*] our brethren how testimonies of godliness are not always infallible protections either against schism or heresy, least it should be judged a casting of *odium* to tell them that men who have been not only esteemed the authors of schism in the ancient churches, have had great testimony of their strictness and integrity of life, as Meletius, Lucifer, Audæus; but even such as have been condemned justly by the ancient councils for heresy; our brethren know what testimony in this respect has been given by Cyril of Alexandria to Nestorius, and by Augustine to Pelagius.[1] But we desire to know unto whom this testimony shall be given; and what assurance may be had that all they whom the brethren or others of their way shall gather into their congregations, whether ministers or others, have used all means, yea all means in faithfulness to know the mind

---

1. [Melitius (died after 325), Bishop of Lycopolis; Lucifer Calaritanus (d. 370 or 371), Bishop of Cagliari in Sardinia; Audius (fourth century); Cyril of Alexandria (c. 376–444), Patriarch of Alexandria; Nestorius (c. 386–c. 451); Augustine, Bishop of Hippo; Pelagius (fl. c. 390–418).]

of Christ? May we not suggest to our brethren one means which has been earnestly desired, and that many years, and never yet to this day by them attempted, namely a free and clear setting forth of their whole way and grounds out of Scripture for it, unto their brethren: by which means, either the weakness of their reasons might have been so fully discovered, as that thereby they might have been moved to forsake this way, and continue in communion with us: or they might have discovered so much light unto us, beyond what has upon any search of our own yet appeared, as that the rule might have been framed unto a general content? Or who shall keep the door of this forbearance being once set open, to prevent the entrance of such as are not in this manner qualified? especially considering that the grant of toleration to all which will make use of it, is like[ly] to take off many from seeking satisfaction in their scruples, and using all means in faithfulness to know the mind of Christ, if they may without due trial betake themselves immediately to the indulgence. And so the toleration may become a sanctuary for such of our churches to fly unto at pleasure from the government, upon such ends as are not at all conscientious, but carnal and corrupt. We therefore conceive it necessary for preventing manifold inconveniences that amongst all other means used in faithfulness, this be one, that each person give account of his scruples to the eldership or congregation where he dwells, that so he may either receive satisfaction or have from them a testimony of godliness and peaceableness.

2. They propound the case of persons thus qualified, "They cannot without sin to them enjoy all the ordinances of Christ and partake of all the duties of worship as members of that congregation where their dwelling is."

If they cannot in all, let them partake in as many duties and ordinances as they can, and let the indulgence only supply that wherein they cannot, and not exempt them universally in that wherein they can. But we desire our brethren to speak clearly and candidly. Can they enjoy any one ordinance, or partake in any one duty in our congregations as members of them? We shall be glad to hear from our brethren that they can be members of that congregation where their dwelling is; if otherwise, to say they cannot partake in all, or enjoy all, is but concealedly spoken, since in truth they will partake in none at all as members.

3. They therefore desire, "They may not live without ordinances, but for the enjoyment of them for their edification in their spiritual good they may join in another congregation."

This desire of joining in another congregation, is but *petitio principii*, and *begging the question* no answer to our reason against it. And whereas they say they must live without ordinances if they join with us as members in our congregations, (1) This implication is very aspersive, it being said indefinitely "without ordinances." (2) It will not follow upon their own concession; for they confess, they can occasionally join with us without sin, and if the occasional joining be lawful, we cannot see why the constant [joining] should be sinful. (3) When they say they cannot enjoy ordinances without sin, if this sin be founded upon an error of conscience, as we are persuaded it is, our brethren know that an erroneous conscience can so hamper and perplex a man, as that during such an error, he shall be bound under sin every way, whether he cross the dictate of his conscience, or follow it; in which case further means and inquiry are to be used how to extricate the conscience out of these straits, and the person erring is bound to put away such an error, as being a sinful infirmity, and the church no way bound to indulge a liberty of persisting in it, especially to the evident disturbance of her own peace.

4. They propound certain limitations in the case; yet so they say, "as not condemning those churches they join not with as false, but still preserving all Christian communion with the saints as members of the same body of Christ of the church catholic, and join with them in all duties of worship that belong to particular churches so far as they are able."

We *answer:* (1) Whatever indulgence shall be granted, let this be the boundary of it which is given by the brethren themselves; that such as give not testimony of their godliness and peaceableness, as have not used all means in faithfulness to know the mind of Christ, as do not condemn those churches which they join not with as false, as do not preserve all Christian communion with the saints, nor join with them in all duties of worship that belong to particular churches, as far as they are able, shall not have the benefit of this indulgence; and to the end that those words, *so far as they are able,* may not stand for a mere cipher, and signify nothing, let each man particularly declare in what ordinances or duties they are able to join that so all total separation may be prevented.

(2) The not condemning of our churches as false, does little extenuate the separation; for divers of the Brownists who have totally separated in former times, have not condemned these churches as false; though they do not pronounce an affirmative judgment against us, yet the very separating is a tacit and practical condemning of our churches, if not false, yet as impure, *eousque* as that in such administrations they cannot be by them as members communicated with without sin. *in so far*

(3) As touching that expression of "preserving all Christian communion with the saints, as members of the same body of Christ," it is no vindication of our churches at all when they depart from us. The same may be said of any saints living in Sodom, in Caesar's household, *in fæce Romuli,*[1] in false churches: we do not find our brethren willing to have communion with the saints as members of our congregations, but as members of the church catholic, which is as full a declining of communion with us as churches, as if we were false churches.

---

1. ["The dregs of Romulus." Cf. Cicero, Letters to Atticus (2.1 {XXVI}). "... the dregs of humanity collected by Romulus...."]

(4) And whereas our brethren say that the forbearance they desire "will countenance only this," which is speciously represented with all favorable circumstances in the case: we conceive under favor that the desire of theirs in their third proposition goes somewhat further. For there they desire a liberty to have congregations which themselves have explained to be, to hold those congregations they already have, or to gather members into a congregation, or to add to those they have already. Now it is one thing for a scrupulous conscience to have liberty to join in another congregation, as it is said in the case, and another thing to have liberty to be active, and to gather members out of our churches, as is implied in the desire. For that would be to desire not only a liberty for consciences that are scrupulous, but a liberty to make consciences scrupulous by preaching or any other way infusing their principles into them, in order to the gaining of them into their congregations; nor can we yet see how our brethren, looking on their way as the counsel of God, and on the rule as not founded on divine right, can allow themselves not to be in this manner active and sedulous to promote that which they judge God's way, and to disparage that which they judge but man's.

The brethren having framed a case which is less than their desire in the third proposition (yet we fear, will not be the case of many who will make use of this indulgence), conclude thus, "If this be called schism or countenance of schism, it is more than yet we have learned either from the Scriptures, or any approved author."

We *answer:* That it is not this new formed case, but the granting of our *in the terms* brethren's desire in the third proposition as it stands *in terminis*, whereof *See note, 313* we say that it would give countenance to a perpetual schism and division in the church, which we do still aver is a thing of itself manifest; not that we think differences in judgment in this or that point to be schism, or that every inconformity unto everything used or enjoyed is schism, so that communion be preserved, or that separation from idolatrous communion or *in itself* worship *ex se* unlawful, is schism, but:

1. We find our brethren desire not only that they may be free from communicating as members in those parishes where they dwell, but may have liberty to have congregations of such persons who out of tenderness of conscience cannot communicate with us, but do voluntarily offer themselves to join in separate congregations of another communion, which secession of our members from us is a manifest rupture of our societies into others, and is therefore a schism in the body. And if the Apostle calls those divisions of the church, wherein Christians did not separate into diverse formed congregations of several communion[s] in the sacrament of the Lord's supper, schism, much more may such separation as this desired be so called (1 Corinthians 1:10, 11; 1 Corinthians 11:18).

2. We find it not alleged as a cause of this separation, either that our churches are false, or our communion in ordinances *ex se* unlawful, but only

"scruple of conscience that a man cannot without sin as to him partake in all duties, and enjoy all ordinances," which is no cause of separating, nor does it take off causeless separation from being schism, which may arise from errors of conscience as well as carnal and corrupt reasons; therefore we conceive the causes of separation muſt be shown to be such as *ex natura* *in reality* *rei* will bear it out, which has not yet been done by our brethren, nor we think can be. And therefore we say that the granting of the liberty desired will give countenance to schism.

3. We cannot but take it for granted upon evidence of reason and experience of all ages that this separation will be the mother and nurse of contentions, ſtrifes, envyings, confusions, and so draw with it that breach of love, which may endanger the heightening of it into formal schism even in the sense of our brethren.

And we desire our brethren to show out of scriptures and approved authors what they have learned concerning schism; for the breaking of members from their churches which are lawfully conſtituted churches, and from communion in ordinances diſpensed according to the Word, without juſt and sufficient cause *ex natura rei,* to juſtify such secession, and to join in other congregations of separate communion, either because of personal failings in the officers or members of the congregation from which they separate, or because of causeless scruple of their own conscience, has been accounted schism, and the setting up *altare contra altare*, as the expression of *altar againſt* former times was;[1] and what is it else that approved authors do call schism? *altar* *Schisma, ni fallor* (said Auguſtine) *eſt eadem opinantem, & eodem ritu utentem solo congregationis deleĉtari dissidio, & schismaticos facit non diversa fides, sed communionis disrupta societas.*[2] Agreeable whereunto is that definition of schism by Cameron, *eſt schisma secessio in religionis negotio vel temeraria, vel injuſta, sive faĉta sit, sive continuata,*[3] and concurrently do other approved

---

1. ["And this is exclaimed against and regretted by the Fathers, under the expression of erecting *altare contra altare,* that is, *altar againſt altar,* whenas the Lord allowed but one, even in reference to His own worship. Schism may be in worship, that is when, it may be, both the same doctrine and government is acknowledged, yet there is not communion kept in church ordinances, as in Prayer, Word and Sacraments, but a separate way of going about these is followed…. This kind of schism has been frequent in the church, and has flowed not so much from dissatisfaction with the doctrine and government thereof, as with the constitution of the members, or failings of the governors. Thus it was in the case of the Novatians, Donatists, Meletians, Cathari, and others, of whom it is recorded that their fault did not consist in setting up any strange doctrine, or in rejecting of the truth (at least at the first) but in breaking the band of communion, as Augustine has it often. For says he, *Schismaticos*…." James Durham, *Concerning Scandal* (Naphtali Press: 1990), p. 227.]

2. Contra Faustum, lib. 20, cap. 3. Qu. Evang. in Math. qu. 11. & de fide & operib. cap. 5. [Augustine, *Contra Fauſtum Manichaeum, PL* 42:369. *NPNF1* 4, p. 253. "As to your calling us a schism of the Gentiles, and not a sect, I suppose the word schism applies to those who have the same doctrines and worship as other people, and only choose to meet separately." *Quæstionum Evangeliorum, PL* 35.1367; *De Fide et Operibus, PL* 40:201.]

3. De Schismate. [John Cameron, ΤΑ ΣΩΖΟΜΕΝΑ *sive opera partim ab auĉtore ipso edita*

authors say, and we likewise conceive that it is the cause of the separation from communion which gives both name and nature to schism; for if that cause be unjust or insufficient according to the rule of the Word of God, let our brethren tell us what such a separation is.

In their third paragraph our brethren proceed, "And as for that irritation our brethren speak of, we humbly conceive it will be according to the temper of men's hearts. If such a practice meet with men whose hearts are gracious, it will only irritate them to search further into the mind of Christ, and to walk before their brethren with more exactness, and to exercise love, meekness and forbearance towards those brethren who differ from them; and such irritation there is no great cause that either we or our brethren should make complaints of. If," etc.

Answer. We know no evil which may not be excused by such a dilemma as this. What scandal, what heresy can arise, which will not operate upon men according to the temper of their hearts? Which will not irritate those who are gracious to search the Scriptures, etc.? For even heresies, said the Apostle, must be that *they who are approved may be made manifest; we may not do evil,* nor plead for evil, nor take it for granted that a thing is not evil, *because good may come of it.*

"If this liberty," they say, "meet with corruption, it is like[ly] enough there may be accidentally an irritation to sin; but the way then to oppose such corruption is by instruction, prayer, walking convincingly before them, etc., if they grow turbulent, to call in the help of the civil magistrate; but not to give that respect to their corruptions, as to deny to men who give undeniable testimony of their godliness that use of the ordinances of Christ that they may with the peace of their consciences enjoy."

Answer. The irritation is not accidental where the cause is *causa per se.* We cannot conceive that this irritation will be *extra semper & frequenter,* as accidental effects are.[1] For to omit the corruptions which this liberty may meet with in such as are not truly godly, will not this be an irritation of their corruptions that are true members of the church? Yea haply, not only of their corruptions, but of their consciences and zeal to oppose such separation and drawing away of their members as this is? The Corinthians were saints, and yet by reason of the schism, contentions, and strife among them, they are charged to be yet carnal, and to walk as men; and if we consult our own experience already, this liberty meets with more whose corruptions are too strong for their graces, than whose graces do make only good use thereof. And because we already find this assumed liberty to be

intrinsic cause

(Frankfurt: 1642) *De Ecclesia,* "De Schismate," p. 323. "Schism is a separation in religious matters {which is} either rash or unwarranted, whether at its making or in its continuance."]

1. [Cf. Aquinas on Aristotle's *Physics,* II. *In octo libros Physicorum expositio,* II, lecture 9, n. 4, 220"For every per se cause produces its effect either always or in most cases" ("omnis enim causa per se producit effectum suum vel semper, vel ut frequenter"). *Commentary on Aristotle's Physics,* translated by Richard J. Blackwell, et al. (Yale, 1963), p. 104.]

an irritation to the worse, and not to the better, we have little reason to expect that being made more confident and bold by a toleration, it should be otherwise hereafter; nor do we think but such separation of church members has been heretofore, and therefore may further be an irritation of corruptions amongst themselves.

To the way they suggest of opposing such corruptions, however it may be good to prevent the evil effects it may have upon a man's own heart; yet so long as the cause of all does remain, which is separation, and so long as men are men, we cannot conceive it will be otherwise, nor can we find in any age or history, but the like cause has had the like effects. And though we acknowledge the magistrate's power to bridle turbulence, and to prevent or heal the breach of peace, yet the irritations will remain, and be often breaking forth to the scandal of religion; and the trouble of the magistrate is not likely to be so great in taking away the fuel, as in coming always in, to pour water upon the fire when it breaks out.

And so to that which they say, "that such respect is not to be given to men's corruptions as to deny," etc: This implication is scandalous that the denying of this liberty is a giving respect to men's corruptions; for it is out of respect to the church's peace and communion, and the covenanted uniformity; and yet doubtless though we may not give respect, yet we may have respect to men's corruptions so far as to prevent the irritation of them; else by this reason we must hand over head grant a universal toleration of all that are any way conscientiously scrupled, without looking to the probable events and consequences thereof, which may follow either by reason of the corruptions of others, or of the men themselves who use this liberty; for it may be as well indulged with respect to men's corruptions, as denied, except it can be undertaken that there shall be no corruption in them that desire and use it. It is our earnest desire and prayer that our brethren might enjoy the ordinances with the peace of their consciences, and of the church also, or that they would rather deny themselves of their full liberty in every point, than redeem it at the price of so much danger and disquiet to the churches of God.

TO THE SIXTH REASON

To the Sixth Reason our Brethren answer, "First in general, our judgments do thus far agree with yours that except upon very weighty considerations, husband and wife, master and servants should partake together in the same ministry."

We take what they grant us, and cannot but think it strange that when our brethren account us true churches, agree with us in substance of doctrine and worship, in the most, and most substantial things of the rule for government, can occasionally join with us in the sacraments, can hear [the Word preached] with us and pray with us, there should yet be such weighty considerations behind (though they call the difference between us, *lesser matters*) as to necessitate separation, and to ground an allowance for wife, child, servant, to withdraw from that authority, which the master of the house has to rule and oversee them in religious duties; but they proceed:

"II. If it should happen to be otherwise, 1. All manner of confusion would not hereby be introduced into families; for can our brethren think that persons agreeing in all the fundamentals of their faith, and who in their judgment and practice join in all the same duties of piety in the family, and also agree in the same duties of public worship for the substance, though not living under the same individual ministry, yet unless they do agree also in a uniformity in everything, both public and private, they must needs run into all manner of confusion: has either nature or the gospel put such a necessity upon uniformity in lesser things to keep families from confusion? If this were the rule of the gospel, then except it prevail upon the opinion of those whom it converts to such a uniformity (which it seldom does) it must by this principle of necessity subvert human society by bringing confusion into families, which we conceive to be a great derogation to the gospel."

Hereunto we *answer*: (1) The common people are not very likely from agreement in fundamentals, to draw consequences of mutual forbearance, when they see ministers, notwithstanding this, for these lesser matters, withdraw and set up separate churches, unto which they following them upon opinion of sin, and that in the worship of God, which is heightened with the notion of *will worship*, and even of *idolatry* and *antichristianism*, must needs greatly endanger heavy contentions and confusion: no animosities being so great as those which rise out of differences in religion, specially among those that live near together.

Nor is it the mere want of uniformity (as our brethren would infer) which does necessitate this, but such a positive deformity in opinion and practice, as that they who live together, and lie in the bosoms of one another, *cannot* (which is more than simply *do not*), serve God together in public, but divide asunder, not unto a several ministry only, but which is much more dangerous, unto a separated ministry, wherein so often as the doctrines which tend to justify that separation shall be taught on the one side, and the contrary thereunto on the other, it is impossible for a family thus contrarily in the members thereof instructed, to join together in mutual edification at home, without confusion.

(2) If any differences in a family should arise, especially growing out of divided opinions in this matter of a church way, as is most probable may, and that frequently, and such as may break forth into public scandal, and require the care of ministers and eldership to heal them, whither can they repair in such a case for help, whose very disagreements are about the remedies that should cure them?

(3) Where husband and wife are divided into separated congregations,

they will certainly endeavor to draw children and servants to their way, whence favors and disfavors are likely to grow, and thereupon such jars and contentions in the family, as may quickly amount to much confusion.

(4) The very several contributions unto the maintenance of several ministers, when a man must [contribute] to his own minister, to his wife's, to his children's, as they severally shall scatter themselves, may not only be a burden to the state of a man, but much more to his mind, when being persuaded his wife or children are in a sin of separation from him, he must yet be at charges to allow them therein; differences that strike this string, do often beget jarring discords, to say nothing of the bad uses, which ill minds, or the many fears, which jealous minds may draw from hence, when young women or children shall constantly depart for the ordinances, it may be some miles from one another, out of the sight, and from under the inspection and care of their parents or husbands, when it is certain they should enjoy as powerful and edifying a ministry by staying at home.

Lastly, if a wife or child should be censured in their separated congregations that also might be a rise of domestical contentions. In his own congregation the husband should hear and understand the case, and have satisfaction in the known integrity of his own eldership, or at least might have the benefit of an appeal, none of which he can have in a separated congregation of which he has no knowledge.

2. "Neither would it" (say our brethren) "exceedingly, much less altogether hinder the mutual edification that might be afforded and received among them. For first although persons of the same family not living under the same ministry, may in some respect of family duties not so fully edify as otherwise, yet in a great measure they may, and if there be a zeal and good conscience in any of the family to be helpful in good conference, it is no such great hindrance to hear in several places, or several preachers, as scholars reading several books and then conferring; many good Christians have for edification purposely practiced it, and it has some advantages for edification which the other way has not."

Answer. Our brethren grant that this course hinders such full edification in some respect, as might otherwise be had; and surely this some respect is a very great one, when there shall be none to help the memories, to clear the doubts, to remove the mistakes, to supply the defects of the rest, none to inculcate the duties, to kindle and mutually warm the affections, or to whet [*hone*] the things which might jointly have been learned, upon the consciences of one another, and having been more jointly affected in the public dispensation of them, to be the better enabled with joint fervency of spirit to beg a blessing upon them. And verily, when we are commanded to do all things unto edification, and to follow those things whereby one may edify another, if any course be more a hindrance than a furtherance unto edification, we know not how upon principles of conscience, a man should constantly be bound unto such a course. Scholars may better profit by conferring their observations out of several books, than ordinary people by bringing broken, and it may be mistaken and incoherent notes from several sermons. In that of scholars there is nothing but speculative or intellectual benefits aimed at; here the heart, conscience, affections are to be kindled, and further quickened by mutual conference, and assistance in the duties they heard before, which is more effectually done when several persons have been jointly warmed and stirred up in the same congregation. Besides, books in that case may agree, when in our case, sermons may not; for one may hear a sermon for separation, another for communion, and so conferring of notes will be but the repeating of contradictions in the family. And though some in the family may have zeal and good conscience to help the rest, yet what will this avail those whose understandings and memories being weak have none to improve and further them in the things which they heard themselves? We are confident, no humble Christians who know their own weakness, and are tender of the weakness of others, will dare to pretend their getting advantage in matter of edification from the ordinances by thus [*this*] constant dividing and scattering the family into several congregations; and therefore our brethren do confess that there is a further degree of edification which comes to persons in a family by going all to the same ministry.

But then they further proceed and say,

[Secondly,] That this "amounts not to that proportion as to countervail the want of enjoying the public ordinances forever, which compared with family duties simply considered, have had the preeminence, both in respect to God's glory, and the edification of souls, in all men's concessions, which cannot be enjoyed by many that yet are truly conscientious, except the liberty petitioned be granted."

Answer. What ordinances must our brethren want [*lack*] forever? They have told us they could not join in some ordinances without sin; here they speak plainer, and if that they say be pertinent to the argument, they tell us they cannot enjoy the ministry of the Word without sin in our congregations. For if they can, and if by their own confession there is a further degree of edification by going all of a family to the same ministry, than by dividing, with what warrant do they divide, in that wherein they can join, even to the prejudice of edification? They have told us before, they can hear our ministers, and allow them to preach among *them* as ministers, and occasionally receive the Lord's Supper with us, and admit us with them; and if all this may be without sin, must yet the toleration desired be upon this ground granted, because else many truly conscientious must want the public ordinances, and that forever. We understand neither the logic, nor divinity of this answer.

We confess to family duties simply considered, public ordinances are to be preferred; but if one muſt be loſt for the other, we think that which is *intrinsic cause* *causa per se* of such an inconvenience, to wit such a separation, is even *eo* *on that account* *nomine* unjuſt.

3. They add, "'for the account governors in great families are to take of all in their families attending upon the ordinances and of their profiting thereby.' We *answer*: The churches we desire being conſtant and fixed, it is no more impossible than it was for a godly tutor in the university to take account of his pupils having liberty to go to several churches."

To which we reply; the case is different. Scholars can write, and give a ready account; every child or servant in a family cannot do so, nor be by the governor helped who heard not with him. 1. Scholars sometimes have deceived their tutors with false notes, and so may children or servants; what security is or can there be that they will go conſtantly to their congregation, and not to taverns, alehouses, or some other ill employment? 2. What time will there be for receiving an account of so many sermons? Add hereunto the different hours of going and returning, which may exceedingly hinder family duties, none of which inconvenience will be remedied by the fixed-ness of the separated churches.

4. They say, "whereas it is heightened that twenty of one family may pos-sibly be of twenty churches, we suppose if the ſtate be pleased to grant us the liberty we petition for that they in their wisdom (to which we have re-ferred ourselves) will take into consideration the limiting such congrega-tions unto a certain number, and there may not then be twenty churches in any city or town to divide themselves into."

To this we *answer*: That it is true according to the judgment of our breth- {See p. 74} ren, who make those many thousands of Chriſtians which were converted at Jerusalem, to have been no argument of more than one congregation in that city, that conformably thereunto a very few congregations may serve together a great multitude of members; but we know not how the princi-ples and grounds of our brethren's desire can allow them to reſt in any set number, if they prove too few for such multitudes as they may gather out of our churches into them. For their petition being indefinite for multi-tudes of persons, cannot be well definite for number of places or congrega-tions. But whether they be more or fewer, they will be abundantly enough to diſtract even a very great family and hinder their mutual edification, and the taking and giving of the sure and profitable account, to the great grief of the husband, parent, and governor, to have his family so authorized to forsake him, and that he (to add that to all the other considerations) who for his own benefit would be glad of their help, muſt want [*lack*] that, as well as they want his.

Our brethren conclude their answer thus: "But the truth is, those that thus plead againſt this permission which we desire as insufferable, muſt certainly suppose that men are to be tied throughout this kingdom to their own parish churches where they live, both masters and servants, and that not only for sacraments, but for constant hearing, which how burdensome it was in former times, the godly people are very sensible of; and now in the time of reformation, it finds many ministers who cannot be cast out by order of law, though bad and unprofitable, as appears by the leaving them out of the classes; and shall the people be tied to live under them as their ministers, who are not worthy to join in government with yourselves? And for time to come as places are void, they must be supplied by the choice of other for them, or by themselves; *if by themselves,* all parishes are not reformed as concerning the people, and the major part being generally the worse, the ministers chosen by them, will be such as the godly cannot live under their ministry; *if by others,* those who are the choosers may also be such, as they cannot be denied by law their right in choosing, and so also unprofitable ministers may be put upon the godly people; and the inconveniences presented will fall more heavy upon the numerous multitude of parishes, in city and country."

Answer. To the pains which this paragraph our brethren have taken in setting forth for the present, and prophesying for the future of the unprofitableness and unworthiness of the ministers in many of our parochial congregations under which godly men cannot live, we will reply no more but this, that it [is] a crimination which might well have been spared in a time of endeavored and covenanted reformation. For it seems to intimate one of these two things, either that there is an impossibility *in natura rei* for a profitable ministry to be for the time to come generally settled in our churches, or that being possible in itself, there would be some defect in those by whose zeal, power and wisdom, this so important a particular of reformation should be promoted: neither of which we think our brethren either will or can affirm.

in the nature of
the matter

Neither is it equal to argue from the former times of unjust vexation, when men were tied to their parishes, though there were no preaching minister, or one who preached errors, or opposed godliness, unto these times wherein men have covenanted against everything that is of this nature.

Nor do we believe that our brethren mean that only such should be allowed to gather into their congregations who live under bad and unprofitable ministers, though that be the only *medium* here used against our reason.

But to the whole we *answer* in brief thus [*this*] much: 1. That we never did, do, nor shall deny any members of our congregations to hear or communicate occasionally elsewhere. And 2. That we doubt not, but by the blessing of God upon the reformation to be settled, there will be that concurrent care of patrons, people, classes, as that there shall be no such unworthy ministers from whom any conscientious Christian shall be forced constantly to withdraw himself; and where the ministry is without just exception, we refer it to our brethren's own consciences, and to the practice of their congregations, to say how fit it is that the members should ordinarily, much less constantly seek the ordinances elsewhere.

February 2, 1645. The committee met again; and the dissenting brethren brought in a paper containing a reply to a second part of the answer of the subcommittee to the desires of the dissenting brethren, December 15, 1645. Which is as follows.

[The Fourth Paper: The Dissenting Brethren's Reply to a second part of the Answer of the Subcommittee, February 2, 1645]

Though it is our desire rather to answer to the papers brought in by our brethren, before we go on any further; yet because the committee requires us to go on, we humbly submit these papers to the consideration of this honorable committee.

Our brethren say,

"II. That none are to be allowed upon differences only in matters of government, to withdraw communion from us in things wherein they declare an agreement: but seeing it is confessed in worship and doctrine we are one, and have covenanted to endeavor the nearest conjunction and uniformity, there may be no such indulgence granted to any as may constitute them in distinct separate congregations, as to those parts of worship where they can join in communion with us, but only some expedient may be endeavored how to bear with them in the particulars, wherein they cannot agree with us.

"III. For this purpose we humbly offer.

"1. That such as through scruple or error of conscience, cannot join to partake of the Lord's Supper, shall repair to the minister and elders for satisfaction in their scruples, which if they cannot receive, they shall not be compelled to communicate in the Lord's Supper: provided that in all other parts of worship, they join with the congregation wherein they live and be under the government of that congregation.

"2. That such as in this matter are under the government of that congregation wherein they live, and are not officers therein, being of the independent judgment, shall seek satisfaction as in the former proposition, which if they cannot receive, they shall not be compelled to be under the power of censures from classes or synods: provided that they continue under the government of that congregation, and that no man who has submitted to classis and synods, shall decline them, in any case, *pendente lite*." *pending case*

Answer. 1. This supposes what our professed judgment is and has been against, namely, to be members or pastors of the parishes as now they are; for the Honorable Houses think not meet [*suitable*] as yet to give power to the ministers by a law to purge the congregations so far as the assembly itself desires; and we have not as you know, presumed to seek the alteration of the rule established; and the rule for purging the parishes given up by the assembly itself, to the Honorable Houses, is not only short, but exclusive of what we in our consciences think is required by God for the qualification of members: so that it is not to us in view, how the parishes shall be reformed, to that which will satisfy our consciences. And as the divines of the reverend assembly have said, *they cannot without sin administer the ordinances to the parishes as they stand;* so neither can we continue or become members or pastors according to our principles; and we humbly desire that our consciences may be considered herein for forbearance, as our brethren desire that theirs may for power by a law.

2. If we could, yet according to what is proposed, we must forever want [*lack*] that great ordinance of the Lord's Supper, which cannot but much prejudice us to the elders and members of the congregation, from whose communion we thus separate; and yet we must be under their government and censures thus prejudiced by us; which how unreasonable it will be, we desire our brethren to consider.

3. All this supposes also that we are to be under the government of a church whereof we are not members; for we account not living in the parishes to be sufficient to make a member of a church; nor did many of you.

4. It supposes this ground (the reason of which we see not, only the charity of it we cannot but wonder at) that because we come so near in doctrine and worship and communion with you, therefore we must not have an indulgence in a difference which yet concerns the edification of our souls by ordinances that are so necessary,

For the reasons the reverend brethren do give, "That seeing it is confessed in worship and doctrine we are one, and have covenanted to endeavor the nearest conjunction and uniformity, there may be no such indulgence granted to any as may constitute them in distinct separated congregations as to those parts of worship where they can join in communion with us;"

We *answer:* Whereas the uniformity sworn to in the covenant is now urged here upon this occasion, and continually upon the like turned as the great argument against us in pulpits, presses, and ordinary treaties, as if what we desired were contrary thereunto: this argument cannot hold against us, without affixing an interpretation upon that part of the covenant, and that according to our brethren's principles only, to the prejudice of ours; who when we took this national covenant were known to be of the same principles we now are of; and yet this covenant was professedly so attempered in the first framing [of] it, as that we of different judgments might take it, both parties being present at the framing of it in Scotland: and if this should be the way of urging, it is as free for us to give our interpretation of the latitude or nearness of uniformity intended, as for our brethren. We have been present at the debates of the assembly about it, and well know and remember the sense that there was held forth thereof; and further the *Minutes, 2.124* assembly being appointed by order of the Honorable House of Commons bearing date September 15, 1643, *To set forth in a declaration the grounds that have induced the assembly to give their opinions that this covenant may be taken in point of conscience,* according to which, some of us were by a committee entrusted to bring in materials to that purpose, and accordingly did, which materials were committed to one of us, by a subcommittee to draw up; and among many other things that which follows, as grounds of taking the covenant, as touching that first article, *viz. that we shall endeavor to bring the churches of God in the three kingdoms to the nearest conjunction and uniformity in religion, confession of faith, form of church government, directory of worship and catechism that we and our posterity after us, may as brethren live in faith and love, and the Lord may delight to dwell in the midst of us.*

This endeavor in our places and callings for uniformity, we apprehended the meaning of it to be:

That as in our ranks and stations we should endeavor it: so according to those general warrants of the Word, to regulate such an endeavor in the use of means, whereby to accomplish it. And therefore, as for the pattern, the Word of God is to be in our eye: so, for the way and means and progress in reducing the churches to such an uniformity, such rules are to be observed, as the nature of such a work will bear; and which the apostles (who had infallibility) observed in reducing the Jews, and those of the circumcision, and the Gentiles to an uniformity; and without tyranny and pressing men's consciences beyond the several degrees of light, which God vouchsafes to several churches more or less. So that although there be one pattern in our eye in common, which all our consciences swear to bring all to; yet *de facto* and in the providence of God, it so falls out, in the reforming of churches (now after Anti-Christianism has over-spread and corrupted all), that the light grows every age more and more, to the perfect day and the coming of Christ, who is to melt that man of sin, by the increasing brightness of his coming: and so both of persons and churches, some see more, some see less; and as we see in the Reformed churches at this day; and will certainly fall out thus, in these of ours. Now therefore in this case that rule for effecting this uniformity must certainly be no other than what the apostle gives (Philippians 3[:16]), *As far as we have attained; let us walk by the same rule.* And therefore the way is to see how far we have attained, and set down wherein we agree (as in all substantials of faith and worship it is certain we shall), and so to walk by that as the same rule; and then in such matters wherein men are otherwise minded, to leave it to God and such good means that God may reveal it to them in his time, as his promise is.

But if a uniformity for uniformity's sake (and so the argument of our brethren here runs); that is, affecting uniformity so much as not to regard men's consciences, should be pressed and urged by such means, as formerly without reſpect had to that variety of light, in matters of a lesser nature, this were beyond the callings and warrants of the Word; and will prove a perfect tyranny; and will be so far from being a means of love, which it aimed at, that it will lay the foundation of confusion and dissension, as formerly it did. It is with churches as with men and particular saints: they are of several sizes and growth, of several ſtatures, and as men are left to be more or less holy, as God by good means shall make them, so muſt churches. As it were againſt nature to ſtretch a low man to the same length with a taller, or to cut a tall man to the ſtature of one that is low for uniformity's sake: so to bring both more grown, or more reformed churches to a middle ſtature for compliance with others, and for *mere uniformity's* sake.

And this suits as with the rules of the Word, so with the *scope of the article.* For firſt look what kind of uniformity in confession of faith, the like in matter of worship and government is to be intended; and that the rather because directions for government and worship are the more remote from all Chriſtian's knowledge, and perhaps more obscure in the Word; and are the ſpecial controversies of the times. Now as in matters of faith you would not for uniformity's sake, determine all *differences in judgment but fundamentals* (and an uniformity therein is all intended), so by analogy in point of worship and government. And secondly, the end is *that God may dwell amongſt us,* which is the Author of peace, not of confusion in all the churches: which peace (while in His providence men's judgments do and will differ) will never be attained by a rigid uniformity.

But this order of the Honorable House of Commons, so necessary for the satisfaction of all differing judgments: as at firſt to take the covenant, so to continue ſteadfaſt therein; and which would in all likelihood have laid a foundation of this and other differences, was superseded to this day.

II. We *answer:* That we willingly again do profess that in the subſtance of worship and doctrine, we are one, and of the same judgment with our brethren, yet to practice and enjoy those parts of worship, as ordinances of a church, there is (as to our consciences) necessarily required, as the seat and subject of worship and other ordinances, a church-ſtate; and those such churches, as where we may be members and join in communion therein as members without sin, which we cannot do as we have all along professed, and such churches, as wherein we can enjoy all ordinances, which is denied us here in this paragraph. So that the only way left to reduce us to a uniformity and conjunction in the same practices, is to allow us such diſtinct churches from yours, according to our principles, in which and by means of which, we shall hold all possible communion and conformity with yours: whereas otherwise, we shall only retain a uniformity in judgment, whereas that uniformity the covenant much rather obliges you and us all unto, is that which may be a uniformity in practice with satisfaction to all men's consciences, and their edification.

March 9, 1645. The committee met again, and the subcommittee presented an answer to the laſt paper of the dissenting brethren, which is as follows.

The Answer of the Subcommittee of Divines unto the Fourth Paper of the Dissenting Brethren, presented to the Honorable Committee

Our brethren being ordered by the honorable committee to go on upon the paper brought in by the subcommittee touching indulgence, are not pleased to take notice of those particulars of forbearance, which are therein offered to consideration; though this would much have conduced unto the expediting of the business of this honorable committee, and encourage us to have ſtudied some further means for their accommodation; neither do they bring in any reasons out of Scripture to juſtify their desire of that which we say cannot be granted them *in terminis.* But thus they begin: See p. 313

"Though it is our desire, rather to answer to the papers brought in by our brethren, before we go on any further; yet because the committee requires us to go on, we humbly submit these papers to the consideration of this honorable committee."

To which we *answer:* That before our laſt papers were brought in, they were ordered by the committee to consider of this former paper, and had a month's time so to have done, but have ſtill declined it upon other reasons than they here express, and seem more willing to lengthen the work into tedious and fruitless diſputes againſt those things which do not please them, than to express a real endeavor of bringing things to an agreement so far as may be, by so much as taking notice of those parts of our paper, which tend thereunto; leaving therefore the two laſt paragraphs of our paper utterly unobserved, they single out only one proposition, againſt which this present paper of theirs is wholly directed, wherein our words are these:

"That none are to be allowed upon differences in matters only of government, to withdraw communion from us in things wherein they declare an agreement; but seeing it is confessed in worship and doctrine we are one, and have covenanted to endeavor the neareſt conjunction and uniformity; there may be no such indulgence granted to any as may conſtitute them in diſtinct separated congregations, as to those parts of worship wherein they can join in communion with us, but only some expedient may be endeavored how to bear with them in the particulars wherein they cannot agree with us."

Hereunto they reply diſtinctly: 1. To our advice; 2. To the reasons of it. Againſt our advice they have four paragraphs, the firſt of which is in these words:

"[1.] This supposes what our professed judgment is and has been against, namely to be members or pastors of the parishes as now they are; for the Honorable Houses think not meet [*suitable*] as yet to give power to the ministers by a law to purge the congregations so far as the assembly itself desires; and we have not (as you know) presumed to seek the alteration of the rule established, and the rule for purging the parishes given up by the assembly itself to the Honorable Houses, is not only short, but exclusive of what we in our consciences think is required by God for the qualification of members: so that it is not to us in view how the parishes shall be reformed to that which will satisfy our consciences. And as the divines of the reverend assembly have said, *they cannot without sin administer the ordinances to the parishes as they stand,* so neither can we continue or become members or pastors according to our principles; and we humbly desire that our consciences may be considered herein for forbearance, as our brethren desire that theirs may for power by a law."

Whereunto we *answer:* What that is which they call their professed judgment, would much more clearly appear unto us, if we could ever obtain that which has been so long and so much desired, namely a full and distinct model of their way. But for the thing in hand we had no reason to suppose that what we advised was contrary to the judgment of our brethren; sure we are when at this honorable committee it was pressed upon our brethren then present to declare whether they could join in communion with us in those things wherein they doctrinally agreed; they did not then declare it to be contrary to their professed judgment; nay, the vote which was then made to be reported to both houses, namely that if the congregations were purged, it would very much tend to accommodation, was passed, *nemine* *contradicentes.* And why our brethren should make the notion of parishes, *as* *now they are,* as a ground of separation, when they know further reformation is covenanted, and intended, we know no reason. Must the communion of true churches be forsaken in all things, because in some things they want [*lack*] reformation, and that even then when reformation is endeavored? Must a man refuse to live in any part of his house, because some one chamber or other is out of repair, and about to be mended? It is no good logic as to our own houses, and we think it is no better as to God's. We could not but look upon it as reasonable (whatever our brethren's judgment is) that in those things wherein there is a doctrinal agreement (as in faith and worship, our brethren profess) there might be among men so agreeing, a practical communion; especially considering that they can occasionally join with us in those other things, concerning which their principles differ, which could not but put us in hope that some expedient to salve [*dress;* or *sic* solve?] that difficulty might the more easily have been provided. And if our brethren may be neither members nor pastors of any of our congregations, how come they, or what calling have they to have any ministerial

nobody
contradicting

relation at all unto them? They preach to them, they receive maintenance from them, when a delinquent pastor has been sequestered, they have entered upon his place, and received the profits of it; we know our brethren do not preach to our people as apostles, evangelists, or prophets; nor without any ministerial mission: and if they preach the Word to them *virtute* *by virtue of* *muneris*, as the ministers of Christ, and as unto professed Christians, not *office* as unto pagans (as we hope they do), why they may not stand in relation of membership as well as ministry or teaching, *eousque* at least as they do *in so far* doctrinally agree with us, we know no cause. We look upon preaching the Word as an office, which no man ought to exercise except he be sent (Romans 10:15). If our brethren may be unto our congregations *aliquousque &* *to some extent* *quoad hoc* officers, why not in like manner members? Especially since we *and thus far* believe our brethren's judgment is that men may be members in a church wherein there are not (either out of the exigency, or out of the iniquity of the times) all the ordinances distinctly to be found in being, much less in perfection. The church of Israel was forty years together without circumcision in the wilderness: and is it unlawful for Christians who live in kingdoms where there are not in ecclesiastical congregations every office or ordinance, suppose deacons, or ruling elders, or the like (the doctrine and worship being otherwise pure), to live as members of those churches? If they may so do notwithstanding the total want of one ordinance, why may not our brethren do the like with us, notwithstanding a gradual defect only in another, especially when some expedient is endeavored to cure that defect as to them; and when separation, both by the intrinsical evil of itself, and by the example which is thereby given unto as many as will to despise our churches, and by the pernicious use which ill minded men may make of it to hinder both reformation in the church and tranquillity in the state, does evidently threaten so much danger unto us.

They tell us: "that the Honorable Houses think not meet [*suitable*] as yet to give power to the ministers by a law to purge the congregations so far as the assembly itself desires." They herein intimate that the assembly has desired a power to be given to the ministers more than the Houses think fit to grant. We desire our brethren to show where the assembly has desired or advised the power which they conceive needful for ordering of the church to be placed in the ministers, without mentioning of others who concur with them. If they cannot, they must give us leave to look on such expressions, rather as artifices than as arguments. But have our brethren at all waited to see what the Honorable Houses with the advice of the assembly would do in the reformation of the church? Did they forbear separation till it appeared what power the houses would grant? Did not they anticipate the advice of the assembly, and the resolutions of the Parliament in gathering churches out of ours, before they could foresee, or be able with a judgment either of truth or charity to conclude that our churches notwithstanding reformation begun, promised, covenanted, would continue indeed as to them unreformed[?] [S]till why do they argue from what the houses think not meet to do, or from what the assembly has thought fit to advise, when themselves thought meet to separate before the one or the other was known? Sure we are that we are little beholding to our brethren, for helping forwards those desires of ours for such a measure of reformation as themselves acknowledge to be good, and we believe to be sufficient, when one of them has publicly professed *that he would not join with us while he lived,* and it was said in the open assembly that *though the thing we desire was good, yet they would not concur with us in it, because it would be an hindrance unto them.* But for our parts, though our brethren refuse to join with us in what themselves acknowledge to be good, yet we doubt not but God who has ſtirred up the Honorable Houses to begin so happy a reformation, will by them in His good time consummate it, though our brethren withdraw their assiſtance. And yet we cannot see what singular excellency the reformation which our brethren would seem to aim at, has above what the assembly has advised. For they have told us that they would admit Anabaptiſts (and we suppose upon the same grounds Antinomians and Arminians) into communion; and one of our brethren has said *that in their way, if a man declare himself willing to join with them in all the ordinances of Chriſt so far as he knows, this is covenant sufficient to join himself with them.*[1] We think that moſt in our churches within the power of the Parliament have undertaken as much, as this comes to, in the national covenant.

They add, "that they have not presumed to seek the alteration of the rule eſtablished." 1. They endeavor to make it void in all reſpeċts unto themselves. 2. They presume to praċtice contrary to it without civil sanċtion or toleration, which we conceive comes much nearer to the formal nature of a *in process* presumption, than when a reformation is but begun, and *in fieri,* for those who are called together to advise about it, by way of humble petition, to desire not the alteration, but the further perfeċtion of the rule. 3. To seek a total exemption from a rule, has surely more of confidence in it, than to desire that, unto that which is done already, more may be added with a purpose to submit to all. Our brethren seek no alteration in the rule, because they intend not to be subjeċt to it. 4. The more defeċtive the rule is, the more color will they have for separation and gathering of churches, and are likely to gain the more people from us: we wonder not at all that our brethren being vigilant enough upon their own intereſt, do not seek *for the better* an alteration of the rule *in melius* when it might tend to the prejudice of that; we believe their piety would diċtate and juſtify as great a presumption as this they ſpeak of, if their wisdom did not look upon it as inconvenient to themselves.

---

1. [Jeremiah Burroughs, *Irenicum: To the Lovers of Truth and Peace* (1645; London: Dawlman, 1653), p. 70.]

They say, "The rule for purging the parishes given up by the assembly itself to the Honorable Houses, is not only short, but exclusive of what we in our consciences think is required by God for the qualification of members."[1]

Though our brethren tell us in their paper afterwards that a short man is not to be stretched to the length of a taller; yet we cannot but wonder at their modesty, which—when the rule given is not only short, but exclusive of what God requires—does not presume to seek the alteration of it; we assure ourselves that the Honorable Houses are so tender of the truth of God, as never to esteem that presumption which seeks the alteration of that that is exclusive of what God requires; but withal we wonder likewise at this whole expression of theirs. In their last paper they told us that they had the same rule for qualification of members which the assembly itself holds forth. Here they say our rule is exclusive of what they in conscience think is required, *nemo tam prope tam proculque nobis*;[2] this constrains us to importune them for their rule for qualification of members that it may be clearly laid down and debated.

"So that it is not in view," they say, "to us how the parishes shall be reformed to that which will satisfy our consciences;" we think this is no good argument for separating from true churches, because it is not to us in view how they shall be reformed; but so long as reformation is *in fieri*, we judge it more consonant to piety and Christian unity, to wait upon God, till we see what issue His power and providence will bring things unto. In the meantime we long to know, and have desired in the assembly, what reformation of our parishes will satisfy our brethren's consciences, or how this kingdom may be made the kingdom of the Lord and of his Christ, better than by dividing the inhabitants of it into several parts by the bounds of their dwelling that all who give up their names to Christ, may be taught and governed, and have all ordinances administered among them suitable to their condition.

---

1. [The assembly had been debating the directory for excommunication since October 14, 1644 and intensely in January, approving advice and directory on February 3, 1645, the day after the brethren drafted their fourth paper (*Minutes*, 3.399, 524; Doc. 57–58, 5.167, 168–172). On February 2, the accommodation committee had reported a vote of January 23 to the Commons, "That, there being an Inclination to bear with our Brethren in the Matter of Subordination, both for People and Ministers, a very great Impediment, likely to hinder the Work committed to this Committee, is the Want of a full Rule for purging the Congregations, in point of receiving the Sacrament, and choosing fit Officers; and therefore it is desired, That the Members of the Honourable Houses, who are Members of this Committee, do communicate so much to the several Houses respectively: And do desire that some effectual and speedy Course may be taken herein, as may seem best to the Wisdom of the Honourable Houses" (*Journal*, 4 February 1645, vol. 4, p. 428). On February 4, the Commons declined to take up the question. The period was apparently a tense one. In the debate of January 3, the "whole Assembly cried" out perhaps not with little frustration, that Goodwin and Burroughs were misconstruing their intent regarding the minister's "voice" in excommunication (Gillespie, 99).]

2. [*nemo tam prope tam proculque nobis*. "*So near and yet so far*." "Quisquam est tam prope tam proculque nobis." Marcus Valerius Martialis, Epigram 87, line 10. Lightfoot uses the phrase in a sermon. *Works* (1822), volume 6, Sermons, 112.]

REPLY TO THE FOURTH PAPER OF THE DISSENTING BRETHREN

They allege the example of the assembly; "As the divines," they say, "of the reverend assembly have said *they cannot without sin administer the ordinances to the parishes as they stand,* so neither can we continue or become members or pastors according to our principles and we humbly desire that our consciences may be considered herein for forbearance, as our brethren desire that theirs may for power of a law." What sect in the kingdom is there which may not plead exemption from the rule, and liberty to act what itself thinks fit by such an argument as this? The assembly never refused communion in parochial churches, nor disliked the distinguishing of congregations by local bounds; but they cannot administer to wicked and scandalous persons in those parishes. Such men are on all hands confessed to be apparently unworthy—does it follow that because we do desire a power to keep away those who are truly scandalous upon principles confessed by all; therefore they upon error of judgment (as we suppose) may desire a power to keep away those who are not scandalous, but as to knowledge and visible conversation duly qualified? They would fain make our desire look like a desire of power, theirs only as a desire of forbearance, when in truth they desire a greater power than we either do or dare desire. We desire to keep away only those that are scandalous, and to have a rule to strengthen us therein. They do not only keep all such away, but many more, without either rule warranting them, or a forbearance permitting them. Some better way would be found out to further their own desires, than by misrepresenting ours.

Their second paragraph is in these words: "If we could, yet according to what is proposed, we must for ever want [*lack*] that great ordinance of the Lord's Supper, which cannot but much prejudice us to the elders and members of the congregation from whose communion we thus separate, and yet we must be under their government and censures thus prejudiced by us, which how unreasonable it will be, we desire our brethren to consider."

We *answer:* 1. That it does not follow if they be members of our congregations that they must for ever want the Lord's Supper; except they will say that unto the receiving of the Lord's Supper, it is necessarily requisite that a man be a formal member of that congregation where he receives it. If they affirm this, what then becomes of their occasional communion? If not, why may not some expedient satisfy them in this to prevent so great an evil as separation? For they here do themselves profess separation from communion with us.

2. We may not do evil for any good end, if a man should be brought to such a strait, as that either he must want the Lord's Supper, or separate from the congregation whereof he is a member, he may here want the ordinance (during this error of his conscience) with less danger, than to purchase it by a sinful separation. This is a strange and dangerous way of arguing, which may open a gap to as many divisions and subdivisions in the church as

the errors are unto which the minds of men are subject. If one man's conscience cannot allow the Word preached but according to a diverse fancy which he has framed to himself, another not hold communion where infants are baptized, another not receive the Lord's Supper but after his own supper, or in such kind of bread or wine as is not in use or the like; if such persuasions of conscience, when men cannot receive the ordinances but according to their own private principles, shall be sufficient ground for renouncing of membership, we desire our brethren to consider how long not our churches only, but their own, or any other churches in the world, shall be free from incurable unquietness.

3. If our brethren's consciences through error do cause prejudice against them, is it unreasonable for them to be under the government of that church which is prejudiced by them? May they with good reason scandalize the church by separation, and the church have no reason to govern them? Then prejudicating or scandalizing errors are a *supersedeas* to all govern- *stay of* ment—we do not then wonder that error and perverse opinions so much *suspension* abound; it may be they are all but the *mediums* to liberty, and exemptions from government.

4. There can no such prejudice remain against them, if what they do, they do only by virtue of a special indulgence.

In their third paragraph they say, "All this supposes also that we are to be under the government of a church whereof we are not members, for we account not living in the parishes to be sufficient to make a member of a church, nor did many of you."

What our brethren mean by *all this* we know not; we are sure there is no such supposition can be drawn out of the words of our proposition against which this paper of our brethren does militate. It has not one word of government to this sense in it, but only of communion. It does not suppose men to be under the government of a church whereof they are not members, but it does expressly suppose that they may be members in a church, and hold a practical communion so far as they do doctrinally agree, and to those purposes having forbearance as to those other ordinances wherein they differ: But it is worth the observing how our brethren avoid government by withdrawing of membership, cut out their names as it were out of the college book, that they may free themselves from the discipline thereof. What heresy, schism, or scandal has not by this means a ready way to escape all government? We grant that living in parishes is not sufficient to make a member. A Turk, or pagan, or idolater may live within the bounds of a parish, and yet be no member of a church. A man must therefore first in order of nature be a member of the church visible, and then living in a parish, and making profession of Christianity, he may claim admission into the society of Christians within those bounds, and enjoy the privileges and ordinances which are there dispensed.

In their fourth paragraph they say, "It supposes this ground, the reason of which we see not, only the charity of it we cannot but wonder at, that because we come so near in doctrine and worship and communion with you, therefore we must not have an indulgence in a difference which yet concerns the edification of our souls by ordinances that are so necessary."

We think our proposition was not so destitute either of reason or charity as our brethren would seem to charge upon it. The reason in it was this: that doctrinal agreement should preserve practical communion in the things wherein that agreement stood. The charity this: 1. That we did desire to continue fellow members with our brethren in church unity and to prevent separation. 2. That for that purpose we did advise some expedient to be endeavored how to bear with them in the particulars wherein they cannot agree with us; if not withstanding our agreement in most things, and those most substantial, nothing will satisfy our brethren, but a separation from us (the word is their own in the second paragraph) and they cannot be edified without scandalizing the church of God, we leave it to all men to judge whose charity is greatest— theirs who labor to preserve union, or theirs who resolve to separate and break it. We think that charity binds Christians to prevent all unjust and needless separation; and suppose Brownists, Anabaptists[1] or Antinomians were in our brethren's congregations, and they should find out some expedient to hold communion still with them, and so prevent their separation, would this be esteemed a breach of charity? Or is all expedient to this purpose impossible, save only renouncing of membership? Our brethren must give us leave to wonder at their charity as well as they do at ours that coming so near to us in doctrine and worship, nothing should content them but a separation.

Thus far our brethren have made observations upon our advice; in all that follows they endeavor to answer the reasons of it; where we cannot by the way but take notice what an edge our brethren have against uniformity, and how hastily (as it is said of Benhadad's servants) they catch at that word to make a large discourse upon it, although had that word been left out of our paper, the force of the reason would have been the very same which now it is.

---

1. ["Thomas Goodwin one day was exceedingly confounded. He has undertaken a publick lecture against the Anabaptists: it was said, under pretence of refuting them, he betrayed our cause to them. That of the Corinthians, our chief ground for baptism of infants, 'Your children are holy,' he exponed of a real holiness, and preached down our ordinary and necessary distinction of real and federal holiness. Being posed hereupon, he could no ways clear himself, and no man took his part. God permits these gracious men to be many ways unhappy instruments. As yet their pride continues; but we are hopeful the parliament will not own their way so much as to tolerate it, if once they found themselves masters. For the time they are loth to cast them off, and to put their party to despair, lest they desert them. The men are exceeding active in their own way. They strive to advance Cromwell for their head." Baillie, to Spang, August 10, 1644, 2.49.]

Their answer to our reasons is partly argumentative, and partly historical; we shall briefly consider both. They tell us, 'That the uniformity sworn in the covenant is not only here upon this occasion, but continually, on the like, turned as the great argument against them in pulpits, presses, and ordinary treaties, as if what they desired were contrary thereunto.' How it is elsewhere turned against them by others we know not. If any do it either uncharitably or irrationally (which we believe none that are wise and fear God would do), let them answer for themselves; but sure[ly] by how much the more they hear of it abroad, by so much the more reason have they to lay it to heart, and to consider whether that great growth of sects and errors in the church, under which it so much groans at this day, have not occasionally, at the least and in part, grown out of that liberty, and those principles for latitude and deformity as well in practice as in judgment, which our brethren so much plead for and allow unto themselves. But for our mentioning it in this paper, we think it very seasonable and suitable to the matter for which we allege it, not with any desire of opposition, or to turn it against our brethren as their phrase is, but out of a sincere zeal to the peace of God's church, and to the preventing of unnecessary separation, which we cannot but think would in time prove the occasion of schisms and errors against which we have covenanted.

They tell us, 'that this argument cannot hold against them without affixing an interpretation upon that part of the covenant, according to our own principles only, to the prejudice of theirs.'

Our proposition was never intended for an argument against them, but for a means of accommodation between them and us; and that reason and argument which is in them, is not drawn from any private interpretation of the covenant (which we dare not assume the liberty to affix thereunto, however our brethren would insinuate the contrary), but from the words themselves. The words are that *we will endeavor the nearest conjunction and uniformity;* now we think from the immediate and grammatical sense of these words without any explication at all, the evidence of our reason does appear: That since we have covenanted to endeavor the nearest conjunction and uniformity, therefore in those things wherein we profess to be of one mind and judgment that conjunction should be practically preserved.

They add, 'When we took this national covenant, we were known to be of the same principles we now are of; and yet this covenant was professedly so attempered in their first framing of it, as that we of different judgments might take it, both parties being present at the framing of it in Scotland.'

We know not how far their principles were then known. They might have been much better known would they have given a free and full account of their judgment to the world in an affirmative way, and not always kept themselves on the negative part, to object and dispute against the affirmations of others; nor do we know how their principles could then well be known, matters of government not being then when the covenant was debated before the assembly till afterwards. But we wonder our brethren should be so intimately acquainted with negotiations of ſtate, as to tell us that the covenant was professedly attempered to different principles and to different parties. It seems to us an indecent assertion, and tending rather to division than union that commissioners were sent into the kingdom of Scotland as different parties to be treated with under such a notion; sure *reservation* we are, our brethren did not take the covenant with any *salvo* to their own principles; and if it were made as a national covenant (as we know it was) what reason is there to think that it was particularly attempered to them, more than others who have consciences as well as they? Does not this seem to lay an implicit obligation upon the parliaments of both kingdoms, as if neither of them might do anything in prejudice of our brethren's principles, leaſt it be interpreted as done contrary to the professed temper of the covenant, and consequently to the scope of it? These to us are ſtrange intimations.

They further add, "if this should be the way of urging, it is as free for us to give our interpretation of the latitude on nearness of uniformity intended, as for our brethren, we having been present at the debates of the assembly about it, and well know and remember the sense which was there held forth thereof."

For our parts, as we think it not free either for us or them or any private person, to make interpretations of the covenant, so we deny that we have done it; we have argued from the very words themselves, and so we all muſt do, or else we can make no use of it. As for the sense held forth in the assembly, which our brethren so well know and remember, we remember *Lightfoot, 11* indeed that the assembly gave their sense by vote touching prelacy, which was after inserted into the body of the article; but for other particulars concerning which no vote passed, this we know, that no member of the assembly could give any other sense but their own as single persons, nothing being the sense of the assembly, but what appears to be so by their order or resolve; and that if one ſpeak anything as his sense, the reſt being silent, their silence is not to be taken for a consent.

They tell us, "That further when the assembly was appointed by an order of the Honorable House of Commons bearing date September 15, 1643, to *Minutes, 2.124* set forth in a declaration the grounds that have induced the assembly to *Lightfoot, 14* give their opinions that this covenant may be taken in point of conscience; accordingly some of them were by a committee entruſted to bring in materials to that purpose, and accordingly did, which materials were committed to one of them by a subcommittee to draw up, and among many other things that which follows as grounds of taking the covenant, as touching that firſt article that we shall endeavor," etc.

Whatever was done by one or more of these brethren by way of comment upon the covenant or any article thereof, was not done according to the fore-mentioned order, seeing it requires only a declaration of the grounds upon which the assembly gave their opinion concerning the lawfulness of taking the covenant, not an explication of what private men conceived to be the meaning of it; and surely that which is here obtruded as the sense, and the only sense in which these brethren judge it lawful, never passed the vote, never was so much as debated in the assembly, and therefore cannot possibly come within the compass of those grounds which the order relates to. But that which we wonder most at, is that our brethren should a little before charge us without cause (as has been showed) of a crime, and should presently fall into the same themselves; for what is, if this be not, to affix an interpretation upon the covenant suitable to the principles of one party, and exclusive to those of another? But we proceed to the explication itself.

"This endeavor," they say, "in our places and callings for uniformity, we apprehended the meaning of it to be that as in our ranks and ſtations we should endeavor it, so according to those general warrants of the Word to regulate such an endeavor in the use of means whereby to accomplish it; and therefore as for the pattern, the Word of God is to be in our eye, so for the way and means and progress in reducing the church to such an uniformity, such rules are to be observed as the nature of such a work will bear, and which the apoſtles who had infallibly observed in reducing the Jews and those of the circumcision, and the Gentiles to a uniformity, and without tyranny or pressing men's consciences beyond the several degrees of light, which God vouchsafes to several churches more or less," etc.

Our brethren here give us such an explication of uniformity, as indeed may suite to any the moſt difformous [*deformed*] churches that are, who will all tell us that they propose to themselves the right pattern, rules and examples, and from thence are inſtructed unto deformity with others; it is not an uniformity of endeavor which we are bound only unto, but to endeavor an uniformity in the particulars expressed, namely, *as in doctrine and worship, so in form of church government.* We all moſt readily agree that the Word of God is the rule in all reſpects for reformation, and the apoſtles examples to be followed in all things of perpetual equity, but does not the Word of God *press upon us unity of judgment and practice, to be of one mind, of one accord, not to cause divisions and offenses contrary to the doctrine which we have learned; to ſpeak the same things, to be perfectly joined together in the same judgments; that there be no divisions among us* (2 Corinthians 13:11; Philippians 2:1, 2; Romans 16:17; 1 Corinthians 1:10)? Or did the apoſtles ever endeavor such a uniformity, or so much as call it so, as was nothing else but a doing every man according to his own light, or to use the phrase of the Old Teſtament that *which is right in his own eyes?*[1] Did they not suppress the contentions of men by *the cuſtom of the churches of God* (1 Corinthians

---

1. [Deuteronomy 12:8; Judges 17:6; Judges 21:25; Proverbs 12:15; Proverbs 21:2.]

11:16), and ordain the same practice in all the churches, not withstanding our brethren's distinction of difference of light (1 Corinthians 7:17)? For the case which our brethren mention of reducing those of the circumcision and the Gentiles to a uniformity, were they not thereunto brought by a synodical determination (Acts 15)? And did not the apostles bind the burden of some necessary things on the churches, albeit there were in those churches gradual differences of light?

We could be glad our brethren had explained themselves when they speak of "tyranny and pressing men's consciences," because under that pretense many oppose all kind of government, and many most injuriously represent presbyterial government as formidable and tyrannical. Our brethren in their way exercise the same kind of power, and that with more rigor; the relief which the law of nature allows to appeal from an unjust sentence, to a power which may correct it, they deny. Christian professors, though neither ignorant nor scandalous, they shut the door against, and keep out of communion. They do doctrinally and practically condemn all churches which are not independent, refusing all membership and ordinary communion in them, and may according to their principles assume a power to inflict the heavy sentence of *non-communion* upon them, when we suppose our brethren will grant these two things: 1. That a member of a particular congregation may be excommunicated for heresy or schism. 2. That the officers of several churches may convene, and pronounce a sentence of non-communion upon other churches. Surely except our brethren resolve to tolerate all sects and heresies, whatsoever, they also may soon lie under the charge and *odium* of tyranny.

They proceed and tell us: "Although there be one pattern in our eye in common, which all our consciences swear to bring all to; yet *de facto*, and in the providence of God, it so falls out in the reforming of churches (now after antichristianism has overspread and corrupted all), that the light grows every age more and more to the perfect day, and the coming of Christ, who is to melt that man of sin by the increasing brightness of his coming [2 Thessalonians 2:8], and so both the persons and churches, some see more, some see less, as we see in the Reformed churches at this day, and will certainly fall out thus in these of ours. Now therefore in this case, the rule for effecting uniformity must certainly be no other than what the Apostle gives (Philippians 3[:16]). *As far as we have attained let us walk by the same rule.* And therefore the way is to see how far we have attained, and set down wherein we agree (as in all substantials of faith and worship it is certain we shall) and so to walk by that as the same rule; and then in such matters wherein we are otherwise minded, to leave it to God, and such good means that God may reveal it to them in His time as His promise is."

We easily understand what our brethren mean by the overspreading of antichristianism, and how they do tacitly charge all who dissent from them with no meaner a guilt; and they tell us of the *increase of light, which must melt the man of sin*. If our brethren mean by *Antichrist* or the *man of sin* that which the Reformed churches have generally understood, namely, the Papacy, we do not think but that in the great differences between them and us, the light already revealed is clear and sufficient enough for conviction, and manifesting of the errors thereof; and we believe if our brethren were employed in that conflict, notwithstanding they appropriate the increase of light unto their way at this time, yet they would not use any more convincing weapons against the man of sin than the champions of the Reformed churches both in these and other kingdoms have formerly used. We shall not at this time curiously examine whether the Apostle by ἐπιφάνεια τῆς παρουσίας [2 Thessalonians 2:8], which they render the increasing brightness of his coming (we know not upon what either ground or authority), means light of the gospel, or the second coming of Christ to judgment, or some other notable manifestation of Christ's presence in ways of power and justice and shaking the earth. But let us admit what our brethren say, that antichristianism is to be melted away by a growing light, does any such growing light appear at this time? We confess there is great crying up of new lights; but under that notion do not old and decried errors of Anabaptism, Antinomianism, Brownism, yea Arrianism and Photinianism, break forth to the great scandal of the church? Surely the new lights we now hear of in the most places are no other in the church than a comet in the heavens, which does only ill lighten men to foresee calamities. Whatever this light is, must it not increase in the next age as well as in this? and must that new light then melt away the antichristianism of Independency as that does in this age the antichristianism of presbytery? and shall government in every age be changed according to differences of light? Have not our brethren found out a *jus divinum* for their way in Scripture? We so understand them; and must some increasing brightness hereafter abolish that? To us such principles tend to very skepticism and to a floating suspense and continual uncertainly and unpersuasion of judgment.

We heartily embrace the rule which our brethren give us out of the apostle (Philippians 3:15, 16), and desire to walk by it. But did the apostle ever intend out of that place to allow brethren who agree in all substantials of faith and worship to separate from one another, etc., to deny fellowship and communion with one another, even in those very substantials wherein they agree? Is this to walk by the same rule, and to mind the same things, to separate from churches in those very things wherein we agree with them? Or shall every circumstantial difference be a sufficient ground to withdraw communion totally and to all purposes? When there were differences of judgment among the Corinthians and Romans, did not the Apostle write to them as one church, as one body? Did he ever suppose that a few differences should be sufficient grounds for extinguishing the mutual relation of membership which they had in those churches? Besides, may not the magistrate out of a care to preserve the churches which are under his government and protection, in unity, and free from schisms and divisions, allow one way of government, and disallow another, as they have done in the case of the liturgy and directory, and in the case of episcopacy and presbytery, without reserving a *salvo* for such as shall in judgment differ from the alteration which they have made? Or must episcopal men be indulged separated dioceses wherein to worship God and enjoy ordinances suitably to such principles as they hold, distinctly from the churches under another rule? Surely if our brethren's principles extend to such a latitude for other men's judgments as well as for their own, which we know no reason why they should not, they put them in a fitter temper to covenant multiformity than uniformity.

They go on: 'But if a uniformity for uniformity's sake (and so the argument of our brethren here runs); that is, affecting uniformity so much as not to regard men's consciences, should be pressed and urged by such means as formerly, without respect had to the variety of light in matters of a lesser nature, this were beyond the callings and warrants of the Word, and will prove a perfect tyranny; and will be so far from being a means of love, which is aimed at, that it will lay the foundation of confusion and dissension as formerly it did. It is with churches as with men, and particular saints, they are of several sizes and growth, of several statures; and as men are left to be more or less holy, as God by good means shall make them, so must churches; as it were against nature to stretch a low man to the same length with a taller, for uniformity's sake, so to bring both more grown or more reformed churches to a middle stature for compliance with others for mere uniformity's sake?'

We know not what our brethren mean by "uniformity for uniformity's sake." We think they asperse us in such expressions as if we laid grounds for tyranny, or intended not to respect the consciences of men. We desire uniformity for order, and order for edification. We desire it as is expressed in the letter of the covenant, by which our brethren are bound as well as we.

But they say "to desire it without respect to variety of lights in lesser *in the nature* matters," etc. Certainly separation is not either *in natura rei* or in the con*of the case* sequences of it so small a thing as our brethren make it. But we wonder our brethren should mention variety of light here so often, when it is plain that the mention we make of uniformity covenanted, was in order unto their communion with us in those things only wherein they and we have an unity of light, *viz.* in the substantials of faith and worship, wherein we desire no more of them than we are confident was practiced by the saints of Philippi, to whom the apostle directs that rule our brethren make mention of, namely, to hold practical communion in things wherein they doctrinally agree; certainly this can never prove a perfect *tyranny;* though for aught we perceive, anything which is *one* must be judged the foundation of *tyranny*. But to touch that point of variety of light, we desire our brethren to answer us in this one thing: whether some must be denied the liberty of their conscience in matter of practice, or none? If none, then we must all renounce our covenant, and let in prelacy again, and all others' ways. If a denial of liberty unto some may be just, then uniformity may be settled notwithstanding variety of lights, without any tyranny at all.

We acknowledge degrees of light and growth among men, and do not affirm that some must be kept under for conformity's sake with those who are worse than themselves; or that all matters of difference in judgment must be authoritatively decided for uniformity's sake; yet hence it does not follow but that as *one confession of faith and one directory of worship, so also one form of government and constitution of churches* may be settled. For we are sure that in this general our brethren agree with us that one way for the substance of it is necessary for all, though touching the particulars we are at difference; and the oneness of the way (if it be right) can be no hindrance to Christian growth, nor the diversities of growth unto it. Are not Christians of several statures in France, Holland, Scotland, where the government is but one? May not churches differ in light and agree in government?

They say, "As men are left to be more or less holy, as God by good means shall make them, so are churches." Must men be left to themselves to be more or less holy as they please, under no discipline to further holiness in them? If not, what argument can our brethren draw from such a proposition between men and churches? We embrace the proportion, and from thence argue, as men though of different growth in light, ought not to be independent and exempt from government, so neither particular churches; and as men thus differing may be under one uniform government, so also may churches.

For our brethren's similitude of low men and tall men, though it be pretty and plausible, yet our brethren know such are but popular and inartificial arguments, which have more of flourish than of substance in them. For would our brethren apply this argument against endeavoring to bring low and middle statured churches to a more grown and more reformed condition, because a low body is not to be stretched to the stature of a taller? Why then do they so much endeavor to gather churches out of ours unto themselves? Or if the magistrate should think fit to settle their way by a law, would they allow a toleration to Episcopacy, Presbytery, Brownism, Erastianism, or any other government excogitable [*contrived*] by the fancies of men upon this reason, because men must not for uniformity's sake be pared or stretched to the measure of other men? Would they endure the lower suckers at the roots of their tree to grow till they had killed the tree itself? *Ad populum phaleras.*[1] But since they will use such kind of

---

1. [*Ad populum phaleras.* "Ad populum phaleras. Ego te intus et in cute novi." Persius

arguments, we muſt needs learn of them who is the low man, and who the tall, leaſt the low man be cut yet shorter by uniformity, or the tall man ſtretched taller; though they know without ſtretching or cutting, long and short timber may be employed in one and the same building, and tall men and little children be members of one and the same family without separating from one another. But did the apoſtles and elders of Jerusalem cut tall men and ſtretch low men when they ordered necessary things for mutual peace? We will not envy our brethren their tallness; we will desire to be low in our own eyes as well as we are in theirs. We confess *our day* is but *the day of small things* [Zechariah 4:10]; yet we hope it is a time of love; far be it from us to say we are rich and ſtand in need of nothing; yet we hope when presbyterian government is [set] up, we shall labor both by our miniſtry and discipline *to present our members blameless before Chriſt*. Our brethren have nothing but what they have received; and time was when he who was taller than all his brethren by the head was laid aside, and a low and lowly person came in his room.

It follows in our brethren's paper: "And this suites as with the rules of the Word, so with the scope of the article; for look what kind of uniformity in confession of faith, the like in matter of worship and government is to be intended; and that the rather because directions for government and worship are the more remote from all Chriſtian's knowledge, and perhaps more obscure in the Word, and are the ſpecial controversies of the times; now as in matters of faith you would not for uniformity's sake determine all differences in judgment, but fundamentals, and as uniformity therein is all intended; so by analogy in point of worship and government. And secondly, the end is that God may dwell amongſt us, Who is the Author of peace and not of confusion in all the churches, which peace (while in His providence men's judgments do and will differ) will never be attained by a rigid uniformity."

We alleged uniformity covenanted for this end, that in those things wherein we agree doctrinally we might agree practically, and not separate as to those purposes; and our brethren throughout this paper diſpute againſt it with reſpect to variety of lights; surely they will not easily persuade us, or (we think) any indifferent men to believe that it was not the scope of the covenant that where there was unity in judgment, there should be at leaſt so far forth uniformity in practice and communion; surely if the covenant intend but one confession of faith and one directory for worship, we cannot see how our brethren can make the scope of it to favor diverse
for granted ways of discipline and church government. But taking all *pro concesso*, we further answer that as in matters of faith we do not for uniformity's sake determine all differences in judgment but fundamentals; so when all do

---

Flaccus, *Satires*, III.30. "Away with those trappings to the vulgar; I know thee both inwardly and outwardly." i.e. 'I know the man too well to be deceived by appearances.']

agree in fundamentals, if any should for some small differences in judgment separate from communion with true churches, we should think that those men did sin against that unity which ought to be amongst Christians so fundamentally agreeing. In like manner, though in matters of government being more obscure and remote from Christian knowledge, difference of judgment, and haply in some things of practice also, may be allowed; yet when in the most things and those most substantial, there is an agreement, for brethren upon smaller differences not to content themselves with such expedients as may be provided to reconcile those differences, but to separate from communion with true churches of Christ, we cannot but believe it to be contrary to the Word of God and to the scope and letter of the covenant. And we would willingly understand from our brethren what disjunction or deformity is contrary to the covenant, if this be not, to have divided practice and separated communion even in those things wherein men have united judgments, or when the peace of the church is likely to be preserved, if men will not keep communion with one another, no not in those things wherein they do doctrinally agree; for our brethren do all along insist upon a wrong ground, namely, difference of judgment, when in our proposition the uniformity mentioned is evidently restricted unto unity of judgment.

Our brethren conclude this long paragraph thus: "But this order of the Honorable House of Commons so necessary for the satisfaction of all differing judgments, as at first, to take the covenant, so to continue steadfast therein, and which would in all likelihood have laid a foundation of ending this and other differences, was superseded to this day."

That there was an order, and superseded, we acknowledge; but that it was intended for the satisfaction of different judgments we deny. It is but their presumption so to affirm. The use these brethren made of it was upon pretense of such a declaration to have given in their private sense of the covenant, which they very much contended for, and the committee of the assembly together with the commissioners from the church of Scotland opposed as destructive and inconsistent with the end of the covenant.

For the *superseding* of it, we give this account:

1. Whereas other orders from the Honorable House were wont to be sent by members of their own, this was given by one of the under clerks to one of the messengers, who brought it to the scribe of the assembly after it had lain in the office many days.

2. Upon debate it was found that these brethren (whose great care to secure their own principles, and long travail to be delivered of that private sense, which themselves had conceived, were sufficiently known) labored to turn it to a wrong use for their private interest and advantage, as appeared *Minutes, 3.283* by many circumstances, and in this especially that one of them though he was in Scotland, or in his journey from thence, and not at the assembly

when they debated and resolved the case of conscience touching the covenant, would yet undertake to set down the reason which moved the assembly to judge the covenant lawful to be taken in point of conscience.

3. It was the advice and counsel of some eminent members of the Honorable House of Commons, who were of the committee from the house to join with the divines of the assembly, and the commissioners from Scotland, about the business that this order should not be proceeded upon without further direction from the house.

4. There was an ordinance of Parliament bearing date February 2, 1643, wherein among other things it was ordained Article 10: *That for the better encouragement of all sorts of persons to take the covenant, it be recommended to the assembly of divines to make a brief declaration by way of exhortation to all sorts of persons to take it, as that which they judge not only lawful, but (all things considered) exceeding expedient and necessary for all that wish well to religion, the King and kingdom to join in, and to be a singular pledge of God's gracious goodness to all the three kingdoms.* And in Article 14, it is again remembered that *the assembly of divines do prepare an exhortation for the better taking of the covenant,* in obedience whereunto the assembly did draw up such an exhortation to satisfy the consciences of men for the taking of it; which exhortation being sent to, and read in the House of Commons, they made this order upon it, *viz. Die Veneris 9.* February 1643. *An exhortation touching the taking of the Solemn League and Covenant, and for satisfying of such scruples as may arise in the taking of it, was this day read the first and second time, and by vote upon the question assented unto, and ordered to be forthwith printed.* So

Minutes, 2.124 that in obeying that latter ordinance we conceive that both that and the
Lightfoot, 14 former order of September 15, then foregoing, and now insisted so much upon by our brethren, were fully satisfied.

Our brethren conclude thus: "2. We answer that we willingly again do profess that in the substance of worship and doctrine we are one and of the same judgment with our brethren, yet to practice and enjoy those parts of worship as ordinances of a church, there is (as to our consciences) necessarily required as the seat and subject of worship and other ordinances, a church-state; and those such churches as where we may be members, and join in communion therein as members without sin, which we cannot do as we have all along professed; and such churches as wherein we can enjoy all ordinances, which is denied us here in this paragraph. So that the only way left to reduce us to a uniformity and conjunction in the same practices, is to allow us such distinct churches from yours according to our principles, in which, and by means of which we shall hold all possible communion and conformity with yours: whereas otherwise we shall only retain a uniformity in judgment, whereas that uniformity the covenant much rather obliges you and us all unto, is that which may be a uniformity in practice, with satisfaction to all men's consciences and their edification."

Upon their professed unity with us in judgment our desire was they might continue communion and membership with us in those things wherein they so agree; here they answer, "No, they cannot do it without sin," and intimate two reasons of it: 1. Because to practice and enjoy those parts of worship as ordinances of a church, there is necessarily required as the seat and subject of worship and other ordinances, a church-state. 2. Those churches must be such, as wherein they may enjoy all ordinances, which is denied them, they say here. 1. This to us voids their occasional communion quite, for can they occasionally practice and enjoy worship and ordinances out of the seat and subject of that worship and ordinances? Or, when they preach and pray with our churches, do they not dispense those ordinances to our people as to churches of Christ who come unto the ordinances as in their proper seat to be edified and comforted by them? 2. They tell us not what their church-state is which they make the seat of ordinances, and which we want [lack], and consequently enjoy ordinances out of their right seat. They acknowledge us true churches of Christ, have not true churches the state of churches? Are not true churches the seat and subject of worship?

But they say, "They must be where they may enjoy all ordinances, which here is denied them." 1. We know not any ordinance which will be denied them in our congregations. 2. Have they all ordinances in their own churches? Do not they hold ruling elders to be an ordinance? Have all their churches ruling elders? Or may they be in their own churches without some one ordinance, and not in ours? If they should think anointing of the sick with oil, or washing of feet be an ordinance, will they be no members where they cannot enjoy these? To determine controversies of faith and cases of conscience judicially, is an ordinance. If they be of no church but where that is exercised, and the liberty of opinions judicially restrained, their churches would soon be dissolved, and they would find it we believe difficult to gather more.

As for their own expedient for uniformity and conjunction with which they conclude, namely, "to allow them distinct churches according to their own principles," we look upon it but as a riddle, and wonder how disjunction can be an only way of conjunction, and multiformity of uniformity, and separation of communion, and different principles and practices of conformity; what churches under heaven may we not hold conjunction, uniformity, communion with upon such terms?

They say, "They agree with us in judgment, but will not join in practice, but persuade us that not joining in practice is the best, the only means to attain unto that practical uniformity which the covenant principally intends," and close all up with this gloss upon uniformity in practice, "that it must be with satisfaction to all men's consciences and their edification." This to us sounds as if they did not only desire "liberty of conscience for themselves, but for all men," and would have us believe that this is all the uniformity which the covenant requires that we should "endeavor to bring the churches of God in the three kingdoms to the nearest conjunction and uniformity, yet so as that we may leave all men to the liberty of their consciences." We hope our brethren have some other meaning, yet at present these their expressions favor so much of such a sense that we cannot understand what they do mean less than this; and whether that be the sense of the covenant; we humbly leave together with this whole paper unto the consideration of this honorable committee.

After the delivery of this paper, the committee of Lords and Commons, and the Assembly of Divines adjourned to a day, but being diverted by other occasions, have not since had any meeting, and so there was no further proceeding in that business.[1]

Finis

---

1. [The Scottish edition of these documents published by Evan Tyler in addition to dropping the various orders to publish and some front matter such as the articulation of the propositions, and some of the over used italics, changed the final note to read: "The Dissenting Brethren demanded a copy of this Answer, which they were allowed to take, they promised also a Copy to it, but never performed unto this day: and so that committee gave over the business." *The Reasons of the Dissenting Brethren* ... (Edinburgh: Evan Tyler, 1648), p. 408. Cf. *The Grand Debate* (1648/1652) Committee of Accommodation Papers, p. 123. My thanks to Wayne Sparkman, Director of the PCA Historical Center, for examining the example of the Tyler edition held by the J. Oliver Buswell, Jr. Library, Covenant Theological Seminary.]

Appendix

Westminster Abbey Library:

And Other Theological Resources of the
Assembly of Divines (1643–1652)

The Westminster Assembly's Need for Books

The Westminster Assembly of Divines was preeminently a gathering of scholars, a "theological think-tank" made up of prominent theologians of the time. A "thorough study of the books available to" these divines is therefore of interest, and their *Grand Debate* affords such an opportunity.[1] However, those members of the assembly who were not from London clearly missed the use of their personal libraries. John Lightfoot raised this early in their proceedings in August 1643, and in October the divines made a request for remedy to the House of Commons.[2]

> Lightfoot, Munday. Aug. 31 [sic 21]. "The first Committee reported the aspersions upon the 3 first Articles [of the 39 Articles] & this forenoone was taken up in concluding which way to take about aspersions, whether to name the errors in the Authors owne words & under their name, which thing I vehemently opposed for this would be a worke long & tedious, & we should be sure to misse of many Authors that were enemies to these truths of our Articles, because of the distance of us all from our libraries, and the exunpectednesse [unexpectednesse] of this taske layd upon us; & so should we be censured either of incogetency or connivence: therefore I desired that we might onely name erronious opinions, but let names & their owne words alone, for opinions I knew we could not misse, but Authors we should be sure to misse of. But it was carried the other waie & voted that every Comittee should bring in aspersions under the

---

1. Chad B. Van Dixhoorn, *Reforming the Reformation: Theological Debate at the Westminster Assembly 1643–1652*. Ph.D. dissertation, University of Cambridge, 7 vols., 2004, 1.121, note 20. (Hereafter <u>Minutes</u>). This appendix is based upon previous research dealing with the fast sermons of the Scottish Commissioners. Cf. "Westminster Abbey Library and other Theological Resources of the Assembly of Divines (1643–1652)," *The Confessional Presbyterian* 6 (2010): 263–282; and *Sermons Preached Before the English Houses of Parliament by the Scottish Commissioners to the Westminster Assembly 1643–1645* (2011). *The Grand Debate* bibliography has been collated against the resources noted in this study.

2. Van Dixhoorn, Lightfoot's first journal, August 21, 1643, 2.37; <u>Minutes</u>, October 17, 1643, 3.183–184. Cf Van Dixhoorn, *The Minutes and Papers of the Westminster Assembly 1643–1652*, 5 volumes (Oxford University Press, 2012) 2.206 (hereafter *Minutes*).

379

aspersers name & wordes & the bookes also quoted for the thing, for the Assemblies ocular & full satisfaction."

[Minutes, Oct. 17] 76 Sess. 17th 1643: Tuesday Morning. "Mr Ley: A motion to disperse the bookes of a church government to the severall members of the Assembly.
Mr Goodwin: Many ministers severed from their bookes; that ther may be a provision of all those bookes in some publique place.
Mr Seaman: A request to have liberty to have some designed together out of those libraryes that are sequestered [in order to have] bookes for this purpose.
Mr White: I will move the house in this."

Lightfoot recorded for the same day as the Minutes: "Then it was propounded that we should get books of the questions that are like to fall under our hands, out of the archbishop's library, and out of the sequestered libraries, laid up in some place where we might have public and common use of them."[3]

SEQUESTERED LIBRARIES

At the outbreak of war, Parliament issued orders for the sequestration of delinquent estates.

> *Resolved*, &c. That the Fines, Rents, and Profits, of Archbishops, Bishops, Deans, Deans and Chapters, and of such notorious Delinquents, who have taken up Arms against the Parliament, or have been active in the Commission of Array, shall be sequestered for the Use and Service of the Commonwealth.[4]

The Commons had set up a committee to handle the seized estates, but also subsequently set up a committee for handling just the books of the acquired properties, and a few months later they also insisted on a careful review of any books before they were sold off. John Selden, one of the Erastian divines attending the Westminster Assembly, was on this committee for managing the sequestered libraries.

> *Ordered*, That no Books, Records, Writings, or Manuscripts, shall be sold without the Perusal, Viewing, and Directions of the Committee appointed to that Purpose, or any Two of them, according to the Ordinance, 8 *Novembris* last, notwithstanding any Order whatsoever heretofore made for the Sale of Goods sequestered: And that the Sequestrators do not sell any Books, Records, Writeings, or Manuscripts, seized by Sequestration, until they receive Order and Direction from the said Committee, or any Two of them, according to the Ordinance aforesaid.[5]

---

3. "Journal of the Proceedings of The Assembly of Divines," in *The Whole Works of the Rev. John Lightfoot*, volume 13 (London: Printed by J. F. Dove, 1824) 21.
4. *House of Commons Journal*, volume 2, 14 October 1642 (1802), 808. Hereafter HCJ.
5. HCJ 3, 13 February 1644 (1802), 398.

> *Ordered*, That Mr. *Selden*, Mr. *Rous*, Mr. *Hill*, Mr. *Young*, Sir *Simonds D'Ewes*, Mr. *Sam. Browne*, Mr. *Prideaux*, Mr. *Millington*, or any Two of them, do peruse all such Books and Manuscripts, Records, and other Monuments of Antiquity, as have been, or shall be, sequeſtred; and are now, or shall be, laid up at *Campden* House, *Savoye*, or any other Place; and to give Order, that they may not be sold, or any way embezzled or defaced; but laid safe up in such Places as they shall think fit, until further Order: And they are to certify their Proceedings herein, from time to time, to the House.[6]

Ten days previous to the forming of the committee to manage the sequeſtered books, the Commons answered the assembly's requeſt and ordered: "That the Assembly of Divines shall have Liberty and Power to go to the several Libraries within the Power of the Parliament; and to have the free Use of such Books as they shall think fit; and to have such Books brought unto them, where they sit, as they shall appoint; provided that they leave Inventories of such Books as they shall remove out of any of the said Libraries, to the end they may be well and safely reſtored unto the said Libraries, and undefaced."[7]

On 26 October the assembly received the order from the House and the Minutes note: "An order read: for sending for bookes." Lightfoot elaborates: "When we were ready to rise, there came in an order from the Parliament, which giveth the Assembly leave to fetch books out of any library forthwith in the power of the Parliament for our use, leaving an inventory of what books are fetched away; and there was a committee appointed to see what books there were to be had."[8] The Minutes then go on to note: "Mr Seaman, ~~Mr Walker, Mr Calamy, Mr Carroll~~. 4 for the citty. For Weſt[minſter]: Mr Young, Mr Hill, Mr Herle, Mr Ny or any 2 of them to search."[9]

BOOKS TAKEN BY THE ASSEMBLY FROM LAUD'S LIBRARY

One record may indicate that the number of volumes collected by these divines on their book search was not insignificant. Ann Cox-Johnson noted that Archbishop Laud's personal library fell under the sequeſtration order, of which as recorded in Lightfoot's journal, the divines were aware, and "on 20 January 1643/44 Mr Nye, accompanied by another gentleman and supported by the authority of Parliament which had so ordered on 23 October of the previous year, entered the Archbishop's private ſtudy and removed some ninety-seven books for the use of the Assembly of Divines at Weſtminſter. A hurried, almoſt illegible liſt was made of them and signed by Walter Dobson."[10]

---

6. HCJ 3, 2 November 1643 (1802), 298.

7. HCJ 3, 23 October 1643 (1802), 285. <u>Minutes</u>, 3.206; *Minutes*, 2.228.

8. "Journal of the Proceedings of The Assembly of Divines," 29–30.

9. The names are crossed out in the manuscript.

10. Ann Cox-Johnson, "Lambeth Palace Library, 1610–1664," *Transactions of the Cambridge Bibliographical Society*, volume 2 Part 2 (1955) 112. Walter Dobson was one of Laud's servants and had served the previous two Archbishops. He also helped draw up the inventory of Archbishop Bancroft's books (Cox-Johnson, 107).

As noted this liſt survives amongſt the manuscript letters of the Archbishop.[11] The liſt is more legible than Ann Cox-Johnson's brief description indicated, and a majority of the books are identifiable. The pages of the liſt are roughly size A4, with a little wear at the edges.[12] The liſt extends from fol. 130r, 130v, to half of 131r. The paper making up the pages had previously been folded into eighths (in half lengthways and then in quarters), and there are three bookworm holes near the bottom of the folio. The script is generally legible as said, but some lines are very difficult to interpret. There is some smudging on the second side of fol. 130, and the script gets more cramped towards the bottom of sides fol. 130r and 130v. The handwriting gets bigger on fol. 131r towards the end of the liſt. The following is a transcription / interpolation of the liſt. Where the text is difficult a beſt guess is given if possible.[13] Braces {} denote text that is difficult to make out or interpret, and "[?]" indicates some queſtion on letters in words so flagged. The liſt was not numbered in the manuscript, but these have been added for ease of reference. If a work is referenced in the Assembly Minutes, the session is noted in brackets.

[fol. 130r]

**Bookes taken out of the ArchB^{pp}s owne Library att
Lambeth Jan: ^{20th} 1643: for the use of the Assembly
of Devines nowe sitting att Westminster**

1. Binnius de Concily's Tom: 5 fol°[14]
2. Sr Tho: Ridley vewe of the civil lawe 4°[15]
3. Crakenthorp on the 5th general Council 4°[16]
4. Linwood Ecclesiastical laws – 3 vol: one in fol: othere in 4° and in 16°[17]
5. Grotius de Jure Belli et Pacis fol[18] [Sess. 114, 157.]
6. Tena on Epist: ad Hebreos[19]

---

11. Bodleian Library, S.C. 14994, fo. 130–131. The tally is ninety-eight entries with one possible duplication, 1–40 on 130r, 41–84 on 130v, and the remaining on the top portion of 131r.

12. This list was the only matter in the volume relative to the assembly. My thanks to Jonathan Vaughan for gaining access to the manuscript list and providing a description and rough transcript with detailed photographs. From the photographs I have refined the transcription significantly and provided the interpolations. I also thank David C. Lachman and Chad Van Dixhoorn for their aid with several of the difficult entries.

13. Of the 98 titles, the majority are fairly identifiable. I could not identify the work by Thomas Browne in #90, and #86 remains uncertain. For almost all the remaining, excepting the tract bundles, I was at least able to offer suggestions or possibilities.

14. Severin Binius, *Concilia generalia, et provincilia.*

15. Sir Thomas Ridley, *A View of the Civile and Ecclesiaſtical Law.*

16. Richard Crakanthorp, *A treatise of the fiſt general councel held at Conſtantinople, anno 553, under Juſtinian … Pope Vigilius.*

17. Apparently William Lyndwood, *Conſtitutiones Angliæ prouinciales ex diuersis Cantuariensium Archiepiscoporum synodalibus decretis, per Guilielmum Lyndewode Anglum iam olim collectæ.* The canon law of the ecclesiastical province of Canterbury, collected and abridged in 1433.

18. Hugo Grotius, *de Jure Belli ac Pacis libri tres.* Cf. *Minutes,* 2.447, 509.

19. Luis de Tena, *Commentaria et diſputationes in epiſtolam. D. Pauli ad Hebræos.*

7.   Pamelij Lyturgica 2 vol: 4°[20]
8.   Dornavius his Amphitheater fol[21]
9.   De Jurisdictione Imperial et Ecclesl: varis fol[22]
10.   M Bucer Script: Anglicani fol[23]
11.   Andreas Massius on Joshua[24]
12.   Hystoria Lyturgica in 3 vol: 8°[25]
13.   Haynes Pax in Terris Octavo[26]
14.   Disaplina Ecclia Scotica 8°[27]
15.   Mitigation towards Cathol: subiects 8°[28]
16.   Ceremonia sacræ 8°[29]
17.   Tortura Torti 4°[30] [Possibly Sess. 232.]
18.   Selden of Tythes – 4°[31]
19.   Mystery of Gentiles 4°[32]
20.   Grotius de satisfact: Christi 4°[33]
21.   Answ: to Cookes reports 8°[34]
22.   Carlson of Jurisdiction 8°[35]
23.   Fitzherbert of Polic: and religion 4°[36]
24.   Icon Animorum 16°[37]

---

20. Jacobus Pamelius, *Liturgica Latinorum*.

21. Caspar Dornau, *Amphitheatrum sapientiæ Socraticæ joco-seriæ*

22. Apparently: Simon Schard, *De Jurisdictione, Auctoritate, et Præeminentia Imperiali, ac Potestate Ecclesiastica…*, though the work is one volume folio.

23. Martin Bucer, *Scripta Anglicana fere omnia*.

24. Andreas Masius, *Iosuæ Imperatoris historia illustrata atque explicate*.

25. The one work found that generally goes by *Historia Liturgica* is by Petri Laurentius and Abraham Andre Angermannus and is one volume quarto (1588); however, the *Antiquitatum Liturgicarum Arcana* of Floris vander Hær (Duaci: Belleri, 1605) is three volumes octavo.

26. Thomas Haynes, *Pax in Terra; seu Tractatus de Pace Ecclesiastica*.

27. Daniel Tilenus, *De disciplina ecclesiastica brevis & modesta dissertatio ad Ecclesiam Scoticam*.

28. Robert Parsons, *A treatise tending to mitigation towardes Catholike-subiectes in England*.

29. Probably, Augustinus Patricius, *Sacræ Ceremoniæ: sive rituum ecclesiastorum: libri tres*, i.e. *Sacrarum ceremoniarum sive rituum ecclesiasticorum Romanæ ecclesiæ libri tres*: 1516. A 1572 edition is in octavo.

30. Possibly Lancelot Andrewes, *Tortura Torti: siue ad Matthæi Torti*. Cf. *Minutes*, 2.232.

31. John Selden, *History of Tythes*.

32. Possibly, or part of John Yates, *Imago mundi, et regnum Christi. The foure monarchies, and Christs two-fold kingdome, Dan. 2.31, to the 36. Regnum lapidis et montis. The Gentiles converted, and the Jews restored. Lapis e monte excisus. The Gentiles converted, collected and governed by the Apostles, apostolicall men and bishops. 1. The mystery of the Gentiles, 1 Tim. 3.16…. 1640*, in quarto.

33. Apparently, Hugo Grotius, *Defensio Fidei Catholicæ De Satisfactione Christi Adversus Faustum Socinum Senensem*.

34. Apparently, Robert Parsons, *An answere to the fifth part of Reportes lately set forth by Syr Edward Cooke Knight, the Kinges Attorney generall. Concerning the ancient & moderne municipall lawes of England, which do apperteyne to spirituall power & iurisdiction*. 1606; however, in 4°.

35. George Carleton, *Jurisdiction, Regall, Episcopall, Papall*.

36. Thomas Fitzherbert, *The First to second part of a treatise concerning policy and religion*.

37. John Barclay, *Icon Animorum*.

Other Theological Resources of the Assembly of Divines   383

25.   Dangerous Positions 4°[38]
26.   Survay[?] of Discipline 4°[39]
27.   Trial of the privait spirit 4°[40]
28.   Mocket[?] 4°[41]
29.   Burges his Defense of Ceremonyes 4°[42]
30.   Answere to Martins Libell[43]
31.   Troubles of Frankford about English Liturgy 8[44] [Sess. 383?]
32.   Peregrin Letteres patents of presbitery 4°[45]
33.   Barrowe and Greenwood 4°[46]
34.   Cartwright ag[t] Whitgift 4°[47]
35.   Puritan Tracts 4[?] parcells bound togeather 4°
36.   Dispute ag[t] English Ceremonyes 4°[48]
37.   Duplyes of Schotts Ministers 4°[49]
38.   A Conference touching Succesion 16°[50]
39.   Kellisons[?] {Hierarchy?} 8[51]
40.   Abridgment of the Lincolneshyre[?] ministers Petition 16[52]

[fol. 130v]
41.   An Assertion for Church Pollicy 16°[53]

---

38. Richard Bancroft, *Dangerous Positions and Proceedings*.

39. Possibly, Richard Bancroft, *Survay of the Pretended Holy Discipline*. The supposition is bolstered by the immediately preceding work by Bancroft.

40. Possibly, James Sharp, *The Triall of the Proteſtant Priuate Spirit*.

41. Possibly, Richard Mocket's *Doctrina et Politia Ecclesiæ Anglicanæ*, or Thomas Mocket, who wrote favorably on the National and Solemn League and Covenant (the latter in 1644).

42. John Burges, *An Answer Rejoined to that much applauded pamphlet A reply to Dr. Morton's General Defense of three nocent ceremonies* (1631); *The Lawfulness of Kneeling in the act of receiving the Lord's Supper* (1631).

43. Apparently, Thomas Cooper, *An Admonition to the People of England: Wherein Are Answered, Not Onely the Slaunderous Vntruethes, Reproachfully Vttered by Martin [Marprelate], the Libeller, …*.

44. William Whittingham, *A brieff discours off the troubles begonne at Franckford in Germany A. Domini 1554. Aboute the book off common prayer and ceremonie*. Cf. *Minutes*, 3.545.

45. James Peregrin, *The Letters Patents of the Presbyterie: with the plea and fruits of the prelacie…*.

46. Henry Barrow, John Greenwood, *A Plaine Refutation of M. Giffards booke, intituled, A short treatise gainſt the Donatiſtes of England …*.

47. See Thomas Cartwright's exchanges with John Whitgift over the "Admonition Controversy."

48. George Gillespie, *A Diſpute Againſt the English Popish Ceremonies*.

49. Apparently, John Forbes, *Duplyes of the Miniſters & Professors of Aberdene, to … some reverend brethren, concerning the late covenant*.

50. Possibly, *A Conference about the next succession to the crowne of Ingland*.

51. Matthew Kellison, *A Treatise of the Hierarchie and Diuers Orders of the Church againſt the Anarchie of Calvin* (1629), octavo.

52. Apparently, *An abridgement of that booke which the miniſters of Lincolne diocess deliuered to His Maieſtie vpon the firſt of December 1605*.

53. William Stoughton, Francis Knollys, *An Assertion for True and Chriſtian Church-Policie*.

42. Puritane Tracts 3 parcells 16°

43. Lombards Sentences – 8°54

44. Salmeron on the Parables 4°55

45. Attestation of church gouvmt 16°56

46. Machiavels prince 8°57

47. Appology of English Arminianisme 8°58

48. Victory Rebellions[?] 8°59

49. Travers of Discipline 16°60 [Sess. 180.]

50. Sa's Aphorismes 16°61

51. Lucas Brugensis on the Gospells 2 vol: fols62

52. Tappers works[?] fol63

53. Cardinal Peron Answ: to K James fol64

54. Vicars his Decapla on the Psalms fol65

55. Service booke Corrected Jacobi fol66

56. Alvarez de Auxilis gratiae67

57. Ames agt Burgesse 4°68 [Sess. 88?]

58. Parker de Politia Ecclias 4°69 [Sess. 85, 156, 160, 295.]

59. Lesly de Authoritate Eclia[?] a Sermon 4°70

60. Syons Plea 4°71

---

54. Peter Lombard, *Sentences*.

55. Alfonso Salmerón, *Sermones in Parabolas evangelicas totius anni*.

56. Henry Jacob, *An Attestation of many learned, godly, and famous divines ... church government ought to bee alwayes with the peoples free consent....*

57. Niccolò Machiavelli, *The Prince*.

58. O. N., *An apology of English Arminianisme*.

59. Perhaps one or more of several tracts relating to the Protestant victory in Ireland.

60. Walter Travers, *A full and plaine declaration of ecclesiastical discipline....* Cf. *Minutes*, 2.272.

61. Manoel de Sa, *Aphorismi confessariorum ex doctorum sententiis collecti....*

62. Francisci Lucæ Brugensis, *In sacrosancta quatuor Iesu Christi evangelia*.

63. *Rvardi Tapperi Abenchvsia ... Opera* (Coloniæ Agrippinæ, 1582–1583).

64. Jacques Davy Du Perron, *The Reply of the Most Illustrious Cardinal of Perron, to the Answeare of the Most Excellent King of Great Britaine*.

65. John Vicars, *Decapla in Psalmos*.

66. Possibly Laud's 1637 service book imposed upoon Scotland, with corrections in hand?

67. Diego Alvarez, *De auxilus divinæ grattiæ et humani arbitii*.

68. William Ames, *A fresh suit against human ceremonies in God's vvorship, or, A triplication unto D. Burgesse his rejoinder for D. Morton....* See #73. This title may have been collected in duplicate by mistake and this may be a double entry. Cf. *Minutes*, 2.272.

69. Robert Parker, *De politia ecclesiastica Christi....* Cf. *Minutes*, 2.250, 501, 538, 3.361.

70. John Leslie, *De illustrium fœminarum in repub. administranda, ac ferendis legibus authoritate ... nunc verò Latino sermone ....* This is Leslie's reply to John Knox's *First Blast of the Trumpet against the monstrous regiment of women*.

71. Alexander Leighton, *An Appeal to the Parliament; or Sions plea against the prelacie*. Alexander Leighton was given charge of Lambeth Palace, but I have not found anything noting he had anything to do with the Lambeth library or Laud's personal library. He had been severely treated by Laud and the Star Chamber. "Lambeth Palace Library," III.

61. Helvicus[?] Vindication of Scripture 8°[72]

62. Charity Mistaken 8°[73]

63. Demands agt the Covenant 4°[74]

64. Forbes Irenicum 4°[75]

65. Colloquy att Wormes 4°[76]

66. Henry {Dunelmensis?} agt Scots Covenant 4[77]

67. Saravia de obidentia Christiana 4°[78]

68. Remonstrance to the Remonstrators 4°[79]

69. Saravia de divsis Ministrorum gradibus 4°[80]

70. Mason de Je{iunio} 4°[81]

71. Sprint, necesity of Conformity 4°[82]

72. Johnsons Chrian Plea 4°[83]

73. A ffresh suit agt Ceremonyes 4°[84]

74. Important Considerations 4°[85]

---

72. There is no title in English that matches "Vindication of Scripture" for the period in question. If the author name is indeed Christopher Helvicus (Helwig), then the title may possibly be his *Vindicatio Locorum Potissimorum V. T. a corruptelis Pontificiorum, Et In His Præcipue Bellarmini; Calvinianorum, Photinianorum, Judæorum &c. Ex originali textu, Linguæ Hebrææ proprietate, Chaldaicis Paraphrasibus, ad perpetuam fidei analogiam; Cum appendice de Genealogia Christi; adornata ; Additus est in fine geminus Index* (1620) which was indeed published in octavo.

73. Anonymous, Edward Knott (i.e. Matthew Wilson), *Charity mistaken, with the want whereof, Catholickes are vniustly charged for affirming, as they do with grief, that Protestancy vnrepented destroies salvation.*

74. *Generall demands concerning the late Covenant: propounded by the ministers and professors of divinity in Aberdeen.*

75. John Forbes, *Irenicum amatoribus veritatis et pacis in ecclesia Scoticana.*

76. Possibly, *Colloquium Wormaciense institutum*, 1542, in quarto.

77. There is a long word that is difficult to make out. The "D" may be an overwritten "L." This may be a reference to Henry Leslie, *A full confutation of the covenant lately sworne and subscribed by many in Scotland; delivered in a speech, at the visitation of Downe and Conner, held in Lisnegarvy the 26th. of September, 1638.* Or it may be Dobson added unpublished information on the author and this refers to the anonymous, *A Briefe discovrse declaring the impiety and unlawfulnesse of the new covenant with the Scots* (Oxford: 1643, printed by Henry Hall).

78. Hadrian Saravia, *De imperandi authoritate, et Christiana obedientia, libri quatuor.*

79. Neither a search of Copac nor Worldcat, nor the Thomason tracts, revealed a title for this period using the term "remonstrators." This may reference one or more of the exchanges between Joseph Hall and Smectymnuus (Stephen Marshall, Edmund Calamy, Thomas Young, Matthew Newcomen and William Spurstowe).

80. Hadrian Saravia, *De diversis Ministrorum Evangelii gradibus.*

81. This would appear to be Henry Mason, *de Jeiunio* [on fasting]: *Christian humiliation, or, the Christians fast. A treatise declaring the nature, kindes, ends, uses, and properties of a religious fast: together with a briefe discourse concerning the fast of Lent* (1625; 2nd edition, 1627).

82. John Sprint, *Cassander Anglicanus: shewing the necessity of conformitie....*

83. Francis Johnson, *A Christian Plea conteyning three treatises.*

84. William Ames, *A fresh suit against human ceremonies in God's vvorship, or, A triplication unto D. Burgesse his rejoinder for D. Morton....* Possibly a duplicate or a double entry. See #57.

85. Either Thomas Bluet, *Important considerations, which ought to moue all true and sound Catholikes, who are not wholly Iesuited* (1601), or possibly John Ley, *Defensive doubts, hopes, and*

75. Montanus de Regalibus fol[86]

76. Gergorey de Valentia 4 vol: fol[87]

77. Durandas – fol[88]

78. A{ltissiodorensis} fol[89]

79. Alcoran [The Koran.]

80. Erasmus fol[90]

81. Spelman Concilia Bretanica 4°[91]

82. Cardan de prudentia Civili 16[92]

83. Celsus de hæreticis combur:[?] 8[93]

84. Saris[?] {buriensis?} 8°[94]

[fol. 131 side 1]

85. Spelman de non Temerandis Ecclips 8°[95]

86. Seutus[?] Regius[?] 8°[96]

87. Cunæus de Rep: Hebr: 8°[97]

88. Sigonius de Rep: Hebr: 8°[98] [Sess. 112, 378.]

89. vossius Idololatria progressu 4°[99]

90. Tho: Browne[?] Concio in Act 1.20. 4°[100]

---

reasons, for refusall of the oath, imposed by the sixth canon of the late synod: with important considerations, both for the penning and publishing of them at this time (1641).

86. Horatius Montanus, *De Regalibus Tractatus.*

87. Gregorio de Valencia, *Commentariorum theologicorum tomi quatuor. In quibus omnes quæstiones, quæ continentur in Summa theologica D. Thomæ Aquinatis.*

88. Possibly, Durandus of Saint-Pourçain, Bishop of Meaux, *In Petri Lombardi sententias theologicas commentariorum libri IIII.*

89. There are only a few works I could identify associated with Altissiodorensis: Bishop Claudius Taurinensis, commentary on Galatians (1542/43), Robertus Altissiodorensis, *Chronologia seriem temporum et historiam rerum in orbe gestarum continens ab eius origine usque ad annum a Christi ortu 1200* (1608), and Gulielmus, Altissiodorensis, Archdeacon of Beauvais, *Summa aurea in quattuor libros sententiarum [of Petrus Lombardus] … Guillermo altissiodorensi edita* (Paris: 1500). Only the last title is in folio and aligns subject-wise with #76 and #77.

90. Possibly one of five one volume folio editions of Erasmus' *Novum Testamentum.*

91. Henry Spelman, *Concilia, decreta, leges, constitutiones in re ecclesiarum orbis Britannici.*

92. Girolamo Cardano, *Hieronymi Cardani … Proxeneta seu de prudentia ciuili liber.*

93. Minus Celsus Senensis [Celsus Socinus], *Mini Celsi Senensis de hæreticis capitali supplicio non afficiendis. Adiunctæ sunt eiusdem argumenti Theodori Bezæ & Andreæ Dvditii epistolæ duæ contrariæ.*

94. Possibly *Ioannis Ivelli Angli: Episcopi Saris-buriensis vita & mors* (1573), but in quarto.

95. Henry Spelman, *De non temerandis Ecclesiis.*

96. Possibly Dobson may have intended *Scutum Regium* by George Hakewill for which there is a 1612 edition in octavo; otherwise this is a mystery.

97. Petrus Cunæus, *Petri Cunæi De republica Hebræorum libri III.*

98. Carlo Sigonio, *De republica hebræorum libri VII.* Cf. *Minutes,* 2.431, 3.532.

99. Gerardus Joannes Vossius, *Theologia Gentili … Sive De Origine Ac Progressu Idololatriæ.*

100. This may be an unpublished sermon by Thomas Browne (1604?–1673) who served as Laud's chaplain. A sermon of his on Job 11:4 preached at Aldermary (whose pulpit would subsequently be filled by Edmund Calamy) was judged blasphemous by the Puritans who complained to Laud, who immediately made him Canon of Windsor. A copy was found on

91. Fulleri. Miscel[101]

92. Rothioford[?] Cont Armin.[102]

93. Grager(?) logie[103]

94. Corpus Confessionum[104]

95. Spanhemii[?] Dubia Evan.[105]

96. Paræus de potesate Erra[?][106]

97. {Sententia de pace?}[107]

98. Theologia chounei[?][108]

Walt: Dobson

On fol. 131v there is a note in small script which reads: "Ye names of some bookes taken out of ye Archbp of Cant primate ſtuddy at Lamb. by Mr Nye & Mr [blank] by of our Order of pliant this 23. Octob. 1643"

The collection tends to be largely made up of works on ecclesiology, worship, and the covenant; more than several are on the nature of the goſpel (e.g. contra Catholicism, Arminiasm, etc.), with a ſprinkling of general use titles (a couple of commentaries on individual books of the bible, logic, church councils, schoolmen) and perhaps a few eclectic titles that simply may have caught Nye's party's intereſt. It is intereſting to note three or four of the divines' individual works were taken from Laud's ſtudy: Selden's *Hiſtory of Tythes* (18), Gilleſpie's *English Popish Ceremonies* (36), Rutherford's *Exercitationes Apologeticæ Pro Divina Gratia* (92), and possibly John Ley's *Defensive doubts, hopes, and reasons, for refusall of the oath* (74).

How much the collection was used is not certain; it may have been more of a diſtraction than a benefit for the assembly.[109] Of seventy titles referenced in *The Grand Debate*, only three are found on Dobson's liſt (31. Troubles at Franckford;

Laud's desk when his papers were seized. A sermon preached in 1634 while at the University of Oxford is not on the text in question. A Latin sermon entitled *Concio Ad Clerum* (discourse of the revenues of the clergy) preached in 1637 apparently existed in MS but was not published until 1730. However the text is also not Acts 1:20. His only other published work prior to 1644 was a translation out of Camden's Annals, on the *Life and Reign of Princess Elizabeth*, published in 1629. See *The Present State of the Republick of Letters* (1730) 201, 218.

101. Nicolai Fulleri, *Miscellaneorum*.

102. Samuel Rutherford, *Exercitationes Apologeticæ Pro Divina Gratia*.

103. Possibly, Thomas Granger, *Syntagma logicum, or, The diuine logike*.

104. Gaspard Laurent, ed., *Corpus et syntagma confessionum fidei* (1612).

105. Friedrich Spanheim, *Dubia evangelica in tres partes diſtributa*.

106. David Paræus, *De Poteſtate ecclesiaſtica et civili propositiones theologico-politicæ*.

107. Possibly, John Davenant, *De Pace Inter Evangelicos procuranda Sententiæ Qvatvor*.

108. Possibly, Thomas Chouneus, *Collectiones theologicarum quarundam conclusionum ex diversis authorum sententiis, perquam breves ſparsim excerpt. Opera, et induſtria Thom Chounei*.

109. Session 455, June 17, 1645. "Upon the motion for the better ordering of the Assemblies, *Ordered*—That the members of the Assembly do not bring any ~~news books or other books into the Assembly to read privately during the sitting of the Assembly,~~—books or papers to read privately in the Assembly during the sitting of the Assembly." The first version was crossed out by the scribe. Alexander F. Mitchell and John P. Struthers, *Minutes of the Sessions*

34. Cartwright v. Whitgift; and 58. Parker's *Politeia Ecclesiaſtica*). It is also unclear how ſtable a collection it was. The Parliament was in the habit of beſtowing seized books upon individuals in payment or recognition of service rendered. To the chaplain of the army, Hugh Peters, they granted the whole ſtudy or library of books belonging to the former Archbishop. So it is not certain whether the 97/98 books were turned over to Mr. Peters some months later in June, 1644. It could be the divines' book collection remained in a ſtate of flux.

> Whereas formerly Books, to the Value of an Hundred Pounds, were beſtowed upon Mr. *Peters*, out of the Archbishop of *Canterbury*'s particular private Study: And whereas the said Study is appraised at a matter of Forty Pounds more than the said Hundred Pounds; It is this Day *Ordered*, That Mr. *Peters* shall have the whole Study of Books freely beſtowed upon him.[110]

THE ABBEY LIBRARY

While it is not certain how large a collection the divines amassed from the sequestered libraries, or how much flux the collection experienced, it is clear they did not need to gather a large general theological library. The abbey did have a subſtantial collection on the premises, and while it was a chained library, prohibiting borrowing, and apparently noisy and not ideal, the divines did resort to it.

> The key resource for this theological think-tank [Weſtminſter Assembly] was the abbey library…. The library is a little known treasure but was very important in the seventeenth century. Dean John Williams's ambitious and beautiful renovation of the thirty by sixty foot chapter library was complete in 1626. The library is ſtill impressive and contains Williams's original presses…. Williams is reported to have given a vaſt library, worth £2,000, with many of the books purchased at "a cheap peny worth for such precious ware." According to my title count of the Weſtminſter Abbey Library's Benefactors' book,[111] Williams donated around 2,200 titles, many of them multi-volume works. He ſtocked the library with editions of works of the church fathers and medieval authors published throughout the sixteenth century and the beginning of the seventeenth. Williams inſpired others to imitation, and by the time the Assembly met, the library had 3,821 titles in its Benefactors' book and perhaps 5,000 volumes on the library shelves.

---

of the Weſtminſter Assembly of Divines (Edinburgh: W. Blackwood and Sons, 1874), 105. Cf. *Minutes* (Oxford, 2012) 3.620–621.

110. *HCJ* 3, 27 June 1644 (1802) 544. Cox-Johnson notes that at the Restoration of the monarchy it had been ordered "that all books and papers belonging to the late Archbishop Laud but in the possession of John Thurloe, once Secretary of State, and the unfortunate cleric, Hugh Peters, should be secured" ("Lambeth Plaace Library," 119). Some books and/or papers must have been held over from Laud's trial by the Secretary, or possibly Thurloe had obtained whatever may have been retained by the Assembly.

111. *Benefactors' book*, Westminster Abbey Library MS 46.

A complaint by the abbey librarian to Parliament teſtifies that the divines used the library.[112] He had ſtayed on at the library after the prebends had left, and argued that Parliament ought to pay him for his work. The main argument for immediate payment was that the Weſtminſter divines and other "persons of quality" used the library regularly and heavily. Although the library was useful, it was busy. Furthermore, it was a chained library and the inability of the library to lend its books presented a problem for the Assembly-men.[113]

The library was originally ordered in 1549 but nothing seems to have been done at that time. In 1574 Dean Goodman gave towards a library a set of the Complutensian Polyglott and a Hebrew grammar. In 1587 rules were adopted including an order to keep an inventory and regiſter of gifts of or towards books, and orders to weed out duplicates and triplicates. The Complutensian set given in 1574 was defeƈtive but later completed/repaired in 1812. It is ſpeculated it remained from that time in the Deanery and was deſtroyed by German bombing, May 10/11, 1941.[114] Another set survives in the library, given by Thomas Mountford in 1631.[115] As noted the library was refurbished by John Williams, who also donated a large number of volumes over whatever had been accumulated prior to that date.

THE BENEFACTORS' BOOK

Compiled in 1651–52 and subsequently augmented, the Weſtminſter Abbey Library *Benefaƈtors' book* liſts donations of books (and occaionally other items) or money given toward the purchase of them from 1623 to about 1710. It is a large folio sized volume in a thick tan leather binding which appears to be Viƈtorian, judging from the decorative endsheets. The binding itself is not particularly decorative, but does have some lines and minor decorations coming off the five main binding threads.

---

112. "That the Place of Library-keeper aforesaid was and still is a Place of Necessity, and of Daily Attendance; many of the Reverend Divines of the Assembly and other Personages of Quality frequently repairing to the said Library, and making great Use thereof." *House of Lords Journal*, volume 8, 1 December 1645 (1767–1830), 17–20. Hereafter HLJ.

113. <u>Minutes</u>, 1.120–121; compare with, *Minutes*, 1.41.

114. *The Firſt Collegiate Church: 1543–1556. Aƈts of the Dean and Chapter of Weſtminſter: 1543–1609, Part 1*, ed. C. S. Knighton. Westminster Abbey record series (Woodbridge [u.a.]: Boydell, 1997) lv. *Part 2, 1560–1609* (Woodbridge: Boydell, 1997) 71, fn 350.

115. *Benefaƈtors' book*, MS 46, page 49r (r=recto; v=verso). Thomas Mountford apparently wished it to be clear which volumes he had donated as the binding holds notice that the set was given by him in 1631. According to Christine Reynolds, Assistant Keeper of Muniments, this was not necessarily a regular or consistent practice (Email correspondence, July 28, 2010). Some works may have been present before the first date in the book, July 20, 1623. Lines, columns and benefactors are unnumbered in the MS and have been supplied in the following bibliography (404ff). A title may be present in different forms and editions. Many entries are not dated and most listings are in two columns (denoted "a" for left, "b" for right). The first entry records John William's significant donation (1-John Williams, July 20, 1623). Except for one clear case that would date to 1645 or later (39-Anton Sousa, undated, 67r), it is presumed that entries date prior to the Assembly through page 68r, encompassing 40 benefactors.

The vellum pages have been padded front and back with a few paper pages in the binding, possibly dating to the rebinding. The dimensions of the volume are 43cm tall by 33cm wide (including the curvature of the ſpine). The volume is 6cm thick at the binding and curves out to 8 or 9 cm across the middle of the volume in a relaxed position. The pages are in good condition and legible.

There is a note in pencil written in a modern hand that dates the volume as follows:

> This book was not written in 1623, but in 1651–2, by Matthew Roydon (WAM 57167, 57168).[116] He presumably compiled it from earlier liſts. His work goes as far as f. 68.
>
> ff. 69–87 (1ſt two lines) were evidently entred in 1673 (WAM 33706—Treasurers Account—f. 7b For recording ye names in ye Library ijlb:vs[)]
>
> ff. 87 (Rich. Perrincliefe—10 Nov 1675) & 88 (George Stradling—6 Nov 1682) both written and signed by Peter Smart.

BENEFIT OF THE BENEFACTORS' BOOK

We learn from the *Benefaċtors' book*, that of seventy works cited in their *Grand Debate*, twenty-nine were possibly "available to the Assembly-men"[117] in the abbey's library at the time of the Weſtminſter Assembly.[118] Again, one can imagine the initial disadvantage experienced by those miniſters away from home and their libraries to which they may have been accuſtomed. Working in close proximity to such a subſtantial library, as the Abbey colleċtion surely was at the time, may have been a providential advantage. Many of the divines wrote subſtantial treatises during this period, and particularly we know the Scottish Commissioners wrote significant scholarly works while in London at the Weſtminſter Assembly. For inſtance, George Gilleſpie may have made use of the Abbey library with ready access to works he likely would not have had otherwise. During this period he wrote his magnum opus *contra* Eraſtianism, and it would be an intereſting line of research to trace the works referenced in it, to see what percentage he could have found in the abbey and elsewhere.[119] Samuel Rutherford also wrote several works during this period.[120] The Weſtminſter divines were also routinely called upon to preach

---

116. WAM=Westminster Abbey Muniments Manuscripts collection.

117. <u>Minutes</u>, 1.121, note 20.

118. My thanks to Christine Reynolds, Assistant Keeper of Muniments, and the Abbey Library for providing a microfilm copy of MS 46. While some of the pages on the film are not legible, the volume itself can be read with little difficulty. However, many of the books are not described or titled sufficiently to identify editions and perhaps in some cases even the actual work. Thanks also go to Dr. Joel Halcomb for examining the *Benefaċtors' book* and providing the description, and for researching some titles in the Abbey library card catalogue, and examining various individual volumes.

119. George Gillespie, *Aaron's Rod Blossoming* (1646).

120. Samuel Rutherford, *Due Right of Presbyteries* (1644); *Lex Rex* (1644); *Tryal and Triumph of Faith* (1645); *Divine Right of Church Government … Diſpute againſt Scandall* (1646); *Chriſt Dying and Drawing Sinners to Himself* (1647); *Survey of Spiritual Antichriſt / Survey of*

sermons for official and unofficial occasions. Including the Scots, two divines at least were called upon each month to preach, often highly scholastic sermons, before Parliament for the regular fast instituted at the outbreak of civil war, and it would seem the Abbey library was suitable for at least some sermon preparation.

But the abbey's thirty by sixty foot chapter library may not have always been convenient. The library was "chained" at the time of the assembly. The now commonplace lending library did not come into existence in England until the early 1700s, when chaining fell from use.[121] While other libraries may not have been as bold as the Bodleian, whose keeper famously refused to let Charles I remove a volume, it is hard to imagine the keeper of the abbey library throwing off the chains and allowing over 100 divines to remove volumes at will. It would be safe to presume if one of the divines wished to do research in any of the abbey's volumes the days he was attending the assembly, he would have had to do so within the library. Clearly though, a single chained library would seem less than sufficient for such a number of divines as made up the assembly on a regular basis during the week.[122] This, and that as fine a collection as it was, it was still lacking in some materials, and that it was not necessarily a quiet place for study, may explain the request for the sequestered books the divines might have more regularly consulted in their diliberations.[123] Despite these disadvantages, the divines' study library made up of the borrowed volumes, clearly was not intended to take the place of a preacher's study. And the divines far from home and their studies, had to make use of some resource at hand. One may certainly deduce some serious use of the abbey library from the fact that many of the books referenced for instance by the Scottish Commissioners in their fast sermons, could have been found there.[124] But others could not.

OTHER POTENTIAL RESOURCES

There were other potential resources to which the Scottish Commissioners and other divines may have had access. Some of the London ministers with good libraries may have been willing to loan books out to other assemblymen. Auction catalogues can give a sense of what books may have been owned at the time such as those of a prominent English "Jus Divinum" Presbyterian, Lazarus Seaman, and of one of the Independent Brethren, William Greenhill. For recent and even older publications, including foreign works, books may have been purchased from the London

---

Antinomianism (1648 [Nov. 1647]). Samuel Rutherford left the assembly on Nov. 9, 1647 (*Minutes*, 4.703).

121. Clearly at the time of the Westminster Assembly chaining was the rule, as "chaining remained commonplace in institutional libraries throughout the seventeenth century…." Daniel R. Woolf, *Reading History in Early Modern England* (Cambridge UP, 2000) 197.

122. *Minutes*, 1.41.

123. "The library was also not completely free from distraction for 'the distant shouts of the Westminster scholars' which Washington Irving heard from the abbey library in 1818 would likely have been heard in the mid-seventeenth century as well." <u>Minutes</u>, 1.121, fn 23.

124. Cf. *Sermons Preached Before the English Houses of Parliament*, Bibliography.

bookshops clustered at St. Paul's Churchyard. However, even better resources potentially lay with the other public libraries. "London's institutional libraries, most of which were open to the professional clergy and lawyers, consisted of the Sion College Library, the libraries of the Inns of Court, Lambeth Palace library, and the library of Westminster Abbey."[125]

WORCESTER HOUSE: RESIDENCE OF THE SCOTTISH COMMISSIONERS

As we look at these other resources, it perhaps would be helpful to have in mind a bit of geography of the city where the Scots Commissioners in particular found themselves, since we know where they were living the whole time while in London. This enables us to place them geographically in relation to Westminster Abbey and other locals of interest, such as the public libraries, booksellers, and the churches and dwellings of other of the Westminster divines.

> *Ordered*, That Mr. *Holland* and Mr. *Oldisworth* do accommodate Lodgings in *Worcester House*, for the Reception and Entertainment of such of the *Scotts* Commissioners as are to come, or are lately arrived, in like manner as formerly: And that the Committee of the King's Revenue do take care to defray the Charge thereof out of the said Revenue.[126]

There has been some confusion regarding the location of this place, because of another house known as Worcester House, which was over in the Strand. In the memoir of Robert Baillie prefixed to his edition of the *Letters and Journals*, Laing clarified which house, but misidentification persisted.[127] "This was not the house of the Earls of Worcester, which Lord Clarendon afterwards inhabited, on the site of the present Beaufort-buildings in the Strand; but Worcester Place, the house of John Tiptoft, Earl of Worcester, Lord High Treasurer of England, also on the banks of the Thames, but nearer the Tower."[128] We find letters by Gillespie and the Scottish Commissioners with the notation "Worcester House" throughout the years they resided in London,[129] and they and their families when with them, resided

---

125. Minutes, 1.120, n17
126. HCJ 3, 17 October 1644, 668.
127. "During the Usurpation, Worcester House in the Strand was furnished by Parliament for the Scotch commissioners…." Peter Cunningham, *Handbook of London: past and present* (J. Murray, 1850) 1.559. *The Diplomatic Correspondence of Jean De Montereul … 1645–48*, Scottish History Society XXX (Edinburgh: Printed at the University Press by T. and A. Constable for the Scottish History Society, 1899) 569, note 1.
128. *The Letters and Journals of Robert Baillie, A.M. MDCXXXVII–MDCLXII*, 3 vols., edited by David Laing (Edinburgh: Printed for Robert Ogle, 1841–1842) 1.li, n2.
129. See the Scottish Commissioners' correspondence and some of Gillespie's letters appended to Baillie's *Letters and Journals*. Laing, 2.490, 500–503, 3.541–343. See also: *The Diplomatic Correspondence of Jean De Montereul*, 569; Reports from Commissioners, Inspectors, and Others: 1877 (volume 30), *Sixth Report of the Royal Commission on Historical Manuscripts* (London: London: Printed by George Edward Eyre and William Spottiswoode, 1877) 89, 98, 112, 116, 117, 120, 123, 130, 137, 139, 142, 157, 162, 165, 169, 174, 181, 183, 184, 191, 216; Publications of

at Worceſter House or Place, the whole time they were in London.[130] Baillie puts it out of queſtion as well:

> For Mr. Thomas Fuller,
>
> Reverend Sir,
>
> Having latelie, and but latelie, gone through your Holy Warr and Description of Paleſtine, I am fallen so in love with your pen, that I am sorry I was not before acquaint with it, and with your self, when from the 1643 to 1647, I lived at Worceſter House, and preached in the Savoy....[131]

Worceſter house no longer exiſts. On the Agas map of old London,[132] the house is located between Queenhithe to the weſt and the Three Cranes Wharf to the eaſt, on the bank of the Thames. Juſt up the ſtreet was the Vintners' Hall. Also, a few

---

the Scottish History Society volume XI. General Assembly Commission Records. May 1892. *The Records of the Commissions of the General Assemblies of the Church of Scotland Holden in Edinburgh in the Years 1646 and 1647, edited from the Original Manuscript by Alexander F. Mitchell, D.D., LL.D. and James Chriſtie, D.D. with an Introduƈion by the former* (Edinburgh: Printed at the University Press by T. and A. Constable for the Scottish History Society, 1892) xxiv, 12, 99, 162, 182, 187, 189, 200, 210, 223, 233, 257, 274, 275, 310, 312, 326.

130. The exception was Lord Warriston who had a separate house. See, Royal Commission on Historical Manuscripts, "The Manuscripts of The Honourable Mrs. Isabella Erskine-Murray of Aberdona, in the County of Clackmannan " *Report of the Royal Commission on Hiſtorical Manuscripts*. Issue 4 (London: [H.M.S.O.], 1874), 522–523. Amongst these papers this 1874 report noted there were "Correspondence and papers of Sir Charles Erskine as commissioner to the Assembly of Divines at Westminster." Erskine was trying to persuade his wife to stay in London and noted these facts: "Writing on 13th July 1647, he says that Mr. Gillespie and his wife were to come to Scotland either by coach or by sea. They were to depart within eight days from London…. He hoped to get her lodged in Worcester House as well as others, or at least in that house Warriston had, for there was room enough in both. Lord Lauderdale had his own family; so had all the rest."

131. *Letters and Journals*, 3.265. The Savoy Chapel was part of the Savoy Hospital built by Henry VIII replacing the Savoy Palace destroyed in the peasant revolt of 1381. The hospital was demolished in the 19th century but the chapel, which dates to the 1490s, still survives. At the time Baillie was in London, the congregation of St. Mary le Strand held worship services there, which they did from 1549–1714. Thomas Fuller was appointed lecturer in 1642, but when the Solemn League & Covenant was drawn up he would not sign without reservation and left Savoy and attended upon the king at Oxford. He was reinstated at the Savoy at the Restoration (*The Colleƈed Sermons of Thomas Fuller, D.D., 1631–1659*, volume 1 [London: The Gresham Press, 1891] xxiii; ccxcii).

132. *Civitas Londinium*, published sometime between 1570 and 1605, is attributed to Ralph Agas. A later 17th century copy of the map was preserved in the Guildhall Library which is now in the collection of the London Metropolitan Archive. A detailed scan of the latter with various locations and buildings identified has been constructed by Dr. Janelle Jenstad, Associate Professor, Department of English, University of Victoria. Worcester House appears in panel C4. See *The Map of Early Modern London*. http://mapoflondon.uvic.ca (accessed April 25, 2013). My thanks to Seth Stark for creating the map, which contains Ordnance Survey data © Crown copyright and database rights 2010. See Worcester House/Place at 14 on the map. Ed. 2024: Prior corrections misstated that the map itself is incorrect. The correction needed is to assign location 1 to Calamy instead of 11. Distances on page 396 have been revised.

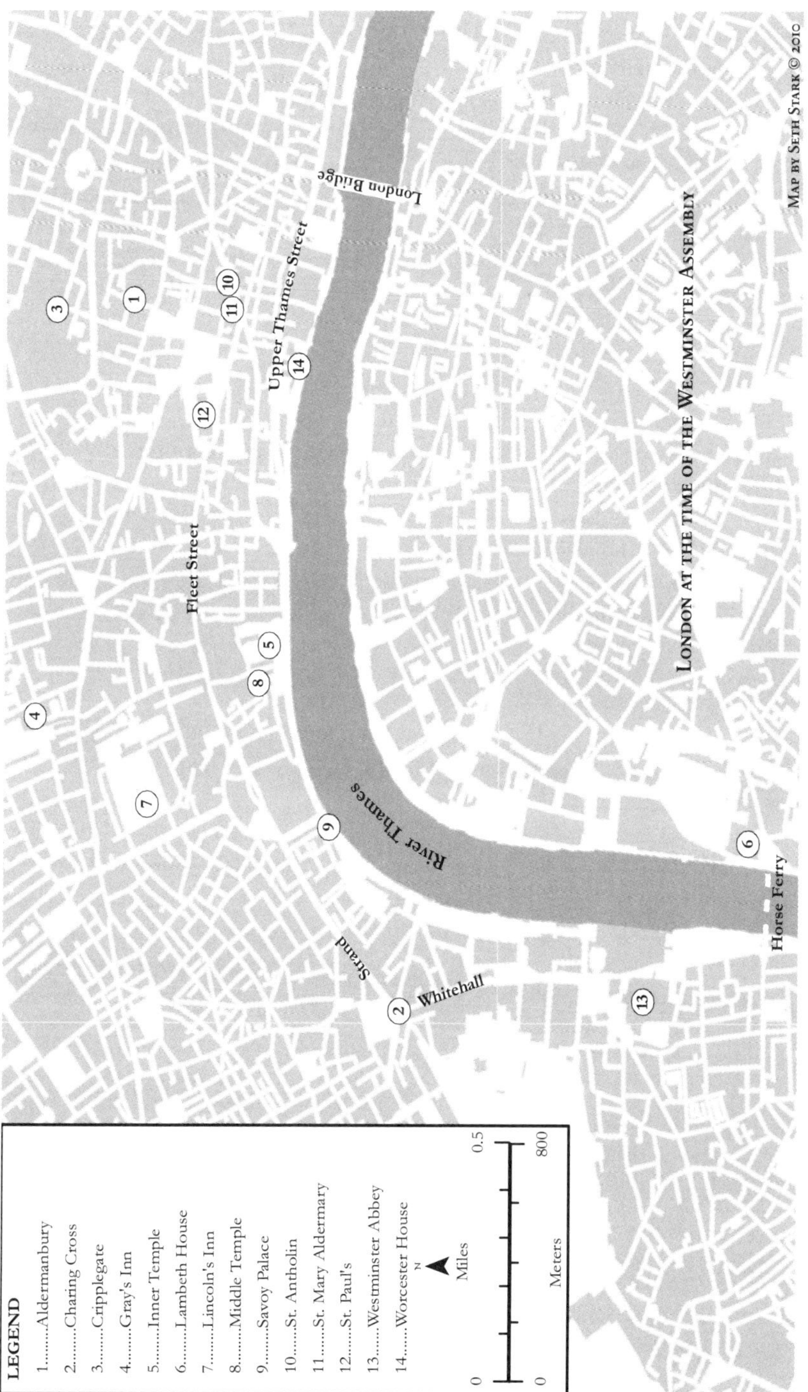
London Bridge
Upper Thames Street
Fleet Street
River Thames
Strand
Whitehall
Horse Ferry
London at the time of the Westminster Assembly
Map by Seth Stark © 2010
LEGEND
1........Aldermanbury
2........Charing Cross
3........Cripplegate
4........Gray's Inn
5........Inner Temple
6........Lambeth House
7........Lincoln's Inn
8........Middle Temple
9........Savoy Palace
10......St. Antholin
11......St. Mary Aldermary
12......St. Paul's
13......Westminster Abbey
14......Worcester House
N
Miles
Meters
0.5
800
0
0

blocks north was St. Antholins [Anthony's] Church (see Map, #10, page 395), which "was set apart for their [the Scottish Commissioners] use, the ministers preaching in their turn, for a time, at least, to very crowded audiences."[133] Saint Mary Aldermanbury, where Edmund Calamy was pastor, was about a mile due north (Ed. 2024: Map, location 1; see fn 132, p. 394). Four blocks north and one block west from Worcester house was All Hallows, Bread Street (Ed. 2024), where Lazarus Seaman was pastor. To the east of Worcester house, was the only bridge across the Thames (until Westminster bridge was built in 1748), old London Bridge. At the time travel by horse was probably the most likely means of getting around the city. There were also hackney-coaches for hire.

> Hackney-coaches were first used in London in 1625. They were then only 20 in number, and were kept at the hotels, where they had to be applied for when wanted. In 1635 an attempt was made to restrain their use by a proclamation of Charles I.; but, this being found unsuccessful, their number was limited, and a commission was given to the Master of the Horse to grant licenses for their use. In this year only 50 were licensed. In 1634 one Capt. Baily, who had formerly been a sea-captain, hit upon the plan of keeping a number of hackney-coaches, with drivers in livery, standing at a particular place (the "Maypole," in the Strand), where they might be had whenever they were wanted. Hackney-coaches now rapidly became more general. The four started by Capt. Baily in 1634 had increased to 200 in 1652, to 800 in 1710, and to 1,000 in 1771.[134]

THE OTHER PUBLIC LIBRARIES: INNS OF COURT

The Inns of Court libraries included the collections of the Inner Temple, Middle Temple, Lincoln Inn and Gray's Inn (Map, 4, 5, 7, 8). The Gray's Inn collection was largely destroyed by fire in 1684[135] and most older records were lost, including the earliest catalogue of books dating to 1669.[136] The whole library was again destroyed during the Blitz in WWII. Catalogues of printed books held in the other three libraries were printed in the nineteenth century and while there are some religious and

---

133. Laing, 1.li. The church was destroyed by the great fire of 1666, and afterwards rebuilt. However, the "church was taken down in September 1874 to make way for the new Queen Victoria Street, and the site is marked by a memorial with a painting of the church." Henry Benjamin Wheatley and Peter Cunningham, *London, Past and Present: Its History, Associations, and Traditions* (London: John Murray, 1891) 1.51.

134. *The Americana: A Universal Reference Library, comprising the arts and sciences, literature, history, biograhy, geography, commerce, etc., of the world,* Volume 4 (New York: Scientific American compiling dept., 1907) "Coach."

135. Reginald J. Fletcher, *The Pension book of Gray's Inn* (records of the honourable society) 1669–1800 (1910) xiv.

136. *Catalogue of the Books in the Library of the Honourable Society of Gray's Inn* compiled by W. Douthwaite (London: C. Roworth & Sons, 1872) iv. Whether the 1669 book list was destroyed in the 1684 fire is uncertain; at least in 1872 Douthwaite simply notes that the catalogue could not be found.

theological books, the collections are largely law books, as might be expected.[137] While these were nearby to the west of Worcester House,[138] it does not seem likely that the Scots would have found these libraries useful when they had the Abbey library as a resource, and possibly the other two public libraries, which were huge theological resources in comparison to those of the Inns of Court.

LAMBETH PALACE LIBRARY

Of the other two libraries, the one at Lambeth Palace was founded in 1610 by Richard Bancroft, and is the historic library of the Archbishops of Canterbury. Almost anything found at Westminster might have been found there as well. The palace is located across the Thames from Westminster Abbey (Map, 6, 13). If any of the divines wished to use the palace library, they could have taken a ferry known as the Horseferry.[139] From their residence at Worcester House, the Scots Commissioners could have taken the two-mile trip by horse or coach, crossing over old London Bridge.

However, it appears that the House of Commons shut down the Lambeth library and locked it up, and therefore it would not have been generally accessible during the time of the assembly. Whether an individual divine might have been granted access is not clear and seems unlikely given the circumstances.

On 18 December 1640 William Laud was accused of high treason by the House of Commons, and was committed to the custody of James Maxwell, Officer of the Upper House. On 1 March 1640/41 he was taken to the Tower.

During 1641 and 1642 the Palace was twice searched for arms. After the second search, the House of Commons ordered on 9 November 1642[140] that 'It be referred to the Committee for Propositions, to consider making the Bishop of Canterbury's House

---

137. *A Catalogue of the Printed Books and Manuscripts in the Library of the Inner Temple* (London: T. C. Hansard, 1833). *A Catalogue of the Printed Books: To which is Prefixed a Short Account of the Manuscripts in the Library of Lincoln's Inn* (London: Printed by G. Davidson, 1835). *A Catalogue of the Library of the Middle Temple* (London: 1845).

138. On the map the Middle and Inner Temple are shown at 5 and 8 (Agas map C3) where Fleet Street turns into the Strand, the same as modern maps today. Lincoln and Grey's Inn are shown at 4 and 7 (Agas, B3). http://mapoflondon.uvic.ca [accessed April 25, 2013

139. The ferry is shown at the bottom of panel D1 on the Agas map across the Thames from Westminster Abbey. "The Ferry at Lambeth was a Horseferry between Lambeth Palace and Millbank. The memory of it is retained in the name 'Horseferry Road', in Westminster. The following is extracted from an interesting paper on [old] Westminster Bridge ... 'Those who may have occasion to cross the river by wherry from the stairs at the foot of the fine old gateway of Lambeth Palace to Millbank on the opposite side, are landed on a shelving slope, directly opposite the end of Market Street, and a little southward of the church of St. John the Evangelist." William Brenchley Rye, *England as seen by foreigners in the days of Elizabeth and James the First: comprising translations of the journals of the two Dukes of Wirtemberg in 1592 and 1610* (London: John Russell Smith, 1865) 60, note. Cf. "Westminster Bridge," in *The Penny magazine of the Society for the Diffusion of Useful Knowledge*, new series XI (London: 1842) April 16, 150.

140. In Cox Johnson (*Journal of the House of Commons*, II, 839).

at Lambeth … a prison to secure prisoners in,' and one Captain Brown was instructed to take over the place.

As soon as Laud heard what was intended, he petitioned the Upper House for the safety of the Library, as well as of his own books and other personal possessions.[141] The Lords granted his request and ordered:[142] 'That the Person that hath the Custody of that House shall take that the Public Library at Lambeth, and also his Grace's Library, be locked up and secured, that they may be preserved from Violence or Imbezzling; and that his Grace shall have liberty to remove his goods he hath there to Croiden or some other place.' (Cox-Johnson, III)

On December 23, 1642, "soldiers and prisoners occupied the Palace" (Cox-Johnson, III). The Commons ordered: "That Mr. *Glyn*, Mr. *Whitlock*, and Mr. *Hill*, do take Care for the Securing of the publick Library belonging to the See of *Canterbury*, the Books, Writings, Evidences, and Goods, in *Lambeth House*; and to take the Keys of the Libraries, and other Rooms, where the Books, Writings, Evidences, and other Goods are, into their Custody. And it is referred to the Committee that is appointed to consider of fit Places for Prisons to prepare an Ordinance for the Regulating of *Lambeth House*, in the like Manner as *Winchester House* is regulated."[143]

Lambeth has manuscript catalogues of the libraries of Archbishops Richard Bancroft and George Abbot. Cox-Johnson noted that in 1633 the library contained 6,065 books that belonged to Bancroft and 2,667 which were Abbot's.[144] When Lambeth was shut up, both Cambridge and Sion College took a keen interest in obtaining the Lambeth collection. Sion College lost the contest and when the Lambeth Library books were moved to Cambridge a catalogue was ordered made in 1647, "A true catalogue of all the Books sent from Lambeth Library to the University of Cambridge by Order of both Houses."[145] A copy of this catalogue was made and used to check in the books on their arrival at Cambridge.[146] These lists would indicate all the books that were at Lambeth prior to the move to Cambridge. The earlier catalogues of the Archbishops' books are Lambeth manuscripts, F.1 through F.4.[147] The library was subsequently restored to Lambeth Palace.[148]

Ann Cox-Johnson notes: "Captain Manwaring and the London militia were ordered to keep a guard in continual readiness. The Library was locked up."[149] So

---

141. In Cox Johnson (*The History of the Troubles and Tryal of William Archbishop of Canterbury*, ed. H. Wharton, I, 197).

142. In Cox Johnson (*Journal of the House of Lords*, V, 439).

143. HCJ 2, 23 December 1642, 900.

144. Ann Cox-Johnson, 108

145. Bodleian Library, MS 3335.

146. Cambridge University Library, MS Oo.7.51. Cox-Johnson, 115–117.

147. Cf. O. S. Pickering and V. M. O'Mara, *The index of Middle English prose. Handlist 13, Manuscripts in Lambeth Palace Library, including those formerly in Sion College Library* (Cambridge: Brewer, 1999) xiii, n3.

148. Ironically, in the late 1990s the Sion College Library was transferred to Lambeth.

149. Ann Cox-Johnson, 112.

while it is the library with the most accurate description of what was in the collection at the time of the assembly, it appears unlikely the divines had access to the Lambeth books; at least it seems they would have needed special permission for access, a record of which has not turned up at the time of this writing. However on the possibility it was accessible in some way, the collation in the bibliography of *The Grand Debate* will include the Lambeth library using the Cambridge catalogue (MS Oo.7.51). Of the approximately seventy works referenced in *The Grand Debate*, forty-eight are found in the Lambeth catalogue.

SION COLLEGE LIBRARY

Whether or not Lambeth was accessible, there was a closer option for the Scottish Commissioners. From Worcester House, the Sion College Library was only about half a mile due north. The old location of the college was in the Cripplegate Ward, essentially where Aldermanbury Square is now (Map, 3). Sion College was founded by provisions in the will of Thomas White (d. 1624), and while the will did not provide for a library, by 1631 the institution's hall, hospital and library had been built.[150] Apparently, though there are scanty records, the library was well furnished by that date and "was well known to one great Orientalist…. In the Life of John Lightfoot prefixed to the folio edition of his works,[151] it is stated that between May 1628, when he married, and the spring of 1630, when he settled in Staffordshire, Lightfoot 'removed to Hornsey, near the city of London, for the sake of the library of Sion College, to which he often resorted.'"[152] The college became an important institution for the Puritans. The London ministers had been meeting informally at Sion College prior to the formation of the London Provincial Assembly in 1647. The house belonging to Edmund Calamy abutted to the college and he had his own entrance into the college gardens from his house. A catalogue of the the contents of the library was published in 1650 and works listed may possibly have been available to the Westminster divines.[153] Of the approximately seventy works referenced in *The Grand Debate*, forty-four are found in the catalogue for Sion College.

PRIVATE LIBRARIES

As already noted, it may be that those divines who had good personal libraries gave aid to the transplanted divines and commissioners by giving them access to their own books. Certainly it was not uncommon for divines to have substantial

---

150. E. H. Pearce, *Sion College and Library* (Cambridge: 1913) 233.

151. Cf. *Works* (1825), 1.47

152. Pearce, 233, n1.

153. John Spencer, *Catalogus universalis libroum omnium in bibliotheca Collegii Sionii apud Londinenses* (Londini: Ex officina typographica Rob. Leybourni, 1650). There are no acquisition dates, so of titles in this study it can only be concluded that books *may* have been present in the Sion College Library during the time the Scots commissioners resided in London.

libraries. While we do not know what may have been in his library at the time, it
is said Thomas Goodwin lost half his books in the fire of London in 1666 which
amounted to £500.[154] Neither do we not know what was in Edmund Calamy's library, but it was not unusual for him to open up his home to guests. As already
noted, he was minister at St. Mary Aldermanbury. "Prior to the assembly Calamy
worked from his home with his fellow 'Smectymanuans'—Stephen Marshall, Thomas
Young, Matthew Newcomen and William Spurstowe [all would be appointed to
the Westminster assembly]—to produce two concerted attacks against episcopacy.
It was in his Aldermanbury home that an agreement was reached between presbyterians and leading congregationalists which delineated the parameters of their ecclesiological differences."[155] On at least one occasion a committee of the assembly
met in his home.[156] So it is possible he could have loaned books out of his library;
except that we have no record of what he owned or how extensive a collection it
may have been. However, there is a bit more known about libraries belonging to
two other of the Westminster divines. There are auction catalogues for the libraries
of Lazarus Seaman and William Greenhill.

THE LIBRARIES OF WILLIAM GREENHILL
& LAZARUS SEAMAN

The collection of William Greenhill was by far the smaller of the two libraries. The
catalogue is only 26 pages, listing 690 lots. "The contents are Bibles and commentaries, the large folio editions of the works of the Fathers, English Puritan Divines, and
a few secular books of no prominence."[157] Greenhill was not a prominent speaker
at the Westminster Assembly, speaking mostly during debates over ecclesiology,
and the Minutes do not note that he referenced any books which might have been
checked against the catalogue to see what he may have owned at the time.[158] Given
its size, of the collections analyzed Greenhill's had the fewest matches to the titles

---

154. James Reid, *Memoirs of the lives and writings of those eminent divines who convened in
the famous Assembly at Westminster* (1811) 1.339. Reid writes that the sale of Seaman's library
brought £700, which may indicate the size of Goodwin's. It is estimated Seaman had 15 to 20
thousand volumes.

155. *Minutes,* 1.III.

156. Lightfoot wrote, "our commitee remooved to Mr. Calamies in London." "Calamy's
home was in Aldermanbury and probably a large one." Chad Van Dixhoorn, "Reforming the
Reformation: Theological Debate at the Westminster Assembly 1643-1652," Volume 2, Appendix A: Lightfoot's Journal, p, 25 and note.

157. *Book Auctions in England in the Seventeenth Century (1676–1700)* (London: Elliot Stock,
1898), 117. Cf. Zacharias Bourne, *Catalogus variorum & insignium liborum selectissimæ bibliothecæ reverendi viri Gulielmi Greenhill: theologi doctissimi & pastoris olim ecclesiæ de Stepney
in comitatu de Middlesex. Quorum auctio habebitur in vico vulgo dicto Breadstreet, in Ædibus
Ferdinandi Stable cossipolæ ad insigne Capitis Turcæ. Per Zachariam Bourne. Catalogi gratis distribuentur ad insigne Unicornu in vico dicto Breadstreat* (London: Tho. Hodgkins, [1678]).

158. *Minutes,* 1.121, 148–161.

referenced in *The Grand Debate*.[159] His catalogue perhaps is more useful for giving an idea of what the average pastor's library for London divines may have been like in the mid-seventeenth century.

The unusually large private library of Lazarus Seaman was the first such collection sold at auction in London (in 1676). The published catalogue extends to 137 pages listing approximately 5,639 lots,[160] amounting to a "collection of 15,000 or 20,000 volumes."[161] Van Dixhoorn notes that by "1643 Seaman was made minister of All Hallows, Bread Street, London. The following year he was appointed master of Peterhouse, Cambridge. Neither pastoral nor academic duties kept Seaman away from the assembly and he ranks as the second most frequent speaker in the assembly with over 400 speeches. He was also a member deemed exceptionally useful in committee, with around eighty appointments during the course of the assembly. Seaman was respected for his learning and had a vast library, the first to be sold by public auction in England."[162]

Some evidence suggests that Seaman may have already collected a good number of volumes for his library at the time of the assembly. Seaman referred to about 18 authors and works explicitly during debates at the assembly, which can be gleaned from the Minutes, Gillespie and Lightfoot:[163] Balsalmon on Acts (Lightfoot, 100), Beza's *Annotationes*, Calvin on Galatians, Cameron's *Prælectiones*, Cartwright's *Confutation*, Chrysostom (*Minutes*, 2.135, 2.187, 2.597, 3.370, 4.47), Cotton's *Keys of the Kingdom of Heaven* (Gillespie, 72), Estius on Acts (*Minutes*, 2.367), Estius "on the seat" likely from his comment on the Sentences (Lightfoot, 125), Festus Hommius, *Harmonia Synodorum Hollandicarum* [i.e. *Belgicarum*] (Gillespie, 73), Ignatius (Lightfoot, 125), Luther on Galatians (*Minutes*, 2.187), Lydius (*Minutes*, 2.633), Guilliame Parisiensis (Gillespie, 96),[164] Savonarola (*Minutes*, 2.36), Symmachus (Lightfoot, 175), Whitaker (*Minutes*, 3.312), and Scotus (*Minutes*, 2.36). Only the Balsalmon on Acts,

---

159. Of about seventy works referenced in *The Grand Debate*, twenty are found in the Greenhill catalogue, and of those referenced by the Independents in their papers, Greenhill owned at one time, works by Budé, Chamier, Davenant, Estienne, Tremellius, Voetius, and Zanchius.

160. *Catalogus Variorum & Insignium Librorum Instructissimæ Bibliothecæ … Lazari Seaman* (London: Ed Brewster & Guil. Cooper, 1676). There is a misnumbering of pages and either a misnumbering of Octavo commentaries or about two pages are missing from the example in Early English Books. Several libaries note the misspagination, [6], 1-64, 57-112, 109-128, 131-137, [1] . The numbering of commentaries jump from 81 on page 112 to 151 on the facing page 109.

161. *Book Auctions in England*, 6.

162. *Minutes*, 1.136.

163. Minutes, "Register of Citations," 1. 148–161. "Notes of Debates and Proceedings of The Assembly of Divines and other Commissioners at Westminster. February 1644 to January 1646," ed. David Meek, *The Presbyterian's Armoury, The Works of George Gillespie* (Edinburgh: Robert Ogle, and Oliver & Boyd, 1846). "The Journal of the Proceedings of the Assembly of Divines: From January 1, 1643, to December 31, 1644," *The Whole Works of the Rev. John Lightfoot, D. D.*, ed. John Rogers Pitman, volume 13 (London: Dove, 1824).

164. The Seaman auction catalogue lists "87. Guil. Parisiensis Episcopi de septem Sacramentis Libellus," page 132. Seaman adduced "De Sacr. Ordinis" according to Gillespie's assembly notes, page 96.

Luther on Galatians, and the Cotton, are not listed amongst the auctioned books. The Cotton would have been generally available at the assembly given that Goodwin and Nye published it with a preface under their own hand. The other two are listed in the Sion College catalogue.[165] The other fifteen are found in some form in the Seaman catalogue (distinct works or collections, etc.). This would indicate that Seaman's library (which assuming he lived near All Hallows, Bread Street, was not that much further from Worcester house than Calamy's house and Sion College), could have been of a significant size and resource at the time for the visiting divines. Of the approximately seventy works referenced in *The Grand Debate*, forty-three are found in the Seaman catalogue, compared to Greenhill's twenty, the twenty-nine found at Westminster Abbey, forty-four at Sion, forty-eight at Lambeth, and three that could be found in the assembly's collection made out of Laud's study. While it cannot be known which works were in Seaman's collection during the assembly, this nevertheless gives an indication just how significant a private collection it was.

THE LONDON BOOK SHOPS

It is possible that the Scottish Commissioners and other divines purchased some of the older as well as newer books not found in the libraries in the London book houses. They would have been able to find some foreign published works as well. Books from the Netherlands could certainly have been on sale in London. It "was not at all unusual for Dutch seventeenth century booksellers to trade in Poland, Lithuania, Denmark, Germany, France, Italy, Smyrna, Spain, Portugal, Hungary, Czechoslovakia, England and Scotland."[166] John Milton owned a copy of Rivet's *Prælectiones* and did reading in it between 1643 and 1646 according to his commonplace book. "The biblical commentaries include Peter Martyr, *In Librum Judicum*, Basil, *Homiliae, In Psalmum I, In Hexameron VIII, In Principium Proverbium*; Chrysostom, *In Genesim Homiliae*, Rivetus (André Rivet), *Praelectiones in Caput XX Exodi*; Peter Martyr (Vermigli), In *Librum Judicum* [sic]."[167]

At the time almost all of the booksellers where located in St. Paul's Churchyard (Map, 12), which was within an easy distance from Worcester House, slightly more distant a few blocks to the northwest than Saint Antholins was to the northeast.[168]

---

165. *Catalogus universalis*, p. 29, item 12. Seaman owned a copy of the Sion College catalogue.

166. David Davies, "The Geographic Extent of the Dutch Book Trade in the Seventeenth Century," *Het Boek* 31 (1952–54): 22, cited in Laura Cruz, "The Geographic Extent of the Dutch Book Trade in the 17th Century an Old Question Revisited," *Boundaries and their meanings in the history of the Netherlands*, ed. Benjamin J. Kaplan, Marbeth Carlson, and Laura Cruz (Brill, 2009) 119.

167. Barbara Kiefer Lewalski, *The Life of John Milton: a critical biography* (Wiley-Blackwell, 2002) 160, 593, note 28. Cf. James Holly Hanford, "The Chronology of Milton's Private Studies," *Publications of the Modern Language Association of America*, volume 36 (Baltimore: Published Quarterly by the Association, Printed J. H. Furst Company, 1921) 279.

168. See location 12 on the map (Agas Map, C5, http://mapoflondon.uvic.ca [accessed April 25, 2013]).

Scottish Agent in Campvere: William Spang

Another possible source for the Scottish Commissioners was Baillie's cousin William Spang. It is clear from their correspondence the cousins were exchanging and obtaining books for each other. Through Spang, Baillie had access to Rivet, whom he had actually met, as well as Voetius and other contemporary Reformed divines on the continent. He begged Spang a number of times to get Rivet and Voet involved writing on the Presbyterian side, and they corresponded often about books.[169] It is at least possible given the flow of books from Spang, that he was a source of books for the Scots while in London, in addition to the other sources at their disposal.

Conclusion

It is clear that the divines attending upon the assembly at Westminster had available to them several significant theological resources. On the premises where they met most days of the work week, they had at least the books from Laud's study at hand (and that at least from January until June 1644) and possibly more books for a longer period from other sequestered libraries. We also have testimony that the divines made heavy use of the Westminster Abbey library. Across town near Worcester House and Edmund Calamy's church and residence, there was the somewhat smaller library at Sion College, and across the Thames there may have been some possible access to the largest library of the three at Lambeth Palace, though at this writing that seems a remote possibility given its apparent closing by the Parliament. The divines also had access to the London book marketers clustered around Saint Paul's, which offered for sale new and old domestic and foreign books. And the Scottish Commissioners had access as well to the Dutch and potentially also the Continental publishers through Baillie's cousin William Spang. And there were the personal libraries of various London divines such as those of Seaman and Greenhill, which may have been available to the Scots and other divines away from their studies and personal libraries while in the city attending upon the assembly. All of these were potential sources for the divines during the "Grand Debate," and the following bibliography has been collated with the transcribed list of books from Laud's library, the Westminster Abbey *Benefactors' book*, the catalogue for the library at Sion College, the MS catalogue for Lambeth Palace Library, and the published auction catalogues for the private libraries belonging to assemblymen William Greenhill and Lazarus Seamen.

---

169. Spang became the minister of the Scotts church in Campvere in 1630 (Memoir of Robert Baillie, *Letters and Journals,* 1.cxiv). In 1637 Baillie is found writing to him to aid in obtaining some books, at that time apparently for his own study. In 1642 Baillie was called to join David Dickson as a professor in Glasgow and much of the later correspondence with Spang about books concerns getting titles for the university. Regarding their book discussions see, *Letters and Journals,* 2.158, 175, 239, 250, 251, 275, 290.

Bibliography

This is a listing of all works cited by the authors of the papers making up *The Grand Debate*. Editions are not necessarily those the Westminster divines may have been referencing. If a title was potentially accessible in various collections of the time, this is noted with more detail in the entry. The numbers (1–7) refer to the libraries which may have been available to the assembly.[1]

Source libraries

[1]Collection of 98 books taken from Laud's study for use by the assembly: **Laud**
[2]Westminster Abbey Library Benefactors' Book: **MS 46**[2]
[3]Westminster Abbey Library, present in collection: **Abbey Library**
[4]Sion College Library 1650 Catalogue: **Sion**
[5]Lambeth Palace Library, MS Catalogue: **Lambeth**
[6]Lazarus Seaman Library: **LS**
[7]William Greenhill Library: **WG**

[2,4-6]Ambrose (Ambrosiaster). Fourth century commentator of Paul's Epistles (fl. 366–384). Cf. *Commentaries on Romans and 1–2 Corinthians*. Translated and edited by Gerald L. Bray. Downers Grove: InterVarsity Press, 2009. This work was attributed to Ambrose (now assigned to Ambrosiaster) and included in his works at the time of the assembly. [**MS 46:** *Opera*, 2v.a9. **Sion:** *Opera* (Paris: 1614; Basil: 1538). **Lambeth:** *Opera* (1603; 1506), 1r, 27r. **LS:** *Opera* (1614), p. 2.]

[5,6,7]Ames, William. Puritan divine (1576–1633). *Bellarmine Enervatus*. 1625; London: Apud Johannem Humpfridum, 1632. [**Lambeth:** 153r. **LS:** 1628, p. 128. **WG:** 1628, p. 25 ("vol. 2," i.e. 2 vols.]

---

1. For more background see the previous appendix, "Westminster Abbey Library: The Theological Resource of the Assembly of Divines (1643–1652)." **Laud:** see "Westminster Abbey Library," 382–388. **MS 46:** *Benefactors' book*, Westminster Abbey Library MS 46. **Abbey Library:** Card catalogue. **Sion:** John Spencer, *Catalogus universalis libroum omnium in bibliotheca Collegii Sionii apud Londinenses* (Londini: Ex officina typographica Rob. Leybourni, 1650). **Lambeth:** Cambridge University Library, MS Oo.7.51. **LS:** *Catalogus Variorum & Insignium Librorum Instructissimæ Bibliothecæ …Lazari Seaman* (London: Ed Brewster & Guil. Cooper, 1676). **WG:** Zacharias Bourne, *Catalogus variorum & insignium liborum selectissimæ bibliothecæ reverendi viri Gulielmi Greenhill…Per Zachariam Bourne. Catalogi gratis distribuentur ad insigne Unicornu in vico dicto Breadstreat* (London: Tho. Hodgkins, [1678]). My thanks to Roy Middleton for obtaining photos of the extremely rare Greenhill catalogue, and to the John Rylands Library, Special Collections, for allowing examination of their copy.

2. Unless noted otherwise, the benefactor was 1–John Williams, July 20, 1623. See page 390, footnote 115 for more information on MS 46.

[4] Apolonius, William. Dutch Reformed theologian (1600–1657). *Consideratio quarundam Controversiarum ad Regimen Ecclesiæ spectantium, quæ in Angliæ regno hodie agitantur.* London, 1644. English: *A Consideration of Certaine Controversies at this time agitated in the Kingdome of England: concerning the government of the church of God, written at the command and appointment of the Walachrian Classis, by Guilielmus Apollonii … and sent from the Walachrian churches, to declare the sense and consent of their churches, to the Synod at London, Octob. 16, 1644, stilo novo; translated out of Latine, according to the printed copy.* London 1645. [**Sion:** p. 10.]

[56] Aretius, Benedictus. Swiss Reformed theologian (d. 1574). *Commentarii In Sacram Actuum Apostolicorum Historiam.* 1579; le Preux, 1607. [**Sion:** *Com. in No. Test. Gen. 1618; In Acta Apost. Laus. 1589.* **Lambeth:** *in Nov. Test: vol: 2. 1607.* 6(2)r. **LR:** *in Novum Testamentum,* Paris, 1607.]

[245] Arias Montano, Benito. Spanish Roman Catholic orientalist (1527–1598). *Biblia Sacra Hebraice, Chaldaice, Græce & Latine* [Antwerp polyglot]. Antwerp: Plantin: 1569–1573. [**MS 46:** *Biblia … Interlinearis. Plantin.: 1584,* 2r.a3. **Sion:** p. 20. **Lambeth:** 125r.]

[2456] Augustine, Bishop of Hippo (354–430). *Contra Faustum Manichæum.* Cf. *Patrologiæ cursus completus, series Latina (PL),* ed. J. P. Migne. 217 volumes. Petit-Montrouge, Apud J.-P. Migne, 1844–1855. Volume 42. Cf. *A Select Library of the Nicene and Post-Nicene Fathers, first series,* ed. Philip Schaff. Buffalo: CLC, 1886–1890. Volume 4. [**Abbey Library:** *Omnia opera D. Aurelii Augustini,* 10 vols. in 9 (Basil: 1543) inscription, "Omptus Capero[?] 27 Maie 1567," G.1.21; *Omnium operum D. Aurelii Augustini,* 10 vols. in 5 (Paris: 1555), G.3.33. Acquisition dates unknown. **Sion:** *Opera* (Basil: 1543; Paris: 1637), p. 14. **Lambeth:** *Opera* (1556; 1563), 1r, 42r. **LS:** *Opera,* 8 vol., 1569, p. 2.]

————. *De Fide et Operibus. PL* 40.

————. *In Joannis Evangelium Tractatus CXXIV. PL* 35.

————. *Quæstionum Evangeliorum, PL* 35.

[456] Bacon, Francis. English philosopher, statesman, scientist (1561–1626). *Sylva Sylvarum, or, A Natural History: in ten centuries.* 1627; 1661. [**Sion:** 1631, p. 15. **Lambeth:** 110r. **LS:** p. 16.]

[245] Baronius, Cardinal Cæsar. Ecclesiastical annalist (1538–1607). *Annales Ecclesiastici,* volume 1. 1614; Paris: 1666. [**MS 46:** *Baroni Annales,* 2r.b22; *Baronius His Workes of the Edition of Coleyn,* 40–John Spirer, 68r.line 1. (apparently the Cologne edition of the *Annales*). **Sion:** *tom. 12, 1607,* p. 17. **Lambeth:** 1591, 136r.]

[24-7] Bellarmine, Cardinal Robert. Jesuit apologist (1542–1621). *Disputationes de Controversiis Christiane Fidei.* Lutetiæ Parisiorum, 1620. *Opera Omnia.* Paris: Vives: 1870. [**MS 46:** *Opera, 4 vols.,* 2–Julius Cralar, 18v.a1. **Sion:** *Opera* (1620), p. 18. **Lambeth:** 4 vols. 1608, 9r, 62r. **LS:** *Disputationes,* 1569, p. 8. **WS:** (1620), p. 6.]

[456] Bertram, Cornelius Bonaventura. Professor of Hebrew at Geneva and Lausanne (1531–1594). *De Politia Judaica.* Geneva, 1580. [**Sion:** 1577, p. 20. **Lambeth:** 1580, 45r. **LS:** *de Republic Ebreorum*, 1641, p. 132.]

[2 4–7] Beza, Theodore. French Reformer (1519–1605). *Novum Testamentum … Annotationes.* Cambridge: 1642. [**MS 46:** 4v.a8. **Sion:** 1642, p. 2. **Lambeth:** 1565, 1598, 1582, 1559, p.6(2)r. **LS:** 1589, p. 11. **WG:** 1638 *sic?* 1633, p. 1.]

[2 4 5 6] Brentius (Brenz), Johann. German Reformer, commentator (1499–1570). *Commentarii in Acta Apostolorum. In Operum … D. Joannis Brentii….* Tübingten, 1576–1590, 8 vols. [**MS 46:** *John. Brentius in Acta: Apos.:*, 7–Sir Francis Leigh, 26r.b8. **Sion:** p. 24. **Lambeth:** 6(2)r. **LS:** *Commentarii in Novum …*, p. 11.]

[2] Brerewood (or Bryerwood), Sir Edward. Antiquary and mathematician (1565–1613). *De ponderibus et pretiis veterum nummorum, eorumque cum recentioribus collatione liber unus.* Londin: Apud Ioannem Billium, 1614. [**MS 46:** 20–William Camden, 44v, line 8.]

[2 4–7] Budé, Guillaume. French scholar, linguist (1468–1540). *Commentarii Linguæ Græcæ.* 1529; Basil: 1556. [**MS 46:** 1548 ed., 3v.a6; *Gul. Budæus, 8°,* 12–Robert Jewell, . **Sion:** p. 27. **Lambeth:** *Budæi Tusani constantini lexicon 1562.* **LS:** 1568, p. 5. **WG:** 1556, p. 2.]

[2 4 5 6] Bullinger, Johann Heinrich. Swiss Reformer (1504–1575). *In Acta Apostolorum.* Zurich, 1533. [**MS 46:** *In Bullinger in Matth.: Johan: et Act: Apost,* 7–Sir Francis Leigh, 26r.a2; *Bullinger in Acta,* 10–John Parker, 28r.a3. **Sion:** *In Marc. Luc. & Acta. 1545.* **Lambeth:** *Marc et Acta 1554.* **LS:** 1546, p. 13.]

[5 6] ————. *In omnes Apostolicas Epistolas.* Tiguri: C. Froschoverum, 1558. [**Lambeth:** *Epist: Tig: 1582.* **LS:** 1582, p. 13.]

Burroughs, Jeremiah. Puritan divine (b.1601?–1646). *Irenicum: To the Lovers of Truth and Peace: Heart-divisions opened in the causes and evils of them.* London: Dawlman, 1645; 1653.

[4 5 6] Calvin, John. Genevan Reformer (1509–1564). Acts. In *Calvin's Commentaries.* 45 volumes. Edinburgh: Calvin Translation Society, 1844–1858; repr. Grand Rapids: Baker Book House, 1983. [**Sion:** *In Evangel. & Acta,* p. 30. **Lambeth:** *Acta. 1572. 6v.* **LS:** *Jo. Calvini Opera 10. vol. Geneva, 1600,* p. 11.]

[4–7] Camerarius, Joachim. German Reformer (1500–1574). *Commentarius in Novum Fœdus.* Cambridge: Roger Daniel, 1642. [**Sion:** p. 30. **LS:** p. 12. **WG:** p. 5]

[4–7] Cameron (Camero), John. Scottish synergistic theologian (c.1579–1625). *Amica Collatio de Gratiæ et Volunt. Humanæ concursu in vocatione … instituta inter … D Tilenam et J. Cameronum.* Leyden, 1621. [**Sion:** p. 31. **Lambeth:** 17v. **LS:** 1622, *Amica collatio de gratiæ et volunt. humanæ concursu,* p. 40. **WG:** 1622, p. 10.]

[4 5 6] ————. "Prælectiones: De Nomine Ecclesiæ, De Schismate." In TA ΣΩΖΟΜΕΝΑ *sive opera partim ab auctore ipso edita.* Frankfurt: 1642. [**Sion:** p. 31. **Lambeth:** *Prælectiones,* 1628, 17v. **LS:** 1642, p. 8.]

[4 5 6] Cartwright, Thomas. Puritan divine (1535–1603). *A Confutation of the Rhemish Testament.* 1618; repr. Da Capo Press, 1971. [**Sion:** p. 35. **Lambeth:** 4v. **LS:** p. 15.]

[156] ————. *The Second Replie of Thomas Cartwright: agaynst Maister Doctor Whitgiftes second answer, touching the Church discipline.* Heidelberg: Imprinted by Michael Schirat, 1575. [**Laud:** "Cartwright agt Whitgift 4°" (Item 34). **Lambeth:** 157v. **LS:** p. 57.]

[2] Casaubon, Isaac. French humanist scholar (1559–1614). *Strabonis Rerum Geographicarum libri XVII.* 1587; Paris: 1620. Cf. *The Geography of Strabo,* translated by H. C. Hamilton and W. Falconer. 3 vols. London: Bohn, 1854–1857. [**MS 46:** *Strabo, gr: Lat: cum Annot: Casauboni: Par:.,* 3r.b14.]

[2457] Chamier, Daniel. French Protestant divine (1565–1621). *Panstratiæ Catholicæ sive controversiarum de religione adversus pontificios corpus.* 4 vols. Geneva: Roverianis, 1626. [**Sion:** *Controversiæ contra Pontificios* (Geneva: 1624), p. 37. **Lambeth:** 4 vols. (1626), 4v. **LS:** p. 7. **WG:** p. 6. **MS 46:** 38-Thomas Merill (Merrill, d. 1631), chief butler Westminster College, undated, 66r, last line. Merrill bequeathed money to purchase books for the library. Merrill's nephew of the same name also served as chief butler (d. 1664). Location in the Benefactors' book and handwriting indicate this was the elder Merrill. See Joseph Lemuel Chester, *The Marriage, Baptismal, and Burial Registers of the Collegiate Church or Abbey of St. Peter* (London: {Private Edition}, 1876) 163, n4.]

[2456] Chrysostom, Greek Father (347–407). *Homilies on the Acts of the Apostles. A Select Library of the Nicene and Post-Nicene Fathers, first series,* ed. Philip Schaff. Buffalo: CLC, 1886–1890. Volume 11. [**MS 46:** *Opera,* 2r.a21; *Homiliæ: grk: lat: Pariis,* 22v.a18; *Chrysostomi Florus,* gr. Lat., 6r.a34; Grk., 6v.b5; *Homiliæ* [Greek], 10r.a14; *Operum* undated (cf. Paris: Frontonis Ducæi, 1614), 26-John Willim, 52r, last line. **Sion:** *Opera* (Paris: 1621; Basil: 1525; Etonæ: 1613), *Homiliæ Græce* MS, p. 38–39; *Catalogus Interpretum S. S. Scripturæ,* p. 21. **Lambeth:** *Opera* (Venice: 1548–49; Paris: 1536; Basil: 1539; 1558), iv, 27r, 42r. **LS:** 11 vols, Paris, 1636, p. 1.]

Cotton, John. New England divine (1584–1652). *The Keyes of the Kingdom of Heaven.* London, 1644; Boston: repr. Tappan and Dennet, 1843.

————. *The True Constitution of a Particular Visible Church, Proved by Scripture. Wherein is Briefly Demonstrated by Questions and Answers what Officers, Worship, and Government Christ Hath Ordained in His Church.* London: 1642.

[46] Cudworth, Ralph. English divine and philosopher (1617–1688). William Perkins, *A Commentarie or Exposition, upon the Five First Chapters of the Epistle to the Galatians .... Now published for the benefit of the Church, and continued with a supplement upon the sixth chapter, by Rafe Cudworth.* Cambridge: John Legat, 1604. [**Sion:** *Catalogus Interpretum S. S. Scripturæ,* p. 21. **LS:** Perkins' Works, 3 vols., p. 13.]

[4-7] Davenant, John. Bishop of Salisbury (1576–1641). "De Judice ac Norma Fidei et Cultus Christiani Disputatio." In *Prælectiones de duobus in Theologia Controversis Capitibus: de Judice Controversiarum, primo; de Justitia Habituali et Actuali, altero.* Canterbury, 1634. [**Sion:** p. 46. **Lambeth:** 1631, 4v. **LS:** *Opera Omnia, 4 vols.* (Cambridge; volumes of varying date), p. 8. **WG:** p. 6.]

de Dieu, Louis (Lodewÿk). Dutch Reformed theologian and linguiſt (1590–1642). *Animadversiones in Aſta Apoſtolorum* (1634).

Diodati, Giovanni. Reformed divine (1576–1649). *Giovanni Diodati, I Commenti Alla Sacra Biblia Con Le Introduzioni E I Sommari.* Firenze: 1880.

————. *La Sacra Biblia.* 1607; 1641.

[6] ————. *La Sainte Bible.* 1644. [**LS:** *Gallice, Gen.* 1643.]

Dissenting Brethren {Thomas, Goodwin (1600–1680) Philip Nye (b.1595–1672), Sidrach Simpson (c.1600–1655), Jeremiah Burroughs (b.1601?–1646) and William Bridge (1600/1–1671)}. *An Apological Narration.* London, 1643.

[2467] Drusius, Joannes. Reformed divine; professor of Hebrew (1550–1616). *Veterum interpretum græcorum in totum vetus Teſtamentum Fragmenta, colleſta.* Janssonius, 1622. [Seaman cited Symmachus in debate and the citation appears in *The Grand Debate* (see p. 114), and the source would likely have been either Drusius or the Greek and Latin bible authorized by Sixti V. Seaman owned a copy of the 1628 edition of the bible at one point as well as the 1622 work by Drusius. **MS 46:** 5v.b2. **Sion:** p. 50. **LS:** p. 3, 22. **WG:** p. 12.]

[124-7] Erasmus, Desiderius. Dutch Catholic Theologian and Humaniſt (1466–1536). *Novum Teſtamentum omne.* Basil: 1519. [**Laud:** Possibly item 80. **MS 46:** *Novum Teſtamentum, Græc.: of Stephanus,* 2r.a5. **Sion:** 1582, p. 52. **Lambeth:** Basil, 1550, 126v. **LS:** 1542, p. 11. **WG:** 1605, p. 3.]

[4-7] Eſtienne, Henri (Henricus Stephanus). Parisian printer and classical scholar (1528?–1598). *Thesaurus Linguæ Græcæ.* Geneva: 1572–1573; Paris: Didot, 1831–1865. [**Sion:** p. 137. Lambeth: 151v. **LS:** 5 vols., p. 5. **WG:** p. 3.]

[2] Euſtathius of Thessalonica (c. 1115–1195/6). *Commentarii in Homeri Iliadem et Odysseam.* Rome, 1542–1550; Lipsiæ: Weigel, 1827. [**MS 46:** *in Homerum 4:vol. Edit: Romanæ,* 21–Henry King, 49r. The entry notes King was archdeacon of Essex and afterward Bishop of Chicheſter. As noted in the Appendix, MS 46 was compiled from earlier records and the reference is therefore likely in retroſpeſt. King became bishop February 6, 1642.]

Gilleſpie, George. Second Reformation Scottish Presbyterian divine (1613–1648). *An Assertion of the Government of the Church of Scotland, in the points of ruling elders, and of the authority of presbyteries and synods.* Edinburgh, 1641; Naphtali Press, 2008. Cf. *Works: A Presbyterian's Armoury.* 1846.

[2457] de Gorran(us), Nicolaus. French theologian (1230?–1295). *In Aſta Apoſtolorum, et singulas apoſtolorum Jacobi, Petri, Johannis et Judæ canonicas Epiſtolas, et Apocalypsin commentarii, authore R. P. F. Nicolao Gorrano.* Antwep, 1620. [**MS 46:** 19–Charles Serjeants, 40v.a12. **Sion:** *Elucidatio in Aſta, Epiſtolas canonica, & Apocalypsim,* 54. **Lambeth:** 13v. **WG:** p. 3.]

[245] Gwalther, Rudolf. Reformed theologian, successor to Bullinger (1519–1586). *In Divi Pauli Apoſtoli Epiſtolas Omnes.* Tiguri: In Officina Froschoviana, 1589. [**Sion:** p. 66; *Catalogus Interpretum S. S. Scripturæ,* p. 22. **Lambeth:** *Opera,* 1582 6(1)v. **LS:** *Opera,* 1578, p. 11.]

[2456] Jerome (Eusebius Sophronius Hieronymus). Roman Christian theologian and translator of the Vulgate (c.345–c.419). *In Isaiam. PL* 24. [**MS 46:** *Opera*, 2v.a10. **Sion:** *Opera* (1546, 1456, 1533), p. 70. **Lambeth:** *Opera* (1553; 1579), 2v. **LS:** *Opera, Coloniæ, 1616*, p. 2.]

Johnson, Francis. Separatist; Brownist (1563–1618). *An Inquirie and Answer of Thomas White: his Discoverie of Brownisme.* Amsterdam: 1606.

[2456] Josephus, Titus Flavius. Romano-Jewish historian (37–c.100). *Antiquities of the Jews.* In *Works.* Translated by William Whiston. Halifax: 1864. [**MS 46:** *Opera*, 2r.a22; anr. ed., 3v.b5; anr. ed., 9r.a26. **Sion:** *Opera* (Geneva, 1611; MS), p. 77. **Lambeth:** *Opera*, 131r. **LS:** *Opera, Gr' & Lat',* 1616, p. 1. *Lat.,* p. 99.]

[24-7] à Lapide, Cornelius. Jesuit, commentator (1567–1637). *Commentaria in omnes Divi Pauli Epistolas.* Antwerp: Nutii and Meursium, 1617. Cf. *Commentarii in Sacram Scripturam*, volume 9. 10 vols. Melitæ: 1843–1851. *The Great Commentary of Cornelius à Lapide.* Volume 7, 1 Corinthians. Translated by W. F. Cobb. Edinburgh: John Grant, 1908. [**MS 46:** 2–Julius Cralar, 18r.a9. **MS 46: Sion:** p. 81. **Lambeth:** *Epist.* (Antwerp, 1614), 13v. **LS:** Seaman owned a 1648 edition at some point which postdates *The Grand Debate* papers. **WG:** *Opera* (Paris, n.d.), possibly various volumes published between 1621–38?]

[245] de Lorin (Lorinus), Jean. French Jesuit commentator (1559–1634). *In Actus Apostolorum Commentaria.* 1607; Colonia Agrippina; 1621. [**MS 46:** 4v.a1. **Sion:** 1621, p. 89. **Lambeth:** 1605, 13v.]

[456] de Lyra, Nicholas. Franciscan, Bible exegete (1270–1340). *Biblia Latina cum postillis Nicolai de Lyra,* 4 vols. Nuremberge: Anthonij Kobergers, 1497. [**Sion:** p. 21. **Lambeth:** *Biblia, 7 vols. Ludg: 1500,* 14r. **LS:** 1508, p. 3.]

[245] ————. *Bibliorum Sacrorum Glossa Ordinaria.* 6 vols. Venice: 1603. [**MS 46:** 24.a4. **Sion:** pp. 21, 90. **Lambeth:** *idem* {Biblia sacra cum glossa ordinaria}, *Par. 1590,* 14r.]

[456] *Ecclesiasticæ Historiæ [Centuriæ Magdeburgenses].* Basil: Oporinus, 1559–74. [**Sion:** p. 37; **Lambeth:** 8 vols., 132r. **LS:** p. 7.]

[2567] Maldonatus, Joannes. Spanish Jesuit, commentator (1534–1583). *Commentarii in Quatuar Evangelistas.* Edited by Franciscus Sausen (Franz Sausen). Moguntiæ: 1844. [**MS 46:** 4r.b29. **Lambeth:** 1602, 7r. **LS:** 1624, p. 12. **WG:** 1624, p. 7.]

Mather, Richard. New England Puritan divine (1596–1669). *Church-government and church-covenant discussed: in an answer of the elders of the severall churches in New-England, to two and thirty questions….* London, 1643.

Mede, Joseph. Puritan divine (1586–1638). *Churches, that is, appropriate places for Christian worship both in and ever since the Apostles times: a discourse at first more briefly delivered in a colledge chappell and since enlarged.* London, 1638. Cf. *The Works.* 1672.

————. *Diatribæ: Discourses on Divers Texts of Scripture: delivered upon severall occasions.* London: 1642.

Mercator, Gerhardus (1512–1599). Flemish mathematician, geographer and map maker. *Claudii Ptolemæi Alexandrini Geographiæ….* Amsterodammi, 1605.

[2456] *Novum Jesu Christi Domini Nostri Testamentum.* 1586; Paris: Boun, 1628. [See Drusius above. **MS 46:** *Biblia Sixti quintir,* 8v.bii; *Biblia 6:": Romæ Fol',* 19–Charles Serjeants, 4ov.a (neither of these give a date nor whether the volume is the version of just the Latin or both the Greek and Latin). **Sion:** p. 20. **Lambeth:** 1628, p. 125r. **LS:** *Gr' & Lat' Autoritate Sixti Quinti 2 vol. Pariis 1628,* p. 3.]

[2456] Oecumenius (10th century, now believed late sixth or early seventh century commentator). *Commentaria.* In *Patrologiæ cursus completus, series Græca (PG),* ed. J. P. Migne. 166 volumes. Petit-Montrouge, Apud J.-P. Migne, 1857–1866. volume 118. Cf. *Oecumenii Commentaria in Hosce Novi Testamenti Tractatus.* Paris: 1630. *Pars Altera.* Paris: 1631. [**MS 46:** *Oecumenius,* 2 *vols,* 2r.a19; *In Acta,* 8v.b19. **Sion:** p. 103. **Lambeth:** 3v. **LS:** 1630, p. 1.]

[124-7] Parker, Robert. Puritan divine (1564–1614). *De Politeia Ecclesiastica Christi, et hierarchica opposita, libri tres.* Frankfurt: Basson, 1616. **Laud:** "Parker de Politia Ecclias 4°" (Item 58). **MS 46:** 12–Robert Jewell, 29v.b8. **Sion:** p. 107. **Lambeth:** 156v, 157v. **LS:** p. 35. **WG:** p. 9.]

[45] Pelargus, Christoph. German Protestant theologian (1565–1633). *Historiæ Sacræ quam Liber Actuum Apostolicorum.* Francofurti, 1602.

[45] de Pineda, Juan. Spanish Jesuit theologian and exegete (1558–1637). *De Rebus Salomonis Regis vel Salomon Prævius.* Moguntiæ: Antonij Hierati, 1613. [**Sion:** 1613, p. 114. **Lambeth:** 1609, 14v.]

[6] Robinson, John. English Separatist; pastor of the Pilgrims of the *Mayflower* (c.1575–1625). *Justification of the Separation from the Church of England.* Amsterdam, 1639. Cf. *Works.* 3 vols. London: Snow, 1851. [**LS:** 1609, p. 60.]

[56] Salmeron, Alphonso. Papal theologian at Trent (1515–1585). *Commentarii in Evangelicum Historiam et in Acta Apostolorum.* Coloniæ, 1612–15. [**Sion:** *Com. in Script. No. Test. tom. 16. Col. 1612,* p. 128. **Lambeth:** *Opera, vol. 16, Ven. 1601,* 15r. **LS:** 1599, p. 11.]

Solemn League and Covenant. Cf. *The Confession of Faith, the Larger and Shorter Catechism … Covenants, National and Solemn League.* Edinburgh: Johnstone and Hunter, 1855; repr. Free Presbyterian Publications, 1976; 1994; 1997.

[6] Thorndike, Herbert. English Caroline divine (d.1672). "Of the Government of Churches; a Discourse Pointing at the Primitive Form." In *The Theological Works,* Volume 1, Part 1. Oxford: John Henry Parker, 1844. [**LS:** 1641, p. 121.]

[56] Toussain (or Tussanus), Daniel. French Protestant Theologian and commentator (1541–1602). "Commentaria in Acta Apostolorum" In *D. Danielis Tossani S. Theologiæ in academia Heidelbergensi doctoris et professoris: primarii operum theologicorum* Hanoviæ: 1604. [**MS 46:** *Opera* {3 vols. 4to}, 2–Julius Cralor, 3v.a14. **LS:** *Opera, 1604,* p. 50.]

[3-7] Tremellius, Emmanuel. Reformed Hebrew Scholar (1510–1580). [H Kainê Diathêkê] … *Syriaca Novi Testamenti.* Stephanus: 1569. And *Novum domini nostri Jesu Christi Testamentum Syriacè.* Cothenis Anhaltinorum: [Fürstliche Druckerei], 1621. And *Biblia Sacra, sive, Testamentum Vetus* (1592; multiple

editions). [*Syriaca Novi Testamenti:* **Lambeth:** 1569, 125r. *Novum … Syriacè.* **LS:** 1621, p. 3. *Biblia Sacra:* **Abbey Library:** Genevæ: 1630, acquisition date unknown. **Sion:** page 2, n.d. **Lambeth:** mulitiple editions, 125v; 126r. **LS:** Genevæ: 1630, p. 3. **WG:** Genevæ: 1630, p. 1.]

[3-7] Vermigli, Peter Martyr. Reformed theologian and commentator (1499–1562). *In Epistolam S. Pauli apostolic ad Romanos … commentarii.* Heidelberg: Andreæ Cambieri, 1613. [**Abbey Library:** *In epistolam S. Pauli Apostoli ad Romanos* (1570), acquisition date unknown, S.4.44. **Sion:** *In Romanos* (1613), p. 94. **Lambeth:** *ad Romanos* (1570), 7r. **LS:** *Opera,* p. 11. **WG:** 1568, p. 3.]

[3-7] ————. *In … S. Pauli Priorem ad Corinthios Epistolam commentarij.* Tigvri, 1572. [**Abbey Library:** *In D. Pauli Apostoli priorem ad Corinthios Epistolam Petri Martyris Vermilii commentarii. Editio tertia* (Apud C. Froschoverum. Tiguri: 1579), V.4.44, acquisition date unknown. **Sion:** p. 94, *Catalogus Interpretum S. S. Scripturæ,* p. 22. **Lambeth:** *priorem ad Corinthios* (1570), 7r. **LS:** *Opera Omnia,* p. 11. **WG:** 1567, p. 3.]

[67] Voetius, Gisbertus. Dutch Calvinist theologian (1588–1676). *Desperata Causa Papatus, novissime prodita a Cornelio Jansinio, ubi imprimis magna illa præjudicia de Reformatorum vocatione: de Magia, aliisque abominationibus Papatus.* Amstelodami: 1635. [**LS:** p. 37. **WG:** *Amstel. 1648 {sic 1635},* p. 11.]

————. *Disputatio Theologica ex Politiâ Ecclesiasticâ de Unione Ecclesiarum earumque Regimine in Classibus & Synodis* (Ultraiecti: ex officinâ Ægidii Roman, Academiæ typographi, 1641). Cf. *Gisberti Voetii, Theologiæ in Academ. Ultrajectinâ Professoris, Politicæ Ecclesiasticæ,* volume 3. Amsterdam: Johannem Jansonium à Wæsberge 1676. *Gisberti Voetii Tractatus selecti de politica ecclesiastica Series Prima,* edited by F. L. Rutgers. Amsterdam, 1885. [While no copy was traced in the collections, this work was known to the Scots (Baillie complained about the work before his arrival at the assembly) and the Independents and Presbyterians of the assembly clearly had access to copies of it. See pp. 97, 170.]

[24-7] Whitaker, William. English Calvinist theologian (1548–1595). *Prælectiones … In quibus tractatur Controversia de Conciliis contra … Robertum Bellarminum….* Cambridge, 1600. *Opera Theologica.* Geneva, 1610. [**MS 46:** *Opera,* 21–Richard Burrell, 47r.b8. **Sion/LS/WG:** *Opera,* p. 151/p. 8/p. 6.]

[24-7] Zanchi, Jerome. Reformed Theologian (1516–1590). *Operum Theologicorum.* 8 vols. Geneva, 1605; 1613; 1619. [**MS 46:** *Opera, 3 vols folio,* 21–Richard Burrell, 47r.a5. **Sion:** 1619, 154. **Lambeth:** 1605, 6r. **LS:** 1605, p. 8. **WG:** 1613, p. 8.]

[456] Zepper, Wilhem. German Reformed theologian (1550–1607). *De Politia Ecclesiastica.* Herbornæ, 1595. [**Sion:** p. 154. **Lambeth:** 55r. **LS:** 1607, p. 95. **WG:** 1595, p. 18.]

Primary Historical Sources

Baillie, Robert. *The Letters and Journals of Robert Baillie,* ed. David Laing, 3 volumes. Edinburgh: Printed for Robert Ogle, 1841–1842.

Gillespie, George. "Notes of Debates and Proceedings of The Assembly of Divines and other Commissioners at Westminster. February 1644 to January 1646," ed. David Meek. In *The Presbyterian's Armoury, The Works of George Gillespie*. Edinburgh: Robert Ogle, and Oliver & Boyd, 1846.

Lightfoot, John. "The Journal of the Proceedings of the Assembly of Divines: From January 1, 1643, to December 31, 1644." In *The Whole Works of the Rev. John Lightfoot, D. D.*, vol. 13, ed. John Rogers Pitman. London: Dove, 1824.

Van Dixhoorn, Chad. *The Minutes and Papers of the Westminster Assembly 1643–1652*. 5 volumes. Oxford University Press, 2012.

————. "A Breife Journal of Passages in the Assembly of Divines by John Lightfoot." In *Reforming the Reformation: Theological Debate at the Westminster Assembly 1643–1652*, volume 2. Ph.D. dissertation, University of Cambridge, 2004, 7 vols.

————. "Minutes of the Westminster Assembly." In *Reforming the Reformation: Theological Debate at the Westminster Assembly 1643–1652*, volume 3–7. Ph.D. dissertation, University of Cambridge, 2004, 7 vols.

Westminster Assembly. Braye volume, Confession, Westminster College, Cambridge. See "The Assembly's Confession of Faith presented to the Parliament (Braye volume: Confession)," https://cudl.lib.cam.ac.uk/view/MS-WESTMINSTER-CONFESSION-00001/1 (accessed October 17, 2023).

Secondary Sources

Aquinas, Thomas. Dominican scholastic (1225–1274). *In octo libros Physicorum exposition*. Cf. Richard J. Blackwell, et al., *Commentary on Aristotle's Physics*. Yale, 1963.

Aristotle. *The Ethics of Aristotle illustrated with essays and notes*. Edited by Alexander Grant. Third Edition Revised and Partly Rewritten in two volumes. London: Longmans, Green, and Co. 1874.

[46] Ball, John. Puritan divine (1585–1640). *A Tryall of the New Church Way in New England and in Old*. London: 1644. [**Sion:** p. 16. **LS:** p. 54.]

Bannerman, James. *The Church of Christ: A Treatise on the Nature, Powers, Ordinances, Discipline, and Government of the Christian Church*. Edinburgh: T & T Clark, 1868.

Baillie, Robert. *A Dissuasive from the Errours of the Time*. London, 1645.

Blades, William. *The Enemies of the Book*. London: Trubner & Co., 1880; revised and enlarged, London: Elliot Stock, 1888.

Baxter, Richard. *A Plea for Congregationall Government: or, A defence of the Assemblies petition, against Mr. John Saltmarsh*. London: Tho. Underhill, 1646.

Burroughs, Jeremiah. *Irenicum, to the Lovers of Truth and Peace: heart-divisions opened in the causes and evils of them, with cautions that we may not be hurt by them, and endeavors to heal them*. London: Drawman, 1645/6; 1653.

Cicero, *Epistulæ ad Atticum* (Letters to Atticus). Cf. *Cicero's Letters to Atticus*. Edited by D. R. Shackleton Bailey. Volume 1. Cambridge: At the University Press, 1965.

————. "In Verrem." *M. Tulli Ciceronis Scripta Quæ Manserunt Omnia.* Edited by C. F. W. Mueller. Teubner, Leipzig; 1901. *The Orations of Marcus Tullius Cicero,* translated by C. D. Yonge. George Bell & Sons, London; 1903.

Coldwell, Chris. "*Antiquary*: The Identity of W. A. & Other Bibliographical Mysteries in *Jus Divinum Regiminis Ecclesiastici* (1646–1654)," *The Confessional Presbyterian* 16 (2020): 258.

Cotton, John. *The Way of the Churches of Christ in New-England.* London: Matthew Simmons, 1645.

de Witt, J. R. *Jus Divinum, The Westminster Assembly and the Divine Right of Church Government.* Kampen: Kok, 1969

Durham, James. Scottish Presbyterian minister (1622–1658). *Concerning Scandal.* 1659; Naphtali Press: 1990; revised, 2014.

Eyre, G. E. Briscoe. *A Transcript of the Registers of the Worshipful Company of Stationers; From 1640–1708 A.D. in three volumes.* London: 1913.

Field, Fridericus. *Origenis Hexaplorum.* Oxford: 1875.

Goodwin, Thomas. Puritan divine (1600–1680). "Of the Constitution, Right, Order, and Government of the churches of Christ." In *Works*, vol. ii. Edinburgh: James Nichol, 1865.

Laniak, Timothy. *Shepherds After My Own Heart: Pastoral Traditions and Leadership in the Bible.* Downers Grove, IL, InterVarsity Press, 2006.

[6] London, Ministers of the City of. *A Letter of the Ministers of the City of London, presented the First of January, 1645, to the Reverend Assembly of Divines sitting at Westminster … against Toleration. 1645; repr. in A Fourth Collection of Scarce and Valuable Tracts.* London: 1751. [**LS:** p. 59.]

Mather, Richard, et al. *Church-government and church-covenant discvssed: in an answer of the elders of the severall churches in New-England to two and thirty questions, sent over to them by divers ministers in England, to declare their judgments therein. Together with An apologie of the said elders in New-England for church-covenant, sent over in answer to Master Bernard in the yeare 1639. As also in an answer to nine positions about church-government.* London, 1643.

Neal, Daniel. *History of the Puritans.* 3 vols. 1837.

Persius Flaccus, *Satires.* Cf. *The Satires of A. Persius Faccus.* Edited by Basil L. Gildersleeve. New York: Harper & Brothers, 1875.

Selden, John. Erastian divine, jurist and orientalist (1584–1654). *De Synedris et Præfecturis Juridicis veterum Ebræorum.* 3 vols. London: Flesher, 1650–1655.

[15] Whittingham, William. English biblical scholar and reformer (c.1524–1579). *A brief discours off the troubles begonne at Franckford in Germany A. Domini 1554. Aboute the book off common prayer and ceremonie.* Cf. *A Brief Discourse of The Troubles Begun at Frankfort in the year 1554.* London: 1846; John Knox, *Works*, volume 4, edited by David Laing. Edinburgh: Printed for the Bannatyne Club, 1845. [**Laud:** "Troubles of Frankfort about the English Liturgy 8" (Item 31). **Lambeth:** 158v.]

Author

COMMENDATIONS

Recent years have witnessed a marked increase of interest in Calvinistic soteriology, much of it from those self identified as "young, restless, and Reformed." A corresponding interest in Presbyterian ecclesiology and polity remains largely dormant among these Reformed novitiates. Additionally, a not insignificant number of Christians in communions other than Reformed and Presbyterian ones who do not style themselves as restless have embraced soteriological Calvinism. Thus there is the need for Reformed and Presbyterian works that speak not only to the question of salvation but also to matters pertaining to the church and its organization. As Presbyterians, we do not permit ecclesiology to swallow soteriology, as does Rome, nor do we marginalize ecclesiology, as do many evangelicals in the current day. We affirm the importance of both soteriology and ecclesiology and desire that those who come to the Reformed faith espouse both.

The Westminster Assembly of Divines certainly concerned itself with both soteriology and ecclesiology, not only in the doctrinal standards that it adopted but also in 1645 in the "Form of Presbyterial Church Government" and the "Directory for the Publick Worship of God." As a part of addressing matters ecclesiological, the Assembly engaged, beginning on 2 February 1644, in what became known as the "Grand Debate," the dispute between the Presbyterians and the Independents, particularly the "Five Dissenting Brethren" (Thomas Goodwin, Philip Nye, Jeremiah Burroughs, William Bridge and Sidrach Simpson). There were a series of papers presented by both sides in the debate. The Independents argued in the negative a series of propositions: that presbyteries were proved from the churches at Jerusalem and Ephesus; that there was a due subordination of church synods; and that ordination should be performed by a presbytery. The Committee for Accommodation sought to compose the differences which were sharp, with politics and the success of Cromwell's army, which favored the Independents, playing no small part in the negotiations.

The important papers addressing the details contained in this significant debate have long been unavailable. In this splendid volume, ably edited by Chris Coldwell and helpfully introduced by Rowland Ward, these important papers are once again made available to modern readers. One might wonder why dusty old historical artifacts as these merit our attention. They do because the church needs to be reformed in all her doctrine, including ecclesiology. This beautifully produced and well-bound volume should garner interest and pay rich dividends to those who study them. This is the fullest expression of the differences between those who both otherwise hold to the same doctrinal standards but differ as to church government. Much remains in our own day to address with respect to ecclesiology and many people who are convinced Calvinists with respect to soteriology are not such with respect to ecclesiology. This is the perfect volume for such, or for any, who would see the biblical roots of Presbyterianism. Examine *The Westminster Assembly's Grand Debate* carefully and you'll learn more than you've ever known about why we are Presbyterians and not Independents.

Alan Strange, Professor of Church History, Registrar, and Theological Librarian, Mid-America Reformed Seminary, Dyer, Indiana.

The Westminster Assembly's *Grand Debate* is not reading for the timid or easily distracted. With that out of the way, I commend it to the teachers and pastors of the church. For every one who believes that God loved the church and gave her gifts, this book is well worth the read. Did God care enough to instruct Christ's church in how she should be ordered for her betterment and beauty? Is there such a thing as *jure divino* church government? Many in the history of the church have believed so. A goodly number have even suffered for this cause. This book displays the arduous work of men, godly men, who believed God had spoken to the Bride about her order, and, thus, her well-being on this earth. If we believe that the gospel message is primarily communicated through the church, then her well-being in all respects is essential. One cannot be for preaching the gospel to the world, and care nothing for the church and her decency and order. *The Grand Debate* displays the concerns of Congregationalists and Presbyterians as they were debated during the Westminster Assembly. The 21st century reader will not only learn history here, but ecclesiology that touches matters of the soul. This book will force the patient and discerning reader to examine his own heart and his love for the brethren; even those with whom he may disagree. We are called to unity in the Holy Scriptures and this volume, though polemical in degree, stands in that apostolic tradition.

C. N. Willborn, Adjunct Professor of Historical Theology, Greenville Presbyterian Theological Seminary.

How the Lord would have his visible church organized and governed may not interest all evangelicals today but it was a question of great practical and doctrinal interest in the British Isles, in the period leading up to and including the Westminster Assembly in the 1640s. Presbyterians and Congregationalists should especially appreciate the publication of these papers as they shed much light on the concerns (e.g., Christian liberty and the limits of ecclesiastical authority) that animated both movements in the sixteenth and seventeenth centuries. This first edition of *The Grand Debate*, since 1648, of those papers circulated at the Assembly, with its excellent introduction by Rowland Ward, is much to be welcomed by all who would know the background of the language adopted by the Assembly and who wish to take a peek through this window into the working of the Westminster Divines.

R. Scott Clark, Professor of Church History and Historical Theology, Westminster Seminary California